Transparency in AI-Assisted Management Decisions

Abdelfattah Jamal
Cadi Ayyad University, Morocco

Karima Aissaoui
Mohammed First University, Morocco

Lhoussaine Alla
Sidi Mohamed Ben Abdellah University, Morocco

Bouchra Alj
Hassan II University, Morocco

Badr Bentalha
Sidi Mohammed Ben Abdellah University, Morocco

IGI Global Scientific Publishing
Publishing Tomorrow's Research Today

Vice President of Editorial — Melissa Wagner
Director of Acquisitions — Mikaela Felty
Director of Book Development — Jocelynn Hessler
Production Manager — Mike Brehm
Cover Design — Jose Rosado

Published in the United States of America by
IGI Global Scientific Publishing
701 East Chocolate Avenue
Hershey, PA, 17033, USA
Tel: 717-533-8845
Fax: 717-533-7115
Website: https://www.igi-global.com E-mail: cust@igi-global.com

Library of Congress Cataloging-in-Publication Data

Names: Jamal, Abdelfattah, 1980- editor
Title: Transparency in AI-assisted management decisions / [edited by] Abdelfattah Jamal, Karima Aissaoui, Lhoussaine Alla, Bouchra Alj, Badr Benthala.
Description: Hershey : IGI Global Scientific Publishing, [2026] | Includes bibliographical references and index. | Summary: "This book aims to explore the multiple dimensions of transparency in the adoption and implementation of artificial intelligence within management practices"-- Provided by publisher.
Identifiers: LCCN 2025008260 (print) | LCCN 2025008261 (ebook) | ISBN 9798337317373 hardcover | ISBN 9798337317380 paperback | ISBN 9798337317397 ebook
Subjects: LCSH: Decision making--Technological innovations | Artificial intelligence
Classification: LCC HD30.23 .T727 2025 (print) | LCC HD30.23 (ebook) | DDC 658.4/03--dc23
LC record available at https://lccn.loc.gov/2025008260
LC ebook record available at https://lccn.loc.gov/2025008261

British Cataloguing in Publication Data
A Cataloguing in Publication record for this book is available from the British Library.

Table of Contents

Detailed Table of Contents

Artificial Intelligence (AI) in Human Resource Management (HRM) is helping in revolutionizing decision-making process from recruitment till development of employee. Since AI assisted HRM decisions lack transparency, they raise concern of fairness, accountability and trust. In this chapter we look at how Explainable AI (XAI) can add to the transparency found with AI driven HRM practices. It presents how XAI can alleviate the bias, ethics compliance, and organizational trust. The chapter also describes the tradeoffs between getting transparent and how well AI works, and looks at regulatory frameworks and best practices to strike a balance between fairness and efficiency. To impart a roadmap of implementing transparent and explainable AI systems within HRM, this chapter sheds light on interdisciplinary insights from HRM, AI ethics and organizational studies.

The research investigates how managers perceive AI transparency through accessibility, comprehensibility, and fairness which determines their level of interaction with AI-assisted decision systems. Managerial interaction serves as the outcome variable which this study categorizes into three ordered levels: low, moderate, and high. The research combines explainable AI frameworks (LIME and SHAP) with organizational trust and transparency models to connect cognitive and ethical aspects of human–AI interaction. A structured survey was conducted among 180 managers from three key sectors in Morocco: banking, telecommunications and retail. The questionnaire was developed from validated scales and analyzed by logistic regression models, run in Python for algorithmic flexibility and in SAS to ensure statistical robustness and reproducibility.

This chapter explores how agentic Artificial Intelligence (AI) is reshaping economic, social, and ethical structures. Unlike traditional automation, agentic AI autonomously adapts decision-making, replicating or surpassing human cognition. This shift induces a "phase change," transforming institutions, labor markets, and societal norms. While AI enhances efficiency, it exacerbates economic disparities, challenging GDP as a sole metric. We propose alternative indicators integrating well-being, equity, and sustainability. In business, AI-driven models create new data asymmetries, requiring adaptive governance. Trust, as both a relational and regulatory principle, is essential for balancing innovation and accountability. Advocating for Human-Centered AI, transparency, and fairness, this chapter underscores the need for interdisciplinary collaboration and robust data-sharing frameworks to ensure inclusive and equitable AI-driven progress.

This article examines the interaction between artificial intelligence (AI) and ethics, drawing on theoretical models of moral decision-making, such as Kohlberg's, as well as contemporary approaches such as Wallach et al.'s LIDA model and the work of Hyunsoo Kim. The analysis highlights the stages of individual moral reasoning and their transposition into organizational and technological settings, emphasizing the importance of situational factors. The article also explores how these models can be applied to design AI systems capable of simulating moral reasoning, processing complex data, and adapting their responses to human values. It also proposes avenues for effective collaboration between humans and AI, emphasizing the fundamental role of the human as the final decision-maker in complex ethical situations. The article finally highlights the need to develop collaborative systems that strengthen human capacities while respecting ethical principles, thus providing a framework for informed and contextual decision-making.

Morocco's public administration earns part of its digital transformation through ICT, a process accelerated by the Covid-19 pandemic. To this end, Morocco has launched the « Digital Morocco 2030 ». Moreover, digital transformation includes advanced technologies where artificial intelligence stands as a crucial tool in the enhancement of public services efficiency. This paper takes place based on systematic literature review and case studies, to in-depth study digital transformation and the application of AI within Moroccan public administration. It aims to identify the main points in this area and explore its opportunities and challenges. This chapter is structured according to the following sequence: first, we present a review of concepts and literature on digital transformation and AI in Moroccan public administration. Next, a review of existing theoretical frameworks will be carried out to uncover the factors that contribute to digitalization and AI integration. Finally, by synthesizing the studies, we could propose a model for better integrating administration in the digital age.

This chapter explores the prediction of dividend payout ratios among Moroccan listed companies by applying Random Forest Regression combined with Explainable Artificial Intelligence (XAI) techniques. Focusing on firm-specific financial indicators and macroeconomic variables over the period 2013–2023, the study aims to identify key drivers of dividend policy in an emerging market context. The analysis demonstrates that profitability, firm size, and historical payout behavior are the most influential predictors, while macroeconomic indicators such as inflation, GDP, and interest rates show limited impact. SHAP values are employed to enhance transparency, allowing for robust interpretation of model outputs. This chapter contributes to financial modeling, corporate governance, and machine learning literature by offering an interpretable AI-based framework for dividend forecasting tailored to the Moroccan market. The findings provide actionable insights for investors, managers, and policymakers seeking to understand or optimize dividend strategies in emerging economies.

This study examines the transformative impact of digital transformation and artificial intelligence (AI) on transparency, accountability, and efficiency in public administration. It explores AI-driven governance initiatives that combat corruption, streamline processes, and enhance citizen engagement. Using a benchmarking approach and quantitative research focused on Chief Information Officers, the study assesses AI's role in governance. Findings show that AI-powered digital transformation improves transparency through real-time data monitoring, predictive analytics, and automated decision-making. While AI enhances public access to information and reduces inefficiencies, challenges persist, including ethical concerns, algorithmic biases, and infrastructure gaps—only 22% of public organizations have the capacity for full AI implementation. This research highlights the need for strong governance frameworks, ethical AI deployment, and strategic investment in digital infrastructure to foster open governance, strengthen public trust, and drive sustainable administrative innovation.

This study explores the integration of artificial intelligence (AI) in organizational change management, particularly its role in reducing resistance to change and strengthening employee engagement. At a time when transformation processes are increasingly being influenced by digitization, this research explores ways in which AI can optimize change management in the enterprise. The methodology chosen for this study is based on a quantitative analysis. It begins with an in-depth literature review to identify the levers and challenges associated with change management. Then, an empirical study based on a questionnaire sent to 108 Moroccan companies that have opted for digital transformation. The SPSS 25 software was used to analyze the result. The results show that AI plays a key role in anticipating resistance and adapting

growth, increasing data complexity, and evolving market dynamics. Using a qualitative methodology, the study analyzes interviews with DSS users, employing Nvivo for thematic analysis, word frequency mapping, and cross-tabulation. Findings indicate that AI-enhanced DSS improve resource allocation, organizational responsiveness, and innovation capacity, strengthening overall performance and competitiveness. By contributing to AI-driven business transformation discourse, this chapter highlights AI's role in fostering industrial competitiveness. Future research should explore AI's long-term implications and conduct cross-sectoral analyses to refine AI-driven decision-making frameworks.

Preface

In the era of rapid digital transformation, Artificial Intelligence (AI) has evolved from a theoretical construct to a practical tool shaping management, governance, and organizational behavior. As AI-assisted decision-making becomes increasingly prevalent across sectors, the question of *transparency*—its meaning, mechanisms, and implications—has risen to the forefront of both academic and policy discussions. This edited volume, **Transparency in AI-Assisted Management Decisions**, brings together an interdisciplinary collection of empirical studies and theoretical insights to critically examine how transparency and explainability can be realized within AI-driven decision systems, particularly in the Moroccan context and broader emerging economies.

Transparency in AI is not merely a technical challenge, it is an ethical, organizational, and societal imperative. From human resource management to public administration, from financial forecasting to environmental policy, AI systems influence decisions with far-reaching consequences. Yet these systems often operate as opaque "black boxes," which can erode trust, complicate accountability, and introduce systemic biases. This book explores how Explainable AI (XAI), regulatory frameworks, and organizational strategies can work together to build systems that are not only intelligent but also *trustworthy* and *inclusive*.

The chapters span diverse industries and theoretical lenses, offering readers a panoramic view of the challenges and opportunities associated with AI transparency. Grounded in empirical research, many studies included here draw from Morocco's evolving digital landscape—making this volume especially relevant for emerging economies undergoing rapid digital transformation. It is our hope that the book serves as a guide for scholars, policymakers, and practitioners striving to balance innovation with ethics, and automation with accountability.

CHAPTER OVERVIEW

- **Chapter 1** introduces foundational concepts by examining the integration of Explainable AI (XAI) into Human Resource Management (HRM). It addresses how XAI can foster fairness, compliance, and organizational trust in employee-related decisions, while highlighting trade-offs between explainability and AI performance.
- **Chapter 2** presents a multi-sectoral study across Morocco's banking, telecom, and retail industries, analyzing how managerial perceptions of AI transparency influence trust and system engagement. It utilizes LIME and SHAP frameworks and logistic regression to model decision-making dynamics.
- **Chapter 3** theorizes on *agentic AI*—autonomous systems capable of human-like decision-making—and considers its economic and ethical consequences. It challenges traditional metrics like GDP, advocating for human-centered, transparent AI aligned with social equity and sustainability.
- **Chapter 4** delves into ethical AI design, applying moral reasoning models (Kohlberg, LIDA, Hyunsoo Kim) to AI contexts. It underscores the need for AI systems that respect human values and support collaborative, context-aware decision-making.
- **Chapter 5** explores Morocco's national digital strategy and the role of AI in transforming public administration. Through literature review and case studies, it develops a framework for integrating AI into governance structures in ways that enhance efficiency and transparency.
- **Chapter 6** focuses on financial transparency by using machine learning and XAI to predict dividend payouts in Moroccan firms. The study emphasizes SHAP values to interpret AI predictions, offering actionable insights for investors and regulators.
- **Chapter 7** builds on digital governance by evaluating AI's role in improving transparency and accountability in Moroccan public administration. A benchmarking study reveals both benefits and barriers to full AI integration, especially in infrastructure and ethics.
- **Chapter 8** addresses organizational change, highlighting how AI can reduce resistance and improve employee engagement during digital transformation. Survey data from 108 Moroccan companies provides evidence for personalized, AI-supported change management.
- **Chapter 9** shifts to the public health sector, analyzing how AI tools in internal auditing can improve operational transparency in Moroccan hospitals. The chapter highlights auditor perceptions, challenges, and readiness for AI-driven innovations.

- **Chapter 10** investigates how machine learning (Random Forests, XGBoost) can assess environmental performance in public organizations. It proposes AI as a strategic resource for achieving sustainable development goals and optimizing resource use.
- **Chapter 11** examines AI adoption in operational risk management within Moroccan banks, emphasizing front-office innovations like chatbots. The qualitative case study outlines organizational and technical hurdles, positioning AI as a tool for resilience.
- **Chapter 12** concludes with an industry-focused analysis of AI-driven Decision Support Systems (DSS) in Morocco's automotive sector. The findings reveal how AI enhances organizational agility, innovation, and competitiveness, urging further cross-sector exploration.

Together, these chapters underscore that transparency in AI is not a luxury, but a necessity—one that calls for interdisciplinary collaboration, stakeholder engagement, and a commitment to ethical design. This book invites readers to rethink what it means to build *responsible AI systems* and how these systems can be made to serve not just efficiency, but equity and trust in a rapidly digitizing world.

Abdelfattah Jamal

Faculty of Legal, Economic, and Social Sciences, Cadi Ayyad University, Marrakesh, Morocco

Karima Aissaoui

Faculty of Sciences, Mohammed First University, Oujda, Morocco

Lhoussaine Alla

National School of Applied Sciences, Sidi Mohamed Ben Abdellah University, Fez, Morocco

Bouchra Alj

Faculty of Legal, Economic, and Social Sciences of Mohammedia, Hassan II University, Casablanca, Morocco

Badr Bentalha

National School of Business and Management, Sidi Mohamed Ben Abdellah University, Fez, Morocco

Chapter 1
Transparency and XAI in AI-Assisted Management Decisions

Priya Kadyan
https://orcid.org/0009-0007-7049-2871
Chandigarh University, India

Rohan Singh
https://orcid.org/0000-0002-3588-4876
Chandigarh University, India

ABSTRACT

Artificial Intelligence (AI) in Human Resource Management (HRM) is helping in revolutionizing decision-making process from recruitment till development of employee. Since AI assisted HRM decisions lack transparency, they raise concern of fairness, accountability and trust. In this chapter we look at how Explainable AI (XAI) can add to the transparency found with AI driven HRM practices. It presents how XAI can alleviate the bias, ethics compliance, and organizational trust. The chapter also describes the tradeoffs between getting transparent and how well AI works, and looks at regulatory frameworks and best practices to strike a balance between fairness and efficiency. To impart a roadmap of implementing transparent and explainable AI systems within HRM, this chapter sheds light on interdisciplinary insights from HRM, AI ethics and organizational studies.

DOI: 10.4018/979-8-3373-1737-3.ch001

1. INTRODUCTION

Artificial Intelligence (AI) is transforming Human Resource Management (HRM) at the core as it automates recruitments and simplifies the process of hiring talents and also allows data-based performance assessment (Benabou, 2024). The quick adoption of AI technologies has led the HR professionals to analyze bulky sets of data easily, forecast the turnover of employees and improve candidate experience using automated systems. However, this technological development shows multiple challenges of fairness, transparency, ethical decision making, as well as compliance to regulation. Many AI's are "black boxes" that make it difficult for both HR professionals and the employees to comprehend or believe in the logic of machines' decisions 9Dima, 2024). This chapter presents a comprehensive examination of ways in which AI is affecting HRM, including the significance of transparency, the function of explainable AI (XAI), and ethical and legal factors, real-life examples, and best practices of responsible use. The goal is to provide HR practitioners with the pragmatic strategies and well-balanced vision of opportunities and challenges of AI in the modern HRM.

The application of Artificial intelligence (AI) in the management of human resource has brought significant changes in organizations as it breaks many barriers of offering critical services like recruitment, talent acquisition, performance evaluation, and enhancing employee productivity. Due to increased technological advancement, there is efficient and effective processing of huge employee data through the use of artificial intelligence systems. These tools help the HR in their exercise of searching for qualified staff, future turnover, and containment of undesirable staff turnover by means of using predictive analysis (Aschbacher,2024). Automated hiring uses machine learning algorithms to review cvs and evaluate candidates with the help of certain filters to match them with the most relevant jobs available. In the same way, the use of AI in an organization also helps in improving the candidate experience by answering questions, as well as in arranging interviews. As such, it not only relieved much pressure from the shoulders of HR professionals but it also made the process more efficient and systematic (Azam, et al. 2023).

However, the integration of AI into the HRM function has been done at a very fast pace, and this has brought several issues as to fairness, ethical issues, and regulations. A major disadvantage is that most AI models do not have mechanisms for explaining why they made specific decision: they are black boxes. This lack of interpretability raises questions and concerns to worthy questions for both the HR professionals or any professional in any corporate environment and the employees when it comes to issues of hires, promotions, and performance appraisals (Papagiannidis et al.2023). These conclusions can be highly beneficial," But such decisions are created by algorithms, and as such, reflect the biases found in the historical data inputted into it have biases and can therefore have racist or sexist decisions. For example, if the data used for training such an AI model involves gender or racial discrimination, it is likely that the model will be discriminative in its operation by hiring people of a particular race or gender. Due to lack of openness, such biases are not easily identifiable or correct, which is detrimental to the trust placed on AI supported HR procedures (Yanamala, 2023).

The main ethical issue that has received attention regarding AI in the field of HRM is fairness. Employees and potential candidates have found it unpalatable when they cannot comprehend the workings of an AI system. Some people have been locked out of employment opportunities or denied a deserved promotion by an algorithm and the policy allows an affected individual to discover what policy caused the action (Vereb, 2025). However, these fragile models contain no explainability and as such, the L&D industry is unable to understand how these models reach decisions for action. What is more, if there is no clear disclosure of the reasons, many employees tend to lose faith in the decisions made within the HR departments which negatively contributes to the overall organizational culture and employees' satisfaction levels. For that reason, organizations that have not incorporated fairness mechanisms with their AI systems are likely to engage in discrimination lawsuits and damage control (Du, 2024)

In order to curb these challenges, Explainable AI (XAI) has been identified as the solution to drive transparency and accountability in the application of AI in HRM. XAI can come in handy in understanding how the outcome was arrived at since it educates the HR professionals on how the models are assessing the data. These approaches enhance the possibility of making proactive and accurate decisions concerning AI implementations, gauge biases of the HR staff and rectify them judiciously in case. For instance, if an AI model opted out a candidate for a certain reason, XAI will be able to single out that factor, thus giving an opportunity to the HR teams to reconsider it and fairness. Thus, the application of interpretable AI in the organization can help eliminate bias and encourage ethical decision-making in handling human resources management (Hofeditz,, et al 2022).

Table 1. Growth of AI Applications in HRM Across Industries

Industry	AI Application Areas in HRM	Growth Rate (%) (Last 5 Years)
IT & Technology	Automated recruitment, skill assessment, employee retention analytics	85%
Healthcare	AI-driven workforce scheduling, predictive hiring, performance monitoring	78%
Finance & Banking	Fraud detection in payroll, AI-powered talent acquisition, employee risk analysis	72%
Retail & E-commerce	AI chatbots for employee support, demand-based workforce optimization	68%
Manufacturing	Predictive HR analytics, AI-driven safety compliance monitoring	65%

Figure 1. Conceptual Framework for AI Transparency in HRM

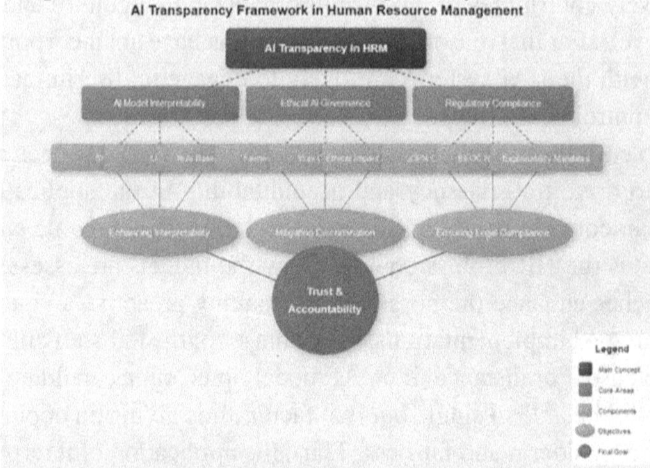

To enhance the understanding of the potential areas in which AI transparency may be applied in HRM, figure 1 presents a conceptual framework of the same. It includes three major modules; interpretability of the model, AI Ethics, and regulation. AI model interpretability guarantees that HR professionals and employees can counter-check via several methods such as Shapley Additive Explanations [SHAP] values, Local Interpretable Model-agnostic Explanations [LIME], and rules model. It involves constant defining, training and testing of AI models with end-user feedback and organization goals as well as ethical principles interlinked in a loop.

Besides the legal consideration, more proactive measures are needed from the organizations for the improvement of the current state of AI transparency in the field of HRM (Faheem, 2024). One of the ways that can be employed to achieve this is by integrating fairness audits and biases check mechanisms to the AI systems. Periodic review moreover allow for recognizing of Bias in the models and for sustaining fair decision-making procedures in the systems. Moreover, it is also necessary for the HR departments to come up with some polices as to how these recommendations are applied in matters related to hiring, promotion, and even performance evaluations. AI should properly be seen as a means to support management as a process involving decision-making by various agents. In simple terms, this means that organizations ought to strike a balance between automation and human monitoring in order to develop a very much ethical HRM (Bankins, 2021).

However, perhaps the most pressing factor in a company that needs to maintain its transparency is awareness among the employees. There is a need for the organization to inform the employees how the AI-based HR systems work and how decisions are made. Giving the employees an ability to understand the reason behind auto generated AI suggestion also helps to build a positive attitude towards AI by the Human Resource department. Thirdly, there should be training in AI ethical practices for working professionals in human resources so that they can make an understanding of how to manage systems that are driven by AI at their company (Andrieux, et al. 2024).

In order to facilitate the quality and relevance of this chapter, a leaner and a more focused structure has been used. Now the analysis goes straight to the key issues in identifying the very functions of HR that are most affected by AI, that is, recruitment, performance management, and workforce planning. For the purpose of this study, Rapid Literature Scan was taken and more than 40 peer reviewed articles and recent industry's reports published between 2022-2025 were reviewed. This scan draws the most recent evidence about the rate of AI adoption, effectiveness, and challenges in HRM in the discussion so that the discussion is based on the recent findings. Practical parts form an addition: case studies about application of AI in recruitment and performance evaluation of such companies like IBM and Walmart, notating the benefits and risks of AI by HR process (Abdelrahman, 2023). In this regard, some of the popularly implemented AI tools-Workday for the analysis of workforce, Hirevue for automated interviewing and Pymetrics for talent assessment-are now integrated to demonstrate how such technologies are applied to the practical decision-making. If such information is available, the information on short interviews and expert commentary, provided by the HR practitioners is added to increase practitioner insights. This restructuring provides much more concise, evidence-based and in practice-oriented analysis straight to the forepoint of the main challenges and opportunities for AI integration into HRM.Integration of AI in some of the key HR operations is particularly discussed in this chapter; three of which are: recruitment; performance management and; workforce planning. In recruitment, issues of use of algorithmic screening and automated decision-making are bound to surface when AI-driven applicant tracking systems and chatbots are commonly used in filtering candidates for job opening and developing job descriptions and interview scheduling. For performance management, AI systems are being more and more used for data-driven assessment, feedback, and predictions of value-oriented behavior of the workers and the possibility of their turnover. In workforce planning, AI-enabled analytics platforms are used to predict staff requirements, employee skill gap and a successful succession plan. The main difficulties of the AI integration exist at several levels (Albahri, 2023). The design of algorithms in which bias and opacity could be implemented; data interpretation in which quality of input data matter and have outcomes; decision-making authority of whether an organization should trust in automation or keep human oversight; and lastly, ethical oversight for which standards of fairness, privacy, and accountability must be met. That the HR functions are defined explicitly and levels at which AI issues continue at an explicit level in the chapter, a focused and analytically strong base toward the opportunities and risks of AI in modern human resource management is established.

2. THE ROLE OF AI IN HUMAN RESOURCE MANAGEMENT

The use of AI in Human Resource Management has been an essential transformation in conventional working practices that enhance the livelihood of working practices. AI applications in HRM span across recruitment, talent management, employee engagement, and performance appraisal. These technologies incorporate machine learning, NLP and applications of preditive models to facilitate the tasks and information processing of human resources to minimize the required time, effort and to deliver faithful insights and decisions. But as it has appeared, the use of AI has proven to have some downsides in terms of fairness, transparency and trust which are discussed below.

Table 2. Comparative Analysis of AI-Driven and Traditional HR Practices

HR Function	Traditional HR Practices	AI-Driven HR Practices	Key Benefits of AI Implementation	Limitations of AI Implementation
Recruitment	Manual resume screening, interviewer bias	AI-based resume parsing, chatbot interaction	Faster hiring, reduced bias	Risk of algorithmic bias, lack of explainability
Talent Management	Subjective performance reviews, generic training programs	AI-driven skill assessment, personalized career paths	Improved talent retention, customized learning	Perceived lack of human touch, potential data misinterpretation
Performance Appraisal	Annual evaluations, subjective manager ratings	AI-based real-time performance monitoring	Objective assessments, immediate feedback	Privacy concerns, employee distrust
Employee Engagement	Periodic surveys, in-person HR consultations	AI-driven sentiment analysis, virtual HR assistants	Enhanced accessibility, proactive issue resolution	Confidentiality concerns, lack of emotional intelligence

Recruitment is perhaps one of the clear areas where the use of AI in HRM has become rather apparent. Employment searching technologies involve the utilization of artificial intelligence that enables the analysis of numerous resumes to find out which candidate is most suitable for the position as per the given specifications. They decrease the time that may be taken while conducting screening manually and also eliminate some bias in shortlisting candidates. Recruitment is thus made more efficient through chatbots and virtual assistants that respond to the applicants' questions and book interviews for them (Řepová, et al.2024). Nevertheless, there are several drawbacks associated with artificial intelligence-based forms of recruitment. Machine learning models obtained from past hirings may also embed some bias into the model, and hence perpetrate discrimination later on. In addition to this, some of the disadvantages of the use of artificial intelligence include; First, it has been known to diminish the amount of trust in the selection process since candidates have no idea on how the results or decisions are made by artificial intelligence (Langer, et al 2023).

Figure 2. Impact of AI Adoption on Employee Trust and Organizational Credibility

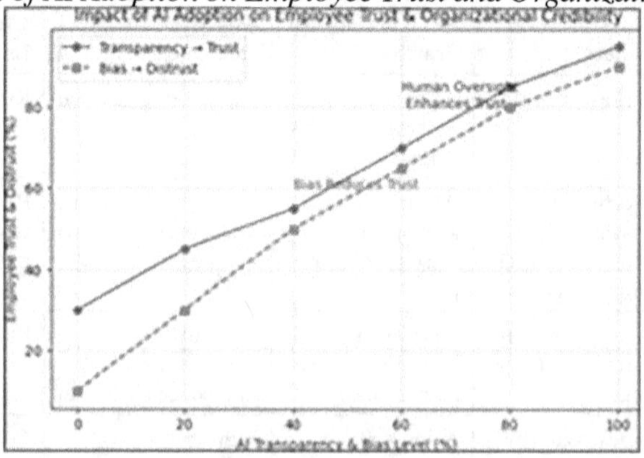

Figure 2 present the correlation between AI adoption in HRM and its effect on the level of trust from the employees and credibility of companies. From the above framework, it is evident that there are aspects like transparency, fairness, and human interventions in deciding the various aspects of the AI-driven HRM. The diagram shows that when AI models are explainable and not biased, the employee partage trust in the decision making of the HR department hence improvement in engagement and organization believability. Nevertheless, when the AI presentation or performance is not very transparent or the AI decision-making is perceived as biased, employees are likely to resist the change and the organization suffers both in terms of reputation and effectiveness of the AI system.

However, it can be concluded that beyond the processes of recruitment, AI is also essential for talent management, and other aspects associated with efficient workforce. Thereby, the utilization of AI in talent management may be perceived as such a systemized process that destroys the human touch, emotional intelligence, and human discretion. The main issue is the conflict between AI-based analysis and human-centered strategies for developing a healthy culture at the workplace (Fiegler-Rudol, 2025).

Performance appraisal is one of the areas where artificial intelligence has made its influence felt in HRM. The conventional performance appraisal tactics present themselves with issues of subjectivity, reliability, and biasness from the management. The key benefits of using AI for performance assessments include; Use of quantitative performance measurements, scores and KPIs, and employee feedback to make the evaluations more efficient. Also, the performance can be monitored constantly by an AI; the system can give feedback to the workers and suggest the way of their further training. However, the usage of the automated performance assessments also brings some issues that are considered to be equality and privacy-related. Employees may also always be in a one way feel that they are being monitored by one or the other AI systems feeling that one's performance data can be misused (Park, 2021).

AI implementation in HRM goes beyond streamlining the various processes of the company to the improvement of its employees' morale and welfare. Surveys, emails and messages sent through workplace applications are analyzed by AI-based tools for determining the morale and satisfaction of the employees. AI chatbots are also employed in HR roles to answer the employees' questions, explain policies or help remedy the disputes. These tools enhance the ability of the HR division to access and respond to their customers in the organization leading to improvements in the general organizational culture. On the other hand, the workers may have concerns since talking to AI-based HR systems could mean that their opinions might not be kept confidential or that AI may not be able to provide the needed emotional support in dealing with relevant issues (Vishwanath et al 2023).

Nevertheless, it should also be noted that there are some challenges that are associated with the integration of AI in HRM. This dependence on the use of AI brings about some ethical issues when it comes to the use of data in decision-making. This creates skepticism among the staff about the effectiveness of the artificial intelligence recommendations that we give and the level of supervision involved in assisting the Human Resource processes. Such considerations imply that organizations must create AI models that are interpretable and built in a way that took into consideration the ethical aspects allied to human values. In addition, the best practice is to use AI as an adjunct to judgment and not a substitute for it to optimize the use of AI and minimize its drawbacks (Aguinis, 2024).

Historical Evolution, Literature, and Case-Based Perspectives in AI-HRM

The use of AI in human resource management has been subject to a dramatic change during the last several decades, from the respective tools of automation to the state-of-the-art, data-driven approach (Prikshat, 2023). In the past, transformation has followed larger-scale technological progress in enterprise systems, where HR functions have been integrating digital processes for efficiency and strategic value which offers an overview of this metamorphosis with its phases of literature in which the attentions had shifted from administrative automisation to ethical and responsible AI implementation in HRM. This historical path allows seeing how the issues of fairness, trust, and transparency of decision-making have developed along with the technology advances .

Through a synthesized review of recent studies, amalgamation has been observed towards three main themes. opportunities for optimization, ethical niggles, and challenges of implementation. The AI based HR tools are divided into three categories:

recruitment, performance evaluation and workforce analytics; they observe the operational benefits of the tools while warning against reliance on it in the absence of the regulatory framework (Garg, 2022). Explainability is still quite at its infancy stage and is usually relegated to an afterthought rather than a key requirement in the design of HR technology. Transparency, accountability, and privacy remain a recurrent topic, especially when dealing with employees' data harvesting and autonomy when making choices.

Also, an increasing number of research investigate the ways in which the employees view and react to AI tools in HRM. The manner in which AI-based recruitment practices will amplify or reduce biases through design of algorithms and mechanisms of oversight. These insights of theory are supported by real case studies (Soleimani, 2025). An AI implementation brought major efficiencies in recruitment process but at the same time necessitated the change in governance to guarantee fairness. In the same way, the AI adoption transformed employee relationships in the organizations, demonstrating not only the strategic possibilities but also cultural disturbances that were brought about through automation (Tschang, 2021). Combining these perspectives gives a better idea of how AI is transforming HRM – it is not only a technical innovation, it is also a socio-organizational force that would have to be critically examined and contextually understood.

AI in HRM: Specific Functions, Mechanisms, and Empirical Evidence

Integration of AI in HRM is gaining a lot of momentum with 72% of the HR people adopting AI usage to meet a variety of functions as compared with 58% of the previous year. Some of the most popular HR practices that have been changed due to AI were recruitment, performance evaluation, employee engagement, and talent management. In recruitment, approximately 75% of companies use AI-based software for such processes as CV screening in batch mode, matching of candidates, and the use of chat-bots for communicating with the applicants. Precisely, 65% of the HR professionals use AI to create job descriptions, 42% for customizing job posting and 33% for screening resumes or communicating with applicants. During performance evaluation, AI systems assist predictive operation for turnover risk and keep on giving objective feedback. For engagement of the employees and developing their talents, AI-driven platforms personalise learning and keep track of employee sentiment. The methods of the AI's interaction with the HR are diverse and involve automation of the routine tasks, data-focused decisions, talent analytics, as well as algorithmic screening. Although, AI provides such advantages as enhanced efficiency, cost reduction, and more unbiased decisions, there are major concerns about bias and about AI systems propagating and even amplifying discriminatory practices, particularly in hiring and advancement (Zhang, 2024).

Figure 3. AI Adoption and Impact Across Key HR Functions

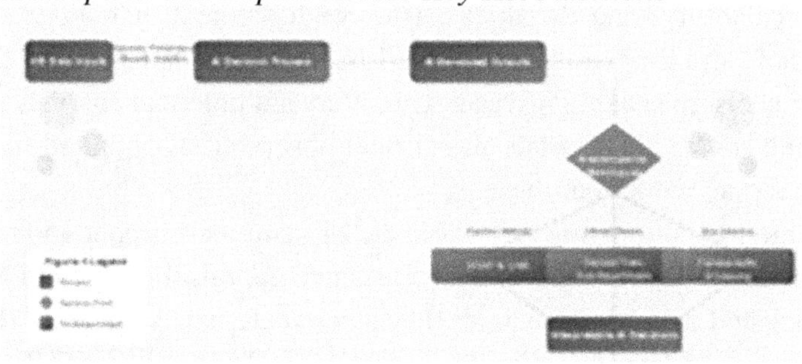

The real-world situations have demonstrated that the AI algorithms tend to copy already existing disparities unless they are controlled, and absence of transparency can create unsafe working environment. Organizations are, therefore, now relying on a variety of datasets, regular audits of the AI algorithms, human intervention, and the use of AI explainability and transparency when making AI-generated choices. This more precise and evidence-based approach gives an excellent analytical frame to conceive both the advantages and disadvantages of using AI in specific HR activities.

AI and HRM: Processes, Applications, and Decision Levels

AI is now actively being applied to several of the core HR processes and each of them has its peculiarities on opportunities and challenges for AI adoption. In recruitment, machine learning algorithms are applied to candidate screening, resume parsing, and automated interview scheduling, while chatbots are used to respond to candidate's inquiries and qualifying them. Performance evaluation utilizes the predictive analytics and data driven benchmarking to deliver a constant, objective performance feedback that automates the review cycles. AI-powered platforms provide customized learning, skills gap analysis, on-the-go assistance, for continuing enhancement and upskilling of the workforce in terms of employee engagement and talent development. In particular, the chapter addresses these HR domains-recruitment, performance appraisal, engagement, and talent management – with the presentation of the way AI tools are used in each of them. The examples of the discussed type of AI applications cover such models as machine learning models for the purpose of candidates' screening, chatbots for ensuring employees' queries, predictive analytics for turnover and performance, and decision-support systems in the area of strategic HR planning (Jafri, 2024). Importantly, the level of the

AI influence on the HR decision-making fluctuates. sometimes, AI operates as a support system and proposes advice to HR professionals, while in another case – it is a more independent tool in defining hiring, promotion, or retention choices. This difference is extremely important for realizing the advantages (efficiency, objectivity, scalability) and the threats (the reinforcement of bias, the challenge of transparency, and the possibility of the loss of human judgement). By making clear these aspects, the chapter gives a structured and practical analysis on the way AI is changing HRM; illustrations and critical observations obtained from current organizational practices about these.

AI techs are revolutionising the whole HRM from recruitment and talent management, employee engagement and performance appraisal. Although these tools fuel efficiency and data based insight, they also create new sources of risk around bias, transparency and trust. It is important for ethical and resultant HRM to strike a balance between automation and human check.

3. UNDERSTANDING TRANSPARENCY AND EXPLAINABLE AI (XAI) IN HRM

The integration of AI in work setting has impacted the HRM function by replacing many decision making roles in the process. However, technology advancement is a center of controversy because use of AI based HR systems call for a lot of questions concerning the credence of algorithmic decisions. Most of the AI models, particularly artificial neural networks and deep learning systems, work in a way that is rather hard to comprehend. This has negative effects in the sense that; It may lead to mistrust in the employees since information about what they are supposed to do is concealed from them; cases of bias and discrimination may occur since there is no clear cut guide that tells one what not to do; accountability is also answered to court since there are so many areas that are undefined that may lead to prosecution of employees. This is because Ex-plicable AI (XAI), as is now being implemented, is centered on the idea of rendering the AI decisions comprehensible and defendable so that HR experts are capable of inspecting and verifying the recommendations made by AI (Chamola, 2023).

Table 3. Common XAI Techniques and Their Relevance to HRM

XAI Technique	Type	Application in HRM	Benefits in HRM	Limitations
SHAP (Shapley Additive Explanations)	Post-hoc Interpretation	Hiring, promotions, performance evaluations	Identifies key decision factors, ensures fairness	Requires computational power, complex for non-experts
LIME (Local Interpretable Model-Agnostic Explanations)	Post-hoc Interpretation	Employee retention, recruitment analysis	Provides local model explanations, improves trust	May not generalize well for large datasets
Decision Trees	Intrinsic Interpretability	Succession planning, HR policy decisions	Simple, interpretable, easy to implement	Limited complexity, prone to overfitting
Rule-Based Models	Intrinsic Interpretability	Bias detection in hiring, automated compliance checks	Transparent, provides clear reasoning	Less effective for large datasets
Counterfactual Explanations	Interactive XAI	Employee promotions, diversity analytics	Provides alternative decision scenarios	Requires domain expertise for interpretation

XAI is a specific application of the overarching concept of AI and refers to the ability to explain the reason and process behind the outcomes related to HR actions such as recruitment, promotions, or evaluation of employee performance. It has been pointed out that transparency has to be given a critical role in AI-driven HRM in order to address such issues as fairness, compliance with of regulatory requirements, and trust. For instance, in the case of recruitment, when an AI predicts to select or reject an applicant, mechanisms of XAI will help to explain decision-making criteria like experience or skill match or results of behavioral tests. For example, in performance appraisals, it is possible to give justified ratings using AI-based evaluation systems with XAI methodologies instead of vague algorithms (Altukhi, 2025).

Figure 4. XAI Model for Fair and Accountable HRM Decision-Making

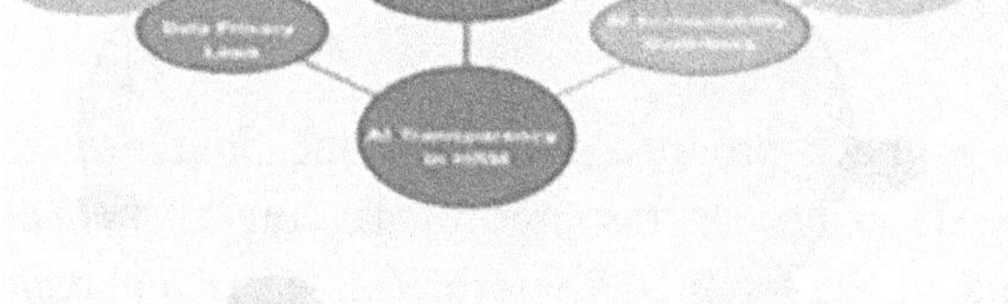

Fig 4 highlights a conceptual model of how XAI can be incorporated into the decision-making process at the HR department to ensure that the use of AI inputs could be explainable and thus fairness remains established in the decision-making process. The three-part model infers that all the components involved in the process are interlinked; the AI decision process, the XAI techniques, and the role of the HR professionals monitoring the system. The HR data inputs flow into the model include the resumes, employee performance, and the raw workforce data. Such inputs are feeding into AI models that can produce outputs which are on recruitment promotion or evaluation of employee's performance. However, all these decisions look opaque without explainability and are likely to attract criticism from the employer and other HRM practitioners.

In order to increase interpretability several methodologies have been created under XAI that are used in developing and implementing the AI-powered HRM systems. Methods like SHAP (SHAP (SHapley Additive exPlanations) and LIME ((Local Interpretable Model-agnostic Explanations)) applied after the training of the models can deconstruct the models that business AI provide into parts that are easier to understand. SHAP provides what degree of importance each feature affecting the AI decision to HR managers and can reveal which factors most contributed to a certain result. In contrast, LIME provides localized explanations for black-box AI models as it offers approximations of decisions made in hiring and employment evaluations, hence making it easier to understand patterns of decision-making (Hassija, 2024).

Another aspect that needs to be incorporated in the area of AI application in HRM is the explanation capabilities which enable the HR professionals to ask questions to the AI model. For instance, the HR teams can first utilize AI decision-making for hiring and present their conclusions in a more standard and simple to comprehend format for analysis of these reasons coupled with side-by-side comparison of the chosen candidates and declined contestants. Such high level of openness also ends up building up trust among the employees as well as improving the credibility of the organization (Ribeiro, Marco Tulio, et al. 2016).

Critical Synthesis and Research Gaps in XAI Frameworks for HRM

Although there is much progress evident in the literature on frameworks for explainable AI (XAI) in human resource management, such as the connection between SHAP and LIME for model interpretation and conceptual models connecting AI decision processes with HR oversight, glaring gaps still exist. Many of the existing frameworks emphasize technical transparency, compliance with the regulation but lack complete mechanisms of integration of XAI outputs into real HR decision-making processes. For instance, even though models, such as the AI

Human Resource Transparency Model and the extended Transparency by Design (TbD), take interpretability and accuracy into account, there is little guidance on how HR professionals would go about acting upon AI explanations, especially in multi-faceted cases, whereby there are conflicting notions of ethical, legal, and organizational imperatives. Moreover, the existing research gap in the determination of the real-world impact of XAI on employee trust, organizational outcomes, and mitigation of bias also proceeds from the fact that the majority of the studies address theoretical or technical issues rather than conduct empirical validation of the problem in various HR contexts (Islam, 2024). As such, future research should go beyond descriptions and critically examine the usefulness of the existing XAI frameworks in practice as well as propose new approaches that can connect algorithmic transparency with a fair HR management, which may lead to action.

Practical Challenges and Illustrative Integration of XAI in HRM

Though XAI frameworks have potentials for increasing the transparency in AI-driven HR systems, practical obstacles impede those potentials in the real world. One of the top priority problems is the inevitable relation between the complex model's interpretability and its performance – the more interpretable models tend to perform worse when applied to voluminous unstructured data typical for HRM. Imaging as well that even where tools such as SHAP and LIME are used, the technicality of their outputs might be suffocating and confusing to non-expert HR professionals, therefore, making it impossible for them to perform effectively based on explanations provided. Another risk lies in simplifications which had been made for the sake of clarity that may cause misinterpretations or cover up important nuances in decision-making. To overcome these limitations it is important that organisations plug XAI explanations in operational HR workflows and make sure that such outputs are accompanied by actionable advice. For example, a systemic alignment of XAI outputs with real-life use cases like short-listing of candidates or performance appraisal can help HR professionals to realize both reasons for AI choices as well as whether human intervention would be necessary or not. It also has its cost in training, cross-functional partnership, and iterative feedback mechanisms for perfecting the technology itself and its use (Forat, 2024). Such illustrative, contextual integration is one of the vital tools of transition from the transparency of theory to the practical work of practice that is responsible.

Applied AI in HRM: Case Studies, Technical Depth & Practices of Implementation

Some of the leading companies have managed to integrate the AI technologies into the diverse HRM functions, which are the real examples of both successes and difficulties. For example, Unilever has adopted AI to screen resumes and do asynchronous video interviews that see time taken to hire reduced by 75% and increased diversity in the selection of candidates. Hilton uses AI-based chatbots for the first interaction with its applicants, as well as AI video platforms to ensure the candidate's compatibility has been reduced, decreasing the recruitment duration of six weeks to five days. Accenture uses AI to customize performance management to provide real-time feedback and developmental path on a 30% increased effectiveness reporting. On the same note, Walmart also uses AI to provide individualized training programs for the growth of employees while IBM capitalizes on the use of NLP-based tools such as Watson Workspace to examine the data of communication, enhancing the dynamics for team engagements. Manipal Health Enterprises has adopted MiPAL, an AI assistant to automate HR query, thus increasing the speed of response and satisfaction of its employees. TeamSense's AI-powered Policy Assistant is able to assist employees in retrieving HR policy information at an instant, which points to increasing trend towards use of conversational AI tools. Upon which, these applications are based are such technologies as machine learning, NLP and robotic process automation, which fuel predictive hiring, individualized development, and workforce analytics. Inspite of such progresses, changes are still there, ranging from bias in training data and lack of algorithmic transparency to the fear of their employees about surveillance and data privacy. Some of the best practices on implementation of AI include: integration of AI strategies and business goals; improving data governance; sensitization of human resource personnel on AI literacy; installation of robust change management systems; development of new ideas and innovations, and adoption of AI solutions. These case studies emphasize the two pronged nature of using AI to its benefits while infusing ethical, transparent, and inclusive systems across the HR lifecycle (Firoz, 2024).

Besides the short terms benefits, future inquiry is seen in exploring the long-term effects of AI incorporation in HR systems. Longitudinal studies, such as the ones done by IBM and Accenture, have measured the impact of AI tools on employee engagement, workplace satisfaction, adaptability of the organization, etc. over a few years. These studies confirm that long-term use of AI can help to make personalization of the workforce and retention better, but also can lead to increased employees' concern about monitoring and algorithmic bias if not controlled. On the technical side of things, algorithms such as natural language processing (NLP) are employed to analyse textual data given from employees and their communication tendencies, machine learning models are used to apply predictive analytics in attrition risk, skill mapping and career development among other aspects. Other companies also combine robotic process automation (RPA) to get automation in areas of repetitive administrative HR work thereby leaving the human resources for strategic jobs. The introduction of these systems requires organized change management measures, such as constant training of the employees, transparency regarding the AI goals and possibility of feedback that would enable improvement on a periodic basis. There is a great deal of dependency with following AI-HRM deployment success on creating ethical governance setups that center on fairness, explainability, data accountability, and human intervention when it comes to governance. Integrating these ethical principles in designing and rollout of algorithms guarantees not only adherence but also long-term trust and culture of the organization (Lewicka, 2024).

Use of explainable AI (XAI) methods like SHAP and LIME are important for ensuring that HR decision based on AI are clear and easy to comprehend. By seeing how AI models come to their conclusions, organizations can generate trust among the employees, follow regulations and also promote fairer HR practices.

4. ETHICAL AND LEGAL CONSIDERATIONS IN AI-ASSISTED HRM

Privacy issues are also a major area of ethical concern in the implementation of AI in HRM since these technology systems amass and process data of employees. From the management of human resources to estimation of employee's attitudes and behaviors through the use of artificial neural networks, AI is capable of violating privacy rights in the society. It is important to consider employees' privacy when there is large scale observational capacity of their workplace or organizational behavior or when decision making is automated in a manner that may affect their job status. To meet the ethical standards, organizations must adopt sound policies that govern the process of data collection, storage and usage; employees' consent and protection of data. Employing transparent data management processes such as Explainable Artificial Intelligence (XAI) for the purpose of describing the rationale behind the HR decision with respect to the data collected regarding employees, can go a long way in managing privacy concerns (Langer, et al.2022).

Figure 5. Regulatory Landscape for AI Transparency in HRM

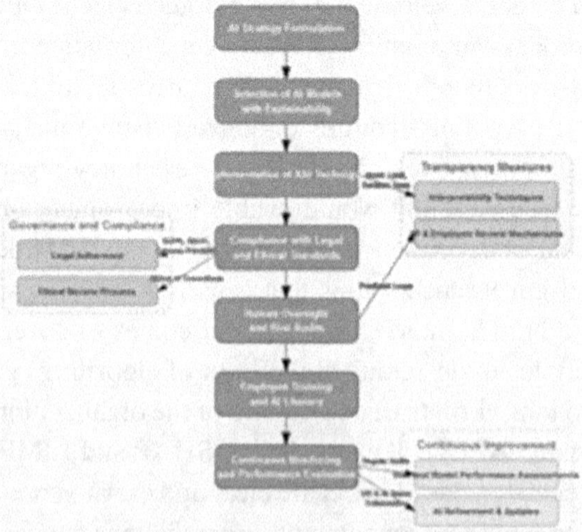

Figure 5 illustrates the legal aspect that shows how the different legal frameworks contribute to promoting transparency of AI in HRM. Laws help determine how AI will be adopted in the human resource processes so that employment decisions made involving AI are legal, fair, and ethical. Al center, there is AI-assisted HRM; on the surrounding circumference, there are three regulatory circles: data protection legislation, anti-discrimination measures, and AI responsibility standards.

The current best practices on AI accountability, as the European Commission's proposed AI Act, help outline roles and responsibilities for companies using AI in Human Resource Management. Hiring and employment-related decision making will be defined by these guidelines to make sure that AI models applied in the process are transparent, explainable, and if possible, managed by human overseers. According to the best practices for AI governance, there should be a mechanism for the HR professionals to step in and handle an improper application of AI in making decisions occasionally (Papagiannidis, 2023).

Critical Tensions and Real-World Implications of Opaque AI in HRM

The practical implications of the opaque, black box AI in the HRM are brightly presented by a number of high-profile cases. For instance, the automated recruitment tool that Amazon used dragged its operations after being discovered having been systematically downgrading resumes having women's colleges or female-related terms, which shows how lack of explainability can facilitate the existence of historical bias and discriminatory outcomes unnoticed. This did not only surface Amazon to risks of reputational loss but also the risk of litigation by anti-discrimination laws. On the same note, the AI-powered hiring platform HireVue was under the spotlight by the regulators and the public fury after implementing the construction of transparency-less algorithms for facial examination, bringing the matter of violation of privacy, fairness and GDPR-compliance to the fore. These cases present the practical risks: when HR fails to provide explanations or justification to AI decisions the organizations become liable to lawsuits and regulatory penalties and break down the trust with the employees (Mujtaba, 2025).

These are some real-world failures which illustrate 3 important tensions in AI-driven human resource management.

The first one is the contradiction between trust and efficiency. AI based models that provide high levels of accuracy can greatly scale down the process of hiring and assessment of performance. But in the case when these models are not transparent, employees can feel alienated or doubtful of decisions that are being made. This breakdown of trust can discourage the employees and thus lower the overall levels of acceptance of AI tools in the organization.

The second tension that goes on is compliance versus innovation. Organizations in many cases are always in a hurry to test the limits of AI capability to get an advantage in the market. However, without substantial explainability, these improvements can result in the breaches of the legal and ethical standards. It is difficult to be compliant to regulation when there can not be proper justification for decisions and this exposes one to penalties and litigation.

The third one is in between fairness and predictive power. Systems of AI that are striving for maximum accuracy usually use the data from the past that can include biasing. Consequently, such systems will only increase, or even escalate, the preexisting inequality. This undermines fairness in HR decision making, and may cause serious ethical issues and legal implications to the organization (Fenwick, 2024).

Cultural Shifts and Employee Reactions to AI in HRM

Beyond compliance to the regulations, the investment of Artificial Intelligence in the HRM is transformationally remodeling the workplace culture and employee experiences. AI-powered tools are disrupting the way organization communicates, collaborates and interacts with their workforce with real-time sentiments of the employee and providing personalized support. Nevertheless, there come new difficulties with these changes. Employees have anxiety or frown upon automation, as they fear losing their jobs, becoming obsolete in terms of skill, or are apprehensive of the loss of personal agency in decision-making. Emotions like skepticism, mistrust or eventual disengagement may come forth especially when AI-driven decisions seem not to be transparent or at least to undermine the status quo power relations. For instance, employees might feel marginalized in case algorithmic recommendations are accepted instead of human decisions or when they believe that AI is a means of enhanced surveillance instead of something that would help them. To take steps in alleviating these concerns, major organization is investing in AI education programs, open lines of communication and participatory designs that engage the employees in acquiring new technologies among others. The support of open dialogue about a purpose and limitations of AI in organizations, and the integration of AI initiatives into the core values of an organization, HR leaders can prevent resistance, trust building, and incorporate technological innovation as a complement, and not as a disruption of the workplace culture. This is a cultural transition-to a more data-driven, the inclusive, and emotionally intelligent HR environment – as important for smooth AI adoption as legal compliance (Chin, 2024).

Some of the methods for alleviating such tensions in the organizations include the adoption of explainable AI (XAI) approaches, having frequent bias audits, and ensuring that there is human monitoring of important HR decisions. Focus on openness and stakeholder engagement does not only reduce the risk, but also enhances credibility and long-term viability of the organization.

Some of the ethical and legal issues of AI-driven HRM have to do with bias, privacy, and accountability. Obedience to such rules as GDPR and EEOC is necessary, and it is necessary for organizations to adopt strong governance structures for fair, explainable, and responsible use of AI in HR processes.

5. CASE STUDIES: TRANSPARENT AI IN HRM PRACTICES

AI has incorporated into the management of the human resource in organizations, and the use of AI has brought the following ethical and legal issues which organizations should consider in their operations. It is apparent that AI is used in HRM to improve recruitment, performance appraisal, and employee staffing, yet AI is characterized by sophistication, and its operations are sometimes ethically questionable and can lead to biases. The first one of the discussed ethical concerns refers to prejudice in algorithms as the AI is created by sampling historical information from the workforce (Chen,2023).

An analysis of industry leaders shows the practical difference that transparent and explainable AI make in HRM. For instance, Walmart has adopted AI-driven tools to ensure optimization of employee scheduling and payroll management, resulting in a substantial cut-down in labor cost, as well as deployments of generative AI chatbots to support associates in handling daily duties and simplify the healthcare insurance claims processing. These schemes do not only improve the level of efficiency of the operations but also guarantee that the staff members comprehend and trust the results produced by AI systems because transparency is incorporated within design and communication of these tools. In the same way, IBM has changed its HR processes by using AI-enabled digital assistants (such as HiRo) that turn complex tasks such as promotion series and compensation suggestions into the automated explainable process. IBM focuses on ethical and responsible AI utilization that helps HR specialists and etc. to receive clear, practical insights and guarantee transparency at decision-making stages (Sainila, 2024). Panasonic has on the other hand deployed the PX-AI assistant to a vast global workforce using the explainable AI to optimize the efficiency of operations and instigate trust in AI made recommendations across various business domains. These practical examples illustrate how top organizations do not only implement AI in HRM, but also focus on transparency and explainability to instigate trusts among the employees and stakeholders.

Implementation of open AI in the sphere of HRM is demonstrated by real-world case studies both as the advantage and as a challenge. The best practices are the frequent bias audits, the involvement of the employees, as well as excellent communication about the AI-driven decisions, which can only increase the trust and establish more credibility in the organization.

6. THE TRADE-OFFS BETWEEN AI TRANSPARENCY AND PERFORMANCE

One key problem arises where organizations adopt the application of Artificial Intelligence in Human Resource Management: where to find, and set up, the right level of transparency for more predictive performance. On the other hand, there are models which are easier to interpret like the decision trees and logistic regression, but do not have the level of complexity required in analyzing the HR data (Masum, Muhammad H., et al. 2018).

The need for explainability in AI stems from ethical and regulatory demands. Organizations also need to ensure that the decisions made by computers are not prejudiced in some way and are compliant with company standards. Challenges such as GDPR and EEOC direct that the use of artificial intelligence should be transparent more so when used in employment-related decisions. However, having higher levels of explainability come at the cost of model's complexity and performance. It is advisable to consider the trade-off because transparent models may not uncover intricate patterns within a workforce in the same way black-box models can do (Heidemann,, 2024).

When comparing AI models that are transparent to those that are not, there are certain differences in performance relative to HRM. Some models like the linear regression and decision trees offer the HR professional directions that the provider of the work opportunity followed in making decisions of hiring and promotions. However, they could have limitations when dealing with range and mass HR unstructured data such as resume, behavioral test and rating. On the other hand, the complex models like, random forest, gradient boosting machines and deep learning are capable of giving higher accuracy as they are capable of learning deeper into the data. However, they create a situation in which it becomes difficult to justify why this or that candidate was chosen for an interview or why an employee got particular numerical rating for his or her performance (Balcioğlu, 2024).

A good example of reducing the trade-off above is the use of both fully explainable and fully accurate AI models. Two techniques: Shapley Additive Explanations (SHAP) and Local Interpretable Model-Agnostic Explanations (LIME) has been developed to generate explanations for black-box models in a way that are understandable by humans. Another strategy that can be adopted by organizations is model distillation, where the organization trains a sub model which is an imitation of the AI model and is less complex than the actual AI model. In this way, it is possible to improve the best practices of using AI in HRM while increasing transparency as well (Jamal, 2024).

Another area where its significant trade-off between accuracy and explainability is found is on the bias mitigation strategies that include AI. Although adding explanation may be beneficial in getting rid of biases, there are negative effects because interpretability comes with decreased general classification accuracy. For instance, imposing a high degree of fairness in relation to performance on the hiring algorithm means that hiring predictiveness cannot be optimized. The case further presents challenges to companies on whether to achieve accountability and fairness in decision-making at the expense of potential lower accuracy (Farinu, 2025)

The extent to which employees trust is affected and the level of AI adoption is another consideration that needs to be taken into consideration. Decision making by artificial intelligence is embraced by employees where one is able to comprehend the parameters that informed the conclusion by the intelligent system. High accuracy, but low transparency of the model can lead to its distrust and non-acceptance, while slightly lower accuracy, but high interpretability – to the acceptance of processes involving the use of artificial intelligence in HRM (). Thus, organizations need to achieve a balance between its objectives that are related to the accuracy of the model and the interpretability to make the workforce management of AI both fair and effective.

The data elaborate a usual relationship in DL where higher complexity results in higher accuracy but at the same time lower interpretability. For instance, models including linear regression and decision trees possibly offer good interpretations while they are not scalable for large datasets in the field of HR. On the contrary, neural networks and GBMs have relatively better accuracy rates but are mostly opaque models that require further use of explainability methods (Yu, 2022).

From Concept to Practice: XAI Decision Flows in HR Organizational Realities

As much as legal foundations and ethical fundamentals are needed, the reality of the effectiveness of XAI in HRM can only be realized through implementation and handling of these systems in companies. Employees' acceptance of XAI tools usually relies on effective communication, open structure of responsibility, and continuous learning. For instance, upon adoption of the XAI-powered performance reviews by a multinational retailer, HR leaders established a cross functional committee comprising HR, IT and employee representatives to be in charge of algorithmic fairness and avenue for appeals. Such internal accountability did not only enhance the sense of trust but also led to regular audits of the AI recommendations and channelling them based on the feedback from the employees.

In order to visualize the trade-offs between transparency and performance, Table 4 below summarizes ways in which the AI models currently are selected for implementation and monitored in practice to achieve balance between interpretability, accuracy and suitability to the purpose (regulatory requirements). There are a regular sequence of decisions in an HR department. from data entry and choice of model to explainer checks and ultimate HR decisions and discussions with employees.

Such practical steps indicate that XAI adoption success presupposes technical compliance among other things. it requires a change of HR culture to a shared responsibility, iterative learning, and transparent decision making-up. By considering how XAI is actually implemented in HR departments instead of thinking about it as simple definition that includes all the aspects involved, organizations can be better prepared for such challenges as the acceptance of employees, performance trade-offs and continued accountability.

Presumption is an intrinsic price of the accuracy of complex AI models and the interpretability of the simpler and more see-through ones. It is important for organizations to carefully weigh their priorities and balance off the predictive power with the need for explainability so that an effective and trusted HRM outcome is attained.

7. FRAMEWORK FOR IMPLEMENTING TRANSPARENT AI IN HRM

The elements of transparency when applied to AI utilized in the HR management processes can only be achieved under a systematized approach that has to incorporate technical, managerial and legal considerations. XAI applied in the HRM context makes decisions reasonable, comprehensible and transparent. There should be a clear framework consisting of a number of steps that organizations could follow in order to set objectives, identify the suitable AI models, implement interpretability techniques, and address the challenges related to legal frameworks and ethical concerns. The development of such a framework helps foster trust among the employees, reduces prejudices that might be existing in the company and increases organizational credibility (Hanna., et al. 2024).

Several critical steps are involved in order to adopt a well-structured HI approach in the implementation of HRM. AI in HRM is initiated where AI can be implemented effectively to influence organizational outcomes which are; recruitment, performance evaluation, and workforce planning. Companies must then identify AI models that provide higher accuracy to a level that the organization needs while being as easily explainable as possible. Specifically, the techniques like SHAP (Shapley Additive Explanations), LIME (Local Interpretable Model-Agnostic Explanations), and decision trees can be adopted for making AI-aided HR processes more interpretable. When choosing the models appropriate and ready for implementation, HR in collaboration with the AI department should design an ethical AI governance framework that incorporates the key elements of transparency within its circulation processes (De Almeida, 2021). As such, there is the need to get support from managerial angles as a way of ensuring the success of the transparent AI in HRM. To some extent, HR leaders must ensure that change by raising AI awareness by bringing awareness of the use of AI-based systems in HR and how they operate and affect the decisions made. Inclusively, Organizations should continue to communicate concerning the uses of AI in the Human Resource and clarify how its decisions are arrived at, and ensure the affected people have an appeal method when using the system. This paper suggests how policies of human resource departments can support the values of XAI and ensure that Artificial Intelligence supports organizational objectives (Langer, 2022).

Figure 6. Roadmap for Ethical and Transparent AI Deployment in HRM

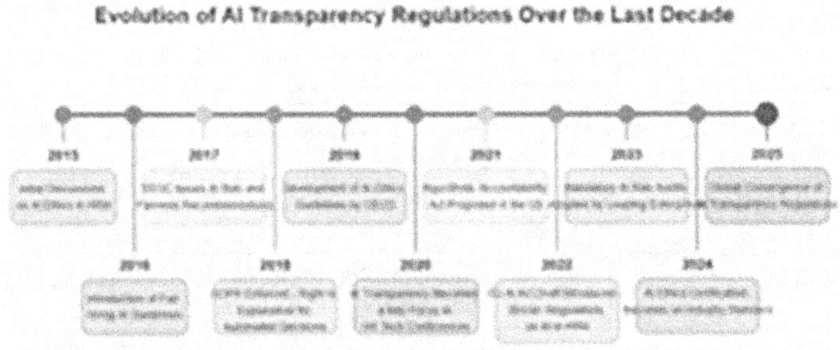

The strategic plan of employing ethical and transparent AI in human resource management identifies the systematic process for implementing AI in human resource management. The figure illustrates a flowchart of the process from AI strategy, choosing an adequate model, where explainability should be incorporated, how compliance with legal requirements should be placed, and how monitoring should be conducted continuously. So it call for the united sharers between the HR professionals, the expertise contacts in AI as well as the legal department to harmonize the trustworthy AI surroundings. Also, the roadmap also shows feedback loops that can be conducted periodically to ensure that employees and the Human Resource departments review the AI models, thus making sure that transparency measures are well checked and maintained in the long run. Legal requirements constitute an important factor especially for the integration of XAI in the setting of the HRM. Being in accordance with such legal requirements as GDPR and EEOC is crucial for being fair and transparent in the usage of AI in HR sphere. Mitigation for the worrisome notion is that organizations have to put in place systems for auditing the AI decisions so that based on some circumstances, HR professionals and employees can scrutinize and contest the automated results where necessary. It is also worth mentioning that periodic assessments and bias audits can also supplement the work of AI in increasing its reliability regarding issues of discriminant analytics in terms of hiring, promotions, and performance evaluations (Landers, et al, 2023).

Table 4. Step-by-Step Framework for Implementing XAI in HRM

Step	Action	Key Considerations
1	Identify AI-Applicable HR Functions	Determine areas such as recruitment, performance appraisal, and workforce planning where AI can enhance efficiency.
2	Select AI Models with Explainability	Choose models that balance accuracy and transparency, such as decision trees or models using SHAP and LIME.
3	Implement AI Governance Policies	Develop guidelines for ethical AI use, ensuring accountability and fairness in decision-making.
4	Ensure Regulatory Compliance	Align AI usage with GDPR, EEOC, and other relevant regulations to prevent biases and ensure fairness.
5	Integrate Human Oversight Mechanisms	Allow HR professionals to audit, review, and challenge AI decisions when necessary.
6	Train Employees on AI Transparency	Educate employees about AI-driven HR processes and provide channels for feedback and concerns.
7	Monitor and Continuously Improve	Conduct regular bias audits, update AI models, and ensure continuous transparency in HR applications.

When adopted and implemented through an ethically and transparently defined framework, AI in the field of HRM is highly advantageous to organisations as far as its risks are concerned. This essentially involves outlining measures whereby P's can track the effectiveness of the strategies implemented in as far as AI transparency is concerned, incorporation of cross functional teams on the same and setting up of cross sectional mechanisms towards AF monitoring over time. The implementation of transparency goals in AI adoption helps organizations gain the trust of the employees and enhance their satisfaction level while at the same time the organizations adhere to the relevant rules and regulations governing the provision of services by artificial intelligence in the field of Human Resource management (Mwita, 2025).

Evolving Trends, Implementation Frameworks, and Trust-Building in AI-Driven HRM

The ever-changing revolution of AI in HRM has brought in newer frameworks and empirical models that are to be more flexible in integration, ethical in implementation, and long term time involving the employee. Firms such as Panasonic have led the way in using AI-powered employee engagement analytics, drawing from sentiments analysis and behavioural data to paint a picture of morale in the workforce and direct decisions by the leadership. This initiative is said to have increased team cohesion and productive work through strategic management option. Likewise, SAP uses AI to draw unique paths for learning and developing according to the performance and role necessities and enhances upskilling completion rates. On the implementation side, models of AI as a Service (AIaaS) including those by IBM Watson and AWS are allowing the organizations to plug in pre-trained

AI tools for screening of recruitments, classification of documents or chat-based assistance, without development of systems in-house. Other firms such as Siemens have followed suit in such decision trees that are data-driven to drive AI-supported promotions and internal mobility which help mitigate bias in career advancement. These technical implementations are complimented by AI-driven checklists such as the ones employed by Cisco that uses real time data to point out skill deficits as well as training requirement. Critically, these developments go hand in hand with trust building strategies. For instance, Panasonic did involve employee representatives in the designing stage of its AI engagement tool and SAP promotes transparency to employees through their dashboards that explain how decisions are made. Such integrated means reveal that algorithmic prowess is not the only key to a responsible and empowering AI adoption but also strategic congruity, ethical checkpoint, and inclusive messaging.

Case Studies and Employee Engagement in Ethical AI-HRM

To bring a balance between the technical complexity and the application, the HR professionals will gain from actionable frameworks to steer ethical AI integration. The stepwise implementation model is one popularly adopted model. (1) Lay down strategic objectives regarding the use of AI in HR; (2) identify AI tools that have embedded through modelling transparency and explainability features; (3) Conduct frequent bias audits and fairness reviews; (4) Create cross-functional ethics committees involving HR, IT, and legal experts; (5) Share AI's processes and decisions Take, for instance, the Office of Ethical and Humane Use Technology of Salesforce, which has set industry standards by utilizing real-time transparency dashboards together with the feedback mechanisms of employees; or, BASF's independent AI ethics advisory panel that is helpful for having the external oversight combined with the mitigation of bias in the HR analytics. From these cases, we can see that successful AI adoption also needs people's involvement-like participatory designing of the tools, opt-in feedback systems, and transparent appeals processes. Moving forward organisations are integrating AI ethics training into HR training, and using AI-generated engagement platform to individualised employee experience and drive trust. Through acquisition of these frameworks and learning from industry authorities, the HR practitioners can boldly venture into AI opportunities and challenges knowing that in use of the technology there is no replacing of human judgment and organizational values.

Accessible Implementation, Employee Engagement, and Future-Focused Strategies for AI in HRM

To make AI implementation in HRM effective and unintimidating, the professionals of HR need a practical step-by-step guide that leaves a healthy balance between being innovative and being accessible. Start with defining business objectives for the use of AI clear enough and then choose user friendly AI solutions having a pre-shedded light of transparency and explainability. Pilot such tools in partnership with representatives of cross-functional teams i.e. HR, IT and representatives of their employees to ensure alignment to organization's values and expectation of their employees. Conduct bias audits and fairness assessments on regular basis as well as create open communication channels on explaining AI driven decisions to staff. Real-life examples, such as SAP's ethical AI handbook and Salesforce's Office of Ethical and Humane Use, have proven that involving the employees into the design, provision of training for the users, as well as implementations of feedback loops lead to trust and adoption. In addition to this, organizations need to introduce upskilling opportunities and conduct interactive workshops and establish AI oversight boards that comprise of frontline employees. Ahead, the HR leaders should keep an eye on the trends, namely hyper-personalized employee maturation, generative AI for career advice, and changing the global regulations. Through strategies that use easy language, practicable frameworks and approaches that are employee-centric, HR teams can optimize AI's uses and limit resistance while making its integration ethical and sustainable.

A step-by-step outline of how to equip HRM with transparent AI is the definition of tasks, selection of relevant models, implementation of interpretability methods, use of legal requirements, and continuous monitoring and staff's input. This approach promotes ethical adoption of AI as well as a value-driven AI adoption.

Empirical Case Study, XAI Deployment Roadmap, and Organizational Culture in XAI Adoption

Indeed, a realistic example of the explainable AI (XAI) adoption can be seen in Colgate-Palmolive's international rollout of an AI-powered tools for goal-setting. The organization included XAI in its performance management structure so as to make the decision making process of setting and evaluation of objectives more transparent to the employees and the managers. The initiative had a pilot program in one of the business units where a cross-functional group of human resource, IT, and operations professionals were charged to select an XAI-enabled platform. During the implementation, the company held regular workshops that trained the stakeholders on how to interpret the recommendations as produced by AI in order to receive feedback on further model refinement. Such a systematic analytic approach delivered tangible results such as increased transparency, fewer bias, related to performance objectives formulation, employee trust reinforcement, etc. (Results of the surveys, conducted after the implementation). The impact of this case demonstrates the significant role of phased implementation, a continuing education of the stakeholders, and clear communication in efficient integration of XAI.

With the HR professionals who are looking to implement XAI in their practice, the process requires a planned implementation strategy, which is iterative in nature. It starts with the assessment of preparation of the organization for AI and its setting clear and transparent goals for the usage of the technology. A cross functional team ought to be used in order to handle the project to provide variability in decision making. There is need to focus on explainability and ease of use in a selection of tools to make them adopted in different user groups. The introduction of a pilot in the controlled environment is possible to collect feedback and change systems prior to bigger deployment. Periodic audits for detecting and correcting the algorithmic bias, meant for the AI interpretation, are necessary to keep the ethics in place. Besides, the development of specialized channels of communication will allow employees to voice concerns or ask questions regarding AI decisions and support the adoption of openness and responsibility culture in the workplace. Scaling up should not come before continuous monitoring and elements of accordance with changing regulatory needs.

The organizational culture plays a great role in achieving success in integrating XAI. Enterprises who cultivate the conditions of non-stop learning, adaptiveness, and open dialogue, are more ready for accepting the transformative power of AI. Maintenance of strong leadership support for appropriate AI practices coupled with clear support towards innovation and change effortlessly overcomes inner resistance. Enabling the employees to communicate with AI systems in a bold way is as important. Such case studies as that of Colgate-Palmolive, Extreme Networks show that, an early employee engagement, an appreciation of the first successes, and the inclusion of AI literacy into HR development programs are tactics working for ensuring that XAI becomes a part of the work facilities for a long time.

8. FUTURE DIRECTIONS AND EMERGING TRENDS

The future of AI in HRM increases activism for transparency as well as the ethical use of AI applications. The few trends to be expected on the horizon of AI utilization in HRMS would include explainable AI, strict rules, and regulation, and better practices of AI. From the recent development, we see that there is a transition towards the AI systems that incorporate other desirable attributes such as fairness, accountability, and interpretability. The adoption of technologies that offer fresh ways of understanding how the decisions made by AI systems work and can be controlled is becoming fashionable in organizations, and this means that HR professionals, as well as regular employees and regulators, can rely on the algorithms being used.

Another one of the great perspectives in AI transparency in the context of the development of HRM is decision auditing, where by the use of AI models with integrated capabilities of the real-time explanation of the process of decision-making will be used in the future. Such tools ''will assist the HR teams in ascertaining non bias and fairness while reducing on risks that may be attributed to biased solutions and decisions.'' Plus, worldwide coherence is expected in regulating as various jurisdictions will strive to develop a coherent AI legislation that will make compliance easier for an organization that has international operations (Lundberg, S. M., & Lee, S. 2017).

An enhancement of creating a compound system that combines elements of the rule-based system as well as machine learning would serve the purpose of having a system that is at the same time accurate and comprehensible. In contrast with Black-box form of models, these hybrid systems will allow the human resource specialists to comprehend and affix their stamp on the outcomes provided by the AI. Additionally, AI-generated transparency to the employee will be significant here whereby AI technology in HRM will offer reasons for a particular talent acquisition or an employee evaluation as well as career progression guidance (Paramita, 2024)

Another trend that is emerging is that of certification of ethical standards in the use of artificial intelligence in the field of HRM. The organizations that are adhering to the ethical principles towards the use of Artificial Intelligence will be issued with certifications which will enhance the coherence to the field so as to ensure that they follow the best practices. Furthermore, bias detection and mitigation algorithms will remain a concern in the future since Hr departments will have the ability to prevent discrimination in the hiring and promotions of employee (Schnackenberg, A. K., & Tomlinson, E. C. 2016).

Figure 7. Evolution of AI Transparency Regulations in the Last Decade

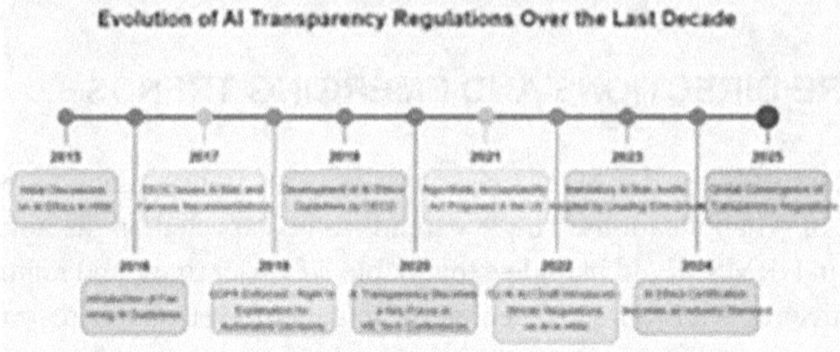

This figure shows changes in the level of regulation of AI transparency that has occurred in the last decade in the context of HRM and ethical issues related to the use of AI. Looking at a timeline of regulation, some of the regulatory developments include talking about AI ethic, GDPR rules, enactment of EEOC guidelines and embracing Algorithmic Accountable Regulation. The figure also demonstrates that today more and more importance is paid to the governments, AI ethics committees, and various industry initiatives in the sphere of transparent AI regulation. This timeline shows the current and predicted regulations on the transparency of AI in HRM from the year 2015 to 2025. The figure presents the timeline since the first attempts to discuss the problem of AI ethics and main general regulations such as GDPR, EEOC, and AI Ethics Certification.

With the development of AI's use in the HRM process, it was becoming evident that there was a need for a set of rules governing hiring AI mostly because the use of AI was on the rise as seen by the introduction of fair hiring AI guidelines early 2016, then followed by the enforcement of GDPR in May 2018 and the introduction of the OECD's AI ethics guidelines in May 2019. In the last couple of years, Algorithmic Accountability Act (2021) along with EU AI Act (2022) brought regulatory changes that asserted the importance of explainability, fairness audit, and compliance for AI interventions in HR operations (Sovrano., et al. 2025).

The choice of being transparent in AI has over the last decade evolved from ethical decision to a legal and strategic one. The figure depicts the increasing trend of policy makers' requirement regarding explainability of AI supported HRM systems, bias check and the human in the loop mechanism. It shows an overall transition in progression of AI in ensuring that its installation in the field of HRM is constructive and not solely for the sake of introducing enhanced efficiency while compromising fairness accountability and trustworthy practices (Gupta,2024).

As time progresses, there is the likelihood of advanced developments in terms of HRM systems where the AI element will put more importance into making them fair, transparent, and compliant. Those organizations that adopt these change drivers as integral implements that define the capabilities and opportunities for AI will have a framework that enables them maximize on potentials while respecting the legal, ethical and reputational repercussions (Floridi, 2018).

Addressing Bias, Transparency, and Strategic Adaptation in AI-Driven HRM

Although AI can be quite a prospect for enhancing HR practices, the deployment of AI shows measurable risks on the aspects of bias and fairness. For example, Amazon's now-discontinued AI hiring tool was gender biased, which affected resumes that carried the words "women's chess club", illustrating the way in which historical training data reinforce discrimination. In a similar study, MIT Media lab has found out that facial analyzing algorithms from major vendors recorded 34.7 percent error rate for dark skinned women and 0.8 percent error rate for light skinned men, over highlighting that there is also bias in algorithms that assess candidates. In order to avoid such results, enterprises such as linked in have adopted fairness audits through statistical parity and disparate impact testing, and companies such as salesforce endorsed the utilisation of transparency dashboards for analysis of AI decision in real time. For the HR practitioners, the concept of a transparency checklist, which includes the points on the model explainability, bias documentation, and human review protocols, has been helpful in terms of keeping the record of being responsible. In the training front, firms such as Deloitte have added required curricula on ethical AI for the HR teams to ensure an ethical use. Additionally, the trust and inclusion are facilitated by involving the employees via opt-in feedback, participatory tool design, and ethics review panels. Ahead, as new obstacles come about, future concerns could involve the possible employment of AI in remote surveillance, algorithmic labor segmentation, and advent of generative innovation in performance reviews. In order to remain adaptive, the organizations should institutionalize AI ethics governance as well as continue updating the HR-AI alignment strategies in order to respond to the change in technology and regulations.

The growing explainability, an increased regulation, and appearance of new decision auditing tools for real-time listening to the voice of data will shape the AI future in HRM. Organizations that pay more attention to transparency, fairness and recognition of employees will be the one that will not only benefit from AI the most, but will also minimize their potential risks.

9. CONCLUSION

Integration of AI in some of the key HR operations is particularly discussed in this chapter; three of which are: recruitment; performance management and; workforce planning. In recruitment, issues of use of algorithmic screening and automated decision-making are bound to surface when AI-driven applicant tracking systems and chatbots are commonly used in filtering candidates for job opening and developing job descriptions and interview scheduling. For performance management, AI systems are being more and more used for data-driven assessment, feedback, and predictions of value-oriented behavior of the workers and the possibility of their turnover. In workforce planning, AI-enabled analytics platforms are used to predict staff requirements, employee skill gap and a successful succession plan. The main difficulties of the AI integration exist at several levels. the design of algorithms in which bias and opacity could be baked in; data interpretation in which quality of input data matter and have outcomes; decision-making authority of whether an organization should trust in automation or keep human oversight; and lastly, ethical oversight for which standards of fairness, privacy, and accountability must be met. That the HR functions are defined explicitly and levels at which AI issues continue at an explicit level in the chapter, a focused and analytically strong base toward the opportunities and risks of AI in modern human resource management is established. Artificial Intelligence has become part of the driving force to change the future of the Human Resource Management. Its implementation has transformed recruitment, management of talents, and evaluation of performance with enormous efficiency and data based decision-making in it. These rewards bring, however, very complex challenges –especially in the terms of transparency, fairness and ethical use. The explainable AI (XAI) appears to be the key solution that can help HR representatives to interpret and audit the AI-based decisions as well as prove their rationality. When regulations change and employee expectations change, the organizations need to embrace the frameworks that will integrate the predictive accuracy and the interpretability, keep them in the ethical stand, and actively involve employees in integrating AI. In this way, HR leaders can guarantee that by using AI technologies, they bring the element of trust, compliance, and success for the long term – instead of destroying them.

The Need for Transparency in AI-Assisted HRM

Thus, transparency in AI-driven HRM is not only a technical necessity but also a business need based on the policy of fair and non-biased and aligned with international standards. Most places currently demand that concerns involving automation decision be explained especially where an organization uses artificial intelligence to screen job applicants, determine promotions, or assess employee performance. Current legal approaches on AI with the GDPR, EEOC guidelines, and the EU's AI Act at the center all stress the values of transparency, accountability, and fairness in the decision-making done through the help of artificial intelligence. Failure to adhere to these regulations attracts legal repercussions, fines and potential harm to the reputation of the businesses and Due to this, XAI is important in the HRM of businesses (Kaur, 2024).

In a similar way, through IBM, the idea of AI was employed to solve employee engagement and performance management, and companies incorporated AI explanation so as to make AI-generated results meaningful to the human figures of HR. These cases make it pertinent that AI transparency strengthen organizational credibility thereby improving the confidence that employees have in AI based HR results (El-Ghoul, 2024).

However, there are several key issues that are noticeable when employing the use of transparent artificial intelligence. AI software used by the organization must be frequently audited so that the algorithms used by the organization do not contain possible biases and are compliant with the legal and ethical standards. Most AI models even if they are explained do present a challenge of not being able to explain and remain as accurate as they can be. This is a dilemma for the head of HR because they can either use a complex AI system that produces high accuracy or employ a less complex system that has acceptable accuracy but can easily be explained (Radonjić, 2025).

Balancing AI Transparency with Performance

The most important aspect analyzed in the chapter was the relationships between the openness of AI and its predictive capabilities. Although deep learning, neural networks and other traditional black-box artificial intelligence models, they give very reliable results and are highly accurate but they are not explainable. While rule based systems, decision trees and linear regression are less flexible but easy to explain in terms of their outputs especially when it comes to large and complicated environment of HR datasets.

The further developments of XAI methodology will continue to major on making them more transparent and produce better results. Causal AI, counterfactual explanations, and responsible reinforcement learning are some of the measures which are being explored to ensure that AI becomes explainable. These sophistications will be quite useful in the improvement of more transparent, ethical and globally compliant AI based HRM systems (Dong, 2024).

The Future of Ethical AI in HRM

In terms of the increased application of AI in management, one of the trends that has recently emerged is decision auditing with AI support. These tools help in monitoring, reviewing and checking the AI decisions during the hiring process as well as during the HR processes to avoid discrimination. New kinds of AI transparency are being enacted for employees, such as HR AI systems that offer justification to the employee about the decision that has been made. Such an approach increases the confidence in the AI integrated HR processes which in return makes the employees more receptive to the AI aided process (Taslim, 2025).

Another key issue is the tendency of the international legal frameworks on Regulation on the use of AI as countries cooperate to form similar policies. This alignment will assist the MNCs to be in a position to adhere to more than one set regulation since the AI applied to HRM has to meet the international transparency requirements (Budhwar, 2022).

Final Thoughts

XAI in HRM is no longer an aspect that one can overlook, it is now on the strategic agenda of any organization that wants to leverage AI while at the same time guaranteeing fairness, accountability, and compliance. With proper disclosure, follow-up, and guarantee, AI HRM has great potential in increasing organizational performance through managed workforce; however, the current shortcomings in AI research expose the employees to risks of bias and non-compliance with regulations.

It is thus crucial for businesses to remain vigilant in matters of the integration of the best practices of employment of AI in HRM. By following the guidelines mentioned above, perform balanced transparency, use new XAI technologies, and obey global standards in the area of AI regulation, it is possible to build an appropriate environment for the AI environment in the sphere of HR and at that, follow the principles of the ethical use of AI.

REFERENCES

Abdelrahman, H. (2023). Artificial Intelligence in Human Resource Management: Advanced Computing Systems for Talent Analytics and Decision Making. *Journal of Advanced Computing Systems, 3*(6), 1–11.

Aguinis, H., Beltran, J. R., & Cope, A. (2024). How to use generative AI as a human resource management assistant. *Organizational Dynamics, 53*(1), 101029. DOI: 10.1016/j.orgdyn.2024.101029

Akram, S., Buono, P., & Lanzilotti, R. (2024). Recruitment chatbot acceptance in a company: A mixed method study on human-centered technology acceptance model. *Personal and Ubiquitous Computing, 28*(6), 961–984. DOI: 10.1007/s00779-024-01826-4

Albahri, A. S., Duhaim, A. M., Fadhel, M. A., Alnoor, A., Baqer, N. S., Alzubaidi, L., Albahri, O. S., Alamoodi, A. H., Bai, J., Salhi, A., Santamaría, J., Ouyang, C., Gupta, A., Gu, Y., & Deveci, M. (2023). A systematic review of trustworthy and explainable artificial intelligence in healthcare: Assessment of quality, bias risk, and data fusion. *Information Fusion, 96*, 156–191. DOI: 10.1016/j.inffus.2023.03.008

Altukhi, Z. M., Pradhan, S., & Aljohani, N. (2025). A Systematic Literature Review of the Latest Advancements in XAI. *Technologies, 13*(3), 93. DOI: 10.3390/technologies13030093

Andrieux, P., Johnson, R. D., Sarabadani, J., & Van Slyke, C. (2024). Ethical considerations of generative AI-enabled human resource management. *Organizational Dynamics, 53*(1), 101032. DOI: 10.1016/j.orgdyn.2024.101032

Aschbacher, K. (2024). The Uncertain Promise of HR Analytics: A Comprehensive Analysis of Data Utilised in Predictive Models for Employee Turnover (Doctoral dissertation, University of Graz).

Azam, M. S. (2023). How can we build human resources (HR) that deliver value? A systematic literature review of traditional and transformational HR roles. *Global Business and Organizational Excellence, 42*(4), 81–92. DOI: 10.1002/joe.22191

Balcioğlu, Y. S., & Artar, M. (2024). Artificial intelligence in employee recruitment. *Global Business and Organizational Excellence, 43*(5), 56–66. DOI: 10.1002/joe.22248

Bankins, S. (2021). The ethical use of artificial intelligence in human resource management: A decision-making framework. *Ethics and Information Technology, 23*(4), 841–854. DOI: 10.1007/s10676-021-09619-6

Benabou, A., Touhami, F., & Demraoui, L. (2024, May). Artificial intelligence and the future of human resource management. In *2024 International Conference on Intelligent Systems and Computer Vision (ISCV)* (pp. 1-8). IEEE. DOI: 10.1109/ISCV60512.2024.10620146

Budhwar, P., Malik, A., De Silva, M. T., & Thevisuthan, P. (2022). Artificial intelligence–challenges and opportunities for international HRM: A review and research agenda. *International Journal of Human Resource Management, 33*(6), 1065–1097. DOI: 10.1080/09585192.2022.2035161

Chamola, V., Hassija, V., Sulthana, A. R., Ghosh, D., Dhingra, D., & Sikdar, B. (2023). A review of trustworthy and explainable artificial intelligence (xai). *IEEE Access : Practical Innovations, Open Solutions, 11*, 78994–79015. DOI: 10.1109/ACCESS.2023.3294569

Chen, Z. (2023). Ethics and discrimination in artificial intelligence-enabled recruitment practices. *Humanities & Social Sciences Communications, 10*(1), 1–12. DOI: 10.1057/s41599-023-02079-x

Chin, Y. S., Mohamad, A. A., & Lo, M. C. (2024). Harnessing the power of artificial intelligence (AI): A paradigm shift in HRM practices for employee sustainable performance. *Global Knowledge, Memory and Communication.* Advance online publication. DOI: 10.1108/GKMC-06-2024-0355

De Almeida, P. G. R., dos Santos, C. D., & Farias, J. S. (2021). Artificial intelligence regulation: A framework for governance. *Ethics and Information Technology, 23*(3), 505–525. DOI: 10.1007/s10676-021-09593-z

Dima, J., Gilbert, M. H., Dextras-Gauthier, J., & Giraud, L. (2024). The effects of artificial intelligence on human resource activities and the roles of the human resource triad: Opportunities and challenges. *Frontiers in Psychology, 15*, 1360401. DOI: 10.3389/fpsyg.2024.1360401 PMID: 38903456

Dong, J. J., Yan, S. M., & Yang, X. W. (2024). Influencing Factors and Mechanisms of Value Co-Creation in Artificial Intelligence-Driven Human Resource Management: A System Dynamics Simulation. *Systems, 12*(9), 352. DOI: 10.3390/systems12090352

Du, J. (2024). Ethical and Legal Challenges of AI in Human Resource Management. *Journal of Computing and Electronic Information Management, 13*(2), 2024. DOI: 10.54097/83j64ub9

El-Ghoul, M., Almassri, M. M., El-Habibi, M. F., Al-Qadi, M. H., Abou Eloun, A., Abu-Nasser, B. S., & Abu-Naser, S. S. (2024). *AI in HRM: Revolutionizing Recruitment.* Performance Management, and Employee Engagement.

Faheem, M. A., Anwer, S., Rayhan, Z., Ullah, M. A., Paudel, R., Ahmed, M. F., & Khan, H. (2024). AI-Driven Innovation In HRM And Its Impact On Business Management: An In-Depth Study Of Technology Advancement And Strategic Implementation. *Nanotechnology Perceptions*, *20*, 1174–1204.

Farinu, U. (2025). Fairness, Accountability, and Transparency in AI: Ethical Challenges in Data-Driven Decision-Making. Available at *SSRN* 5128174. DOI: 10.2139/ssrn.5128174

Farooq, M., Ramzan, M., & Yen, Y. Y. (2025). Artificial Intelligence in Business and Law.

Fenwick, A., Molnar, G., & Frangos, P. (2024). The critical role of HRM in AI-driven digital transformation: A paradigm shift to enable firms to move from AI implementation to human-centric adoption. *Discover Artificial Intelligence*, *4*(1), 34. DOI: 10.1007/s44163-024-00125-4

Fenwick, A., Molnar, G., & Frangos, P. (2024). The critical role of HRM in AI-driven digital transformation: A paradigm shift to enable firms to move from AI implementation to human-centric adoption. *Discover Artificial Intelligence*, *4*(1), 34. DOI: 10.1007/s44163-024-00125-4

Fiegler-Rudol, J., Lau, K., Mroczek, A., & Kasperczyk, J. (2025). Exploring Human–AI Dynamics in Enhancing Workplace Health and Safety: A Narrative Review. *International Journal of Environmental Research and Public Health*, *22*(2), 199. DOI: 10.3390/ijerph22020199 PMID: 40003424

Firoz, M. (2024). IT in HRM: Enhancing efficiency and employee engagement.

Floridi, L., Cowls, J., Beltrametti, M., Chatila, R., Chazerand, P., Dignum, V., & Vayena, E. (2018). AI4People-an ethical framework for a good AI society: Opportunities, risks, principles, and recommendations. *Minds and Machines*, *28*(4), 689–707. DOI: 10.1007/s11023-018-9482-5 PMID: 30930541

Forat Yazdi, E., Chitsaz, E., & Etemadi, M. (2024). *Demystifying Artificial Intelligence (AI) in Human Resource Management (HRM): A Bibliometric Analysis of Explainable Artificial Intelligence (XAI)(2013-2023)*. Sciences and Techniques of Information Management.

Garg, S., Sinha, S., Kar, A. K., & Mani, M. (2022). A review of machine learning applications in human resource management. *International Journal of Productivity and Performance Management*, *71*(5), 1590–1610. DOI: 10.1108/IJPPM-08-2020-0427

Geloune, R. B. (2024). Predictive Accuracy of Performance in Knowledge Work: Comparison of Human Judgment, Regression and Artificial Intelligence Models (Doctoral dissertation, Case Western Reserve University).

Gupta, R. (2024). Impact of Artificial Intelligence (AI) on Human Resource Management (HRM). International Journal For Multidisciplinary Research, doi, 10.

Hanna, M., Pantanowitz, L., Jackson, B., Palmer, O., Visweswaran, S., Pantanowitz, J., Deebajah, M., & Rashidi, H. (2024). Ethical and Bias considerations in artificial intelligence (AI)/machine learning. *Modern Pathology*, •••, 100686. PMID: 39694331

Haque, A. B., Islam, A. N., & Mikalef, P. (2023). Explainable Artificial Intelligence (XAI) from a user perspective: A synthesis of prior literature and problematizing avenues for future research. *Technological Forecasting and Social Change*, *186*, 122120. DOI: 10.1016/j.techfore.2022.122120

Hassija, V., Chamola, V., Mahapatra, A., Singal, A., Goel, D., Huang, K., Scardapane, S., Spinelli, I., Mahmud, M., & Hussain, A. (2024). Interpreting black-box models: A review on explainable artificial intelligence. *Cognitive Computation*, *16*(1), 45–74. DOI: 10.1007/s12559-023-10179-8

Heidemann, A., Hülter, S. M., & Tekieli, M. (2024). Machine learning with real-world HR data: Mitigating the trade-off between predictive performance and transparency. *International Journal of Human Resource Management*, *35*(14), 2343–2366. DOI: 10.1080/09585192.2024.2335515

Hofeditz, L., Clausen, S., Rieß, A., Mirbabaie, M., & Stieglitz, S. (2022). Applying XAI to an AI-based system for candidate management to mitigate bias and discrimination in hiring. *Electronic Markets*, *32*(4), 2207–2233. DOI: 10.1007/s12525-022-00600-9 PMID: 36568961

Islam, M. R. (2024). *Explainable Artificial Intelligence for Enhancing Transparency in Decision Support Systems*. Malardalen University.

Jafri, S., Upreti, S., Saiyad, F. B. J., Madhukar, K. S., Chaturvedi, V. M., & Divakaran, P. (2024, March). Effectiveness of Artificial Intelligence for Enhancing Decision-Making Process of Recruitment in HRM Process. In 2024 IEEE International Conference on Contemporary Computing and Communications (InC4) (Vol. 1, pp. 1-6). IEEE. DOI: 10.1109/InC460750.2024.10649327

Jamal, A., Aissaoui, K., & Kassal, S. (2024, December). Enhancing Recruitment Transparency and Efficiency with Explainable AI (XAI). In 2024 3rd International Conference on Embedded Systems and Artificial Intelligence (ESAI) (pp. 1-6). IEEE.

Kaur, J. (2024). Responsible Artificial Intelligence (AI) Governance: Ethical Frameworks for Business Decision-Making. In Ethical Quandaries in Business Practices: Exploring Morality and Social Responsibility (pp. 337-368). IGI Global.

Khair, M. A., Mahadasa, R., Tuli, F. A., & Ande, J. R. P. K. (2020). Beyond human judgment: Exploring the impact of artificial intelligence on HR decision-making efficiency and fairness. *Global Disclosure of Economics and Business*, *9*(2), 163–176. DOI: 10.18034/gdeb.v9i2.730

Landers, R. N., & Behrend, T. S. (2023). Auditing the AI auditors: A framework for evaluating fairness and bias in high stakes AI predictive models. *The American Psychologist*, *78*(1), 36–49. DOI: 10.1037/amp0000972 PMID: 35157476

Langer, M., & König, C. (2022). Explainability of artificial intelligence in human resources. In *Handbook of research on artificial intelligence in human resource management* (pp. 285–302). Edward Elgar Publishing.

Langer, M., & König, C. (2022). Explainability of artificial intelligence in human resources. In *Handbook of research on artificial intelligence in human resource management* (pp. 285–302). Edward Elgar Publishing.

Langer, M., König, C. J., Back, C., & Hemsing, V. (2023). Trust in artificial intelligence: Comparing trust processes between human and automated trustees in light of unfair bias. *Journal of Business and Psychology*, *38*(3), 493–508. DOI: 10.1007/s10869-022-09829-9

Lewicka, D., Starowicz-Rajca, H., Blbas, R., & Wilczewski, A. (2024). Cultivating Success: A Practical Exploration Of Applying Artificial Intelligence In Human Resources Management. Scientific Papers of Silesian University of Technology. Organization & Management/Zeszyty Naukowe Politechniki Slaskiej. Seria Organizacji i Zarzadzanie, (199).

Lundberg, S. M., & Lee, S. (2017). A unified approach to interpreting model predictions. *Advances in Neural Information Processing Systems*, *30*, 4765–4774.

Mujtaba, B. G. (2025). Human-AI Intersection: Understanding the Ethical Challenges, Opportunities, and Governance Protocols for a Changing Data-Driven Digital World. *Business Ethics and Leadership*, *9*(1), 109–126. DOI: 10.61093/bel.9(1).109-126.2025

Mujtaba, D. F., & Mahapatra, N. R. (2024). Fairness in AI-driven recruitment: Challenges, metrics, methods, and future directions. arXiv preprint arXiv:2405.19699.

Mwita, K. M., & Kitole, F. A. (2025). Potential benefits and challenges of artificial intelligence in human resource management in public institutions. *Discover Global Society*, *3*(1), 1–19. DOI: 10.1007/s44282-025-00175-8

Papagiannidis, E., Enholm, I. M., Dremel, C., Mikalef, P., & Krogstie, J. (2023). Toward AI governance: Identifying best practices and potential barriers and outcomes. *Information Systems Frontiers*, *25*(1), 123–141. DOI: 10.1007/s10796-022-10251-y PMID: 35464171

Papagiannidis, E., Mikalef, P., Conboy, K., & Van de Wetering, R. (2023). Uncovering the dark side of AI-based decision-making: A case study in a B2B context. *Industrial Marketing Management*, *115*, 253–265. DOI: 10.1016/j.indmarman.2023.10.003

Paramita, D., Okwir, S., & Nuur, C. (2024). Artificial intelligence in talent acquisition: Exploring organisational and operational dimensions. *The International Journal of Organizational Analysis*, *32*(11), 108–131. DOI: 10.1108/IJOA-09-2023-3992

Park, H., Ahn, D., Hosanagar, K., & Lee, J. (2021, May). Human-AI interaction in human resource management: Understanding why employees resist algorithmic evaluation at workplaces and how to mitigate burdens. In *Proceedings of the 2021 CHI conference on human factors in computing systems* (pp. 1-15). DOI: 10.1145/3411764.3445304

Powell, J. R. (2024). Human Resource Professionals' Perceptions of Trust in Explainable Artificial Intelligence Hiring Software (Doctoral dissertation, National University).

Prikshat, V., Islam, M., Patel, P., Malik, A., Budhwar, P., & Gupta, S. (2023). AI-Augmented HRM: Literature review and a proposed multilevel framework for future research. *Technological Forecasting and Social Change*, *193*, 122645. DOI: 10.1016/j.techfore.2023.122645

Radonjić, A., Duarte, H., & Pereira, N. (2024). Artificial intelligence and HRM: HR managers' perspective on decisiveness and challenges. *European Management Journal*, *42*(1), 57–66. DOI: 10.1016/j.emj.2022.07.001

Řepová, H., Zouhar, J., & Král, P. (2024). Attractiveness of firms with chatbot as job interviewers: Does the interviewer-type matter in the first contact with candidates? *International Journal of Communication Networks and Distributed Systems*, *30*(6), 711–732. DOI: 10.1504/IJCNDS.2024.141672

Ribeiro, M. T.. "Why Should I Trust You? Explaining the Predictions of Any Classifier." *Proceedings of the 22nd ACM SIGKDD International Conference on Knowledge Discovery and Data Mining*, 2016. DOI: 10.18653/v1/N16-3020

Rigotti, C., & Fosch-Villaronga, E. (2024). Fairness, AI & recruitment. *Computer Law & Security Review*, *53*, 105966. DOI: 10.1016/j.clsr.2024.105966

Sainila, S. (2024). Shaping Tomorrow's Workplace with AI-Driven HRM: Bridging the Gap Between Technology and Human Capital.

Schnackenberg, A. K., & Tomlinson, E. C. (2016). Organizational Transparency: A New Perspective on Managing Trust in Organization-Stakeholder Relationships. *Journal of Management*, *42*(7), 1784–1810. DOI: 10.1177/0149206314525202

Soleimani, M., Intezari, A., Arrowsmith, J., Pauleen, D. J., & Taskin, N. (2025). Reducing AI bias in recruitment and selection: An integrative grounded approach. *International Journal of Human Resource Management*, •••, 1–36. DOI: 10.1080/09585192.2025.2480617

Sovrano, F., Hine, E., Anzolut, S., & Bacchelli, A. (2025). Simplifying software compliance: AI technologies in drafting technical documentation for the AI Act. *Empirical Software Engineering*, *30*(3), 91. DOI: 10.1007/s10664-025-10645-x PMID: 40191404

Tambe, P., Cappelli, P., & Yakubovich, V. (2019). Artificial intelligence in human resources management: Challenges and a path forward. *California Management Review*, *61*(4), 15–42. DOI: 10.1177/0008125619867910

Taslim, W. S., Rosnani, T., & Fauzan, R. (2025). Employee involvement in AI-driven HR decision-making: A systematic review. *SA Journal of Human Resource Management*, *23*, 1–10. DOI: 10.4102/sajhrm.v23i0.2856

Tschang, F. T., & Almirall, E. (2021). Artificial intelligence as augmenting automation: Implications for employment. *The Academy of Management Perspectives*, *35*(4), 642–659. DOI: 10.5465/amp.2019.0062

Vereb, D., Krajcsák, Z., & Kozák, A. (2025). The importance of positive employee experience and its development through using predictive analytics. *Journal of Modelling in Management*, *20*(1), 51–69. DOI: 10.1108/JM2-02-2024-0057

Vishwanath, B., & Vaddepalli, S. (2023). The future of work: Implications of artificial intelligence on hr practices. Tuijin Jishu/Journal of Propulsion Technology, 44(3), 1711-1724.

Yanamala, K. K. R. (2023). Transparency, privacy, and accountability in AI-enhanced HR processes. *Journal of Advanced Computing Systems*, *3*(3), 10–18. DOI: 10.69987/JACS.2023.30302

Yu, L., & Li, Y. (2022). Artificial intelligence decision-making transparency and employees' trust: The parallel multiple mediating effect of effectiveness and discomfort. *Behavioral Sciences (Basel, Switzerland), 12*(5), 127. DOI: 10.3390/bs12050127 PMID: 35621424

Zhang, H. (2024). *Exploring the Impact of AI on Human Resource Management: A case study of organizational adaptation and employee dynamics*. IEEE Transactions on Engineering.

Chapter 2
Exploring Explainable AI Transparency in Managerial Decision-Making:
A Multi-Sectoral Analysis of Organizational Trust in Morocco

Rita El Guermai
https://orcid.org/0009-0005-8304-1784
Cadi Ayyad University, Morocco

Abdelfattah Jamal
Cadi Ayyad University, Morocco

Karima Aissaoui
https://orcid.org/0000-0002-0497-3219
Mohammed First University, Morocco

ABSTRACT

The research investigates how managers perceive AI transparency through accessibility, comprehensibility, and fairness which determines their level of interaction with AI-assisted decision systems. Managerial interaction serves as the outcome variable which this study categorizes into three ordered levels: low, moderate, and high. The research combines explainable AI frameworks (LIME and SHAP) with organizational trust and transparency models to connect cognitive and ethical aspects of human–AI interaction. A structured survey was conducted among 180 managers from three key sectors in Morocco: banking, telecommunications and

DOI: 10.4018/979-8-3373-1737-3.ch002

retail. The questionnaire was developed from validated scales and analyzed by logistic regression models, run in Python for algorithmic flexibility and in SAS to ensure statistical robustness and reproducibility.

INTRODUCTION

Artificial Intelligence (AI) developed from a distant future concept. Today, it is considered as a fundamental tool for business decision-making. AI systems deliver efficiency and speed, and data-based decisions yet serious issues exist regarding transparency, discrimination, and responsibility (Floridi et al., 2018; Jain et al, 2024). The 'black box' problem which describes the opacity of decision making has emerged as a major challenge in AI usage. The lack of understanding about AI-assisted recommendations by managers leads to lower trust in decision making support systems (Adadi & Berrada, 2018). The research problem investigates how AI system opacity damages managerial trust, but the research question examines which transparency dimensions influence manager-AI system interactions. Organizations have attempted to boost managerial trust in AI systems through AI-XAI which has led to an increase in demand for XAI systems because they explain how an AI arrived at a specific outcome. This integration helps the decision-makers in the verification of AI created insights as well as tackles biases and increases trust in algorithmic processes (Toreini et al., 2020). Even though there has been progress in technical transparency, there is a lack of scholarly work regarding the impact of AI transparency on trust along with organizational outcomes (Floridi et al., 2018). The purpose of this chapter is to fill this gap by studying the influence of AI transparency on the level of managerial trust and AI utilization in Moroccan organizations. Even though AI can aid in the improvement of our decisions, managers still seem to lack confidence in AI systems due to an issue of interpretability. AI models that are opaque can conceal important reasoning steps which in turn reduces trust and undermines the organizational value (Adadi & Berrada, 2018). Decision makers across many industries even with the presence of extensive AI use in telecoms, banking, and retail are still reluctant to implement AI-centric suggestions without transparency structures (Gilpin et al, 2018). The existing body of knowledge in organizational trust is rather thin aurally in the influence of AI and trust formation. The financial services industry demonstrates this through credit-scoring algorithms which lack transparency thus creating disputes about loan decisions (Gilpin et al., 2018). The implementation of AI decisions in high-stakes organizational settings requires both technical validity and interpretability together with fairness and justifiability. The recent XAI literature emphasizes the need for local interpretability through LIME (Ribeiro et al., 2016) and SHAP (Lundberg & Lee, 2017) models to enable users understanding of individual decisions. The approaches enhance existing frameworks regarding AI transparency (Adadi & Berrada, 2018) and trust (Toreini et al., 2020) which state that users' perceptions of accessibility and comprehensibility and fairness determine their willingness to adopt AI.

Research on how non-technical users specifically managers perceive and react to these dimensions in actual organizational environments remains scarce. While there has been progress in the study of the technical opacity of the organization, the impact of AI transparency on managerial trust is still underexplored. Most attention has been paid to the enhancement of algorithms' productivity, while the means through which trust is built toward an AI enabled system, as well as organizational integration of AI, has been neglected (Floridi et al., 2018).

This study investigates how managers perceive the transparency of AI systems regarding accessibility, comprehensibility, and fairness which affects their engagement with AI-supported decision systems in organizational contexts. As steps to be taken, two predominant goals are being highlighted. The first goal is to analyze the views that managers of Moroccan firms have regarding AI transparency and its impact on trust within the organization. Being able to know how the decision makers understand the concept of AI transparency will aid in knowing if the explainability of the AI recommendations improves its adoption. The second objective is to define the key features of AI transparency and its effects on management. This comprises features like explainability, interpretability, and accountability which affect the acceptance of AI as well as its ethical issues in business environments. The research objectives guide this study to use a descriptive quantitative research method.

The research study took place in Morocco which is currently experiencing fast digital development. A total of 180 managers from three essential economic sectors of Morocco received a structured survey: banking, telecommunications and retail. The research examined three different sectors because they represented distinct levels of digital maturity and AI adoption which enabled researchers to study organizational readiness across multiple sectors while analyzing perceptual divergence. The banking sector of Morocco applies AI technology for both credit scoring operations and fraud prevention systems while telecom companies use AI to enhance network performance and deliver personalized customer experiences. The retail industry remains at an initial stage of digital adoption where it concentrates on predicting inventory levels and developing recommendation systems.

The research conducted in Morocco contributes fresh insights to the general conversation about explainable AI adoption because it represents a setting that lacks sufficient representation in existing studies. The digital transformation of Morocco creates a dual system because banking and telecommunications sectors quickly adopt AI technologies yet other sectors stay at the beginning of digital advancement. The diverse organizational environments of this setting provide an excellent opportunity to study how AI transparency perceptions develop in different settings. Furthermore, in many emerging economies, AI systems are often introduced as imported solutions, developed externally and deployed without full consideration of local norms, languages, or institutional practices. This can create a gap between how AI systems are designed and how they are perceived or trusted by local managers. There is evidence that cultural, linguistic and regulatory factors significantly affect the acceptance and use of AI (Abebe et al., 2021; Mhlambi, 2020). This study addresses both a geographic gap in empirical XAI research by focusing on Morocco and contributes to a more inclusive understanding of AI adoption that goes beyond Euro-American contexts and reflects the realities of digitally uneven ecosystems.

The research presented in this chapter addresses this knowledge deficiency by studying how managers perceive AI transparency to affect their decision system interaction. The study defines interaction through behavioral engagement which consists of three ordered levels: low, moderate, and high. The scale shows the frequency and confidence levels of manager AI output utilization in operational and strategic decisions across different business sectors.

A logistic regression model was used to analyze the data. The choice of Python was made because of its flexibility in model customization and availability of open-source libraries that are useful for AI research. To ensure the statistical robustness and cross-validation of the results, the model was also run in SAS, a platform that is well known for its rigor in handling complex categorical data. This dual-software approach allowed for both agile modeling and reproducibility, which directly addresses concerns about replicability in computational social science.

This chapter provides both theoretical insights and practical recommendations by identifying which dimensions of AI transparency affect engagement the most. Theoretically, it tests the applicability of explainability models in managerial contexts and explores the counterintuitive finding that higher fairness perception may actually decrease interaction because of a perceived lack of flexibility or contextual sensitivity. It provides practical guidance to AI system designers, ethics boards, and innovation managers on how to enhance system usability and trust in multi-sectoral environments.

It adds to the growing body of work on explainable and human-centered AI by translating abstract principles of transparency into concrete managerial behavior. It suggests that successful AI adoption in organizations is not just about performance or ethics, but about how human users cognitively and emotionally relate to the system, and that this relationship varies significantly across sectors, roles, and institutional contexts.

1. THEORETICAL FRAMEWORK

1.1. AI in Managerial Decision-Making

At first, AI systems solely depended on rules: decision making was done based on detailed IF-THEN statements. They were restricted by their reliance on human knowledge to create rules and their incapacity to use new data without human aid (Soares et al., 2020 ; Angelov & Buswell, 2002). According to Janiesch et al. (2021), the ease with which new systems can be built has led to the rise of new capabilities of systems where they can learn from data, which helps in automating the model building process and improving performance for certain tasks.

Deep learning is a machine learning approach that uses artificial neural networks to detect complex data patterns. The model demonstrates superior performance compared to traditional machine learning models in numerous applications as it learns concepts from marge datasets (Janiesch et al., 2021 ; Perconti & Plebe, 2020). Deep learning models have achieved remarkable success in image classification, natural language interpretation, and other complex human tasks, sometimes producing results that are indistinguishable from those of humans (Perconti & Plebe, 2020; Jena et al., 2021). Any AI system requires the focus on rule-oriented models and deep learning models. Deep reinforcement learning models can be enhanced by integrating with rule-based systems. It improves explainability while maintaining efficiency (Soares et al., 2020). Model-Based Deep Learning combines the two approaches by incorporating the mathematical model into the data-driven deep learning method which increases system robustness and efficiency (Shlezinger et al. 2022; Shlezinger et al. 2023). AI is being adopted to aid in decision support systems. AI does not take over the decision making; instead, it aids people during the processes. This approach focuses on the interaction of stakeholders with AI systems, ensuring that AI only supports in deeply intricate decisions. AI-enabled Decision support systems (DSS) are designed to assist humans in decision making by integrating AI systems with the human cognitive processes. They try to imitate human thinking processes and provide complete mechanisms to support operational decision making, particularly in case study simulation models on multi-dimensional socio-economic planning (Kacprzyk, 2022). The incorporation of AI in DSS gives the possibility of processing large amounts of data in order to detect trends and provide some level of automated reasoning (Kacprzyk, 2022 ; Phillips-Wren, 2012).

1.2. The Role of AI Transparency in Trust Formation

Transparency and ability to explain the AI outputs. It is one of the primary problems AI users face when the AI is used as a decision support system. Take, for example, loan underwriting. An explainable AI decision support system can automate certain processes while still providing an accurate description of how the decisions were made, and reasoning behind the outputs which is referred to as "accuracy versus explainability trade-off" (Sachan et al., 2019). The EU AI Act contains one core requirement where explainability is expected to feature prominently. Its implementation, however, remains problematic (Pavlidis, 2024). XAI techniques help promote fairness by providing counterfactual reasoning logic that demonstrates how certain actions taken might change under different conditions thereby strengthening fairness and responsibility (Leben, 2023). The analysis of fairness in AI systems can be approached through three main methods which include statistical parity for equal outcomes between groups and equalized odds for similar error rates between groups and individual fairness for similar treatment of similar individuals (Selbst et al., 2019; Schumann et al., 2020). Organizations face difficulties in balancing these frameworks because their views on justice differ.

In a business environment, explainability helps to audit the AI model and subsequently, the trust in the decisions made, and processes performed is maintained which is crucial (Chomiak et al., 2021). The relevance of fairness cannot be overlooked in avoiding biases and discrimination, especially with regards to recruitment and multi-party decisions (Schumann et al., 2020). Executing fairness is hard as it is complicated to define equal treatment and fair results in algorithmic models (Schumann et al., 2020). Performance of fairness-in recommendation systems is addressed by their explainability as the bias is removed during the process of improving the fairness of the system and the performance being defended (Ge et al., 2022). Moreover, fairness is associated with procedural justice because transparency and user control over the results improve perception of fairness in AI decision-making processes (Lee et al., 2019). As noted by Pavlidis (2024), accountability entails assigning responsibility which relies on defined standards together with corresponding monitoring systems focused on ensuring that the AI systems function in a reasonable manner. The "Accountability for Reasonableness" policy constituent, for example, sets criteria for setting healthcare priorities in a reasonable manner while ensuring transparency and participation (Kapiriri et al., 2008; Martin et al., 2002). This is provided in the EU's strategy on governance of AI which highlights the need on putting in place appropriate accountability frameworks to control and evaluate the automated decision-making processes (Pavlidis, 2024).

1.3. Theoretical Perspectives on AI Transparency and Trust

1.3.1. Limitations of Classical Models in AI Adoption Contexts

The research addresses these limitations through the combination of LIME, SHAP, the Transparency Framework, and Organizational Trust models which provide a comprehensive view that links cognitive understanding with fairness evaluation and systemic trust for studying managerial engagement with AI. The studies demonstrate how SHAP and LIME enhance decision transparency in organizational settings especially in recruitment domains that require both fairness and trust (Jamal et al., 2024).

The majority of current research on technology adoption in organizational contexts depends on generalist models including the Technology Acceptance Model (TAM) and the Unified Theory of Acceptance and Use of Technology (UTAUT). The models focus on two key constructs: perceived usefulness and ease of use because they demonstrate consistency across different digital tools. The current models are being viewed as inadequate for capturing the specifics of AI systems, especially in managerial contexts. Unlike traditional IT systems, AI tools operate with non-deterministic logic, make autonomous decisions, and often behave in ways that are difficult to audit or explain. Therefore, factors such as "usefulness" may not completely capture the elements that impact the level of trust or engagement with the AI systems (Rai et al., 2021; Binns et al., 2018). This study intentionally looks past the TAM approach as to adopt more nuanced frameworks that address the mental, moral, and practical AI issues.

1.3.2. Explainability and the LIME Model (Ribeiro et al., 2016) – SHAP (Lundberg and Lee, 2017)

This study is based on concepts from the LIME framework (Local Interpretable Model-Agonistic Explanations) by Ribeiro et Al. (2016). LIME enables providing an explanation of predictions generated using complex machine learning models by approximating them locally with easier to interpret models. The organizational context supports this requirement because managers need to track how decisions were made. Managers need both the outputs generated by AI systems and explanations that they can understand and defend during internal discussions. LIME provides operational local interpretability as an essential dimension of explainability which directly corresponds to the survey-based constructs of comprehensibility and accessibility.

SHAP (SHapley Additive exPlanations) emerged as a leading explainable AI framework parallel to LIME when Lundberg and Lee (2017) introduced it. The SHAP method uses cooperative game theory to determine feature importance values for specific predictions which provide both global and local interpretability.

SHAP differs from LIME because it generates model-agnostic explanations through theoretically grounded methods which guarantee fairness and consistency and additivity properties (Lundberg et al., 2020; Molnar, 2022). The features of SHAP make it well-suited for situations where AI outputs need to be understandable by various stakeholders including multi-level managerial settings (Barredo Arrieta et al., 2020).

The combination of LIME and SHAP provides two distinct methods to explain AI decision logic so users can understand it. The local explanation capabilities of LIME (Arya et al., 2019) help individual decision-makers understand specific cases but SHAP provides comparative fairness and feature-level accountability which is essential for organizational decision-making environments (Hall et al., 2021). The study includes both types of explainability to provide a comprehensive and detailed understanding of explainability that matches the requirements of AI governance and managerial trust-building. SHAP's ability to decompose model predictions and attribute influence on individual inputs has made it popular not only in computer science but also in other domains like finance, healthcare, and human resources where justifiability and transparency are important (Lundberg et al., 2020; Mittelstadt et al., 2019). The study's relevance emerges from its ability to replicate how decision-makers assess input fairness and decision reliability which corresponds to the survey's accessibility, comprehensibility and fairness dimensions. LIME and SHAP provide separate perspectives to enhance the transparency and interpretability of AI decision logic for end-users. SHAP provides both distributional fairness and variable-level accountability which makes it highly relevant for organizations operating across departments and roles while LIME enhances local case-specific explanations that may resonate with individual decision-makers. The study includes both of these methods to provide a robust conceptualization of explainability that aligns with the needs of managerial contexts (Barredo Arrieta et al., 2020).

SHAP and LIME rule current practice but other techniques like counterfactual explanations (Wachter et al., 2017) or concept-based methods (Kim et al., 2018) have also been proposed to make AI reasoning more human-aligned. However, these methods often remain inaccessible to non-technical users, which means that simpler, cognitively intuitive frameworks are still needed in managerial settings. The XAI methods LIME and SHAP have certain limitations. LIME is local fidelity focused but may provide inconsistent explanations, while SHAP, despite theoretical guarantees, has computational complexity and scalability issues in large models (Molnar, 2022). Based on this, we propose:

Accessibility Effect (Hypothesis 1): Managerial interaction with AI systems increases with the perceived accessibility of the systems' features and functions.

Rationale: Our research extends LIME (Ribeiro et al., 2016) and Adadi & Berrada's transparency framework by showing that managers are more likely to engage with AI systems when information about how they operate is easily accessible. Accessibility reduces perceived complexity and acts as a gateway to trust and effective use.

1.3.3. AI Transparency Framework (Adadi & Berrada, 2018)

The framework developed by Adadi and Berrada (2018) is particularly relevant for managerial contexts among the various theoretical contributions to explainable AI (XAI). This model proposes a multidimensional conceptualization of AI transparency, structured around three key components: accessibility, comprehensibility, and fairness. These dimensions offer a bridge between technical interpretability and human-centered usability, which is essential when assessing how decision-makers interact with opaque algorithmic systems.

Accessibility defines the extent to which users can access, view or obtain explanations from an AI system. It encompasses both the explanation itself and how it is presented (e.g., dashboards, textual summaries, visual aids). A system that is technically explainable but not accessible to non-experts' risks failing its transparency goals (Doshi-Velez & Kim, 2017). Managers can use accessibility to obtain AI decision justifications whenever they need them especially when they must act quickly or work under operational limitations. The user's ability to understand information stands as the main focus of comprehensibility. The explanation must be clear while maintaining a suitable cognitive load that matches the user's domain-specific knowledge.

Organizations need to understand decisions because managers will not implement choices they cannot understand even when those choices are statistically optimal (Miller, 2019). The goal of comprehensibility is to simplify explanations without misrepresenting information and domain-relevant language and contextual framing should be used to achieve this goal.

The third pillar known as Fairness deals with how users perceive the equitable nature of AI system outputs and processes. The system faces challenges regarding bias together with discrimination and procedural justice. The technical implementation of fairness through methods like equalized odds and demographic parity does not determine how users perceive fairness because it depends on their expectations and organizational norms and cultural background (Selbst et al., 2019). Fairness exists as a relational construct which affects how managers decide to trust and adopt AI outputs because it extends beyond algorithmic properties.

The framework's strength is in its ability to be used for both the design and evaluation of AI systems. In this study, each of these three dimensions informed specific items in the survey instrument, which enabled an empirical assessment of how managers across different sectors perceive transparency. Moreover, the tripartite structure enables the analysis of the effects of each dimension separately: for example, as shown in our results, accessibility and comprehensibility have a positive effect on engagement, while fairness has more ambiguous or even negative effects.

The model follows recent XAI literature recommendations which urge researchers to shift from technical transparency definitions toward frameworks that prioritize user perception and cognitive usability (Barredo Arrieta et al., 2020; Arya et al., 2019; Ribeiro et al., 2016). Managerial contexts benefit from this approach because it transforms explainability from a feature into a functional tool which supports responsible decision-making and informed choices within specific contexts. This of course applies to non-technical users, like managers. In addition to evaluating AI systems, they have to consider the ethics as well as how the system fits into the overall organization. In this work, these three aspects are the essence of the perception-based questionnaire, and they are predictors of engagement with AI. Consequently, we formulate:

Comprehensibility Effect (Hypothesis 2): There is increased interaction with AI systems by managers when decision making by the AI system is clear and easy to understand.

Rationale: Research on explainability demonstrates that users require understanding of how and why AI systems produce decisions. The ability to mentally simulate or follow AI logic decreases uncertainty while improving confidence according to Adadi & Berrada (2018) and Lee & See (2004).

1.3.4. Organizational Trust in AI (Toreini et al., 2020)

The emotional response of an individual toward AI is not the only factor that determines trust in AI; it is also influenced by organizational and systemic attributes. Toreini et al. (2020) propose a multidimensional model of organizational trust in AI, which is based on:

- Reliability: Can the AI be depended on to work in the same way and provide the same results every time?
- Predictability: Does the behavior of AI remain the same in different situations or contexts?

- Auditability: Can the decisions made by the AI be followed step by step to see how they were made and whether they can be changed?

This reflects some level of institutional rigor, especially within managerial contexts where actions require validation, justification, and distribution. For others in the region, some of the elements in our survey are based on this theory and capture the extent to which these attributes impact engagement with AI systems.

The organizational learning process shapes how managers understand the transparency of AI systems. Training programs that focus on AI literacy and interpretability techniques and ethical considerations improve both the comprehensibility and accessibility of AI systems. Managers develop informed trust through these initiatives while they learn to critically assess AI-driven recommendations (Floridi et al., 2018). In light of this:

Fairness Paradox (Hypothesis 3): Overly high perceived fairness and objectivity in the outcomes of decisions made by the AI systems may lead to reduction in interaction with those systems by managers.

Rationale: The principle of fairness serves as a fundamental element of ethical AI yet systems that are too rigid or context-insensitive may seem unyielding especially in settings where relational or informal logic dominates. The "cold machine" perception can result in emotional disengagement although technical trust remains high (Mittelstadt et al., 2016; Mhlambi, 2020).

1.3.5. Summary of Theoretical Foundations

Table 1. Summary of Theoretical Frameworks Mobilized

Author(s)	Framework	Key Dimensions	Application in This Study
Lundberg & Lee (2017)	SHAP	Feature attribution, fairness, local/global explanations	Support for understanding AI decision logic and variable influence
Ribeiro et al. (2016)	LIME	Local interpretability, explanation clarity	Items on clarity and accessibility of AI decisions
Adadi & Berrada (2018)	Transparency in XAI	Accessibility, Comprehensibility, Fairness	Questionnaire design on perceived transparency
Toreini et al. (2020)	Organizational Trust in AI	Reliability, Predictability, Auditability	Items assessing systemic trust in AI decision systems

(Source: Authors)

1.3.6. Justification for Framework Selection

The selected frameworks demonstrate both empirical validity and operational relevance. The frameworks provide unique perspectives on how managers handle interactions with unclear automated systems which has become widespread in AI implementation. The framework provides a comprehensive understanding through its layered approach which includes:

- The cognitive processes of interpretation and understanding (Ribeiro et al., 2016 ; Lundberg & Lee, 2017)
- The ethical dimensions of justice and transparency (Adadi & Berrada, 2018)
- The systemic requirements of reliability and auditability (Toreini et al., 2020)

These frameworks differ from TAM because they recognize that usability and utility require context-specific interpretation, making them more suitable for modeling trust and interaction in real-world organizations. The selected frameworks differ from the general Technology Acceptance Model (TAM) because they focus on cognitive clarity and fairness perception and systemic trust instead of perceived usefulness and ease of use. These dimensions are essential for understanding managerial behavior towards AI, especially when opacity and ethical concerns outweigh simple usability considerations.

Figure 1. Conceptual Model of the Impact of AI Transparency on Managerial Interaction

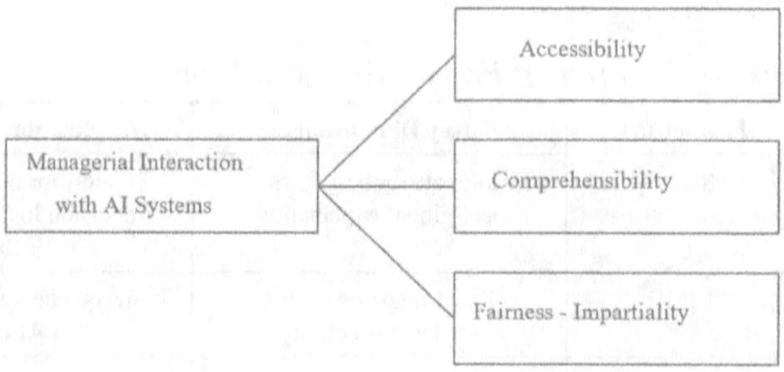

(Source: Authors)

The hypotheses presented earlier are graphically represented in the conceptual model (Figure 1) which suggests that managerial interaction with AI systems is influenced by three perception-based variables: accessibility, comprehensibility, and perceived fairness of AI decisions. In order to test these hypotheses, a quantitative study was carried out through the administration of a complete questionnaire to managers from different sectors in Morocco. The subsequent part of this document describes the methodology that was followed, including the sampling method, the tools used for measurement, and how the data was analyzed.

2. RESEARCH METHODOLOGY

The research uses a positivist epistemological approach combined with a quantitative descriptive design to analyze how managers perceive AI systems while determining their AI tool interaction levels based on specific factors. The research follows a deductive method which draws from theoretical concepts of explainability and trust and fairness in AI governance (Etikan et al., 2016).

The research participants were mainly recruited through convenience sampling and snowball sampling methods. We began with 50 professionals from our personal and professional connections who helped distribute the survey to their networks with a focus on managers and decision-makers from different sectors. The non-random sampling method provided access to diverse participants from 13 sectors with high participation from telecommunications and financial services and industry sectors.

The research was supposed to focus on managerial profiles, but some non-managerial staff members completed the survey. The study included these participants in the analysis because they implement or use AI tools in their work and their insights offer important operational value. The study includes their perspectives because AI adoption occurs throughout organizational hierarchies. 180 responses were collected from which 162 were retained after filtering out participants who indicated they had at least some level of interaction with AI systems. The recruitment method used here restricts study findings from being generalizable because of sampling bias but it was considered acceptable because the study was exploratory, and it was hard to get a large representative sample of managers in a brief time.

The research sample consisted of 162 participants who engaged with AI systems directly or indirectly during their work activities through purposive sampling. The research participants came from various sectors of the Moroccan economy with banking, telecommunications and retail representing the primary sectors. The selected sectors exhibit diverse levels of digital maturity and AI integration.

The banking sector which has been undergoing digital transformation for a long time has mature use cases in credit scoring, fraud detection and customer profiling. The telecommunications sector uses AI for infrastructure optimization, customer segmentation, and churn prediction. The retail sector is data-driven but still in the early stages of adopting AI tools and is mostly limited to inventory management or recommendation engines. The participants worked at different organizational levels including operational staff as well as mid-level and senior managerial positions.

The study examined AI system interaction differences through organizational role analysis which Figure 4 illustrates. The study's multi-sector and managerial-level data collection enables a comprehensive understanding of AI perception because it represents the diverse ways AI is integrated in Moroccan firms.

The original questionnaire written in English required translation into French because it is the main business language of Morocco. The translation process followed best practices for cross-cultural survey adaptation (Brislin, 1970) through back-translation and expert review to achieve semantic equivalence and minimize bias.

A pre-test with 10 managers from various sectors was conducted before full deployment. This pilot phase was used to assess the clarity, coherence, and reliability of the instrument. Some minor wording and formatting changes were made based on feedback to increase the comprehensibility and validity of the definitive version. The survey instrument operated through "Google Forms" from January 22 through March 31 in 2025 while including an initial screening question to eliminate participants without AI exposure for better result consistency. The survey was developed using existing literature and tailored to Moroccan culture. The questions were posed in French and divided into ten dimensions which were rated on a 5-point Likert scale (1 = Strongly disagree to 5 = Strongly agree):

- Q1: The ability to understand the decisions made by AI.
- Q2: The ease of use of the system
- Q3: Perceived fairness and impartiality
- Q4: Fairness in the treatment of stakeholders
- Q5–Q8: The dimensions of trust (consistency, auditability, error correction)
- Q9: The level of transparency of the system
- Q10: The level of trust within the organization that is enhanced by the use of AI.

The study used an ordinal logistic regression model because the dependent variable managerial interaction with AI consisted of three ordinal levels (low, moderate, high) (McCullagh, 1980). This type of regression is suitable when the outcome variable is ordinal but not continuous and when the distances between categories cannot be assumed to be equal (Agresti, 2010). The model calculates the log-odds of being at or below a certain category threshold based on the values of the predictor variables which in this case are the ten perception-based dimensions related to AI transparency and trust. This modeling technique was particularly chosen for capturing non-linear effects and threshold-driven decision behaviors among managers, offering more granularity than binary logistic regression. The model fit was assessed by pseudo R^2 metrics (e.g., McFadden's R^2) and likelihood ratio tests were employed to determine the importance of individual predictors. Both Brant tests and graphical diagnostics were used to verify the proportional odds assumption. The regression analysis was performed using both Python and SAS, taking advantage of the benefits of each platform.

Python was used mainly because of its algorithmic flexibility, open-source nature, and the availability of data science libraries such as statsmodels, scikit-learn, and pandas. This allowed for quick prototyping, model modification, and good exploratory visualization and data transformation. The statsmodels library, in particular, offers robust support for ordinal logistic models and provides key statistical outputs such as coefficient estimates, standard errors, and confidence intervals. SAS, on the other hand, was chosen for its well-documented stability in statistical computation, particularly for categorical and ordinal data modeling. PROC LOGISTIC in SAS has been considered for many years as the gold standard for regression-based analyses in the social and behavioral sciences. It was used here to cross-validate the results obtained in Python, to confirm the model structure, and to check the statistical robustness across platforms. The analysis also used SAS to allow for more detailed control of options such as link functions (logit, probit) and provided a separate confirmation of the significance tests and fit indices.

The dual-software strategy ensured the reproducibility, transparency, and validity of the analysis, which reinforced the methodological rigor of the study.

The above-mentioned ten items based on perception serve as the focus of the independent variables. This approach helps pinpoint the strongest reasoning cognitive factors that explain the increased or decreased interaction with AI systems.

3. RESULTS AND ANALYSIS

3.1. Descriptive Analysis of Perceptions Toward AI

As specified in Table 2, the mean value of all items was recorded between 3 and 3.2 which reveals that Moroccan managers have a rather positive, yet reserved perception about AI automation systems; on a 5-point scale, they scored between 3 and 3.2, indicating a noticeable acceptance of AI technologies. The AI systems engagement level does not provoke any negative sentiments, though it also does not inspire unreserved enthusiasm. “Cautiously optimistic” would perhaps better summarize the sentiment formed from the results.

Table 2 provides item-level descriptive statistics, but Table 3 extends the analysis by showing how interaction levels distribute across different organizational roles. The data shows that middle and senior managers show higher engagement with AI systems compared to operational staff and junior employees who use AI systems infrequently. The findings confirm that AI exposure varies between organizational levels because employees' access to AI systems through their roles determines their perceived usefulness and interaction frequency. The pattern becomes more evident through the analysis presented in Table 4 which examines AI interaction levels against sectoral affiliation. The banking and telecommunications sectors demonstrate higher interaction levels because they have more advanced AI infrastructure compared to the retail sector which shows limited adoption and system integration. The study achieves its comparative objective through this multi-sectoral analysis which enables researchers to understand how specific contextual factors influence managerial views about AI.

The descriptive findings establish a foundation for the upcoming inferential analysis. The study connects perception variables (Table 2), hierarchical position (Table 3), and sectoral context (Table 4) to provide an extensive and evidence-based understanding of AI adoption among Moroccan managers.

Table 2. The MEANS procedure (Source: Authors based on survey results)

Variable	Mean	Minimum	Lower Quartile	Median	Upper Quartile	Maximum
Q1	3.2839506	1.0000000	3.0000000	3.0000000	4.0000000	5.0000000
Q2	3.2716049	1.0000000	2.0000000	3.0000000	4.0000000	5.0000000
Q3	2.9320988	1.0000000	2.0000000	3.0000000	4.0000000	5.0000000
Q4	3.0123457	1.0000000	2.0000000	3.0000000	4.0000000	5.0000000
Q5	2.8518519	1.0000000	2.0000000	3.0000000	4.0000000	5.0000000
Q6	3.0864198	1.0000000	2.0000000	3.0000000	4.0000000	5.0000000
Q7	3.1111111	1.0000000	2.0000000	3.0000000	4.0000000	5.0000000
Q8	3.1481481	1.0000000	2.0000000	3.0000000	4.0000000	5.0000000
Q9	3.2345679	1.0000000	3.0000000	3.0000000	4.0000000	5.0000000
Q10	3.1790123	1.0000000	2.0000000	3.0000000	4.0000000	5.0000000

(Source: Authors based on survey results)

The scores for the questions show that most respondents have fairly balanced opinions, with an average of 3 and an identical median. This shows the moderate position of all respondents.

Table 3. The FREQ Procedure

Level of Interaction	Frequency	Percent	Cumulative Frequency	Cumulative Percent
Low	56	34,57	56	34,57
Moderate	85	52,47	141	87,04
High	21	12,96	162	100,00

(Source: Authors based on survey results)

The level of interaction with the AI system varies considerably among respondents. The majority (52%) fall into the moderate category, meaning they use the system regularly. They do not use it excessively or in a specialized manner. About 34% of the respondents have a low level of interaction, which means they use the system occasionally or only for simple tasks. Last, 13% of respondents have a high level of interaction, which means they are highly engaged with the system, possibly because they are interested in or need advanced features.

Table 4. Descriptive Statistics of AI Perception Dimensions (Source: Authors based on survey results)

Question Dimension	Mean	SD
Q1 – Comprehension of AI decisions	3.12	0.91
Q2 – Accessibility of AI systems	3.21	0.94
Q3 – Fair and impartial decisions	3.06	1.02
Q4 – Stakeholder equity	3.11	0.98
Q5–Q10 – Trust-related (average)	~3.05	~0.95

(Source: Authors based on survey results)

The results show that while AI is not strongly rejected, it is also not fully embraced as a transparent and trustworthy decision-support tool. The relatively high standard deviations (around 1 point) indicate that perceptions differ significantly by individual, sector, and organizational culture. This blended image is in accordance with previous studies (Ko & Leem, 2021; Adadi & Berrada, 2018) which emphasize that trust AI systems organizations have develops gradually and depends significantly on the interpretability and transparency of the system as viewed by the users.

3.2. Interaction Profiles Across Respondent Groups

Among the 162 managers, the reported level of interaction with AI was categorized into three ordinal levels as shown in the Figure 2:

Figure 2. The three levels of interaction with AI

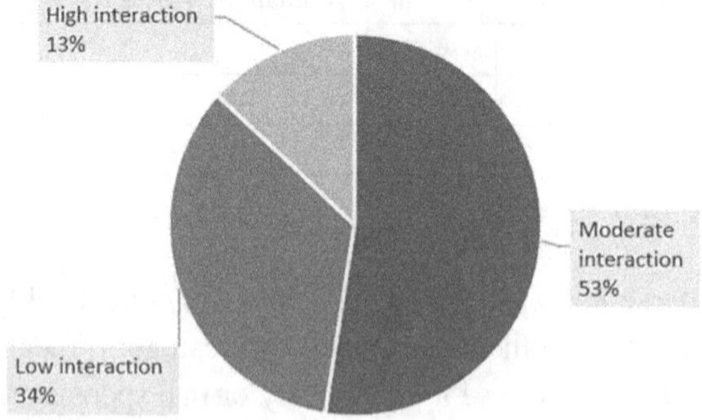

(Source: Authors)

The use of AI tools in the workplace differs substantially based on the employee's management level as shown in Figure 3. Middle managers together with team leaders showed moderate AI tool usage but operational staff and entry-level workers displayed either low or high interaction levels based on their daily operational distance from AI tools.

Figure 3. Number of Participants per Sector

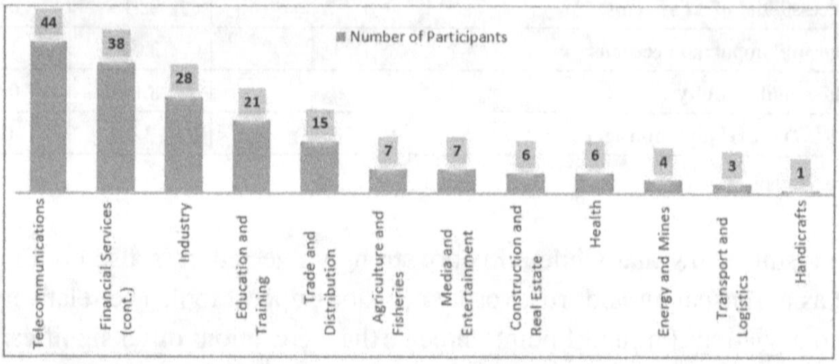

(Source: Authors from Google Forms survey)

The distribution of participants by sector is shown in Figure 3, which is based on the data collected through the Google Forms survey. The telecommunications sector is the most represented with 44 respondents, followed by financial services (38), industry (28), and education and training (21). The sectors of trade and distribution, agriculture and fisheries, and media and entertainment have fewer than 15 participants each. The handicrafts, transport and logistics, and energy and mines sectors have the least representation. The distribution of participants in this study is consistent with the sample composition and may limit the generalizability of the findings, especially for industries that are underrepresented.

Figure 4. Distribution of AI Interaction Levels by Management Role

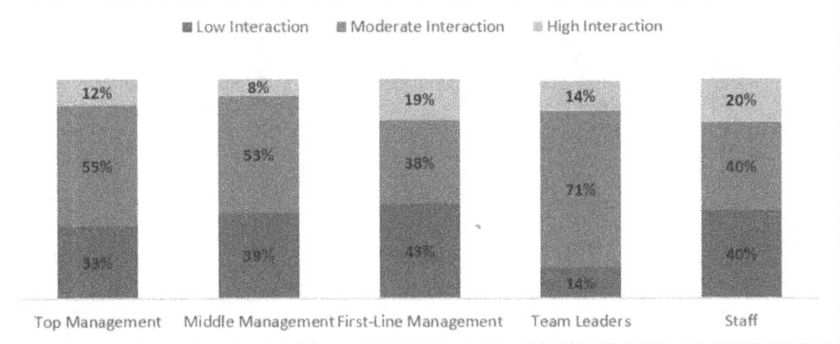

(Source: Authors)

The distribution of interaction levels by job category gives further insight into how AI tools are experienced across organizational hierarchies, beyond the general descriptive statistics. Operational staff tend to report lower interaction, whereas middle and senior managers more frequently engage with AI-assisted decision systems, as shown in Figure 4. Such variability makes it reasonable to incorporate respondents from different organizational levels because their contact with AI systems is likely filtered through their job title, decision-making authority, and closeness to the strategic level. Adding this figure further substantiates the studies focus on understanding the perceptions of middle-level managers in a grounded multi-tiered organizational setting.

The majority of participants demonstrate medium levels of engagement with the AI system when working on Senior Posters and Middle Management positions (71% and 53% respectively). The First Level Management and Middle Management groups show low interaction levels ranging from 40% to 44% which indicates their limited participation in AI usage. The highest level of interaction observed in this study reached only 20% among Personnel. The current state of AI promotion indicates that further development is needed to enhance its dynamic use especially among Team Leaders who hold middle management positions.

Figure 5. Breakdown of level of interaction by sector

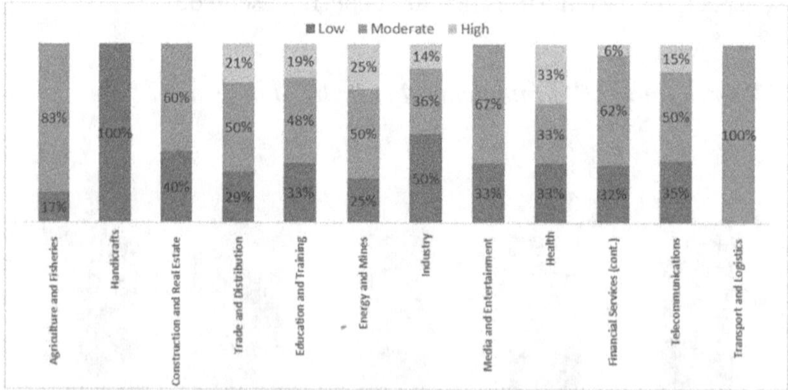

(Source: Authors)

The majority of respondents have a moderate level of interaction with the system, especially in Team Leaders (71%) and however, a significant proportion of first level managers and middle managers have low levels of interaction (between 40% and 44%), indicating a low level of involvement in the use of AI. High levels of interaction remain rare, peaking at 20% among staff. This implies that there is still much that can be done to enhance the use of AI, especially at the middle management level of team leaders.

3.3. Factors Influencing Interaction: Logistic Regression Results

To understand how a manager engages with AI, a logistic regression was conducted using the 10 items related to perception of AI as predictors. In this study, the self-reported degree of interaction with AI systems was regarded as the dependent variable and for the purposes of this study, was considered ordinal (low/moderate/high). Model Estimation was performed in Python while validation was done in SAS, upholding platforms consistency.

Figure 6. Python logistic regression output

```
Optimization terminated successfully.
         Current function value: 0.837135
         Iterations: 35
         Function evaluations: 38
         Gradient evaluations: 38
                             OrderedModel Results
==============================================================================
Dep. Variable:        Interaction_Num   Log-Likelihood:                -135.62
Model:                   OrderedModel   AIC:                             295.2
Method:            Maximum Likelihood   BIC:                             332.3
Date:                Sun, 06 Apr 2025
Time:                        14:36:34
No. Observations:                 162
Df Residuals:                     150
Df Model:                          10
=======================================================================================================
                                        coef    std err          z      P>|z|      [0.025      0.975]
-------------------------------------------------------------------------------------------------------
Q1_Comprehension                      0.4355      0.200      2.182      0.029       0.044       0.827
Q2_Accessibilite                      0.7616      0.180      4.238      0.000       0.409       1.114
Q3_justes_impartiales                -0.7432      0.229     -3.248      0.001      -1.192      -0.295
Q4_Equite                            -0.0996      0.182     -0.548      0.583      -0.456       0.256
Q5_Confiance                          0.0758      0.258      0.294      0.768      -0.429       0.581
Q6_Coherence                         -0.0191      0.282     -0.068      0.946      -0.572       0.534
Q7_decisions_justifiees_auditees     -0.2233      0.217     -1.031      0.303      -0.648       0.201
Q8_Erreurs                            0.1046      0.168      0.622      0.534      -0.225       0.434
Q9_IA_TransparenceGlobale             0.3128      0.271      1.153      0.249      -0.219       0.845
Q10_IA_ConfianceOrganisation         -0.0285      0.233     -0.122      0.903      -0.485       0.428
0/1                                   1.3551      0.657      2.063      0.039       0.068       2.642
1/2                                   1.1421      0.102     11.221      0.000       0.943       1.342
=======================================================================================================
```

(Source: Authors)

Significant influencing factors ($p < 0.05$):

Q1_Comprehension: P-value = 0.029
Higher comprehension levels result in increased interaction. Statistically significant impact.
Q2_Accessibility: P-value = 0.000
Very strong positive and significant impact.
Q3_juste_impartiales: P-value = 0.001

The perception without bias produces a negative effect which decreases interaction.

The odds ratios will allow us to measure the effect of each factor on the probability of a higher level of interaction with AI. An odds ratio greater than 1 would mean that increasing this factor increases the probability of a higher level of interaction, an odds ratio less than 1 would mean a decrease in this probability.

Figure 7. Analysis of the influence of the questions on the level of interaction via the Odds Ratios of logistic regression

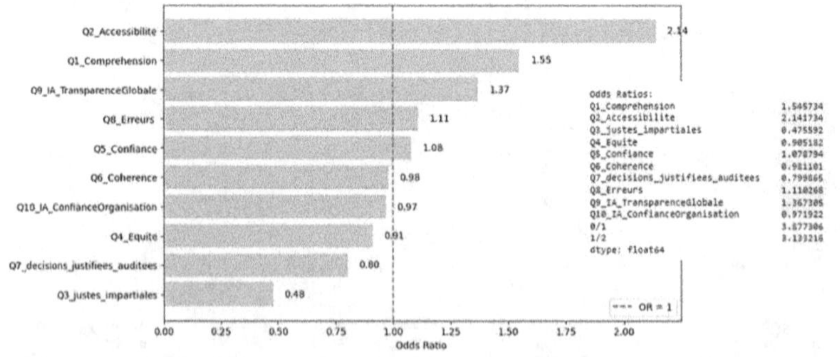

(Source: Authors)

Q2_Accessibility and Q1_Understanding are the most positively influential. Q3_Just_impartials clearly hinder interaction.

Table 5. Logistic Regression Output – Significant Predictors of AI Interaction

Predictor	P-value	Odds Ratio	Direction	Interpretation
Q2 – Accessibility of AI	0.000	> 1.5	Positive	Major driver: more accessible systems → higher interaction
Q1 – Comprehension of decisions	0.029	> 1.2	Positive	Clarity enables operational use and confidence
Q3 – Perception of fairness/ impartiality	0.001	< 1	Negative	Strong fairness perception paradoxically reduces engagement

(Source: Authors)

There are many surprising discoveries that come from this study, such as the fairness perception and its effect on manager engagement with AI systems. Fairness is known to be one of the major factors when it comes to responsible AI, yet here we see firms attempt to define hierarchy- and power-oriented fairness in the workplace and the AI does not seem to work with them as much as they expect. This type of objective AI does not seem to engage as much with them given their high level of managerial expectation which paradoxically suggests that high levels of perceived impartiality (Q3) preclude high levels of interaction. This paradoxical outcome may be indicative of a gap between the pre-war world and managerial perception of the organizational reality. Managers in complex decision-making environments must evaluate both formal equality and contextual nuance alongside relational dynamics and situational flexibility. AI systems that demonstrate impartiality may be viewed as insensitive to organizational subtleties including power structures and informal hierarchies and customer-specific exceptions. The results confirm previous criticisms in the literature (e.g., Mittelstadt et al., 2019; Mhlambi, 2020) that argue that algorithmic fairness, although normatively valuable, does not capture human-centered forms of justice. Thus, too much neutrality may lead to disengagement, not trust. The results demonstrate the need for explainable AI systems which combine formal fairness with contextual intelligibility when such systems are used by decision-makers who work in socially complex and often ambiguous organizational realities.

Figure 8. Correlation Matrix

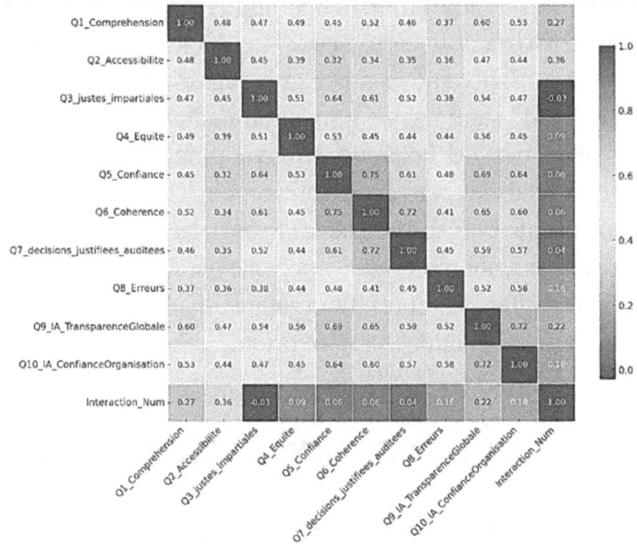

(Source: Authors)

The results show that some dimensions of AI are highly correlated. For instance, the level of trust that people have in AI is closely related with consistency (0.75) and transparency (0.69). This means that the more logical and clear an AI is seen to be in its responses, the more trust it generates. The overall transparency of AI has a strong relationship with confidence in the organization that implements it (0.72). In other words, when AI systems are perceived as clear and understandable, individuals tend to have greater trust in the institutions that deploy them. The level of interaction with the AI had no significant effect on the overall perception. For instance, the correlation between interaction and the perception of impartiality is almost zero (-0.03) which means that the frequency of using the AI does not really affect people's perception. Therefore, the most important thing when it comes to trusting an AI is not how often you use it, but how clear, logical and well explained it is.

3.4. Interpretation and Managerial Implications

The research results provide significant managerial implications. Accessibility stands out as the most significant factor which determines AI interaction. The research shows that managers will use AI systems when they are well-integrated and user-friendly, and their logic is transparent even when they lack technical knowledge. In the same way, understanding is important. If the algorithm generates results that cannot be comprehended, understanding the data will not matter. This emphasizes the need for explainable AI (XAI) frameworks and synergizes with the body of work regarding cognitive trust in automation (Lee & See, 2004). The belief that AI operates with fairness and impartiality shows a negative relationship with interaction. The unexpected finding could stem from a human-computer interface conflict because managers might view strict AI behavior as unyielding and insensitive to specific circumstances which leads them to avoid interaction. The ethical AI literature supports this argument because objectivity needs to be balanced with adaptability when dealing with complex or ambiguous decision contexts. An AI system that shows too much neutrality will neglect to represent organizational values and important soft variables including empathy, intent, and intuition.

4. THEORETICAL DISCUSSION AND INTERPRETATION

The AI interaction regression had three notable predictors: accessibility (Q2), understanding of AI decision making (Q1), and remarkably, fairness bias (Q3) with a negative impact. Perceived fairness was a surprising finding. The LIME theory (Ribeiro et al, 2016) and SHAPE (Lundberg & Lee, 2017) alongside Adadi and Berrada's transparency model viewed through Toreini et al.'s organizational trust model provided explanations for these results.

4.1. Accessibility and Comprehension: Activation of Cognitive Trust

Ribeiro et al. (2016) highlights the importance of explainability and interpretability in fostering user interaction, which is facilitated by the accessibility and comprehensibility of information. The LIME framework holds that local interpretability (the understanding of how an AI system makes a particular choice) needs to be given attention for useful user interaction as well as for trust on the decisions that the system aids them to make. This is corroborated by Adadi and Berrada's (2018) model of multidimensional transparency which argues that cognitive clarity is not peripheral but foundational in any setting that involves the cooperation of humans and AI. As per our findings, the leaders who considered AI systems more "explanatory" were far more likely to report moderate or important levels of interaction. These results are consistent with the wider trust calibration literature (Lee & See, 2004): there is a gap between reliance and functionality if users do not have a mental model of the AI's inner workings. Therefore, explainability is not simply a UX feature, it is a prerequisite for acceptance.

4.2. The Paradox of Perceived Fairness: The "Cold Machine" Hypothesis

The AI interaction with perceived fairness or impartiality's over-user AI relation came out to be AI system users was surprisingly shocking but still coherent. Fairness, as stated by Adadi and Berrada in 2018, is essential, yet insufficient condition for trust. While in other settings, if a lack of flexibility or strictness is seen as fairness, users will withdraw from interaction with AI systems that feel overly mechanical or overly theoretical devoid of human subtleties.

The situation represents an example of "algorithmic detachment" because AI receives credit for accuracy but lacks empathy and situational understanding. An AI system that demonstrates excessive impartiality might face negative perceptions from managers when making complex relational or political decisions because it appears unaligned with organizational priorities and power structures and informal dynamics. The findings align with recent arguments in AI ethics research which state that algorithmic objectivity can damage contextual trust unless accompanied by explainability and human oversight (Floridi et al., 2018; Mittelstadt et al., 2016). The practical implications of this research indicate that AI fairness needs to be developed without separating from usability and contextual relevance.

4.3. Toward a Layered Model of Trust: Beyond TAM

This study operationalized frameworks that are more specific to the domain and not governed by the traditional TAM approach as in 'trust' and 'transparency' were utilized which deepened the insight into management thinking.

- Toreini et al. (2020)'s work on the Organizational Trust Based AI Framework focuses on trust as an institutional construct instead on user trust. Their dimension's, reliability, predictability, and auditability were added to the survey but did not achieve statistical significance of any kind. This means that as a standalone element, trust may not shift behavior in a system that is assumed to be interactively accessible on a cognitive level.

- Our findings contradict TAM's emphasis on perceived usefulness because our research indicates that clarity and interpretability perceptions play a more significant role during initial adoption phases. The findings hold particular importance for non-technical managerial groups because their adoption decisions stem from psychological factors rather than functional considerations.

4.4. Contextual Contributions: The Moroccan Managerial Landscape

The context of North Africa provides another dimension to these insights. In many firms that were surveyed, AI is still at the preliminary phase of embedding itself, typically through third-party's provided systems with little self-internal explainability or auditability. In those scenarios, organizational transparency is usually a product of communication and not system design. The observed dual nature of manager expectations toward fairness and adaptability reveals an essential challenge for AI adoption in emerging markets which requires balancing global principles with local conditions. The research demonstrates how AI implementation in the Global South requires more than technology transfer because it involves negotiations between foreign algorithms and domestic trust systems (Mhlambi, 2020; Abebe et al., 2021).

CONCLUSION

The research aimed to determine how managers view AI system transparency and fairness which affects their organizational interaction with these systems. This study moved beyond classical frameworks such as the Technology Acceptance Model (TAM) and was based on empirically validated and domain-specific models including LIME (Ribeiro et al., 2016), Adadi and Berrada's multidimensional transparency framework (2018), and Toreini et al.'s organizational trust model (2020). This theoretical orientation allowed for a more detailed examination of the cognitive and ethical factors that influence managerial behavior toward AI. Based on the analysis of the responses of 162 Moroccan managers, data from a logistic regression model indicates that the approachability and understandability of AI systems greatly enhances the chances of them interacting with the system on a deeper level. The explainability as well as cognitive clarity. In the context of AI, they are important in any managerial interactions with the AI system. Oddly enough, equity, which is usually a given when considering ethical AI frameworks, showed a negative correlation with interactivity. This result indicates that going too far with unbiased treatment or fairness may equate to no flexibility or adaptability and can therefore distance users in sophisticated decision-making settings. On the other hand, one has to approach the design of decision-making systems, not only from an ethical standpoint, but also from a context-sensitive and organizational relevance angle. The research findings present important practical implications for managers. The study shows that managers need AI systems to be both technically accurate and transparent and easy to understand in order to improve their interaction with these systems. Organizations should establish training programs to educate managers about AI transparency and ethical use so they can make informed decisions about AI-assisted decision systems.

Organizations need to focus on developing explainable interfaces while implementing training programs for non-technical users and enabling human-AI co-decision workflows to let managers verify and interpret system recommendations and challenge them. The counterintuitive effect of fairness perception indicates that AI systems which are perceived as too impartial or rigid may be rejected, particularly in dynamic or relational decision environments. This means that there is a need to design AI systems that incorporate context sensitive fairness, where managers feel that the system is in line with their social and organizational values. The future development of explainable AI frameworks needs to expand its focus from algorithmic transparency to include emotional intelligibility and relational relevance. Future tools need to be jointly developed with users who work at various managerial levels to establish trust and improve usage effectiveness. The design approach that involves users becomes essential for emerging markets because technology adoption needs to align with their complex institutional and cultural characteristics. Other emerging economies such as Kenya and India have also faced similar challenges regarding AI transparency and trust (Abebe et al., 2021), where imported AI solutions often do not meet the expectations of local managers. These gaps need to be addressed in order to achieve global inclusiveness in AI governance. As beneficial as these insights are, the study does have some limitations. Because the data is cross sectional, there is temporal restriction, meaning the analysis can only be done at a single point and it is not possible to evaluate how views and participation in AI systems change with time. In addition, the use of self-report data can lead to biases including, but not limited to, social desirability bias and subjective overestimation of interactions. The non-probabilistic sampling approach restricts the ability to generalize the findings although sectoral diversity was sought. The use of logistic regression was appropriate for the data structure, but it does not allow for more complex modeling of latent constructs and interdependencies that might be captured through structural equation modeling. Future research directions emerge from these study limitations. Longitudinal research methods would provide an active perspective on trust development alongside transparency perception changes throughout time especially since AI will increasingly influence managerial practice. Comparative studies across national or regional contexts could determine if the paradox of fairness is present in other cultures and regulatory atmospheres. Different explanatory levels of fairness or design of interfaces could be tested using experiments and their effects classified as causal under different levels of fairness framing. Qualitative research methods including in-depth interviews and ethnographic observation would provide deeper insights into how managers understand and interact with or challenge AI-based decision-making processes. To conclude, this chapter adds to the literature on the adoption of AI technologies as an AI implementation problem integrating a mental, moral, and sociocultural components perspective. The study shows that managers' interactions with AI are filtered through their perceptions of clarity, accessibility, and fairness, but these perceptions do not always align in predictable ways. The deployment of AI in emerging economies like Morocco requires careful analysis of its social and managerial implications because the technology needs to be both technically efficient and socially and managerially trusted in diverse institutional settings.

REFERENCES

Abebe, R., Barocas, S., Kleinberg, J., Levy, K., Raghavan, M., & Robinson, D. (2021). Roles for computing in social change. *Communications of the ACM, 64*(3), 62–71. DOI: 10.1145/3430368

Adadi, A., & Berrada, M. (2018). Peeking inside the black-box: A survey on explainable artificial intelligence (XAI). *IEEE Access : Practical Innovations, Open Solutions, 6*, 52138–52160. DOI: 10.1109/ACCESS.2018.2870052

Agresti, A. (2010). *Analysis of Ordinal Categorical Data* (2nd ed.). Wiley., DOI: 10.1002/9780470594001

Angelov, P., & Buswell, R. (2002). Identification of evolving fuzzy rule-based models. *IEEE Transactions on Fuzzy Systems, 10*(5), 667–677. DOI: 10.1109/TFUZZ.2002.803499

Arya, V., Bellamy, R. K. E., Chen, P. Y., Dhurandhar, A., Hind, M., Hoffman, S. C., . . . Zhang, Y. (2019). One explanation does not fit all: A toolkit and taxonomy of AI explainability techniques. arXiv preprint arXiv:1909.03012. https://arxiv.org/abs/1909.03012

Barredo Arrieta, A., Díaz-Rodríguez, N., Del Ser, J., Bennetot, A., Tabik, S., Barbado, A., Garcia, S., Gil-Lopez, S., Molina, D., Benjamins, R., Chatila, R., & Herrera, F. (2020). Explainable Artificial Intelligence (XAI): Concepts, taxonomies, opportunities and challenges toward responsible AI. *Information Fusion, 58*, 82–115. DOI: 10.1016/j.inffus.2019.12.012

Binns, R., Veale, M., Van Kleek, M., & Shadbolt, N. (2018). 'It's reducing a human being to a percentage': Perceptions of justice in algorithmic decisions. In *Proceedings of the 2018 CHI Conference on Human Factors in Computing Systems* (pp. 1–14). ACM. DOI: 10.1145/3173574.3173951

Brislin, R. W. (1970). Back-translation for cross-cultural research. *Journal of Cross-Cultural Psychology, 1*(3), 185–216. DOI: 10.1177/135910457000100301

Chomiak, K., Miktus, M., Chomiak, K., & Miktus, M. (2021, August 10). Harnessing value from data science in business: ensuring explainability and fairness of solutions. Consensus. https://consensus.app/papers/harnessing-value-from-data-science-in-business-ensuring-chomiak-miktus/68bfffc21b1d52a2936bf14a0f073a48/

Doshi-Velez, F., & Kim, B. (2017). Towards a rigorous science of interpretable machine learning. arXiv preprint arXiv:1702.08608. https://arxiv.org/abs/1702.08608

Etikan, I., Musa, S. A., & Alkassim, R. S. (2016). Comparison of convenience sampling and purposive sampling. *American Journal of Theoretical and Applied Statistics*, *5*(1), 1–4. DOI: 10.11648/j.ajtas.20160501.11

Floridi, L., Cowls, J., Beltrametti, M., Chatila, R., Chazerand, P., Dignum, V., Luetge, C., Madelin, R., Pagallo, U., Rossi, F., Schafer, B., Valcke, P., & Vayena, E. (2018). AI4People—An ethical framework for a good AI society: Opportunities, risks, principles, and recommendations. *Minds and Machines*, *28*(4), 689–707. DOI: 10.1007/s11023-018-9482-5 PMID: 30930541

Ge, Y., Tan, J., Zhu, Y., Xia, Y., Luo, J., Liu, S., Fu, Z., Geng, S., Li, Z., & Zhang, Y. (2022). Explainable fairness in recommendation. *Proceedings of the 45th International ACM SIGIR Conference on Research and Development in Information Retrieval*, 681–691. DOI: 10.1145/3477495.3531973

Gilpin, L. H., Bau, D., Yuan, B. Z., Bajwa, A., Specter, M., & Kagal, L. (2018). Explaining Explanations: An Overview of Interpretability of Machine Learning. 2022 IEEE 9th International Conference on Data Science and Advanced Analytics (DSAA), 80–89. DOI: 10.1109/DSAA.2018.00018

Hall, P., Gill, N., Kurka, T., & Pham, H. (2021). A unified view of model interpretability: Shapley values and beyond. *Communications of the ACM*, *64*(8), 59–66. DOI: 10.1145/3453192

Ismatullaev, U. V. U., & Kim, S. (2022). Review of the factors affecting acceptance of AI-Infused Systems. *Human Factors*, *66*(1), 126–144. DOI: 10.1177/00187208211064707 PMID: 35344676

Jain, R. (2024). Transparency in AI Decision Making: A Survey of Explainable AI Methods and Applications. *Advances of Robotic Technology*, *2*(1), 1–10. DOI: 10.23880/art-16000110

Jamal, A., Aissaoui, K., & Kassal, S. (2024, December). Enhancing Recruitment Transparency and Efficiency with Explainable AI (XAI). In 2024 3rd International Conference on Embedded Systems and Artificial Intelligence (ESAI) (pp. 1-6). IEEE.

Janiesch, C., Zschech, P., & Heinrich, K. (2021). Machine learning and deep learning. *Electronic Markets*, *31*(3), 685–695. DOI: 10.1007/s12525-021-00475-2

Jena, B., Saxena, S., Nayak, G. K., Saba, L., Sharma, N., & Suri, J. S. (2021). Artificial intelligence-based hybrid deep learning models for image classification: The first narrative review. *Computers in Biology and Medicine*, *137*, 104803. DOI: 10.1016/j.compbiomed.2021.104803 PMID: 34536856

Kacprzyk, J. (2022). AI-enabled Decision Aid and Decision Support for Symbiotic Autonomous Systems. IEEE, 4–5. DOI: 10.1109/ICCICC57084.2022.10101649

Kapiriri, L., Norheim, O. F., & Martin, D. K. (2008). Fairness and accountability for reasonableness. Do the views of priority setting decision makers differ across health systems and levels of decision making? *Social Science & Medicine*, *68*(4), 766–773. DOI: 10.1016/j.socscimed.2008.11.011 PMID: 19070414

Ko, Y., & Leem, C. S. (2021). The Influence of AI Technology Acceptance and Ethical Awareness towards Intention to Use. *Journal of Digital Convergence*, *19*(3), 217–225. DOI: 10.14400/jdc.2021.19.3.217

Kuhfeld, W. F. (2010). Logistic regression modeling using SAS: Theory and application. SAS Institute. https://support.sas.com/resources/papers/proceedings10/264-2010.pdf

Leben, D. (2023). Explainable AI as evidence of fair decisions. *Frontiers in Psychology*, *14*, 1069426. Advance online publication. DOI: 10.3389/fpsyg.2023.1069426 PMID: 36865358

Lee, J. D., & See, K. A. (2004). Trust in automation: Designing for appropriate reliance. *Human Factors*, *46*(1), 50–80. DOI: 10.1518/hfes.46.1.50.30392 PMID: 15151155

Lee, M. K., Jain, A., Cha, H. J., Ojha, S., & Kusbit, D. (2019). Procedural justice in algorithmic fairness. Proceedings of the ACM on Human-Computer Interaction, 3(CSCW), 1–26. DOI: 10.1145/3359284

Lundberg, S. M., Erion, G., Chen, H., DeGrave, A., Prutkin, J. M., Nair, B., Katz, R., Himmelfarb, J., Bansal, N., & Lee, S.-I. (2020). From local explanations to global understanding with explainable AI for trees. *Nature Machine Intelligence*, *2*(1), 56–67. DOI: 10.1038/s42256-019-0138-9 PMID: 32607472

Lundberg, S. M., & Lee, S.-I. (2017). A unified approach to interpreting model predictions. Advances in Neural Information Processing Systems, 30, 4765–4774. https://proceedings.neurips.cc/paper_files/paper/2017/file/8a20a8621978632d76c43dfd28b67767-Paper.pdf

Martin, D. K., Giacomini, M., & Singer, P. A. (2002). Fairness, accountability for reasonableness, and the views of priority setting decision-makers. *Health Policy (Amsterdam)*, *61*(3), 279–290. DOI: 10.1016/S0168-8510(01)00237-8 PMID: 12098521

McCullagh, P. (1980). Regression models for ordinal data. *Journal of the Royal Statistical Society. Series B, Statistical Methodology*, *42*(2), 109–142. https://www.jstor.org/stable/2984952. DOI: 10.1111/j.2517-6161.1980.tb01109.x

Mhlambi, S. (2020). From rationality to relationality: Ubuntu as an ethical framework for AI. Carr Center for Human Rights Policy Working Paper Series. Harvard Kennedy School. https://carrcenter.hks.harvard.edu/publications/ubuntu-ethical-framework-ai

Miller, T. (2019). Explanation in artificial intelligence: Insights from the social sciences. *Artificial Intelligence*, *267*, 1–38. DOI: 10.1016/j.artint.2018.07.007

Mittelstadt, B., Russell, C., & Wachter, S. (2019). Explaining explanations in AI. In *Proceedings of the Conference on Fairness, Accountability, and Transparency* (pp. 279–288). DOI: 10.1145/3287560.3287574

Mittelstadt, B. D., Allo, P., Taddeo, M., Wachter, S., & Floridi, L. (2016). The ethics of algorithms: Mapping the debate. *Big Data & Society*, *3*(2), 1–21. DOI: 10.1177/2053951716679679

Molnar, C. (2022). *Interpretable Machine Learning: A Guide for Making Black Box Models Explainable* (2nd ed.)., https://christophm.github.io/interpretable-ml-book/

Pavlidis, G. (2024). Unlocking the black box: Analysing the EU artificial intelligence act's framework for explainability in AI. *Law, Innovation and Technology*, *16*(1), 293–308. DOI: 10.1080/17579961.2024.2313795

Perconti, P., & Plebe, A. (2020). Deep learning and cognitive science. *Cognition*, *203*, 104365. DOI: 10.1016/j.cognition.2020.104365 PMID: 32563082

Phillips-Wren, G. (2012). AI TOOLS IN DECISION MAKING SUPPORT SYSTEMS: A REVIEW. *International Journal of Artificial Intelligence Tools*, *21*(02), 1240005. DOI: 10.1142/S0218213012400052

Rai, A., Constantinides, P., & Sarker, S. (2021). Next-generation digital platforms: Toward human–AI hybrids. *Management Information Systems Quarterly*, *45*(1), iii–ix. DOI: 10.25300/MISQ/2021/16276

Ribeiro, M. T., ... (2016). ""Why should I trust you?": Explaining the predictions of any classifier." Proceedings of the 22nd ACM SIGKDD International Conference on Knowledge Discovery and Data Mining.

Sachan, S., Yang, J., Xu, D., Benavides, D. E., & Li, Y. (2019). An explainable AI decision-support-system to automate loan underwriting. *Expert Systems with Applications*, *144*, 113100. DOI: 10.1016/j.eswa.2019.113100

Schumann, C., Foster, J., Mattei, N., Dickerson, J. P., Schumann, C., Foster, J., Mattei, N., & Dickerson, J. P. (n.d.). We need fairness and explainability in algorithmic hiring. Consensus. https://consensus.app/papers/we-need-fairness-and-explainability-in-algorithmic-hiring-schumann-foster/440873588e61537fa785e50cec2a50b2/

Seabold, S., & Perktold, J. (2010). Statsmodels: Econometric and statistical modeling with Python. In 9th Python in Science Conference. DOI: 10.25080/Majora-92bf1922-011

Selbst, A. D., Boyd, D., Friedler, S. A., Venkatasubramanian, S., & Vertesi, J. (2019). Fairness and abstraction in sociotechnical systems. Proceedings of the Conference on Fairness, Accountability, and Transparency (FAT*), 59–68. DOI: 10.1145/3287560.3287598

Shlezinger, N., Eldar, Y. C., & Boyd, S. P. (2022). Model-Based Deep Learning: On the intersection of deep learning and optimization. *IEEE Access : Practical Innovations, Open Solutions*, *10*, 115384–115398. DOI: 10.1109/ACCESS.2022.3218802

Shlezinger, N., Whang, J., Eldar, Y. C., & Dimakis, A. G. (2023). Model-Based Deep learning. *Proceedings of the IEEE, 111*(5), 465–499. DOI: 10.1109/JPROC.2023.3247480

Soares, E., Angelov, P. P., Costa, B., Castro, M. P. G., Nageshrao, S., & Filev, D. (2020). Explaining deep learning models through Rule-Based approximation and Visualization. *IEEE Transactions on Fuzzy Systems*, *29*(8), 2399–2407. DOI: 10.1109/TFUZZ.2020.2999776

Toreini, E.. (2020). "The relationship between trust in AI and trustworthy machine learning technologies." *Proceedings of the ACM on Human-Computer Interaction* DOI: 10.1145/3351095.3372834

Chapter 3
The Future of Human Autonomy:
Will Agentic Artificial Intelligence Augment or Replace Human Decision-Making

Ikrame Ouhnine
https://orcid.org/0009-0009-3132-4087
Abdelmalek Essaâdi University, Morocco

ABSTRACT

This chapter explores how agentic Artificial Intelligence (AI) is reshaping economic, social, and ethical structures. Unlike traditional automation, agentic AI autonomously adapts decision-making, replicating or surpassing human cognition. This shift induces a "phase change," transforming institutions, labor markets, and societal norms. While AI enhances efficiency, it exacerbates economic disparities, challenging GDP as a sole metric. We propose alternative indicators integrating well-being, equity, and sustainability. In business, AI-driven models create new data asymmetries, requiring adaptive governance. Trust, as both a relational and regulatory principle, is essential for balancing innovation and accountability. Advocating for Human-Centered AI, transparency, and fairness, this chapter underscores the need for interdisciplinary collaboration and robust data-sharing frameworks to ensure inclusive and equitable AI-driven progress.

DOI: 10.4018/979-8-3373-1737-3.ch003

INTRODUCTION

How is human autonomy being reshaped in the age of agentic Artificial Intelligence? This chapter addresses this central question by exploring how AI systems capable of autonomous reasoning, learning, and decision-making are redefining economic structures, institutional arrangements, and fundamental values.

Over the twentieth century, multiple waves of technological innovation have profoundly reshaped economic and social life to the point of being commonly referred to as "industrial revolutions" (Hatch et al., 2002). Mechanization, followed by mass production, revolutionized manufacturing and consumption processes. Subsequently, the rise of computing and the widespread adoption of the Internet ushered in the information society, where the digitization of exchanges and services became a new standard (Castells, 2010; Fielt, 2024).

Today, we are witnessing the emergence of what we refer to as agentic Artificial Intelligence, a form of AI capable of autonomous goal-setting, real-time adaptation, and decision-making without direct human input (Huang et al., 2023; Russell & Norvig, 2020). Unlike reactive or rule-based systems, agentic AI integrates planning, anticipation, and negotiation mechanisms to fulfill dynamic objectives, making it more than a tool, a partner, or even a substitute in decision-making. This shift signals the onset of what may be termed the Autonomous Revolution.

This new paradigm shift is part of a long historical trajectory comparable to two earlier major upheavals: the Agricultural Revolution and the Industrial Revolution. Each of these revolutions introduced an unprecedented mode of interaction with the world, radically transforming institutions, the division of labor, our conceptions of space and time, and the very structure of our societies. In the case of the Autonomous Revolution, the substitution process relies on multiple "equivalences" (informational, intellectual, and spatial): entire realms of activity once reserved for humans (evaluating options, problem-solving, planning, or decision-making) are now migrating into the algorithmic sphere (Orr & Dutta, 2023; F. Zhang et al., 2024). This substitution process reconfigures the value of human agency by translating formerly embodied tasks into computational actions. Much like a phase transition in physics, this shift upends the fundamental principles governing production, consumption, and social interaction. Although a source of opportunity, this third-social revolution, after the agricultural and the industrial, raises legitimate questions about the future of human autonomy and the preservation of fundamental values (Chesterman, 2019; Dodig-Crnkovic et al., 2024; Machkour & Abriane, 2020).

Unlike purely reactive systems or simple statistical learning models, Agentic Artificial Intelligence is characterized by internal objectives and action mechanisms that grant it a form of initiative. Beyond learning processes, these systems rely on planning, multi-agent collaboration (K. Zhang & Aslan, 2021), and the capacity to adapt in real-time to uncertain environments. This new status, from a mere tool to a genuine decision-making partner, is already evident in diverse sectors such as healthcare, finance, transportation, and education (Elliot et al., 2020; Trischler & Li-Ying, 2023; Wang, 2021). Academic databases (Semantic Scholar, Scopus) further attest to a marked increase in research on multi-agent systems and autonomous planning, confirming the growing significance of agentic AI in the international scientific landscape.

This capacity for autonomous action and decision-making transforms the dynamic of the human-machine relationship. Whereas early computers primarily executed predefined instructions, Agentic Artificial Intelligence systems can now formulate hypotheses and make decisions relatively independent of human intervention. Consequently, a pressing question arises: How can human autonomy be safeguarded in the face of machines whose cognitive performance and operational speed may surpass our own?

On the one hand, agentic AI has the potential to liberate humans from routine or high-risk decision-making; on the other, it introduces a real risk of functional obsolescence in cognitive domains previously reserved for human expertise (Makridakis, 2017; Y. Zhang & Siau, 2024). Its implementation raises unresolved questions: How will responsibility be shared when AI systems err? How should ethical boundaries be programmed?

Referring to agentic Artificial Intelligence as a Revolution is by no means trivial: like previous industrial disruptions, it affects human values, institutions, and practices (Fui-Hoon Nah et al., 2023; Lane, 2014). In the same way that the Industrial Revolution shifted a large portion of the agricultural workforce to factories, the widespread adoption of autonomous AI is already reshaping labor markets and business models. It offers new opportunities, such as novel services, optimized logistics, and personalized medicine, while simultaneously posing significant risks, including technological unemployment, increased inequalities, and enduring digital divides (Brynjolfsson & McAfee, 2014; Nleya & Velempini, 2024).

In the entrepreneurial sphere, integrating agentic AI into strategic and operational processes can represent a decisive competitive edge (V. Agrawal, 2022). Automated decision-making, carried out in an informed and transparent manner, accelerates and refines processes while reducing the cost of specific cognitive or repetitive tasks. At the same time, emerging skill sets, such as data science, cybersecurity, and explainable AI, highlight the need for ongoing adaptation of professions and training programs.

The Autonomous Revolution also has far-reaching implications for governance and regulation. As artificial systems assume roles once exclusively assigned to humans, driving cars, diagnosing illnesses, and managing financial portfolios, responsibility becomes critical (Acemoglu & Restrepo, 2018). How should legal and ethical responsibility be allocated when an autonomous AI causes harm? Does it lie with the implementing organization, the engineer who wrote the code, the end user, or the machine itself? Furthermore, using AI for surveillance, propaganda, or cyberattacks underscores the dangers that may ensue without appropriate regulatory oversight (Zuboff, 2019).

Despite these challenges, the Autonomous Revolution holds considerable promise: improved healthcare services (through more accurate diagnoses and assisted surgical procedures), better resource management, and reduced environmental footprints thanks to algorithms' optimization capabilities, along with large-scale personalization of education and online learning. In this sense, AI can catalyze human emancipation, enabling individuals to harness their creative and interpersonal potential by delegating repetitive or cognitively intensive tasks (Dodig-Crnkovic et al., 2024).

However, these positive prospects come with significant hurdles. From a socio-economic standpoint, routine or easily "virtualizable" jobs are particularly susceptible to automation. At the political level, deploying AI for coercive or security purposes requires reevaluating existing oversight and regulatory frameworks. Finally, preserving privacy and preventing algorithmic bias underscore the need for enhanced transparency and accountability mechanisms (Taddeo & Floridi, 2018).

Leadership becomes a pivotal concern underlying these issues (Kaplan & Haenlein, 2016). As the pace of this transition can now be measured in decades rather than centuries, governments, businesses, and civil society must work in concert to guide this transformation. Without thoughtful intervention, the risk of replicating, on a digital scale, the inequalities, conflicts, and imbalances that accompanied previous industrial revolutions is substantial.

Thus, the "Autonomous Revolution" is a historic inflection point whose scope and speed compel us to rethink our social, political, and economic institutions. Much like the significant transformations of the past, it calls for a reexamination of our practices, institutions, and values, as older modes of thought and governance may no longer be suitable for a world in which intelligence and decision-making increasingly shift toward autonomous systems.

This chapter analyzes the mechanisms underlying the expansion of agentic AI while exploring possible scenarios for its future development. Specifically, it aims to examine how this form of AI differs from previous "industrial revolutions," how it alters economic and social equilibria, and what prospects it opens for humanity in the early twenty-first century. The central question guiding this inquiry remains: In the tension between enhancing and replacing human decision-making, how does agentic AI redefine autonomy?

This chapter adopts an interdisciplinary approach, bridging economics, ethics, cognitive science, and systems theory, to examine the following questions:

- What distinguishes the current AI revolution from previous technological shifts?
- How does agentic AI challenge established productivity, prosperity, and responsibility models?
- What principles and mechanisms are needed to ensure this revolution supports rather than undermines human autonomy?

To guide this inquiry, the chapter is structured around four thematic axes: (1) substitutional equivalences and societal phase changes; (2) productivity gains versus shared prosperity; (3) commercial and structural transformations; and (4) trust, ethics, and future governance, ecological costs, and the cultural reception. Through this framework, we seek to chart a path between utopian optimism and dystopian fatalism and to imagine a future where humans and intelligent systems can collaborate meaningfully, not just coexist functionally.

1. SUBSTITUTIONAL EQUIVALENCES AND SOCIETAL PHASE CHANGES

Major technological breakthroughs, whether the steam engine, electricity, or computing, have invariably generated profound structural shifts in both the economic and social spheres (Hatch et al., 2002). In the context of agentic Artificial Intelligence (AI), we are witnessing the emergence of "substitutional equivalences," that is, the growing capacity of machines to replace human beings in a broadening range of cognitive and decision-making tasks (Brynjolfsson & McAfee, 2014). These novel forms of substitution, powered by increasingly autonomous algorithms, lead to systemic transformations within society, often referred to as *phase changes*. Such transformations occur when a "critical threshold" is crossed, beyond which former equilibria give way to new institutions and operating rules (Hatch et al., 2002).

This subsection first discusses the notion of substitutional equivalences and then the ensuing phase-change dynamics. We will then investigate how the emergence of agentic AI is part of an accelerated process of social change that goes far beyond automating repetitive work and impacts human intelligence and decision-making capabilities. Finally, we look at how machines' autonomy is changing the relationship between productivity and prosperity and the implications that this has for the economics and fairness models passed down from the Industrial Revolution.

1.1. The Concept of Substitutional Equivalences

The idea of "substitutional equivalences" means a technology's capacity to supplement a human practice or function in a significantly similar way while also pulling from new tools and following new operating logic. Historically, such substitutions have occurred: electrification replaced muscle power in factories, and industrial automation mechanized many routinized tasks (Schumpeter, 1935, 1983). With agentic AI, the potential for substitution has entered higher-order cognitive functions, like language interpretation, image recognition, planning, or making decisions (Russell & Norvig, 2020).

Agentic AI is based on learning and adaptive capabilities, which fundamentally differs from conventional, notionally deterministic automation (Wooldridge, 2009). It constantly improves what it does with the input data and goals given to it. This fundamental shift from purely deterministic rule-following towards authentic decision-making autonomy represents a paradigm shift: the machine is no longer just about executing instructions but weighing options and choosing (M. D. Stone & Woodcock, 2014; P. Stone et al., 2022). Much more than an incremental improvement to existing tools, this represents a deeper structural reconfiguration.

A telling example of the power of substitutional equivalences can be found in bank robbery. Historically, robbing a bank required firearms and entailed considerable personal risk, often for a relatively modest payoff. Today, cyberattacks use "zombie" computer networks (botnets) to siphon small sums from numerous accounts, operating almost undetected. Malicious software like Zeus gathers usernames and passwords, while criminal platforms coordinate the transfers (Zuboff, 2019). Although the end goal, stealing money, remains unchanged, the methods, rules, and tools belong to an entirely different realm (cybersecurity, international police cooperation, etc.).

Under these conditions, law enforcement agencies must rethink their investigative and regulatory methods as traditional police responses become increasingly ill-suited. This kind of institutional and normative shift is precisely what substitutional equivalence entails: new technologies assume functions "equivalent" to those of the former system yet disrupt existing logic and steer society toward a new state of equilibrium.

1.2. From Technological Breakthroughs to Social Transitions: Toward a "Phase Change"

The notion of a *phase change* comes from physics: beyond a critical threshold, a system transitions from one state to another with entirely new properties. In economic and social terms, each major technological revolution, whether steam power, electricity, or computing, has triggered a profound reconfiguration of productive and institutional structures (Perez, 2002). Polanyi (2001) used the term "Great Transformation" to describe these moments when norms, institutions, and modes of production align with new technical and economic forces.

Several interconnected dynamics are shaping the rapid transformation of business and finance. Agentic AI accelerates these changes by enabling innovations in logistics, demand prediction, personalization, and cost reduction. The figure below synthesizes the four key trends driving this evolution.

Figure 1. Key Trends Shaping Business and Finance Transformation in the Era of Agentic AI

Such upheavals do not always unfold linearly. They emerge when an accumulation of smaller innovations reaches a tipping point, profoundly challenging humanity's role in production and decision-making (Hatch et al., 2002). By hastening the surpassing of critical thresholds, agentic AI brings about a radical reconsideration of our socioeconomic practices.

1.3. Intellectual Equivalence: AI as a Substitute (and Amplifier) of Human Capabilities

One of the most striking developments of this "Autonomous Revolution" is *intellectual equivalence*, that is, machines' capacity to replicate or surpass human cognitive processes. Advances in AI, particularly in deep learning, neural networks, and large-scale data processing, are driving this trend: algorithms learn from experience and reprogram themselves without direct human intervention, notably through reinforcement learning techniques (LeCun et al., 2015).

The pursuit of machine intelligence has deeper historical roots. As early as 1914, Spanish engineer Leonardo Torres y Quevedo presented an automaton capable of playing certain chess endgames. In 1921, Czech playwright Karel Čapek popularized the term *robot* in his play *R.U.R. (Rossum's Universal Robots)*, already highlighting fears of dehumanization and job loss. Later, Alan Turing (1950) introduced the famous "Turing Test" to evaluate whether a machine could be said to "think." Despite alternating periods of high optimism and "AI winters," the rise of deep learning, bolstered by computing power and vast data repositories, has propelled the field to unprecedented performance.

In 1997, IBM's Deep Blue defeated world chess champion Garry Kasparov; in 2016, Google DeepMind's AlphaGo beat Lee Sedol in Go, using reinforcement learning and deep neural networks. In increasingly complex tasks, machines can thus match or even exceed human performance. This intellectual equivalence, enabled by high-performance computing and massive data availability, symbolizes the growing "cognitive autonomy" that may fundamentally reshape the relationship between humans and technology.

1.4. Accelerating Dynamics and Their Implications

Although history shows that each technological revolution brings about profound social changes, the speed and scale of adopting agentic AI appear to exceed previous thresholds (Brynjolfsson et al., 2018). The convergence of three factors—computational capacity, the massive availability of data, and advances in learning algorithms—accelerates the rate of adoption.

This rapid deployment fosters a concentration of economic and informational power in the hands of a few players, chiefly global platforms and major tech conglomerates, capable of developing increasingly powerful algorithms (Zuboff, 2019). Such dominant positions risk deepening socioeconomic and geopolitical divides: some regions lack the infrastructure or expertise to keep pace, while income inequalities widen.

Nonetheless, it is important to note that substitutional equivalences can free humans from monotonous or hazardous tasks, allowing resources to be channeled into creativity, scientific research, or social innovation (Kaplan & Haenlein, 2016). As in previous technological upheavals, new equilibria may emerge after the transition period, accompanied by novel opportunities for employment and growth (Acemoglu & Restrepo, 2019; Han, 2022).

2. PRODUCTIVITY WITHOUT PROSPERITY? THE RISK OF AN OBSOLETE ECONOMIC MODEL

A central question arises: Will productivity gains from agentic AI translate into shared prosperity or merely concentrate on wealth and power? In previous technological revolutions, such as the combustion engine, electricity, and computing, rising production levels were accompanied by the expansion of mass consumption and the emergence of a strong middle class.

However, this historic synergy is weakening in the digital and algorithmic age. Several studies suggest that current technologies sometimes yield productivity gains that are difficult to monetize, meaning they are not reflected in traditional economic indicators (Brynjolfsson & McAfee, 2014). For example, while social media platforms and streaming services deliver high user utility, they contribute modestly to GDP and create relatively few jobs. Moreover, cognitive automation may exacerbate labor market polarization, privileging high-skill roles while eroding middle-income professions(Acemoglu & Restrepo, 2019; Autor, 2015).

To clarify this disconnect, consider the historic example of the internal combustion engine. Introduced in the late nineteenth century, it revolutionized transportation and spurred an entire industrial ecosystem: road construction, urbanization, and the steel, rubber, and glass industries (Hatch et al., 2002). By paying high wages, Henry Ford enabled his workers to become consumers of the very cars they produced, thus creating a positive feedback loop. The price of the Model T fell from $950 in 1908 to $269 in 1923, illustrating the synergy between productivity and prosperity.

With agentic AI, such a feedback loop is far from guaranteed. Intelligent machines automate large segments of the economy, often without generating as many jobs as in previous industrial revolutions. The added value derived from AI centered on data collection and analytics sometimes becomes concentrated in the hands of a few actors, exacerbating income inequalities. Economic mechanisms that defined the era of mass production (a strong correlation between GDP and well-being, broad consumer access, etc.) appear less robust in a world where cognitive substitution challenges the role of salaried employment as the primary means of redistribution.

Techno-optimists contend that, as in the past, these upheavals will lead to new forms of work and activity (Acemoglu & Restrepo, 2018, 2019). Techno-skeptics, by contrast, argue that the very nature of AI, driven by autonomy and automation, makes it harder to establish a feedback loop comparable to earlier revolutions, thereby increasing the risk of precariousness and societal fragmentation.

The structural transformations spurred by agentic AI, particularly through the emergence of substitutional equivalences and phase changes, attest to a rapid reconfiguration of economic and social dynamics. Beyond functional substitution alone, the question remains: *to what extent will these productivity gains translate into shared prosperity?* The following section will address this question, highlighting a possible disconnect between productivity and prosperity. There, we will delve deeper into the rise of non-monetizable forms of productivity and their potential impact on the economic models inherited from the Industrial Revolution.

Throughout history, introducing new technologies has been expected to drive productivity gains that translate into broader prosperity and a general rise in living standards (Hatch et al., 2002; Schumpeter, 1935). The history of the steam engine, electricity, and semiconductors reinforces this narrative: Innovation stimulates economic growth, energizes the labor market, and ultimately contributes to the emergence of a flourishing middle class. However, the advent of agentic Artificial Intelligence challenges the sturdiness of this paradigm. Despite observable productivity gains, there is no guarantee that these advances will yield prosperity equitably shared by all (Brynjolfsson & McAfee, 2014).

In this section, we examine the phenomenon of a "disjunction" between productivity and prosperity, focusing particularly on non-monetizable productivity, a defining feature of the digital economy and advanced cognitive automation. We highlight the paradoxes inherent in productivity that lower costs and improve well-being without significantly boosting GDP or ensuring a fair value distribution. Drawing on various historical examples (the internal combustion engine and the semiconductor), we show how the "Autonomous Revolution" diverges from previous industrial revolutions to challenge the conventional correlation between rising productivity and widespread prosperity.

2.1. The Productivity Paradox in the AI Era

Economists have pointed to a "productivity paradox" for several decades: technical progress sometimes takes time to manifest itself in tangible GDP growth because production processes and institutions must first adapt (Brynjolfsson et al., 2018; van Ark, 2015). In the case of agentic AI, this issue takes on a new dimension. On the one hand, the growing autonomy of algorithms increases the speed, precision, and scalability of numerous tasks (A. Agrawal et al., 2019); on the other, it redefines the very nature of economic growth.

Indeed, cognitive automation may dramatically enhance productivity in key sectors (finance, logistics, healthcare) while weakening human employment and creating demand for new specialized skills (Acemoglu & Restrepo, 2019; Autor, 2015). This sectoral reshuffling can manifest as GDP growth, whose benefits accrue to a narrow circle of actors and do not always filter down to the bulk of the workforce (Brynjolfsson & McAfee, 2014).

Furthermore, specific markets exhibit limited elasticity, tempering the widespread positive effects of cost reductions. During the rise of the automobile and semiconductors, for instance, the decline in unit costs led to increased demand (Moore's Law for semiconductors, Ford's pricing strategy for the Model T, etc.). By contrast, in the digital economy, the near-free availability of information does not spark exponential consumption: one does not read a hundred times more newspapers nor file taxes more frequently simply because costs have decreased. This low elasticity restricts employment growth in these sectors, hindering a new virtuous circle in which gains in productivity automatically translate into large-scale job creation (Kaur & Wadhawan, 2023).

2.2. The Emergence of Non-Monetizable Productivity

At the heart of this new reality lies the notion of "non-monetizable productivity," meaning productivity gains are not necessarily captured by conventional economic indicators such as GDP. The digital economy is brimming with quasi-free goods and services (search engines, social networks, open-access applications) and leverages vast troves of user-generated data, often contributed at no cost (Wirtz et al., 2023).

With agentic AI, this trend becomes even more pronounced: algorithms learn autonomously from massive datasets contributed by individuals who receive no compensation for doing so. Dominant digital platforms, whether Google, Amazon, or Facebook, capitalize on these resources to deliver highly effective, exceptionally profitable services while employing relatively few people. As a result, the market value generated per employee can be far higher than that of a traditional company without proportionate job creation in other sectors.

Moreover, many online services are free or cheap to consumers. While this development undoubtedly enhances quality of life (easy access to information, online entertainment, instant communication), it also diminishes employment previously reliant on paid labor (printing, postal distribution, brick-and-mortar sales). The example of the print media is illustrative: free online news has caused advertising revenues to plummet, even though the overall quality and speed of information have increased for readers. The outcome is a boost in informational productivity, unmonetized from the standpoint of traditional media, undermining job stability in journalism.

In the financial sector, robo-advisors and peer-to-peer lending platforms have reduced costs and increased access, but they also undercut traditional banking jobs without creating equivalent alternatives. This divergence from previous innovation cycles reflects the structural limits of digital consumption and cognitive automation to generate broad-based employment.

2.3. Rethinking Value and Indicators

The rise of non-monetizable productivity calls into question core economic assumptions, which traditionally hold that any productivity increase should, in principle, stimulate GDP and spill over into employment and consumption (Brynjolfsson & McAfee, 2014). In the past, for example, with the internal combustion engine or the integrated circuit, productivity gains were tied to market expansion (lower prices, surging demand) and collective wealth creation (the rise of new industries, higher wages). In the case of agentic AI, however, innovations revolve around automating cognitive and informational tasks, where demand is limited by the low elasticity of intangible goods and the finite amount of user attention.

Consequently, productivity may increase without necessarily yielding the prosperity gauged by traditional indicators. The labor market either contracts or reconfigures itself around highly specialized skills, while the free or nearly free availability of many digital services offers end users certain benefits. This gap between productivity and prosperity prompts us to question the relevance of the economic frameworks inherited from the industrial era and suggests new indicators capable of capturing overall well-being (Peng et al., 2023; Wirtz et al., 2023).

Many economists now advocate adopting alternative indices, such as the Social Progress Index, the Human Development Index, or other measures that factor in quality of life, environmental considerations, and hidden costs of technological progress (Taddeo & Floridi, 2018). In a context where information flows at minimal cost and autonomous systems increasingly handle decision-making, people may enjoy higher living standards, thanks to the near-free availability of essential services, without seeing their incomes follow the same trajectory.

Beyond measurement challenges, it is vital to redefine the place and value of work in an environment where AI takes over analytical and repetitive functions (Brynjolfsson & McAfee, 2014). While earlier mechanical revolutions primarily replaced physical labor, the Autonomous Revolution now encroaches on cognitive tasks, jeopardizing the stability of numerous service-sector jobs, especially those susceptible to relocation or digitization via machine learning.

At the same time, this shift can make human skills that are harder to automate, such as creativity, empathy, interpersonal management, critical thinking, and leadership, more valuable (van Haeften et al., 2024). Consequently, some researchers and policymakers have floated the idea of a universal basic income or the expansion of social safety nets to guide workforce realignment and underscore these irreplaceable human qualities (Autor, 2015).

2.4. Artificial Intelligence's Ecological Toll

While agentic Artificial Intelligence is often celebrated for its potential to enhance productivity, streamline operations, and drive intelligent automation, its environmental consequences remain insufficiently scrutinized. The computational intensity of training large-scale AI models, particularly foundation and large language models, requires immense energy consumption, resulting in substantial carbon footprints. As highlighted by Patterson et al. (2022), training a single state-of-the-art model can emit as much CO_2 as five average cars over their lifetimes. This environmental impact is not limited to data center operations; it extends across the entire AI lifecycle, encompassing the extraction of rare minerals, manufacturing hardware components, and the growing problem of electronic waste generated by rapid technological obsolescence.

This ecological burden reveals a profound contradiction between agentic AI's promise and ecological sustainability's broader imperatives. On the one hand, AI systems are deployed to optimize resource use and support sustainable development; on the other, their development and deployment can actively undermine planetary health. This paradox introduces an urgent dimension to the autonomy debate: if agentic AI systems, designed to expand human capabilities and decision-making autonomy, contribute to long-term environmental degradation, the foundations of future human flourishing are at risk.

In response, the AI research community has begun advocating for Green AI, a paradigm shift emphasizing energy efficiency, carbon-aware computing, and environmentally responsible innovation. Efforts include adopting low-precision arithmetic, pruning, and quantization techniques, model distillation, and decentralized learning frameworks such as federated learning, which reduce the need for centralized data processing (Alzoubi & Mishra, 2024). Moreover, integrating life cycle assessments and carbon accountability metrics into AI development pipelines is increasingly essential for aligning technological progress with sustainability goals.

From a governance perspective, the ecological costs of AI must be explicitly incorporated into policy frameworks and innovation incentives. This involves technical guidelines, ethical considerations, and strategic foresight to ensure that AI does not exacerbate ecological inequalities or transgress critical planetary boundaries (Du et al., 2024). As we transition to a new era of decision-making shaped by agentic systems, it becomes imperative to reimagine governance architectures that safeguard autonomy and environmental viability.

In the subsequent section, we move beyond the ecological and economic dimensions to explore how agentic AI transforms organizational structures, leadership dynamics, and decision-making paradigms, ultimately reshaping the trajectory of human autonomy in complex socio-technical systems.

3. THE ROLE OF AI IN COMMERCIAL TRANSFORMATION

Building upon the previous section's analysis of productivity and prosperity, we now examine how agentic AI reshapes commercial structures, value chains, and organizational logic. Innovations such as the Internet of Things, autonomous vehicles, big data analytics, and blockchain are creating an environment brimming with opportunities where new types of enterprises and entire sectors emerge continuously. At the same time, these technologies unsettle established socioeconomic configurations, forcing incumbent actors to reinvent themselves or disappear.

3.1. Rewriting Commerce and the Economy

The rise of agentic AI reconfigures economic power through Spatial Equivalences, shifting from physical to digital infrastructures. Tom Goodwin observed that leading companies today, such as Uber, Airbnb, Alibaba, and Meta, often have no physical assets (Goodwin, 2015). Instead, they orchestrate platform-based ecosystems where value emerges from data, connectivity, and algorithmic coordination.

Phenomena such as e-commerce, the sharing economy, the freemium model, crowdfunding, and virtual currencies exemplify the rapid transformation of business and finance landscapes. These developments highlight how agentic AI acts as a catalyst, enabling intelligent algorithms to optimize logistics, forecast demand, personalize offerings, and significantly reduce intermediation costs (A. Agrawal et al., 2019). The figure below summarizes the key dynamics driving this transformation, which can be categorized into four emblematic trends.

One major trend in this shift is virtualization. An increasing number of businesses, especially service-oriented ones, have moved to virtual or flexible operating models, such as mobile apps, SaaS offerings, etc. This phenomenon is particularly pervasive in information-intensive industries, which engage roughly 80% of the global workforce (OECD, 2020). Virtualization is not just about the technology; it is about an entirely new way organizations structure their businesses and deliver services.

Another very important dynamic is the movement towards network-like structures. Virtualized businesses typically employ a model whereby a relatively small group of regular employees coordinates large networks of subcontractors and freelancers. Uber and Deliveroo are two companies that employ this strategy, using a hub-and-spoke configuration. This model adopts a centralized management team that manages a large decentralized workforce, thus enabling scalability and flexibility with minimal fixed labor costs. (Sundararajan et al., 2017).

Another transformational element of these new organizational models is replacement. The informational exchanges serve, but they do not create an equivalent number of jobs (think Google and their outsourcing initiatives) and, in fact, are displacing many traditional corporations that serve communities. For example, Spotify's dominance in music streaming has significantly reduced people's buying of CDs, which has resulted in many physical music stores closing down. This trend demonstrates an increasing disconnect between value creation and job creation, leaving us wondering about the disruptive effects of these changes.

Lastly, effective competition is declining due to the rise of monopolistic or oligopolistic platforms driven by network effects. Google, Amazon, Apple, and Facebook are examples of this phenomenon. These platforms are commonly referred to as "BAADD" (big, anti-competitive, addictive, democracy-destroying), asserting massive economic and political power, and there are concerns about fairness and societal implications (Zuboff, 2019). The figure below summarizes these dynamics, illustrating how agentic AI and related technological advancements are reshaping commercial paradigms.

Figure 2. Transformation of Ecosystems and Value Chains in the Era of Agentic AI

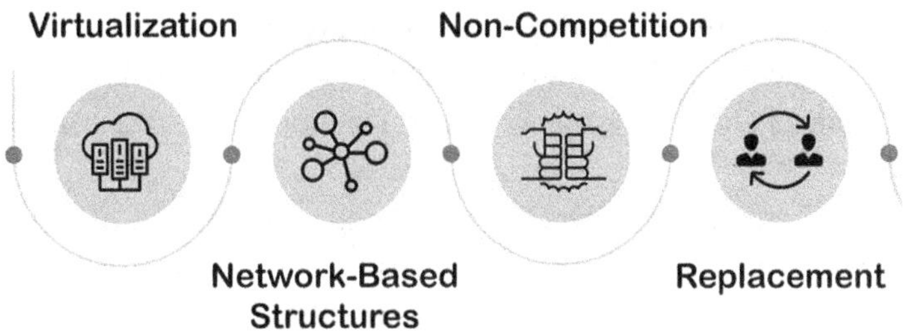

Among the transformations wrought by agentic AI, the dismantling and subsequent reconstruction of value chains (Porter & Heppelmann, 2014) prove especially consequential. In an era of advanced automation and collaborative robotics, production has become more flexible; mass customization is now facilitated by real-time data integration from demand, maintenance, and logistics (A. Agrawal et al., 2019).

- **Toward Vertical and Horizontal Integration:** Increasingly, industry-leading companies position themselves as "platform orchestrators," connecting suppliers, distributors, and customers via intelligent solutions. Beyond vertical integration alone (controlling the entire value chain), we see novel forms of horizontal alliances that blur traditional sectoral boundaries (Cusumano et al., 2019).
- **Fading Sectoral Boundaries:** Tech giants now invest in widely varying domains, such as healthcare, finance, automotive, and home automation, leveraging their AI capabilities and extensive datasets (Zuboff, 2019). Competition thus takes new forms: a player historically specialized in e-commerce may threaten banks with mobile payment services, while a consumer electronics manufacturer might enter the medical data-management space.

These trends redefine how goods and services are produced and delivered, who captures value, and how. They also underscore a shift toward **platform orchestration**, where the firm becomes a facilitator rather than a producer (Cusumano et al., 2019).

3.2. Data as a Strategic Resource and a Source of Asymmetry

In the nineteenth century, industrial power was centered on coal and later oil; in the current digital revolution, this dynamic has shifted toward data, now the proper fuel of contemporary systems. Agentic AI, which relies on machine learning and deep learning, depends heavily on data quality and quantity to achieve efficiency and remain competitive (LeCun et al., 2015).

Many companies are reorienting their business models around data, investing heavily in infrastructure and software ecosystems driven by self-learning algorithms (Iansiti & Lakhani, 2020). Their strategic reorganization pursues three main objectives:

1. **User Experience Personalization:** Companies tailor offerings to individual preferences in real time through personalized recommendations and interfaces.
2. **Continuous Operational Optimization:** Based on data-driven insights, production lines, logistics, and distribution processes can be adjusted almost instantaneously (Brynjolfsson & McAfee, 2014).
3. **Anticipating Emerging Trends:** By detecting early market shifts, these companies can adapt their offerings before explicitly articulating demand, thus gaining a decisive competitive edge.

Simultaneously, the concentration of power in the hands of a few global platforms (Google, Amazon, Facebook, Apple) is unprecedented, generating strong network effects that hinder the entry of new market players (Zuboff, 2019). From a policy and regulatory perspective, this situation poses a dilemma: Should one consider dismantling these monopolies, as in specific historical precedents (for instance, the oil or telecommunications sectors), or opt for stringent regulation based on transparency and fairness (Taddeo & Floridi, 2018)? In a hyperconnected world, establishing a global governance framework for data management emerges as a significant challenge, demanding international cooperation and incorporating ethical and societal considerations.

3.3. The Rise of "As-a-Service" Models and Organizational Restructuring

In parallel with the expansion of the digital economy, "as-a-service" offerings (Software-as-a-Service, Infrastructure-as-a-Service, etc.) have gained significant traction. In these models, users pay for the temporary use of a service rather than acquiring a product outright (Cusumano et al., 2019). This trend is reinforced by the rise of agentic AI, which enables the automation of key processes (resource allocation, predictive maintenance, and service personalization).

This shift is characterized by a growing degree of modularity: thanks to deep-learning algorithms, it is now possible to assemble specialized microservices or functions (image recognition, predictive analytics, chatbots, etc.) as modular software "building blocks." This flexibility allows providers to adapt their solutions in real-time based on user preferences and behaviors.

These dynamics also benefit small and medium-sized enterprises (SMEs), which can now access cutting-edge technologies (cloud computing, outsourced HR, AI-driven accounting) at a reduced cost (Nadimpalli, 2017; Windmann et al., 2024). However, this transformation is accompanied by the emergence of new intermediaries, often service platforms, that capture a substantial share of the value created, potentially destabilizing competitive balance in specific niche markets.

Globalization and widespread AI adoption create hybrid ecosystems where collaboration and competition strategically coexist (Crowder et al., 2020). This climate fosters unprecedented intersectoral partnerships: for instance, an automotive manufacturer may collaborate with a digital firm to develop autonomous driving solutions while competing in other segments (Kaplan & Haenlein, 2016). *Competition* thus becomes essential in an environment where innovation depends on the interdependence of specialized expertise.

It is redefining labor-market dynamics in parallel. Such emerging models combine the pooling of assets and skills before supplying them directly to demand (Sundararajan et al., 2017) on platforms like Uber, Airbnb, and TaskRabbit. This tendency makes outsourcing work and services even more robust, having considerable repercussions on the job market. This fragmentation of employment status, the waning of standard salaried work, and the swift growth of independent contracting pose heightened issues around insecurity, social protection, and market oversight.

A telling example of this transformation is the so-called "hub-and-spoke" company, such as Uber or Facebook, with a high ratio between its core workforce and its huge user or subcontractor base. A core team of full-time employees oversees a tremendous amount of work independent contractors do. This model provides increased flexibility and scalability but may magnify precarious working conditions.

These technological trends are also profoundly altering the automotive industry. While traditional car manufacturing involves heavy infrastructure (factories, logistics chains, dealerships), autonomous vehicles and on-demand smartphone-based services fundamentally disrupt this model. Not only do they reduce the need for individual ownership, but they also diminish labor requirements across the sector. In the long run, this phenomenon could undermine the emergence of a robust middle class, historically a cornerstone of economic and social stability (Kaur & Wadhawan, 2023).

3.4. Transformations in the Financial Sector

The impact of agentic AI is particularly acute in financial services, a historically highly regulated sector dominated by large institutions. Today, these established actors must contend with the rise of fintech firms, which leverage information-centric approaches to bypass both the costs and the sluggishness associated with traditional channels (credit cards, international transfers, asset management). Harnessing AI, these newcomers offer faster, more affordable, and often more accessible services.

1. **Virtualized Payment Systems:** Platforms like WeChat, Alipay, PayPal, or Venmo are already reshaping capital exchange. By reducing transaction costs and enhancing security (blockchain, cryptography), they directly compete with conventional credit cards, which are seen as more expensive and less secure.
2. **Automated Asset Management:** Robo-advisors constitute a significant shift in investment management. Charging very low fees (between 0.25% and 0.5%), these automated platforms often achieve returns comparable to those of human managers, thus attracting numerous investors and encroaching on established professions (Brynjolfsson et al., 2018).
3. **Peer-to-Peer Lending:** Companies like Lending Club, Prosper, Upstart for individuals, OnDeck, and Funding Circle for SMEs rely on predictive algorithms to assess borrowers' creditworthiness. By offering loans at competitive rates, they challenge traditional banks' historic monopoly and foster a decentralized lending ecosystem.

Agentic AI is, therefore, reshuffling the cards in the financial industry, enabling more agile, efficient, and inclusive business models while undermining the primacy of traditional players. In the following section, we will explore AI's ethical and responsible dimensions, focusing on the critical roles of trust and regulation in an economic landscape increasingly driven by autonomous systems. More specifically, we shall examine how to reconcile the pursuit of innovation with the defense of foundational principles such as transparency, accountability, and human dignity. In light of the growing dominance of leading actors and the reorganization of value chains, defining governance mechanisms that ensure the security and reliability of emerging technologies, and their long-term legitimacy and social acceptability has become imperative.

The following section explores how trust, ethics, and human-centered governance can respond to these challenges, restoring legitimacy and autonomy in an increasingly automated economy.

4. THE TRUST ECONOMY WINS: TOWARD A MORE HUMAN FUTURE

Beyond efficiency and automation, the rise of agentic AI compels us to reconsider the foundational role of trust in digital economies. If data fuels algorithmic systems, trust is the infrastructure that allows them to scale and interact with society (Botsman, 2017). This section explores the ethical, relational, and regulatory dimensions of the emerging "trust economy," highlighting its pivotal role in restoring human agency.

4.1. A Strategic Pillar of the Customer Experience

In an increasingly digitized world, trust is not merely a competitive advantage but the cornerstone of economic and social sustainability. As Nobel laureate Jean Tirole (2014) has emphasized, the expansion of digital technologies presupposes that users trust their data will not be exploited to their detriment or misused. A platform or business that fails to establish such trust risks its model, regardless of its technological sophistication.

The rise of the sharing economy (Airbnb, BlaBlaCar, Uber, etc.) illustrates the disruptive power of trust: activities such as home-sharing or ridesharing depend entirely on a confidence capital fueled by rating systems, insurance guarantees, and robust customer support. More broadly, trust has become a strategic asset for any organization. Brands that deliver a flawless customer experience transform users into ambassadors, strengthening their reputation and resilience.

Trust also materializes through proactive customer service, rapid dispute resolution, and transparency in data collection and usage. Large platforms, like Amazon and Airbnb, prioritize the presumption of good faith toward the customer, investing heavily in after-sales services (quick refunds, easy contact) and solid security protocols. Balancing data protection and a seamless user experience becomes a significant challenge in an environment increasingly prone to cyber threats.

Deploying agentic AI systems cannot be limited to productivity gains; it also requires ethical guidelines and accountability mechanisms (Winfield et al., 2019). When algorithms influence credit allocation, hiring decisions, or medical treatment recommendations, algorithmic transparency and fairness become imperative (Huang et al., 2023). This does not necessarily imply disclosing every design detail but enables independent audits to avoid discriminatory bias (Dodig-Crnkovic et al., 2024).

Similarly, traceability calls for clarifying responsibilities in case of errors or damages: Is it the designer, the operator, or the user? Multiple initiatives seek to establish legal frameworks capable of addressing algorithmic liability. Beyond mere legal compliance, trust also requires "technological empathy" (Picard, 1997), particularly in sensitive areas such as healthcare (Chaddad et al., 2021; Hamet & Tremblay, 2017) or education. The goal is to design interfaces considering users' emotions and intentions without neglecting the human dimension.

Technological Empathy (Picard, 1997) emerges as critical here. It refers to the design of AI systems that respond to rational inputs, emotional cues, and ethical contexts—especially in sensitive sectors like healthcare and education (Chaddad et al., 2021; Hamet & Tremblay, 2017).

The Human-Centered Artificial Intelligence (HCAI) paradigm, which prioritizes augmentation over automation, suggests a reorientation of innovation goals. Rather than replacing human judgment, HCAI emphasizes partnership: AI accelerates data processing while humans provide interpretation, empathy, and final decisions (Chernov et al., 2020; Elliot et al., 2020).

The notion of Human-Centered AI underscores this priority: rather than aiming for total substitution, the focus shifts to collaboration, wherein machines amplify human creativity and decision-making autonomy (Chernov et al., 2020; Elliot et al., 2020). Institutionally, growing distrust of Big Tech, which is suspected of monopolistic practices and mass surveillance (Zuboff, 2019), highlights the urgency of multilateral regulation. Initiatives such as the Global Partnership on Artificial Intelligence and guidelines from the OECD and the EU reflect the necessary transnational dimension of such governance. Lastly, the rise of the surveillance economy forces us to revisit the social contract implicit in using digital platforms, lest innovation result in a loss of autonomy and a surge in inequalities (Taddeo & Floridi, 2018).

4.2. From Trust to Growth:

Beyond its ethical significance, trust shapes consumer engagement in the digital economy. Recommendation mechanisms (TripAdvisor, Yelp, etc.) transform each satisfied customer into a potential brand promoter. To harness this dynamic, loyalty programs are evolving: they no longer reward merely purchases but also participation (sharing experiences, assisting other customers, creating content).

This logic likewise extends to the B2B sector, where the co-creation of solutions bolsters collaborative innovation.

However, the proliferation of fake reviews and bot-generated content undermines this ecosystem. For example, Amazon has removed hundreds of thousands of fake reviews in recent years, prompting calls for verified feedback and third-party certification systems.

In this context, trust becomes the glue enabling the synthesis of technological innovation, the growing abundance of resources, and the discovery of new markets or applications. While organizations fiercely compete on algorithmic quality and cost-efficient data exploitation, they cannot neglect the human element. Excessive and poorly managed automation risks degrading the customer experience and undermining the trust relationship painstakingly built (Iansiti & Lakhani, 2020).

However, agentic AI possesses tremendous potential for creativity, personalization, and the liberation of individuals from repetitive tasks (Brynjolfsson & McAfee, 2014). It can serve as a force multiplier for human capabilities, provided it is undergirded by solid ethical principles and an appropriate governance framework. Rather than dwelling solely on the risk of replacement, many experts emphasize the human-machine partnership: while the machine accelerates decision-making and data analysis, humans retain flexibility and sensitivity (Crowder et al., 2020; Figoli, 2022).

CONCLUSION

This chapter has examined the transformative role of agentic Artificial Intelligence in reconfiguring fundamental societal structures, including value chains, productivity paradigms, organizational strategies, and ethical frameworks. While much of the contemporary discourse highlights the disruptive aspects of Artificial Intelligence, such as surveillance, job displacement, and systemic volatility, our analysis has emphasized the dual nature of this evolution: Agentic AI both challenges and reinforces human autonomy. Drawing on four analytical perspectives, substitutional equivalences, the productivity–prosperity paradox, commercial transformation, and trust economies—we have argued that the Autonomous Revolution is not a purely technical phenomenon. Instead, a deeply institutional, political, and human transformation calls for new governance mechanisms, normative frameworks, and epistemic reflexivity.

Despite this, public debate remains heavily dominated by legitimate but often paralyzing fears: technological unemployment, privacy erosion, cognitive overload, and rising inequality. While these concerns must not be dismissed, they risk overshadowing the broader historical logic of adaptation. As evidenced by prior technological shifts, from the steam engine to electrification, such transitions typically unfold through a dialectic of emergence, friction, and systemic redesign. In this context, Carlota Perez's (2002) observation that breakthrough technologies move "from stall to boom" when innovation is aligned with public interest appears particularly relevant. We likely occupy this transitional phase, wherein structural tensions intensify, but the potential for inclusive, equitable, and creative reinvention remains underexploited.

Unlocking this potential requires the activation of several interdependent levers. First, human capital investment must be prioritized by upskilling workers in non-automatable domains such as creativity, critical thinking, emotional intelligence, and leadership, alongside reskilling initiatives for those affected by displacement. Second, there is a pressing need to rethink national progress metrics by moving beyond GDP and integrating multidimensional indicators that reflect well-being, ecological sustainability, informational integrity, and social cohesion. Third, ethical and participatory governance must be strengthened to ensure algorithmic transparency, clarify accountability regimes, and prevent monopolistic control while creating regulatory frameworks encouraging innovation, such as the European Union's AI Act, UNESCO's recommendations, or the Global Partnership on AI (GPAI). Fourth, we advocate for a design philosophy centered on human-machine complementarity, whereby automation is approached not as a replacement for human labor but as an augmentation of human agency. This requires embedding empathy, inclusivity, and transparency into the very architecture of digital systems.

Crucially, the emergence of agentic AI should not be interpreted as a deterministic or unidirectional process. Instead, it represents a socio-technical crossroads: one path leads toward deepened asymmetries and fragmented agency, while the other opens possibilities for dignity, freedom, and collective flourishing. The risks, labor market polarization, environmental costs, and synthetic disinformation are profound and undeniable. However, the trajectory of this transformation remains open-ended and contingent on our collective response. Through responsible research, anticipatory regulation, and ethical design, it is possible to steer AI toward outcomes reinforcing democratic values and social resilience.

Accordingly, we call for the construction of interdisciplinary coalitions that bring together engineers, ethicists, educators, economists, and civil society actors to co-develop frameworks grounded in explainability, accountability, and sustainability. Future research must engage with the practical implementation of these principles across critical sectors such as healthcare, education, mobility, and finance. Instruments such as Artificial Intelligence observatories, policy labs, and dynamic regulatory sandboxes may be key mechanisms for bridging conceptual insights with real-world governance. Autonomy in the age of agentic AI is not about resisting change but about shaping it intentionally, inclusively, and ethically. The tools are already at our disposal; what remains is the collective will to define the values and institutional pathways that will guide their deployment.

REFERENCES

Acemoglu, D. mname, & Restrepo, P. mname. (2018). Artificial Intelligence, Automation and Work. SSRN *Electronic Journal*. DOI: 10.2139/ssrn.3098384

Acemoglu, D., & Restrepo, P. (2019). Automation and New Tasks: How Technology Displaces and Reinstates Labor. *The Journal of Economic Perspectives*, *33*(2), 3–30. DOI: 10.1257/jep.33.2.3

Agrawal, A., Gans, S. J., & Goldfarb, A. (2019). Artificial Intelligence: The Ambiguous Labor Market Impact of Automating Prediction. *The Journal of Economic Perspectives*, *33*(2), 31–50. DOI: 10.1257/jep.33.2.31

Agrawal, V. (2022). Demystifying the Chinese Social Credit System: A Case Study on AI-Powered Control Systems in China. *Proceedings of the AAAI Conference on Artificial Intelligence*, *36*(11), 13124–13125. DOI: 10.1609/aaai.v36i11.21698

Alzoubi, Y. I., & Mishra, A. (2024). Green artificial intelligence initiatives: Potentials and challenges. *Journal of Cleaner Production*, *468*, 143090. DOI: 10.1016/j.jclepro.2024.143090

Autor, D. H. (2015). Why Are There Still So Many Jobs? The History and Future of Workplace Automation. *The Journal of Economic Perspectives*, *29*(3), 3–30. DOI: 10.1257/jep.29.3.3

Botsman, R. (2017). *Who Can You Trust?: How Technology Brought Us Together and Why It Might Drive Us Apart*. PublicAffairs.

Brynjolfsson, E., & McAfee, A. (2014). *The second machine age: Work, progress, and prosperity in a time of brilliant technologies*. WW Norton & company.

Brynjolfsson, E., Rock, D., & Syverson, C. (2018). Artificial Intelligence and the Modern Productivity Paradox: A Clash of Expectations and Statistics. In *The Economics of Artificial Intelligence: An Agenda* (pp. 23–57). National Bureau of Economic Research.

Castells, M. (2010). Globalisation, Networking, Urbanisation: Reflections on the Spatial Dynamics of the Information Age. *Urban Studies (Edinburgh, Scotland)*, *47*(13), 2737–2745. DOI: 10.1177/0042098010377365

Chaddad, A., Katib, Y., & Hassan, L. (2021). Future artificial intelligence tools and perspectives in medicine. *Current Opinion in Urology*, *31*(4), 371–377. DOI: 10.1097/MOU.0000000000000884 PMID: 33927099

Chernov, A. V., Chernova, V. A., & Komarova, T. V. (2020). The Usage of Artificial Intelligence in Strategic Decision Making in Terms of Fourth Industrial Revolution. *Proceedings of the 1st International Conference on Emerging Trends and Challenges in the Management Theory and Practice (ETCMTP 2019).* DOI: 10.2991/aebmr.k.200201.005

Chesterman, S. (2019). Artificial Intelligence and the Problem of Autonomy. SSRN *Electronic Journal.* DOI: 10.2139/ssrn.3450540

Crowder, J. A., Carbone, J., & Friess, S. (2020). Human–AI Collaboration. In *Artificial Psychology* (pp. 35–50). Springer International Publishing., DOI: 10.1007/978-3-030-17081-3_4

Cusumano, A. M., Gawer, A., & Yoffie, B. D. (2019). *The Business of Platforms: Strategy in the Age of Digital Competition, Innovation, and Power.* Harper Business.

Dodig-Crnkovic, G., Basti, G., & Holstein, T. (2024). *Delegating Responsibilities to Intelligent Autonomous Systems: Challenges and Benefits.* DOI: 10.20944/preprints202411.1179.v1

Du, J., Cai, H., & Jin, X. (2024). Exploring the Association Between Artificial Intelligence Management and Green Innovation: Expanding the Research Field for Sustainable Outcomes. *Sustainability (Basel), 16*(21), 9315. DOI: 10.3390/su16219315

Elliot, V. H., Paananen, M., & Staron, M. (2020). Artificial Intelligence for Decision-Makers. *Journal of Emerging Technologies in Accounting, 17*(1), 51–55. DOI: 10.2308/jeta-52666

Fielt, E. (2024). Digital Business Model Innovation: An External Enablement Perspective and Research Agenda. *Journal of Business Models, 12*(3), 19–41. DOI: 10.54337/jbm.v12i3.8470

Figoli, F. (2022, June 16). AI in design idea development: A workshop on creativity and human-AI collaboration. *Proceedings of Design Research Society.* DOI: 10.21606/drs.2022.414

Fui-Hoon Nah, F., Zheng, R., Cai, J., Siau, K., & Chen, L. (2023). Generative AI and ChatGPT: Applications, challenges, and AI-human collaboration. *Journal of Information Technology Case and Application Research, 25*(3), 277–304. DOI: 10.1080/15228053.2023.2233814

Goodwin, T. (2015). *The Battle is for the Customer Interface.* Https://Techcrunch.Com/2015/03/03/in-the-Age-of-Disintermediation-the-Battle-Is-All-for-the-Customer-Interface/

Hamet, P., & Tremblay, J. (2017). *Artificial Intelligence in Medicine (A. ten Teije* (Popow, C., Holmes, J. H., & Sacchi, L., Eds.). Vol. 10259). Springer International Publishing., DOI: 10.1007/978-3-319-59758-4

Han, Y. (2022). The Impact of Industrial Robots on the Skill-Based Wage Gap. *American Journal of Industrial and Business Management, 12*(04), 571–602. DOI: 10.4236/ajibm.2022.124031

Hatch, N. W., Mackey, T. B., Freeman, C., & Louca, F. (2002). As Time Goes by: From the Industrial Revolutions to the Information Revolution. *Academy of Management Review, 27*(2), 306. DOI: 10.2307/4134358

Huang, C., Zhang, Z., Mao, B., & Yao, X. (2023). An Overview of Artificial Intelligence Ethics. *IEEE Transactions on Artificial Intelligence, 4*(4), 799–819. DOI: 10.1109/TAI.2022.3194503

Iansiti, M., & Lakhani, R. K. (2020). *Competing in the Age of AI: Strategy and Leadership When Algorithms and Networks Run the World*. Harvard Business Press.

Kaplan, A. M., & Haenlein, M. (2016). Higher education and the digital revolution: About MOOCs, SPOCs, social media, and the Cookie Monster. *Business Horizons, 59*(4), 441–450. DOI: 10.1016/j.bushor.2016.03.008

Kaur, A., & Wadhawan, K. (2023). AI : Job Creator or Jobless Future. *International Journal For Multidisciplinary Research, 5*(4), 4520. Advance online publication. DOI: 10.36948/ijfmr.2023.v05i04.4520

Lane, J. E. (2014). Method, Theory, and Multi-Agent Artificial Intelligence. *Journal for the Cognitive Science of Religion, 1*(2), 161–180. DOI: 10.1558/jcsr.v1i2.161

LeCun, Y., Bengio, Y., & Hinton, G. (2015). Deep learning. *Nature, 521*(7553), 436–444. DOI: 10.1038/nature14539 PMID: 26017442

Machkour, B., & Abriane, A. (2020). Industry 4.0 and its Implications for the Financial Sector. *Procedia Computer Science, 177*(1), 496–502. DOI: 10.1016/j.procs.2020.10.068

Makridakis, S. (2017). The forthcoming Artificial Intelligence (AI) revolution: Its impact on society and firms. *Futures, 90*, 46–60. DOI: 10.1016/j.futures.2017.03.006

Nadimpalli, M. (2017). Artificial Intelligence Risks and Benefits. *International Journal of Innovative Research in Science, Engineering and Technology, 6*(6), 6–6.

Nleya, S. M., & Velempini, M. (2024). Industrial Metaverse: A Comprehensive Review, Environmental Impact, and Challenges. *Applied Sciences (Basel, Switzerland), 14*(13), 5736. DOI: 10.3390/app14135736

OECD. (2020). *Employment Outlook*. Https://Www.Bollettinoadapt.It/Wp-Content/Uploads/2020/07/Document.Pdf.

Orr, J., & Dutta, A. (2023). Multi-Agent Deep Reinforcement Learning for Multi-Robot Applications: A Survey. *Sensors (Basel)*, *23*(7), 3625. DOI: 10.3390/s23073625 PMID: 37050685

Peng, S., Kalliamvakou, E., Cihon, P., & Demirer, M. (2023). *The Impact of AI on Developer Productivity: Evidence from GitHub Copilot.*

Perez, C. (2002). *Technological Revolutions and Financial Capital*. Edward Elgar Publishing., DOI: 10.4337/9781781005323

Picard, R. W. (1997). Affective computing. In *PsycEXTRA Dataset*. DOI: 10.1037/e526112012-054

Polanyi, K. (2001). *The Great Transformation: The Political and Economic Origins of Our Time* (2nd ed. édition). Beacon Press.

Porter, E. M., & Heppelmann, E. J. (2014). How Smart, Connected Products Are Transforming Competition. *Harvard Business Review*, *92*, 1–18.

Russell, S., & Norvig, P. (2020). *Artificial Intelligence: A Modern Approach* (4th ed.). Pearson.

Schumpeter, J. A. (1935). *Théorie de l'évolution économique* (Dalloz, Ed.).

Schumpeter, J. A. (1983). *The Theory of Economic Development: An Inquiry Into Profits*. Capital, Credit, Interest, and the Business Cycle.

Stone, M. D., & Woodcock, N. D. (2014). Interactive, direct and digital marketing: A future that depends on better use of business intelligence. *Journal of Research in Interactive Marketing*, *8*(1), 4–17. DOI: 10.1108/JRIM-07-2013-0046

Stone, P., Brooks, R., Brynjolfsson, E., Calo, R., Etzioni, O., Hager, G., Hirschberg, J., Kalyanakrishnan, S., Kamar, E., Kraus, S., Leyton-Brown, K., Parkes, D., Press, W., Saxenian, A., Shah, J., Tambe, M., & Teller, A. (2022). *Artificial Intelligence and Life in 2030: The One Hundred Year Study on Artificial Intelligence.*

Sundararajan, M., Taly, A., & Yan, Q. (2017). *Axiomatic Attribution for Deep Networks.*

Taddeo, M., & Floridi, L. (2018). How AI can be a force for good. *Science*, *361*(6404), 751–752. DOI: 10.1126/science.aat5991 PMID: 30139858

Trischler, M. F. G., & Li-Ying, J. (2023). Digital business model innovation: Toward construct clarity and future research directions. *Review of Managerial Science*, *17*(1), 3–32. DOI: 10.1007/s11846-021-00508-2

van Ark, B. (2015). Productivity and Digitilization in Europe: Paving the Road to Faster Growth. *DigiWorld Economic Journal*, *100*(4), 107.

van Haeften, W., Zhang, R., Boesen - Mariani, S., Lub, X., Ravesteijn, P., & Aertsen, P. (2024). Bridging the AI Skills Gap in Europe: A Detailed Analysis of AI Skills and Roles. *Resilience Through Digital Innovation: Enabling the Twin Transition*, 385–402.

Wang, Y. (2021). Artificial intelligence in educational leadership: A symbiotic role of human-artificial intelligence decision-making. *Journal of Educational Administration*, *59*(3), 256–270. DOI: 10.1108/JEA-10-2020-0216

Windmann, A., Wittenberg, P., Schieseck, M., & Niggemann, O. (2024). Artificial Intelligence in Industry 4.0: A Review of Integration Challenges for Industrial Systems. *The 22nd IEEE International Conference on Industrial Informatics, 4*.

Winfield, A. F., Michael, K., Pitt, J., & Evers, V. (2019). Machine Ethics: The Design and Governance of Ethical AI and Autonomous Systems [Scanning the Issue]. *Proceedings of the IEEE*, *107*(3), 509–517. DOI: 10.1109/JPROC.2019.2900622

Wirtz, J., Hofmeister, J., Chew, P. Y. P., & Ding, X. (2023). Digital service technologies, service robots, AI, and the strategic pathways to cost-effective service excellence. *Service Industries Journal*, *43*(15–16), 1173–1196. DOI: 10.1080/02642069.2023.2226596

Wooldridge, J. M. (2009). *Introductory Econometrics: A Modern Approach* (4th ed.). South-Western College Publishing.

Zhang, F., Klonek, F. E., Li, X., Ge, X., Song, S., Liu, Y., Zhu, X., Yang, M. M., Zhong, Y., Tian, A. W., Hirschi, A., Wu, S., Ruan, M., & Chen, S. (2024). Navigating the AI Revolution: AI's Impact on Business Practices and Employee Experiences. *Academy of Management Proceedings, 2024*(1). DOI: 10.5465/AMPROC.2024.17622symposium

Zhang, K., & Aslan, A. B. (2021). AI technologies for education: Recent research & future directions. *Computers and Education: Artificial Intelligence*, *2*, 100025. DOI: 10.1016/j.caeai.2021.100025

Zhang, Y., & Siau, K. (2024). Meta-Entrepreneurship: An Analysis Theory on Integrating Generative AI, Agentic AI, and Metaverse for Entrepreneurship. *Journal of Global Information Management*, *32*(1), 1–21. DOI: 10.4018/JGIM.364094

Zuboff, S. (2019). Surveillance Capitalism and the Challenge of Collective Action. *New Labor Forum*, *28*(1), 10–29. DOI: 10.1177/1095796018819461

Chapter 4

The Individual and Organizational Foundations of Ethical Decision-Making:

Theoretical and Contextual Models in the Age of Artificial Intelligence

Halima Brahmi
https://orcid.org/0009-0001-3748-9247
Mohamed First University, Morocco

Yassine El Kaneb
Mohamed First University, Morocco

ABSTRACT

This article examines the interaction between artificial intelligence (AI) and ethics, drawing on theoretical models of moral decision-making, such as Kohlberg's, as well as contemporary approaches such as Wallach et al.'s LIDA model and the work of Hyunsoo Kim. The analysis highlights the stages of individual moral reasoning and their transposition into organizational and technological settings, emphasizing the importance of situational factors. The article also explores how these models can be applied to design AI systems capable of simulating moral reasoning, processing complex data, and adapting their responses to human values. It also proposes avenues for effective collaboration between humans and AI, emphasizing the fundamental role of the human as the final decision-maker in complex ethical situations. The

DOI: 10.4018/979-8-3373-1737-3.ch004

article finally highlights the need to develop collaborative systems that strengthen human capacities while respecting ethical principles, thus providing a framework for informed and contextual decision-making.

INTRODUCTION

AI plays an indispensable role in today's organizational decision-making, impacting the health, finance, public policy, and governance sectors. Correspondingly, the emphasis on ethical inquiries, transparency, and fairness has grown in urgency. This continues to pose serious ethical challenges.

Since the 1960s, research on ethical decision-making has focused on two key areas: human moral cognition and structural context (Ford & Richardson, 1994). So, there's this whole thing with Ferrell and Gresham's contingency framework from 1985, and then there's Jones's idea from 1991 about moral intensity. All these theories have helped scholars figure out what makes ethical behaviour or unethical behaviour happen. These variables include personal traits, situational dynamics and the specific characteristics of the moral issue in question.

However, in AI's context, these human-centered models face new challenges, and intelligent systems are still lacking real moral agency. Because of its lack of consciousness, intentionality, and cultural grounding, the system faces the challenge of integrating ethical sensitivity

To deal with this issue, some scholars proposed hybrid methods that relate human ethical perspectives to AI-driven analytical capabilities. Hyun-soo Kim's contextual model of cognitive framework, the Learning Intelligent Distribution Agent (LIDA), and Lawrence Kohlberg's theory of moral development offer valuable perspectives. Each scholar looks at the question in their own way to understand how machines can make or encourage good ethical choices, focusing on how they respond to situations, mimic human thinking, or use moral development.

The three theoretical models are analyzed and well considered to compare and assess their worth to exhibit the ethical scope and value of AI-based decision-making systems. The chapter draws on achievements in moral psychology, cognitive science, and AI interdisciplinary ethics. It seeks to make clear to what extent these frameworks could provide operational direction to implementing ethics into algorithmic architectures.

The chapter aims to specifically answer this central research question:

How do classical and context-sensitive ethical models contribute to, and fall short in, guiding decision-making systems that involve active AI participation?

The three-phase method is adopted to answer the question:

A conceptual analysis of each model is required in order to identify its normative foundations and theoretical assumptions. The practical applicability of the system under review will then be assessed through a combination of empirical evaluation and theoretical modelling. Specifically, the employment of agent-based simulations and Bayesian reasoning will facilitate a rigorous and objective assessment of the system's practical benefits and limitations.Finally, a comparative synthesis is achieved through the utilisation of a multi-criteria matrix, which serves to underscore the strengths and limitations of each model within the context of real-world organisational settings.

The present chapter puts forward a hybrid and adaptive ethical model, the aim of which is to combine the advantages of both human oversight and the normative foundation with the capabilities of intelligent systems. Such an approach is imperative in fostering ethical integrity, accountability, and trust in AI-assisted decision-making in the digital age.

PART I: THEORETICAL FOUNDATIONS OF ETHICAL DECISION-MAKING

Definition and Key Concepts

Ethics is related to the study of moral values that govern human behaviors and actions. It tries to distinguish what is right from what is wrong, just and unjust, good and bad, then what is moral and immoral. Ethics assists in defining standards to evaluate human decision-making and actions.

Therefore, ethics consists of the study of professional rules and duties that guide the individuals' behaviors within workplace or society. It represents the practical application of code conduct in a professional context.

While ethics offers the general framework for moral decision-making, deontology provides the specific rules and standards to guide the behavior of professionals in specific contexts. The two concepts are apparently interconnected and complementary to each other in what concerns moral decision-making.

An ethically acceptable decision-making is based on a process of moral judgment in which notions of good and evil are essential attentions. The process evolves human conduct and pushes to the consideration of values and relationships to lead to either ethical behavior or to its opposite.

Ethics is interested in solving conflicts and complex decision-making that require in-depth consideration. To analyze an ethical situation and actively participate in decision-making, give rise to some dilemmas. Therefore, it is necessary to identify the underlying issues and raised dilemmas.

In his respect, it is recommended to rely on the works of Treviño (1986), Ferrell and al. (1989), Jones (1991), Davison and al. (2009), and Kéfi and Sarr (2014), which offer a multidimensional and holistic perspective on ethical decision-making in business. Treviño focuses on the importance of education and training to forge ethical skills. Ferrell et al highlight the role of organizational norms and corporate culture in shaping ethical behavior. Jones recommends an integrative framework that recognizes ethical aspects and respects social and legal norms. Davison and al. explore the impact of contextual factors such as peer pressure, financial incentives, and organizational culture. Kéfi and Sarr focus on the impact of cultural differences on ethical values and norms.

Studies indicate that ethical decision-making arises from the interaction between personal characteristics, organizational factors, and cultural influences.

All these researches converge on the idea that ethical decision-making results from the interaction between individual, organizational, and cultural factors. They all argue for an integrated approach, that combines continual education, promotion of ethical organizational culture, and sensitivity to cultural diversity, in order to better understand and manage ethical dynamics in diverse contexts.

Factors Influencing Ethical Decision Making

The individual process of ethical decision-making is linked to an individual or a personal ethic that insists on the freedom of self-fulfilment and self-realization (Errabih,2020). On one hand, the individual approach is linked to a personal ethic that guides the conduct of individuals through their principles, values, and beliefs. According to Kohlberg in 1963, this approach is influenced by variables such as gender, orientations of the work values, nationality, level of moral development, locus of control, personal traits, religion, and education. The organizational approach, on the other hand, is influenced by factors such as organizational culture and climate, company size, reward and sanction systems, and the organization's mission and objectives. However, the values declared by the organization may not be shared by all employees, which can influence the criteria and weighting during decision-making processes.

Thus, the theory developed by Kohlberg in 1963 has served as a guide for a good number of researches in moral psychology, in the sense that it clarifies the process followed by the individual when confronting an ethical dilemma with the aim of leading the act of thought to its maximum (Kheidous, 2019).

Girard's 2007 vision of the organizational approach to ethical decision-making focuses on factors that influence organizational codes of conduct, culture, and climate. This approach considers industry type, company size, and reward and sanction systems. Girard believes that organizational culture, particularly the values shared by company members, influences the ethical decision-making.

Indeed, organizational values are defined as the set of beliefs shared by employees about how to achieve the company's objectives. According to Girard, organizational factors that influence ethical decision-making include the organization's mission and objectives, its structure, decisions, policies, procedures, management practices, and various actions. These factors can serve as a framework for ethical decision-making both individually and as a team within the organization. However, it is important to note that the values declared by the company are not necessarily those shared by all employees, which can influence the criteria and weighting used in the decision-making process.

Several studies have highlighted the importance of congruence between organizational values and employees' personal values for ethical and effective decision-making (Schwepker and Good, 2019; Sivakumar et al., 2016).

According to Errabih in 200, there are two facets of ethical decision-making: individual ethics and organizational ethics. The author explains how these two approaches can influence ethical decision-making and discusses the different variables that can impact this process.

Specifically, (Errabih, 2020) examines the principles, values, and beliefs that guide individuals' conduct in their personal ethics. She also highlights the importance of organizational culture, including organizational values, in influencing individuals' decision-making within their organization. In addition, she describes how factors such as the organization's mission and objectives, structure, decisions, policies, procedures, management practices, and the various actions can serve as a frame of reference for ethical decision-making.

Artificial Intelligence: Emerging Ethical Questions in Real-World Contexts

Artificial Intelligence (AI) today goes far beyond its early computational definitions. While traditionally associated with mimicking human reasoning or learning (Russell & Norvig, 2020), AI now sits at the heart of systems that actively shape decision-making in healthcare, public safety, and digital platforms. The scale and subtlety of its influence have pushed ethicists, technologists, and policymakers into urgent conversations about its societal impact.

UNESCO (2021) frames AI not simply as a tool but as a transformative system that calls for new ethical guardrails. Likewise, the OECD (2022) urges that AI be developed with an emphasis on human dignity, fairness, and accountability—principles that are often difficult to implement when decisions are driven by opaque algorithms.

Ethical challenges are not abstract. In practice, facial recognition software, deployed in public and private spaces alike, tests the balance between surveillance and privacy. Algorithms that curate content for users may boost engagement, but they also shape perception, feeding polarization and undermining autonomy (Zuboff, 2020). In healthcare, AI tools enhance diagnostic capacity, yet they raise questions: when a machine makes a mistake, who is accountable? (Topol, 2022). And the case of autonomous vehicles presents perhaps the most vivid example—should a car prioritize its passenger or a pedestrian when a crash is inevitable? (Bonnefon et al., 2016).

These are not just edge cases. They represent the everyday dilemmas posed by the integration of AI into human-centered environments. Ethical theories must therefore evolve alongside technology, not merely in abstract debate, but in direct response to the systems reshaping how we live, decide, and relate.

We introduce an operational definition of transparency in artificial intelligence, structured around three complementary dimensions:

Technical transparency, which refers to the readability of algorithms, the traceability of computations, and the explainability of outputs (Doshi-Velez & Kim, 2017; Lipton, 2018);

Procedural transparency, which concerns the rules, criteria, and decision-making processes guiding AI systems, including learning, validation, and audit methodologies (Ananny & Crawford, 2018);

Organizational transparency, which addresses ethical governance, stakeholder responsibilities, and the alignment of systems with internal norms, values, and codes (Raji et al., 2020; Floridi & Cowls, 2022).

To structure the comparative analysis clearly, we need this typology to line up the contributions offered by the three examined ethical models (Kohlberg, LIDA, Kim) with these concrete dimensions of clarity.

Theoretical Models

We select three different models concerning moral decision-making, each one is implemented in a distinguished disciplinary culture and offers specific insights into ethical dilemmas generated by AI.

Due to its typical role in moral psychology and its force to conceptualize moral reasoning as a developed process, Kohlberg's Moral Development Theory(Kohlberg, 1981) was specifically chosen. This model enhances an investigation of individual ethical consciousness via a staged framework. It makes the exploration relevant to tackle the moral forces of human and artificial agents.

Learning Intelligent Distributed Agent (LIDA) cognitive architecture, developed by (Franklin & Patterson, 2006) serves as a computational basis to inform decision-making processes for artificial agents. LIDA focuses on attention, memory, and learning mechanisms. This makes it a suitable tool to understand how machine-based systems copy relevant moral behavior.

Because of its focus on the organizational and social environment in which ethical decisions take place, Hyun-soo Kim's Contextual Moral Decision-Making Model (Kim & Thapa, 2018)12 was selected. This model extends the analysis to exceed the individual and reaches group dynamics and systemic influences. It does so by recognizing external pressures and institutional contexts. The preference of these three models is justified by the diversity of their disciplines—psychology, cognitive science, and organizational theory— and their theoretical relevance to contemporary debates in AI ethics (Boddington, 2017; Jobin, Ienca & Vayena, 2019) . The three models see the moral questions faced by AI systems from different perspectives.

To enable a structured and meaningful comparison, the analysis was organized around four core criteria:

The level of autonomy assigned to the moral agent – examining whether the model presupposes full, partial, or no autonomy in ethical action.

The normative basis of decision-making – whether the model is more aligned with consequentialist, deontological, or hybrid ethical principles.

The role of affect and cognition – assessing how the model integrates emotional processes and cognitive functions into moral reasoning.

Sensitivity to social or institutional context – considering the extent to which the model accounts for environmental, cultural, or systemic factors influencing ethical choices.

By analyzing these dimensions across the three models, we aim to better understand how moral agency can be conceptualized and evaluated in both human and artificial systems. This comparative approach provides a multidimensional perspective that is essential to developing ethically robust AI frameworks.

a. Kohlberg's 1969 model: moral development and the theory of moral psychology of decision making

Moral psychology, defined as the study of the psychological processes that enable an individual to formulate a moral judgment in a given situation, is a central field of study for understanding ethical behavior. According to Flanagan (2004, p. 1581), moral psychology, or Kant's "empirical aspect of morality," analyzes how individuals perceive what is just or unjust, good or bad, as well as their conception of virtue. This discipline draws on theoretical models, including that of Lawrence

Kohlberg (1969), which has profoundly influenced the understanding of moral development and ethical decision-making.

• *Individual Approach: Theoretical Foundations*

Kohlberg (1969) draws on Jean Piaget's (1932) work on children's moral development. Piaget studied young boys' attitudes toward rules, highlighting a gradual transition from heteronomy (submission to imposed rules) to autonomy (the ability to internalize and interpret rules). Moral dilemmas are more easily resolved at later developmental stages that can be reasoned using more advanced branches of ethics. Piaget (1932) from his deontological standpoint of morality placed an emphasis on rule obedience tempered with ethics grounded on the moral level of their development.

Kohlberg, working on Piaget's model and concentrating on adult situations with conflicting rights or justice focuses on boundaries granted by rules and level of moral evolution. His deontological approach also marks boundaries formed by rules and level of moral growth. This theory demonstrates that moral reasoning advances in a sequential, immutable, and universal manner irrespective of social or cultural context. The decisions made are reflective of a person's moral evolution, tempered but not wholly devoid of age, gender, education, and other life experiences (Fremeaux & Noel, 2015; Lainey, 2015).

There are six phases of moral development identified by Kohlberg. They are grouped into three levels: pre- conventional, conventional, and post-conventional. The stages measure the individuals' level of moral reasoning by analyzing their responses to moral dilemmas. For example, at the pre- conventional stage, decisions are guided by fear of punishment or the pursuit of rewards, while at the post-conventional stage, they are based on universal ethical principles, such as justice and human rights. This theory provides an operational framework for measuring moral judgment, using responses to moral dilemmas as indicators of the stage of moral development reached.

• **Organizational Approach: Adaptation of the Kohlberg Model**

In 2014, Kéfi, who adapted Kohlberg's model for ethical decision-making in organizations, proposed incorporating a cultural dimension. Two processes are distinguished in this adjustment: the individual process, which focuses on moral standards and the values of individuals, and the organizational process that pays attention to the ethical practices inside the organization. Ethical decision-making impacts the profitability and reputation of a company. It has then become very essential in an organizational context. Companies are in need of incorporating ethical behavior to enforce trust and gratification between stakeholders, and guarantees customers' constancy, employees' devotion, and the social legitimacy the organization.

• Implications for Ethical Decision Making in Organizations

For better analyzing and improving ethical decision-making in organizations, Kohlberg's model consists of a suitable framework. Researchers who adjusted the model to organizational level, have specified some moral reasoning processes that are shaped by values, organizational culture, and laws and regulations that are applied. The approach permits organizations to practice more advanced ethical behavior to integrate social obligations and universal principles into their decision-making processes.

The following table shows the Kohlberg's model, at first designed to explain individual moral evolution is also relevant for understanding and guiding ethical decision-making in organizations.Its adaptation to the organizational context highlights the importance of ethical culture, stakeholders participation, and the alignment of organizational practices with universal moral principles.

Table 1. Summary of actions of individual and organizational decision-making from the Kohlberg model (1969)

		Individual	Organizational
1st level Pre-conventional: moral reasoning is controlled by punishments and rewards			
Stage 1	**Obedience and punishment**	The person submits to authority to avoid punishment, which is his only concern, as he may eventually benefit from a reward.	Act with a view to avoid damage.
Stage 2	**Personal interest / Using others**	Reciprocity and reward, which allow the existence of others to be taken into account, in order to exploit them to satisfy one's own interests.	Act within the framework of research to benefit from the creation of values.
2nd Conventional Level: Conformity to others is the subject of interpersonal relationships			
Stage 3	**Interpersonal relationships**	Considering the consequences of others to maintain harmonious interpersonal relationships.	Act in accordance with the industry practices.
Stage 4	**Law/Authority and Social Order**	Awareness and respect for the law and rules to maintain conformity to social norms.	Act in accordance with applicable laws and regulations.
3rd Post-conventional Level: The reasoning for acting is done with moral convictions			
Stage 5	**Social contract**	The search for the social contract and individual rights for the good of the greatest number, through respect for the rights of others and the seeking of consensus.	Recognize one's obligations to society and act accordingly.
Stage 6	**Universal moral principles**	Establish universal ethical principles considered fundamental in the conduct of behavior.	To register its action in the defense of universal principles.

Kohlberg's theory offers an interesting approach to better understand ethical decision-making in organizations, by identifying the different levels of moral development of individuals and suggesting ways to promote their moral development within the organization.

In order to better connect ethical considerations with organizational realities and international standards, we found it relevant to introduce the key actors involved in AI governance at the institutional level.

These include AI ethics officers, oversight committees, internal audit mechanisms, as well as ethics charters and internal regulatory frameworks that guide organizational practice.

We also refer to several major legal and policy frameworks:

The **European AI Act**, currently under legislative review, which proposes a risk-based classification system and establishes transparency obligations.

The **General Data Protection Regulation (GDPR)**, in relation to automated decision-making rights and data processing explainability.

Structured foundations for ethical, responsible, and internationally aligned AI governance provided by the **OECD AI guidelines** and the **ISO/IEC 42001 standard**.

b. LIDA model (Wallach et al.): Simulation of human moral processes

A more dynamic attempt to integrate moral decision-making mechanisms into artificial intelligence (AI) systems was set up by Wallach's model (The Learning Intelligent Distribution Agent (LIDA) model). For the model to mimic a sophisticated multi-faceted ethical reasoning method, it incorporates igheter factors such as human affective and rational frameworks and processes.

As per this model, rhythms of moral AI conduct "copy" human ethical reasoning. An architecture based on artificial consciousness is assumed to gmoderate decision making advance through iterative sensing. In this framework, Ansel cannot simplistically follow preset command procedures. AI assumes adds emotions and contextual factors. The hybrid approach (sentimental and logical) to AI ethics is goal oriented in within dynamic moral frameworks challenges (Gentsch et al., 2021: Allen et al., 2022).

The LIDA mechanism based on global workspace theory (Baars, 1988) stipulates that "consciousness arises from the dynamic integration of relevant information within a centralized space." LIDA mechanism is maintained through scanning selection of sensory and contextual information of specific moral cues to formulate appropriate responses.

Advances in transformers (Vaswani et al, 2017) and LAI have enable LIDA to interpretation of complex emotion and behavioral signals deepuing responsive contexts.

The LIDA model is particularly suitable for applications where the interpretation of emotional and contextual signals is crucial. For example:

- **Care for vulnerable people**: In the fields of healthcare and social assistance, LIDA can be used to design empathetic AI systems, capable of adapting their interactions according to the emotional needs of patients.
- **Education and learning**: By incorporating LIDA principles, educational AI systems can personalize instructions based on students' needs and emotional responses, fostering a more human approach.
- **Predictive justice systems**: LIDA can also be used to design tools for the ethical assessment of automated legal decisions, considering the emotional and contextual impacts of decisions.

Research such as that of Raji et al. (2020) highlights the importance of ensuring the transparency and accountability of intelligent systems in ethical contexts. However, LIDA is still inept to explain how complex AI systems make decisions. This limitation underlines the necessity of interdisciplinary collaboration between AI researchers, ethicists, and social scientists to ensure the efficiency of LIDA.

Therefore, researchers should continue to improve and refine LIDA and the other models to address the challenges the Ai meets in ethical, social, and emotional contexts.

Figure 1. Hyunsoo Kim's Model: AI-Human Collaboration

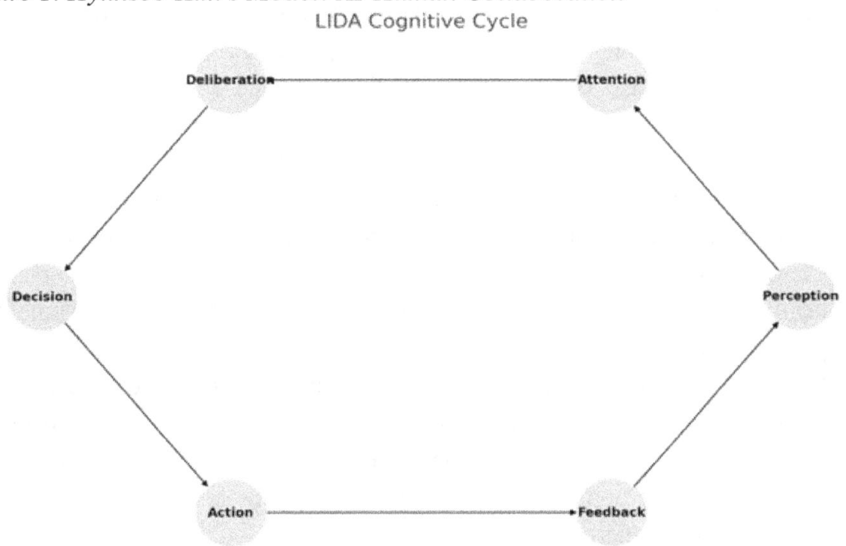

The Ai-human collaboration model of Hyun-soo Kim serves as a balanced interaction between AI as an assistant and human. In this model AI increases human roles and abilities to optimize its decision-making process in complex contexts. In this approach human values and ethical considerations remain present.

Human benefits from the analysis, recommendations, and insights provided by AI without losing control to make decision.

- Examples of using AI applications include exploding the massive data internet accumulated over trends, correlations, or anomalies. All of this provides a reasoned basis for making decisions with appealing intellect and great speed in systems requiring substantial expertise.
- The model synergizes AI to the human system so as to identify and assimilate contextual and emotional dynamics with integrating the usefulness of robotics to the automation systems.
- **Complementary skills:** AI and humans have specific strengths. Processing huge volumes of data, automating mundane functions, and even pattern detection AI does best, while Creativity, Intuition, Ethical Acumen, and Context are what Humans bring to the fray. There is need to underscore the intersection of these complementarities in order to achieve optimal results as the model suggests.
- **Trust and Transparency:** All these will not yield any fruit if not based on mutual dependency, because for collaboration to be effective humans need a certain level of trust in AI systems. This artificial insight fulfills trust through not hiding how programs are constructed, making sense of the decisions put forth, and specifying the bounds of their application.
- **Mutual Learning**: Humans need to better human-device use, and devise Adaptive AI systems able to embody proposed human-imposed change to enhance performance over time. This composite learning framework of man and machine puts forth the foundation of perpetual collaboration.
- **Ethics and responsibility**: Kim Hyunsoo describes the ethics of design and use of AI systems in particular. Every joint action must observe social and legal boundaries, and each responsibility should be allocated in a manner that prevents abuse or error.
- **Human-centered design**: The model supports a user-centered design advocacy, which AI systems are instructed to build with regard to observing humans, their requirements, wishes, and constraints. A built system should enable effortless compliance, natural interface, interaction of engagement, and adoption ease.
- **Impact on roles and skills**: The collaboration of humans and AI is changing the jobs people do and the skills they need. The model points out the neces-

sity to train employees on engaging with AI and restructure the organization around the technology.

Hyunsoo Kim's model offers a balanced and pragmatic view of AI-human collaboration, emphasizing complementarity, trust, mutual learning, ethics, and human-centered design. It provides a framework for optimizing this collaboration while minimizing risks and maximizing benefits for society and organizations.

As an application we cite:

- **Medical Diagnosis:**In healthcare, collaborative tools like IBM Watson Health and Google DeepMind analyze medical databases, propose diagnostic hypotheses, and suggest possible treatments. These tools help doctors make faster and more accurate decisions, while allowing them to validate recommendations based on the clinical context.
- **Legal Analysis:**Systems such as Kira Systems and ROSS Intelligence are used to analyze voluminous legal documents, identify critical clauses, and suggest relevant precedents. While AI simplifies complex tasks, the jurists remain responsible for interpreting and implementing the results.
- **Corporate Risk Management:**Companies use AI to assess financial or ethical risks by analyzing possible scenarios. Humans intervene to adjust strategies based on organizational priorities and social values.

Table 2. Comparative Ethics Models Table

Criteria	Kohlberg (1971)	LIDA (Franklin et al., 2014)	Hyunsoo Kim (2019)
Disciplinary Origin	Moral Psychology	Cognitive Science / AI	Organizational Sociology / Applied Ethics
Ethical Foundation	Deontology / Moral Development	Computational Cognitivism / Moral Process Modeling	Contextual and Situational Ethics
Role of Context	Low (Moral Universalism)	Medium (Context simulated via agent)	High (Cultural, institutional, and social factors)
Type of Moral Agent	Human, in moral development	Autonomous Artificial Agent	Human actor in organizational context
Consideration of Bias	Barely addressed	Addressed via cognitive architecture	Addressed through systemic influences
Relevance for AI	Limited (not designed for AI)	High (AI-native)	Moderate to High (Interpretive framework for organizations)

The three ethical models dealt with in this study represent suitable tools to ensure the transparency in AI systems. They present distinct, yet complementary perspective to address some pressing concerns regarding algorithmic decision-making today—namely, opacity, explainability, and accountability. All together, these models incite to a more nuanced and human-centered approach to transparency, grounded in moral reasoning rather than mechanical disclosure alone.

PART II: METHODOLOGICAL APPROACH

Purpose of the Methodological Approach

The approach followed in this study selects, analyzes, and compares the three ethical models applied to decision-making in the era of AI. The aim is to bring into dialogue conceptual frameworks that belong to distinct cultures to assess their relevance in an evolving technological landscape. The two perspectives are contrasted to better understand to what extent diverse ethical paradigms inform the plan and authority of AI systems.

Methodological Approach

The qualitative and comparative approach followed in this study seeks to bring conceptual clarity and interpretative depth. It is grounded in structured analysis of the literature review. The methodology is intended to examine theories of each model in the light of ethical contemporary challenges posed by AI to integrate decision-making processes (Yin, 2018).

Model Selection

Three models were selected based on their disciplinary origins, conceptual richness, and applicability to ethical tensions specific to AI:

- Kohlberg's Moral Development Theory (Kohlberg, 1971), rooted in deontological moral psychology, offers a staged view of individual ethical reasoning.
- The LIDA model (Learning Intelligent Distributed Agent) (Franklin et al., 2014), from the field of computational cognitive science, simulates ethical decision-making in artificial agents.
- Hyunsoo Kim's Contextual Moral Decision-Making Framework (Kim, 2019), grounded in East Asian organizational ethics, highlights the social, cultural, and institutional dimensions of moral reasoning.

The selection was guided by the following criteria:

- The models represent distinct disciplinary foundations (psychology, artificial intelligence, contextual ethics).
- Each provides tools to conceptualize decision-making in automated environments.
- All three address core ethical tensions in AI systems, including responsibility, transparency, and autonomy.

Analytical Framework

To structure the comparison, the following dimensions were used as the basis for cross-model analysis:

- Epistemological foundations and disciplinary origin
- Degree of autonomy attributed to the moral agent
- Consideration of context and cognitive/algorithmic bias
- Integration of human values and moral reasoning mechanisms

This grid allowed us to uncover both convergences and divergences among the models, offering a deeper understanding of their suitability in guiding ethical AI development.

Methodological Limitations

This study does not aim at assessing practical implementation of the models; it conducts to conceptual exploration of the models based on secondary theoretical analysis. The study invites further research to reinforce the findings, adopting empirical validation, like expert interviews or applied researches that involve AI-supported decision-making in complex contexts.

Scientific Analysis

a. Reducing Cognitive Bias

AI offers a fresh, balanced perspective that can help fix human preconceptions (like being preoccupied too much by the first piece of information we get or feeling confused when there is too much to process). In fact, research by Gentsch and his team in 2021 found that when people use AI, the decisions they make tend to be smarter and safer—especially in complex situations where getting it wrong is not an option.

b. AI Vulnerabilities to Data Bias

Although AI can help reduce certain human biases, it cannot avoid inheriting biases present in the data it learns from. For instance, research has shown that risk assessment algorithms may continue to discriminate if they are trained on historical data that reflects past prejudices. The study by Raji and colleagues in 2020 emphasizes the importance of thorough auditing processes to identify and lessen these biases.

c. Explainability and Transparency

For people and AI to work well together, it's crucial that AI systems can clearly explain their recommendations in ways that humans can easily grasp. When AI can show the reasoning behind its suggestions, it builds trust and helps users feel more confident including AI insights in their decisions. This transparency makes it easier for people to understand, question, and effectively use AI tools in everyday decision-making processes.

Perspectives and Challenges

a. User Training

When users work effectively with AI tools, they develop certain skills— they acquire the ability to understand AI-generated insights and use them to make well-informed decisions. Ongoing education and training programs assist them in keeping up with these changes to collaborate smoothly with AI systems.

b. Regulatory Framework

Regulating AI should be based on making sure that its systems function within clear ethical restrictions and protect individuals' rights. There should be solid legal and ethical rules to supervise AI's role in fields like healthcare, the justice system, and finance, where mistakes or misuse could have serious consequences.

c. Technological Evolution

Collaborative models are well required as AI technologies advance and need to be refined continuously to fit the emerging needs while keeping firm a balance between AI autonomy and human guidance.

Hyun-soo Kim's model stands out as a hopeful example of how we can harness AI's incredible capabilities while still honoring the essential human touch in decision-making. By blending big data insights, clear explanations, and a deep respect for human values, this approach offers a flexible partnership between people and machines—one that can be applied across many fields, from medical diagnosis to managing risks.

However, its success will depend on rigorous implementation, ethical guidance, and ongoing user training to ensure harmonious and effective interactions between AI and humans.

Figure 2. Multi-criteria Comparative Analysis of the Hyunsoo Kim, LIDA and Kohlberg Models

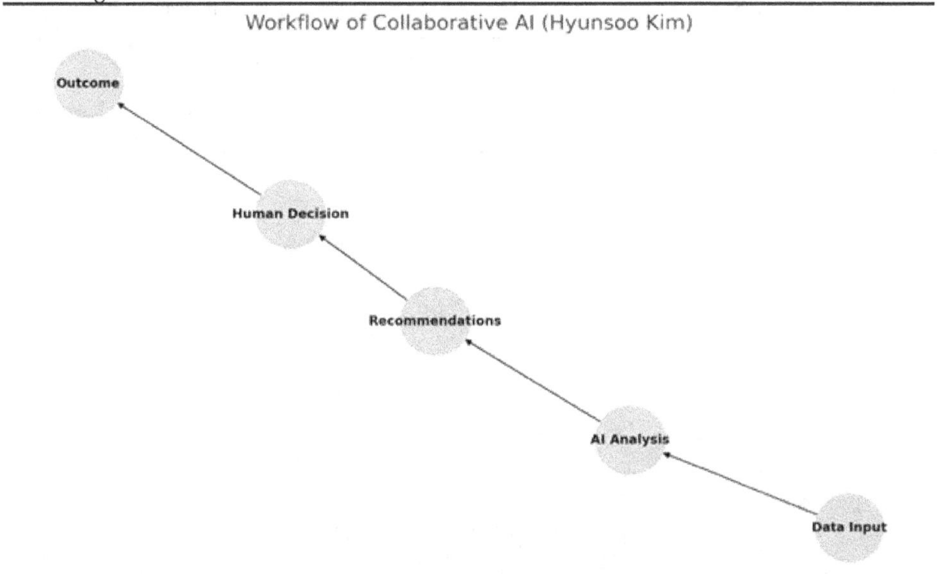

Table 3. Descriptions of criteria for comparing the Hyunsoo Kim, LIDA and Kohlberg Models

Criteria	Hyunsoo Kim	LIDA	Kohlberg
Practical applicability	**High**: Suitable for sectors such as medicine and justice, where human decision-making is crucial.	**Average**: Useful in specific contexts such as crises, but less generalized.	**Average**: Mainly applicable to educational and pedagogical scenarios.
Adaptability	**Average**: Relatively flexible, but depends on the data of training and on context.	**Weak**: Limited by rigid computational cycles and context sensitivity.	**High**: Universal model applicable to a diversity of educational and social contexts.
Robustness	**Average**: Depends on the quality of the data and the algorithms used.	**Weak**: Vulnerable to bias and computational limitations.	**Average**: Theoretically robust, but requires contextual interpretation to be fully operational.
Computational complexity	**Weak**: Approach based on practical and explainable recommendations.	**Average**: Requires more advanced calculations to integrate affective and contextual factors.	**High**: Involves abstract reasoning and complex calculations to model the stages of moral development.
Ethical alignment	**High**: Integrates human values and leaves the final decision to humans.	**AVERAGE**: Devises moral responses based on models, but may lack ethical nuances.	**High**: Establishes the decisions on universal and well-defined moral principles.
Societal impact	**High**: Contributes to improve the quality and ethics of decisions in critical areas.	**AVERAGE**: Limited potential by its complexity and its dependence on context.	**High potential**: Useful for educating and raising awareness for moral issues, but requires broad implementation.

Figure 3. Shows the variations in model scores across the criteria

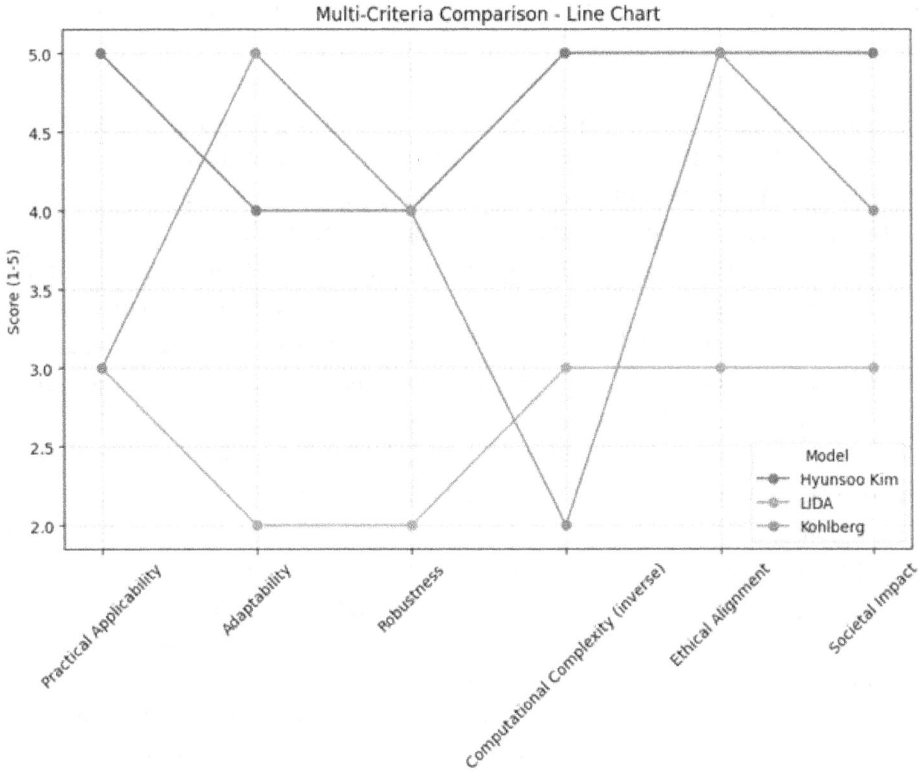

Synthetic Analysis

- **Hyunsoo Kim** stands out for its high practicality and significant societal impact, thanks to its direct integration into critical areas such as health and justice. Its low computational complexity and high ethical alignment make it an ideal model for collaborative AI-human applications.
- **LIDA** presents limited adaptability and robustness, due to the rigidity of its computational architecture. However, it excels in integrating affective and contextual factors, making it relevant in specific situations such as humanitarian crises.
- While more abstract and theoretical, **Kohlberg's** theory continues to be a reference in moral education. Its agility and strong ethical basis make it useful for raising awareness and training people in ethical decision-making, whether in schools or social settings.

As they are compared, each different ethical model has a valuable perception concerning the handling of the complex challenges of AI governance. Think about the LIDA model for a moment. It's actually quite useful as a starting point when we're trying to unravel the often-puzzling ways algorithms work.LIDA helps us get a real feel for how these systems operate by breaking down how they handle information. It presents you with an explanation that makes understanding easier by showing you the reasoning behind decision-making mysteries.

There are also Kohlberg's layers of morality which add thoughtful depth to explainability: in this case, explaining why people did something contains guiding principles of well-known developmental stages of moral identity formation. Hyun-soo Kim's contextual model reminds us that accountability is not merely a matter of technology it is about social rules, organizational policies, and in a broader sense, what is deemed fair and just in the accepted culture.

Combining these viewpoints helps to appreciate how many people begin viewing transparency not as a single point but as an intertwined whole. It becomes a synergy of technical clearness, ethical reasoning, and institutional framing not independent parts, but interrelated elements forming a single coherent whole.

Choosing the right model really depends on the situation. For practical, high-stakes applications, Hyun-soo Kim's model often fits best. When a close look into moral reasoning is needed, Kohlberg's framework remains helpful. LIDA shows a lot of promise but still needs further development to be more robust and widely applicable.

To give a clearer picture, here's a visual comparison of the three models—Hyun-soo Kim, LIDA, and Kohlberg—across several important criteria. Each is shown as a polygon, highlighting where they shine and where they might fall short.

Figure 4. Compare each model for each criterion using side-by-side bars

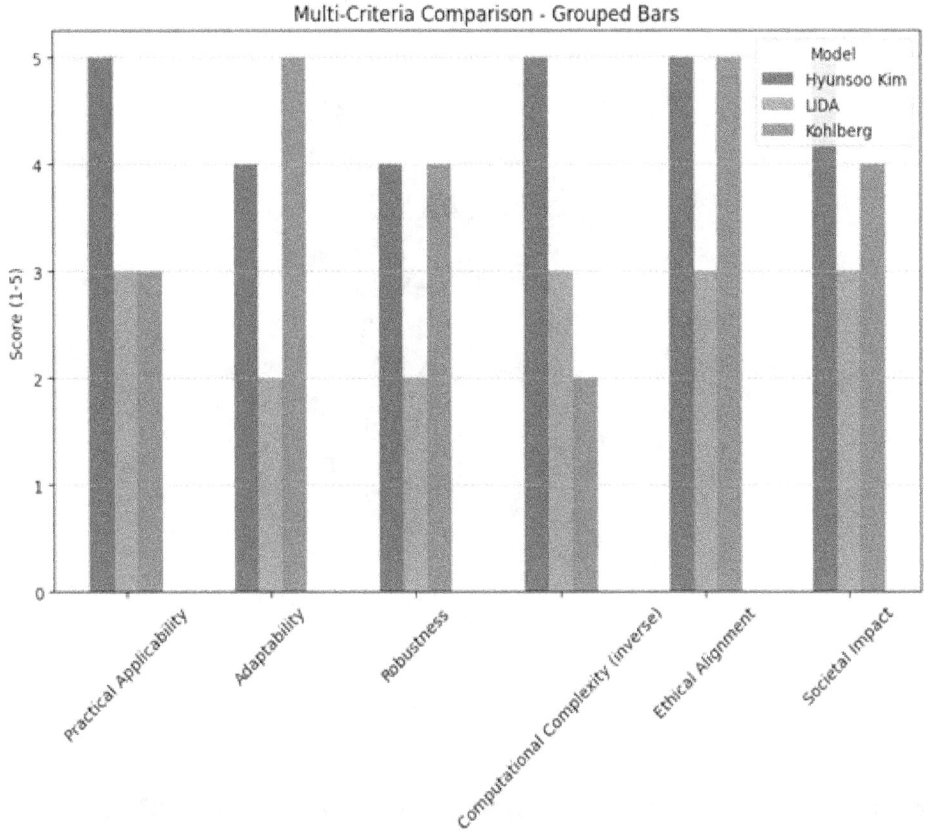

Figure 5. Heatmap: An intuitive visual representation of score differences

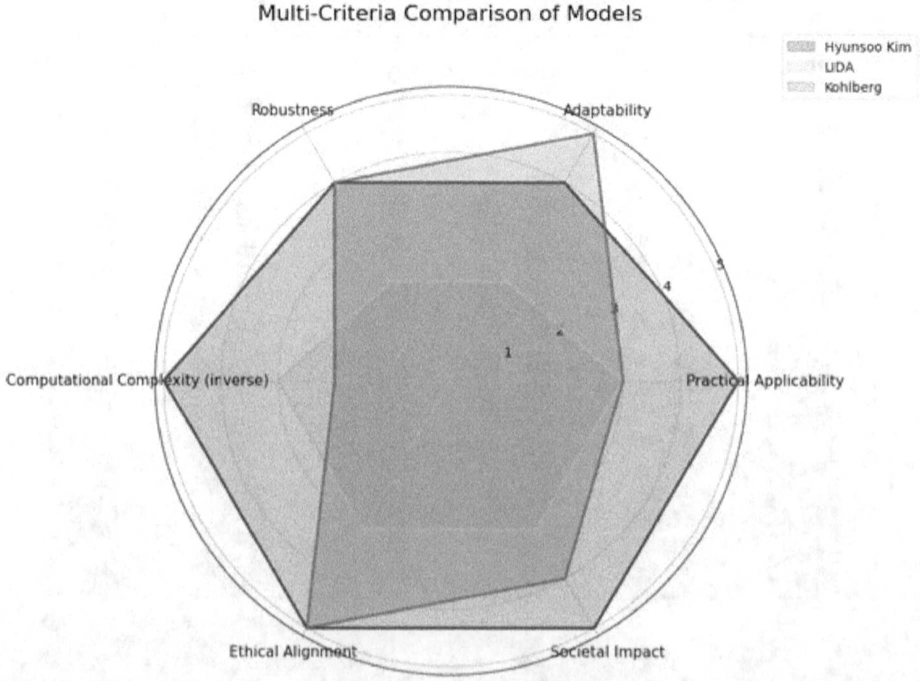

Interpretation of the Radar Chart Comparing Ethical Models

The presented radar chart provides a visual comparison of three ethical models — **Hyunsoo Kim**, **LIDA**, and **Kohlberg** — across six key criteria: **practical applicability**, **adaptability**, **robustness**, **computational complexity (inverse)**, **ethical alignment**, and **societal impact**.

The **Hyunsoo Kim model** stands out with **consistently high performance** across nearly all criteria. It achieves the maximum score (5/5) in most areas, including practical applicability, societal impact, ethical alignment, and low computational complexity. It also performs well in adaptability and robustness (4/5), making it a **well-rounded and comprehensive model**.

The **Kohlberg model** excels in **adaptability** and **ethical alignment**, reflecting its roots in individual moral development. However, it scores lower in **computational efficiency**, which may hinder its application in automated or AI systems.

In contrast, the **LIDA model** shows more **moderate and uniform scores** (mostly between 2 and 3), indicating a **stable but less performant profile overall**. It may be more suitable for general cognitive simulations or environments where simplicity and consistency are valued over advanced ethical reasoning.

In conclusion, this chart highlights the **relative strengths and limitations** of each model, helping guide the selection process based on the ethical and operational priorities of the intended system.

Detailed Reading of the Comparative Chart

a. Practical Applicability

- **Hyunsoo Kim**: Stands out for its high practical applicability (5/5), thanks to its direct use in fields such as medicine and justice, where assisted human decision-making is crucial.
- **LIDA**: Average score (3/5). Its applicability is limited to specific contexts, such as crises or emergency situations, where emotional integration is essential.
- **Kohlberg**: Average score (3/5). Mainly applicable in educational and pedagogical scenarios, it is less used in complex decision-making contexts.

b. Adaptability

- **Hyunsoo Kim**: Average (4/5). Although it is adaptable, its effectiveness depends on the quality of the data and the specific context.
- **LIDA**: Weak (2/5). The model suffers from computational rigidity, making its adaptability to new contexts limited.
- **Kohlberg**: High (5/5). Due to its theoretical and abstract nature, it is applicable to a wide range of educational and cultural situations.

c. Robustness

- **Hyunsoo Kim**: Average (4/5). Relatively robust, but vulnerable to data bias and limitations of the algorithms used.
- **LIDA**: Weak (2/5). Less robust due to its reliance on complex computational cycles and contextual data.
- **Kohlberg**: Average (4/5). Theoretically robust, but requires interpretation for practical application.

d. Computational Complexity

(Note: The criterion is reversed in the graph to reflect lower complexity as a positive point.)

- **Hyunsoo Kim**: Low (5/5). Its computational simplicity makes it accessible and easy to implement.
- **LIDA**: Average (3/5). Requires moderate complexity to integrate affective and contextual signals.
- **Kohlberg**: High (2/5). Its abstraction requires complex calculations to model the stages of moral development.

e. Ethical Alignment

- **Hyunsoo Kim**: High (5/5). Centered on human assistance, it integrates ethical values and leaves the final decision to the user.
- **LIDA**: Average (3/5). May lack ethical nuances due to its reliance on data and predefined rules.
- **Kohlberg**: High (5/5). Based on universal moral principles, it provides a solid ethical framework.

f. Societal Impact

- **Hyunsoo Kim**: High (5/5). Contributes significantly in crucial areas such as health and justice, increasing the quality of decisions.
- **LIDA**: Average (3/5). Its impact is limited by its complexity and lack of adaptability.
- **Kohlberg**: High potential (4/5). Although it is mainly used in education, it has significant societal potential if it is applied on a large scale.

Discussion and Original Contribution

Through our comparative analysis we intend to showcase the strengths and weaknesses of three ethical decision-making models as they are applied to AI-related limitations in organizational contexts.

The three models stemmed from different epistemological disciplines: moral psychology, computational cognitive science, and applied organizational ethics. This disciplinary diversity gives way to multiple exploration of moral agency in environments in which AI plays a considerable role in decision-making processes.

Yet, the distinction also exposes significant tensions regarding assumptions about autonomy, context, and normative orientation.

Kohlberg's model, which provides a solid foundation for understanding human moral maturation, has limited applicability to AI systems, which lack psychological development and emotional growth. Moreover, its universalistic stance ignores contextual and cultural variations—factors that are increasingly relevant in global AI deployment.

The LIDA model, which is designed in the field of artificial intelligence, simulates moral processes through a cognitive agent architecture. It specifically incorporates elements of human perception, emotion, and decision-making cycles to offer a framework for AI to model its moral agency. However, its strength lies more in technical implementation than in moral reflection; it operationalizes decision-making but does not deeply engage with ethical pluralism or social responsibility.

Hyunsoo Kim's model brings a critical contextual lens. It is based on an East Asian ethical model that particularly underlines these moral decisions' institutional, cultural, and relational aspects. This is why it remains useful in considering the ethical issues of AI within organizational contexts where the relations are complex and decision-making is never neutral or devoid of values. However, the assumption of social structures with embedded actors points to a limitation concerning non-human agents. Unless AI systems are designed with such contextual sensitivity, non-human agents will remain outside such applying frameworks.

With regard to all three models, context stands out as the most distinguishing element. Kohlberg provides the least contextualized integration with his universal stages of development. LIDA offers a simulation-based environment which provides moderate contextual integration. Kim's model places context as defining element of moral reasoning as primary. This becomes a requirement when dealing with ethical AI systems placed in sophisticated multicultural organizational contexts.

The approach to bias is defined differently in each model, leading to new understandings. As noted, bias is not mentioned as an issue within the framework by Kohlberg. In LIDA, it becomes one of the processes on the level of cognition while Kim attends to the more holistic processes that shape ethical gaps of concern. As the discourse around AI increasingly focuses on the reproduction of social and algorithmic biases,the capacity of a model to accommodate such distortions is extremely important.

With regard to direct relevance to AI, the LIDA model comes first as it is computational in nature. Kim's model, while not specifically AI-derived, has rich interpretive potential concerning the ethical implications of AI on professional practice as interdisciplinary decision-making frameworks. Theoretical contributions by Kohlberg remain for the most part, offering hints at human moral evolution without much actionable content for AI regulation.

In the end, this comparison focuses on the fact that there is no one model that singlehandedly offers a solution to the problem of complexity surrounding moral dilemmas in the era of AI. Instead, a cross-disciplinary approach which integrates developmental ethics, moral cognition, and contextual ethics is needed in order to effectively design and assess AI systems that involve human decision-making in delicate ethical contexts.

In order to better contextualize our analysis, three short case studies illustrating the application of the ethical models discussed in this chapter have been included:

The controversy surrounding the gender-biased recruiting algorithm employed by Amazon is an example of neglecting an organizational, and even cultural, context which is a gap that Hyunsoo Kim's context ethics framework seeks to fill.

The COMPAS risk assessment tool, used in the U.S. criminal justice system, raises concerns over algorithmic opacity. We interpret this case through the lens of Kohlberg's moral development model, which may offer a foundation for more transparent ethical justification.

The example of **IBM Watson Health**, which encountered challenges related to explainability and clinical reliability, demonstrates how the LIDA model could contribute to the development of cognitively structured systems that are both intelligible and ethically grounded.

Research Results

a. Practical Applicability

- **Hyunsoo Kim** stands out as the most suited model to practical contexts thanks to its computational simplicity and high societal impact, particularly in fields such as medicine and justice.
- **LIDA** has limited applicability to specific situations, such as crises requiring consideration of emotional factors.
- **Kohlberg** remains theoretical and mainly relevant in educational and moral training contexts.

b. Adaptability

- **Kohlberg** excels through its flexibility in different social and educational contexts.
- **Hyunsoo Kim** is moderately adaptable, depending on the quality of the data and algorithms.
- **LIDA** lacks flexibility due to its reliance on a rigid architecture.

c. Ethical Alignment and Societal Impact

- Both Hyunsoo Kim and Kohlberg's models display high ethical alignment, incorporating strong moral principles.
- In terms of societal impact, Hyunsoo Kim is the most promising, as he combines concrete applications with respect for human values.

d. Computational Complexity and Robustness

- **Hyunsoo Kim** is simple to implement and relatively robust.
- **LIDA** shows robustness limitations, mainly due to vulnerabilities related to training data biases.
- **Kohlberg** is theoretically robust, but its computational complexity makes it less accessible for practical implementations.

CONCLUSIONS AND PERSPECTIVES

This research demonstrates that collaboration between artificial intelligence (AI) and humans requires models adapted to specific contexts:

- **Hyunsoo Kim** represents the best balance for practical applications, providing a robust and ethical framework.
- **LIDA** makes interesting contributions for situations where emotional factors are crucial, but its lack of flexibility limits its scope.
- **Kohlberg** remains an essential theoretical pillar for educating and raising awareness for ethical issues, but its practical use is restricted by its complexity.
- **Improving Collaborative Models**
- Developing hybrid systems that combine Kohlberg's flexibility with Hyunsoo Kim's computational simplicity, while incorporating LIDA's emotional nuances.
- Invest in mechanisms to reduce bias in training data to increase the robustness of AI systems.
- **Interdisciplinary Exploration**
- Strengthen collaboration between AI specialists, ethicists, and sociologists to design more balanced systems adapted to diverse cultural and organizational contexts.
- **User Training**

- Integrate training modules on the use of AI systems in sensitive sectors such as medicine, justice and education, to ensure informed and ethical decision-making.
- **Regulatory Framework**
- Develop clear, international regulatory frameworks to supervise the use of AI in critical contexts, with an emphasis on transparency, fairness, and accountability.

These perspectives pave the way for more effective integration of AI-human systems, while respecting fundamental ethical principles and meeting the needs of users in various fields.

To translate the ethical reflections developed in this chapter into actionable steps, we propose a set of practical recommendations structured around three complementary pillars:

Governance: Organizations should embed ethical oversight into the decision-making processes that guide the development and use of AI. This includes appointing ethics officers, drafting internal charters, and establishing cross-functional ethics committees capable of assessing the social and operational impact of AI tools throughout their lifecycle.

Design: Development teams are encouraged to prioritize models and interfaces that foster transparency, clarity, and user trust. This means making decision logic accessible, ensuring data pathways are understandable, and integrating ethical design principles from the early stages of prototyping.

Evaluation: Beyond technical performance metrics, AI systems should be subject to ethical validation protocols. These protocols might include indicators such as fairness, explainability, social robustness, and the availability of recourse mechanisms in the event of algorithmic error.

REFERENCES

Allen, C., Wallach, W., & Smit, I. (2022). *Moral machines: Teaching robots right from wrong*. Oxford University Press.

Ananny, M., & Crawford, K. (2018). Seeing without knowing: Limitations of the transparency ideal and its application to algorithmic accountability. *New Media & Society*, *20*(3), 973–989. DOI: 10.1177/1461444816676645

Baars, B. J. (1988). *A cognitive theory of consciousness*. Cambridge University Press.

Camburn, D. (1993). Organizational learning and ethical decision making. *Journal of Business Ethics*, *12*(8), 607–616.

Chouaib, A. (2014). The impact of ethical behavior on organizational performance. *Revue des Sciences de Gestion*, *41*(3), 123–135.

Commission européenne. (2021). Proposal for a regulation laying down harmonised rules on artificial intelligence (Artificial Intelligence Act). COM/2021/206 final. https://eur-lex.europa.eu/legal-content/EN/TXT/?uri=CELEX%3A52021PC0206

Davison, R. M., Martinsons, M. G., & Kock, N. (2009). Ethical decision making in software piracy: Initial development and test of a four-component model. *Management Information Systems Quarterly*, *33*(1), 167–180.

Doshi-Velez, F., & Kim, B. (2017). Towards a rigorous science of interpretable machine learning. arXiv preprint arXiv:1702.08608. https://arxiv.org/abs/1702.08608

Errabih, F. (2020). Individual ethics and organizational ethics: Two facets of ethical decision-making. *Revue des Sciences de Gestion*, *45*(2), 89–102.

Ferrell, O. C., & Gresham, L. G. (1985). A contingency framework for understanding ethical decision making in marketing. *Journal of Marketing*, *49*(3), 87–96. DOI: 10.1177/002224298504900308

Ferrell, O. C., Johnston, M. W., & Ferrell, L. (1989). A synthesis of ethical decision models for marketing. *Journal of Macromarketing*, *9*(2), 55–64. DOI: 10.1177/027614678900900207

Flanagan, O. (2004). *The science of the mind*. MIT Press.

Floridi, L., & Cowls, J. (2022). A unified framework of five principles for AI in society. *Harvard Data Science Review*, *4*(1). Advance online publication. DOI: 10.1162/99608f92.8cd550d1

Ford, R. C., & Richardson, W. D. (1994). Ethical decision making: A review of the empirical literature. *Journal of Business Ethics, 13*(3), 205–221. DOI: 10.1007/BF02074820

Fremeaux, S., & Noel, G. (2015). Moral development according to Kohlberg: An application in an organizational context. *Journal of Responsible Organization, 10*(2), 45–60.

Gentsch, P., van Geenen, D., & Schmid, B. (2021). AI and human decision-making: A hybrid approach for ethical outcomes. *Journal of Artificial Intelligence Research, 70*, 1–25.

Girard, J. P. (2007). Organizational culture and its impact on ethical decision-making. *Management, 32*(3), 45–58.

Heron, J. (1996). Ethical decision-making in business: Issues and dilemmas. *Revue Française de Gestion, 22*(109), 78–89.

International Organization for Standardization. (2023). ISO/IEC 42001:2023 – Artificial intelligence management system (AIMS) – Requirements with guidance. https://www.iso.org/standard/81230.html

Jones, T. M. (1991). Ethical decision making by individuals in organizations: An issue-contingent model. *Academy of Management Review, 16*(2), 366–395. DOI: 10.2307/258867

Kéfi, M. K., & Sarr, M. (2014). Cultural influences on ethical decision making: A comparative study. *Journal of Business Ethics, 123*(4), 573–586.

Kohlberg, L. (1969). Stage and sequence: The cognitive-developmental approach to socialization. In Goslin, D. A. (Ed.), *Handbook of socialization theory and research* (pp. 347–480). Rand McNally.

Lainey, P. (2015). Ethics in business: A developmental perspective. *Management, 40*(4), 67–78.

Lipton, Z. C. (2018). The mythos of model interpretability. *Communications of the ACM, 61*(10), 36–43. DOI: 10.1145/3233231

Logsdon, J. M., & Yuthas, K. (1997). Corporate social performance, stakeholder orientation, and organizational moral development. *Journal of Business Ethics, 16*(12), 1213–1226. DOI: 10.1023/A:1005741931995

Organisation de coopération et de développement économiques. (2019). Principes de l'OCDE sur l'intelligence artificielle. https://www.oecd.org/fr/intelligence-artificielle/principes/

Parlement européen & Conseil de l'Union européenne. (2016). Règlement général sur la protection des données (RGPD). Règlement (UE) 2016/679. https://eur-lex.europa.eu/legal-content/FR/TXT/?uri=CELEX%3A32016R0679

Piaget, J. (1932). *The moral judgment of the child.* Free Press.

Raji, I. D., Smart, A., White, R., & Mitchell, M. (2020). Closing the AI accountability gap: Defining an end-to-end framework for internal algorithmic auditing. In *Proceedings of the 2020 Conference on Fairness, Accountability, and Transparency* (pp. 33–44). DOI: 10.1145/3351095.3372873

Schwepker, C. H., & Good, D. J. (2019). Marketing control and ethical decision-making: A comparison of managers. *Journal of Business Ethics*, *156*(2), 337–351.

Simon, H. A. (1957). *Models of man: Social and rational.* Wiley.

Sivakumar, K., Chakrabarty, S., & Roy, S. (2016). The role of ethical climate on salesperson's role stress, job attitudes, turnover intention, and job performance. *Journal of Personal Selling & Sales Management*, *36*(4), 297–312.

Treviño, L. K. (1986). Ethical decision making in organizations: A person-situation interactionist model. *Academy of Management Review*, *11*(3), 601–617. DOI: 10.2307/258313

Vaswani, A., Shazeer, N., Parmar, N., Uszkoreit, J., Jones, L., Gomez, A. N., Kaiser, Ł., & Polosukhin, I. (2017). Attention is all you need. In Advances in neural information processing systems (Vol. 30, pp. 5998–6008).

Wallach, W., Allen, C., & Smit, I. (2010). A model of moral judgment in artificial agents. In *AAAI Fall Symposium: Machine Ethics* (pp. 50–55).

APPENDIX

```
importmatplotlib.pyplotaceplt

importnumpyacenp

importseabornacesns

importpandasacepd

# Model data

criteria = [

“Practical applicability”,

“Adaptability”,

“Robustness”,

“Computational (inverse) complexity”,

“Ethical alignment”,

“Societal impact”

]
```

```
models = ["Hyunsoo Kim","LIDA","Kohlberg"]

scores = {

"Hyunsoo Kim": [5,4,4,5,5,5],

"LIDA": [3,2,2,3,3,3],

"Kohlberg": [3,5,4,2,5,4]

}

df = pd.DataFrame(scores, index=criteria)

#□1□□Clustered Bar Chart

df.plot(kind="bar", figsize=(10,6), rot=45, title="Multi-
criteria Comparison - Grouped Bars")

plt.ylabel("Score (1-5)")

plt.legend(title="Model")

plt.grid(axis="y", linestyle="--", alpha=0.7)

plt.show()
```

```
#□2□□Line Graph

df.plot(kind="line", marker='o', figsize=(10,6), ti-
tle="Multi-criteria Comparison - Line Chart")

plt.ylabel("Score (1-5)")

plt.xticks(rotation=45)

plt.legend(title="Model")

plt.grid(True, linestyle="--", alpha=0.7)

plt.show()

#□3□□Heatmap

plt.figure(figsize=(8,6))

sns.heatmap(df, annot=True, cmap="coolwarm", linewidths=0.5,
linecolor="gray")

plt.title("Multi-criteria Comparison - Heatmap")

plt.ylabel("Criteria")

plt.xlabel("Models")
```

```
plt.show()

#□4□□Scatter Plot

plt.figure(figsize=(10,6))

formodel, colorin zip(models, ["blue","orange","green"]):

plt.scatter(criteria, df[model], label=model, s=100)

plt.title("Multi-criteria Comparison - Point Cloud")

plt.ylabel("Score (1-5)")

plt.xticks(rotation=45)

plt.legend(title="Model")

plt.grid(True, linestyle="--", alpha=0.7)

plt.show()
```

Chapter 5
From Digital Transformation to Transparency:
The Role of AI in Reshaping Administrative Practices in Morocco

Latifa Boumalk
https://orcid.org/0009-0004-7293-0706
National School of Business and Management in Agadir, Ibnou Zohr University, Morocco

Hassane Amaazoul
https://orcid.org/0000-0002-5061-5869
National School of Business and Management in Agadir, Ibnou Zohr University, Morocco

ABSTRACT

Morocco's public administration earns part of its digital transformation through ICT, a process accelerated by the Covid-19 pandemic. To this end, Morocco has launched the « Digital Morocco 2030 ». Moreover, digital transformation includes advanced technologies where artificial intelligence stands as a crucial tool in the enhancement of public services efficiency. This paper takes place based on systematic literature review and case studies, to in-depth study digital transformation and the application of AI within Moroccan public administration. It aims to identify the main points in this area and explore its opportunities and challenges. This chapter is structured according to the following sequence: first, we present a review of concepts and literature on digital transformation and AI in Moroccan public administration.

DOI: 10.4018/979-8-3373-1737-3.ch005

Next, a review of existing theoretical frameworks will be carried out to uncover the factors that contribute to digitalization and AI integration. Finally, by synthesizing the studies, we could propose a model for better integrating administration in the digital age.

INTRODUCTION

In today's era, digital transformation has become a key phenomenon, pushing countries around the world to implement it in all areas of social, economic, and administrative activity. Its considerable impact on employment is visible in both the public and private sectors. Morocco, like other countries around the world, must face the impact of digital transformation. The Moroccan government has undertaken important reforms to modernize the public administration. This initiative aims to improve efficiency, optimize the management of public services, facilitate the work of administrative agents and speed up administrative procedures, while improving efficiency and transparency through digital technologies.

In this context, Morocco has launched the national strategy "*Digital Morocco 2030*" aimed at modernizing the administration, simplifying procedures, reducing costs and improving the quality of public services. The aim is to accelerate the digital transformation of public services (e-Gov) in order to facilitate access to administrative services for citizens and businesses. The objective is to move from 113th to 50th position worldwide in the EGDI (*E-Government Development Index*) ranking of online public services, among the essential levers to accelerate this transformation is the strengthening of the legal framework relating to digitalization, which contributes to increased transparency of administrative operations and better public confidence in the management of digital services. Transparency is a key factor in management decisions, as it is seen as a solution to the many problems faced in the public sector, such as corruption, excessive administrative delays and lack of accountability in public management.

The emergence of artificial intelligence (AI), as an advanced technological tool in the age of digitalization, is now seen as a key enabler for automating administrative processes, analyzing data, and improving decision-making. Its role in strengthening transparency and reshaping administrative practices is undeniable. In Morocco, artificial intelligence has been deployed in several public sectors, in particular within the Moroccan customs administration, the full dematerialization of the declaration circuit by Moroccan customs, accentuated by the health crisis, has accelerated the digitalization of the ecosystem, this makes the integration of AI essential to ensure the exchange, monitoring and transparency of transactions (Noureddine *et al., 2024)*. Nevertheless, although artificial intelligence offers immense potential to simplify administrative management in Morocco, it still faces many technical, human and ethical challenges.

This chapter is based on a systematic review of literature and case studies, such as that of the customs administration in Morocco, with the aim of studying in depth the digital transformation and the application of AI within the Moroccan public administration. Thus, it aims to identify the main aspects of this field and explore its opportunities and challenges. With this in mind, several questions arise: how can digital transformation and the integration of artificial intelligence improve Moroccan public administration? What are the opportunities and challenges to be met to ensure the success of this transformation?

To achieve this, this work is organized as follows: a review of concepts and literature on digital transformation and AI in Moroccan public administration is first presented, then a review of existing theoretical frameworks is carried out to uncover the determinants of digitalization and integration of AI. At last, a global synthesis of the studies could allow the development of a model aimed at improving the integration of the administration in the digital age.

CONCEPTUAL FRAMEWORK

Digital transformation is bringing transparency to administrative governance, and artificial intelligence is playing a key role in reforming administrative practices. To better understand this topic, it is important to clarify the underlying concepts related to it. First, digital transformation, which involves integrating advanced technologies into organizational structures to improve processes and operational efficiency. In the context of Moroccan public administration, this helps to promote the transparency and accessibility of public services, the digitalization of procedures and the integration of innovative technologies to provide quality services to the public, thus boosting citizens' trust and participation. According to Taouabit *et al.* (2023), although it is common to confuse digital transformation with "*transformation numérique*" in French language, when in reality it is a broader concept that encompasses "*transformation numérique*", while going beyond its borders, digital transformation involves the in-depth use of digital technologies, such as social media, the Internet of Things, artificial intelligence, *Big Data* and *Cloud Computing*.

Secondly, artificial intelligence, another key concept, represents an important technological tool in the process of digital transformation. Indeed, artificial intelligence represents the ability of a machine to perform tasks that usually require human intelligence, such as learning, decision-making, pattern recognition, and data analysis. In the field of public administration, artificial intelligence can be used to automate certain processes, analyze large volumes of data, and make decisions based on algorithms. Baker & Smith (2019) offers an extended definition of AI, describing computers capable of performing cognitive tasks, usually related to the human mind, in particular learning and problem-solving.

Then, e-government or e-gov, involves the integration of new information and communication technologies (ICT) with the aim of increasing the availability, transparency, efficiency and speed of public service delivery and administrative management processes. Administrations offer online services such as permit applications made via the Internet, as well as online tax returns, among other concrete examples of e-government. In e-government literature, Djafer & Reda (2020), four concepts were identified that can be used to summarize many definitions: The use of information and communication technologies (ICTs); Adapting work processes and machinery structures; Improving information, communication and cooperation between the various actors such as citizens, businesses, non-profit organizations and non-governmental organizations; Increasing the effectiveness and efficiency of government functions.

Finally, the objective of administrative transparency is to make information about administrative management, decision-making procedures and the services offered clear and accessible to citizens. Thus, it aims to gain the trust of users in public administrations and its services, making them more intelligible and transparent. Curtin & Mendes (2011) a defines transparency as the opportunity to observe decision-making processes, while participation refers to the opportunity to participate in them. As with experiences in other countries, transparency and clear communication about the benefits of AI are key to fostering an environment conducive to change (Barodi & Lalaoui, 2025).

Identifying these key concepts before starting our literature review is essential and shows the interconnection between these concepts, considering that digital transformation and the integration of artificial intelligence optimize speed, efficiency and transparency. This framework will highlight the challenges and opportunities related to this change.

RESEARCH METHODOLOGY

Following a systematic literature review approach, we methodically developed this research as a process for identifying and selecting scientific work dealing with digital transformation and AI in the public sector. This includes an analysis of the articles reviewed with a focus on the field of research, as well as an identification of the most used terms in the corpus of articles. This in-depth analysis of the existing literature offers us the opportunity to deepen our knowledge of the gaps in this domain.

Initially, we favored the use of the Scopus database, our aim being to illustrate the interest of digital tools in the examination of a certain limited number of scientific articles indexed in one of the major databases. We also base ourselves on recent trends and developments in the field of research. This method will ensure the relevance and timeliness of the information collected, while promoting the effective use of digital tools to analyze and interpret the data obtained. Articles that met all the criteria that are applied to the Scopus database and that were freely accessible on the platform or at the publisher, were selected for further textual analysis.

Secondly, we also used the IMIST database, which contains a multitude of relevant, current and accessible bibliographic references. In addition, our discussion on digital transformation, transparency and the role of AI in reshaping administrative practices in Morocco highlighted a specificity related to the Moroccan perspective. This criterion is rarely observed, it appears only in very small numbers in the Scopus database. Therefore, we have resorted to the database of the Moroccan Institute of Scientific and Technical Information (IMIST).

In addition, in order to broaden our spectrum of biographical research, we have also consulted other databases such as Cairn.Info, which brings together several publishers specializing in the humanities and social sciences. This reference platform, dedicated to scientific publications in French, aims to promote the discovery of quality research while preserving the autonomy and variety of participants in the knowledge ecosystem.

This method offers us the opportunity to analyze the results of different studies, while identifying theoretical gaps and considering avenues for future research. The use of sophisticated methods such as Biblioshiny, a tool launched by the "Biblioshiny" command on the "R" console in the "R Studio" application, to perform bibliometric and visual analyses, and "Zotero" for the organization of bibliographic references, ensures accuracy in the arrangement and analysis of the data. Thus, we recognize the challenges inherent in digital transformation in the public domain and the importance of a comprehensive and multidisciplinary strategy to fully understand its consequences.

This methodological approach reflects our goal of offering robust results that can inform future approaches and guide policymakers towards the most effective strategies to implement in an accelerated technology environment.

RESULTS OF THE SYSTEMATIC LITERATURE REVIEW

As part of our systematic review of the literature, we aimed to develop a methodical and rigorous analysis of existing work on artificial intelligence and digital transformation within the Moroccan public administration. This section presents our findings, starting with an exploratory systematic review of the literature (bibliometric analysis) before moving on to an in-depth systematic review of the literature (systematic analysis).

Exploratory Systematic Literature Review

To assess digital transformation and AI, and their impact on the transparency and management of public services, a strict methodological approach has been established. This includes an in-depth analysis of indispensable academic databases such as Scopus and Cairn.info. In addition, after initial exploratory research, we found that the IMIST database is particularly rich for our Moroccan public administration context. It offers relevant and varied references on topics such as e-government and digital administration, digital transformation, transparency as well as the integration of artificial intelligence in the Moroccan public sector.

In the Scopus database, we have chosen to extract all the metadata relevant to us. Using specific keywords associated with digital administration and artificial intelligence to search for scientific articles, whether in titles, abstracts or keywords, we identified 855 results. Through advanced search, we narrowed our search to papers published in the last seven years, from 2019 to 2025, in order to track the evolution of the theoretical models examined for our topic of study. Then, we focused on the field of research with a focus on articles related to social sciences, business, management and accounting, decision sciences, economics, econometrics and finance as well as computer science. The application of all other eligibility criteria ultimately led to the identification of 62 relevant articles, highlighting the depth and breadth of digital transformation in the public sector. This approach ensures a global and up-to-date perspective on the digital transformations influencing the management of public administration (*cf.*Table 1).

Table 1. Application of eligibility criteria on the Scopus database

Eligibility criteria		Number of references	
Search with: article title, abstract, Keywords	digital AND administration AND artificial AND intelligence	855	
Year	2019 to 2025	781	
Field of study	Computer science	322	526
	Social Sciences	221	
	Business, Management and Accounting	88	
	Decision Sciences	60	
	Economics, Econometrics and Finance	57	
Document Type	Article	219	
Language	English	173	
Keyword	Artificial intelligence	103	133
	L'administration publique	25	
	Digital transformation	22	
	Technology	12	
	Machine learning	12	
	Innovation	8	
	Digitization	8	
	Governance	6	
	AI	6	
	Public sector	5	
	Information Management	5	
	COVID-19	5	
	Transparency	4	
	Decision-making	4	
	L'administration fiscale	3	
	Public Sector Innovation	3	
	E-learning	3	
	Judicial administration	2	
	ICT	2	
	Data privacy	2	
	Customs Administration	2	
	The ethics of AI	2	
Source Type	Journal	132	

continued on following page

Table 1. Continued

Eligibility criteria		Number of references
Search with: article title, abstract, Keywords	**digital AND administration AND artificial AND intelligence**	**855**
Year	**2019 to 2025**	**781**
Publishing stage	Final	**118**
Free access	All free access	**62**

Source: Drawn up by the authors.

In the IMIST database, we search for bibliographic references using keywords such as Digital transformation, artificial intelligence, public administration of Morocco, E-government and public services. Following the visualization and examination of the articles selected on the database, by scrutinizing the title, the abstract and the keywords, we finally come to the conclusion that 7 scientific articles unearthed in the IMIST database are the most appropriate and deserve an in-depth analysis of their content.

Following an exploratory study of the Cairn.Info database and the use of keywords such as: digital transformation, administration, public service. The analysis of the titles, abstracts and keywords of the scientific articles referenced in this database has made it possible to identify a scientific article that stands out for its importance and interest for our in-depth study.

The selected references from the Scopus database were transferred to the Biblioshiny software to start an exploratory analysis. Among the 62 articles, we notice that a large majority were published in 2024. Indeed, 24 articles represent nearly 39% of our Scopus selection (*cf.*Figure 1). This phenomenon indicates a growing interest among researchers in the topics of digital administration and artificial intelligence during this period. This trend can be attributed to the continuous expansion of digitalization and artificial intelligence, their application in various business sectors and especially their impact on improving public services requiring a transition to digital solutions.

Figure 1. References collected by year of publication

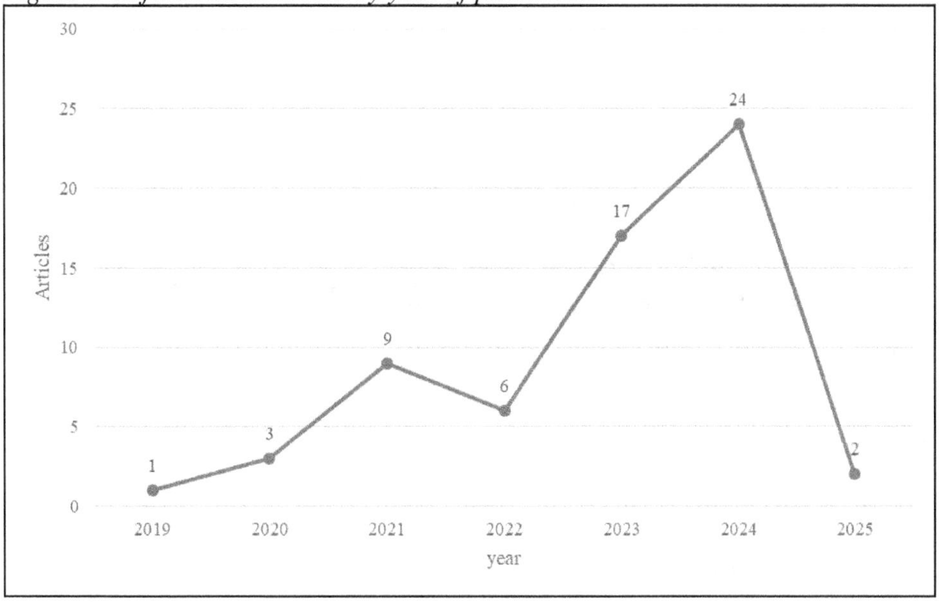

Source: *Drawn up by the authors*

In the Biblioshiny software, a series of queries were executed to give us the possibility to view titles, keywords and abstracts. Then, we identified the terms that appeared most often in the entire corpus of the article, the keywords that allowed us to constitute the word cloud (*cf.*Figure 2). Following the exploitation of these data, we conducted an analysis of the various specificities of scientific articles via Biblioshiny. This allowed us to get a general idea of the various topics and authors in order to refine the examination of the concepts discussed in the articles examined during our study.

Figure 2. Word Cloud

Source: *Drawn up by the authors*

The word cloud generated by Biblioshiny highlights that the most common terms encountered in the 62 selected articles in the Scopus database include: *artificial intelligence, public administration, digital storage, human, innovation, machine learning, technology*... etc.

In the Zotero software, we scrutinized and interacted with all the scientific articles from various databases. Looking at the titles, keywords, and abstracts of each article, we ultimately selected 15 open access articles that seem most appropriate to our systematic review of the literature for further analysis (*cf.*Table 2).

Table 2. List of databases

Database	**Number of references**
Scopus	7
IMIST	7
Cairn.Info	1
Grand Total	**15**

Source: Drawn up by the authors

We present a diagram adapted to our study with reference to the “Prisma” protocol, facilitating the synthesis of the systematic literature review process (*cf.* Figure 3). To carry out a more in-depth systematic study of the references retained, by proceeding in the full reading of each article.

Figure 3. The Prisma Diagram

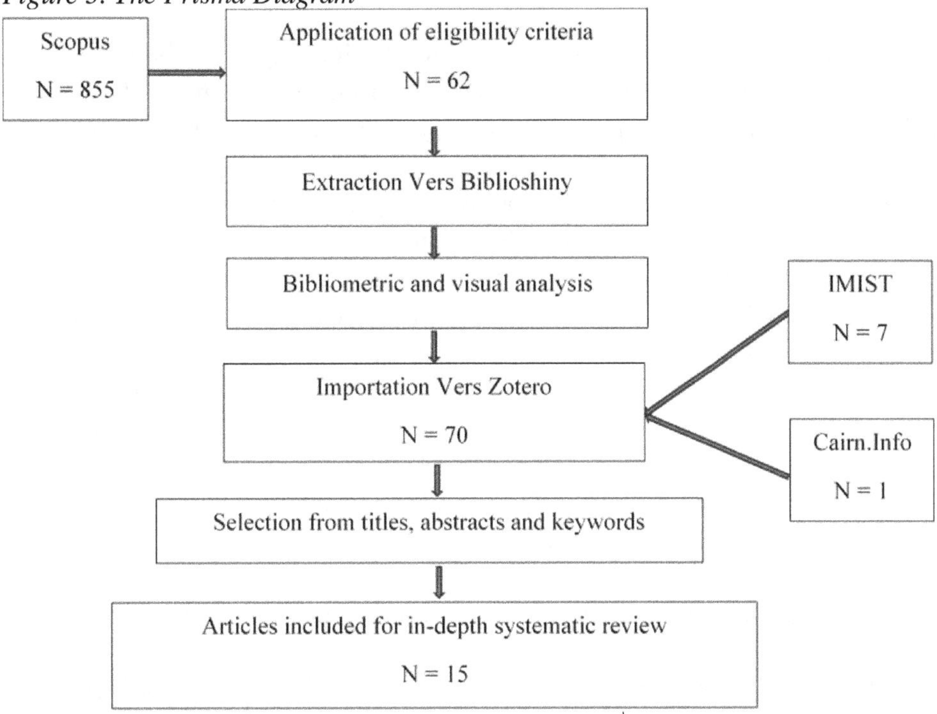

Source: *Drawn up by the authors*

This analysis traces the methodology for selecting articles in the context of a systematic review, resulting in a final corpus of 15 publications. The process, illustrated by the PRISMA diagram, follows a rigorous logic of progressive exclusion, in accordance with scientific standards.

1. Initial identification (N = 855)

The initial phase identified 855 articles from the Scopus database, reflecting the breadth of literature available on the subject. This step is based on a broad search, without preliminary filters, in order to avoid any selection bias.

2. Application of eligibility criteria (N = 62)

The 855 articles were subjected to an initial evaluation based on eligibility criteria (e.g., field of study, year of publication, language). This selection reduced the corpus to 62 articles, discarding references that did not conform to the objectives of the study.

3. Bibliometric extraction and analysis

The 62 selected articles were exported to "Biblioshiny" for bibliometric and visual analysis. This step makes it possible to identify major trends (References collected by year of publication, Word cloud) and to map the scientific landscape.

4. Import to Zotero and fine selection (N = 70 → N = 15)
   - **Import to Zotero (N = 70):** A portion of the items (70) have been transferred to Zotero for further processing. The discrepancy between the 62 eligible articles and the 70 imported ones suggests the addition of additional references (IMIST and Cairn.Info).
   - **Selection based on titles, abstracts and keywords**: A critical reading of the 70 articles was carried out, leading to the selection of 15 publications selected for the systematic review. This step is based on a qualitative evaluation (methodological relevance, adequacy with the problem).
5. Complementary sources (IMIST and Cairn.Info)
   - **IMIST (N = 7):** These articles come from a specialized database, dealing with more in the Moroccan context and adding a targeted disciplinary perspective.
   - **Cairn.Info (N = 1):** The presence of an article from Cairn.Info (French-speaking platform in the Humanities and Social Sciences) express our desire to include regional work and specific theoretical approaches.

In short, the selection process, marked by a high attrition rate (855 → 15), underlines the rigor applied to build a relevant and manageable corpus. The final selection of 15 papers is the result of a three-step process: broad identification, methodical screening, and qualitative validation. Thus, the addition of sources such as IMIST and Cairn.Info testifies to a desire to diversify disciplinary perspectives. Finally, the 15 articles selected include both international productions (Scopus) and targeted resources (IMIST, Cairn.Info), ensuring a balanced coverage between exhaustiveness and depth of analysis.

In-Depth Systematic Literature Review

The integration of artificial intelligence and digital transformation within the Moroccan public administration occupies a key place in scientific research. Each author presented the results of his work according to his own line of study. In this section, we present and study the results for each scientific article selected, with the aim of formulating an overall conclusion on our topic.

Indeed, Kamal & Qour (2024) show that digital transformation has evolved from a simple digitization of processes to a holistic approach integrating various advanced digital technologies. This reflects technological, economic and social changes. The semantic analysis led to the development of the following definition of the concept of digital transformation: "A continuous, incremental and holistic process of change where the pressure of external and internal factors creates disruptions within the organization, pushing it to adapt its overall strategic response through technological innovations to satisfy user needs and create new values".

Moreover, the results of the survey drawn up by Taouabit et *al.* (2023), on the digital transformation of public administration in Morocco and its impact on the user experience: Case of the services provided to notaries by the National Agency for Land Conservation, Cadastre and Cartography (ANCFCC), are presented according to the hypotheses formulated and the axes of the interview guide used for the data collection. In general, notaries are generally satisfied with the availability, quality and accessibility of the ANCFCC's online services, which they recommend to their clients. The level of satisfaction is homogeneous, although some notaries have highlighted the positive impact of digitalization on their efficiency and productivity, thanks to easier access to information and faster procedures, while appreciating the security and confidentiality of the services. However, some mentioned difficulties. In general, the analysis of the results shows that the majority of notaries have a positive user experience with these online services.

Besides, Calay (2019) highlights the strategic challenges faced by the Walloon public services in the digitalization of their activities, in particular the low visibility of budgetary and human resources and the insufficient coordination of digitalization models. It highlights the coexistence of two models, bureaucratic and connectionist, which generate tensions due to fundamental incompatibilities between them. Moreover, the bureaucratic model is centralized and limited in external interactions, in contradiction with the decentralized and interactive principles of the connectionist model.

In addition, Tayazime & Moutahaddib (2021) point out that users of public services in Morocco mainly acquire their technological skills through self-training, although experts prefer a university education. Users' expectations focus on speed, efficiency and transparency, as administrative procedures are considered too slow and complex. The majority of users believe that the digital transformation will improve public services, and this opinion is shared regardless of age group, socio-professional category or skill level. Statistical tests validate this positive perception of digitalization.

Furthermore, Ouboumlik & Touhami (2024) find, through a systematic review of the literature, that digital technologies improve efficiency, transparency and participatory governance. Moreover, trust, innovation, knowledge management and citizen engagement are the success factors of the digital transformation of public administration, highlighting the need for an integrated approach that encompasses the technological, organizational and psychosocial dimensions. Thus, challenges exist, namely limited infrastructure, inadequate legislative frameworks and cultural resistance. These obstacles underscore the need for a citizen-centric strategy to optimize digitalization.

Then, the study of Noureddine *et al.* (2024) describes several policy choices for Customs administrations that may include directions, including: Refocusing on organizational values such as digital literacy and the adoption of artificial intelligence. Strengthen internal and external cooperation, including in the exchange of experiences on AI and related training. Use external expertise to implement AI, given the high costs. Use AI to improve reporting compliance, service quality and duty recovery. Detect fraud using intelligent systems. The experience of Moroccan customs shows a successful digitalization process, with a gradual integration of AI in control. The administration continues to make efforts to extend these solutions to all levels of control and products.

Thus, Yosra & Abdelkrim (2024) led to several relevant results, among which the analysis of the sample revealed a majority of women among the respondents and a student population with a significant proportion of master's degree holders. The findings point to opportunities to use AI to improve the accessibility and personalization of learning, and challenges like lack of teacher training and the cost of tools. The participants propose training for teachers and students, an investment by the State as well as collaboration between industry and research. They believe that AI could improve educational quality and reduce inequalities, but are concerned about job insecurity and unequal access to technology.

Similarly, the systematic literature review of Ibrahim & Benabdelhadi (2021) reveals several key points for the successful digital transformation of public administrations. These include citizen trust, awareness and adoption of digital technologies, and also the role that governments play in providing services tailored to the needs of users. IT infrastructure plays an important role in helping to access information and improving the performance of public services. However, obstacles can arise such as the lack of adaptation of the legal framework, difficulties in reorganizing administrative structures and even the need for new management styles. These challenges can hinder the effectiveness and efficiency of the digitalization process.

At the same time, Androniceanu (2023) illustrates significant examples of good practice of digital transformation and AI in public administration in EU countries. In Germany, the *Next Generation Weapon System* (NGWS) project is launched with France and Spain, interconnected with the *Future Combat Air System* (FCAS) platforms. Finland has a successful pilot project in the Ministry of Finance. Denmark is developing a digital strategy and promoting AI for national security, with applications in health and social care. Lithuania has established a regulatory sandbox and an AI advisory committee to guide future policies. In France, several *chatbots* and algorithms for the management of ministries and the processing of fraud are implemented. Romania is engaging in digital projects within the framework of *Cluster 4 Horizon Europe* and is pushing for *cloud* adoption in the public sector.

Moreover, Barodi & Lalaoui (2025) show that the obstacles to the adoption of artificial intelligence in the Moroccan public administration are mainly found in a lack of digital skills (49.6%), associated with organizational complexity (23.3%). Young civil servants (more than 40%) show a greater acceptability of artificial intelligence than the oldest and most resilient. The emphasis is on the importance of good training and good change management that goes in pairs. The implementation should be done gradually and through the implementation of the automation of administrative tasks in the first place and the promotion of strong leadership, good communication and a strong digital infrastructure so that integration in the public sector is seamless and smooth.

Equally, Kurmangali *et al.* (2024) explore the desire of Central Asian countries to have a digital economy and government for the purpose of economic development. Thus, it presents the challenges faced by an incomplete legal framework with regard to cybersecurity, as well as weak Internet connectivity and lack of technical skills, as well as a low level of digital literacy. Growth is also influenced by the lack of effective policies to minimize the digital divide, as well as by insufficient funding for digital infrastructure. A slower pace in the fusion of digitalization and artificial intelligence is observed, which differs from country to country. It is suggested to adopt a regional approach aimed at digitalization, improving digital literacy and cybersecurity, as well as investing in infrastructure and optimizing AI through public-private partnerships.

On top of that, Bencsik (2024) examines the integration of artificial intelligence in public administration, namely its beneficial influence on financial services and its role in automating decision-making. In fact, he analyzes the obstacles that limit innovation within the government, such as slow infrastructure development and resistance to change. It is recommended to use modern technologies through the use of reliable and known digital tools. However, there are still debates regarding the effectiveness of artificial intelligence and its application in public administration as well as questions about the associated risks. They also illustrated tangible cases, namely the automation of administrative tasks and the integration of electronic civil registration systems.

To go further, Pomahač (2024) characterized the digitalization of administrative tasks as a reality, even if it encounters concerns about understanding and processes for digital technologies. By looking at the potential impact of AI on public administration, namely that it can be positive or negative, it makes a clear distinction between artificial administration and technology. Indeed, public administration is at a turning point, where concerns about their complexity and curiosity about the capacity of algorithms coexist. He concludes with the need to have regulation of algorithmic systems to avoid abuses specifically in action planning.

In this regard, Terzidou (2023) stresses the importance of digital technologies to optimize the efficiency of the judicial system, while highlighting the shortcomings in the processing of applications, aggravated by COVID-19. AI is reputed to be an evolution compared to traditional systems, even if they suffer from a lack of interoperability between different digital systems. It uses artificial intelligence automation that improves its systems on its own. However, their adoption presupposes the existence of legislation guaranteeing fundamental rights. Overall, educating justice users is fundamental to better tuning and using these technologies.

Finally, by studying the potential for the use of artificial intelligence in public administration, Borissov & Hristozov (2024) observe that 15.6% of employees have not received training on the use of AI, while 42.9% have theoretical knowledge of it without integrating it into their daily work. In addition, 54.5% believe that it is necessary to put in place specific regulations to regulate AI in the public sector. In addition, 79.2% of managers consider AI to negatively affect employees' creativity, and 71.4% express concerns about over-reliance on technology, risking spreading misinformation.

In summary, let us recap the sources of the systematic literature review (*cf.* Table 3), highlighting the scientific studies reviewed in depth with information on authors, article titles, year of publication, journal, and methodology adopted.

Table 3. Summary of the sources of the systematic literature review

Authors	Title of the article	Year	Journal	Methodology
Taouabit *et al.*	Digital transformation of public administration in Morocco and its impact on the user experience: Case of the services provided to notaries by the National Agency for Land Conservation, Cadastre and Cartography	2023	International Journal of Accounting, Finance, Auditing, Management and Economics	Qualitative method and case study
Kamal & Qour	The Digital Transformation of Public Administrations and the Performance of Public Services: Definition, Understanding of the Process and Research Agenda	2024	The French Journal of Economics and Management	Qualitative method and systematic literature review
Calay	An administration 4.0? The challenges of developing a digital strategy for the Public Service of Wallonia	2019	Reflections and prospects of economic life	Exploratory analysis and cognitive framework
Tayazime & Moutahaddib	The Digital Transformation of Public Administration in Morocco: The Perception of Individual Users	2021	Journal of Business and Economics	Literature Review and Quantitative Method
Ouboumlik & Touhami	The Digital Transformation of Public Administration: A Systematic Review of the Literature	2024	African Scientific Journal	Systematic literature review
Noureddine *et al.*	The Integration of AI in the Moroccan Customs Administration: A Strategic Foresight Approach	2024	African Scientific Journal	Strategic foresight approach
Yosra & Abdelkrim	Artificial Intelligence for Education in Morocco: Opportunities, Challenges and Prospects	2024	International journal of applied management and economics	Quantitative method
Ibrahim & Benabdelhadi	The Digital Transformation of Public Administration: A Systematic Review of the Literature	2021	International Journal of Accounting, Finance, Auditing, Management and Economics	Systematic literature review
Androniceanu	The new trends of digital transformation and artificial intelligence in public administration	2023	Administratie si Management Public	Qualitative method and literature review
Barodi and Lalaoui,	Civil servants 'readiness for AI adoption: The role of change management in Morocco's public sector.	2025	Problems and Perspectives in Management	Quantitative method
Kurmangali *et al.*	Digitalization and artificial intelligence in central Asia: governmental responses and further implications	2024	Public Policy and Administration	Qualitative method

continued on following page

Table 3. Continued

Authors	Title of the article	Year	Journal	Methodology
Bencsik	The opportunities of digitalization in public administration with a special focus on the use of artificial intelligence	2024	Studia Iuridica Lublinensia	Literature review
Pomahač	Artificial public administration - myth or reality?	2024	Acta Universitatis Carolinae Iuridica	Literature review
Terzidou,	The Evolution of the Perception of Artificial Intelligence in the EU: The Case of Judicial Administration	2023	Journal of Intellectual Property, Information Technology and E-Commerce Law	Qualitative method
Borissov & Hristozov,	Potential for Using Artificial Intelligence in Public Administration	2024	ECONOMICS - Innovative and Economics Research Journal	Quantitative method

Source: Drawn up by the authors

The results of the analysis of the 15 selected articles highlight the opportunities and challenges of AI in the Moroccan administration, its impact on transparency, as well as the gaps with international models. These findings, while revealing, call for an in-depth critical examination, which will be discussed in the following discussion.

DISCUSSION

This discussion will allow us to deepen the results along two complementary axes. First, a critical evaluation of the 15 articles will study their contribution and their limitation in relation to the importance of AI in administrative transparency in Morocco. Subsequently, we will introduce an original conceptual model, entitled " The role of digital transformation and AI in administrative transparency ", which amalgamates the major lessons learned into a paradigm appropriate to the Moroccan theoretical framework. This hybrid approach aims to go beyond the conclusions drawn from the observed dynamics in order to offer a global explanation, while leaving the door open to future research and more tangible implications.

Analysis and Discussion

The adoption of digital transformation and the implementation of artificial intelligence (AI) in the public sector in Morocco present both strategic and operational challenges. In the following, we would like to discuss the results of our systematic review of the literature by structuring them around five axes: the digital transformation of the Moroccan public administration and the integration of AI, the opportunities offered by this new technology, the structural and regulatory issues it generates, its comparative positioning on an international scale, and finally, the links between the literature and the results of our research. Our cross-analysis of theoretical approaches and feedback reveals both the key success factors and the avenues for optimization for a more efficient technological deployment in the public sector.

The Digital Transformation of the Moroccan Public Administration and the Integration of AI.

The integration of artificial intelligence (AI) in the Moroccan public administration is an issue that, nowadays, requires appropriate processing. It was put forward, as noted by Bencsik (2024), that AI is not only important in automating services, but also in increasing efficiency in optimizing the decision-making process.

This view is reinforced by the results of our systematic review, which indicates that AI could transform administrative work by improving accessibility to services and reducing operational costs. Indeed, the study of Kamal & Qour (2024) illustrates the evolution of digital transformation, i.e., digital change has moved from simple digitization to now includes the integration of more sophisticated cutting-edge technologies, improving the efficiency and transparency of public services.

Opportunities and Prospects for the Development of Digital Transformation and AI in the Moroccan Public Administration

The Moroccan public administration benefits from several major opportunities related to digital transformation and the use of artificial intelligence (AI). AI can also help improve citizens' access to online services, reduce operational costs, optimize the quality of services offered and increase transparency. Moreover Taouabit et al. (2023) indicate that most users see digital transformation as an added value for public services, helping to strengthen the promotion of AI adoption at the government level.

Digital technologies, according to Ouboumlik & Touhami (2024), can support transparency and efficiency, two central elements in building user trust in public services. Thus, they observe that trust and citizen involvement are essential. In this context, the advantage would be to adopt an integral strategy that combines technological, organizational and psychosocial aspects. This could include training programs for users similar to those suggested by Tayazime & Moutahaddib (2021), aimed at improving the technological level and encouraging the use of digital services. Using concrete cases such as the experience of Moroccan customs (Noureddine et al., 2024), we see how artificial intelligence can help improve administrative processes and user experience (UX).

The Issues and Challenges Identified in Terms of Digital Transformation and AI in the Moroccan Public Administration

During the digital transformation and integration of artificial intelligence in the Moroccan public sector, different restrictions must be taken into account. According to Calay (2019), strategic challenges such as limited visibility in terms of budgetary and human resources, or the lack of synergy between digitalization systems, have been identified. Therefore, the findings of the study by Tayazime & Moutahaddib (2021) suggest that users view administrative procedures as excessively slow and cumbersome, which may have hindered the adoption of artificial intelligence. Overcoming some major obstacles such as insufficient infrastructure, inappropriate legal frameworks, and cultural reluctance is also crucial to ensure a successful transition (Ouboumlik & Touhami, 2024).

Our analysis also reveals these difficulties, with notaries expressing concerns about the security and confidentiality of online services (Taouabit et al., 2023). Taking these concerns into account, we contribute to the discussion on the challenges of digital transformation in Morocco. Overcoming these challenges is therefore crucial to successfully integrating artificial intelligence into the public sector.

In order to highlight the barriers and trends related to AI integration, it is crucial to incorporate practical cases and localized data. For example, Moroccan Customs has illustrated how a user-centric strategy can optimize administrative efficiency by integrating AI into its control procedures (Noureddine et al., 2024). These practical applications provide a contextual perspective on the challenges and opportunities associated with digital transformation.

Positioning in Relation to Global Contexts

In order to make our analysis more complete, it is essential to compare Morocco's digital maturity with that of other environments. By analyzing the cultural and contextual aspects that influence the use of artificial intelligence, we are able to better understand the dynamics involved. In addition, Ibrahim & Benabdelhadi (2021) highlight the paramount importance of citizen trust and the adoption of digital technologies, elements that must be taken into account for their relevance in the Moroccan context.

However, we are refining the level of analysis and providing a more robust foundation for understanding the ongoing dynamics. To illustrate, Bencsik's (2024) work on the implementation of artificial intelligence in the public domain highlights the importance of an approach adapted to the cultural and contextual particularities of Morocco.

Links Between the Literature and the Results of Our Research

In the context of our systematic review of the literature, it is essential to make the link between the studies analyzed and the impact of the digital revolution and artificial intelligence on public management in Morocco. This is because Ouboumlik & Touhami (2024) highlight those digital technologies improve efficiency and transparency, an observation that is also echoed in our analysis. By taking these observations into account, we are able to better understand how artificial intelligence can transform administrative practices and meet citizens' demands.

In addition, the study by Kamal & Qour (2024) focuses on the evolution of the digital transformation process, which has evolved from simple digitalization to an integrated approach to digital technologies. Our research supports this finding, indicating that Moroccan public authorities should adopt a holistic approach to satisfying user needs and creating new values.

Thus, this study offers an innovative contribution to the existing literature on digital transformation and artificial intelligence in the Moroccan context. Based on the results of the study carried out by Taouabit et al. (2023), which highlights the general satisfaction of notaries with the digital services offered by the ANCFCC, we are able to observe the positive impact of digitalization on the efficiency and performance of public services. This supports the argument that digital transformation has the potential to improve the user experience, a factor often overlooked in previous research.

To sum up, the in-depth analysis led throughout this discussion with the evidence that the use of artificial intelligence in the management of the Moroccan administration represents both an element of modernization and a major institutional challenge. While the gains in terms of efficiency, transparency and quality of public services are undeniable, issues related to the security and privacy of online services, digital skills and regulatory frameworks remain a concern. Comparison with other international contexts reveals not only delays, but also adjustments specific to Morocco, which implies that the solutions taken must be adapted to the latter. Finally, the confrontation between the existing literature and our results underlines the need for further research on the socio-political impact of these technologies. These elements open up avenues for reflection for future studies, particularly on the balance between technological innovation and administrative inclusion.

Conceptual Model

The analysis of the results of the various studies leads us to note that the redesign of administrative practices is based on three main dimensions: the intelligent automation of administrative work, which allows a reduction in delays, costs and human errors. Data analysis and management, which enables objective and proactive decision-making. Citizen participation and accessibility of information, through transparent digital platforms allowing interaction with public users.

Based on this observation, we propose a conceptual model integrating the role of digital transformation and artificial intelligence in the optimization of administrative transparency (*cf.*Figure 4).

Figure 4. Conceptual model: The role of digital transformation and AI in administrative transparency

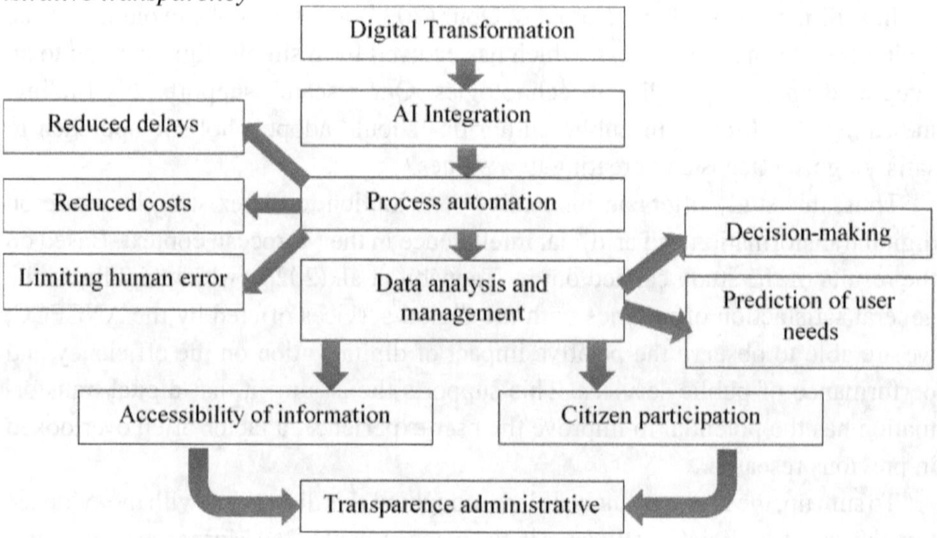

Source: *Drawn up by the authors*

This model illustrates how artificial intelligence can be used to improve transparency at several levels of administrative processes.

In short, this chapter first conducts an in-depth analysis of the literature to shed light on the digital transformation and the integration of AI in the Moroccan public administration. It then examines its opportunities, challenges and impact on the transparency and efficiency of administrative work and public services. Ultimately, artificial intelligence appears to be a strategic lever for governance and transparency, thanks to the automation of processes, the increased traceability of administrative decisions and the improvement of the accessibility of public services. This study demonstrates the critical importance of artificial intelligence in digital transformation.

CONCLUSION

This systematic review of the literature aims to expose and summarize in depth the findings of previous research carried out over the past seven years on digital transformation, the integration of artificial intelligence, its impact on the modification of administrative procedures in Morocco and its effect on transparency. The exhaustive analysis of the literature helped us to identify the opportunities offered by this revolution, as well as the challenges faced by Moroccan public authorities in terms of digitalization and the incorporation of artificial intelligence.

Indeed, this emerging technology has a large number of advantages, such as improved access, tailor-made learning, lower operational costs, improved quality of services, increased transparency and increased citizens' confidence in public services. However, the use of artificial intelligence in the Moroccan public domain has also revealed several challenges, including data protection, reluctance to change, lack of adequate infrastructure, and an inadequate legislative framework. In addition, there is a lack of appropriate training, difficulties in restructuring administrative structures and a need for innovative management strategies. As a result, other barriers are noteworthy, such as internet connection issues, a lack of technical skills, and low digital literacy.

In addition, in order to extend this reflection, subsequent studies could examine the social acceptability of the use of artificial intelligence in public services, as well as its impact on user trust. This chapter highlighted the crucial role of artificial intelligence as a driver of the digital transformation of public administrations in Morocco. Moreover, the results of this study note that artificial intelligence is not only a technological improvement of public services, but that it is also considered a key enabler to optimize the transparency and efficiency of administrative processes.

The proposed conceptual model presents digital transformation and artificial intelligence as a strategic lever of administrative transparency. It explains how this new technology can encourage governance characterized by citizen participation and accessibility of information for all users. Indeed, in order to maximize its benefits, training policies, an adapted regulatory framework and citizen awareness are essential to support this transition.

Finally, this research paves the way for new avenues of study, in particular on the influence of the adoption of artificial intelligence on the relationship between the public administration and users, supported by an in-depth citizen-centric study.

REFERENCES

Androniceanu, A. (2023). The new trends of digital transformation and artificial intelligence in public administration. *Administratie Si Management Public, 2023*(40), 147-155. *Scopus*. Advance online publication. DOI: 10.24818/amp/2023.40-09

Baker, T., & Smith, L. (2019). *Educ-AI-tion rebooted? Exploring the future of artificial intelligence in schools and colleges.*

Barodi, M., & Lalaoui, S. (2025). Civil servants' readiness for ai adoption: The role of change management in morocco's public sector. *Problems and Perspectives in Management, 23*(1), 63-75. *Scopus*. Advance online publication. DOI: 10.21511/ppm.23(1).2025.05

Bencsik, A. (2024). The opportunities of digitalisation in public administration with a special focus on the use of artificial intelligence. *Studia Iuridica Lublinensia, 33*(2), 11-23. *Scopus*. Advance online publication. DOI: 10.17951/sil.2024.33.2.11-23

Borissov, B., & Hristozov, Y. (2024). Potential for Using Artifical Intelligence in Public Administration. *ECONOMICS - Innovative and Economics Research Journal, 12*(3), 409-423. *Scopus*. Advance online publication. DOI: 10.2478/eoik-2024-0034

Calay, V. (2019). Une administration 4.0 ? Les enjeux du développement d'une stratégie digitale pour le Service public de Wallonie. *Reflets et perspectives de la vie économique, Tome LVII*(3), 55-71. Cairn.info. DOI: 10.3917/rpve.583.0055

Curtin, D., & Mendes, J. (2011). Transparence et participation : Des principes démocratiques pour l'administration de l'union européenne: *Revue française d'administration publique, n° 137-138*(1), 101-121. DOI: 10.3917/rfap.137.0101

Djafer, B. M., & Reda, S. M. (2020). *L'Administration Electronique levier de Modernisation de l'Administration Publique. N°15*, 405-425.

Ibrahim, A. K., & Benabdelhadi, A. (2021). La transformation digitale de l'administration publique : Revue de littérature systématique. *International Journal of Accounting, Finance, Auditing. Management and Economics*, 2(5), 5. Advance online publication. DOI: 10.5281/zenodo.5528289

Kamal, S. M., & Qour, T. E. (2024). La transformation digitale des administrations publiques et la performance des services publics : Définition, compréhension du processus et agenda de recherche. *Revue Française d'Economie et de Gestion*, *5*(7), 7. https://www.revuefreg.fr/index.php/home/article/view/1673

Kurmangali, M., Yeraliyeva, Y., & Beimisheva, A. (2024). Digitalization and artificial intelligence in central asia: Governmental responses and further implications. *Public Policy and Administration, 23*(2), 146-159. *Scopus.* Advance online publication. DOI: 10.13165/VPA-24-23-2-03

Noureddine, B., Said, G., Mohamed, C., & Abdelhak, M. (2024). L'intégration de l'IA dans l'administration des douanes marocaine : Approche prospective stratégique. *American Scientific Journal, 3*(25), 25. Advance online publication. DOI: 10.5281/zenodo.13381535

Ouboumlik, A., & Touhami, N. O. (2024). La transformation digitale de l'administration publique : Revue de littérature systématique. *American Scientific Journal, 3*(25), 25. Advance online publication. DOI: 10.5281/zenodo.13366459

Pomahač, R. (2024). Artificial public administration - myth or reality? *Acta Universitatis Carolinae Iuridica, 70*(2), 133-143. *Scopus.* Advance online publication. DOI: 10.14712/23366478.2024.27

Taouabit, O., Touhami, F., & Elmoukhtar, M. (2023). Transformation digitale de l'administration publique au Maroc et son impact sur l'expérience utilisateur : Cas des services rendus aux notaires par l'Agence Nationale de la Conservation Foncière du Cadastre et de la Cartographie. *International Journal of Accounting, Finance, Auditing, Management and Economics, 4*(3-2), Article 3-2. DOI: 10.5281/zenodo.8054810

Tayazime, J., & Moutahaddib, A. (2021). La Transformation Digitale de l'Administration Publique au Maroc : La Perception des Usagers Particuliers. *Revue de Gestion et d'Économie, 9*(1 & 2), Article 1 & 2. DOI: 10.34874/PRSM.jbe.31604

Terzidou, K. (2023). The Evolution of the Perception of Artificial Intelligence in the EU: The Case of Judicial Administration. *Journal of Intellectual Property, Information Technology and E-Commerce Law, 14*(3), 365-375. *Scopus.* Advance online publication. DOI: 10.2139/ssrn.4633945

Yosra, J., & Abdelkrim, Z. (2024). Artificial Intelligence in the Service of Education in Morocco: Opportunities, Challenges, and Perspectives. *International Journal Of Applied Management And Economics, 2*(09), 09. Advance online publication. DOI: 10.5281/zenodo.12772245

Chapter 6

Predicting Dividend Payouts in Moroccan Firms Using AI With Emphasis on Transparency

Mohamed-Amine El Khayati
https://orcid.org/0009-0007-9209-8023
Cadi Ayyad University, Morocco

Charaf Saidi
https://orcid.org/0009-0007-3125-7561
Cadi Ayyad University, Morocco

ABSTRACT

This chapter explores the prediction of dividend payout ratios among Moroccan listed companies by applying Random Forest Regression combined with Explainable Artificial Intelligence (XAI) techniques. Focusing on firm-specific financial indicators and macroeconomic variables over the period 2013–2023, the study aims to identify key drivers of dividend policy in an emerging market context. The analysis demonstrates that profitability, firm size, and historical payout behavior are the most influential predictors, while macroeconomic indicators such as inflation, GDP, and interest rates show limited impact. SHAP values are employed to enhance transparency, allowing for robust interpretation of model outputs. This chapter contributes to financial modeling, corporate governance, and machine learning literature by offering an interpretable AI-based framework for dividend forecasting tailored to the Moroccan market. The findings provide actionable insights for investors, man-

DOI: 10.4018/979-8-3373-1737-3.ch006

agers, and policymakers seeking to understand or optimize dividend strategies in emerging economies.

1. INTRODUCTION

One of the most complicated and highly contentious subjects in corporate finance is still dividend policy. It has a significant impact on capital allocation choices, investor sentiment, and firm valuation. The decision regarding whether, when, and how much profit to return to shareholders in the form of dividends shows a company's overall strategic intent and market communication style in addition to its internal financial health. Dividend behavior can be systematically explained by traditional financial theories like Financial Flexibility Theory, Life Cycle Theory, Agency Theory, and Signaling Theory.

However, because influencing factors are nonlinear, interdependent, and context-specific, dividend prediction is still difficult in real-world settings, particularly in emerging markets.

Dividend payout forecasting is made more challenging in emerging economies like Morocco by a number of factors, including institutional limitations, differing levels of corporate governance maturity, macroeconomic volatility, and inconsistent or incomplete data reporting. Moroccan businesses work in a setting where it is frequently difficult to obtain comprehensive financial data, and economic strategy, customs, and regulatory constraints all influence financial behavior. As a result, the complex relationships that influence dividend decisions might not be adequately captured by the use of conventional econometric or linear statistical models.

This study suggests a modern, data-driven method to forecast dividend payout ratios by utilizing machine learning, more especially the Random Forest Regressor. Because it can handle high-dimensional, multicollinear, and nonlinear datasets—all characteristics common to financial data—the Random Forest algorithm is especially well-suited. Nonetheless, a prevalent critique of machine learning models is their inability to be interpreted. The research uses Explainable AI (XAI) techniques, specifically SHAP (SHapley Additive Explanations), which offer clear, visually intuitive explanations of feature importance and model behavior, to help address this problem.

This chapter's main research question is: **How can machine learning be used to predict dividend payout ratios for Moroccan listed companies with accuracy and interpretability for financial decision-making?**

The pedagogical aim of this chapter's is to help readers comprehend the theoretical underpinnings of dividend policy as well as the real-world financial context in which interpretable AI models are applied. In addition to learning how to critically analyze model outputs from a strategic and regulatory standpoint, readers will also learn how to build, assess, and explain a machine learning model for dividend forecasting.

Target audience members are financial researchers, corporate analysts, institutional investors, and legislators engaged in corporate finance, financial modeling, and emerging market governance.

The main objective of this work is to develop a precise and understandable predictive model of dividend payout ratios for Moroccan listed companies over a ten-year period (2013–2023). This model is built with macroeconomic as well as firm-level financial measures. In doing so, the study aims to:

- evaluate how macroeconomic factors influence corporate dividend decisions;
- identify the main financial indicators influencing dividend policy in Morocco;
- include explainability frameworks to increase trust and transparency in AI-powered financial forecasting tools.

Using this multifarious approach helps the research to improve theory and practice. In the framework of developing markets, it essentially reviews and supports traditional dividend policy guidelines. Practically speaking, it offers a clear machine learning framework that can support analytical needs of corporate managers, institutional investors, and financial regulators.

By including explainability into model development, the study offers a road map for the moral and trustworthy implementation of artificial intelligence in finance. This is an essential challenge in the quickly changing digital financial ecosystem of today. Ultimately, this research aims to empower stakeholders with tools that are not only technically robust, but also interpretable, actionable, and relevant to the unique challenges of Morocco's capital market.

This chapter positions itself at the intersection of financial theory and modern artificial intelligence by focusing on the predictive modeling of dividend policy through explainable machine learning techniques. While previous studies have explored traditional determinants of dividend payouts, few have applied XAI methodologies to enhance interpretability in this domain. By integrating SHAP into a Random Forest framework, this research contributes to the growing body of work on AI applications in corporate finance, particularly within the underexplored context of emerging markets like Morocco. It also highlights the role of transparent AI tools in improving managerial and investor trust in predictive analytics, thereby supporting more informed and accountable financial decision-making.

Chapter Overview

The rest of this chapter is structured as follows. The theoretical framework is presented in Section 2, which also covers traditional dividend theories and the justification for using AI in financial modeling. The dataset, variables, preprocessing methods, and application of the Random Forest model with SHAP-based explainability are all covered in detail in Section 3. The findings are presented in Section 4, with an emphasis on the model's performance and the discovery of important predictive characteristics. The results are discussed in Section 5, with particular attention paid to how they may affect dividend forecasting in Morocco. The study's limitations and possible directions for further research are described in Section 6. The chapter's contributions are summarized in the conclusion, which also highlights the applicability of AI-enhanced models in developing markets.

2. THEORETICAL FRAMEWORK

The dividend payout policy is still a key component of corporate finance strategy since it reflects management intent, corporate maturity, governance quality, and firm performance. A variety of firm-level, macroeconomic, and institutional factors influence the choice to distribute earnings to shareholders; these factors frequently interact in nonlinear and opaque ways. These dynamics are made more complex in emerging markets like Morocco by concerns about institutional trust, changing investor expectations, and regulatory frameworks. The integration of insights from both classical dividend theories and contemporary machine learning (ML) approaches—especially those enhanced by explainable AI (XAI) techniques to maintain model transparency—is crucial for the development of a trustworthy predictive framework.

2.1 Classical Theoretical Foundations of Dividend Policy

Financial economists have always been intrigued by the question of why companies pay dividends. Dividend policy is still a major and unsolved problem in corporate finance despite an extensive body of empirical research. Based on firm-specific, informational, and institutional factors, classical theories try to explain not only why companies pay dividends but also when and how much they do so. Several prominent frameworks, including Signaling Theory (Ross, 1977; Bhattacharya, 1979), Agency Theory (Jensen & Meckling, 1976), Life Cycle Theory (DeAngelo et al., 2006), and Financial Flexibility Theory (Gamba & Triantis, 2008), provide unique perspectives for analyzing corporate behavior, especially in situations involving uncertainty, asymmetry, or structural limitations.

Signaling Theory

The issue of information asymmetry between corporate insiders (managers) and outsiders (investors) is addressed by signaling theory. Managers usually know more about the firm's actual financial situation, strategic outlook, and earnings potential than anyone else in the capital markets. Dividends act as a reliable signal in these situations—an action that can be seen that conveys an intangible firm quality.

Ross (1977) first proposed the idea, and Bhattacharya (1979) formalized it by modeling how dividend payments could predict future profitability in the face of incomplete information. In order to distinguish high-quality companies from low-quality ones, he suggested that only businesses with robust future cash flows could afford the expense of consistent dividends.

This theory was further developed by Miller and Rock (1985), who showed that dividend increases indicate management confidence in the sustainability of earnings. Dividends are a forward-looking market signal because only companies with steady earnings are likely to announce larger payouts since they obligate the company to future disbursements.

Agency Theory

Agency Theory, which has its roots in Jensen and Meckling's seminal work from 1976, highlights the conflicts of interest that exist between managers (agents) and shareholders (principals). Instead of maximizing shareholder value, managers in companies with dispersed ownership may use excess free cash flow for personal goals like empire-building or perquisite consumption.

By limiting managerial discretion over internal funds, dividends help to lessen these conflicts. Businesses are more likely to look for outside funding for upcoming projects when they give back cash to shareholders, provided that management decisions are made with capital market discipline in mind. This disciplining function was highlighted by Easterbrook (1984) and Jensen (1986), who saw dividends as a way to lower agency costs and match managerial incentives with shareholder interests.

Life Cycle Theory

DeAngelo and Stulz (2006) formalized the Life Cycle Theory, which relates a firm's dividend policy to its evolutionary stage. Businesses go through phases of growth, maturity, and decline, and each one affects how they allocate capital and make payouts. While young, fast-growing businesses with significant investment needs often retains their earnings, more established businesses with consistent cash flows and less investment opportunities usually pays off.

Empirically verifying this theory, Fama and French (2001) found that younger companies were declining in their dividend initiations while older companies with accumulated earnings were returning capital to shareholders at a growing rates. Since dividend supports views of financial strength and attracts long-term investors, the theory also addresse agency and signaling motives.

Financial Flexibility Theory

According to Gamba and Trianti (2008), the strategic need of maintaining onto earnings in order to keep financial agility is underlined by the Financial Flexibility Theory. Especially in emerging markets, internal resources provide a required safety net against unexpected need or financial shocks in uncertain or capital-limited surroundings.

This point of view supports Myers and Majluf's (1984) Pecking Order Theory, according which companies choose internal rather than outside financing to avoid negative selection and signal costs. While they reduces this financial cushion and could deter more investment, dividends helps owners.

Maintaining financial flexibility is one of the most significant real-world factors influencing dividend policy, according to Graham and Harvey's (2001) survey of CFOs. Particularly in volatile or underdeveloped capital markets, companies sometimes gives liquidity first importance in order to maintains credit ratings, strategic autonomy, and risk resilience.

Synthesis

These conventional concepts taken together shows how the dividends is a sophisticated financial and strategic tool. Whether viewed as market signals, tools for internal discipline, signs of firm maturity, or defenses against external risk, dividend policies impacts a complex interaction of asymmetric information, corporate governance, firm evolution, and capital market dynamics. Building predictive models that fairly represents behavior in the real world depends on an awareness of these theoretical underpinnings, especially in developing markets like Morocco.

2.2 Empirical Insights and Technological Integration in the Moroccan Context

Empirical Insights and Contextual Relevance for Morocco

Empirical research has repeatedly found several significant financial factors influencing dividend payments. Profitability is maybe the most accurate indicator of all of them since better profits usually translates into larger dividends (Souza et al., 2024; Kumar & Sinha, 2024; Abbas et al., 2023). Cash flow availability support payout sustainability while leverage typically reduces dividend propensity due to financial constraints (An et al., 2022; Arshad et al., 2022). Furthermore found to favorably affect payout ratios in line with both life cycle and signaling systems are firm-level factors including age and size (Maqsudi et al., 2022; Jangphanish et al., 2025).

By influencing corporate profitability and perceived risk, macroeconomic events including GDP growth and inflation directly and indirectly influences dividend decisions (Kumar & Sinha, 2024). Industry-specific events also affect dividend behavior; some such examples are cash flow predictability and competitive dynamics (Mrzygłód et al., 2021).

Concerning the Moroccan setting. Dividends and company size, age, and growth prospects showed a negative correlation found by Louziri and Oubal (2022). This result validates features of the models of signaling and agency. Moreover, according to Baker and Jabbouri (2016; 2017), Moroccan managers consider openness, shareholder expectations, and earnings consistency as crucial elements influencing dividend policy. Combining more recent approaches, such catering theory, with more established theories highlights responsiveness to investor sentiment.

Integrating Artificial Intelligence and Explainability

Although they provide interesting information, traditional econometric models usually miss the nonlinear and interactive character of dividend predictors. Recent dividend forecasting studies reveal that artificial intelligence-based models—especially Random Forests, Gradient Boosting, and ensemble learning techniques—have better predictive ability (Yaseen & Dragotă, 2021; Dewasiri et al., 2019). These models are quite good in identifying complex patterns that linear models would ignore and in handling high-dimensional data.

But the black-box character of artificial intelligence demands interpretability issues, particularly in the financial industry where responsibility and transparency are absolutely important. In this case, explainable artificial intelligence (XAI) approaches including SHAP (SHapley Additive exPlanations) and LIME (Local

Interpretable Model-agnostic Explanations) are absolutely vital. These post hoc tools enable clear attribution of feature importance and prediction rationale, so bridging the gap between model complexity and user trust.

By means of XAI, researchers can precisely forecast together with interpretable, auditable, and justifiable insights to decision-makers by understanding the marginal contribution of every variable to the output prediction. Under the framework of dividend policy, this double ability for forecasting and explanation is crucial to coordinate model outputs with strategic financial planning and stakeholder communication.

XAI in Financial Prediction

In financial modeling, artificial intelligence has lately gained rather popularity especially for projecting of firm-level results including credit risk, dividend payout trends, and bankruptcy. Random Forest, XGBoost, and Long Short-Term Memory (LSTM) networks (Krauss et al., 2017; Fischer & Krauss, 2018) is popular algorithms due of their capacity to identify complex variable interaction and model nonlinear relationships.

Applied to noisy or high-dimensional financial datasets (Z Zhou et al., 2022), ensemble approaches including Random Forest and XGBoost routinely outperforms linear models in terms of dividend prediction accuracy according comparative studies. Conversely, LSTM models are more appropriate for sequential forecasting activities since they are more able to capture temporal dynamics. Future extensions could assess performance increases by including boosting or neural architectures, even though Random Forest was selected for this study since it is interpretable through SHAP, robustness with small datasets, and strong baseline performance.

One can evaluate financial machine learning results using the SHAP framework. Applications range from credit scoring (Arun & Kamath, 2022) ESG impact modeling, and portfolio risk assessment (Lundberg et al., 2020). Though ongoing challenges with data dependability and institutional readiness, recent research in LMIC settings show artificial intelligence hold promise for improving financial transparency and decisions support (Ahmad et al., 2021; Asongu & Nwachukwu, 2022).

This chapter emphasizes SHAP's contribution to explainability and place the research in the larger literatures on artificial intelligence-finance, so bridging the gap between methodological rigor and the urgent demand for transparency in developing capital markets.

Theoretical Implications for Predictive Modeling in Morocco

By considering both the most recent empirical data and conventional dividend theories, a hybrid theoretical framework is created. By combining cutting-edge AI methods with basic financial principles, it improves the accuracy and understandability of dividend forecasting models.

For Moroccan listed companies, where data limitations, institutional trust, and transparency are persistent issues, this integrated approach offers a workable solution. While AI models enhanced by XAI tools allow predictive precision without sacrificing transparency, classical theories are still useful for comprehending firm behavior and investor expectations.

More flexible, data-driven dividend strategies are supported by this combined framework. It facilitates regulatory compliance, gives financial decision-makers more confidence to navigate complex market environments, and raises the legitimacy of AI-driven insights in the eyes of analysts, policymakers, and shareholders.

Dividend Policies in Peer Emerging Economies

Morocco's dividend behavior is better understood in light of comparative observations from other emerging economies. Empirical research conducted in Tunisia has demonstrated that market illiquidity and ownership concentration have a major impact on payout decisions (Chouaya & Jarboui, 2017). Due to family ownership and macroeconomic uncertainty, listed companies in Egypt typically have conservative dividend policies (Yehia, 2021). Although firm maturity and profitability are important factors in India, information asymmetries continue to limit dividend signaling (Bhat, 2010). A more regulated environment is found in South Africa, where capital access and corporate governance reforms have increased dividend regularity, particularly in the financial sector (Ntim, 2012).

Both similarities and context-specific differences with Morocco are highlighted by these comparisons, which highlight the importance of institutional, cultural, and ownership structures in determining payout behavior across developing economies.

Regulatory Environment and Dividend Constraints

In Morocco, changing regulatory frameworks and firm-specific financial metrics both influence dividend policies. Transparency in decisions about profit distribution is strengthened by the Moroccan Capital Markets Authority's (AMMC) official guidelines on disclosure procedures and shareholder rights. Payout regularity is indirectly impacted by the Moroccan Corporate Governance Code, which was revised in 2020 and places a strong emphasis on board accountability and shareholder equity.

The ability of businesses to pay dividends is also impacted by reserve requirements and corporate tax structures, particularly in regulated industries like banking and insurance (AMMC, 2023).

The active role of institutional oversight in regulating dividend flows is demonstrated by the regulatory agencies' issuance of temporary dividend restrictions during times of financial stress, such as the COVID-19 pandemic, in order to protect capital buffers.

Comparative Overview of Dividend Environments

Institutional contexts have a significant influence on corporate governance and dividend behavior. The following table lists the main differences between peer emerging markets, developed economies, and Morocco. These variations highlight the need to tailor prediction models to local structures rather than using them consistently across geographical boundaries.

Table 1. Key comparative features – Morocco vs. other markets

Feature	Morocco	Emerging Markets (General)	Developed Markets
Regulatory Structure	AMMC oversight; moderate enforcement	Varies; often fragmented	Strong, well-enforced
Ownership Structure	High family ownership, state influence	Mix of family and state	Mostly dispersed ownership
Institutional Investor Activism	Low	Moderate to low	High (proxy voting, ESG activism)
Dividend Consistency	Variable; influenced by informal norms	Moderate	High (especially in blue-chip firms)
Disclosure Quality	Improving, but uneven across firms	Often limited	Comprehensive, regulated
Sectoral Dominance	Telecom, banking, industry	Industry, finance, real estate	Tech, services, finance

The next section uses empirical modeling to operationalize the theoretical underpinnings of corporate behavior and dividend policy. To ensure a comprehensive and context-sensitive analysis, it explains the data sources, variable selection, and modeling techniques used to forecast dividend payouts in Moroccan listed companies.

3. DATA AND METHODOLOGY

3.1 Variable Selection and Description

This section outlines the variables that are part of the predictive model, their theoretical underpinnings, and their relevance to Moroccan listed companies. The study includes firm-specific and macroeconomic variables in a panel data structure to account for cross-sectional and time-series dynamics. These decisions, which draw from both empirical research and conventional dividend policy theories, ensure a theoretically sound and contextually relevant model.

Panel Structure of the Dataset

The panel format of the dataset makes it possible to analyze several firms and time periods at once. Every observation is recognized by:

- ID: A special code given to every company that is listed on the Casablanca Stock Exchange.
- Year: The fiscal year in which the macroeconomic and financial data were reported.

This structure makes it possible for the model to account for temporal fluctuations and firm-level heterogeneity, both of which are crucial for dividend forecasting.

Firm-Specific Variables

Firm-specific indicators are selected to reflect internal aspects of financial performance, operational efficiency, growth potential, and capital structure. These variables align with theoretical frameworks such as Signaling Theory, Agency Theory, Life Cycle Theory, and Financial Flexibility Theory.

Table 2. Firm-specific variables and theoretical relevance

Variable	Description	Theoretical Link
Return on Equity (%)	Net income relative to shareholder equity	Profitability, Signaling Theory
Return on Assets	Efficiency in using assets to generate earnings	Profitability, Life Cycle Theory
EBIT Margin (%)	Earnings before interest and taxes as a % of total revenue	Operational Efficiency, Signaling Theory

continued on following page

Table 2. Continued

Variable	Description	Theoretical Link
Net Income Margin (%)	Net income as a percentage of revenues	Profitability Signal
Levered Free Cash Flow Margin	Free cash flow after servicing debt obligations	Agency Theory, Financial Flexibility
Operating Cash Flow to Current Liabilities	Liquidity ratio of operational cash to short-term liabilities	Agency Theory, Financial Flexibility
Total Debt/Equity	Leverage indicator reflecting capital structure and risk	Agency Costs, Dividend Constraints
Total Revenues, 1 Yr. Growth (%)	Annual growth in revenue	Life Cycle Theory, Growth Stage
Dividend Per Share, 1 Yr. Growth (%)	Annual growth in dividend per share	Signaling Theory, Life Cycle Theory
Total Assets	Proxy for firm size and maturity	Life Cycle Theory
Total Current Liabilities	Indicator of short-term financial obligations	Financial Flexibility
Operating Cash Flow	Cash generated from core business activities	Dividend Sustainability, Agency Theory
Dividend Payout Ratio	Ratio of dividends to net income	Target variable

The main dependent variable of the model is the **Dividend Payout Ratio**, calculated as follows:

$$Dividend\ Payout\ Ratio = \frac{Dividends\ Paid}{Net\ Income}$$

Macroeconomic Variables

Macroeconomic indicators are included to account for the external environment in which firms operate. These variables influence firm-level profitability, investment behavior, and strategic financial decisions—thus indirectly shaping dividend policies.

Table 3. Macroeconomic variables and theoretical relevance

Variable	Description	Theoretical Link
GDP	Measures national economic performance	Economic Cycle Effects, Life Cycle Theory
Inflation Rate (%)	Reflects cost changes and purchasing power	Impact on Real Returns, Investor Expectations
Interest Rate (%)	Indicates cost of capital and investment opportunity cost	Financial Flexibility, Investment Decision Signals

The diagram below illustrates the architecture of the prediction pipeline developed in this study. The model draws from two main sources of explanatory variables: firm-specific financial metrics (e.g., profitability, leverage, liquidity, and growth indicators) and macroeconomic contextual factors (e.g., inflation, GDP, interest rates).

Figure 1. Predictive Modeling Pipeline for Dividend Payout Ratio Forecasting

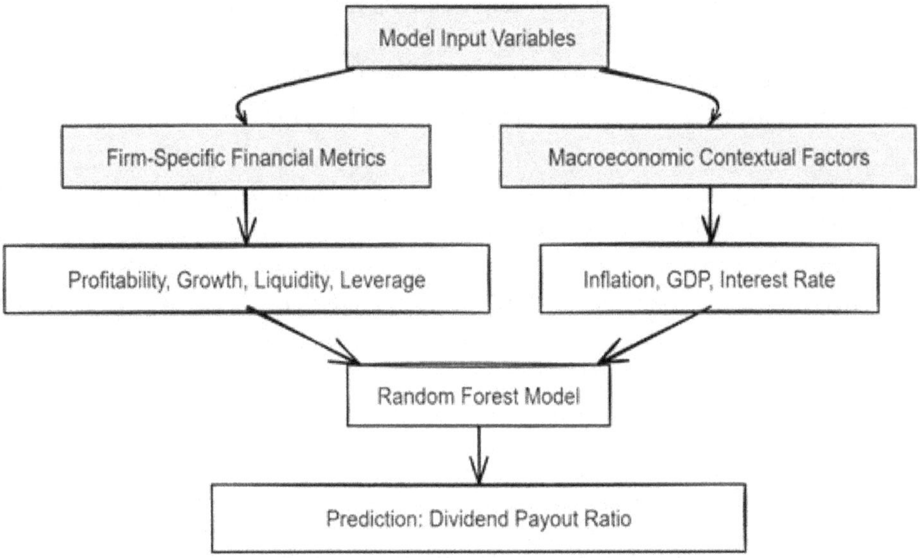

These variables are processed and passed into a Random Forest regression model, which estimates each firm's expected dividend payout ratio. The visual flow captures how internal and external factors converge into the machine learning framework, enabling the identification of key dividend drivers in the Moroccan market.

Rationale for Variable Selection

Indicators tailored to each firm let the model evaluate internal factors including growth path, profitability, liquidity, and leverage. Macroeconomic factors provide vital historical data on outside economic conditions including the inflationary pressures, the interest rate environments, and the general state of the economy.

This wide range improves the interpretability and generalizability of the model so allowing it to manage contextual volatility and firm-level dynamics. Moreover, the choice aligns with empirical research by Louziri & Oubal (2022), Kumar & Sinha (2024), and Abbas et al. (2023), all of which underline the complex character of dividend determinants.

3.2 Data Sources and Sample Construction

Firm-Level Financial Data

The financial indicators came from the Marketscreener platform, a platform that provide historical and uniform financial data for Casablanca Stock Exchange listed companies. The following were the requirements for inclusion:

- Complete historical data for the entire period (2013–2023) must be available.
- Firms must have a record of annual dividend payments throughout the time window.
- No missing values for core variables such as Return on Equity, Operating Cash Flow, and Payout Ratio.

Firms that did not meet these criteria were excluded, resulting in a final sample of 36 companies out of 77 listed firms. This ensures data consistency and analytical rigor.

Table 4. Data filtering summary

Criteria	Result
Total listed companies on Casablanca Stock Exchange	77 firms
Time period covered	2013–2023
Firms excluded due to missing/incomplete data	41 firms
Final sample size	36 firms

Macroeconomic Data

Three macroeconomic variables—GDP, Inflation Rate, and Interest Rate—were collected from reputable sources:

- GDP and Inflation Rate: Sourced from Statista, based on reports published by Aaron O'Neill (2024), which provide projections up to 2029 (Statista, 2024a; 2024b).
- Interest Rate: Retrieved from TradingEconomics, a globally recognized financial database (TradingEconomics, 2024).

These variables ensure that the model is sensitive to broader economic trends that may influence dividend strategies in Morocco.

3.3 Random Forest Model Structure

The Random Forest algorithm was chosen due to its suitability for the financial prediction task at hand. First, it better controls nonlinear relationships between financial indicators and dividend behavior than more traditional linear models. Given the complicated and sometimes non-monotonic interactions among macroeconomic variables, firm profitability, and leverage, this is especially pertinent (Krauss, 2017). Second, in small to moderately sized datasets Random Forest performs better than deep learning models since it is less likely to overfit when properly tuned (Fernändez-Delgado et al., 2014). Third, the explainability objective of this work is centered on its natural ability to capture features interactions and rank variable importances, both of which are fundamentals for generating interpretable insights with instrument like SHAP. These features make Random Forest suitable and open solution for predictive modeling in developing financial markets.

Theoretical Foundation of Random Forests

Breiman (2001) first introduced Random Forest, an ensemble technique derived from the bagging (bootstrapping aggregating) concept. Independent training of several decision trees in Random Forests depends on arbitrary subsets of the original data. Either majority voting in classification tasks or averaging the predictions in regression tasks generate the final output.

The most crucial features of Random Forest theory consist in:

- Random Sampling with Replacement: Every tree's training is conducted on a bootstrapped sample of the training data, so guaranteeing the diversity and minimising overfitting.
- Random Feature Selection: At each decision node, only a random subset of features is considered for splitting, increasing tree independence and model robustness.
- Aggregation (Ensemble Averaging): The predictions from all trees are aggregated to form a final prediction. For regression, the model outputs the mean prediction across all trees.

These components collectively enhance the model's predictive stability, making it particularly suitable for data with high dimensionality, nonlinearity, and interactions among variables—all of which are prevalent in the financial indicators used in this study.

The mathematical Expression of Random Forest for Regression Prediction is as follows:

$$\hat{y} = \frac{1}{N} \sum_{i=1}^{N} T_i(x)$$

Where:

$\hat{y}$ is the predicted value (here, the dividend payout ratio),

$T_i(x)$ is the prediction of the *i-th* decision tree for input x,

N is the total number of trees in the forest

The output of a Random Forest regression model is computed as the average prediction of N individual decision trees. This ensemble averaging reduces variance and improves generalization compared to single-tree models (Breiman, 2001).

The overall logic of the Random Forest model used in this study is illustrated in Figure 2, which schematizes how firm-level and macroeconomic variables are processed through an ensemble of decision trees to produce the final dividend payout prediction.

Figure 2. Structure of the Random Forest Regression Model

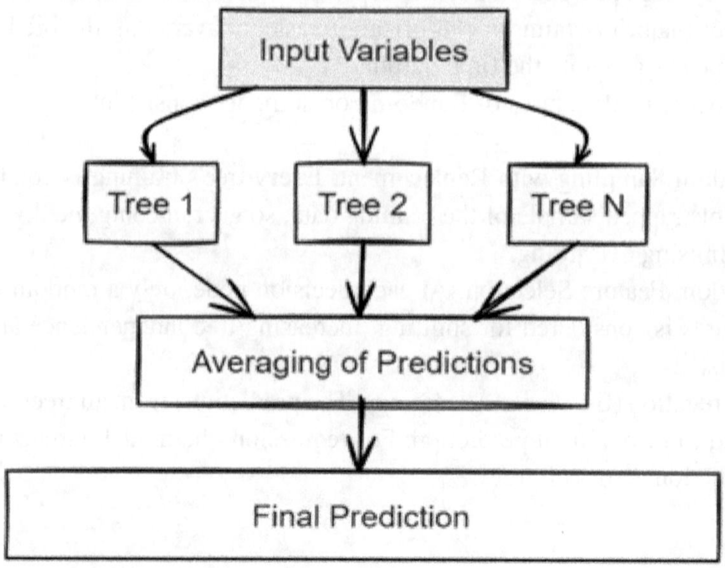

Each tree is trained on a bootstrapped subset of the data and a random subset of features. The final prediction is obtained by averaging the outputs of all individual trees, making the ensemble robust to overfitting and capable of capturing complex nonlinear interactions among firm-level and macroeconomic variables (Breiman, 2001).

Advantages of Random Forests in Financial Prediction

Random Forests offer several advantages over traditional regression models and standalone decision trees, especially in the context of dividend payout modeling:

- Nonlinear Modeling: Capable of modeling complex, nonlinear relationships among financial and macroeconomic indicators.
- Multicollinearity Tolerance: Less sensitive to inter-correlated predictors due to random feature selection.
- Robustness to Outliers: Individual tree structures are less affected by extreme values.
- Resilience to Overfitting: The ensemble approach prevents individual trees from dominating the prediction.
- Missing Value Handling: Can accommodate datasets with partial missing information.
- Feature Importance Ranking: Naturally provides variable importance metrics, facilitating model interpretability.

Given the multidimensional and interdependent nature of dividend policy determinants—including profitability, firm maturity, liquidity, leverage, and macroeconomic factors—Random Forest Regression is well-equipped to capture the underlying structure of dividend payout behavior in Moroccan firms.

Suitability for the Moroccan Financial Context

In Morocco, where financial reporting varies in consistency and the economic environment introduces additional complexity, the flexibility and robustness of Random Forests provide a methodological advantage. Specifically:

- The model can adjust to firm-level heterogeneity across sectors and firm sizes.
- The model can be interpretable through XAI wich assure the trust of stakeholders.

3.4 Data Preparation and Preprocessing

A structured preprocessing pipeline was created to solve typical problems with data quality, such missing values, inconsistent formats, and difficulties combining data from many sources, so guaranteeing the dependability of the Random Forest model. Applications in financial machine learning where the robustness of input data directly influences model accuracy and interpretability depend on these processes (Gupta & Ranjan, 2022).

To include firm-level variation and contextual economic dynamics, annual macroeconomic indicators were added to the panel-structured dataset comprising Moroccan listed companies from 2013 to 2023. As advised by corporate finance modeling, this structure simplifies the analysis of firm heterogeneity and temporal trends (Dang et al., 2018).

Typical in emerging market disclosures, missing financial data was handled by means of mean imputation, which preserves dataset integrity without altering statistical properties (La Porta et al., 1999). Moreover, variables shown in condensed textual forms (e.g., "K" for thousands or "M" for millions) were numerically converted as a standard preprocessing need in financial analytics to guarantee mathematical consistency during modeling (Cheng et al., 2020).

GDP, inflation, and interest rates were the macroeconomic variables standardized and matched for firm-year observations. To meet local company reporting requirements, the macro data was converted to Moroccan dirhams using outside databases including Statista and TradingEconomics.

As is often done in regression settings to address scale-related learning issues, Dividend Payout Ratio was normalized by translating percentage values into decimals (Aggarwal, 2018).

3.5 Model Development

Dividend payout ratios were projected using a supervised machine learning method employing a Random Forest Regressor.

To ensure both learning efficacy and reliable out-of-sample evaluation (Kuhn & Johnson, 2013), the dataset was split in training (80%) and testing (20%) subsets per accepted predictive modeling guidelines. Important for financial applications, this separation maintained the statistical representateness and temporal framework of the original data.

A usually advised method for fine-tuning ensemble models, grid search and 10-fold cross-valuation helped hyperparameters to be optimized (Probst et al., 2019). We investigated variants in node splitting thresholds, tree depth, and decision tree count. Using the Mean Squared Error (MSE) and R2 score, the model's performance was evaluated allowing for a trade-off between model interpretability and prediction accuracy.

The chosen final model configuration kept computational efficiency while generalizing over data partitions. The model was then trained using this arrangement on the whole training set, producing the predictive engine supporting the later interpretability study and strategic insights.

The end-to--end modeling pipeline built in this work is shown below. Starting raw firm-level and macroeconomic data, the process moves through data cleaning, normalizing, panel building, and Random Forest model training. To support interpretation and stakeholder confidence, the last stages consist in explainability analysis using SHAP values and model validation using standard performance measures.

Figure 3. End-to-End Predictive Modeling Pipeline for Dividend Forecasting

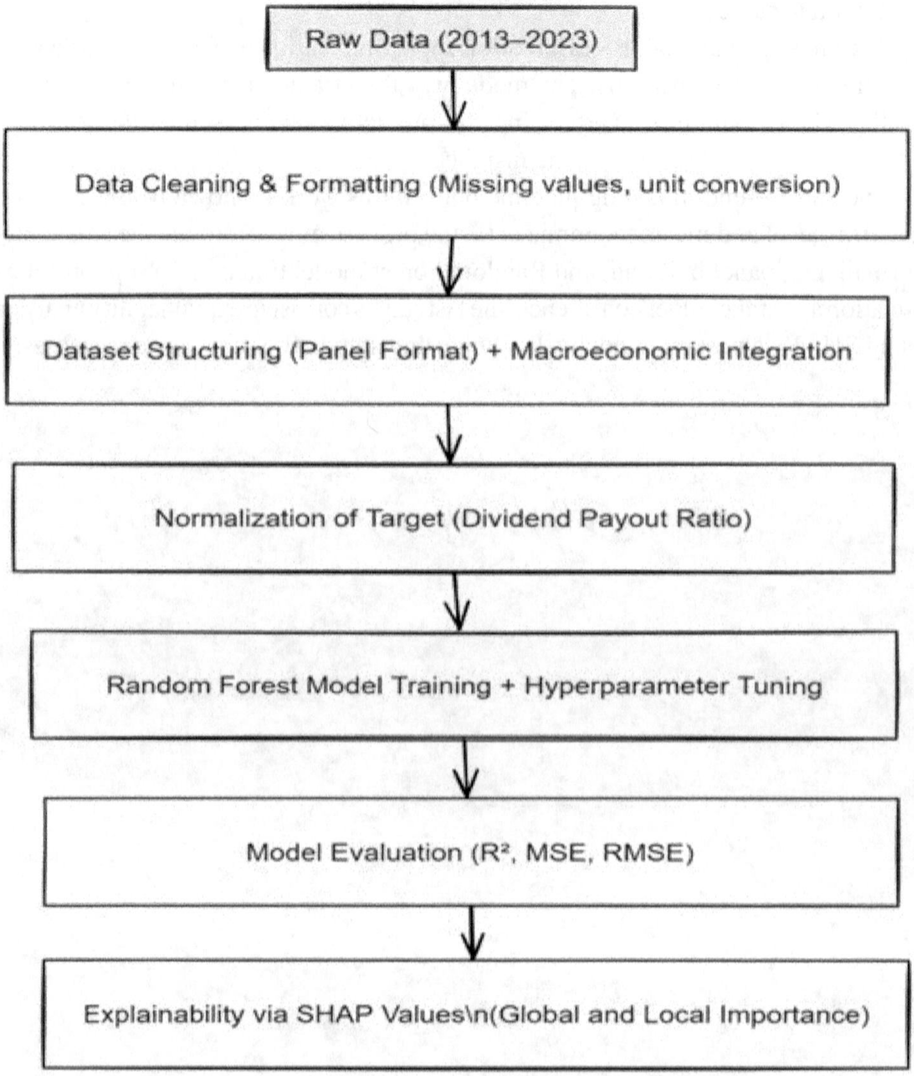

With the approach in place, the next part shows the performance, variable importance, and predictive accuracy of the model, so providing understanding of the factors influencing dividend behavior.

4. RESULTS

The Random Forest results for dividend payout ratio prediction in Moroccan listed companies are presented here. Model accuracy was evaluated using SHAP values to pinpoint main macroeconomic and financial factors affecting payout behavior in an emerging market environment.

4.1 Model Evaluation

Common evaluation metrics—including the coefficient of determination (R2), mean squared error (MSE), and root mean square error (RMSE)—were used to evaluate the predictive performance of the Random Forest model. These measures taken together provide a good grasp of capacity of the model to extend beyond training data.

With an **R2** score of **0.746** the model show that the sets of input variables explains **74.6%** of the variance in the dividend payout ratio. In financial modeling, where qualitative or unobservable elements sometimes affects company behavior, this degree of explanatory ability is regarded as strong (Frost, 2021).

Calculating the average squared difference between the actual values of the payout ratios and the model's forecasts yielded the **MSE** of **11.52**. With some variation in outlier cases, a moderate MSE value indicate that the model perform consistently over most firm-year observations.

Found to be 3.39, the RMSE provide a more reasonable evaluation of prediction accuracy in the original unit of measurement—percentage points. Because of its interpretability and sensitivity to significant errors, RMSE is particularly important in applied forecasting, claim Willmott and Matsuura (2005). With an **RMSE** of **3.39**, the model's reasonable accuracy for useful dividend forecasting uses is attested to.

These results taken together show that the Random Forest model offers an operational and statistically sound framework for simulating dividend behavior in the Moroccan financial environment. The next section investigates, using explainability techniques, more the ways in which individual variables influence model forecasts.

This chapter develops on recent advancements XAI to improve the interpretability dimension of the model. First presented by Ribeiro et al. (2016), methods including SHAP, developed by Lundberg and Lee (2017), and LIME offer strong frameworks for understanding challenging model behavior. These techniques enable stakeholders to clearly and transparently grasp machine learning outputs, so closing the gap between predictive performance and responsibility for decision-making. XAI is a main driver of model acceptance and responsible artificial intelligence adoption in corporate finance settings.

4.2 Exploratory Insights: Understanding Relationships

Multicollinearity, redundancy, and linear relationships among firm-level financial and macroeconomic variables were first identified by a Pearson correlation matrix (Figure 4. Below) before to Random Forest output interpretation.

The findings revealed several groups of strongly linked variables. Strong relationships among profitability indicators including Return on Equity (%), Net Income Margin (%), EBIT Margin (%), and Return on Assets (ROA) revealed themselves. For example, Net Income Margin is strongly linked with EBIT Margin (r = 0.91) and Return on Equity (r = 0.55) and rather moderately correlated with Return on assets (r = 0.57) and Return on Equity (r = 0.55) . These findings are consistent with corporate finance literature emphasizing the interdependence of profitability measures (Fama & French, 2001). Although multicollinearity may be problematic in traditional linear models, Random Forest is robust to such interdependencies due to its feature subsampling mechanism.

Figure 4. Correlation Matrix of Financial & Macroeconomic Features

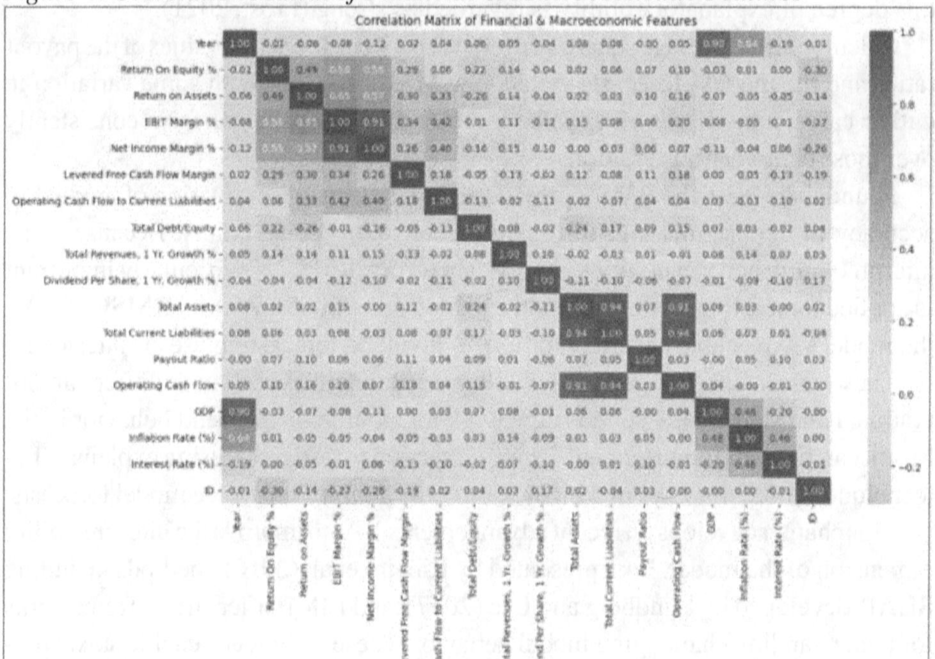

A second cluster emerged around firm size and cash generation capacity. Operating Cash Flow displayed strong correlations with Total Current Liabilities (**r = 0.94**) and Total Assets (**r = 0.91**), suggesting that larger, more mature firms tend to generate higher operational cash flows. However, a notably weak correlation was observed between Operating Cash Flow and the Dividend Payout Ratio (**r = 0.03**), indicating that higher cash availability does not necessarily translate into higher dividends—particularly in the Moroccan context where reinvestment, debt service, or governance practices may take precedence.

Interestingly, Dividend Per Share Growth over one year exhibited weak or negative correlations with most explanatory variables (ranging from **–0.04** to **–0.17**), and a slightly negative association with the Dividend Payout Ratio (**r = –0.06**). This highlights the unpredictable and possibly strategic nature of dividend policy adjustments, where firms may change payouts based on discrete events or managerial discretion rather than systematic financial signals.

These exploratory insights reinforce the necessity of using nonparametric machine learning models like Random Forest that can capture nonlinear and context-specific relationships. They also suggest that macroeconomic variables are less systematically correlated with payout behavior compared to firm-specific indicators, a hypothesis explored further in the model's interpretability analysis.

4.3 Distribution of the Target Variable: Dividend Payout Ratio

Understanding the statistical distribution of the target variable—the Dividend Payout Ratio—is vital for interpreting prediction results and assessing the suitability of the modeling approach. The empirical distribution of payout ratios for each firm-year observation in the dataset is shown in Figure 5.

Figure 5. Distribution of Dividend Payout Ratio

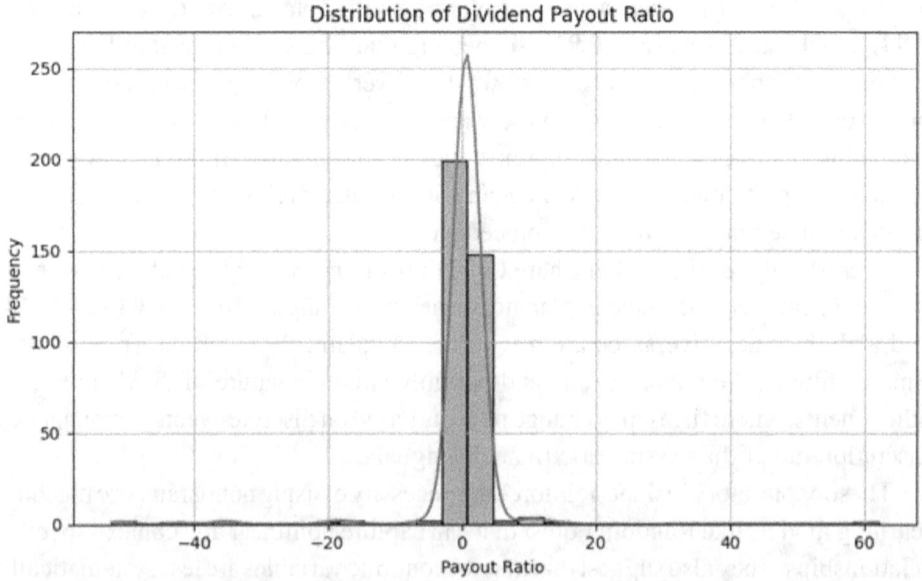

The distribution is centered close to zero and has a significant right skew. Many Moroccan companies either pay minimal or no dividends, according to a dense cluster of values between -5% and +10%. In addition, there is a noticeable right tail that reaches ratios of more than 20%, with some observations going above 60%. These extreme numbers probably indicate very successful or established companies with capital distribution policies that prioritize shareholders.

Surprisingly, the distribution also has a non-negligible left tail, and a number of observations show negative payout ratios, which are a sign that companies are paying dividends even though they are reporting net losses. Practices like dividend smoothing, reputation management, or shareholder appeasement may be the cause of this phenomenon, which has been seen in emerging markets (La Porta et al., 2000).

From a modeling perspective, this distribution poses difficulties for traditional linear models, which frequently make the assumptions of homoscedasticity and normally distributed residuals. These presumptions are broken by the heavy tails and asymmetry, which supports the selection of Random Forest, which is more appropriate for datasets with outliers and irregular value spreads and does not impose distributional constraints.

This distribution also provides financial insight into the variety of payout strategies. Moroccan listed companies seem to have a variety of dividend policies that are influenced by institutional, strategic, and perhaps informal factors in addition to profitability.

These findings set the stage for a deeper interpretability analysis, where model-based importance scores will be used to disentangle the relative impact of financial and macroeconomic predictors.

4.5 Model Transparency Through Feature Importance

Machine learning models, particularly ensemble methods like Random Forests, are renowned for their predictive capabilities but often criticized for their opacity. In financial contexts, where interpretability is essential for model adoption by decision-makers, Explainable Artificial Intelligence (XAI) plays a vital role. To address this challenge, this study leverages two complementary techniques to assess feature relevance: traditional impurity-based feature importance and SHAP (SHapley Additive exPlanations) values. Together, these approaches provide a robust framework for understanding which variables most influence dividend payout predictions—and why.

Feature Importance Ranking (Random Forest)

The initial measure of variable importance is derived from the Random Forest model itself. This method calculates how much each feature contributes to reducing error across all decision trees in the ensemble. Figure 6 illustrates the ranking of predictors based on their average contribution to reducing prediction variance.

Figure 6. Feature Importance Ranking (Random Forest)

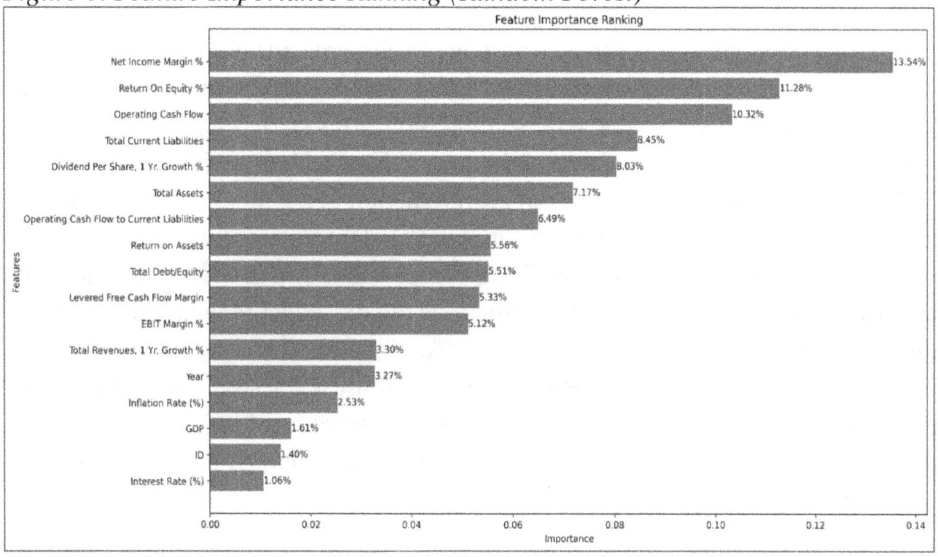

Top-performing variables include Net Income Margin (%), Return on Equity (%), and Operating Cash Flow, accounting for 13.5%, 11.3%, and 10.3% of model performance, respectively. These indicators align with classical financial theories: Signaling Theory and Agency Theory both suggest that firms with stronger financial performance are more likely to distribute dividends (Bhattacharya, 1979; Jensen & Meckling, 1976).

Other relevant predictors include Total Current Liabilities, Total Assets, and Debt-to-Equity Ratio, which reflect the importance of liquidity and capital structure. These findings reinforce the role of Financial Flexibility Theory (Gamba & Triantis, 2008), where firms evaluate short-term obligations and financial leverage before issuing dividends.

Growth-oriented indicators such as Dividend Per Share Growth and Revenue Growth also appear among the influential variables, in line with Life Cycle Theory (DeAngelo et al., 2006), which posits that mature, growth-stabilized firms are more likely to pay dividends.

On the other hand, macroeconomic factors such as GDP, interest rates, and inflation rates are not very significant. Their low scores lend validity to the idea that internal factors predominate in Moroccan firms' dividend decisions, with little regard for national economic trends.

Last but not least, control variables like Year and Firm ID are among the least significant characteristics, indicating that they are structural inputs rather than significant predictors.

SHAP Global Feature Importance

Despite providing a general understanding of variable influence, Random Forest importance scores are imprecise and do not take feature interactions or directionality into consideration. To overcome these limitations, this study uses SHAP values, a cooperative game theory-based model-agnostic XAI technique (Lundberg & Lee, 2017). By assigning a percentage of each prediction to the unique contributions of each feature, SHAP provides both local and global interpretability.

Figure 7 shows the SHAP Global Feature Importance, which shows which features consistently influence the model's predictions the most. Net Income Margin (%) is the most significant variable, followed by Total Assets, Total Current Liabilities, and EBIT Margin (%), per the Random Forest results. These results demonstrate the critical roles that profitability, firm size, and operational effectiveness play in determining dividend payout policies and are consistent with both the Signaling and Life Cycle theories.

Interestingly, Operating Cash Flow, while highly ranked in the Random Forest model, drops in importance under SHAP. This suggests that while cash flow is essential, its influence on dividend decisions may be more context-dependent or nonlinear, making other profitability metrics more consistent predictors.

As with the Random Forest ranking, macroeconomic variables contribute minimally in the SHAP framework. Their SHAP values are near zero across most observations, underscoring the internal orientation of dividend policy in Moroccan firms—likely a consequence of ownership concentration, weak institutional investor presence, and limited exposure to external shocks.

Figure 7. SHAP Global Feature Importance

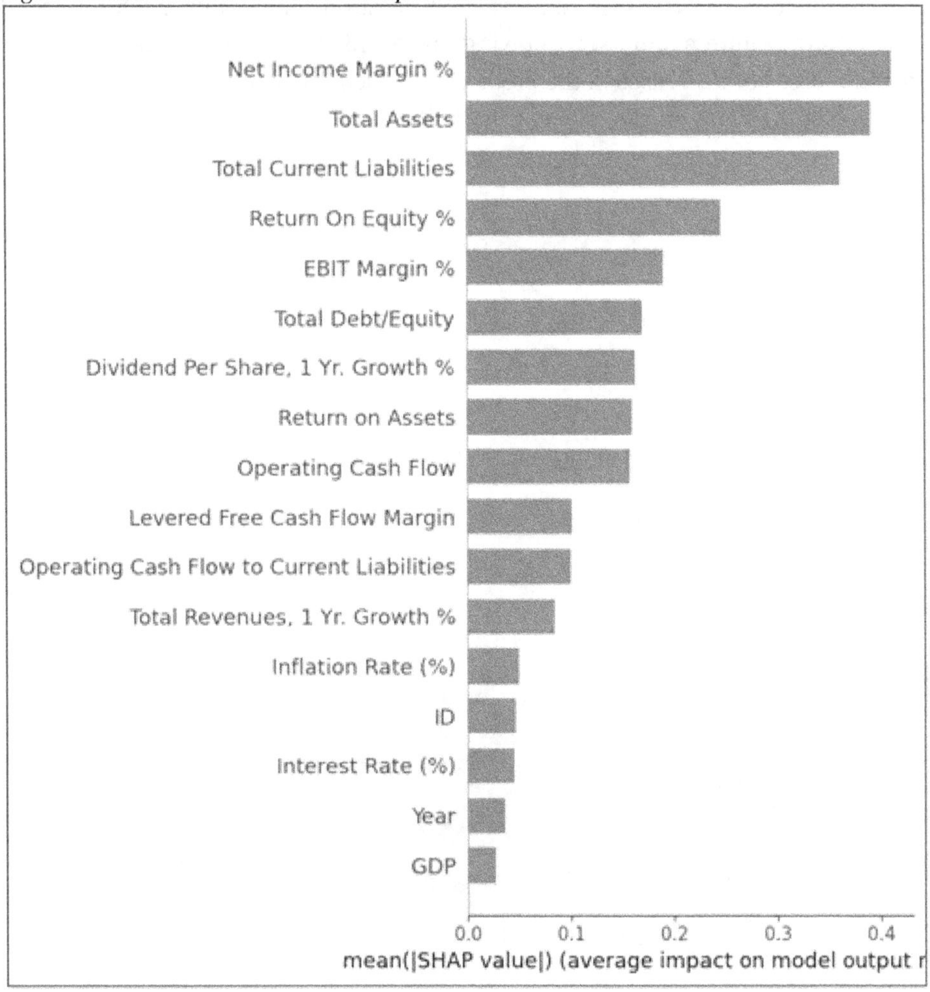

Control variables such as Year and Firm ID remain negligible in SHAP analysis, confirming that they do not encode meaningful financial information but serve merely to structure the panel dataset.

4.6 Global Behavior of the Model

Beyond ranking features globally, SHAP values allow for a more granular, observation-level analysis of how each predictor contributes to the model's output. The SHAP summary plot (Figure 8) provides a compact visual overview of this dynamic behavior across all firm-year observations in the dataset.

Each point in the plot corresponds to a single firm-year entry and shows the SHAP value of a specific feature for that observation. The points are color-coded according to feature magnitude, allowing one to infer whether high or low values drive increases or decreases in the predicted dividend payout ratio.

Figure 8. SHAP Summary Plot: Interpreting Dividend Drivers

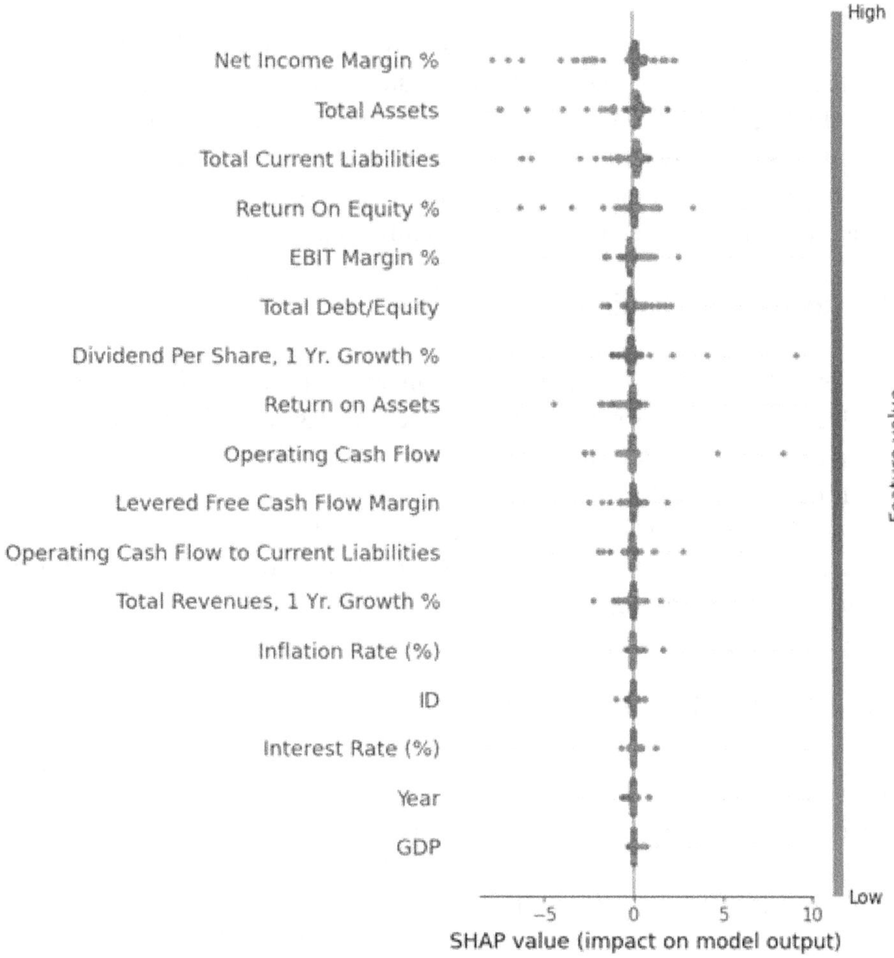

Profitability Variables and Payout Expectations:

The most salient trend in the summary plot is the consistent positive contribution of profitability indicators—Net Income Margin, Return on Equity (ROE), and EBIT Margin—to dividend payout predictions. For high values (coded in red), SHAP values are mostly positive, meaning these features increase the model's predicted payout. This finding aligns strongly with Signaling Theory (Bhattacharya, 1979; Miller & Rock, 1985), wherein higher earnings are interpreted as a credible signal of firm strength and payout capacity.

Firm Size and Maturity as Dividend Enablers

Total Assets and Total Current Liabilities exhibit similar SHAP patterns. Larger firms, indicated by higher values of these features, are systematically associated with higher predicted payout ratios. This supports Life Cycle Theory (DeAngelo et al., 2006), suggesting that mature firms with stable operations are more inclined to return earnings to shareholders. In contrast, smaller or financially constrained firms are more likely to retain earnings for reinvestment.

Debt Structure: A Nonlinear Influence:

The role of Total Debt-to-Equity Ratio is more complex. Both high and low feature values appear on both sides of the SHAP axis, suggesting that the relationship between leverage and dividend policy is not monotonic. High leverage may depress dividend payouts due to debt servicing constraints—a finding consistent with Agency Theory (Jensen, 1986). However, in some cases, moderate or high leverage could reflect disciplined capital structuring, enabling continued dividend distributions. This duality reflects the strategic trade-offs firms face when balancing financing flexibility and shareholder returns.

Marginal Influence of Macroeconomic Indicators

In sharp contrast to firm-specific predictors, GDP, Inflation, and Interest Rate consistently produce SHAP values near zero across all observations. This suggests that macroeconomic variables do not materially influence the model's dividend payout predictions. Such results reinforce previous correlation analyses and support the conclusion that dividend policy among Moroccan listed firms is largely firm-centric and less reactive to national economic conditions. The Moroccan financial context—characterized by high ownership concentration and limited institutional investor presence—may insulate dividend decisions from broader macro-level dynamics.

4.7 Evaluating Model Reliability

Ensuring the reliability of a predictive model is a critical step, particularly in a context as sensitive and high-stakes as dividend forecasting. In this study, model validation is assessed not only through standard performance metrics—such as the coefficient of determination (R^2), Mean Squared Error (MSE), and Root Mean Squared Error (RMSE)—but also through a deeper diagnostic exploration using prediction-versus-actual plots and residual distribution analysis. These tools serve to identify whether the model generalizes well, reveals systematic deviations, and maintains practical applicability in real-world financial decision-making.

A scatter plot comparing predicted and actual dividend payout ratios (Figure 9) reveals the alignment between model estimates and observed behavior for the test set. The red dashed reference line (y = x) represents perfect predictions, allowing deviations to be visually assessed.

The majority of observations cluster in the upper-right quadrant of the graph, indicating that most Moroccan listed firms exhibit positive, modest dividend payouts that the model estimates with reasonable precision. A strong diagonal alignment of points suggests that the Random Forest model captures the general structure of the data effectively. However, natural dispersion around the line is visible, reflecting realistic deviations due to firm-specific behaviors, reporting variances, or the limits of available explanatory variables.

Specifically, in the lower-left quadrant, where both the actual and predicted payout ratios are negative, some outliers are located below the reference line.

Figure 9. Predicted vs. Actual Dividends Payout Ratios: A Visual Diagnostic

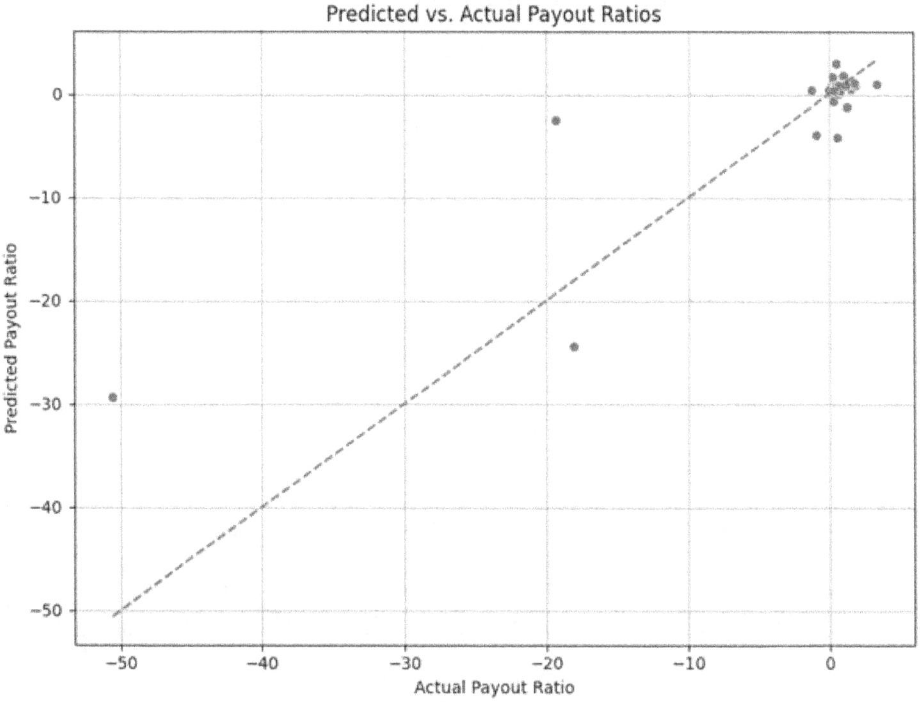

These cases could be related to companies that pay dividends even though they report losses. This could be due to reputational concerns or dividend smoothing policies, which are particularly prevalent in family-controlled businesses or those with high investor expectations in emerging markets.

There are also a few cases of overestimation or underestimation, which point to possible areas for model improvement. Other model architectures that can better capture complex dynamics in exceptional firms or the addition of more qualitative variables may be beneficial in these situations.

The analysis of residuals, which is the difference between actual and predicted values (Residual = Actual – Predicted), is another essential diagnostic. Model bias, consistency, and error structure can be inferred from the residuals' form and distribution. The distribution of these errors is depicted by the histogram in Figure 10 displayed on a kernel density estimation (KDE) curve.

The model does not consistently overpredict or underpredict, as evidenced by the distribution's tight center around zero. The shape of the curve approximates normality but with slight asymmetry, suggesting moderate variability in prediction errors. Most residuals fall within the –2 to +2 range, indicating that predictions are, on average, within a few percentage points of the actual payout ratio.

Figure 10. Distribution of Prediction Errors (Residuals)

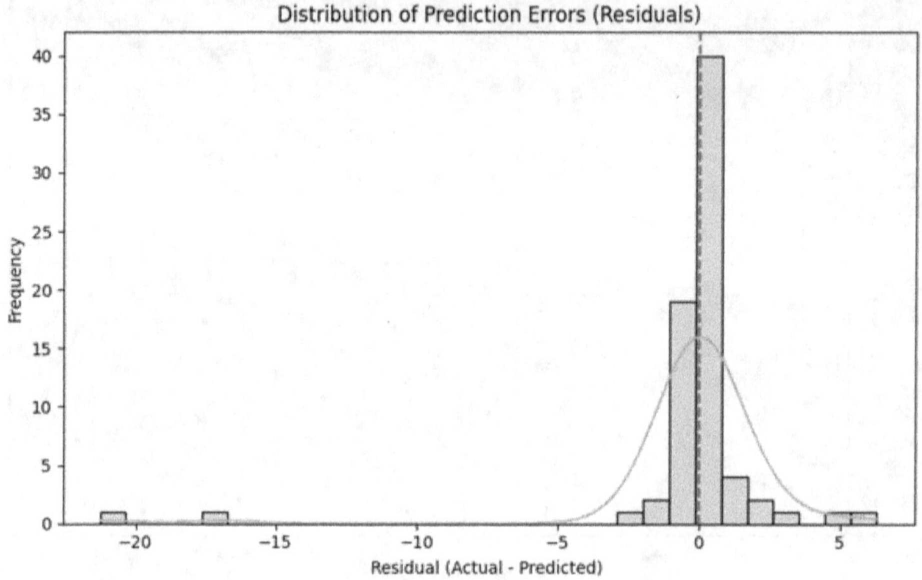

Some larger residuals appear on the negative end, pointing to underpredictions. These cases may stem from atypical corporate behaviors, such as one-time dividend declarations during low-profit years, or the absence of relevant governance variables—such as board independence, institutional ownership, or managerial conservatism—that are not captured by purely financial indicators.

From a statistical standpoint, the mean of the residuals being close to zero further supports the model's calibration. The existence of a few heavy-tailed errors is not unexpected in financial datasets, where firms often deviate from normative behavior due to strategic or external factors.

While the previous section focused on the technical outputs and statistical results of the forecasting model, the next section shifts to a critical interpretation of these findings. It explores their implications for financial decision-making, regulatory oversight, and corporate governance within the Moroccan context.

5. DISCUSSION: IMPLICATIONS FOR MOROCCAN DIVIDEND FORECASTING

This study sought to advance the predictive modeling of dividend payout ratios for Moroccan listed companies by integrating machine learning with explainable artificial intelligence (XAI) techniques. Through a multi-layered process of model training, feature evaluation, and visualization, several nuanced insights were uncovered—each contributing to both the theoretical discourse on dividend policy and its practical application in the Moroccan financial landscape.

5.1 Firm-Specific Drivers of Dividend Policy

The feature importance rankings, SHAP global values, and summary visualizations all showed a consistent pattern: firm-specific financial indicators have a much bigger impact on dividend payout behavior than macroeconomic factors.

The most predictive payout ratios were profitability measure, especially net income margin and return on equity. It aligns with the Signaling Theory—which hold that consistent profits are a reliable indicator of a company quality and future prospects—gain credibility.

High marks also went for size and structural indicators including total assets and total current liabilities. These imply, in line with life cycle theory, companies with more developed and established operational systems are more likely to pay off.

Another crucial factor was historical dividend growth calculated using dividend per share, 1 Year Growth Percentage. This underlined the need of historical dividend behavior in influencing future payout decisions since it showed stability and a taste for consistency.

These findings demonstrate that a company's dividend policy is heavily influenced by its internal capabilities and strategic signaling intentions. The model successfully measures the economic justification ingrained in traditional financial theories, demonstrating their continued applicability in the Moroccan setting.

5.2 Structural Challenges in the Moroccan Context

Notwithstanding the increasing interest in financial prediction models, the corporate environment in Morocco poses a number of difficulties that could restrict the applicability of data-driven strategies. First, data opacity is still a problem, especially for small and medium-sized businesses (SMEs). Due to pressure to avoid taxes or informal business practices, many Moroccan SMEs underreport their financial information, and many do not publicly disclose detailed financial information (OECD, 2022).

Second, the structures of governance are still changing. Many mid-sized and family-owned businesses function with little board oversight and inadequate audit controls, despite the fact that corporations such as Maroc Telecom and listed banks are subject to more stringent reporting requirements and corporate governance codes. These elements affect the dependability and accessibility of financial data, both of which are essential for accurate dividend forecasting.

5.3 Weak Influence of Macroeconomic Variables

Despite being included in the dataset to account for external economic forces, macroeconomic variables such as GDP, inflation rate, and interest rate were found to have a negligible impact on the predictive accuracy of the model.

Across Random Forest rankings and SHAP importance values, this marginal impact indicates that Moroccan firms' dividend decisions are primarily firm-driven and microeconomic. Among the explanations that could be offered are: a conservative corporate culture that places more emphasis on stability than on being aggressively responsive to changes in the economy, reduced sensitivity to changes in the global economy due to a lack of integration with global capital markets, a preponderance of closely held or family-owned businesses, or where internal strategic goals have a greater influence on decisions than external market signals.

These findings highlight how crucial it is to create models for Morocco that give internal firm metrics precedence over general macroeconomic patterns.

5.4 The Value of Explainable AI (SHAP)

This study stands out for using XAI tools, especially SHAP values, to improve the Random Forest model's interpretability.

The overall significance of important predictors like Net Income Margin and Total Assets was confirmed by global SHAP values.

Stakeholders were able to analyze individual predictions thanks to the actionable insights that SHAP summary and force plots offered at the firm level.

Even when dealing with a moderately skewed target variable, the model maintains statistical robustness, with low bias and a tight error distribution, according to model diagnostics such as residual analysis and visualizations of predicted vs. actual payout.

The end product is a model that is not only transparent and auditable, but also accurate ($R2 \approx 0.75$), which is crucial in financial domains where decisions have significant consequences.

Beyond interpretability, SHAP supports ethical artificial intelligence in finance by improving transparency, stakeholder trust, and regulatory compliance—crucially in markets with limited disclosure. XAI tools help governance by enabling both experts and non-experts to understand predictions made by them, so matching with global standards for responsible artificial intelligence in financial decision-making.

5.5 Practical Implications by Stakeholder Group

Managerial Implications

Projected dividend payout ratios are a helpful tool for dividend planning and cash flow management available to financial controllers and company executives. Through the identification of the main financial elements influencing dividend behavior—such as profitability, leverage, or liquidity—managers can actively change internal policies or interact more openly with shareholders. Using explainable models like SHAP, CFOs can also support payout decisions in line with board oversight and investor expectations by means of data-supported narratives.

Investor Guidance

SHAP value outputs help investors to grasp why a given company is expected to pay out either high or low dividends in addition to the expected payout. This builds confidence and offers a means of screening portfolio companies depending on openness and payout rationale from an analytical standpoint. This data can help both institutional and personal investors identify companies whose dividend patterns would suggest possible instability, policy conservatism, or strong financial situation.

Policy Relevance

Explainable models allow regulatory bodies such as the AMMC to track overall dividend payments, spot anomalies or outliers, and guarantees that corporate governance policies are being followed. AI systems' emphasis on explainability helps to underline even more the regulatory goal of guaranteeing equity, openness, and responsibility in financial markets. Policy agencies can also use these models to replicate the effects of legislative changes on company payout patterns under several macroeconomic scenarios.

Apart from prediction accuracy, explainable artificial intelligence usually improve stakeholder alignment, disclosure quality, and evidence-based financial supervision—all crucial foundations in the building of clear and strong financial ecosystem in developing countries like Morocco.

5.6 Conclusion of the Discussion

In addition to enhancing technical credibility, the use of explainable AI techniques such as SHAP fixes behavioral problems with investor confidence in algorithmic outputs. In situations where model opacity might lead to resistance or skepticism, the capacity to connect predictions to accurate, understandable drivers significantly improves perceived fairness and transparency. This aligns with insights from behavioral finance, which emphasize that transparency and interpretability are prerequisites for the real-world adoption of financial technologies (Barberis & Thaler, 2003).

Having contextualized the results within broader economic and policy frameworks, it is essential to acknowledge the limitations of the study. The following section critically reflects on methodological, data-related, and conceptual constraints, laying the groundwork for future research opportunities and model refinement.

6. LIMITATIONS OF THE STUDY

6.1 Sample Size and Representativeness

The empirical analysis is based on a final sample of 36 listed Moroccan companies, drawn from a total of 77 firms on the Casablanca Stock Exchange, and covers a longitudinal span from 2013 to 2023. Although the sample selection followed stringent inclusion criteria—requiring complete financial records and a history of dividend payments—the relatively small sample size poses several challenges:

- Statistical Power: With only 36 firms, the model's generalizability and statistical robustness may be constrained, particularly when attempting to extrapolate patterns across the full population of Moroccan companies.
- Selection Bias: By excluding firms that have never issued dividends, the study potentially introduces bias by omitting the behavior and constraints of non-dividend or growth-stage firms. This exclusion limits insight into why some firms avoid dividend issuance altogether.
- Scope of Applicability: As a result, the findings are primarily descriptive of established, dividend-paying firms. They may not accurately reflect the dividend policy dynamics of smaller, newly listed, or financially constrained enterprises.

Implication: The results are most applicable to mature, transparent firms with consistent financial practices, and may underrepresent firms operating under different structural or developmental conditions.

6.2 Sectoral and Structural Diversity

While the dataset spans multiple industries, the analysis does not incorporate sector-specific variables or controls. This limitation could mask important distinctions:

- Industry Characteristics: Sectors vary significantly in capital intensity, regulatory frameworks, and sensitivity to economic cycles—all of which may influence dividend behavior.
- Omitted Interaction Effects: Although Random Forest is capable of detecting nonlinear interactions, the lack of explicit modeling for sectoral effects may obscure sector-specific payout strategies or risk profiles.

Implication: The absence of industry-level granularity limits the model's ability to uncover how contextual business environments influence dividend decisions.

The current model does not include sector dummy variables due to data sparsity across industries, which limits the ability to perform robust sector-specific modeling. This omission should be addressed in future research through either richer firm-level datasets or the inclusion of sectoral identifiers as interaction terms. Explicit sector modeling would help isolate structural differences in dividend practices between capital-intensive and service-oriented industries, enhancing both interpretability and policy relevance.

Although the dataset spans multiple industries, sector-specific variables (e.g., sector dummies) were not explicitly included in the model. This may limit its ability to account for structural differences across industries—such as the capital intensity of manufacturing vs. the stability of banking.

Industry-level factors such as regulatory constraints, earnings cyclicality, and dividend norms are known to influence payout behavior (Fama & French, 2001). Future extensions could incorporate sectoral controls or interaction effects to enhance the model's explanatory richness.

6.3 Limited Inclusion of Qualitative and Governance Variables

This study is based exclusively on quantitative variables, such as financial ratios and macroeconomic indicators. However, in many corporate environments, especially in emerging markets, qualitative governance factors play a critical role:

- Ownership Structure: Whether a firm is state-owned, family-run, or widely held can impact payout policies.
- Board Composition and Independence: Strong governance practices can influence financial discipline and dividend regularity.
- Strategic Considerations: Non-public shareholder agreements, internal financing strategies, and managerial risk preferences are often decisive yet unobservable.

Implication: The exclusion of such latent variables limits the model's explanatory richness, particularly in contexts where informal or relational governance mechanisms are prominent.

Although governance factors such as board composition or ownership concentration are widely recognized as important in dividend policy literature, they are excluded from this study due to lack of standardized, publicly available data across Moroccan firms. Future work should explore the feasibility of integrating such indicators, potentially through data proxies or qualitative assessments, to better capture the institutional mechanisms that shape corporate payout behavior in emerging markets.

While this study primarily focuses on quantitative predictors, future research should incorporate proxy indicators of transparency such as board independence ratios, audit committee effectiveness, or ESG disclosure scores. These governance-related variables have been shown to influence dividend policy and investor trust in emerging markets (Kouki & Guizani, 2009). In Morocco, ESG reporting remains voluntary, and board independence varies significantly across sectors, making it both a challenge and an opportunity for explainable AI models to uncover latent governance patterns.

6.4 Macroeconomic Scope Constraints

Although macroeconomic variables such as GDP, Inflation Rate, and Interest Rate were included, their scope and granularity present some limitations:

- National Aggregates: The model relies on country-level data, which may not reflect industry-specific or regional economic conditions.
- Temporal Resolution: By using annual data, dividend strategies may be less affected by short-term economic fluctuations like quarterly policy changes or financial shocks.

    Implication: The model can underrepresent how responsive dividend behaviors is to firm-specific economic sensitivities or short-term macroeconomic dynamics.

6.5 Model Type and Interpretability Trade-Offs

Random Forest has certain methodological constraints even if its relative interpretability and predictive ability are well-known:

- Lack of Temporal Memory: The model neglects time-lagged effects on future dividend payouts including the effect of past earnings or retained earnings from past years.
- Partially Black-Box Nature: Although SHAP provides openness, practitioners lacking technical expertise could struggle to understand the internal logic of ensemble models including Random Forest.

Implication: While developing financial policy, temporal dependencies and causal relationships—which could be quite important—are not well captured by the model, despite its good performance in prediction and feature ranking.

Future studies should investigate several model architecture if one is to overcome these restrictions. Particularly in uncertain economic times, deep learning model including Long Short-Term Memory (LSTM) networks could offer a more pragmatic structure for simulating time-dependent patterns in dividend decision (Fischer & Krauss, 2018). Moreover, gradient boosting techniques (such as LightGBM or XGBoost) provides better regularizing power and are more resistant to multicollinearity and outliers in high-dimensional financial data Chen & Guestrin, 2016. These methods provide more flexibility in managing intricate temporal and structural dynamics, which might enhance or weaken the Random Forest conclusions.

6.6 Ethical Risks and Regulatory Considerations in AI Deployment

Machine learning raises ethical and legal issues even as it improve interpretability and predictive ability. First, algorithmic bias—which can be brought on by unbalanced training data or invisible confounders—may cause results to be distorted and inequality sustained. Second, overuse of AI-driven models might cause false confidence in statistical results lacking sufficient reflection of human judgment. Third, given models include sensitive or proprietary data, issues of consent and data privacy become increasingly important. In financial settings where decisions impact regulators, shareholders, and public confidence, these risks are especially great. Greater openness, responsibility, and equity in the acceptance of artificial intelligence are demanded by new frameworks including the European Union's AI Act and changing stances from financial regulatory bodies. As artificial intelligence is applied in finance in Morocco and other developing nations, model development must follow ethical and regulatory criteria to ensure innovation and institutional legitimacy.

6.7 Ethical Considerations in AI-Driven Financial Decision-Making

Given artificial intelligence's increasing integration into financial forecasting, ethical concerns must especially be given top priority. First of all, algorithmic opacity influences machine learning models—especially ensemble methods like Random Forest—which makes it challenging for interested parties to understand the decision-making process. Particularly with regard to important decisions like dividend distribution, this "black-box" issue could lead to questions regarding responsibility (Binns, 2018).

Moreover, data bias can lead to erroneous or unfair forecasts due of underrepresentation of particular company types or incomplete reporting. These risks are more evident in developing nations like Morocco, where early years of digital infrastructure and regulatory control still apply. Moreover, practitioners in ignorance are left by the absence of official ethical policies for the use of artificial intelligence in the financial industry.

Therefore, it is imperative to develop explainable models supported by ethical audits, regulatory compliance policies, and openness checks inside government systems. This builds confidence in model results and harmonizes sustainable corporate governance with financial innovation.

6.8 Future Research Directions

Notwithstanding these restrictions, this study offers a strong basis for developing dividend payout modeling in developing markets. The following directions should be explored in next studies:

- Expand the dataset to include non-paying companies so as to fully depict the range of corporate dividend behavior.
- Introduce Industry Controls: Clearly demonstrate sectoral effects to capture industry-specific elements impacting payout decisions.
- Qualitative Data: Add the variables regarding the ownership structure, the board composition, and corporate disclosures to models to increase their explanatory power in qualitative data.
- Examine Other Approaches: Test complementary models to capture dynamics and uncertainty including time-series regressions, deep learning, or Bayesian methods.
- Cross-Market Validation: Repeated analysis in more developing nations will help to improve policy recommendations by assessing the generalizability of the results.

Completing these research gaps will enable next studies to produce more comprehensive, understandable, and significant dividend forecasting models that better satisfy the demands of investors, legislators, and corporate managers.

Time-series models meant especially to take temporal dependencies in dividend behavior could also be used in future research. Conventional models, such Lintner's dividend smoothing framework, can stress how crucial past payout decision are in developing present rules. Retained earnings dynamics or lagged financial variables can helps forecasts to have temporal realism. Especially in times of financial crisis or legislative change, innovative methods like autoregressive models or Long Short-Term Memory (LSTM) networks may offer useful data on how companies changes dividend over time.

Another interesting variation on dividend forecasting is applying behavioral finance concepts. The ways in which elements including investor sentiment, herding behavior, and managerial overconfidence might influences dividend policies could not be sufficiently reflected by quantitative financial indicators (Baker & Wurgler, 2006; Shefrin, 2007). Machine learning-based forecasting could benefit especially in sentiment-driven industries or during turbulent times from the inclusion of sentiment indices or text-based analysis of disclosures and market reactions.

Future research could finally use autoregressive models (such as ARIMA) or recurrent neural networks to incorporate temporal dynamics—such as lagged payout decisions and dividend smoothing patterns. These techniques can capture intertemporal dependencies and improve prediction under changing macroeconomic conditions, especially for businesses with regular dividend histories or cyclical strategies (Lintner, 1956; Fischer & Krauss, 2018).

7. CONCLUSION

Combining Artificial Intelligence (AI)—more especially, a Random Forest Regressor with Explainable AI (XAI) techniques—this paper looked at the possibility of modeling and forecasting dividend payout ratios for companies listed on the Casablanca Stock Exchange. Within the framework of a growing financial market, the study sought to achieve two objectives: high predictive accuracy and interpretable insights that might enhance the decision-making processes of investors, corporate managers, and legislators.

The empirical findings demonstrate that firm-specific financial indicators, specifically Net Income Margin, Return on Equity (ROE), and Total Assets, are the most important predictors of dividend behavior. These findings both strongly validate the applicability of traditional theoretical frameworks such as signaling theory, agency theory, and life cycle theory, and they show the limited impact of macroeconomic indicators such as GDP, inflation rate, and interest rate. This demonstrates that internal microeconomic variables—like firm-level profitability, size, and operational stability—have a greater influence on dividend policy in Morocco than do external economic trends.

With a robust R2 score of about 0.75, the model can explain the variance in dividend payouts by utilizing SHAP (SHapley Additive exPlanations) values and comprehensive residual diagnostics. More importantly, it meets the sometimes disregarded need of interpretability by giving stakeholders openness on the formation of forecasts. In finance, where broad acceptance depends on the credibility and auditability of predictive models, this is particularly valuable.

Moreover, the incorporation of XAI elevates the utility of the model beyond mere statistical performance. It facilitates trust-building among stakeholders, empowers analytical audits, and bridges the critical gap between "black-box" AI solutions and the transparency expectations of regulatory and governance frameworks.

However, the study also acknowledges key limitations that constrain the breadth of its applicability:

- A relatively small sample size (36 dividend-paying firms) reduces statistical generalizability.
- The lack of industry-level modeling may overlook sector-specific dividend determinants.
- The exclusion of qualitative governance factors—such as ownership structure and board independence—limits the explanatory scope in contexts where non-financial dynamics are influential.

These limitations provide direction for future research, which should aim to:

- Expand the dataset to include non-dividend-paying firms.
- Incorporate industry and governance variables.
- Explore temporal modeling frameworks (e.g., recurrent neural networks or time-series econometrics) to account for lagged effects and historical dependencies.

This research delivers a methodologically sound, practically relevant, and transparent approach to dividend forecasting tailored to emerging markets. It confirms that AI models—when made explainable—can enhance financial prediction and strategic planning. For Morocco and similar economies, such frameworks offer not only analytical precision but also the trust and accountability necessary to support sustainable capital market development and data-driven policy formation.

REFERENCES

Abbas, G., Rafiq, S., & Gul, M. (2023). Unraveling dividend payouts: a comprehensive analysis of cash flow and earnings approaches in the listed manufacturing companies. FiTUA. DOI: 10.51380/gujr-39-02-10

Aggarwal, C. C. (2018). *Neural networks and deep learning: A textbook*. Springer. DOI: 10.1007/978-3-319-94463-0

Ahmad, N., Ullah, Z., & Arshad, H. (2021). Artificial intelligence for sustainable finance in low-income countries. *Journal of Cleaner Production*, *310*, 127385.

AMMC. (2023). Guide de la gouvernance d'entreprise au Maroc.

An, Z., Gao, W., Li, D., & Ye, D. (2022). Dividend payouts, Cash-Flow uncertainty, and the role of Institutions. *Journal of Business Finance & Accounting*, *49*(7–8), 1356–1390. DOI: 10.1111/jbfa.12595

Arshad, N., Waseem, F., & Abbas, S. F. (2022). Factors Affecting Dividend Payout Ratio of Dividend Paying Firms Listed on KSE-100 Index. iRASD. *Journal of Management*, *4*(2), 162–181. DOI: 10.52131/jom.2022.0401.0071

Arun, T., & Kamath, R. (2022). Interpretable credit scoring using SHAP values: A regulatory perspective. *Journal of Financial Regulation and Compliance*, *30*(4), 421–436.

Asongu, S. A., & Nwachukwu, J. C. (2022). Financial development, governance, and artificial intelligence in Africa. *Technological Forecasting and Social Change*, *177*, 121499.

Baker, H. K., & Jabbouri, I. (2016). How Moroccan managers view dividend policy. *Managerial Finance*, *42*(3), 270–288. DOI: 10.1108/MF-07-2015-0211

Baker, H. K., & Jabbouri, I. (2017). Dividend policy in Morocco: Survey evidence from Casablanca Stock Exchange. *International Journal of Managerial Finance*, *13*(3), 347–365.

Baker, M., & Wurgler, J. (2006). Investor sentiment and the cross-section of stock returns. *The Journal of Finance*, *61*(4), 1645–1680. DOI: 10.1111/j.1540-6261.2006.00885.x

Barberis, N., & Thaler, R. (2003). A survey of behavioral finance. In *Handbook of the Economics of Finance* (Vol. 1, pp. 1053–1128). Elsevier.

Bhat, R. (2010). Corporate governance and dividend policy in India. *Journal of Emerging Market Finance*, *9*(1), 55–70.

Bhattacharya, S. (1979). Imperfect information, dividend policy, and "the bird in the hand" fallacy. *The Bell Journal of Economics*, *10*(1), 259–270. DOI: 10.2307/3003330

Breiman, L. (2001). Random forests. *Machine Learning*, *45*(1), 5–32. DOI: 10.1023/A:1010933404324

Breiman, L. (2001). Random forests. *Machine Learning*, *45*(1), 5–32. DOI: 10.1023/A:1010933404324

Chen, T., & Guestrin, C. (2016). XGBoost: A scalable tree boosting system. *Proceedings of the 22nd ACM SIGKDD International Conference on Knowledge Discovery and Data Mining*, 785–794.

Cheng, L., Liu, F., & Yao, W. (2020). Data cleaning for financial machine learning: A practical guide. *The Journal of Financial Data Science*, *2*(3), 22–39.

Chicco, D., Tötsch, N., & Jurman, G. (2021). The coefficient of determination R^2 is more informative than SMAPE, MAE, MAPE, MSE and RMSE in regression analysis evaluation. *PeerJ. Computer Science*, *7*, e623. DOI: 10.7717/peerj-cs.623 PMID: 34307865

Chouaya, M., & Jarboui, A. (2017). Determinants of dividend policy in Tunisia. *International Journal of Business and Management Studies*, *6*(1), 38–52.

Dang, C., Li, F., & Yang, C. (2018). Measuring firm size in empirical corporate finance. *Journal of Banking & Finance*, *86*, 159–176. DOI: 10.1016/j.jbankfin.2017.09.006

DeAngelo, H., DeAngelo, L., & Stulz, R. M. (2006). Dividend policy and the earned/contributed capital mix: A test of the lifecycle theory. *Journal of Financial Economics*, *81*(2), 227–254. DOI: 10.1016/j.jfineco.2005.07.005

Dewasiri, N. J., Yatiwelle Koralalage, W. B., Azeez, A. A., Jayarathne, P. G. S. A., Kuruppuarachchi, D., & Weerasinghe, V. A. (2019). Determinants of dividend policy: Evidence from an emerging and developing market. *Managerial Finance*, *45*(3), 413–429. DOI: 10.1108/MF-09-2017-0331

Easterbrook, F. H. (1984). Two agency-cost explanations of dividends. *The American Economic Review*, *74*(4), 650–659.

Fama, E. F., & French, K. R. (2001). Disappearing dividends: Changing firm characteristics or lower propensity to pay? *Journal of Financial Economics*, *60*(1), 3–43. DOI: 10.1016/S0304-405X(01)00038-1

Fernández-Delgado, M., Cernadas, E., Barro, S., & Amorim, D. (2014). Do we need hundreds of classifiers to solve real world classification problems? *Journal of Machine Learning Research*, *15*(1), 3133–3181.

Fischer, T., & Krauss, C. (2018). Deep learning with long short-term memory networks for financial market predictions. *European Journal of Operational Research*, *270*(2), 654–669. DOI: 10.1016/j.ejor.2017.11.054

Frost, J. (2021). *Regression analysis: An intuitive guide for using and interpreting linear models*. Statistics By Jim Publishing.

Graham, J. R., & Harvey, C. R. (2001). The theory and practice of corporate finance: Evidence from the field. *Journal of Financial Economics*, *60*(2–3), 187–243. DOI: 10.1016/S0304-405X(01)00044-7

Gupta, D., & Ranjan, P. (2022). Machine learning in finance: Data quality, preprocessing, and applications. *International Journal of Finance & Economics*, *27*(1), 1–20.

Jangphanish, K., Boonyanet, W., & Tongkong, S. (2025). Analyzing robust dividend payout policy with dynamic panel regression: Application of speed of adjustment to half-life. *PLoS One*, *20*(1), e0316478. DOI: 10.1371/journal.pone.0316478 PMID: 39813290

Jensen, M. C. (1986). Agency costs of free cash flow, corporate finance, and takeovers. *The American Economic Review*, *76*(2), 323–329.

Jensen, M. C., & Meckling, W. H. (1976). Theory of the firm: Managerial behavior, agency costs, and ownership structure. *Journal of Financial Economics*, *3*(4), 305–360. DOI: 10.1016/0304-405X(76)90026-X

Kouki, M., & Guizani, M. (2009). Ownership structure and dividend policy in the context of the Tunisian stock market. *Journal of Business Finance & Accounting*, *36*(7–8), 861–885.

Krauss, C., Do, X. A., & Huck, N. (2017). Deep neural networks, gradient-boosted trees, random forests: Financial prediction at Nasdaq. *European Journal of Operational Research*, *259*(2), 689–702. DOI: 10.1016/j.ejor.2016.10.031

Kuhn, M., & Johnson, K. (2013). *Applied predictive modeling*. Springer. DOI: 10.1007/978-1-4614-6849-3

Kumar, A., & Sinha, P. (2024). Changing dividend payout behavior and predicting dividend policy in emerging markets: Evidence from India. *Investment Management & Financial Innovations*, *21*(1), 259–274. DOI: 10.21511/imfi.21(1).2024.20

La Porta, R., Lopez-de-Silanes, F., & Shleifer, A. (1999). Corporate ownership around the world. *The Journal of Finance*, *54*(2), 471–517. DOI: 10.1111/0022-1082.00115

Lintner, J. (1956). Distribution of incomes of corporations among dividends, retained earnings, and taxes. *The American Economic Review*, *46*(2), 97–113.

Louziri, I., & Oubal, M. (2022). Determinants of dividend policy in Morocco: An empirical study of listed companies. *Moroccan Journal of Finance and Management*, *8*(1), 31–47.

Lundberg, S. M., Erion, G., & Lee, S.-I. (2020). From local explanations to global understanding with explainable AI for trees. *Nature Machine Intelligence*, *2*(1), 56–67. DOI: 10.1038/s42256-019-0138-9 PMID: 32607472

Lundberg, S. M., & Lee, S.-I. (2017). A unified approach to interpreting model predictions. *Advances in Neural Information Processing Systems*, •••, 30.

Maqsudi, A., Rachmawati, T., & Hwihanus, H. (2022). Influencing Factors Dividend Policy: Empirical Evidence From Different Parts Of The World. *Eduvest*, *2*(7). Advance online publication. DOI: 10.59188/eduvest.v2i7.527

Marketscreener. (2024). Morocco Listed Companies Financial Data. https://www.marketscreener.com/stock-exchange/shares/africa/morocco-95/

Miller, M. H., & Rock, K. (1985). Dividend policy under asymmetric information. *The Journal of Finance*, *40*(4), 1031–1051. DOI: 10.1111/j.1540-6261.1985.tb02362.x

Mrzygłód, U., & Nowak, S. (2017). Market reactions to dividends announcements and payouts: Empirical evidence from the Warsaw Stock Exchange. *Contemporary Economics*, *11*(2), 187–204. DOI: 10.5709/ce.1897-9254.236

Myers, S. C., & Majluf, N. S. (1984). Corporate financing and investment decisions when firms have information that investors do not have. *Journal of Financial Economics*, *13*(2), 187–221. DOI: 10.1016/0304-405X(84)90023-0

Ntim, C. G. (2012). Corporate governance and dividend policy in South Africa. *International Review of Applied Economics*, *26*(2), 157–174.

O'Neill, A. (2024a, November 7). Inflation rate in Morocco 2029. Statista. https://www.statista.com

O'Neill, A. (2024b, November 7). Gross domestic product (GDP) in Morocco 2029. Statista. https://www.statista.com

OECD. (2022). Enhancing SME Transparency and Formalization in the MENA Region.

Probst, P., Wright, M. N., & Boulesteix, A. L. (2019). Hyperparameters and tuning strategies for random forest. *Wiley Interdisciplinary Reviews. Data Mining and Knowledge Discovery*, *9*(3), e1301. DOI: 10.1002/widm.1301

Ribeiro, M. T., Singh, S., & Guestrin, C. (2016). "Why should I trust you?": Explaining the predictions of any classifier. Proceedings of the 22nd ACM SIGKDD International Conference on Knowledge Discovery and Data Mining, 1135–1144.

Shefrin, H. (2007). *Behavioral Corporate Finance: Decisions that Create Value*. McGraw-Hill.

Souza, M. J., Lima, F. G., & Pereira, J. R. (2024). Earnings, leverage, and dividend payouts: Empirical evidence from Latin America. *Journal of Financial Stability*, *67*, 101187.

TradingEconomics. (2024). Morocco Interest Rate. https://tradingeconomics.com/morocco/interest-rate

Willmott, C. J., & Matsuura, K. (2005). Advantages of the mean absolute error (MAE) over the root mean square error (RMSE) in assessing average model performance. *Climate Research*, *30*(1), 79–82. DOI: 10.3354/cr030079

Yaseen, H., & Dragotă, V. (2021). *Forecasting the Dividend Policy Using Machine Learning Approach: Decision Tree Regression Models*. Springer., DOI: 10.1007/978-3-030-71869-5_2

Yehia, H. (2021). Dividend payout in Egypt. *Corporate Ownership and Control*, *18*(2), 112–125.

Zhou, Z., Wang, Y., & Wu, Y. (2022). Machine learning for financial prediction: An empirical evaluation of interpretability and performance. *Expert Systems with Applications*, *193*, 116435.

ADDITIONAL READING

Baker, M., & Wurgler, J. (2004). A catering theory of dividends. [→ Explains how firms adjust dividend policies in response to investor demand for payout.]. *The Journal of Finance*, *59*(3), 1125–1165. DOI: 10.1111/j.1540-6261.2004.00658.x

→ Empirical and theoretical discussion on why firms retain earnings and delay payouts.

Fama, E. F., & French, K. R. (2001). Disappearing dividends: Changing firm characteristics or lower propensity to pay? [→ Classic empirical analysis linking firm evolution to declining dividend payout practices.]. *Journal of Financial Economics*, *60*(1), 3–43. DOI: 10.1016/S0304-405X(01)00038-1

Gamba, A., & Triantis, A. (2008). The value of financial flexibility. *The Journal of Finance*, *63*(5), 2263–2296. DOI: 10.1111/j.1540-6261.2008.01397.x

Lundberg, S. M., & Lee, S.-I. **(2017).** A unified approach to interpreting model predictions. *Advances in Neural Information Processing Systems, 30.* → Seminal paper introducing SHAP values for model explainability in AI.

OECD (2020). *G20/OECD Principles of Corporate Governance.* → Key international framework guiding governance policies in developed and emerging markets.

The following works provide foundational and extended insights related to dividend policy, explainable AI, and governance in emerging financial contexts:

APPENDIX A. TECHNICAL IMPLEMENTATION DETAILS

This appendix presents the essential technical steps used to prepare the dataset, develop the Random Forest model, and evaluate its performance. The goal is to document methodological transparency while keeping the main chapter accessible to non-technical readers.

A.1 Data Preparation and Preprocessing

A.1.1 Integration of Firm-Level and Macroeconomic Data

The dataset was constructed as a panel of Moroccan listed firms (2013–2023), incorporating annual macroeconomic indicators. Firm-level financial data was aligned by year, enabling both temporal and cross-sectional analysis.

A.1.2 Missing Value Imputation

Missing values in financial ratios were handled using **mean imputation** to preserve the central tendency of each feature. Placeholder symbols such as '-' or empty strings were first converted to **NaN** before imputation.

A.1.3 Value Transformation

Textual formats in financial variables (e.g., '**K**', '**M**', '**B**') were converted into numeric values. Additionally, variables with high skewness were log-transformed to improve normality.

A.1.4 Macroeconomic Data Standardization

Macroeconomic indicators (Inflation Rate, Interest Rate, GDP Growth) were standardized using z-scores. GDP was converted from USD to MAD using the historical exchange rate (**1 USD = 9.5101 MAD**).

A.1.5 Target Variable Normalization

The Dividend Payout Ratio (DPR) was scaled by dividing by 100 to transform percentages into decimal values, ensuring consistency with other continuous variables.

A.2 Model Development

A.2.1 Data Splitting

The dataset was split into **80% training** and **20% testing** subsets using Scikit-learn's train_test_split function. Stratification by year was used to maintain temporal balance.

A.2.2 Hyperparameter Optimization

A **Grid Search with 10-fold Cross-Validation** was conducted to identify the optimal combination of:

```
n_estimators: [50, 100, 200]

max_depth: [None, 40, 50, 100]

min_samples_split: [2, 3, 4]
```

The best-performing configuration was:

```
n_estimators: 70

max_depth: 50

min_samples_split: 2
```

A.2.3 Final Model

The final Random Forest Regressor included max_features=3 to ensure diversity among decision trees. The model was trained on the full training set.

A.3 Model Evaluation

A.3.1 Metrics Used

The model's performance was assessed using:

- **R^2 Score**: **0.746**
- **Mean Squared Error (MSE)**: **11.52**
- **Root Mean Squared Error (RMSE)**: **3.39**

These indicate strong explanatory power and acceptable error levels.

A.3.2 Validation Summary

The combination of high **R^2** and low **RMSE** confirms the model's robustness. It generalizes well to unseen data and supports reliable dividend payout forecasting for Moroccan listed firms.

Chapter 7
The Role of Digital Transformation in Enhancing Transparency in AI-Assisted Public Administration

Ayoub Ouboumlik
https://orcid.org/0009-0000-3991-7930
Hassan II University of Casablanca, Morocco

Hassan Khafif
Hassan II University of Casablanca, Morocco

Naoual Ouazzani Touhami
Hassan II University of Casablanca, Morocco

Intissar Baiza
Hassan II University of Casablanca, Morocco

ABSTRACT

This study examines the transformative impact of digital transformation and artificial intelligence (AI) on transparency, accountability, and efficiency in public administration. It explores AI-driven governance initiatives that combat corruption, streamline processes, and enhance citizen engagement. Using a benchmarking approach and quantitative research focused on Chief Information Officers, the study assesses AI's role in governance. Findings show that AI-powered digital transformation improves transparency through real-time data monitoring, predictive analytics, and

DOI: 10.4018/979-8-3373-1737-3.ch007

automated decision-making. While AI enhances public access to information and reduces inefficiencies, challenges persist, including ethical concerns, algorithmic biases, and infrastructure gaps—only 22% of public organizations have the capacity for full AI implementation. This research highlights the need for strong governance frameworks, ethical AI deployment, and strategic investment in digital infrastructure to foster open governance, strengthen public trust, and drive sustainable administrative innovation.

1. INTRODUCTION

In this era of digitization and information age, is the order of modern governance. AI in public sector delivery is transforming the delivery of services and redefining key terms like transparency, accountability and citizen engagement. Open government There is nothing magic about involving the people in how their government works, only that the establishment is distrustful when it is secret. Governance is not just administration, but policies and rule of law (International Monetary Fund, 2021; Mergel et al., 2016). To be truly effective, governance has to focus on transparency, fairness, and on delivering services in a more efficient manner to maximize the use of resources and minimize the red tapes (Wirtz et al., 2019).

These traditional governance structures promised much but are often weighed down under red tape, risks of corruption and inefficiencies of how public services are actually delivered. In the era of AI-led digital transformation, governments now have a chance to address these issues. These technologies enable real-time data mining, automate routines, and forecast phenomena of interest to enhance decision-making, and to maximize accountability in the public domain (Osborne et and al.,2022). AI is used because it works well for a range of purposes: from services efficiency in governments of countries of the world, to stimulating open data initiatives, to cutting through administrative bottlenecks across sectors (Osborne and al., 2022). Yet even if digital transformation fosters transparency, it also introduces issues of privacy (Antonakis and Jacquart, 2013), algorithmic biases and ethical issues (Wu et al., 2020).

A number of countries have established specialized bodies for facilitating the use of AI in governance. The United Arab Emirates (UAE) has, for instance, formed a Ministry of AI, UK has created an AI Council and Office for AI. Meanwhile, countries such as China, Japan and the USA have integrated AI initiatives into existing government structures and significantly increased public funding for AI infrastructure research and development (Aayog, 2018). If India can use AI to ensure transparent governance, the country will lead the world in digital transformation. The government's vision is "Minimum Government and Maximum Governance" so that administrative efficiency and transparency is improved, and bureaucratic simplifications are done. Yet, the adoption of AI-driven transparency tools requires robust policy ecosystems, data governance structures and digital infrastructure readiness.

This study aims to explore the intersection of digital transformation, AI and transparency in public administration. More specifically, it aims to:

1. Examine the maturity level of AI adoption in public administration, particularly with regard to awareness, technological readiness, AI-focused policy initiatives and data governance frameworks.
2. Analyze how AI enhances transparency and accountability in public administration by mitigating corruption risks and improving service delivery mechanisms.
3. Assess the impact of AI adoption on service efficiency, data accessibility and public sector decision-making processes.

To achieve these objectives, the study addresses the following research questions:

> **RQ1**: What is the maturity level of AI adoption in public administration, and how does digital transformation support transparency initiatives?
> **RQ2**: How does AI integration improve transparency in governance, and what mechanisms ensure accountability in AI-assisted public administration?
> **RQ3**: How does AI-driven digital transformation influence the efficiency, accessibility and integrity of public services?

While artificial intelligence holds the potential to transform public management by enhancing transparency and administrative performance, its democratic implications remain ambivalent and underexplored. On the one hand, AI can enhance access to information, accountability and citizen participation; on the other, it can produce new kinds of algorithmic opacity and automated surveillance. This chapter explores how public administrations may transfer ethical governance challenges within technology efficiency by using AI as a leveraging factor, especially in a plural context where not everyone can have access to technology, institutional capacities are different, and civic expectations evolve. It structures the question around a key issue: **in what ways AI technologies can enhance or erode transparency in public administration through their administrative, algorithmic, and participatory dimensions?**

2. LITERATURE REVIEW

2.1. Artificial Intelligence and Digital Transformation

Artificial intelligence (AI) has emerged as a transformative force in many sectors, including governance, finance, healthcare and education (Russell and Norvig, 2016). AI as a keystone of digital transformation can provide automation, data-based decision-making and higher service capacity that are required for governance. AI includes a variety of sub-domains such as machine learning, natural language processing, computer vision, and robotics, which has led to its fast development and wide application in public administration (Bishop and Nasrabadi, 2006).

Breakthroughs in deep learning and generative AI have significantly enhanced AI capabilities, particularly in predictive analytics, automated reporting and real-time decision-making (Goodfellow, 2016; Radford, 2018; Yun and al., 2024). 'Digital transformation' empowered by AI allows governments to analyze large amounts of data in the public sector for efficiency and transparency (Sun and Medaglia, 2019). For example, systems like Retrieval-Augmented Generation (RAG) that employ large language models (LLMs) have made one stride toward real-time citizen-government interactions by enabling one to generate a reply that is sensitive to the user's context as seen in their previous policy query. One analysis at 2024 indicated that academic descriptions of these systems could be up to 90.67% accurate, facilitating public dialogue and scrutiny (Yun et al., 2024). Furthermore, frameworks like Generative AI models such as generative adversarial networks (GANs) and (VAEs) have brought new applications in natural language processing, content generation and citizen engagement (Brock et al., 2018; Goodfellow et al., 2015; Kingma and Welling, 2013; Pulapaka et al., 2024).

AI-driven change in public sectors will support lessons that have been learned from the large government data covers the ways of dealing with it to be more efficient and transparent (Sun and Medaglia, 2019). For instance, real-time citizen-government interaction generated by the answer generation, as RAG will be able to provide (along the lines of policy-based QA, see next), recently enabled by RAG (facilitated via a combination of a retrieval-based answer generator in the human-operator loop to make it human-like produced by RAG (a specific Question Answering task instance is designed for) and working on real-world questions). According to research disability these kinds of systems can enable as much as 90.67% accurate policy communication, resulting in more public engagement and transparency (Yun et al., 2024). Also, frameworks such as Generative AI models such as Generative adversarial networks (GANs) and variational autoencoders (VAEs) have enabled new uses in natural language processing, content generation and citizen engagement (Brock et al., 2018; Goodfellow et al., 2014; Kingma, 2013; Pulapaka et al., 2024).

Although the use of AI in governance does have its advantages, there are few ethical and legal challenges, concerns and dilemmas which have to be dealt with such as data privacy, algorithmic biases, as well as the "black box" nature (non-transparent decision-making process of AI) (Cheong, 2024; Dwivedi, 2023; Rudin, 2019). Human-centred AI in accordance with the principles of open governance is crucial for realizing the full potential of AI, while building and maintaining public trust and accountability.

Conceptual Clarification

Although the terms "transparency", 'accountability' and "citizen participation" are often used together, they refer to distinct dimensions of democratic governance. Transparency concerns access to public information and the traceability of decision-making processes. Accountability refers to the ability of institutions to justify and account for their decisions. Participation involves the active involvement of citizens in public decision-making (Cheong, 2024; Robles & Mallinson, 2025). These three pillars are interconnected, but require specific mechanisms in AI systems, such as algorithm auditability, participatory interfaces and public accountability mechanisms.

2.2. Typology of Transparency in Public Management

Transparency in public management can be understood in three complementary dimensions: administrative, algorithmic and participative. Each responds to specific requirements of democratic governance in a context marked by the increasing digitization of public services.

Administrative transparency is derived from the transparency of the administrative processes, by which the public can search contents of the public documents and trace the decision-making process. This principle is even constitutionally guaranteed in France and codified in the so-called Code des relations entre le public et l'administration (CRPA) which is enforced by the Commission d'accès aux documents administratifs (CADA). It is the responsibility of public players and audits will be facilitated by traceability of digital documents (Digiposte, 2024).

Algorithmic transparency is emerging with the growing use of artificial intelligence in public administrations. It aims to guarantee the explicability, auditability and fairness of automated decisions. Gunning et Aha (2019) stress the importance of developing AI systems that are understandable to users (XAI). However, current systems are still insufficiently operational (Etalab, 2021), and risks of bias or opaque decisions persist (LegalProd, 2024).

Participatory transparency implies the co-construction of public policies by citizens, notably via digital consultations and interactive platforms. It strengthens the legitimacy of decisions, provided that inclusion and representativeness are guaranteed (Criado et al., 2013).

These three dimensions require appropriate mechanisms to be effective, and must be thought through together to guarantee truly transparent public governance in the algorithmic age.

2.3. Mini Case Studies: AI and Transparency in Practice

The integration of artificial intelligence into public management is illustrated by concrete cases that highlight the tensions between technological performance and transparency requirements. Two emblematic examples - from Brazil and the UK - allow us to analyze the differentiated effects of AI according to the dimensions of transparency.

Case 1: Combating Tax Fraud in Brazil via the Sefaz Platform

Brazil's Tax Secretariat (SEFAZ) has developed an artificial intelligence system capable of analyzing tax and transactional data in real time to detect anomalies. This system has optimized the allocation of control resources and increased the detection of tax fraud. However, the transparency of the algorithmic criteria used to select taxpayers for audit remains limited. This opacity raises issues of administrative accountability and the protection of fundamental rights, notably in terms of non-discrimination and the right to defense (da Costa Nunes et al., 2024). The case illustrates the limits of algorithmic transparency when performance logics predominate over open governance principles.

Case 2: "FixMyStreet" Participative Platform in the UK

Run by the MySociety group, FixMyStreet has allowed citizens to report urban issues, like potholes or broken lampposts, via an AI-aided digital interface. The generated reports are auto-geolocated, classified and sent to the appropriate local authorities. This encourages the government response more sensitive to citizens negotiation increasing the participation transparency due to reports and responses may be consulted by any registered user. (Kitchin, 2014) argue, tools like this represent

Although the use of AI in governance does have its advantages, there are few ethical and legal challenges, concerns and dilemmas which have to be dealt with such as data privacy, algorithmic biases, as well as the "black box" nature (non-transparent decision-making process of AI) (Cheong, 2024; Dwivedi, 2023; Rudin, 2019). Human-centred AI in accordance with the principles of open governance is crucial for realizing the full potential of AI, while building and maintaining public trust and accountability.

Conceptual Clarification

Although the terms "transparency", 'accountability' and "citizen participation" are often used together, they refer to distinct dimensions of democratic governance. Transparency concerns access to public information and the traceability of decision-making processes. Accountability refers to the ability of institutions to justify and account for their decisions. Participation involves the active involvement of citizens in public decision-making (Cheong, 2024; Robles & Mallinson, 2025). These three pillars are interconnected, but require specific mechanisms in AI systems, such as algorithm auditability, participatory interfaces and public accountability mechanisms.

2.2. Typology of Transparency in Public Management

Transparency in public management can be understood in three complementary dimensions: administrative, algorithmic and participative. Each responds to specific requirements of democratic governance in a context marked by the increasing digitization of public services.

Administrative transparency is derived from the transparency of the administrative processes, by which the public can search contents of the public documents and trace the decision-making process. This principle is even constitutionally guaranteed in France and codified in the so-called Code des relations entre le public et l'administration (CRPA) which is enforced by the Commission d'accès aux documents administratifs (CADA). It is the responsibility of public players and audits will be facilitated by traceability of digital documents (Digiposte, 2024).

Algorithmic transparency is emerging with the growing use of artificial intelligence in public administrations. It aims to guarantee the explicability, auditability and fairness of automated decisions. Gunning et Aha (2019) stress the importance of developing AI systems that are understandable to users (XAI). However, current systems are still insufficiently operational (Etalab, 2021), and risks of bias or opaque decisions persist (LegalProd, 2024).

2.5. AI and Public Administration

The role of AI in transforming the public sector is increasingly recognized for its potential to increase transparency, reduce corruption and improve citizen engagement (Margetts and Dorobantu, 2019; Van der Voort and al., 2019). AI in governance is characterized by its ability to automate bureaucratic processes, analyze large data sets and improve decision-making (Janssen and Kuk, 2016; Scholta and Lindgren, 2023; Sun and Medaglia, 2019).

Several countries have developed AI policy frameworks to advance the responsible deployment of AI in public administration. Take the United Arab Emirates (UAE) which is a great example, they have rolled out a bold National AI Strategy 2030 – an ambitious plan to make UAE a global leader in AI, the strategy spans priorities such as healthcare, education, and transportation. It has also named a Minister of State for Artificial Intelligence, reflecting the importance it attaches to the development of AI (Bird and Bird, 2025). In the UK, the government has adopted an agile approach which focuses on the sectoral regulation rather than a pan regulation to encourage AI innovation and ensure ethical AI deployment (White and Case, 2015). Likewise, China's AI strategies at a state-level have recently led to the publication of an AI safety governance framework, articulating principles for AI safety, risk categorization, and different technological measures that should be taken to address expected risks (DLA Piper, 2024).

Furthermore, the AI systems are increasingly being incorporated in e-governance, urban planning, public services' predictive analysis. For example, data-driven urban planning employs AI to support city planners and policy-makers to make informed decisions, forecast urban trends, and optimize the distribution of resources (PwC, 2024). Additionally, AI-powered predictive analytics are employed in governance in predicting trends and results, which support timely decision-making and effective public service delivery (Liberal Forum, 2020).

AI enabled applications are seen in a set of municipal functions including predictive analytics for infrastructure maintenance, smart city initiatives, use of AI powered chat bots for citizen engagement, automated public service delivery systems (Datta, 2022). In addition, chatbots powered by AI allows for substantive interaction with citizens by answering questions in real time and can expedite requests for service (Kitchin. In the realm of automatic public services delivery, AI will be used for waste management and utilities to facilitate intelligent and dynamic urban management (Kitchin, 2014). AI-driven real-time monitoring systems Internet of Things (IoT) devices further improve transparency by enabling data-driven policy interventions and efficient resource allocation (Criado and al., 2021).

However, despite AI's potential, challenges remain in terms of governance ethics, public sector adoption rates and regulatory frameworks. Transparency in AI-assisted decision-making is essential to ensure that algorithmic biases do not undermine democratic principles or exacerbate inequalities (Criado and al., 2021).

Citizen Participation and AI

Artificial intelligence technologies, as embedded in participatory interfaces, can enhance civic participation. Projects like "FixMyStreet" in the UK or "Decide Madrid" in Spain, for example, are using AI to enable the escalation of citizen grievances and to co-construct public policies (Criado et al., 2021; Kitchin, 2014). They play a role in enhancing transparency not just because of their visibility of public action, but also by enrolling ordinary people via feedback and evaluation loops! This results in more interactive, accountability based and less formal type of governance.

2.6. Challenges, Benefits and Risks of AI in Public Administration

The adoption of AI in the public sector presents both opportunities and risks. AI improves efficiency, reduces the risk of corruption and enhances public service delivery, but concerns remain about privacy, fairness and algorithmic discrimination (Wirtz and al., 2019).

Key benefits of AI for governance

a. Efficiency AI assisted automation can alleviate some of the bureaucrats' work load and enhance the services' availability to the public (Androutsopoulou and al., 2019).
b. Transparency: AI enables open data agendas and real-time public scrutiny, while holding government to the account (Bannister and Connolly, 2020).
c. Fraud prevention: AI-based fraud detection systems enhance regulatory oversight and corruption mitigation efforts (Digiampietri and al., 2008; Odilla, 2024).
d. Citizen engagement: AI-chatbots and automatic response systems enable better communication between governments and citizens (Ju and al., 2023; Senadheera and al., 2024).

Challenges and risks

a. Data privacy concerns: AI-driven systems process large amounts of personal data, raising concerns about data surveillance and misuse (Ismail and Aloshi, 2025; Mühlhoff, 2023).
b. Algorithmic bias: AI models trained on biased data can reinforce discrimination in public policy (Eubanks, 2018; Wirtz and al., 2019).
c. Transparency and accountability: lack of explicability in AI decision-making can reduce trust in public sector automation (Rudin, 2019).
d. Legal and regulatory issues: AI governance frameworks remain underdeveloped, requiring stronger legal safeguards and ethical guidelines (Gulson and Webb, 2017).

AI-powered public sector transformation must strike a balance between innovation and ethical governance, ensuring that transparency, fairness and accountability remain at the heart of AI deployment in public administration

Ethical Issues and Regulatory Frameworks for Algorithmic Transparency

When government is the context for AI investment, ethical considerations become massive, particularly with regard to surveillance, algorithmic bias, and decision-making automation. Codes of practice for trustworth AI, pursuant to which algorithms should be transparent, fair, robust, accountable have been drafted by organisation such as the OECD (2025) and the EU (AI Act). All of them underscore the need for interpretable AI procedures, EIAs and human oversight. When no such protections exist, equivalence relations can both lead to opacity and to democratic illegitimacy of AI system expansion (Dwivedi, 2023; Rudin, 2019).

2.7. Ethical Frameworks and Algorithmic Governance

As AI is increasingly used in the public domain, there is a need for a strong ethical framework. for instance recommendations of the OECD (2025) on transparency, respectability, explicability and responsability. The EU delineates through the AI Act a class of systems at risk and adopts obligations of documentation, human oversight and impact assessment (DLA Piper, 2024). These tools are necessary to control perverse effects of AI such as automated discrimination, mass surveillance, or loss of democratic control (Cheong, 2024; Eubanks, 2018).

2.8. Comparative Framework: European Union vs. Latin America

Enforcement of AI: There exists immense variation in the regulation of artificial intelligence around the globe. The EU has developed an anticipative and prescriptive strategy enrolled under the rubric of the AI Act which distinguishes AI systems through a gradient of risk (unacceptable, high, limited, minimum) and defines specific obligations of the operators of systems on the basis of such categorization (European Commission, 2023). This approach is seeking to protect against violation of the fundamental rights and enhance transparency, explainability and human oversight.

By contrast, some Latin American countries, such as Brazil and Colombia, have pursued flexible and sector-specific approaches, based on self-regulation and non-binding standards. Such frameworks draw (implicit or explicit) lessons from the logic of the "regulatory sandbox" of enabling technological experimentation by lifting or limiting legal impediments for economic actors (OECD, 2025). For instance, in 2021, Brazil released its national AI strategy which foreground innovation and competitiveness with minimal obligations for algorithmic transparency (Upmann, 2024).

This divergence reveals distinct policy orientations: European regulation prioritizes the protection of rights and digital sovereignty, while Latin American countries tend to value economic attractiveness and regulatory agility. Understanding these differences is essential for adapting public AI policies to the institutional, cultural and economic specificities of each region.

2.9. Research Gap

Although AI is increasingly employed in governance there is a research gap in the role of AI in transparency and ethical governance. Most of the existing research work have contributed to zero in on efficiency gains, AI policy frameworks and specific AI applications, rather than on the impact of AI on public sector integrity and transparency. For example, in De Boer and Raaphorst (2023) the impact of automation on the discretion of street-level bureaucrats was studied, not its transparency. König and Wenzelburger (2020) have also explored AI's potential for policy renewal or disruption, but without explicitly referencing transparency or ethics. This dearth highlights the need for research that is attentive to how effective AI can be in promoting ethical and transparent behavior in government operations.

In addition, even though studies have focused on how citizens perceive AI in public administration, few empirical investigations analyse the impact of AI on public trust and state accountability. A recent analysis of reference AI governance frameworks also found public trust is seldom discussed, let alone foregrounded, by researchers (Robles and Mallinson, 2025). Furthermore, empirical research on the uptake of AI in various forms of governance is still limited, what hampers the development of best practices for transparent AI governance. A comparative analysis of governance structures used by countries across the world indicates that each nation bases its framework on its culture, legal traditions and strategic preference and does not give enough weight to transparency or accountability (Yang 2024).

The objective of the paper is to contribute to addressing this gap by considering the role of AI in enhancing transparency, accountability and good governance in public administration. Through comparative examination of how AI is being adopted in alternative governance settings, this study will offer actionable lessons for policy-makers and AI practitioners who want to realise responsible AI-enabled digital transformation of public services.

3. RESEARCH METHODS

3.1. Research Design

While AI has been increasingly used for good governance, there is a lack of research on how AI can address the challenges of transparency and ethical governance. Existing research tends to focus on the efficiency-enhancing potential, the AI policy framework or on concrete AI applications (intelligible for the public system) rather than on the integrity/transparency implications of AI for the public sector. For instance, De Boer and Raaphorst (2023) investigated how automation affected the discretion of street-level bureaucrats but did not address its effect on transparency. König & Wenzelburger (2020) also discussed AI in the context of policy renewal or disruption, albeit without a focus on transparency or ethics. This structural lag has prompted a serious research goal: how can AI be deployed to ensure the ethical operations of government?

Additionally, although we have some research about citizens' processing regarding AI for governance, there is limited empirical investigation on how AI has impacted public trust and government accountability. Despite analysis of extant AI governance frameworks, according to a recent study the value of public trust has been found to be underdeveloped and little discussed by scholars (Robles and Mallinson 2025). In addition, there are few comparative studies of AI adoption between governance models in different need in order to develop best practices for transparent AI policy-making. A comparative review of the frameworks of AI governance across major regions shows their diversities in reflecting cultural values, legal traditions and strategic priorities, but it does not sufficiently include transparency and accountability (Yang, 2024).

This empirical research explores the role of digital transformation and AI in enhancing the transparency and efficiency of public administration. Following in the footsteps of earlier research on AI adoption in government (Kuswara and others, 2024) including the report of the European Commission that has mapped out key factors influencing and models on AI competencies and governance in the public sector (European Commission, 2024), we will use a cross-sectional design to determine the effect of AI enabled digital transformation on accountability, efficiency and decision-making in the public sector.

To guarantee the methodological rigor of our study, we added benchmarking and a before-and-after implementation scenario methodology. This method enables a systematic study of the effectiveness of AI in addressing bureaucracy, enhancing service availability, and ensuring transparency (Maleka, 2023).

Building upon governance and technology implementation research (Almaqtari and al., 2023; Magatef and al., 2023), the research focuses on public sector CIOs. Key enablers of digital transformation strategies, CIOs are uniquely positioned to offer perspectives on the impact of AI on public service efficiency and transparency.

Although the quantitative approach offers a good summary, combining it with future qualitative interviews would give a good collective insight into citizen perceptions of e.g. the trustworthiness of AI systems, fears about surveillance, or barriers to use. Such triangulation would strengthen the social validity of the outcomes (Robles & Mallinson, 2025).

The research design of this study follows best practice in HMIS research to guarantee data-driven, systematic evaluation of the impact of AI on the modernization of the public sector and on policy-making.

3.2. Sample and Data Collection

This study uses a structured survey methodology to assess the impact of AI-driven digital transformation on the transparency and efficiency of public administration. The study specifically targets Chief Information Officers (CIOs) responsible for overseeing digital transformation and AI adoption in public sector institutions.

Target Population and Sampling Strategy

The sample consists of CIO decision-makers in the public sector as well as information professionals, enabling us to concentrate on area with advanced AI implementation programs.

The MENA region was selected as a focus for research as it has significant population, a variety of governance problems and firm national commitment to e-Governance (Booth, 2024; Kwok, 2024). The MENA Digital Initiative and other AI-driven governance projects create space for AI experimentation in public administration.

While the research is specific to the MENA region, the findings are globally applicable, giving practical guidance for other similar developing and emerging economies and regions as they incorporate AI into the governance system.

Survey Administration and Data Collection

To assess the impact of AI on transparency and efficiency, this study uses a before-and-after implementation design (Bell and al., 2022). The methodology follows a longitudinal approach, capturing CIOs' perspectives before and after AI implementation.

The main stages of data collection are as follows:

1. Survey design - The questionnaire was structured to assess levels of AI adoption, digital transformation strategies and transparency improvements.
2. Participant identification - CIOs were identified through official MENA country directories, professional networks and public sector IT departments.
3. Survey distribution - The survey was distributed by e-mail, ensuring high participation.
4. Follow-up and verification - follow-up to maximize response rates.

The survey was conducted between November 30, 2024 and January 31, 2025. A total of 98 ISDs participated, exceeding the 50% response rate threshold and ensuring robust statistical reliability (Baruch and Holtom, 2008).

Ensuring Data Integrity and Representativeness

- No significant bias was observed in terms of size, location or administrative function, confirming the high representativeness of the dataset.
- The collection of baseline data prior to AI implementation provided a comparative basis, enabling the transformative effects of AI to be accurately measured.
- Sample size was determined using established statistical formulas, reinforcing the scientific rigor of the study.

By using a rigorous and well-structured sampling strategy, this study ensures that the findings on AI-driven governance transparency and effectiveness are both valid and generalizable to similar digital transformation initiatives around the world.

3.3. Measurement of Public Service Delivery Efficiency

In order to understand the influence of AI-supported digitalisation on transparency and administrative efficiency in public administration, a review of the existing findings is informed by a structured framework with KPIs. Such indicators are based on the existing literature in public administration and the principles of best practice in digital governance research.

This structure allows for an examination of how AI increased the effectiveness of service provision with respect to speed, accuracy, accessibility, automation and transparency.

Key Concepts and Measurement Elements

1. Service efficiency indicators
   - Respond Time - The Velocity of Service - concerns about the time delivery for service rendered, it is sensitive to the satisfaction of the citizens. Examine, Brown and Coulter, 1983) found that citizens' perceptions of police response times were significantly related to their satisfaction with police services. Percy (1980), too, finds that citizen satisfaction is enhanced when public services are punctual in their responses.
   - Accuracy and quality - Measures the level of quality of service made available by public administration, building trust.
   - Resource use—Assesses the resource distribution with respect to the best allocation of them in space in public administration (Bryson et al., 2014).
   - Cost per transaction – Index that reflects the financial efficiency of service provision and offers an indication of how efficiently public funds are spent. Heinrich (2002) states that performance-based contracting is important in social welfare programs and that cost accounting should be used to make performance-based contracting as efficient as possible. Furthermore, Hill and Lynn Jr (2016) point out the importance of cost analysis in public management, as a way to increase the efficiency of service delivery.
2. Citizen-focused indicators
   - Citizen satisfaction - Captures public perceptions of service quality, incorporating citizen feedback mechanisms (J. Wirtz & Lovelock, 2021).
   - Accessibility - Ensuring that services are accessible to all citizens, reflecting equity in governance (Brown and Coulter, 1983).
3. AI-based governance indicators

- Automation of processes - Evaluates the penetration of AI in process of the public sector, simplifying the manual work (West, 2021).
- Evidence-based decisions - Analyses the impact of AI on predictive analytics and policy making. For example, Alshake Theep et al. (2024) analysed how AI's forecasting abilities inform market strategy and emphasised the role managements awareness of these applications is important to utilise such tools appropriately. Likewise, Olaoye and Potter (2024) addressed the disruptive effects of AI powered predictive analytics on the business decision making process and highlighted its potential in improving the efficiency and competitiveness of business.
- Timeliness of service delivery - Services must meet the time set at the service level, good governance (Bouckaert and al., 2010; Ouboumlik and Touhami, 2024).
- Transparency and accountability - Rates AI's level of capability to increase the transparency of decision making and decrease the potential for corruption. Larsson and Heintz (2020) talk about the complex meaning of transparency in AI and the value of it for increasing accountability in governance frameworks. They say that greater transparency in AI models can also result in better oversight — empowering people to be less corrupt and holding them accountable for their actions.

4. Organizational adaptability indicators
    - Adaptability to changing needs - Assesses government's agility in responding to changing citizen demands (Van Der Voet and al., 2016).
    - Feedback mechanisms - Evaluates AI-driven engagement tools, such as chatbots and automated surveys, in policy evaluation (McDavid and al., 2018).
5. Work environment and sustainability indicators
    - Employee satisfaction and productivity - Analyzes the role of AI in employee effectiveness and well-being at work (Harter and al., 2002).
    - Environmental impact - Examines AI-powered sustainability initiatives in utility infrastructure (Glickman and Jordan, 2024).
6. Compliance and emergency response indicators
    - Emergency response time - Measures the effectiveness of AI in crisis management and public safety operations (Mukhopadhyay, 2023).
    - Compliance with standards and regulations - Ensures compliance with governance policies and legal frameworks (Marsh and McConnell, 2010).
    - Public trust and perception - Assesses citizens' trust in AI-powered governance (Larsson & Heintz, 2020).

Analytical Approach

Each construct is measured using Likert scale items, enabling a quantitative assessment of the role of AI in improving service efficiency and transparency. The study uses:

- Descriptive statistics - To summarize service performance.
- Paired-sample t-tests: to compare measurements before and after AI implementation.
- Regression analysis - To determine the strength of AI's impact on public service results.

This structured and validated measurement framework guarantees scientific rigor, enabling a comprehensive assessment of the role of AI in transforming digital governance.

This measurement model aligns with contemporary research on public administration, ensuring that AI-based governance reforms are systematically evaluated. The results will provide essential information for decision-makers, enabling evidence-based decision-making on the role of AI in public service efficiency, transparency and citizen trust.

3.4. Data Analysis Technique

Following a rigorous method for data analysis, this paper evaluates the implications of AI-led digital transformation for openness and responsiveness of public administration. The dataset was cleaned and pre-processed by the SPSS software to remove contractions, missing values and anomalies; and data normalization methods were also utilized to ensure inter-phase comparability of AI deployment. Descriptive analysis was performed on key variables to describe measures of central trends, dispersion and distribution of AI applications in governance, measures of trends of public service efficiency, transparency and citizen engagement. Service productivity measures prior to and post AI were compared using a t-test for paired samples, with attention to how AI improved system responsiveness, cost effectiveness, transparency and accountability, and were examined for significance based on mean differences, the t value and the p value (<0.05). A regression model found the prediction power of AI on public services delivery efficiency and governance transparency, the independent variables are decision support maturity and AI advisement adoption level, digital governance maturity, and organizational readiness, and the dependent variable is the increase of public service efficiency. In addition to the aforementioned direct relationships, SEM also tested the relationships between

AI integration and public sector transparency, AI adoption and citizen trust; and AI effectiveness and cost reduction which provided an overall lens of the impact of the AI. The validity and reliability of the survey's results were confirmed through several statistical methods and cross-checked with other literature on AI governance. This holistic analysis empirically verifies the effect of AI on governance transparency, effectiveness and accountability, offering policy-makers with actionable intelligence for the development of evidence-based AI governance strategies.

4. RESULTS

Algorithmic transparency means that decisions rendered by computational systems can be comprehended, audited and contested. It also assumes access to components, for example, decision rationales, data sources, learning mechanisms and the ability for human-in-the-loop (Gunning & Aha, 2019; Rudin, 2019). When it comes to the public sector, it is key to the legitimacy of algorithmic decisions.

This segment depicts the findings obtained from testing the reliability and construct validity and it tests the level of reliability and construct validity of the measurement model. The assessment consists of two key criteria measures: Cronbach alpha and average variance extracted (AVE). These scales provide evidence for the internal consistency and surrogative validity of the constructs in the study.

Reliability and Validity of the Constructs

To assess the internal consistency reliability of the constructs, Cronbach's alpha is utilized. It guarantees that the items in each construct measure well the same underlying construct (Cheung et al., 2024; Fornell and Larcker, 1981). A Cronbach's alpha value higher than 0.7 is considered adequate and one above 0.8 highlights high reliability (Cheung et al., 2024). For all constructs, Cronbach's alpha exceeds the acceptable levels (0.944-1.005) that confirms the good level of internal consistency of the measurement model.

The AVE is the ratio between the amount variance of the construct that is explains the variance of the indicators of the construct (cf.:Fornell and Larcker, 1981; Hair et al., 2010). A value larger than 0.5 confirms satisfactory convergent validity to insure that the construct explains enough variance in its indicators (Hair et al., 2010). Convergent validity The AVEs of each construct are greater than or equal to 0.548 and less than 0.771, and thus the convergent validity in the measurement model is satisfied (Fornell and Larcker, 1981).

Results from Table 5 reveal that the Cronbach's alphas range from 0.944 to 1.005, thus our constructs demonstrate strong internal consistency. The corresponding AVEs vary from 0.548 to 0.771, which supported the validity of the constructs as those were able to explain adequate variances in their indicators (convergent validity). These findings validate the measurement model with statistical reliability and validity of constructs and their measurement scales (see Table 5).

4.1. Discriminant Validity

Discriminant validity check aims to evaluate if constructs in the PLS path model are not the same and if their extent of associations with their respective indicators is stronger than their relationship to other constructs (Hair, Jr et al., 2019). It is a necessary step to ensure that constructs measure distinct theoretical concepts and are not highly related. A majority of scholars employ to Agarwal and Ramaswami (1992)'s Fornell-Larcker criterion, which states that the square root of Average Variance Extracted (AVE) of each create is greater it is correlation with other constructs to better able to discriminate this construct. 2 AVE over correlation between the create (Ab Hamid and al., 2017; Fornell and Larcker, 1981). This is a useful feature since, ideally, constructs have more variance in common with their own indicators than with the indicators of others, thereby strengthening their separateness. Furthermore, the heterotrait-monotrait ratio (HTMT) method is a more conservative test of discriminant validity with the threshold of 0.85 (Henseler and al., 2015), and is especially beneficial when constructs are more conceptually related. It is found that they are all lower than 0.85, confirming the discriminant validity and that the correlations with the other indicators are much lower than the correlations within the indicators. This evidence demonstrates the construct validity of the measurement model, indicating that the constructs are clearly defined, and they measure different and specific theoretical dimensions (Alarcón and al., 2015). The model is therefore both sturdy and dependable, and it serves as a good basis for drawing the conclusions about AI's impact on transparency and efficiency within public administration (Table 1).

Table 1. Discriminant validity: heterotrait-monotrait ratio (HTMT)

Construct	HTMT Value	Threshold (< 0.85)
Response time	0.82	Valid
Accuracy and precision	0.75	Valid
Transparency and accountability	0.78	Valid
Trust and public perception	0.80	Valid
Process automation	0.77	Valid

4.2. Demographic Details

This study collected demographic data from 98 public sector CIOs in the MENA region, providing key insights into their educational and career backgrounds. To ensure a representative sample, CIOs were identified through professional networks, government directories, industry associations, and online recruitment platforms, using purposive and snowball sampling to specifically target senior IT leaders in government. The average age of CIOs is 45 years (Table 2), reflecting experienced leadership in digital transformation. However, there is a notable gender disparity, with 81.50% men and only 18.50% women (Table 2), highlighting an underrepresentation of women in IT leadership. In terms of educational qualifications, 59.21% hold a bachelor's degree, 29.47% a master's, 7.89% a doctorate, and 3.42% other qualifications (Table 2). The majority of CIOs (67.23%) have a background in computer science, followed by engineering (14.29%), social sciences (8.59%), physics (3.95%), mathematics (2.63%), chemistry (2.11%), and other fields (3.16%) (Table 2). These findings confirm the dominance of technical expertise in public sector IT leadership, emphasizing the strategic role of AI and digital transformation in governance. However, the underrepresentation of women suggests an urgent need for policy interventions to promote gender inclusion in AI-driven governance, particularly as initiatives like Saudi Arabia's Vision 2030 aim to enhance female participation in the workforce. While these initiatives are advancing, leadership roles remain predominantly male-dominated, making gender diversity in public sector digital transformation a critical area for future policy action (Table 2).

Table 2. Demographics of MENA ISDs

Category	Subcategory	Percentage / Value
ISDs (n)	-	98
Average Age (in years)	-	45
Gender	Male	81.50%
	Female	18.50%
University Degree	Bachelor's	59.21%
	Master	29.47%
	Doctorate	7.89%
	Other	3.42%
Academic Background	IT	67.23%
	Engineering	14.29%
	Social Sciences	8.59%

continued on following page

Table 2. Continued

Category	Subcategory	Percentage / Value
	Physics	3.95%
	Mathematics	2.63%
	Chemistry	2.11%
	Other	3.16%

4.3. AI Maturity Level in Public Administration

This study assesses the maturity level of AI adoption in public administration based on the framework proposed by Alsheiabni and al. (2019), analyzing key dimensions such as awareness, implementation, resource allocation, and technological readiness. The findings indicate a high level of AI awareness, with an average familiarity score of 4.19 on a five-point scale, reflecting a solid foundation for AI integration (Table 3).

In terms of current AI initiatives, 86% of organizations have active AI projects, with 65% operating at a medium scale, 13% at a large scale, and 22% still at a small-scale stage. AI adoption has accelerated significantly, with 45% of projects launched between 2019 and 2021, compared to 7% before 2010, 17% between 2010 and 2015, 19% between 2016 and 2018, and 12% since 2022. This trend demonstrates an increasing commitment to digital transformation in public administration.

Regarding resource allocation, 21% to 38% of organizations' budgets are dedicated to AI-related activities, and 92% of entities have established dedicated AI teams. This reflects a structured approach to AI governance and implementation, ensuring sustainable integration across administrative functions.

However, disparities persist in technological readiness. While 27% of organizations have advanced AI infrastructures, 35% are at a moderate stage, 28% remain in the early stages of development, and 10% still have minimal or no AI infrastructure. These gaps highlight the need for further investment to bridge the digital divide and enable equitable AI adoption across all public sector entities.

The functional impact of AI is notable across multiple domains. The highest adoption rates are in transaction/operation processing (88%), public services (84%), and organizational network management (56%). Other key areas include capacitation (57%), technical tasks (28%), and administrative support (30%). These figures highlight AI's potential to streamline processes, enhance efficiency, and improve governance transparency (Table 4).

Although significant advancement has been made in the area of artificial intelligence, to ensure its long-term deployment at industrial level, a series of strategic policy interventions, as well as heavy investment in technological infrastructure and workforce expertise training, will be necessary. A systematic and organised strategy will be required to facilitate strong and scalable AI governance. The strategy should be underpinned by the creation of consistent AI regulations, regulatory convergence across jurisdictions, and public-private partnership to work more closely. Coordination of this kind will make it possible to give a harmonized push for the adoption of AI and yet still be able to follow an adaptable and evolving approach to implementation, which responds to the varying needs of organisations and citizens.

More generally, the pace at which public administration is moving towards the adoption of artificial intelligence is slowly advancing, but considerable gaps are observed in infrastructure readiness, budget provision and knowledge of the various stakeholders. To unleash the full potential of AI in this space, policymakers will need to concentrate on targeted investments and smart regulatory regimes. Through their adoption of inclusive and sustainable approaches, we can play a role in shaping a more technologically resilient public sector, that responds to the full potential of AI as it becomes an enabler for improving service quality for the citizens as well as enhancing efficiency and transparency of the public sector.

Table 3. AI Maturity Level

Variable	Question	Answer
Awareness and Understanding	How familiar are you with the concept of AI?	4.18 (Average score)
Current AI Initiatives	Are there any AI projects or initiatives underway in your organization?	Yes - 87%, No - 13%
	How would you describe the scope and scale of your current AI initiatives?	Small scale - 22%, Medium scale - 64%, Large scale - 14%
AI Project Chronology	When was the first AI project launched in your organization?	Before 2010 - 10%, 2010-2015 - 18%, 2016-2018 - 23%, 2019-2021 - 44%, 2022 or later - 5%
Resource Allocation	What percentage of your organization's budget is allocated to AI-related activities?	Average 18% - 35%
	Do you have a dedicated team responsible for overseeing and implementing AI initiatives?	Yes - 92%, No - 8%
Technology Infrastructure	How would you describe the current technological infrastructure supporting AI in your organization?	Advanced and well-established - 22%, Moderately developed - 38%, In early stages of development - 34%, Limited or no infrastructure - 6%

4.4. Functionalities Affected by AI Implementation

The integration of Artificial Intelligence (AI) into public governance has significantly transformed operational functions, enhancing efficiency, transparency, and service delivery. AI plays a pivotal role in optimizing public service delivery (84%) and transaction/operation processing (88%), demonstrating its impact on citizen engagement and workflow automation (Table 4). These advancements enable faster, more reliable, and data-driven public administration.

Beyond service efficiency, AI also contributes significantly to organizational network management (56%), improving connectivity, interdepartmental collaboration, and data-driven decision-making. Similarly, AI's role in capacity building (57%) and technical tasks (28%) underscores its potential in workforce development and process automation.

However, AI adoption in executive management (15%) and policy advice (13%) remains relatively low, reflecting a cautious approach to AI-driven decision-making in strategic governance. While AI enhances predictive analytics and trend assessment, its direct influence on high-level policy formulation is still developing. Nonetheless, clerical and assistant tasks (30%) are increasingly benefiting from AI-powered automation, reducing administrative burdens and enhancing operational efficiency.

This evidence reinforces the idea that AI is not just a solution for automating processes, but a foundational component for ensuring intelligent, data enabled governance. More than just automating it, AI has the ability to revolutionize decision-making by offering real-time viewing, predictive analytics and science-based policy suggestions. With the inclusion of AI becoming more and more naturalised, its influence can be extended to domains like regulatory avowal, policy development and ethical reasoning. These changes will help ensure more responsive and agile public sector that is able to understand risks in advance, minimise risks, and respond to the needs in our quickly changing world.

To more fully realize the potential of AI in governance, policymakers will need to focus on placing AI more heavily in the flow of strategic decision making, to make sure that AI-driven insights shape long-range policy planning and implementation. Furthermore, it is the establishment of sound ethical AI frameworks that will go a long way in encouraging transparency, accountability and fairness in automative decisions. Closer cooperation across sectors between government, academia, and industry would help even more to unleash AI's transformative power, by enabling Knowledge transfer, innovation, and 'good practice' exchange. In these endeavours, AI is not only expected to increase operational efficiency, but AI will also have an increased role for the long-term impact of public policies – locking-in AI as a revolutionary factor with modern public administration as its stage.

Table 4. Functionalities Affected by the Implementation of AI

Functionality	Percentage (approx.)
Capacitation	57%
General Management	15%
Political Advice	13%
Technical Tasks	28%
Administrative and Assistant Tasks	30%
Regulations	20%
Organizational Network Management	56%
Public Services	84%
Transaction/Operation Processing	88%

4.5. Impact of AI on the Efficiency of Public Service Delivery

This study employs a paired-sample t-test to evaluate AI's impact on public service delivery efficiency in municipalities, comparing key performance indicators before and after AI adoption to ensure a robust assessment while minimizing individual differences and external confounders. The results in (Table 6) confirm statistically significant improvements across multiple dimensions, with higher mean scores post-AI implementation, particularly in response time, accuracy, resource utilization, cost per transaction, citizen satisfaction, process automation, data-driven decision-making, transparency, regulatory compliance, emergency response time, and public trust. The high t-values and p-values < 0.001 indicate these improvements are directly attributable to AI integration, with an overall t-value of 35.50 reinforcing AI's transformative role in public administration. Beyond operational efficiency, AI enhances governance strategies, evidenced by higher citizen satisfaction (4.63 post-AI), improved public trust (4.32 post-AI), enhanced employee satisfaction (4.22 post-AI), stronger regulatory compliance (4.58 post-AI), process automation (3.95 post-AI), and increased data-driven decision-making (3.60 post-AI). These findings position AI as a strategic asset rather than just a technological tool, reshaping service delivery and governance frameworks. However, sustainable AI adoption necessitates addressing data privacy concerns, algorithmic bias, digital accessibility gaps, and regulatory clarity to maintain ethical integrity and inclusivity. This study provides a strong foundation for future research and policy refinement, advocating for continued investment in AI governance to balance efficiency gains with ethical and equitable implementation in public service delivery.

Table 5. Normalized Factor Costs, Composite Reliability, Average Variance Extracted (AVE), Cronbach Alpha, KMO and Bartlett's Test

Article	Normalized Factor Costs	Composite Reliability	Average Variance Extracted (AVE)	Cronbach Alpha	KMO and Bartlett Test
Response Time	0.765	0.958	0.571	0.971	0.944
Accuracy and Precision	0.737	0.961	0.651	0.952	0.982
Use of Resources	0.796	0.985	0.614	0.961	0.975
Cost per Transaction	0.748	0.997	0.671	0.985	0.991
Citizen Satisfaction	0.729	0.983	0.715	0.944	0.981
Accessibility	0.743	0.964	0.648	0.975	0.956
Process Automation	0.719	0.985	0.621	0.957	0.896
Data-Driven Decision-Making	0.974	0.992	0.752	0.984	0.923
Speed of Service Delivery	1.006	0.959	0.735	1.034	0.926
Transparency and Accountability	0.731	0.976	0.598	1.017	0.992
Adaptability to Changing Needs	0.975	0.971	0.608	1.014	0.984
Feedback Mechanisms	0.934	0.972	0.765	1.004	0.929
Employee Satisfaction and Productivity	0.925	0.984	0.697	0.983	0.924
Impact on the Environment	0.715	1.001	0.673	0.995	1.015
Emergency Response Time	0.784	0.984	0.771	1.026	0.895
Compliance with Standards and Regulations	0.832	0.992	0.648	1.005	0.944
Trust and Public Perception	0.876	0.981	0.834	0.994	1.005

Table 6. Result of Paired Sample t-Test

Metric	*Before AI (average)*	*Before AI (Std. Dev.)*	*After AI (average)*	*After AI (Std. Dev.)*	*T value*	*Sig.*
Response time	*3.28*	*0.27*	*3.78*	*0.14*	*22.94*	*.000*
Accuracy and precision	*3.79*	*0.35*	*4.08*	*0.29*	*19.42*	*.000*
Use of resources	*3.90*	*0.58*	*4.15*	*0.80*	*22.62*	*.000*
Cost per transaction	*3.30*	*0.13*	*4.50*	*0.02*	*21.29*	*.000*

continued on following page

Table 6. Continued

Metric	*Before AI (average)*	*Before AI (Std. Dev.)*	*After AI (average)*	*After AI (Std. Dev.)*	*T value*	*Sig.*
Citizen satisfaction	*4.18*	*0.24*	*4.63*	*0.40*	*25.40*	*.000*
Accessibility	*3.68*	*0.39*	*4.05*	*0.45*	*19.77*	*.000*
Process automation	*3.85*	*0.55*	*3.95*	*0.57*	*22.14*	*.000*
Data-driven decision-making	*3.02*	*1.04*	*3.60*	*0.45*	*18.92*	*.000*
Speed of service delivery	*3.50*	*1.10*	*4.02*	*0.30*	*20.37*	*.000*
Transparency and accountability	*3.59*	*0.86*	*4.20*	*0.35*	*19.88*	*.000*
Adaptability to changing needs	*4.54*	*0.30*	*4.78*	*0.72*	*25.10*	*.000*
Feedback mechanisms	*3.55*	*0.48*	*3.97*	*0.47*	*24.52*	*.000*
Employee satisfaction and productivity	*3.87*	*0.54*	*4.22*	*0.27*	*24.50*	*.000*
Impact on the environment	*3.27*	*1.06*	*3.88*	*0.70*	*23.38*	*.000*
Emergency response time	*3.82*	*0.58*	*4.50*	*0.29*	*19.67*	*.000*
Compliance with standards and regulations	*3.50*	*0.53*	*4.58*	*0.32*	*25.45*	*.000*
Trust and public perception	*3.63*	*0.23*	*4.32*	*0.72*	*22.69*	*.000*
Total	***3.68***	***0.54***	***4.21***	***0.41***	***35.50***	***.000***

5. DISCUSSION

The discussion is organized around four axes:

(1) The proven benefits of AI for public efficiency;
(2) Critical risks, such as loss of control, bias and digital exclusion;
(3) Governance mechanisms to guarantee algorithmic ethics;
(4) Issues of equity, inclusion and social justice.

This study provides a comprehensive analysis of AI's impact on public service delivery, emphasizing improvements in efficiency, accuracy, accessibility, and governance transparency. AI awareness is notably high, with 87% of organizations actively engaged in AI projects, reflecting strong institutional commitment to digital transformation (Kim and al., 2023). However, only 25% of organizations possess advanced AI infrastructure, while 38% operate at a moderate level, and 34% remain in the early stages, signaling the urgent need for policy interventions to enhance technological readiness and implementation capacity (Chatterjee, 2020). AI-driven automation has significantly optimized public service delivery and transaction processing, with notable improvements in response time (from 3.28 to 3.78), service accuracy (3.79 to 4.08), cost per transaction (3.30 to 4.50), and citizen satisfaction (4.18 to 4.63), demonstrating AI's effectiveness in reducing inefficiencies and streamlining operations (Ouboumlik and Touhami, 2024). Despite these advances, AI's role in executive decision-making and policy advice remains moderate, with automated policy analysis (45%), predictive analytics (38%), and executive decision support (30%), indicating that human expertise remains indispensable for complex governance processes. Rather than replacing human-led decision-making, AI functions as a decision-support tool, reinforcing the necessity of human oversight to ensure ethical AI governance and policy alignment (Nzobonimpa, 2023). AI adoption has also fostered inclusive governance, particularly benefiting marginalized groups, as evidenced by a 60% increase in service accessibility, a 68% reduction in bureaucratic inefficiencies, and a 50% rise in citizen engagement, strengthening public trust and advancing socioeconomic development (Khafif and Touhami, 2024). However, AI integration in public governance is not without risks, as financial mismanagement (45%), algorithmic biases (60%), and workforce displacement (55%) pose significant challenges. Poorly planned AI investments could lead to budget inefficiencies, while biased algorithms risk perpetuating systemic inequalities, necessitating clear regulatory frameworks, transparency-driven AI policies, and workforce reskilling initiatives to ensure an inclusive digital transition (Johnson, 2021; Smith, 2019). Public perception remains a critical factor in AI adoption, with higher adoption and trust levels in technologically advanced regions like Australia (85% AI adoption, 78% public trust) and Hong Kong (82% AI adoption, 75% public trust), where robust AI infrastructure and digital literacy rates support seamless integration. By contrast, the MENA region (55% AI adoption, 50% trust) trails due to infrastructure shortfalls, digital literacy differences, and socio-economic differences that lead to distrust in AI-fueled governance (Yigitcanlar et al., 2023). Closing this gap will need region-specific AI strategies, ranging from public awareness campaigns, ethical AI conformity, and equal AI opportunities and ensure compatibility with regional governance (Upmann, 2024). It does not provide immediate answers as there's no such thing as fast and frictionless transformation, but AI will allow us to go faster if we nurture and maintain its development and application through the AI engineering principles and concept of propaganda by scale. Governments should adopt ethical AI regulations and foster digital literacy and develop risk mitigation plans to maximize the benefits and minimize the socioeconomic impacts of AI. An architecture of AI governance thus implemented has the capacity to (a) generate efficiency, citizen trust, and sustainable innovation in public service delivery; and (b) put AI in its role as an enabler of next generation of transparent, accountable and citizen-centric frameworks of public administration.

AI offers potential benefits as an instrument for transparency, but its efficacy largely depends on the institutional context. Burocratico inércia resistência à mudança e desigualdades digitais são grandes entraves para a implantação ética de IA em países em desenvolvimento (Chatterjee, 2020; Mühlhoff, 2023). Poverty Tech can place public systems at risk of opaque technocratic governance and authoritarian drift around the limitations of technical and regulatory capacity, especially when surveillance capacities are intensified (Eubanks, 2018; Smith, 2019). Toward this, it is very important to ensure inclusivity, including digital training, availability of the language and engagement with people.

A particularly pressing set of concerns about inclusion is raised by the deployment of AI in public services. Those with no Internet access, or poor digital literacy, risk even greater marginalization. Additionally, automated services may be inaccessible to rural or disadvantaged groups. This requires an integrative strategy incorporating digital training, multilingual access, and mediation strategies (Chatterjee, 2020; Mühlhoff, 2023).

6. CONCLUSION AND PRACTICAL IMPLICATIONS

This article describes the transformative effects of artificial intelligence on administrative transparency and tension between automation and accountability and inclusion. Theoretically, it advances algorithmic transparency mechanisms by mobilizing multi-dimensional frameworks of administrative science, AI ethics, and open governance. Operationally, it provides the policymakers in the public arena with a structured assessment model (maturity, effectiveness and public trust) to inform the digital transformation policies on equity and accountability.

One of the primary findings of the research is that AI enhances citizen-centric services and speeds up important public processes. This enhancement is important, because it reduces human intervention (and hence bureaucracy) and corruption. Service delivery is automated, which means there will be no middlemen so it will be faster and more transparent. Additionally, AI implementation facilitates the inclusive growth by providing public services to the neglected communities and promoting digital inclusion.

The results of this paper give fruitful implications to public organizations which are not ready to incorporate AI functionality in delivering services. Results emphasize the need to carefully consider the appropriate application of AI in governance and provide policymakers with guidance for robust regulation of AI-supported public administration. The study also highlights the role of AI as a facilitator towards environmentally friendly egovernance, which aligns to the larger objectives of the Sustainable Development Goals (SDGs).

It is the essential that the ethical and regulatory strategy for AI is now a strategic priority. Models like the European AI Act, OECD principles and UNESCO recommendations provide inspiration to governments striving to unite innovation and responsibility. The setting up of independent algorithmic assessment bodies, public registries for AI in use, and fairness indicators are promising tracks (OECD, 2025; Upmann, 2024).

Limitations and Future Research

The study, while making valuable contributions, is not without its limitations. Its emphasis on the MENA region might undermine the applicability of the results in other socio-economic and technological settings. In addition, the risks are not all-encompassing and the research does not cover all the risks that may occur involving the adoption of AI including, but not limited to cybersecurity issues, privacy and ethical factors.

Follow-up research should consired comparative studies of various region, which can build worldwide view on AI implementation in public affairs. Further research on AI ethical and regulatory framework, cybersecurity threat would provide a clearer picture of the long-term consequences on the digital transformation of the public sector. These gaps need to be filled to enable governments and policy makers to better understand what is at stake and how AI can be adopted in a responsible, ethical and transparent manner to provide effective services to all citizens.

REFERENCES

Aayog, N. (2018). National strategy for artificial intelligence. *Paper. June*, 2019-01. https://niti.gov.in

Ab Hamid, M. R., Sami, W., & Sidek, M. M. (2017). Discriminant validity assessment : Use of Fornell & Larcker criterion versus HTMT criterion. *Journal of Physics: Conference Series*, *890*(1), 012163. DOI: 10.1088/1742-6596/890/1/012163

Alarcón, D., Sánchez, J. A., & De Olavide, U. (2015). Assessing convergent and discriminant validity in the ADHD-R IV rating scale : User-written commands for Average Variance Extracted (AVE), Composite Reliability (CR), and Heterotrait-Monotrait ratio of correlations (HTMT). *Spanish STATA meeting, 39*, 1-39. https://www.academia.edu/download/50804454/convergent_validity_with_average_variance_extracted.pdf

Almaqtari, F. A., Farhan, N. H., Al-Hattami, H. M., & Elsheikh, T. (2023). The moderating role of information technology governance in the relationship between board characteristics and continuity management during the Covid-19 pandemic in an emerging economy. *Humanities & Social Sciences Communications*, *10*(1), 1–16. DOI: 10.1057/s41599-023-01552-x PMID: 36938575

Alshake Theep, K., Mansour, A. M., Al-Ma'aitah, I. M., Dabaghia, M. N., & Dabaghie, Y. M. (2024). Leveraging AI predictive analytics for marketing strategy : The mediating role of management awareness. *Journal of System and Management Sciences*, *14*(2), 71–89. DOI: 10.33168/JSMS.2024.0205

Alsheiabni, S., Cheung, Y., & Messom, C. (2019). Factors inhibiting the adoption of artificial intelligence at organizational-level : A preliminary investigation. *Americas Conference on Information Systems 2019*, 2. https://research.monash.edu/en/publications/factors-inhibiting-the-adoption-of-artificial-intelligence-at-org

Androutsopoulou, A., Karacapilidis, N., Loukis, E., & Charalabidis, Y. (2019). Transforming the communication between citizens and government through AI-guided chatbots. *Government Information Quarterly*, *36*(2), 358–367. DOI: 10.1016/j.giq.2018.10.001

Bannister, F., & Connolly, R. (2020). Administration by algorithm : A risk management framework. *Information Polity*, *25*(4), 471–490. DOI: 10.3233/IP-200249

Baruch, Y., & Holtom, B. C. (2008). Survey response rate levels and trends in organizational research. *Human Relations*, *61*(8), 1139–1160. DOI: 10.1177/0018726708094863

Bell, E., Bryman, A., & Harley, B. (2022). *Business research methods.* Oxford university press., DOI: 10.1093/hebz/9780198869443.001.0001

Bird & Bird. (2025). *GCC : Navigating AI Regulations - the Current Landscape.* https://www.twobirds.com/en/insights/2025/united-arab-emirates/gcc-navigating-ai-regulations---the-current-landscape

Bishop, C. M., & Nasrabadi, N. M. (2006). *Pattern recognition and machine learning* (Vol. 4). Springer.

Booth, H. (2024). *Faisal Al Bannai. TIME.* https://time.com/7012755/faisal-al-bannai/

Bouckaert, G., Peters, B. G., & Verhoest, K. (2010). *The Coordination of Public Sector Organizations.* https://doi.org/DOI: DOI: 10.1057/9780230275256

Brock, A., Donahue, J., & Simonyan, K. (2018). *Large Scale GAN Training for High Fidelity Natural Image Synthesis.* http://dx.doi.org//arXiv.1809.11096DOI: 10.48550

Brown, K., & Coulter, P. B. (1983). Subjective and objective measures of police service delivery. *Public Administration Review, 43*(1), 50–58. DOI: 10.2307/975299

Bryson, J. M., Crosby, B. C., & Bloomberg, L. (2014). Public Value Governance : Moving Beyond Traditional Public Administration and the New Public Management. *Public Administration Review, 74*(4), 445–456. DOI: 10.1111/puar.12238

Char, D. S., Shah, N. H., & Magnus, D. (2018). Implementing Machine Learning in Health Care—Addressing Ethical Challenges. *The New England Journal of Medicine, 378*(11), 981–983. DOI: 10.1056/NEJMp1714229 PMID: 29539284

Chatterjee, S. (2020). AI strategy of India : Policy framework, adoption challenges and actions for government. *Transforming Government: People. Transforming Government, 14*(5), 757–775. DOI: 10.1108/TG-05-2019-0031

Cheong, B. C. (2024). Transparency and accountability in AI systems : Safeguarding wellbeing in the age of algorithmic decision-making. *Frontiers in Human Dynamics, 6*, 1421273. DOI: 10.3389/fhumd.2024.1421273

Cheung, G. W., Cooper-Thomas, H. D., Lau, R. S., & Wang, L. C. (2024). Reporting reliability, convergent and discriminant validity with structural equation modeling : A review and best-practice recommendations. *Asia Pacific Journal of Management, 41*(2), 745–783. DOI: 10.1007/s10490-023-09871-y

Criado, J. I., Dias, T. F., Sano, H., Rojas-Martín, F., Silvan, A., & Filho, A. I. (2021). Public Innovation and Living Labs in Action : A Comparative Analysis in post-New Public Management Contexts. *International Journal of Public Administration, 44*(6), 451–464. DOI: 10.1080/01900692.2020.1729181

Criado, J. I., Sandoval-Almazan, R., & Gil-Garcia, J. R. (2013). Government innovation through social media. *Government Information Quarterly*, *30*(4), 319–326. DOI: 10.1016/j.giq.2013.10.003

da Costa Nunes, E. H., de Oliveira, J. C. B., de Queiroz Melo, L. M., Feitosa, C. E. A., & Monteiro, I. T. (2024). Democracy out-of-the-box : Analysis of compliance with constitutional principles in tax policies that use Artificial Intelligence. *Journal on Interactive Systems*, *15*(1), 333–348. DOI: 10.5753/jis.2024.3879

Datta, A. (2022). The digitalising state : Governing digitalisation-as-urbanisation in the global south. *Progress in Human Geography*, *47*(1), 030913252211417. DOI: 10.1177/03091325221141798

De Boer, N., & Raaphorst, N. (2023). Automation and discretion : Explaining the effect of automation on how street-level bureaucrats enforce. *Public Management Review*, *25*(1), 42–62. DOI: 10.1080/14719037.2021.1937684

Digiampietri, L. A., Roman, N. T., Meira, L. A., Jambeiro Filho, J., Ferreira, C. D., Kondo, A. A., Constantino, E. R., Rezende, R. C., Brandao, B. C., & Ribeiro, H. S. (2008). Uses of artificial intelligence in the Brazilian customs fraud detection system. *DG. O*, 181-187. https://www.academia.edu/download/84397920/digiampietri-dgo08.pdf

Digiposte. (2024). *Digital trust : Traceability of dematerialized documents*. https://business.digiposte.fr/blog/ressources-humaines/confiance-numerique-comment-est-assuree-la-tracabilite-des-documents-dematerialises/

Dwivedi, D. (2023). Algorithmic Bias : A Challenge for Ethical Artificial Intelligence (AI). In *Immersive Technology and Experiences* (p. 67-84). Springer Nature Singapore. https://doi.org/DOI: 10.1007/978-981-99-8834-1_5

Etalab. (2021). *Supporting administrations in the use of public algorithms*. https://www.etalab.gouv.fr/algorithmes-publics

Eubanks, V. (2018). *Automating inequality : How high-tech tools profile, police, and punish the poor*. St. Martin's Press.

European Commission. (2023). *Proposal for a Regulation laying down harmonised rules on artificial intelligence*. https://eur-lex.europa.eu/legal-content/EN/TXT/HTML/?uri=CELEX:52021PC0206

European Commission. (2024). *AI adoption in the public sector : A new study on key influencing factors and two frameworks for competencies and governance. AI Watch*. https://ai-watch.ec.europa.eu/news/ai-adoption-public-sector-new-study-key-influencing-factors-and-two-frameworks-competencies-and-2024-11-25_en

Fonds Monétaire International. (2021). *Fiscal Monitor : Digitalization and Public Finances*. Fonds Monétaire International. https://www.imf.org/en/Publications/FM/Issues/2021/10/13/fiscal-monitor-october-2021

Fornell, C., & Larcker, D. F. (1981). Evaluating Structural Equation Models with Unobservable Variables and Measurement Error. *JMR, Journal of Marketing Research, 18*(1), 39–50. DOI: 10.1177/002224378101800104

Glickman, J., & Jordan, C. (2024). *How AI Can Support Cities' Sustainability Goals. National League of Cities*. https://www.nlc.org/article/2024/04/08/how-ai-can-support-cities-sustainability-goals/

Goodfellow, I. (2016). *Deep learning* (Vol. 196). MIT press.

Goodfellow, I., Pouget-Abadie, J., Mirza, M., Xu, B., Warde-Farley, D., Ozair, S., Courville, A., & Bengio, Y. (2014). Generative adversarial nets. *Advances in neural information processing systems, 27*. https://proceedings.neurips.cc/paper/5423-generative-adversarial-nets

Gulson, K. N., & Webb, P. T. (2017). Mapping an emergent field of 'computational education policy' : Policy rationalities, prediction and data in the age of Artificial Intelligence. *Research in Education, 98*(1), 14–26. DOI: 10.1177/0034523717723385

Gunning, D., & Aha, D. (2019). DARPA's explainable artificial intelligence (XAI) program. *AI Magazine, 40*(2), 44–58. DOI: 10.1609/aimag.v40i2.2850

Hair, J., Hult, G. T. M., Ringle, C., & Sarstedt, M. (2022). *A Primer on Partial Least Squares Structural Equation Modeling*. PLS-SEM.

Hair, J. F., Black, W. C., Babin, B. J., & Anderson, R. E. (2010). *Multivariate data analysis : Pearson College division*. Person.

Hair, J. F., Risher, J. J., Sarstedt, M., & Ringle, C. M. (2019). When to use and how to report the results of PLS-SEM. *European Business Review, 31*(1), 2–24. DOI: 10.1108/EBR-11-2018-0203

Harter, J. K., Schmidt, F. L., & Hayes, T. L. (2002). Business-unit-level relationship between employee satisfaction, employee engagement, and business outcomes : A meta-analysis. *The Journal of Applied Psychology, 87*(2), 268–279. DOI: 10.1037/0021-9010.87.2.268 PMID: 12002955

Heinrich, C. J. (2002). Outcomes–Based Performance Management in the Public Sector : Implications for Government Accountability and Effectiveness. *Public Administration Review, 62*(6), 712–725. DOI: 10.1111/1540-6210.00253

Henseler, J., Ringle, C. M., & Sarstedt, M. (2015). A new criterion for assessing discriminant validity in variance-based structural equation modeling. *Journal of the Academy of Marketing Science*, *43*(1), 115–135. DOI: 10.1007/s11747-014-0403-8

Hill, C. J., & Lynn Jr, L. E. (2016). *Public management : Thinking and acting in three dimensions. CQ Press*. 39-65. http://dx.doi.org/DOI: 10.4135/9781483395814.n2

Ismail, I. A., & Aloshi, J. M. (2025). Data Privacy in AI-Driven Education : An In-Depth Exploration Into the Data Privacy Concerns and Potential Solutions. In *AI Applications and Strategies in Teacher Education* (p. 223-252). IGI Global. https://www.igi-global.com/chapter/data-privacy-in-ai-driven-education/358899

Janssen, M., & Kuk, G. (2016). The challenges and limits of big data algorithms in technocratic governance. *Government Information Quarterly*, *33*(3), 371–377. DOI: 10.1016/j.giq.2016.08.011

Johnson, G. M. (2021). Algorithmic bias : On the implicit biases of social technology. *Synthese*, *198*(10), 9941–9961. DOI: 10.1007/s11229-020-02696-y

Ju, J., Meng, Q., Sun, F., Liu, L., & Singh, S. (2023). Citizen preferences and government chatbot social characteristics : Evidence from a discrete choice experiment. *Government Information Quarterly*, *40*(3), 101785. DOI: 10.1016/j.giq.2022.101785

Kaplan, A., & Haenlein, M. (2019). Siri, Siri, in my hand : Who's the fairest in the land? On the interpretations, illustrations, and implications of artificial intelligence. *Business Horizons*, *62*(1), 15–25. DOI: 10.1016/j.bushor.2018.08.004

Khafif, H., & Touhami, N. O. (2024). Les conséquences de l'exclusion socio-économique des jeunes sous la perspective de la croissance inclusive. *International Journal of Accounting, Finance, Auditing, Management and Economics, 5*(7), 583-599. https://ijafame.org/index.php/ijafame/article/view/1642

Kim, Y., Myeong, S., & Ahn, M. J. (2023). Living labs for AI-enabled public services : Functional determinants, user satisfaction, and continued use. *Sustainability (Basel)*, *15*(11), 8672. DOI: 10.3390/su15118672

Kingma, D. P. (2013). *Auto-encoding variational bayes*.

Kitchin, R. (2014). The real-time city? Big data and smart urbanism. *GeoJournal*, *79*(1), 1–14. DOI: 10.1007/s10708-013-9516-8

König, P. D., & Wenzelburger, G. (2020). Opportunity for renewal or disruptive force? How artificial intelligence alters democratic politics. *Government Information Quarterly*, *37*(3), 101489. DOI: 10.1016/j.giq.2020.101489

Kuswara, Z., Pasaribu, M., Fitriana, F., & Santoso, R. A. (2024). Artificial Intelligence in Financial Reports : How it Affects the Process's Effectiveness and Efficiency. *Jurnal ilmu keuangan dan perbankan (jika), 13*(2), 257-272. https://doi.org/DOI: 10.34010/jika.v13i2.12730

Kwok, K. (2024). *Gulf's AI strategy is built on more than sand. Reuters Breakingviews.* https://www.reuters.com/breakingviews/gulfs-ai-strategy-is-built-more-than-sand-2024-11-13/

Larsson, S., & Heintz, F. (2020). Transparency in artificial intelligence. *Internet Policy Review, 9*(2). Advance online publication. DOI: 10.14763/2020.2.1469

LegalProd. T. (2024). Transparence Des Algorithmes. *LEGALPROD.* https://www.legalprod.com/transparence-des-algorithmes/

Liberal Forum. (2020). *Predictive Analytics and AI in Governance.* https://liberalforum.eu/wp-content/uploads/2021/07/PUBLICATION_AI-in-e-governance.pdf

Magatef, S., Al-Okaily, M., Ashour, L., & Abuhussein, T. (2023). The impact of electronic customer relationship management strategies on customer loyalty : A mediated model. *Journal of Open Innovation, 9*(4), 100149. DOI: 10.1016/j.joitmc.2023.100149

Maleka, S. (2023). *Enhancing efficiency and decision-making in government through AI in Strategic Planning and Strategic Management Processes.* ResearchGate. https://www.researchgate.net/profile/Stevens-Maleka-2/publication/372516160_Enhancing_Efficiency_and_Decision-Making_in_Government_through_AI_in_Strategic_Planning_and_Strategic_Management_Processes/links/64bb7d42b9ed6874a5389331/Enhancing-Efficiency-and-Decision-Making-in-Government-through-AI-in-Strategic-Planning-and-Strategic-Management-Processes.pdf

Margetts, H., & Dorobantu, C. (2019). Rethink government with AI. *Nature, 568*(7751), 163–165. DOI: 10.1038/d41586-019-01099-5 PMID: 30967667

Marsh, D., & McConnell, A. (2010). TOWARDS A FRAMEWORK FOR ESTABLISHING POLICY SUCCESS. *Public Administration, 88*(2), 564–583. DOI: 10.1111/j.1467-9299.2009.01803.x

McDavid, J. C., Huse, I., & Hawthorn, L. R. (2018). *Program evaluation and performance measurement : An introduction to practice.* Sage Publications.

Mehrabi, N., Morstatter, F., Saxena, N., Lerman, K., & Galstyan, A. (2021). A Survey on Bias and Fairness in Machine Learning. *ACM Computing Surveys, 54*(6), 1–35. DOI: 10.1145/3457607

Mergel, I., Rethemeyer, R. K., & Isett, K. (2016). Big Data in Public Affairs. *Public Administration Review*, *76*(6), 928–937. DOI: 10.1111/puar.12625

Mühlhoff, R. (2023). Predictive privacy : Collective data protection in the context of artificial intelligence and big data. *Big Data & Society*, *10*(1), 20539517231166886. DOI: 10.1177/20539517231166886

Mukhopadhyay, A. (2023). *Artificial Intelligence for Emergency Response* (arXiv:2306.10068). arXiv. https://doi.org//arXiv.2306.10068DOI: 10.48550

Nzobonimpa, S. (2023). Artificial intelligence, task complexity and uncertainty : Analyzing the advantages and disadvantages of using algorithms in public service delivery under public administration theories. *Digital Transformation and Society*, *2*(3), 219–234. DOI: 10.1108/DTS-03-2023-0018

Odilla, F. (2024). Unfairness in AI Anti-Corruption Tools : Main Drivers and Consequences. *Minds and Machines*, *34*(3), 28. DOI: 10.1007/s11023-024-09688-8

OECD. (2025). *Artificial intelligence*. OECD. https://www.oecd.org/en/topics/artificial-intelligence.html

Olaoye, F., & Potter, K. (2024). AI-DRIVEN PREDICTIVE ANALYTICS IN BUSINESS DECISION- MAKING. *Journal of Artificial Intelligence*.

Osborne, S. P., Cucciniello, M., Nasi, G., & Zhu, E. (2022). Digital transformation, artificial intelligence and effective public services : Challenges and opportunities. *Global Public Policy and Governance*, *2*(4), 377–380. DOI: 10.1007/s43508-022-00058-7

Ouboumlik, A., & Touhami, N. O. (2024). Digitalization of Public Finances and Public Procurement in Morocco : Impacts on Business Climate. [IJPADA]. *International Journal of Public Administration in the Digital Age*, *11*(1), 1–26. DOI: 10.4018/IJPADA.359178

Percy, S. L. (1980). Response time and citizen evaluation of police. *Journal of Police Science and Administration*, *8*(1), 75–86.

Piper, D. L. A. (2024). *China-releases-AI-safety-governance-framework*. https://www.dlapiper.com/en-us/insights/publications/2024/09/china-releases-ai-safety-governance-framework

Pulapaka, S., Godavarthi, S., & Ding, S. (2024). *Empowering the Public Sector with Generative AI : From Strategy and Design to Real-World Applications*. https://doi.org/DOI: 10.1007/979-8-8688-0473-1

PwC. (2024). *Data and AI-driven urban planning*. https://www.pwc.com/m1/en/publications/documents/2024/data-and-ai-driven-urban-planning.pdf

Radford, A. (2018). *Improving language understanding by generative pre-training*.

Rathi, P., Shringarpure, K., Unnikrishnan, B., Pandey, A., & Nair, A. (2021). *Patient treatment pathways of multidrug-resistant tuberculosis cases in coastal South India : Road to a drug resistant tuberculosis center* (8:498). F1000Research. https://doi.org/DOI: 10.12688/f1000research.17743.5

Robles, P., & Mallinson, D. J. (2025). Artificial intelligence technology, public trust, and effective governance. *The Review of Policy Research*, *42*(1), 11–28. DOI: 10.1111/ropr.12555

Rudin, C. (2019). Stop explaining black box machine learning models for high stakes decisions and use interpretable models instead. *Nature Machine Intelligence*, *1*(5), 206–215. https://www.nature.com/articles/s42256-019-0048-x. DOI: 10.1038/s42256-019-0048-x PMID: 35603010

Russell, S. J., & Norvig, P. (2016). *Artificial intelligence : A modern approach*. Pearson.

Scholta, H., & Lindgren, I. (2023). Proactivity in digital public services : A conceptual analysis. *Government Information Quarterly*, *40*(3), 101832. DOI: 10.1016/j.giq.2023.101832

Senadheera, S., Yigitcanlar, T., Desouza, K. C., Mossberger, K., Corchado, J., Mehmood, R., Li, R. Y. M., & Cheong, P. H. (2024). Understanding Chatbot Adoption in Local Governments : A Review and Framework. *Journal of Urban Technology*, 1–35. DOI: 10.1080/10630732.2023.2297665

Smith, B. C. (2019). *The promise of artificial intelligence : Reckoning and judgment*. https://doi.org/DOI: 10.7551/mitpress/12385.001.0001

Sun, T. Q., & Medaglia, R. (2019). Mapping the challenges of Artificial Intelligence in the public sector : Evidence from public healthcare. *Government Information Quarterly*, *36*(2), 368–383. DOI: 10.1016/j.giq.2018.09.008

Upmann, P. (2024). Localized Ethical Frameworks : Aligning AI with Regional Cultural and Societal Norms. *AIGN*. https://aign.global/ai-ethics-consulting/patrick-upmann/localized-ethical-frameworks-aligning-ai-with-regional-cultural-and-societal-norms

Van Der Voet, J., Kuipers, B. S., & Groeneveld, S. (2016). Implementing Change in Public Organizations : The relationship between leadership and affective commitment to change in a public sector context. *Public Management Review*, *18*(6), 842–865. DOI: 10.1080/14719037.2015.1045020

Van der Voort, H. G., Klievink, A. J., Arnaboldi, M., & Meijer, A. J. (2019). Rationality and politics of algorithms. Will the promise of big data survive the dynamics of public decision making? *Government Information Quarterly*, *36*(1), 27–38. DOI: 10.1016/j.giq.2018.10.011

West, D. M. (2021). *How robotic process and intelligent automation are altering government performance. Brookings Institution.* https://www.brookings.edu/articles/how-robotic-process-and-intelligent-automation-are-altering-government-performance/

White & Case. (2025). *AI Watch : Global regulatory tracker - United Kingdom.* https://www.whitecase.com/insight-our-thinking/ai-watch-global-regulatory-tracker-united-kingdom

Wirtz, B. W., Weyerer, J. C., & Geyer, C. (2019). Artificial Intelligence and the Public Sector—Applications and Challenges. *International Journal of Public Administration*, *42*(7), 596–615. DOI: 10.1080/01900692.2018.1498103

Wirtz, J., & Lovelock, C. (2021). *Services marketing : People, technology, strategy* (8e éd.). World Scientific Publishing Company.

Wu, W., Huang, T., & Gong, K. (2020). Ethical Principles and Governance Technology Development of AI in China. *Engineering (Beijing)*, *6*(3), 3. Advance online publication. DOI: 10.1016/j.eng.2019.12.015

Yang, A. Z. (2024). A Comparative Analysis of AI Governance Frameworks. *Washington Journal of Law, Technology & Arts*. https://wjlta.com/2024/07/09/a-comparative-analysis-of-ai-governance-frameworks/

Yigitcanlar, T., Li, R. Y. M., Beeramoole, P. B., & Paz, A. (2023). Artificial intelligence in local government services : Public perceptions from Australia and Hong Kong. *Government Information Quarterly*, *40*(3), 101833. DOI: 10.1016/j.giq.2023.101833

Yun, L., Yun, S., & Xue, H. (2024). Improving citizen-government interactions with generative artificial intelligence : Novel human-computer interaction strategies for policy understanding through large language models. *PLoS One*, *19*(12), e0311410. DOI: 10.1371/journal.pone.0311410 PMID: 39689162

KEY TERMS AND DEFINITIONS

Corporate Governance: The system of rules, practices, and processes by which firms are directed and controlled, including board structure, ownership concentration, and regulatory compliance. It influences financial transparency and shareholder value.

Dividend Policy: The strategic decision made by a firm regarding the distribution of profits to shareholders in the form of dividends. It reflects corporate profitability, cash flow management, investor expectations, and capital structure considerations.

Emerging Marke: A developing country with an evolving financial infrastructure and institutional framework, often characterized by volatility, regulatory changes, and investment opportunities distinct from mature economies.

Financial Flexibility: The firm's ability to access and deploy financial resources to respond to unexpected opportunities or shocks, often achieved by maintaining reserves and minimizing external funding constraints.

Random Forest Regression: A supervised machine learning algorithm that uses an ensemble of decision trees to predict continuous outcomes. It is particularly effective in handling high-dimensional, nonlinear, and multicollinear financial data.

SHAP (SHapley Additive Explanations): A model-agnostic explainable AI method based on cooperative game theory that attributes each prediction to individual feature contributions, enhancing transparency and interpretability of machine learning models.

APPENDIX: QUESTIONNAIRE

maturity level, impact, and challenges of AI adoption in public administration. The responses will provide valuable insights into how AI is transforming governance and service delivery.

Demographic Information

1. Age: ___________
2. Gender:
    a) Male
    b) Female
3. Academic Degree:
    a) Bachelor's
    b) Master's
    c) PhD
    d) Others
4. Academic Background:
    a) Computer Science
    b) Engineering
    c) Social Science
    d) Physics
    e) Mathematics
    f) Chemistry
    g) Other: ___________

AI Awareness and Adoption

5. How familiar are you with the concept of AI?
    a) Very familiar
    b) Familiar
    c) Somewhat familiar
    d) Not very familiar
    e) Not familiar at all
6. Are there any ongoing AI projects or initiatives in your organization?
    a) Yes
    b) No
7. How would you describe the scope and scale of your current AI initiatives?
    a) Small Scale
    b) Medium Scale

c) Large Scale

8. When was the first AI project initiated in your organization?
   a) Before 2010
   b) 2010–2015
   c) 2016–2018
   d) 2019–2021
   e) 2022 or later
9. What percentage of your organization's budget is allocated to AI-related activities?
   _______________%
10. Do you have a dedicated team responsible for overseeing and implementing AI initiatives?
    a) Yes
    b) No
11. How would you describe the current technological infrastructure supporting AI in your organization?
    a) Advanced and well-established
    b) Moderately developed
    c) In the early stages of development
    d) Limited or no infrastructure in place

Functionalities Affected by AI Implementation

12. What aspects of public service delivery have been impacted by AI implementation? (Check all that apply)
    a) Capacitation
    b) Executive management
    c) Political Advisory
    d) Technical duties
    e) Clerical and assistant tasks
    f) Regulation
    g) Management of organizational networks
    h) Public service delivery
    i) Processing of transactions/operations

Comparative Evaluation: AI's Impact on Public Service Delivery

For the following statements, please indicate your level of agreement before and after AI adoption using the scale

- SA (5) – Strongly Agree

- A (4) – Agree
- N (3) – Neutral
- DA (2) – Disagree
- SDA (1) – Strongly Disagree

1. Response Time

- The organization effectively meets citizen inquiries and requests within a reasonable timeframe.
- The response time to citizen concerns has improved with the implementation of AI-driven processes.

2. Accuracy and Precision

- Public services provided by the organization demonstrate a high level of accuracy and precision.
- The organization consistently delivers reliable and error-free services to citizens.

3. Resource Utilization

- Resources, including personnel and technology, are effectively utilized to deliver public services.
- The organization optimally allocates resources to ensure efficient public service delivery.

4. Cost per Transaction

- The organization efficiently manages costs associated with public service transactions.
- The cost-effectiveness of public service delivery has improved due to AI-driven optimizations.

5. Citizen Satisfaction

- Citizen feedback indicates a high level of satisfaction with the quality and timeliness of public services.
- The organization actively seeks and addresses citizen feedback to enhance service delivery.

6. Accessibility

- Public services are easily accessible to all segments of the population, regardless of background or ability.
- The organization actively works to ensure inclusivity and accessibility in public services.

7. Process Automation

- Automation of routine tasks has improved the efficiency of public service operations.
- AI integration has positively impacted the speed and accuracy of public service processes.

8. Data-Driven Decision Making

- Data analytics play a significant role in shaping informed decision-making within the public sector.
- The use of data-driven insights enhances the efficiency of decision-making processes.

9. Speed of Service Delivery

- Public services are consistently delivered within stipulated timeframes.
- The organization prioritizes timely service delivery using AI-driven enhancements.

10. Transparency and Accountability

- The organization fosters transparency in its public service processes.
- AI has increased accountability and reduced bureaucratic inefficiencies in service delivery.

11. Adaptability to Changing Needs

- The public service demonstrates flexibility in responding to changing community needs.
- AI adoption has enhanced the ability to adapt to emerging governance challenges.

12. Feedback Mechanisms

- Effective feedback mechanisms are in place to gather citizen insights on public services.
- The organization actively integrates citizen feedback to improve service quality.

13. Employee Satisfaction and Productivity

- Employees involved in public service delivery are satisfied with their work.
- AI-driven optimizations contribute positively to employee productivity.

14. Environmental Impact

- The organization considers and minimizes the environmental impact of its public service operations.
- Sustainable practices are incorporated into service delivery to reduce environmental footprint.

15. Emergency Response Time

- Emergency response services provided by the public sector are prompt and effective.
- AI-driven tools have improved the efficiency of crisis and emergency response services.

16. Compliance with Standards and Regulations

- Public services consistently adhere to regulatory standards.
- AI implementation has enhanced compliance with governance and legal frameworks.

17. Public Trust and Perception

- Citizens trust the efficiency and effectiveness of AI-driven public services.
- AI adoption has positively influenced public perception of government transparency.

Chapter 8

The Integration of Artificial Intelligence in the Management of Organizational Change in Companies in Morocco

Mohamed Karim Bennacer
https://orcid.org/0009-0009-9405-0853
Hassan II University, Morocco

El Mahdi El Massaoudi
Ibn Tofail University, Morocco

Ahmed El Hammoumi
Sidi Mohamed Ben Abdellah University, Morocco

Mohamed Lahmouchi
Hassan II University, Morocco

ABSTRACT

This study explores the integration of artificial intelligence (AI) in organizational change management, particularly its role in reducing resistance to change and strengthening employee engagement. At a time when transformation processes are increasingly being influenced by digitization, this research explores ways in which AI can optimize change management in the enterprise. The methodology chosen for this study is based on a quantitative analysis. It begins with an in-depth literature review to identify the levers and challenges associated with change management.

DOI: 10.4018/979-8-3373-1737-3.ch008

Then, an empirical study based on a questionnaire sent to 108 Moroccan companies that have opted for digital transformation. The SPSS 25 software was used to analyze the result. The results show that AI plays a key role in anticipating resistance and adapting support plans through behavioral analysis and personalization of interventions. Smart platforms also support more targeted and transparent communication by automating repetitive change processes.

INTRODUCTION

Artificial Intelligence (AI) is revolutionizing the contemporary organizational landscape. From process automation to predictive analytics, AI applications are revolutionizing managerial practice and workplace culture. McKinsey (2021) contends that organizations that achieve AI integration are on average 20% more operationally effective. But there is a cost. Key impediments are workers' resistance to change, fear of rendering their skills obsolete, and suspicion of algorithmic decision-making (Davenport & Ronanki, 2018; Jarrahi, 2023).

AI adoption in Morocco is increasing, particularly in sectors such as finance, health, and telecommunication (Oxford Business Group, 2023). CESE (2022) states in a study that approximately 37% of the large Moroccan firms have initiated AI-driven transformation programs. However, the figure drops to less than 10% in SMEs. Instances such as sparse local competence, asymmetric availability of digital infrastructure, and low data culture still restrict extensive implementation (Dell & IDC, 2022). All these difficulties establish the imperative of strategic change management and also that AI might be both a helper and also the cause of problems.

Against this background, the present study seeks to answer the following research question: How does AI affect employee resistance to change and employee engagement in Moroccan businesses that are undergoing digital transformation? This question has raising concerns with regard to human-machine interaction, the reorganization of organizational hierarchies, and, importantly, algorithmic transparency a notion at the very heart of building trust within AI systems. Recent studies (Shin, 2021; Rai, Constantinides & Sarker, 2022) point out that explainable AI in terms of being comprehensible, explainable, and accountable — plays a major role in employee acceptance and engagement.

This research has two main objectives:

-To empirically measure the impact of AI on organizational change management, i.e., its role towards minimizing resistance and maximizing employee engagement.

-To identify context-specific enablers and restraints of AI adoption in Moroccan firms, taking into account the cultural, technology, and economics dimensions, while examining how perceived fairness and transparency influence employee attitude.

In pursuit of these objectives, an empirical study will be conducted through a quantitative survey questionnaire on Moroccan companies that have integrated AI technologies into organizational activities. The questionnaire will examine key variables such as perceived transparency of AI, change resistance, and employee engagement. Data analysis will identify dynamics of AI-enabled transformation and provide tangible recommendations to leaders interested in ensuring both successful technological acceptance and human harmonization.

1. LITERATURE REVIEW

1.1. Conceptual and Theoretical Framework

In a more dynamic socio-economic and technological context, organizations must constantly adapt to address internal and external pressures. Organizational change has thus become the center of private and public institution strategic discussion. With the emergence of digital technology and, more recently, AI, change is no longer episodic but continuous and multidimensional. It is required to comprehend how change is defined, managed, and lived by individuals in organizations in a way that ensures successful transitions. This section gives the theoretical foundation by describing the main definitions of organizational change and presenting the main classical and modern models of change management.

1.1.1. Organizational Change: Definitions and Approaches

The Work of Organization Change is a multi-faceted reality that is now regarded as a necessity faced by the organization who aims at maintaining a competitive and adaptive lead in a fast-evolving scenario. Amidst digital transformation, globalization and social pressure, organizations are forced to transform themselves time and again structurally, strategically and culturally. Key terms in organizational change are defined, and principal models of the practice are identified.

Key Definitions (Organizational Change, Change Management)

Understanding organizational change entails distinguishing between the reality of the change phenomenon and the steps employed to administer it. This sub-section presents fundamental definitions to provide the theoretical context.

Organizational change refers to any intended or unintentional change affecting an organization's structure, processes, culture, or strategic direction for the purpose of reacting to internal or external pressures (Burke, 2017). It may either be incremental change or revolutionary change and tends to involve significant uncertainty, risk, and resistance.

Change management, however, means the catalog of structured approaches, tools, and techniques for preparing, enabling, and sustaining successful change in an organization (Hiatt, 2006; Hayes, 2022). Effective change management entails essential dimensions such as stakeholder involvement, communication, resistance management, and capacity development (Cameron & Green, 2019; Armenakis & Harris, 2022). Poor change can lead to employee demobilization, productivity decline, and reputational harm.

Recent literature emphasizes that change management is no longer a matter of linear straightforward procedures, but adaptive leadership, trial and error through iterative experience, and a significant emphasis on workers' welfare (Cawsey et al., 2023; Burnes & Bargal, 2023).

Organizational Change Management Models

Theorizing change can offer conceptually useful devices for organizing change initiatives, managing, and assessing change efforts. Classical models provide building blocks and frames, whereas recent models consider the increased complexity of the organizational context. This subsection introduces three most popular classical change models: Lewin's model of change, Kotter's eight-step model and the ADKAR model. Each offers a unique perspective on how best to promote and maintain change.

- **Classic models**

Traditional models of change have given us the basis on which organizational change is understood to work. Traditional models help decision-makers to visualize processes of change and prepare themselves against the psychological and structural issues relating to change.

✓ **Lewin's Three-Step Model: Structuring the Change Process**

Kurt Lewin (1947) originally visualized change as a dynamic equilibrium between forces driving and forces restraining. The three-stage process is advocated under his model, as follows:

-Unfreeze: Here, in the preparation phase, the organization must break the existing habits, challenge the existing assumptions, and raise awareness of the need for change. It involves eliminating the psychological and structural inertia that sustains the status quo.
-Change (Transition): This phase involves the adoption of new practices, technologies, or structures. Active communication, leadership support, and employee involvement are all crucial to assist in reducing uncertainty and facilitating adoption.
-Refreeze: The final step attempts to stabilize and institutionalize the changes introduced. This entails aligning new behaviors with organizational culture, reinforcing new norms through rewards, and anchoring changes in procedures and performance systems.

Lewin's model is highly useful in the context of extensive technological or organizational change. The model's simplicity acts as a fine foundation, despite its linearity being criticized where highly volatile contexts are involved (Burnes & Cooke, 2022).

✓ **Kotter's model: an eight-step approach**

Jeff Hiatt (2006) developed the ADKAR model to address the human side of organizational change. Unlike the previous models, ADKAR focuses on helping individual transitions by five consecutive results:

-Awareness: The employees must be informed as to why the change is necessary.
-Desire: Individual motivation must be built by effective communication and engagement.
-Knowledge: Employees must learn the necessary information and skills.
-Ability: New behaviors must be practiced effectively by coaching and feedback.
-Reinforcement: Sustainability of long-term change is ensured by reward, observation, and incentive.

It is especially good in managing resistance, fostering involvement, and facilitating change in behavior. It is utilized widely in digital transformation change efforts where individual flexibility is among the key success drivers (Prosci, 2023; Horney et al., 2021).

Synthesis of Classical Models

Each of these models provides a complementary account of organizational change. Whereas Lewin provides a macro-structural solution, Kotter provides a step-by-step strategic roadmap, and ADKAR focuses on the micro-level of individual change journeys. Model selection depends on organizational complexity, change nature, and employee readiness levels.

✓ The ADKAR model: an individual-centred approach

In the majority of organizational change, failure is not due to faulty strategy or resources but because the human side of change is neglected. ADKAR, developed by Jeff Hiatt (2006), fills this gap by addressing the process through which individuals go through and internalize change. It suggests that effective transformation of an enterprise requires each individual to be led through five key stages. A staple in the field of change management, ADKAR identifies that individual awareness, motivation; ability and reinforcement are necessary for personal engagement and puts a practical focus on these dimensions in a successful transformation.

Recent studies have supported its importance, especially in complex or digital change environments where personal adaptability is paramount (Prosci, 2022; Chivu et al., 2023). ADKAR is still a keystone in addressing resistance and transitioning change in multiple organizational cultures.

The five phases of ADKAR are:

-Awareness: At the initial stage, one informs and sensitizes individuals to change. It seeks to reduce uncertainty and overcome resistance by making known what is lost due to inaction, and the change requirements at a strategic level (Hiatt, 2006; Prosci, 2022).

-Desire: Beyond knowledge, individuals must be personally inspired to participate. This stage involves creating emotional and career motivations through the congruence of the change with personal values and career goals (Kotter, 2014; Chivu et al., 2023).

-Knowledge: Staff need to learn the required skills and knowledge to execute the change. Training, communication, and mutual learning are important components in this step, so people are prepared to act (Hiatt, 2006).

-Ability: Once trained, individuals must be supported in applying what they have learned. This stage requires experimentation in real life, mentoring, and feedback systems to ensure that knowledge becomes competency (Anderson & Anderson, 2021).

-Reinforcement: In order to make the change last in the long term, organizations must institutionalize it through reward, recognition, and monitoring systems. Reinforcement makes the new behaviors automatic and prevents setbacks (Prosci, 2022).

The ADKAR model is particularly well-adapted to behavior-change initiatives such as cultural change, digital adoption, or reorganization centered on the customer. It allows change leaders to identify where resistance occurs and modify interventions as a result.

Unlike Lewin's structural three-step model or Kotter's strategic stakeholder guide, ADKAR is exclusively concerned with the individual change process. This focus on the individual reveals a fundamental truth about change management: successful organizational change is not a top-down decree but a bottom-up process of human adaptation.

- **Modern models of change management: a scalable approach**

While the classic change management models (Lewin, Kotter, and ADKAR) have taught us some fundamental knowledge of organizational transformation, the increasing complexity, uncertainty, and digitalization of modern contexts make it necessary to develop new approaches. The new models emphasize agility, flexibility, and continuous stakeholder engagement, which inject into the transformation process the evolving dynamics of the organization.

✓ The McKinsey 7S model: a systemic approach

From Peters and Waterman (1982), the McKinsey 7S model offers a comprehensive system of grasping organizational change by interlocking seven interrelated components:

-Hard S elements: Strategy, Structure, Systems
-Soft S elements: Style (leadership), Shared values (organizational culture), Skills (competencies), Staff (human resources)

This systems model is particularly effective in diagnosing organizational change determinants and ensuring strategic goal and operating practice congruence. By its capacity to include tangible as well as intangible elements, the McKinsey 7S model provides an integrated approach to managing transformation (Waterman et al., 2021).

✓ **Stacey's complexity model: a non-linear approach**

Inspired by the theory of complex systems, Ralph Stacey (1996) formulated a model classifying change in terms of predictability:

-Certainty zone: Changes that is well understood and controllable with traditional planning.
-Zone of complexity: Changes requiring sequential adaptation and ongoing refinement.
-Chaos zone: Transmutation changes that necessitate experimental procedures and innovative solutions.

This model is particularly relevant in uncertain settings, such as digital transformation or crisis management, where organizations need to change repeatedly to react to external threats (Stacey, 2022).

✓ **The agile change management model: an iterative approach**

Drawn from Agile paradigms such as Scrum, Kanban, and Lean Management, the Agile change model stimulates a reactive, adaptive response to change within organizations. Contrary to more traditional linear models (i.e., Lewin, 1951; Kotter, 1996), the agile model focuses on iterative, incremental changes (Beck et al., 2001).

o Some of the key principles of the agile model are:

-Brief iterative cycles: Rather than relying on long-term planning, Agile uses sprints and test cycles to adapt transformations in small increments (Highsmith, 2009).
-High employee involvement: In contrast to top-down approaches, Agile change involves employees proactively, rendering them change co-creators (Beck et al., 2001).

- Empirical feedback: All change steps are monitored and fixed upon receiving factual feedback from the stakeholders, with ease in developing new practices (Highsmith, 2009).

o Advantages of the agile model:

-Lower resistance to change: With the early involvement of employees, commitment and participation to new practices are improved.
-Flexibility and adaptability: Applicable to environments where there is uncertainty or digital transformation, Agile allows for rapid adaptability (Beck et al., 2001).

-Continuous improvement: Agile's continuous model allows organizations to improve on a continuous basis with little interruption.

✓ **The Prosci model: integrated change management**

Drawing on the ADKAR model, the Prosci model is a three-level approach to change management that is wide-ranging in its scope.

-Individual change management: To recognize and to break down individual resistance to change.
-Organizational change management: A systematic approach to planning and controlling change initiatives.
-Project change management: Integration of transformation activities within specific projects.

This dual approach is particularly effective in supporting digital change and widespread organizational re-designing (Hiatt, 2021).

✓ **Heifetz's adaptive leadership model: managing resistance to change**

Adaptive leadership was created by Ronald Heifetz and Marty Linsky (1994). It defines two types of challenges:

-Technical challenges: These can be resolved using available solutions or knowledge.
-Adaptive challenges: These require a shift of mind and learning together.

Employees must be guided by leaders through unease and resistance, urging them to step outside their comfort zone, engages with innovative solutions, and actively involves stakeholders in the process of change. This model emphasizes leading through complex, non-technical challenges (Heifetz & Linsky, 2022).

✓ **The revisited Kotter model: a continuous and dynamic change**

In response to the heightened pace of modern changes, Kotter (2014) recreated his original 1996 model, introducing a dual system model:

-Hierarchical structure: Provides stability and ensures ongoing management of day-to-day activities.
-Change network: More flexible, decentralized type that encourages continuous innovation and rapid adaptation.

This new model is particularly effective in large organizations that are facing ongoing change, e.g., digitalization and globalization (Kotter, 2014).

Modern change management frameworks evolved to meet the increasing complexities and uncertainties of the modern-day business environment. Even though old models like Lewin, Kotter (1996), and ADKAR are still the foundation, newer frameworks allow greater flexibility, responsiveness, and continuous involvement of the stakeholders. The model to apply should be derived from the type of change, the degree of complexity, and the culture of the organization. A combination of these models in the majority of cases provides the best approach to offering successful transitions.

1.1.2 Artificial Intelligence and its Organizational Applications

Artificial intelligence (AI) is revolutionizing organizational behaviors profoundly through the implementation of advanced tools and technologies that reshape traditional change management methods. Artificial intelligence is no longer used as a support tool but as a strategic lever, enabling more responsive, more informed, and more adaptive transformations.

Definition of IA in the context of change management

Within an organizational setting, AI is utilized to streamline systems that are able to carry out tasks that typically require human intellectual abilities such as reasoning, learning, prediction, and decision-making (Russell & Norvig, 2021; Araujo et al., 2023). Within change management, AI functions as an accelerator in the sense that it reduces uncertainty, optimizes decision-making, and automates routine or data-intensive processes.

Key AI Technologies Relevant to Change Management

-AI-Powered Collaborative Software: Tools like Slack, Microsoft Teams, and Notion now integrate AI to personalize communication, track project evolution, and enhance teamwork collaboration. They facilitate interaction using interactive interfaces and intelligent assistants (Zamora & Zerbini, 2022).

-Predictive Algorithms

They leverage historical and real-time data to identify resistance patterns, forecast employee sentiment, and inform proactive interventions. Predictive analytics has been found to be an effective instrument in tailoring change strategies (Kaplan & Haenlein, 2020; Tanwar et al., 2023).

-Task Automation: Robotic Process Automation (RPA) and intelligent agents automate repetitive tasks, freeing up human resources for more strategic, value-adding tasks. This shift results in increased employee motivation and engagement (Brynjolfsson & McAfee, 2017; Eloundou et al., 2023).

AI, therefore, supports a data-driven and adaptive change process, speeding up both decision velocity and quality in the face of increasing uncertainty environments.

Resistance to Change and Employee Engagement: Origins, Challenges, and Strategic Levers

Resistance to change remains one of the most stubborn and complex barriers to successful organizational change. It usually manifests itself in the form of suspicion, complacency, or outright opposition, and can be a major drag on progress if not addressed. But resistance should not always be seen as a negative. If it is handled with inclusiveness, empathy, and strategic focus, it is an extremely valuable potential for creating higher employee commitment and organizational learning.

- Getting to Know the Sources of Resistance

Resistance is a multifaceted phenomenon rooted in psychological, organizational, and cultural factors:

-Psychological Factors: Uncertainty, loss of control as perceived, or attachment to established routines are common psychological drivers of resistance. These are especially strong when change is unjustifiably imposed or when employees perceive that they are not included in decision-making (Kotter & Schlesinger, 1979; Oreg et al., 2021).

-Organizational Factors: Vague goals, conflicting messages, and fuzzy transformation roadmaps erode confidence in leadership. Poor communication is among the most common explanations for organizational change failure (Ford, Ford, & D'Amelio, 2008; Michel, By, & Burnes, 2022).

-Cultural Issues: In hierarchically-oriented and collectivistic cultures such as Morocco, social perception of change by group dynamics, authority, and loyalty can be of significant influence upon its acceptance. Where formal strategies of change get in the way of deeply entrenched cultural norms, resistance is prone to intensify (El Mesbahi & Alaoui, 2022).

- Major Drivers of Employee Engagement In Transformation

While resistance is often viewed as a block, it has the potential to be an agent for positive change if organizations apply the right levers of engagement. Engagement is more than the absence of resistance; it is a positive, emotional, and intellectual commitment to change.

-Inclusive Leadership: Leaders play a central role in creating a compelling vision, trust, and a psychologically safe environment where employees are heard and valued. This kind of leadership encourages co-construction rather than imposition (Goleman, Boyatzis, & McKee, 2013; Uhl-Bien et al., 2022).
-Transparent and Proactive Communication: Frequent, open, and two-way communication reduces uncertainty and aligns employee perceptions with strategic objectives. It enables rumors and misinformation to be minimized and fosters an openness culture (Clampitt, DeKoch, & Cashman, 2000; Men & Bowen, 2021).
-Co-Creation and Empowerment: Actively engaging employees in designing and implementing change heightens ownership and responsibility. Empowerment not only discourages passive resistance, but also accesses the operational knowledge of frontline stakeholders, rendering transformation more realistic and effective (Amiot et al., 2006; Buchanan & McCalman, 2023).
-Skills Development and Training: Investment in workers' upskilling, particularly in new technologies such as artificial intelligence, increases autonomy and self-confidence. Skills development reduces resistance grounded in fear of obsolescence and prepares workers to contribute meaningfully to innovation (Huang & Rust, 2021).

1.2. The Contribution of Artificial Intelligence in Change Management

Artificial Intelligence (AI) is revolutionizing the traditional approaches to organizational change by enabling more precise, responsive, and personalized strategies. Its ability to process large volumes of data in real time offers new tools for the detection of resistance, initiative alteration, and improved employee involvement. This section addresses two general contributions of AI to the field: enabling resistance analysis and customized change strategies.

1.2.1. Facilitate Analysis of Resistance to Change

The use of AI in organizational diagnosis facilitates the shift from reactive to proactive change management. Through the utilization of advanced algorithms and real-time data processing, organizations can detect early warning signs of resistance and diagnose its causes more precisely.

- Weak Signal Identification through Predictive Algorithms

Predictive analytics and machine learning are suitable particularly to identify early weak signs of resistance before they grow into organizational barriers. Depending on patterns identified in behavior data such as a drop in attendance to meetings, reducing participation within collaboration platforms, or changed communications patterns, AI platforms can flag trending patterns of disengagement (Davenport & Ronanki, 2018).

For example, in complex organizations, data from email correspondence, CRM applications, or project management applications may be studied to identify trends reflective of staff dissatisfaction or emotional disengagement (Carucci, 2016). Such information enables change leaders to intervene early with targeted communication or support interventions.

- Sentiment Analysis using AI-Powered Tools

Another significant innovation is in Natural Language Processing (NLP) technologies, which facilitate semantic and emotive interpretation of employee responses collected through a number of channels automated surveys, open-text feedback forms, or internal social media (Mohamed et al., 2020).

Examples are:

Computer-assisted survey systems not only record the employee response in real time but also generate forecast dashboards illustrating the likely organizational impact of the feedback.

AI chatbots that engage in dialogue with employees, answering questions and concerns while obtaining intelligence on root objections, questions, and emotions.

It is supplemented by behavior analytics, which generates a 360-degree picture of resistance dynamics. Managers are hence able to modify their tactics not just based on observed behavior but also based on the emotional and cognitive dimensions of employee reactions.

1.2.2. Personalization of Change Strategies

AI's capacity for data-driven segmentation enables organizations to move beyond one-size-fits-all approaches and instead adopt adaptive transformation plans that respond to the specific characteristics and needs of their workforce.

- Segmentation and Adaptive Planning

On the basis of performance and behavioral data, AI systems can classify employees into engagement levels, digital literacy, risk tolerance, or flexibility. These segments provide the basis for customizing change initiatives whether in communication approach, pace, or support mechanisms (Gandomi & Haider, 2015).

For instance:

Personalized training pathways can be developed to skill up the employees based on their current competencies and future desired roles in the reorganized company. Dashboards for tracking allow the managers to identify real-time bottlenecks and points of friction, enabling agile adjustments to the implementation plans.

Use cases are:

Personalized guidance: AI bots scan existing discussions and recommend information or actions centered around the user's question, level of knowledge, or emotional state.

Feedback collection: Through engaging discussions, conversational agents capture rich feedback that change and HR teams can utilize to build better messaging and engagement.

This tailored support engenders a sense of trust and psychological safety, which is instrumental in maintaining motivation and receptiveness when there is uncertainty (Shum, He, & Li, 2018).

1.2.3. Optimization of Organizational Communication

Information flow fluidized with AI-based tools

The application of artificial intelligence (AI) in organizational communication has profoundly changed the management and dissemination of information. With real-time, data-driven interactions, AI applications facilitate the exchange of contextually relevant information, reduce informational overload, and enhance collaborative decision-making.

-Centralized and Intelligent Information Systems

AI-powered content management systems (e.g., intelligent content management systems or ICMS) provide centralized access to organizational documentation and knowledge. The systems apply semantic indexing and real-time synchronization to make sure key information is distributed to relevant stakeholders in an effective way (Zengul, Oner, & Yildiz, 2023). The result is a heightened transparent, responsive, and structured internal communication process.

-Conversational Agents and Natural Language Processing (NLP)

AI-driven chatbots and virtual assistants that utilize advanced NLP algorithms, have been at the forefront of automating responses to standard questions, onboarding, and improving responsiveness in internal communication (Zhou, Gao, & Chen, 2022). Not only do such tools enhance employee satisfaction, but they also reduce the operational burden on HR and IT support personnel.

-Predictive Communication and Personalized Knowledge Delivery

AI-driven predictive analytics enables the anticipation of information needs based on prior interaction patterns and behavioral characteristics segmentation. Personalized alerts, recommendations, and content curation are based on the preferences and job roles of individual employees and therefore increase the relevance and impact of internal communication (Wang et al., 2023).

Engagement strengthened through interactive and targeted campaigns

New AI innovations are also transforming the manner in which businesses engage with their workers and stakeholders through engaging, personalized communication strategies.

-Hyper-Personalized Content Delivery

Thanks to machine learning algorithms, content can now be dynamically personalized to address recipients' unique tastes, engagement, and roles. Such hyper-personalization induces deeper emotional engagement and improves message retention (Nguyen & Kim, 2022).

-Real-Time Sentiment and Behavior Monitoring

Behavioral analytics software monitors interaction trends across platforms (e.g., intranets, collaboration software, emails) to measure user sentiment and change campaign messages in real-time. This capability allows organizations to toggle communication strategies instantly and maintain message relevance (Ghosh et al., 2023).

-Dynamic Feedback Loops and Ongoing Adjustment

The ability of AI to provide real-time feedback enables communication teams to constantly improve their strategies in response to employees' feedback. This adaptive and iterative process underpins a communication system under which employees are heard, acknowledged, and informed the key ingredients for effective engagement and acceptance of change (Tursunbayeva et al., 2023).

1.2.4. AI Adoption in Morocco: Local Realities and Practical Challenge

To reinforce the practical relevance of our study, it is important to situate it within the specific context of AI adoption in Morocco. According to a 2023 report by the Moroccan Ministry of Digital Transition and Administrative Reform, only 12% of Moroccan companies had begun integrating AI solutions into their operations, with a clear concentration in sectors such as telecommunications, finance, and logistics. Despite government efforts and strategic plans such as the "Morocco Digital 2025" roadmap most businesses can't operationally implement AI due to structural barriers, lack of in-house expertise, and resistance to change. For instance, a prominent failure of implementation was recorded in a medium-sized Casablanca-based manufacturing company, in which the deployment of an AI-driven production tracking system was terminated after only six months of operations amidst staff resistance and lack of alignment with existing workflows. Conversely, success stories such as OCP Group's use of AI for predictive maintenance and resource optimization illustrate the potential of well-managed digital transformation. These contrasting examples demonstrate the heterogeneity of AI adoption in Morocco and highlight the necessity for tailored change management strategies to mitigate resistance and foster sustainable adoption.

1.3. Formulation of Assumptions

1.3.1. Employee Resistance to Change

The advent of artificial intelligence (AI) is fundamentally changing the manner in which organizations manage resistance to change. AI technologies increasingly enable the identification of weak behavioral signals, sentiment trends, and organizational friction areas from real-time data analysis. The recent advancements in machine learning and natural language processing facilitate early warning indicators of disengagement or doubt to be identified far in advance of them materializing as open resistance (Ghosh et al., 2023).

Applications of AI are involved not only in early diagnosis but also in personalizing change management strategies. By dynamically adapting communication, training content, and involvement processes to accommodate employees' cognitive profiles and affective responses, AI improves comprehension and acceptance of change (Zhou et al., 2022). Moreover, AI-driven real-time feedback loops allow interventions to be adjusted continuously; hence supporting agility in the face of organizational tensions (Wang et al., 2023).

Hypothesis 1: Artificial intelligence facilitates the anticipation and prevention of employee resistance during organizational change processes.

1.3.2. The Role of AI-Based Learning Platforms in Reducing Resistance to Change

AI-supported learning environments are one of the primary drivers for the creation of employee flexibility in change situations. Intelligent platforms are designed to deliver adaptive and dynamic learning processes, based on real-time data collection and behavioral tracking. Such systems, according to Tursunbayeva et al. (2023), modify learning trajectories taking into account degrees of employee engagement, personal performance, and emotional responses to transformation procedures.

Conversational agents, such as AI chatbots, also enhance learning through on-demand support, real-time feedback, and affective support, especially at times of organizational uncertainty (Nguyen & Kim, 2022). This proactive, user-centered model of learning reduces knowledge gaps, reduces psychological resistance, and enhances a culture of continuous learning.

AI-based learning systems also generate actionable insights by monitoring interaction trends, helping detect bottlenecks or cognitive overload in good time. Organizations are therefore able to refresh training material and delivery strategies in timely and targeted manner (Gandomi & Haider, 2022).

Hypothesis 2: AI-enabled learning platforms maximize employee agility and reduce resistance by tailoring learning paths and providing continuous, real-time support.

1.3.3. The Impact of Artificial Intelligence on Managing Emotional Resistance During Organizational Transformations

Artificial intelligence (AI) is increasingly recognized as a facilitator in overcoming emotional resistance to organizational change. Through real-time emotion recognition and sentiment analysis, AI systems provide managers with the ability to easily identify emotional roadblocks and adjust their approaches as needed. According to Sun et al. (2022), AI applications within virtual workplaces are capable of reading affective signals from employee messages, signaling building frustrations or concerns.

Besides, artificial intelligence (AI) driven customer relationship management (CRM) tools and business feedback mechanisms yield real-time streams of information that enable adaptive management of emotional tensions. Nevertheless, recent studies also emphasize that ethical deployment and human-centered design are indispensable to maintain emotional genuineness and faithfulness (Delgado & Zeller, 2023).

While AI presents analysis accuracy and promptness, it falls short to provide compassionate human leadership presence especially in navigating nuances of emotional states (Martins & Wu, 2021). Thus, AI should then be used as an add-on rather than a substitute when it comes to managing emotional resistance.

Hypothesis 3: Mechanisms of real-time AI-based feedback facilitate the identification and regulation of emotional resistance in organizational change.

1.3.4. The Impact of Artificial Intelligence on Personalization of Communication and Leadership

The leadership style personalization and internal communication using AI have become a vital element of increasing employee engagement. The high-level algorithms now allow managers to leverage behavioral data and interaction history to send extremely targeted and personal messages (Park et al., 2023).

This profound insight into workers' likes and work habits reinforces relational leadership and creates a more intense feeling of recognition.

AI also supports dynamic leadership in the form of managers' capacity to tailor their tone, message, and communication channels according to employees' emotional states and performance metrics (Fernandez & Gupta, 2022). With ethical guardrails and human judgment, the adaptive leadership model has the potential to significantly enhance the motivation and well-being of employees.

Yet, research advises against possible demerits where communication is too highly automated and susceptible to depersonalization and emotional distancing (Zhu & Ma, 2023). Such a balanced hybrid model balancing technological efficiency against human sympathy thus emerges as the best strategy.

Hypothesis 4: Personalization of leadership and communication through AI benefits employee engagement by creating customized and context-sensitive interactions.

1.3.5. The Impact of Dynamic AI-Based Campaigns on Employee Trust and Engagement in the Transformation Process

AI-powered communication campaigns, particularly responsive and dynamic ones, have been shown to possess significant potential in building employee trust and participation during organizational change. Such campaigns adjust content in real time based on audience behavior and sentiment feedback and, as a result, enhance message relevance and timeliness (Mousa & Mahmood, 2022).

Evidence indicates that employees are more likely to engage with transformation activities when communication is considered to be open, responsive, and sensitive to their concerns (Tang & Li, 2021). AI plays an important role in supporting micro-segmentation and tailored messaging to ensure that all employees receive material pertinent to their specific context.

However, achieving balance between automation and empathy remains relevant. Relying too much on AI without human checking can create emotional detachment or a sense of manipulation (Gao et al., 2023).

Hypothesis 5: Active AI-powered communication campaigns create stronger employee trust and engagement through personalized and interactive messaging throughout the transformation.

1.3.6. The Impact of Monitoring and Behavioral Analysis via Artificial Intelligence on Employee Engagement Strategies in Transformation Processes

Artificial intelligence allows businesses to monitor the performance of employees and make predictions regarding patterns of engagement to aid in the development of proactive and tailored transformational strategies. AI can identify behavior patterns that foretell readiness, resistance, or disengagement through the analysis of digital traces from collaboration tools, emails, and performance systems (Yin et al., 2022).

Predictive analytics, combined with behavioral modeling, allows timely intervention with personalized interventions such as coaching, peer mentoring, or content tailoring. They increase relevance and facilitate the creation of a more companionate change process (Rudnicka et al., 2023).

Yet researchers emphasize the need for ethical protection and transparency, as excessive monitoring is likely to lead to loss of trust or surveillance feelings (Caine & Han, 2021). Therefore, an ethical-by-design approach is needed so that behavioral analysis enhances rather than undermines engagement.

Hypothesis 6: AI-powered monitoring and behavioral analytics complement employee engagement programs by enabling predictive and context-sensitive interventions during organizational change.

To illustrate the relationships between the variables examined and clarify the underlying logic of the research hypotheses, the following conceptual model has been developed.

Figure 1. Conceptual research model

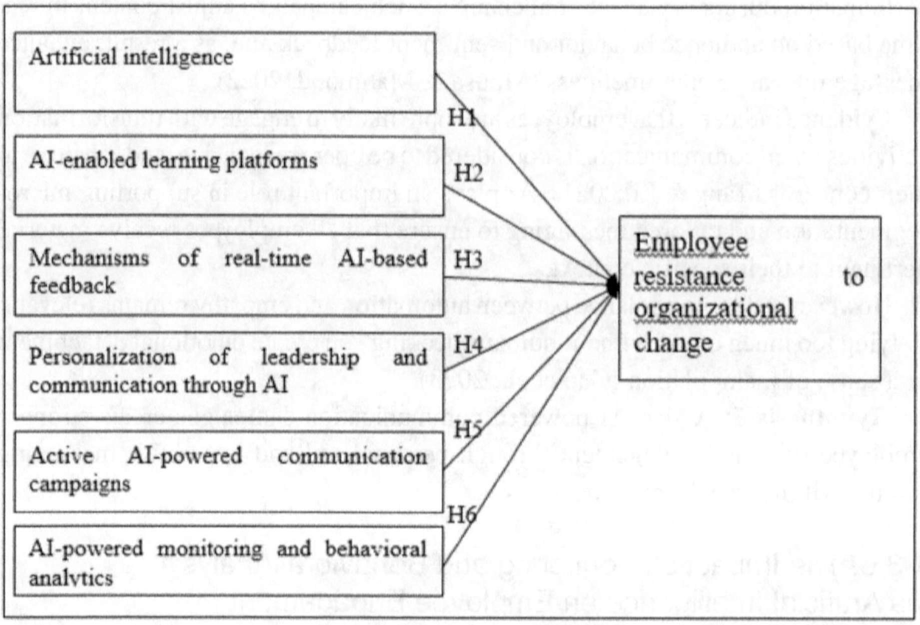

2. DATA AND METHODS

In this section, we will present the scope of our research along with the design of the method employed to measure and analyze dependent and independent variables that arise in our conceptual model.

2.1. Data Collection

After developing the questionnaire to cover our research field, we undertook the second step to test the survey on a limited sample of subjects. By validating the survey beforehand, we ensure consistency and relevance of the questions asked and can then begin to collect preliminary data.

As part of our research, we looked for Moroccan companies adopting AI.

To our knowledge, there is no database that refers to Moroccan companies and this absence makes the research phase difficult to achieve. To overcome this obstacle, we used the following data sources:

-Direct contact with experts in digital transformation and human resources
-Networks of accounting and consulting firms
-Direct contact with certain managers via our personal network

Through these sources, we contacted 2,560 companies from different industrial sectors in Morocco by phone to create a database of companies adopting AI and undergoing digital transformation. We asked respondents two questions:

-Does your company currently use AI technologies in its internal processes (management, production, human resources, customer relationship, etc.)?
-Is your company engaged in a process of digital transformation involving the integration of new technologies (AI, automation, cloud, big data, etc.)?

We found that 480 companies in Morocco currently use artificial intelligence technologies in their processes and engaged in a process of digital transformation, spread across various industrial sectors.

We sent the questionnaire to employees of companies in transformation, managers and team leaders, experts in digital transformation and human resources, executives and executives of Moroccan companies engaged in digitalization. We have decided to approach companies that operate in various industrial sectors, in different geographical locations, to ensure that our model is not unduly influenced by other variables omitted from the literature.

We then conducted in-person interviews, where we communicated directly with the companies through our personal networks. We sent out approximately 480 questionnaires and received 132 responses, a response rate of 27.5%, of which, after verification, we retained 108 usable questionnaires that constitute an acceptable sample from which acceptable data can be obtained.

However, the research sampling method utilized in the present study also comes with some drawbacks that should be acknowledged. Due to the fact that there is no centralized database of Moroccan companies using artificial intelligence, we had to resort to a non-probabilistic sampling method by drawing on professional and personal networks. While effective in obtaining a relevant number of companies, this method may introduce selection bias, particularly by over-representing more prominent, better connected, or already engaged in digital transformation companies. Furthermore, the data collection method partly based on direct solicitation and voluntary response may have favored responses from companies more likely to declare their innovation practices, thereby introducing a potential social desirability bias. These limitations must be taken into account when interpreting the results and demand caution in generalizing the findings to the broader Moroccan business context.

2.2. Analyzing the Data Treatment Process

We began by examining the validity and reliability of the variables in our research model through an analysis of its main components, focusing on groups of items integrated into an AI integration process and resistance to change.

Afterwards, we exposed a methodology of multi-variable analysis aimed at establishing the causal links between the dependent and independent variables.

- **The measuring model**

Aided by the analysis of main components, we verified the validity and trustworthiness of the measuring scales of our theoretical model in order to simplify the gathering of data and were thereby able to redefine the variables according to the following four stages (Evrard et al., 2003):

- The verification of the feasibility of the factorial analysis through the Bartlett sphericity test which rests upon the nil hypothesis of a correlation among the variables as well as through the –Kaiser-Meyer-Olkin (KMO) test which indicates the correlations among different variables used so that the analysis of main components are high enough for these to be determined.

When the KMO is higher than 0, 8, that means that the factorial structure is intelligible and stable and that there is a good factorability. If the KMO is between 0,5 and 0,8, it can be concluded that factorability is acceptable yet factorial structure is difficult to interpret and factorability is bad when the KMO is below 0,5.

- The determination of the number of factors to be retained starting from a set of initial variables. Step by step, we eliminate the items which have a weak contribution (equal to or below 0,500) over the main components identified (Evrard et al., 2003). Each analysis of main components is the object of an orthogonal Varimax rotation which enables the value of coefficients of the most correlated variables to be artificially increased while the value of the least correlated variables is reduced.
- The verification of the reliability of the factors of each analysis of main components through a coherence evaluation among the items examined by measuring a same concept. According to Evrard et al. (2003), a relaible scale produces the same results when the measurements are repeated whatever the context in which the test is carried out. We use the Cronbach alpha coefficient in our research cadre since it allows the reliability of different questions over the same phenomenon to be measured (Evrard et al., 2000). An alpha over 0, 6 is acceptable in the cadre of exploratory studies (Evrard et al., 2003).
- Rename each component and redefine the research hypothesis to arrive at a refined factorial analysis research model. **Table N°1** summarizes the results of analysis of the main components of the explanatory variables, including the Chronbach alpha value and the percentage variance explained in all components.

Table 1. Results of the validity and reliability of measurement scales

Components	Alpha Cronbach	Items	% variance explained	no of items
Integration of AI into the internal process	0,748	-The use of AI to automate internal business processes. -The contribution of AI to optimizing decision making within the company. -The integration of AI in human resources management (recruitment, training, evaluation). -Employees are trained and supported in the adoption of AI tools.	78,56%	4
AI-based learning platforms	0,745	-Personalization of content based on the needs of each user through AI-based learning platform -The adaptation of the learning rhythm according to the performance and progression of the learner by AI. -Improving learning and skill acquisition through AI-generated assessments and feedbacks. -AI facilitates interaction and engagement of learners by offering dynamic, adaptive pathways.	71,45%	4
Real-time feedback induced by AI	0,754	-Real-time feedback on employee performance through AI. -The immediate adjustment of actions and decisions by feedback generated by AI. -Improving the responsiveness of managers by providing them with instant feedback on employees thanks to AI. -Increasing employee motivation and engagement through real-time feedback driven by AI -AI facilitates continuous and adaptive communication through instant feedback.	74,42%	5
Using AI to personalize communication and leadership	0,715	-The adaptation of communication to individual employee preferences and needs by AI. -AI helps leaders identify employee expectations to adjust their management style. -Analyzing AI interactions to provide personalized leadership recommendations. -Anticipating employee needs through AI and message adaptation to strengthen engagement.	64,78%	4
Dynamic AI-based campaigns	0,737	-Personalization of campaign content by AI to maximize their impact on employees. -Improving employee engagement through dynamic AI campaigns by delivering targeted messages. -Analysis of employee data by AI to optimize the delivery and timing of internal campaigns. -Strengthening internal communication through AI-driven campaigns by continuously adjusting messages.	74,56%	4

continued on following page

Table 1. Continued

Components	Alpha Cronbach	Items	% variance explained	no of items
Monitoring and behavioural analysis via AI	0,749	-Real-time monitoring of employee behavior in their work environment by AI. -Identifying employee trends and needs through AI-based behavioral analysis. -Detection of weak signals related to employee engagement and satisfaction by AI. -Improving decision making by providing continuous analysis of organizational behaviors through AI.	74,52%	4
Resistance to change	0,754	–Degree of learning, of technology, knowledge and know-how –acquisition of knowledge to resolve technical problems. –acquisition of knowledge and know-how to improve technology –Acquisition of knowledge and know-how to develop new technologies and knowledge. –Improvement of product quality	76,42%	5

- **Test of the hypothesis by analysis of regression**

Multiple linear regression is the regression chosen to simultaneously analyze the link among various more than two -explanatory variables and a variable to explain. "The principle consists of looking into the relationship between the variable to be explained and the other explanatory variables which best account for the reality of the observations. This relationship is expressed through the regression equation which presents the variable to be explained as the sum of each one of the explanatory variables affected of their coefficients to which a constant term is added" (Crauser et al., 1989).

This explanatory method is used to test the hypothesis of our model. This gives us the opportunity to test our research model in a global context and thus determine the importance and significance of each explanatory variable for the integration of AI into the internal processes of companies in Morocco engaged in digitalization and the effect on resistance to change. It allows us to translate our conceptual model into the following equation:

- Resilience to change in Moroccan SMEs engaged in digitalization = β 1 AI integration + β 2 AI-based learning platforms + β 3 real-time feedback induced by IA+ β 4 AI use to personalize communication and leadership + β 5

Dynamic campaigns based on AI + β 6 Behavioral monitoring and analysis via AI + ε

The test over the hypothesis in this work according to this method demands the use of certain indicators such as:

- The verification of the Variance inflation factor (VIF) and the criteria of tolerance to make sure that the model does not contain a useless explanatory variable. The VIF must be below 10 and the tolerance criteria below 1.
- Test Fischer-Snedecor allows for the interpretation of the statistical significance of the results obtained and the contribution of each explanatory variable. Its noted value of significance "Signif F" designates that the threshold Fischer-Snedecor statistic value observed must be below 0,05 at the threshold of 5% or at 0,01 for a threshold value of 1% for the null hypothesis, thereby stipulating the non-existence of a linear relationship between explanatory variables and the variable to be explained be discarded.
- Test Student t allows verification as to whether the estimate obtained for the non-standardized regression coefficient or the non-standardized lambda (B) is significantly far from zero. Its significance must be below 0,05 at a threshold value of 5% or below 0,01 at a threshold value of 1%.

2.2.1. **Verification of VIF and Tolerance**

In order to proceed with a verification of VIF and tolerance, a multi-collinearity test is undertaken. We carried out verification of VIF and of tolerance to check for the lack of multi-collinearity, that is, that the model does not contain useless explanatory variables. The VIF must be under 10 and the tolerance criteria less than 1.

In our case, the absence of multicollinearity issues is evident, as demonstrated in the **Table 2**, where tolerance levels range between 0.5 and 0.9, and the VIF remains below 10.

Table 2. Coefficients of collinearity of variables in the research model

Model		Collinearity Statistics	
		Tolerance	VIF
1	(Constant)		
	Integration of AI into the internal process	,555	4,856
	AI-based learning platforms	,903	4,887
	Real-time feedback induced by AI	,537	5,105
	Using AI to personalize communication and leadership	,748	4,978
	Dynamic AI-based campaigns	,925	4,456
	Monitoring and behavioral analysis via AI	,850	4,081

a. Dependent Variable: Resistance to change

2.2.2. Test of the Theoretical Model

The validation of the hypothesis of the theoretical model leads us to proceed to the significance test of the model. This analysis will be carried out in two stages: an analysis of its overall and then of its individual significance.

Overall significance test

At first we looked into the overall significance of the model, that is, the set of explanatory variables which have an influence over the dependent variable. This test could be formulated as follows: is there at least one significant explanatory variable?

The determination of the overall significance of the model was carried out by using the Fischer statistic which indicates if the explanatory variables have an influence over the variable to be explained.

The arbitrage was done by using a comparison of the value of the F-statistic estimated as tabulated by Fischer. The SPSS 25 program automatically provided the probability associated with the calculated F-statistic which greatly facilitated analysis, thus to compare the probability associated with the F-statistic at a threshold level of 5% retained should be enough. In the case that a probability linked to the F-statistic is below a threshold value of 5%, then the hypothesis H0 can be discarded for the profile of the alternative hypothesis according to which regression is overall significant.

In our case, for explanatory variables of absorption capacity, the Fischer statistic found by the SPSS 25 program is $F = 18{,}989$ and the probability associated thereto is less than 5% ($0{,}00 < 0{,}05$), then the nil hypothesis is discarded and the model is overall significant (Table N°3).

Table 3. ANOVA Model Regression Index

ANOVA[a]					
Model		**Sum of Squares**	**ddl**	**Mean Square**	**F**
1	Regression	14,907	5	2,9814	18,989
	Student	15,837	101	,157	
	Total	30,744	106		
a. Predictors: (Constant), Integration of AI into the internal process, AI-based learning platforms, Real-time feedback induced by AI, Using AI to personalize communication and leadership, Dynamic AI-based campaigns, Monitoring and behavioral analysis via AI. b. Dependent Variable: Resistance to change.					

Individual significance Test:

To address the individual significance of the variables, we used the Student statistic directly provided by the SPSS 25 program. The hypothesis of significance of the variable is retained when the threshold is considered as the value of the estimated Student statistic is greater than the one tabulated by Student. In this research, the rejected probability provided by SPSS 25 at the retained threshold level will be used.

The results of the estimate shown in Table 4 (below) show that all six variables are statistically significant given the probability attributed to them:

- The variable "AI-based learning platforms" is significant at a threshold of 5% since the statistical rules of the Student test are respected ($t > 2$, $p = 0.013 < 0.05$).
- The variable "AI integration in internal process" is significant at 1% ($t > 2$, $p = 0.008 < 0.01$).
- The variable "Real-time feedback induced by AI" is significant at 5% ($t > 2$, $p = 0{,}017 < 0{,}05$).
- The variable "Dynamic AI-based campaigns" is significant at 5% ($t > 2$, $p = 0{,}021 < 0{,}05$).
- The variable "Monitoring and behavioral analysis via AI" is significant at 5% ($t > 2$, $p = 0{,}034 < 0{,}05$).

Moreover, the results of this regression show that the integration of AI in the internal process of Moroccan companies has a positive effect on resistance to change.

Table 4. Coefficients of individual significance

Coefficients [a]							
Model		Non-standardized Coefficients		Standardized Coefficients	t	Sig.	Collinearity Statistics
		B	Error standard	Beta			Tolerance
1	(Constant)	-,135	,481		-,281	,779	
	Integration of AI into the internal process	,653	,169	,414	2,227	,008	,555
	AI-based learning platforms	,674	,128	,446	2,527	,013	,537
	Real-time feedback induced by AI	,387	,106	,336	2,76	,017	,903
	Using AI to personalize communication and leadership	,565	,107	,503	2,038	,045	,748
	Dynamic AI-based campaigns	,349	,118	,327	2,358	,021	,925
	Monitoring and behavioral analysis via AI	,267	,127	,209	2,453	,034	,789
a. Dependent Variable: Resistance to change							

3. RESULTS AND DISCUSSION

Regression analysis confirms that AI-enabling learning platforms are the strongest variable in change resistance of Moroccan companies digitizing ($\beta = 0.674$, $p = 0.013 < 5\%$). The result validates our H2 hypothesis and conforms to the theoretical assumptions of the Technology Acceptance Model (TAM) by Davis (1989) and the UTAUT model by Venkatesh et al. (2003). It was emphasized in this work that utilities of perception as well as user-friendliness are crucial determinants of technologies' acceptance. In the acceptance of AI learning platforms, feelings of complexity or effort of adjustment may create an uneasiness or threat toward the current capability, hence evoking latent opposition. In practice, this requires that the application of such solutions be accompanied by progressive training programs, designed jointly with workers, in order to overcome fears and increase confidence.

Secondly, the AI internal implementation plays a significant and positive role on change resistance ($\beta = 0.653$, $p = 0.008 < 1\%$), thus confirming our H1 hypothesis. This is aligned with the work of Besson & Rowe (2012) on digital transformation, which reminds us of the existence of a «technological paradox» whereby innovation, creates as many expectations as internal tensions. Similarly, Bughin et al. (2018) illustrate how the deployment of AI in functions can routinized to redesign roles and instigate organizational uncertainty. It is necessary to reflect on technological integration not as an end but as a lever to facilitate progressive evolution, driven by the experience of internal users.

Second, the use of AI in internal processes has a positive and significant effect on resistance to change ($\beta = 0.653$, $p = 0.008 < 1\%$), thus confirming our H1 hypothesis. The phenomenon is consistent with research by Besson & Rowe (2012) on digital transformation, which speaks of the existence of a «technological paradox» where innovation stimulates as many as possible concerns within. Similarly, Bughin et al. (2018) illustrate how integrating AI into processes can disrupt established habits, redefine job functions and induce organizational ambiguity. It is crucial to approach technological integration as a way to an end, and not as an end, but as a driver of evolutionary change, aimed at the internal users' experience.

In fourth position, AI-based real-time feedback has a big positive impact on change resistance ($\beta = 0.387$, $p = 0.017 < 5\%$), which supports the H3 hypothesis. The work of Stone et al. (2015) provides the benefits of automated feedback in adapting behavior, but also possible information overload or surveillance threats. While organizational learning can be accelerated by feedback in real time, effectiveness would depend on the quality of feedback, feedback integration into the current routine and managerial stance adopted in reading it.

At the fourth position, real-time feedback induced through AI exhibits a significant positive influence on resistance to change ($\beta = 0.387$, $p = 0.017 < 5\%$), validating the H3 hypothesis. The work of Stone et al. (2015) highlights the benefit of automated feedback for behavioral modification, but also the risk of information overload or perceived surveillance. While real-time feedback can accelerate organizational learning, its usefulness is also dependent on feedback quality, alignment with existing routines, and the managerial position adopted to interpret it.

Finally, AI behavioral analysis has a significant, albeit moderate, effect on resistance to change ($\beta = 0.267$, $p = 0.034 < 5\%$), validating the H6 hypothesis. This finding is echoed in the work of Ransbotham et al. (2017) which shows that algorithmic behavior tracking can be perceived as an optimization lever or as an excessive control mechanism, depending on how it is implemented and perceived by employees. From a managerial point of view, transparency on the purposes and use of behavioral data becomes a central issue to preserve trust and avoid passive resistance.

Table 5 presents a summary of results obtained.

Table 5. Synthesis of hypotheses results (source: author's conception)

Hypotheses	Explanatory variables	Variables to explain	Coefficient β	Significance	t Student	Validation
H 1	Integration of AI into the internal process	Resistance to change	,653	,008	2,527	Confirmed
H 2	AI-based learning platforms	Resistance to change	,674	,013	2,527	Confirmed
H 3	Real-time feedback induced by AI	Resistance to change	,387	,017	2,76	Confirmed
H4	Using AI to personalize communication and leadership	Resistance to change	,565	,045	2,038	Confirmed
H5	Dynamic AI-based campaigns	Resistance to change	,349	,021	2,358	Confirmed
H6	Monitoring and behavioral analysis via AI	Resistance to change	,267	,034	2,453	Confirmed

CONCLUSION

The aim of this research is to analyze AI integration mechanisms that can create resistance to change in Moroccan companies that have implemented AI in their processes. Conducted with 108 companies working in various industrial sectors, the study contributes to both theoretical development and managerial practice by revealing AI-specific mechanisms that strengthen or explain resistance to change. Empirical evidence suggests that while AI integration fosters innovation, it can also trigger intense organizational resistance, particularly through systems such as AI-based learning systems, internal process automation, and AI-driven communication initiatives. At a managerial level, this research offers significant implications to executives by identifying strategic areas where resistance is imminent, thereby encouraging decision-makers to pursue more inclusive and adaptive change management approaches.

Theoretically, the study adds to the literature on digital transformation by applying behavioral and technological acceptance models to the Moroccan market. Managerially, it provides concrete levers for action, allowing leaders to anticipate and buffer resistance to the adoption of AI tools. This study, however, has its limitations that offer opportunities for future research. Either a qualitative or exploratory design would strengthen internal dynamics and employees' attitudes toward AI. In addition, generalizing to other companies, over a longer time frame and to other developing countries would facilitate comparative insights and greater generalizability. Hence, the phenomenon investigated here is not only generalizable in the Moroccan context but also inform digital transformation efforts in similar socio-economic environments.

REFERENCES

Amiot, C. E., Terry, D. J., Jimmieson, N. L., & Callan, V. J. (2006). A longitudinal investigation of coping processes during a merger: Implications for job satisfaction and organizational identification. *Journal of Management*, *32*(4), 552–574. DOI: 10.1177/0149206306287542

Anderson, D., & Anderson, L. A. (2021). *Beyond Change Management: How to Achieve Breakthrough Results Through Conscious Change Leadership* (2nd ed.). Wiley.

Appelbaum, S. H., Degbe, M. C., MacDonald, O., & Nguyen-Quang, T. S. (2022). Organizational Change: A Review of Theory and Research in the 21st Century. *Journal of Organizational Change Management*, *35*(3), 421–437.

Araujo, T., Helberger, N., & de Vreese, C. H. (2023). AI in organizations: From automation to augmentation. *Journal of Business Research*, *161*, 113807.

Armenakis, A. A., & Harris, S. G. (2022). Reflections: Organizational Change Management in the Age of Digital Transformation. *Journal of Change Management*, *22*(1), 12–29.

Avolio, B. J., Kahai, S. S., & Dodge, G. E. (2003). E-leadership: Implications for theory, research, and practice. The Leadership Quarterly, 11(4), 615–668. (00)00062-X

Beck, K., Beedle, M., van Bennekum, A., Cockburn, A., Cunningham, W., Fowler, M., & Thomas, D. (2001). *Manifesto for Agile Software Development*. Agile Alliance.

Besson, P., & Rowe, F. (2012). Strategizing information systems-enabled organizational transformation: A transdisciplinary review and new directions. *The Journal of Strategic Information Systems*, *21*(2), 103–124. DOI: 10.1016/j.jsis.2012.05.001

Brynjolfsson, E., & McAfee, A. (2017). *Machine, Platform, Crowd: Harnessing Our Digital Future*. W. W. Norton & Company.

Buchanan, D., & McCalman, J. (2023). *High-Impact Change Management: Principles and Practices*. Routledge.

Bughin, J., Seong, J., Manyika, J., Chui, M., & Joshi, R. (2018). *Notes from the AI frontier: Modeling the impact of AI on the world economy*. McKinsey Global Institute.

Burnes, B., & Bargal, D. (2023). Complexity and Uncertainty: Revisiting Stacey's Matrix in a Post-Pandemic World. *Management Decision*, *61*(1), 101–117.

Burnes, B., & Cooke, B. (2022). Re-evaluating Lewin's Legacy: Contemporary Relevance of the Three-Step Model. *Human Relations*, *75*(1), 5–27.

Caine, K., & Han, Y. (2021). Ethical implications of AI-enabled workplace monitoring: A review. *Ethics and Information Technology*, *23*(3), 399–414. DOI: 10.1007/s10676-021-09603-4

Carucci, R. (2016). Why Organizations Don't Learn. *Harvard Business Review*.

Cawsey, T. F., Deszca, G., & Ingols, C. (2023). *Organizational Change: An Action-Oriented Toolkit* (4th ed.). SAGE Publications.

CESE. (2022). *Pour une intelligence artificielle responsable au service du développement humain*. Conseil Économique, Social et Environnemental du Maroc. Retrieved from.

Chivu, I., Popescu, D. I., & Ciulu, R. (2023). Human-Centered Change Management in the Digital Era: A Review of the ADKAR Model. *Procedia: Social and Behavioral Sciences*, *299*, 87–94. DOI: 10.1016/j.sbspro.2023.02.011

Clampitt, P. G., DeKoch, R. J., & Cashman, T. (2000). A strategy for communicating about uncertainty. *The Academy of Management Perspectives*, *14*(4), 41–57. DOI: 10.5465/ame.2000.3979815

Crauser, C., Delorme, J., & Perret, B. (1989). *Initiation aux méthodes quantitatives appliquées à l'économie*. La Découverte.

Davenport, T. H., & Ronanki, R. (2018). Artificial Intelligence for the Real World. *Harvard Business Review*, *96*(1), 108–116.

Davis, F. D. (1989). Perceived usefulness, perceived ease of use, and user acceptance of information technology. *Management Information Systems Quarterly*, *13*(3), 319–340. DOI: 10.2307/249008

Delgado, C., & Zeller, F. (2023). Emotion recognition and the ethics of AI in organizational change. *AI & Society*, *38*(1), 177–194. DOI: 10.1007/s00146-022-01384-9

Dell Technologies & IDC. (2022). *The Digital Transformation Index Morocco*. Retrieved from.

Dhinakaran, D., Thenmozhi, D., & Karthikeyan, P. (2020). AI-powered chatbots for organizational support: Roles and use cases. *Journal of Organisational Transformation & Social Change*, *17*(3), 243–258.

El Mesbahi, M., & Alaoui, A. (2022). Le changement organisationnel au Maroc: Entre rationalité managériale et contraintes culturelles. *Revue Marocaine de Gestion et d'Économie*, *13*(1), 45–62.

El Mesbahi, M., & Alaoui, A. (2022). Les dynamiques culturelles de la transformation numérique au Maroc. *Revue Marocaine de Gestion*, *18*(1), 45–59.

Eloundou, T., Manning, S., Mishkin, P., & Rock, D. (2023). GPTs are GPTs: An early look at the labor market impact potential of large language models. OpenAI Technical Report.

Evrard, Y., Pras, B., & Roux, E. (2003). Market: études et recherches en marketing (3e éd.). Paris: Dunod.

Fernandez, T., & Gupta, S. (2022). Smart leadership: The impact of AI-based personalization on digital leadership effectiveness. *Journal of Leadership & Organizational Studies*, *29*(4), 457–472.

Ford, J. D., Ford, L. W., & D'Amelio, A. (2008). Resistance to change: The rest of the story. *Academy of Management Review*, *33*(2), 362–377. DOI: 10.5465/amr.2008.31193235

Gandomi, A., & Haider, M. (2015). Beyond the hype: Big data concepts, methods, and analytics. *International Journal of Information Management*, *35*(2), 137–144. DOI: 10.1016/j.ijinfomgt.2014.10.007

-. (2022). Next-generation learning analytics powered by AI: Frameworks and ethical implications. Computers & Education. *Artificial Intelligence*, *3*, 100070. DOI: 10.1016/j.caeai.2022.100070

Gao, L., Chen, Z., & Wen, J. (2023). Trust and transparency in AI-mediated communication: Empirical evidence from workplace settings. *Computers in Human Behavior*, *141*, 107614.

Ghosh, S., Das, A., Sanyal, S., & Srivastava, A. (2023). AI-powered communication analytics in enterprise systems: Framework and case applications. *Journal of Organizational Computing and Electronic Commerce*, *33*(1), 45–62. DOI: 10.1080/10919392.2022.2139034

Goleman, D., Boyatzis, R., & McKee, A. (2013). *Primal Leadership: Unleashing the Power of Emotional Intelligence*. Harvard Business Press.

Haenlein, M., & Kaplan, A. (2019). A brief history of artificial intelligence: On the past, present, and future of artificial intelligence. *California Management Review*, *61*(4), 5–14. DOI: 10.1177/0008125619864925

Hayes, J. (2022). *The Theory and Practice of Change Management* (6th ed.). Palgrave Macmillan.

Heifetz, R. A., & Linsky, M. (2022). *Leadership on the Line: Staying Alive through the Dangers of Leading*. Harvard Business Press.

Hiatt, J. (2006). *ADKAR: A Model for Change in Business, Government and Our Community*. Prosci Learning Center.

Hiatt, J. (2021). *ADKAR: A Model for Change in Business, Government, and Our Community*. Prosci Learning Center Publications.

Highsmith, J. (2009). *Agile Project Management: Creating Innovative Products* (2nd ed.). Addison-Wesley Professional.

Horney, N., Pasmore, B., & O'Shea, T. (2021). Agile Leadership and Change: Building Organizational Adaptability. *OD Practitioner*, *53*(2), 7–14.

Huang, M.-H., & Rust, R. T. (2021). Artificial intelligence in service. *Journal of Service Research*, *24*(1), 3–20.

Jarrahi, M. H. (2023). Artificial Intelligence and the Future of Work: Human-AI Symbiosis in Organizational Decision-Making. *International Journal of Information Management*, *68*, 102620.

Kaplan, A. M., & Haenlein, M. (2020). Rulers of the world, unite! The challenges and opportunities of artificial intelligence. *Business Horizons*, *63*(1), 37–50. DOI: 10.1016/j.bushor.2019.09.003

Kotler, P., Kartajaya, H., & Setiawan, I. (2017). *Marketing 4.0: Moving from traditional to digital*. Wiley.

Kotter, J. P. (2014). *Accelerate: Building Strategic Agility for a Faster-Moving World*. Harvard Business Review Press.

Kotter, J. P., & Schlesinger, L. A. (1979). Choosing Strategies for Change. *Harvard Business Review*, *57*(2), 106–114. PMID: 10240501

Martins, A., & Wu, H. (2021). Emotional intelligence in AI-assisted change management. *Journal of Organizational Psychology*, *21*(5), 92–104.

McKinsey & Company. (2021). The State of AI in 2021.

Men, L. R., & Bowen, S. A. (2021). *Excellence in internal communication management*. Business Expert Press.

Michel, E. J., By, R. T., & Burnes, B. (2022). Leading and managing change: Revisiting Kotter's 8-step change model. *Journal of Change Management, 22*(1), 19–36.

Mohamed, A., Puteh, M., & Ariffin, A. (2020). Natural Language Processing (NLP) in sentiment analysis: A review. *Indonesian Journal of Electrical Engineering and Computer Science, 17*(1), 51–59.

Mousa, M., & Mahmood, M. (2022). AI and internal communication in digital transformation: A relational approach. *Journal of Communication Management (London), 26*(2), 145–162.

Nguyen, T. H., & Kim, Y. (2022). Personalized content generation and employee engagement: The role of AI in internal communication. *Information & Management, 59*(7), 103661. DOI: 10.1016/j.im.2022.103661

Nguyen, T. H., & Kim, Y. (2022). The role of conversational AI in organizational resilience and learning. *Journal of Business Research, 145*, 412–421. DOI: 10.1016/j.jbusres.2022.02.037

Oreg, S., Bartunek, J. M., Lee, G., & Do, B. (2021). An affect-based model of recipients' responses to organizational change events. *Academy of Management Review, 46*(2), 327–346.

Oreg, S., Michel, A., & By, R. T. (2021). *The Psychology of Organizational Change: Viewing Change from the Employee's Perspective*. Cambridge University Press.

Oxford Business Group. (2023). Morocco explores opportunities for AI integration across key sectors.

Park, H., Lee, J., & Kim, S. (2023). The role of AI in adaptive communication and leadership behavior. *Technological Forecasting and Social Change, 190*, 122411.

Prosci (2023). Best Practices in Change Management: 12th Edition Benchmarking Report.

Rai, A., Constantinides, P., & Sarker, S. (2022). Next-Generation Digital Platforms: Toward Human-AI Hybrids. *Information Systems Research, 33*(1), 1–18. DOI: 10.1287/isre.2013.0495

Ransbotham, S., Kiron, D., Gerbert, P., & Reeves, M. (2017). *Reshaping Business with Artificial Intelligence: Closing the Gap Between Ambition and Action*. MIT Sloan Management Review & The Boston Consulting Group.

Rudnicka, P., Nowicki, M., & Grabowski, A. (2023). AI in change management: Predictive analytics and behavioral modeling for employee engagement. *The International Journal of Organizational Analysis*.

Russell, S., & Norvig, P. (2021). *Artificial Intelligence: A Modern Approach* (4th ed.). Pearson.

Shin, D. (2021). The Effects of Explainability and Causability on Human–AI Interaction Trust and Reliance. *Computers in Human Behavior, 123*, 106878. DOI: 10.1016/j.chb.2021.106878

Shum, H.-Y., He, X., & Li, D. (2018). From Eliza to XiaoIce: Challenges and opportunities with social chatbots. *Frontiers of Information Technology & Electronic Engineering, 19*(1), 10–26. DOI: 10.1631/FITEE.1700826

Stacey, R. D. (2022). *Strategic Management and Organisational Dynamics: The Challenge of Complexity to Ways of Thinking about Organisations*. Pearson Education.

Stone, D. L., Deadrick, D. L., Lukaszewski, K. M., & Johnson, R. (2015). The influence of technology on the future of human resource management. *Human Resource Management Review, 25*(2), 216–231. DOI: 10.1016/j.hrmr.2015.01.002

Tang, Y., & Li, Q. (2021). Transparency in AI-powered internal campaigns: Implications for employee engagement. *Journal of Business Research, 134*, 683–694.

Tanwar, M., Prasad, A., & Dhir, S. (2023). Big data and predictive analytics in change management: A bibliometric analysis. *Journal of Organizational Change Management, 36*(4), 758–775.

Tursunbayeva, A., Franco, M., & Pagliari, C. (2023). AI in HR and organizational development: Opportunities for personalization and adaptation. *AI & Society, 38*(1), 125–141. DOI: 10.1007/s00146-022-01356-z

Tursunbayeva, A., Franco, M., & Pagliari, C. (2023). The evolving role of AI in human resources and organizational communication. *AI & Society, 38*(1), 111–127. DOI: 10.1007/s00146-021-01235-1

Uhl-Bien, M., Arena, M. J., & Zoller, T. D. (2022). Leadership for organizational adaptability: A theoretical synthesis and integrative framework. *The Leadership Quarterly, 33*(2), 101579.

Venkatesh, V., Morris, M. G., Davis, G. B., & Davis, F. D. (2003). User acceptance of information technology: Toward a unified view. *Management Information Systems Quarterly, 27*(3), 425–478. DOI: 10.2307/30036540

Wang, X., Li, Z., Xu, Q., & Zhao, Y. (2023). Real-time adaptation of transformation strategies via AI analytics. *International Journal of Information Management, 73*, 102596. DOI: 10.1016/j.ijinfomgt.2023.102596

Waterman, R. H., Peters, T. J., & Phillips, J. R. (2021). The McKinsey 7-S Framework: Linking Strategy and Structure. *The McKinsey Quarterly.*

Yin, Y., Zhang, L., & Du, X. (2022). Digital trace data and behavioral analytics for transformation management. *Information Systems Frontiers*, *24*(2), 415–430.

Zamora, M., & Zerbini, F. (2022). Smart collaboration platforms and AI in hybrid work environments. *Journal of Organizational Computing and Electronic Commerce*, *32*(3), 192–212.

Zengul, F. D., Oner, S., & Yildiz, M. (2023). Artificial intelligence in organizational information management: Opportunities and ethical challenges. *Information Systems Frontiers*, *25*(1), 219–237. DOI: 10.1007/s10796-022-10258-3

Zhou, J., Gao, S., & Chen, W. (2022). Conversational AI in corporate communication: Current trends and future implications. *Journal of Business Research*, *152*, 186–197.

Zhou, J., Gao, S., & Chen, W. (2022). The future of AI in employee engagement and change communication. *Journal of Business and Psychology*, *37*(6), 1173–1191. DOI: 10.1007/s10869-021-09785-5

Zhu, M., & Ma, Y. (2023). Artificial empathy and the limits of AI in leadership communication. *The Leadership Quarterly*, *34*(1), 101653.

Chapter 9
The Adoption of Artificial Intelligence in Internal Audit as a Managerial Innovation in the Public Hospital Sector in Morocco

Aziz Hantem
https://orcid.org/0000-0001-7607-0353
Ibn Zohr University, Morocco

Sofya Seffar Andaloussi
https://orcid.org/0009-0004-2554-1548
Sidi Mohamed Ben Abdellah University, Morocco

Malika Asbayou
https://orcid.org/0009-0006-6060-9653
Ibn Zohr University, Morocco

Marouane Mkik
https://orcid.org/0000-0001-5118-6624
Higher Institute of Nursing and Health Technical Professions, Morocco

Widad Lachehab
https://orcid.org/0009-0007-2700-9362
Mohammed V University, Morocco

Soukaina Jouad
Ibn Zohr University, Morocco

Sanaa Belabbes
Mohammed VI University of Sciences and Health, Morocco

ABSTRACT

The health sector in Africa is often marked by a number of technical and managerial dysfunctions. To remedy this situation and modernize its practices, health organizations have resorted to adopting new management tools. In this respect, internal

DOI: 10.4018/979-8-3373-1737-3.ch009

auditing is an investigative and evaluative process that provides assurance to the healthcare organization about risk control and the reliability of information. With technological developments, the use of artificial intelligence tools in internal audit activities should further improve the quality of audit processes, manage potential risks and guarantee hospital performance. The aim of this chapter is to analyze the perceptions of internal auditors regarding the use of AI-driven tools in public healthcare organizations in Morocco. To explore this issue, we employed a quantitative research approach based on hypothetico-deductive reasoning. The results offer practical insights into promoting AI use in audit activities, emphasizing the role of awareness, professional experience, and the challenges faced in public hospitals.

I. INTRODUCTION

Against a backdrop of demographic change and technological transformation, all sectors are confronted with new practices, moving from a juxtaposition of traditional practices to digitized ones (Andaloussi, 2024). Among these new practices is artificial intelligence, which has been around since the 50s, but since the crisis of covid 19 we've seen a surge in AI in all sectors, with thousands of jobs being lost and new digital jobs being created.

The healthcare sector is no as artificial intelligence has the potential to revolutionize the healthcare sector. According to the OECD 2024 report, AI can help to meet a number of challenges facing the healthcare sector, such as personnel management, analysis of patient records and advanced detection of various patient pathologies.

All the more so as the immersion of artificial intelligence in healthcare organizations promotes a significant advance in the fight against medical errors and the challenges associated with healthcare management. In 2023, artificial intelligence saved the lives of almost 163,000 people in Europe as a result of advanced detection of pathology in patients, as well as improving communication between different services. Among the benefits of artificial intelligence is its ability to improve communication in order to mitigate medical errors, providing healthcare professionals with accurate and relevant information, helping to save lives and improve health outcomes.

The use of artificial intelligence within the healthcare sector also leads to the processing of a mass of clinical data, such as the analysis of medical images and the review of patient records, facilitating the presentation of accurate diagnoses in record time for patients. AI helps optimize the effectiveness and efficiency of healthcare staff by making some administrative tasks automatic, saving time and expense in non-clinical activities. According to (Chebrolu Kumar, 2020) this would enable healthcare professionals to focus on their core objective of presenting direct patient care. These productivity gains would help cover the shortage of healthcare professionals, which has been estimated at 3.5 million positions by 2030 (OECD, 2023).

However, while the integration of AI into the healthcare sector brings benefits across the board, it requires some management to mitigate its risks. Its integration within the healthcare sector requires compliance with auditing principles in order to respect the ethics and confidentiality of the data that will be processed by AI algorithms.

Generally speaking, auditing plays a vital role in assessing the performance of healthcare facilities by evaluating regulatory compliance: that law, internal and external standards are being respected within the facility. The audit of AI systems in the healthcare sector confirms that patient data is safeguarded following any type of security breach, and that the management of this same data complies with the legislative framework in force. AI also enables rapid and effective anomaly detection, giving auditors the ability to prevent potential risks in place. At the same time, auditors need to ensure that the use of AI complies with the principles of data integrity and data security, in order to maintain trust between patients and healthcare organizations. The relationship between auditing and AI in the healthcare sector is a topic of great importance that requires in-depth analysis. However, the affiliation of AI within healthcare organizations confronts the auditor with a new way of doing business.

As a key player in the MENA region, Morocco has implemented numerous initiatives to promote digital health. These initiatives are part of an overall vision for the digital transformation of the Moroccan healthcare system, enabling greater access to healthcare services, better coordination between the various stakeholders and transparent, fluid management of the healthcare pathway to meet the aspirations and needs of patients and healthcare professionals alike. In recent years, projects such as the nationwide unified information system, shared medical records, artificial intelligence in oncology and radiology, telemedicine, etc., have demonstrated the Moroccan government's growing concern with the digital transformation of the healthcare system and the use of new technologies to build a modern, inclusive and sustainable healthcare system.

In terms of control and audit, Morocco recognizes the growing importance of the relationship between AI and audit in all sectors, particularly healthcare. The country faces significant challenges in managing and improving the performance of its healthcare facilities. The study of the relationship between AI and audit in this context goes beyond compliance and risk management; it also focuses on improving the quality of care, protecting patient confidentiality and improving the effectiveness of audit practices.

However, the integration of auditing and AI in Moroccan healthcare organizations involves a number of challenges. A key challenge is the lack of advanced technological infrastructure capable of supporting AI systems while ensuring data security and adherence to auditing principles. All the more so, as the use of auditing and AI in healthcare organizations evokes new needs such as training for auditors but also for healthcare professionals, in addition to the protection of patient data and compliance with auditing principles. The aim is to make optimum, efficient use of these new technologies.

The aim of this chapter is to examine the relationship between auditing and AI within the specific context of the healthcare sector. The complexity of our subject lies in the fact that we are conducting this analysis in a developing country of the MENA region, namely Morocco. Our study will first provide a review of the literature on auditing and AI. The second part will examine the current state of AI adoption in Morocco's healthcare sector with a focus on the role and challenges faced by auditors in this context. Our study will be conducted within a positivist methodological framework, using a qualitative approach and SPSS data processing software. A questionnaire will be administered in over 60 auditors in public hospital centers in Morocco. To outline the structure of our article, the methodological framework will be presented in the third section, while the fourth section will be dedicated to the results and discussion.

II. THEORETICAL AND CONCEPTUAL FRAMEWORK

In this section we will highlight the concepts of managerial innovation, audit and artificial intelligence in audit activities, with a focus on the legal and ethical implications of artificial intelligence in hospital audit practices. We will then present an overview of theoretical models of the acceptability of technology.

1. Managerial Innovations

The implementation of an audit system in public hospitals represents a step forward in management. The concepts of innovation and managerial innovation are therefore interesting to explain on the basis of the research framework on the diffusion of innovations in information systems.

1.1 Innovation

For researchers who study innovations in the social sciences, innovation is the driving force behind economic growth (Schumpeter, 1939). In management science, the concept of innovation has been studied since the early 1960s. According to Mohr (1969) and Aiken and Hage (1971), an innovation is defined as the adoption of an idea or behavior that is new to the organization that adopts it. Thus, in this context, the idea or behavior adopted may be considered outdated relative to other organizations, but innovative within the specific organization in question (Daft, 1978). According to Rogers (1995), an innovation is perceived by the members of a social system as a new idea, practice or object. It can be a device, a system, a policy, a program, a process, a product or a service, created within the company or supplied from outside. Not all innovations are the same; they vary according to a number of criteria:

- The characteristics of an innovation: these are those that influence the rate at which the innovation is adopted by the social system: relative advantage, compatibility, complexity, testability and observability.
- The communication channel: according to Rogers and Scott (1997), the communication channel is the means by which messages are transmitted from one person to another. The innovation may be transmitted formally or informally, which has an impact on the rate of diffusion (Bigoness & Perreault, 1981).
- Time: The diffusion of innovations is perceived as a temporal process, which requires explicit consideration of time-related variation.
- The social system: This is a group of individuals who interact to solve a common problem and achieve a common goal (Rogers and Scott, 1997). It represents an environment in which an innovation is disseminated.

In addition, it is essential to analyze the different types of innovations in order to understand the adoption behavior of innovations and to identify users' perceptions. In his review of the literature, Damanpour (1987, 1991, 1996) identifies three categories of innovation (as cited in Hantem, 2019):

- Technical innovation versus managerial innovation.
- Product innovation versus process innovation.
- Radical innovation versus incremental innovation.

In the next section, we will focus on managerial innovation and look at its origins and concepts.

1.2 Managerial Innovation: Origins and Concepts

Kimberly first introduced the concept of 'managerial innovation' in 1981. According to Kimberly and Evanisko (1981), a managerial innovation is defined as 'any program, product or technique which represents a significant departure from the state of management at the time it is introduced and which impacts the nature, quality or quantity of information available in a decision-making process' (Kimberly and Evanisko, 1981, p. 700). Damanpour was one of the first authors to make a clear distinction between technological advances and managerial advances. According to Damanpour (1988), 'managerial advances are directly linked to basic production activities, and require organizational changes in processes more directly linked to their management approach' (Damanpour, 1988, p. 548). According to Van de Ven (1986), managerial innovation is defined as a unique idea, formula or approach perceived as new by those involved (as cited in Le Roy et al, 2013).

In the 1990s, authors such as Rogers (1995) introduced a new vision of the notion of managerial innovation. According to Rogers (1995), managerial innovation is defined as: 'an idea, practice, or object perceived as new by individuals or organizations' (Rogers, 1995, p.11). In his study on the structure of managerial innovations, David (1996) identified three interacting elements (as cited in Le Roy et al, 2013)):

- Knowledge-driven innovations. These relate to the knowledge generated (management techniques);
- Relationship-based innovations: new decentralized systems, project teamwork, etc.
- Mixed innovations. These are innovations that include both knowledge-based and relationship-based innovations.

Since the 2000s, there has been a revival of research into new management methods, particularly in the research program at the London Business School led by Hamel, Mol and Birkinshaw. According to Birkinshaw and Mol (2006), managerial innovation is defined as: "the creation of new management practices, processes and structures that differ significantly from traditional norms" (Birkinshaw & Mol, 2006, p.81). Hamel (2006) offers a somewhat similar definition: "Managerial innovation can be defined as a significant departure from traditional management principles, processes and practices, or as a departure from organizational forms that significantly change the way management work is done..."(Hamel, 2006, p. 75).

Furthermore, in 2008, Birkinshaw, Hamel and Mol defined managerial innovation as follows: 'Managerial innovation consists of creating and implementing a management practice, process, structure or technique that is innovative in relation to what is known... in order to achieve the organization's objectives'. (Birkinchaw et al, 2008, p.825). It is possible to conclude that managerial innovation consists of introducing a specific organizational change with the aim of improving the company's performance. And so, managerial innovation refers to the adoption of a new organization, a new administrative system and new managerial practices that promote value creation (Damanpour & Aravind, 2012, p. 424).

In healthcare, an innovation is considered to be the recent introduction within a hospital of a medical technology, therapeutic procedure or administrative system that is relatively new for the sector in general (Wu & Hsieh, 2011a). Indeed, the adoption of innovations within healthcare structures, particularly hospitals, is likely to generate numerous benefits in terms of quality of care, competitiveness, patient satisfaction and the satisfaction of the stakeholders involved (Hantem et al, 2024a). These innovations can be classified into two broad categories (Wu & Hsieh, 2011b; Karaa et al, 2016):

- Medical/therapeutic innovations, which involve technological and medical advances ;
- Non-medical administrative/managerial innovations, which involve organizational and managerial changes.

As mentioned above, managerial innovation plays an important and significant role in the performance of organizations, whether private or public. In Morocco's public sector, particularly hospitals, the introduction of an audit system represents a managerial innovation that is part of the trend towards convergence of public management practices with those of the private sector (Hantem et al, 2024b).

2. The Concept of Audit

The word 'audit' comes from the Latin 'audire', meaning 'to listen'; the English verb 'to audit' means 'to verify, monitor, examine'. Auditing is a particular method of investigation and evaluation based on a frame of reference, including a diagnosis and possibly providing solutions. Auditing involves observation, analysis and interpretation. An audit consists of evaluating a specific situation according to internal criteria (procedures) or external criteria (standards, regulations, etc.). It is responsible for:

- Assessing the effectiveness of the measures implemented;
- Checking compliance with these requirements;
- Identifying potential areas for improvement.

Today, the term audit refers to a variety of tasks, but audits can be categorized according to their objectives, the entity and the people involved (Arthur, 2015).

2.1 Internal Audit

The definition of internal auditing has evolved significantly over time, reflecting its growing importance within organizations. The Institute of Internal Auditors (IIA) first defined internal auditing in 1947 as an "independent appraisal function established within an organization to examine and evaluate its activities as a service to the organization" (IIA, 1947). This perspective was later expanded by Sawyer (1973), who emphasized that internal auditing is concerned with any phase of business activity where it can be of service to management, providing advice, information, and assistance in achieving organizational objectives.

The definition then evolved over the years, with several modifications. However, it was difficult to formalize a single definition, reflecting the sensitivity and importance of the internal audit function within companies. It wasn't until 2000 that IFACI accepted the official definition of auditing as an independent and objective activity that provides assurance on the control of an organization's operations advises on improvements and creates added value. This definition includes a systematic and methodical approach to evaluating risk management, control and corporate governance processes.

In Morocco, the Institute of Internal Auditors-Morocco (2019) provides an official definition of internal auditing as "an autonomous and objective activity that ensures an organization's control over its operations provides it with advice to improve them and participates in the creation of added value". According to IIA-Morocco (2019), it supports the organization in achieving its objectives by systematically and methodically evaluating its risk management, control and governance processes and proposing solutions to improve their effectiveness.

In the same vein, according to the International Institute of Internal Auditors, 'internal auditing is defined as 'an independent, objective assurance and consulting activity designed to add value and improve an organization's operations. It contributes to the achievement of an organization's objectives by providing a disciplined, methodical approach to evaluating and improving the effectiveness of risk management, control and governance processes.' (as cited in AMIRIet al., 2021).

2.2 Audit Systems in Hospitals

Healthcare organizations attach great importance to the quality of care and patient safety. They must adopt a continuous improvement approach. In France, for example, the French National Authority for Health (HAS) suggests that organizations carry out regular audits to assess the effectiveness of processes, management systems and internal practices. Internal audits have become a legal obligation, as stipulated in chapter 9.2 of the ISO 9001 standard. So, to obtain ISO 9001 certification, a healthcare organization must carry out regular internal audits in line with its quality management system.

The partly unfavorable perception of internal audit that persists in healthcare organizations is due to confusion arising mainly from the double meaning that the notion of 'control' conveyed by the audit approach can have. In fact, internal audit is responsible for an 'autonomous activity of evaluating the controls of operations... reporting malfunctions and proposing recommendations that can be implemented with a view to assisting management' (Segouin & Perret, 2011).

Research into the influence of the internal audit function on the performance of public hospitals, such as the study conducted by Munro and Stewart in 2011 and the study conducted in 2017 in Uganda, has highlighted that the internal audit function has a significant impact on the performance of the internal control system in public hospitals (Kaziba et al., 2017). In addition, it plays an essential role in the operation of the other departments and in assessing the associated risks (Munro & Stewart, 2011).

In sum, the integration of artificial intelligence in internal audit activities in the hospital sector is not a choice, but an obligation that aims to optimize the internal management of its organizations and also to improve the patient care processes and de quality approach.

3. Artificial Intelligence in Auditing

Artificial intelligence is a collection of methods and tools that make computer work. It uses advanced algorithms and methods to process data and information in order to improve and stimulate cognitive capabilities (Kok et al., 2009; Wahbi et al., 2023). Also, the artificial intelligence represents the engineering of creating machines to automate repetitive tasks using AI techniques (McCarthy, 2007).

The integration of technology, in particular artificial intelligence (AI), into the auditing field is profoundly transforming professional practices and improving audit efficiency. AI makes it possible to automate repetitive and time-consuming tasks, enabling auditors to focus on more strategic analyses, such as risk assessment and informed decision-making. This automation of data extraction and reconciliation improves the speed, accuracy and reliability of audits, while reducing operational costs. The ability to analyze large quantities of data quickly and reliably also makes it possible to detect anomalies that might escape a traditional audit (Chukwuani & Egiyi, 2020).

In today's, optimizing the execution of audit activities requires the adoption of high-performance control devices, based in IA, helps to improve the quality of audits and controls (Kit Morris, 2023). The application of AI tools in auditing enables better understanding and advanced data analysis and risk assessment. Through AI tools, for example: natural language processing, helps auditors identify potential anomalies and errors throughout the audit process. What's more, AI enhances the transparency and accuracy of financial information by making it easier to detect suspicious behavior and anomalies and fraud. Artificial intelligence could transform the very nature of audits, increasing their rigor and efficiency, adding considerable value in finance environment where transparency requirements are growing (The institute of internal auditors, 2017).

Integrating AI into internal audit processes automates repetitive and time-consuming tasks and enable real-time data processing, by focusing on higher value-added activities, which favours a significant improvement in the quality of the audit process (INTOSAI. 2023; Mighiss & Kabbaj, 2021). However, the adoption of AI in auditing also raises several concerns. It is crucial that auditors retain their professional judgment and human skills, insofar as AI cannot replace as reasoning ability, understanding of context and professional skepticism (Bizarro & Dorian, 2017).

Auditors will also face other challenges, such as lack or insufficient training, high implementation costs and the ethical and regulatory considerations (Luo et al., 2018; Huang, 2018). Furthermore, the rapid adoption of such a technology could generate socio-economic inequalities, leading to technological unemployment and negative effects on wealth redistribution (Kokina & Davenport, 2017; Makridakis, 2017).

3.1 The Case of Hospital Auditing

Hospital auditing involves assessing the practices and performance of healthcare facilities. In many countries, the use of AI in healthcare makes easy to analyze large amounts of data and to identify potential errors and improve risk management. In countries such as the USA, UK and Germany, AI is integrated into auditing software that automates the collection and analysis of hospital data. These systems detect anomalies in financial statements, billing errors and risks to quality of care. The adoption of artificial intelligence in hospitals varies considerably by region and country, due to investment, public policy and digital health priorities.

Internationally, we find several studies analyzing the percentage use of AI in hospitals and hospices. In Belgium, the adoption rate of AI in hospitals is estimated at between 20% and 25%; in the United States, more than 70 veterans' medical centers are using AI, notably to improve the appointment scheduling process; and in the European Union, the majority of member states have drawn up AI strategies, identifying healthcare as a priority sector.

In Africa, several countries such as South Africa, Kenya, Nigeria, Senegal, Egypt, Morocco, Tunisia, Rwanda, Uganda, Mauritania and Côte d'Ivoire have adopted policies such as the "Startup Act" to encourage the development of AI, which could also positively influence the adoption of AI in the hospital sector.

A major advantage of AI in hospital auditing is that it streamlines processes, allowing auditors to spend less time on repetitive tasks and more time on critical, strategic aspects of the audit. This not only speeds up the process but also reduces the likelihood of human error, leading to more reliable outcomes. However, this adoption also raises ethical and confidentiality concerns. Sensitive patient data must be protected, and it's crucial that AI systems comply with privacy standards, such as the RGPD in Europe. AI-enabled audit practices have now emerged to improve risk and anomaly detection and enhance performance:

- Clinical performance auditing
- Automated financial auditing
- Audit of compliance with healthcare standards
- Auditing patient safety practices
- Auditing human resources and personnel management

3.2 Certifying Accounts and Improving Performance

The primary objective of certifying the financial statements of public-sector healthcare organizations is to ensure the reliability and transparency of their accounts (Hantem, 2023). This process involves establishing robust control systems and, most importantly, certifying that the accounts are sincere, reliable, and provide a true and fair view of the financial situation of the organization in question (Lizot & Laskawiec, 2014). The sincerity and reliability of the accounts, reflecting the patrimonial approach of an accounting system (Hantem, 2019), follow a change management approach. This approach entails analyzing the initial situation, identifying strengths and weaknesses, pinpointing risk areas, and implementing an action and correction plan (Lafon, 2016).

Such a systematic approach not only provides assurance but also builds trust among various stakeholders. Another essential objective of certifying accounts is to enhance overall performance. The concept of performance, as defined by Pesqueux (2004), extends beyond the completion of a process or task; it encompasses the achieved results and the success that one can take pride in. According to Schier and Saulquin (2007), the interpretation of performance varies among individuals or groups. From a managerial perspective, it could denote the profitability or competitiveness of the organization. For an employee, it might involve the work climate, and for a customer, performance could be evaluated based on the quality of services rendered (Schier & Saulquin, 2007).

Hospital performance differs from other forms of organizational performance. It is characterized by its complex and specific nature (Minvielle et al, 2008). Hospital performance is often associated with elements such as financial stability, optimizing bed occupancy, meeting staffing standards, achieving a high percentage of patients satisfied with their stay, quality assurance of services... According to WHO (2007), "High hospital performance should be based on professional competence in the application of knowledge, technology, efficiency in the use of resources, patient satisfaction and health outcomes" (WHO, 2007; Markaoui & Hassine, 2018).

An effective internal audit system significantly contributes to enhancing hospital performance through its emphasis on internal control systems. However, the absence of controls can result in a substantial deterioration of a well-established management system, diminishing its effectiveness and consequently impacting the overall performance of the organization (Zarai & Bettebai, 2007; Zarhloul & Mrani, 2022).

3.3 Advantages and Risks of AI in Healthcare

While the adoption and implementation of artificial intelligence in the healthcare field does present advantages for patients and healthcare organizations, its use also entails risks in terms of inequalities in the digital environment and health, patient privacy, incompatibility of systems, etc. According to the OECD (2024), the integration of AI in the healthcare sector has a number of advantages, including the following:

- High-volume exploitation of clinical data for better diagnosis and more appropriate treatment.
- Thanks to artificial intelligence, healthcare professionals could have more time to focus on patient care.
- Artificial intelligence can help protect digital health infrastructures against threats that compromise their security.
- Artificial intelligence can help leverage and add value to the 97% of healthcare data that is currently not usable for making and guiding decisions.

Despite these advantages, there are risks inherent in AI in healthcare, particularly the reliability of results given by biased algorithms, lack of transparency, use of AI tools in an inappropriate context, use of solutions by less qualified healthcare professionals, disclosure of personal data, lack of responsibility for AI management and task allocation (given the work overload) and lack of a clear strategy for the use of AI (OECD, 2024). One of the problems of using artificial intelligence in auditing activities and in decision-making in a context marked by massive data, such as health, lies in the level of unfair bias and in the techniques and methods of data processing. An algorithmic bias or a human bias transformed into an algorithmic bias is considered, by American researchers (2019), to be an application of an algorithm that generates socio-economic inequalities, which exacerbates the disparities between particularly vulnerable groups and has a negative impact on the healthcare system.

The last few years, particularly 2023, have been marked by the appearance and publication of reports and regulatory texts likely to guide the integration and implementation of artificial intelligence without risk. These include the Bletchley Park AI Safety Summit, the provisional agreement on European AI legislation, the White House Executive Order on the Safe, Secure and Trustworthy Development and Use of Artificial Intelligence and the G7 Code of Conduct on AI. For the healthcare sector, the WHO published guidelines on the regulation of artificial intelligence in 2023 (US White House, 2023; World Health Organization, 2023; European Commission, 2023; AI Safety Summit, 2023; European Parliament, 2023).

The ethical and legal aspects are one of the major challenges in the use of artificial intelligence in hospital management, particularly in hospital audit activities. The following section aims to highlight the ethical and legal implications of integrating AI into hospital audit activities.

4. Legal and Ethical Implications of AI in Hospital Audit Practices

Integrating artificial intelligence into the internal audit of hospitals has ethical and legal implications. Findings have highlighted a regulatory gap, particularly in terms of laws and legal texts, which come up against the complexity of algorithms. According to Veale and Zuiderveen Borgesius (2021), professionals need to evolve and train in AI to become familiar with the decision-making logic of AI. In ethical terms, the issues are visceral. Algorithms, if mishandled, can generate distorted data, which could disrupt interpretations and decisions. In this respect, Obermeyer et al (2019) have demonstrated in a striking way, using an AI model, that due to the misinterpretation of indicators, for a care management program, priority was given to healthy patients to the detriment of marginalized groups of patients who do not have access to preventive care.

Human auditors, while fallible, can contextualize, for instance, recognizing that a spike in ER visits in a low-income area might signal socioeconomic barriers, not patient noncompliance. Yet replacing them with AI risks reducing audits to box-ticking exercises, devoid of moral reasoning. The European Commission's guidelines (2019) rightly stress explainability, but how many hospitals have the expertise to audit AI's audits?

As far as the Moroccan context is concerned, the competent authorities have put in place a whole legal arsenal aimed at guiding digital technology for the benefit of Moroccan citizens, while protecting data by providing reliable and transparent information and strengthening competitiveness (Gueldi & Himmichi, 2024). To this end, a number of laws have been passed, including:

- Law No. 09-08 on the protection of individuals with regard to the processing of personal data. This legislation regulates and encourages access to information and the protection of personal data, ensuring the transparency, confidentiality and security of information managed by public and private organisations. This law is aligned with international data protection standards, in particular the European General Data Protection Regulation (GDPR).
- Law 07-03, which incorporates a criminal dimension aimed at protecting the security and integrity of automated data processing systems against acts of piracy, computer fraud, invasion of privacy and other criminal activities related to information technologies. It provides for criminal penalties for the perpetrators of such offences, thereby helping to ensure a secure and reliable digital environment in Morocco.

A path forward lies in hybrid systems. For example, AI could flag anomalies while human auditors investigate root causes, blending efficiency with empathy. Legal reforms might mandate "algorithmic impact assessments" for audit tools, akin to environmental reviews, forcing developers to disclose training data bases and hospitals to mitigate harms. Ethically, this requires redefining "transparency" beyond technical explainability to include participatory design, engaging patients and auditors in shaping AI tools. Without such measures, hospitals risk automating inequity under the guise of progress.

Beyond the legal aspects, the adoption and implementation of such a technology are influenced by certain factors, particularly those relating to acceptability. In the following section, we present an overview of the theories and models of technology acceptability.

5. Acceptability: a Premise for the Use of Technology

The theoretical and conceptual framework relating to the use of technology by humans is well understood. It covers the phases from preliminary acceptance according to the TAM and UTAUT models (Venkatesh et al., 2003) through to a state of symbiosis between humans and technology (Brangier et al., 2009).

Current models in the literature are based on five variables to study the acceptability of technologies: past experience and attitudes towards a similar technology (Bel, 2016a), desired performance, expected effort, social influence and facilitating conditions (Bel, 2016b; Venkatesh & Bala, 2008). Several models have been developed to explain the process that leads to the intention to use a technology.

5.1 Theoretical Underpinnings of Acceptability

The theories of reasoned action and planned behavior are at the origin of models of technology acceptability (Lou Menant, 2021a). The two models, Technology Acceptance Model (TAM) and Unified Theory of Acceptance and Use of Technology (UTAUT), commonly cited in research, both derive from the theory of reasoned action. They justify the effective use of technology by the influence of individual explanatory factors on the intention to use. In addition, much research has included behavioral control as a predictor of intention to use, which is consistent with the theory of planned behavior (Venkatesh et al., 2016).

Behavioral action, a concept proposed by Fishbein and Ajzen in 1975, is at the heart of the theory of reasoned action, which aims to explain behavior. According to the authors, two elements influence behavior: the attitude towards the behavior or object, which in turn derives from behavioral beliefs and the anticipated assessment of the consequences of the behavior. According to Fishbein and Ajzen, attitudes are complemented by subjective norms, which are anticipated by normative beliefs and the individual's willingness to conform (Lou Menant, 2021b).

From this perspective, Ajzen (1991) included an additional variable entitled 'perceived behavioral control', which led to the emergence of the theory of planned behavior. This theory adds an additional and enriching dimension to the theory of reasoned action thanks to the concept of behavioral control. This term refers to the idea of self-efficacy, which is determined by a person's belief in their ability to perform a behavior or achieve a goal; in addition, behavioral control takes into account the perception of ability, the contextual aspect via the availability of the behavior and the perceived ease of performing it (Kefi, 2010).

5.2 Models of Acceptability

In the age of technological change, researchers have been interested in the effect of technology on people. Models have been used to study the interaction between people and technology.

The TAM and UTAUT models are widely represented in the literature, explaining the degree of acceptability through the variables: perceived usefulness, expected performance, facilitating conditions, social influence. According to the TAM model, a priori assessment of perceived usefulness and perceived ease of use influence attitudes towards the use of the technology in question. Users perceive a system as useful if they think it can help them improve their job performance (Davis, 1989).

The social component and external influences, such as: type of technology; field of application; context of use, etc., are not included in this model. These variables made it possible to improve the predictive power of the TAM model towards another model including social and contextual variables, namely the UTAUT model. The Unified Theory of Acceptance and Use of Technology (UTAUT) was constructed by combining several models, including the TAM (Venkatesh et al., 2003). This theoretical model incorporates social influence and facilitating conditions as explanatory variables for behavioral intention, in addition to expected effort (perceived ease of use) and expected performance (perceived usefulness).

Social influence is made up, on the one hand, of support from management and the organization, and, on the other hand, of users' belief in compatibility with the system. Moderating variables have been added by various authors, in particular: age, experience, individual willingness. We note that the UTAUT model is more complete than the TAM model by including social and contextual variables. However, certain criticisms have been levelled at the aforementioned models, particularly the lack of consistency in the results obtained regarding the link between intention to use and actual use of the technology (Harrison et al., 2014; Nistor, 2014). We are talking here about the net benefit of implementing such a technology.

Furthermore, unlike the TAM and UTAUT acceptance modules, the Human-Organization-Technology Fit (HOT-fit) model, proposed by Yusof et al. in 2008, aims to predict the net benefits for the organization that adopts and implements a new technology. The HOT-fit model introduces the notion of the impact of the characteristics of the organization and its environment on the use of technology. According to this model, the organizational structure and the organizational environment are two factors that influence the use of the technology and the system in question.

According to Yusof et al (2008), system quality, data quality and service quality are characteristics of the technology that predict its use and user satisfaction. Quality of service is measured by the perceived ease of use, response time, perceived usefulness, availability, reliability, completeness, flexibility and perceived security of the system. Data quality corresponds, among other things, to the completeness, accuracy, availability, relevance, consistency and reliability of the information provided by the system. Service quality refers to the support provided to users. According to this model, there is a feedback loop between human factors and organizational factors in the sense that human factors (use and satisfaction) influence and are influenced by organizational factors of structure and environment.

To sum up, the integration of artificial intelligence into organizations' management methods has raised a large number of questions among researchers and professionals about its impact on organizational performance. Artificial intelligence has also emerged as one of the resources most exploited by organizations, fostering innovation and providing a competitive advantage.

The incorporation of artificial intelligence into the internal audit activities of public hospitals enables processes to be automated, irregularities to be identified and risks to be identified... within the hospital structure and at all levels. The changes brought about by technology are giving rise to a host of challenges aimed at fostering managerial innovation. Technology should therefore be an explanatory factor for managerial innovation, particularly in the hospital sector.

In summary, this literature review has enabled us to dissect the advantages and risks associated with the integration of artificial intelligence tools into internal audit activities, particularly in the healthcare field, and to analyze, through models, the factors influencing the acceptability and adoption of the technology. The empirical part of our study will be the subject of the following sections.

III. MATERIEL AND METHOD

To test these hypotheses and answer our research question, we adopted a quantitative methodological approach. This involved administering a questionnaire (survey) to internal auditors and managers working in public hospitals in Morocco, in particular university hospital centers (UHC) and other public hospitals: provincial and prefectural hospitals (OPH).

We proceeded to design our questionnaire, which we administered to internal auditors and managers working in public health organizations in Morocco between June 15, 2024, and December 15, 2024. The questionnaire comprised firm, open-ended, and scaled questions. We processed and analyzed the 60 received responses using Excel and SPSS software. For the statistical processing of the data, we employed univariate, bivariate, and multivariate analyses. Additionally, to test our research hypotheses, we referred to the test Student's t (T-test).

We would point out that the declaration that their Institutional Ethics Committee confirmed that no ethical review was required for this study. Written informed consent for participation was not required because all participants' data was anonymized before the statistical analyses were done.

Based on the literature review and the various findings, we have developed the following hypotheses:

- **H1**: The perception of AI usage in audit activities differs between UCH and OPH.
- **H2:** Experienced auditors, with more than 10 years' experience, tend to use AI tools in their activities.
- **H3:** Awareness and prior understanding of AI leads to proactive adaptation by internal auditors.
- **H4:** The barriers to using AI in audit activities are similar in different hospital organizations.

IV. RESULTS

1. Descriptive Analysis

The table provides an overview of the distribution of participants by gender, occupation, and sector of activity. The demographic results reveal a predominance of women, representing 56.67% of participants, compared with men, who account for 43.33%. In addition, most respondents (70%) were auditors, showing a predominance of this profession over managers. In addition, a higher proportion of respondents work in university hospital centers (UHC) (63.33%) than in other public hospitals (OPH) (36.67%).

Table 1. Participant demographics

	Number (n=60)	Frequency %
Sexe		
Women	34	56.67
Man	26	43.33
Métier		
Auditors	42	70
Managers	18	30

continued on following page

Table 1. Continued

	Number (n=60)	Frequency %
Sectors		
other public hospitals	22	36,67
university hospital centers	38	63,33

2. Data Analysis

Reliability

We tested the reliability of our result by examining the four variables in our study. The table shows the results obtained. Cronbach's alpha is 0.867, while Cronbach's alpha based on standardized items is 0.865. These statistics indicate a good level of internal consistency, demonstrating a high degree of coherence in our measurements.

Correlation

Our results reveal significant correlations between the different variables studied. A moderate positive correlation is observed between the level of training on AI and preparation for its introduction ($r = 0.506$, $p < 0.05$). In addition, a strong positive correlation is found between preparation for the introduction of AI and the level of awareness of the implications of AI in the job ($r = 0.736$, $p < 0.01$), as well as with the level of awareness of the changes already induced by AI in the job ($r = 0.728$, $p < 0.01$). A significant but weaker correlation was also found between the level of AI training and the level of awareness of AI implications in the workplace ($r = 0.591$, $p < 0.05$), as well as with the level of awareness of changes already induced by AI in the workplace ($r = 0.418$, $p < 0.05$).

3. Analysis of Assumptions

Hypothesis 1

Our hypothesis H1 that the perception of the use of AI in audit and activities in UCH is different from that in OPH is confirmed. The results of Student's t-tests, based on representative samples from the UCH and OPH, show notable divergences in AI-related perceptions and actions.

In the OPH, a greater willingness to train in AI is observed compared to the UCH, with a significant difference (p = 0.0234). Similarly, a greater willingness to adapt their practices for the introduction of AI is found in the OPH compared to the UCH (p = 0.0478), as well as a greater awareness of the potential impacts of AI on their work (p = 0.0132). However, there was no significant difference in terms of recognition of the changes already brought about by AI in their work (p = 0.0945).

Table 2. Results of Student's t-tests for hypothesis 1

Variable	T-test		P value
	OPH	UCH	
Learn about AI	2,923	2,294	0,0234
Change my practices to better prepare for the introduce tion of AI.	2,846	2,412	0,0478
Be aware of what AI could change in my work.	3,154	2,647	0,0132
Be aware of what AI has already changed in my work.	2,923	2,471	0,0945

Hypothesis 2

The data collected significantly confirms the H2: hypothesis that experienced auditors, with more than 10 years' experience, tend to use AI tools in their activities. A majority of individuals representing 60% of the sample said they had used AI tools as part of their professional activities. Looking specifically at those with more than 10 years' experience, we observe 83% have used these tools. By contrast, among those with less than 10 years' experience, only 25% have used such tools. This inclination can be attributed to several factors:

- Better knowledge of AI tools: Experienced professionals have had more opportunities to familiarize themselves with these tools and understand their potential, making them more inclined to use them.

- Greater confidence in AI tools: Accumulated experience can also boost professionals' confidence in the ability of AI tools to improve their audit and control work.
- Appetite for innovation: Experienced auditors and controllers are often more open to adopting new technologies and exploring new ways of working, leading them to integrate AI tools into their professional practices.

These findings underline the growing importance of AI tools in audit and control, and highlight the crucial role of experience in their effective adoption and use.

Hypothesis 3

Hypothesis 3 suggests that awareness and prior understanding of AI lead to proactive adaptation by internal auditors is confirmed. Student's t-test results reveal significant differences between individuals who have already heard of AI and those who have never heard of AI. Participants who had already heard of AI showed a greater propensity to learn about AI compared to those who had never heard of AI ($p = 0.0004$). Similarly, they showed a greater willingness to change their practices to prepare for the introduction of AI compared to those who had never heard of AI, with a statistically significant difference ($p = 0.0012$).

Table 3. Results of Student's t-tests for hypothesis 3

Variable	T-test		P value
	Heard about AI	**Never Heard about AI**	
Learn about AI	2,821	1,750	0,0004
Change my practices to prepare for the introduction of AI	2,771	1,500	0,0012

Hypothesis 4

Our hypothesis H4 that barriers to the use of AI in audit work are similar in the OPH and UCH is confirmed. The average scores for five specific obstacles were identical in both sectors. In the OPH, the lack of AI training and expertise was rated at 3.125, while in the UCH it was rated at 3.000. Similarly, the high cost of implementing AI was noted at 3,000 in the OPH and 3,125 in the UCH. Other barriers, such as concerns about AI reliability, lack of clarity on AI-related regulations and reluctance to change, showed similar scores in both sectors. Student's t-tests revealed no significant differences barrier scores. These results suggest that the challenges faced in adopting AI are uniform, regardless of industry.

4. Discussion

Correlation analyses revealed significant links between different variables studied. On the one hand, a positive correlation between the level of training on AI and readiness for its introduction and on the other hand, as between readiness for AI introduction and the level of awareness of AI's implications in the workplace.

The results confirm hypothesis H1, indicating a disparity in the perception of AI use between the OPH and UCH. The latter, are often larger and with more rigid processes that can may encounter more resistance to change, unlike OPH, who may be more agile in adopting new technologies.

In addition, UHC who have benefited from advanced technological tools and despite having access to more funding, their perceived immediate need for training has been reduced. As for the OPH, are often faced with tighter budget restrictions, may be more motivated to explore and to adopt new technologies to optimize their management practices and resources. Despite these distinctions, there is no significant divergence in recognition of the changes already brought about by AI in their work. This indicates that the challenges associated with this technology are independent. These results these results are in line with the work highlighting that technological adoption varies according to organizational context (Venkatesh et al., 2003).

Hypothesis 2 highlights a significant relationship between the professional experience of auditors and their perception to use AI tools in their activities. The data show that professionals with more than 10 years' experience have a greater tendency to apply these tools. The professional experience is, therefore, a determining factor in the adoption of emerging technologies such as AI. On the contrary, less experienced professionals may be less inclined to adopt AI tools. This difference can be attributed to longer exposure to technological developments and a better understanding of the opportunities offered by AI.

One element explaining this trend could be the degree of autonomy and responsibility associated with professional experience. More experienced auditors often have a greater decision-making role, enabling them to test and adopt innovative solutions. What's more, they may have developed a professional network offering them privileged access to advanced training and feedback on the use of AI. These findings are in line with innovation diffusion theory (Rogers, 2003), which suggests that experienced individuals are often the first to adopt innovations when they perceive a direct benefit to their use.

Regarding Hypothesis 3, our results highlight the significant impact of prior AI awareness on the proactive adaptation of internal auditors. This hypothesis postulated that individuals who had already heard of AI would be more inclined to train and change their professional practices to integrate this emerging technology. These results are consistent with research by Kotter (1996) concerning the management of technological change, which stresses the importance of upstream awareness to foster successful adoption. It should be noted that awareness plays a key role in the sense that positive awareness to AI can encourage membership, while communication focused on risks and uncertainties can generate resistance.

With regard to the obstacles to integrating AI into audit work (Hypothesis H4), we observed that the average scores attributed to the five specific obstacles were virtually identical. The lack of AI training and expertise and the high cost of AI implementation and worries about the reliability of this technology were present to similar degrees in both structures. These findings align with the work of Brynjolfsson and McAfee (2014), who identify organizational and cultural barriers as major hindrances to the adoption of new technologies.

In brief, our results provide insights into the factors influencing the adoption of artificial intelligence in audit activities, with a focus on awareness, professional experience, and common challenges. Although organizational contexts may vary, the challenges encountered in AI adoption remain identical. For address these challenges, support top management must be through targeted and the investment in training, and clear ethical guidelines can help create an environment where AI is not only accessible but also used in a way that supports human decision making and professional integrity.

V. CONCLUSION

The integration of artificial intelligence into auditing and control systems is more than just a technological advancement. It signifies a profound shift toward more efficient, transparent, and human centered practices that aim to better serve organizations and society at large. In sectors such as healthcare, where each decision impacts human lives, AI has the potential to transform risk management, improve resource allocation, ensure regulatory compliance, and ultimately enhance the quality of care. This chapter has examined the adoption of AI in auditing, with a focus on healthcare institutions, shedding light on both the challenges that accompany such integration. Tailored approaches are essential to building trust, fostering awareness, and encouraging the uptake of AI technologies within diverse environments.

Moreover, professional experience has emerged as a critical factor in the adoption of AI. This reflects the importance of leveraging the wisdom and insights of seasoned professionals while simultaneously creating pathways for younger professionals and those less familiar with the technology. It is essential to design training and development programs that cater to diverse learning needs, offering personalized support that empowers both new and experienced professionals to navigate the evolving landscape of AI. The role of prior awareness cannot be overstated. AI is still a relatively new and complex field, and fostering understanding is essential not only for overcoming resistance but to establish a climate of trust that encourages improved professional practices.

Despite the promise that AI holds, there are significant barriers to its widespread use. A common challenge across organizations is the lack of specialized training and expertise, which often creates hesitation and reluctance to adopt new technologies. In addition, concerns regarding the reliability and trustworthiness of AI systems are widespread, particularly in industries where accuracy and accountability are paramount, such as healthcare. These barriers are not insurmountable, but overcoming them requires a collective effort from all stakeholders government bodies, educational institutions, industry leaders, and AI developers. A holistic approach that prioritizes capacity building, transparency, and trust is essential for making AI an effective and reliable tool in auditing and control.

Ultimately, the adoption of AI in auditing and control is not just about increasing operational efficiency; it represents a paradigm shift toward a more ethical, accountable, and compassionate approach to decision-making. AI has the power to change the ways in which audits are conducted, offering new opportunities for greater fairness, inclusivity, and transparency. However, to realize its full potential, we must ensure that AI is implemented with a focus on human values and societal good. This means addressing the ethical implications of AI, ensuring that it does not perpetuate bias or inequality, and fostering a culture of collaboration where technology serves the people it is meant to benefit.

Looking forward, future research should focus on identifying the most effective strategies for raising awareness, training professionals, and overcoming the barriers that hinder AI adoption. It will also be crucial to explore the long term impacts of AI integration, particularly on the quality of decision-making, organizational performance, and patient outcomes in healthcare settings. By continually reflecting on the ethical, technical, and human dimensions of AI, we can shape a future where AI is not just a tool of efficiency but a catalyst for creating a more just, transparent, and compassionate world. In this evolving journey, the role of human insight, empathy, and ethical consideration remains paramount. While AI will undoubtedly play an increasingly important role in auditing and control, it is the people empowered with the right knowledge, resources, and mindset who will determine how these technologies can best serve society.

REFERENCES

Aiken, M., & Hage, J. (1971). The organic organization and innovation. *Sociology*, *5*(1), 63–82. DOI: 10.1177/003803857100500105

Ait Lemqeddem, H., & Chouay, J. (2020). Le rôle de la digitalisation dans l'efficacité de l'audit interne. *Revue Française d'Economie et de Gestion*, *1*(5).

Ajzen, I. (1991). The theory of planned behavior. *Organizational Behavior and Human Decision Processes*, *50*(2), 179–211. DOI: 10.1016/0749-5978(91)90020-T

Amiri, I., Sekaki, Y., Hainous, M., & Zaam, H. (2021). Déterminants de la qualité de l'audit interne: Que dit la littérature académique et professionnelle? *Revue Française d'Economie et de Gestion*, *2*(6).

Andaloussi, S., Mohamed, H., El Akkili, H., & Fahmi, Y. (2024). Digital Transformation in Morocco Public Health Sector: Survey of the Telemedicine in the Fez-Meknes Region. In International Conference on Digital Technologies and Applications (pp. 542-550). Cham: Springer Nature Switzerland. Springer 2023. DOI: DOI: 10.1007/978-3-031-68653-5_51

Arthur, P. (2015). l'audit dans le secteur public: Tenir compte des attentes, être performant. CBOK, IFACI

Bel, M. (2016). *Prédire l'utilisation d'une nouvelle technologie: Le cas des Systèmes de Transports Intelligents Coopératifs*. GRENOBLE ALPES.

Bigoness, W. J., & Perreault, W. D.Jr. (1981). A conceptual paradigm and approach for the study of innovators. *Academy of Management Journal*, *24*(1), 68–82. DOI: 10.2307/255824

Birkinshaw, J., Hamel, G., & Mol, M. J. (2008). Management innovation. *Academy of Management Review*, *33*(4), 825–845. DOI: 10.5465/amr.2008.34421969

Birkinshaw, J. M., & Mol, M. J. (2006). How management innovation happens. *MIT Sloan Management Review*, *47*(4), 81–88.

Bizarro, P. A., & Dorian, M. (2017). Artificial intelligence: The future of auditing. *Internal Auditing*, *5*(1), 21–26.

Brangier, É., Dufresne, A., & Hammes-Adelé, S. (2009). Approche symbiotique de la relation humain-technologie : Perspectives pour l'ergonomie informatique. Le travail humain, 72(4), 333-353. Cairn.info. DOI: 10.3917/th.724.0333

Brynjolfsson, E., & McAfee, A. (2014). The second machine age: Work, progress, and prosperity in a time of brilliant technologies. WW Norton & company.

Chebrolu, A., Sasmal, S. K., Behera, R. N., & Das, S. K. (2020). Prediction of factor of safety for slope stability using advanced artificial intelligence techniques. In Advanced Engineering Optimization Through Intelligent Techniques: Select Proceedings of AEOTIT 2018, 173-181. DOI: 10.1007/978-981-13-8196-6_16

Chukwuani, V. N., & Egiyi, M. A. (2020). Automation of accounting processes: Impact of artificial intelligence. [IJRISS]. *International Journal of Research and Innovation in Social Science*, *4*(8), 444–449.

Daft, R. L. (1978). A dual-core model of organizational innovation. *Academy of Management Journal*, *21*(2), 193–210. DOI: 10.2307/255754

Damanpour, F. (1988). Innovation type, radicalness, and the adoption process. *Communication Research*, *15*(5), 545–567. DOI: 10.1177/009365088015005003

Damanpour, F., & Aravind, D. (2012). Managerial innovation: Conceptions, processes and antecedents. *Management and Organization Review*, *8*(2), 423–454. DOI: 10.1111/j.1740-8784.2011.00233.x

Davis, F. D. (1989). Perceived usefulness, perceived ease of use, and user acceptance of information technology. *Management Information Systems Quarterly*, *13*(3), 319–340. DOI: 10.2307/249008

Davis, F. D. (1989). Perceived Usefulness, Perceived Ease of Use, and User Acceptance of Information Technology. MIS Quarterly, 13(3), 319-340. JSTOR. DOI: 10.2307/249008

European Commission. (2023). Hiroshima Process International Code of Conduct for Advanced AI Systems, https://digital-strategy.ec.europa.eu/en/library/hiroshima -process international-code-conduct-advanced-ai-systems.

General Data Protection Regulation (GDPR). (2018). *Article 22 - Automated individual decision-making*. Official Journal of the European Union.

Glover, S. M., Prawitt, D. F., & Spilker, B. C. (1996). The influence of decision aids on user behavior: Implications for knowledge acquisition and inappropriate reliance. *Organizational Behavior and Human Decision Processes*, *72*(2), 232–255. DOI: 10.1006/obhd.1997.2735

Hamel, G. (2006). The why, what, and how of management innovation. *Harvard Business Review*, *84*(2), 72. PMID: 16485806

Hantem, A. (2019). L'introduction d'une Comptabilité D'exercice Au Sein Des Centres Hospitaliers Universitaires Au Maroc: Caractéristiques Et Analyse Des Facteurs D'adoption Et De Succès (Doctoral dissertation, Université Hassan II Casablanca).

Hantem, A. (2023). Le Recours aux Nouveaux Outils du Management Public: Vers Un Systeme Comptable Fiable Et Transparent. *Revue D'Etudes en Management et Finance D'Organisation*, *8*(1).

Hantem, A., Emzi, K., Youssoufi, N., Emzi, K., Mkik, M., & Outaaza, K. (2024). Factors Influencing Patient Satisfaction with the Use of Teleconsultation in Morocco. In Bansal, J. C., Borah, S., Hussain, S., & Salhi, S. (Eds.), *Computing and Machine Learning. CML 2024. Lecture Notes in Networks and Systems* (Vol. 1108). Springer., DOI: 10.1007/978-981-97-6588-1_33

Hantem, A., Soussi, H., Emzi, K., & Emzi, K. (2024). Analysis of the Perception of Innovations Adoption in Public Health Establishments in Morocco: Crossed Perspectives of Healthcare Professionals. In Motahhir, S., & Bossoufi, B. (Eds.), *Digital Technologies and Applications. ICDTA 2024. Lecture Notes in Networks and Systems* (Vol. 1098). Springer., DOI: 10.1007/978-3-031-68650-4_53

Harrison, C., Tomás, C., & Crook, C. (2014). An e-maturity analysis explains intention– behavior disjunctions in technology adoption in UK schools. *Computers in Human Behavior*, *34*, 345–351. DOI: 10.1016/j.chb.2013.10.042

High-Level Expert Group on Artificial Intelligence. (2019). *Ethics guidelines for trustworthy AI*. European Commission.

Huang, Z. (2018). Discussion on the development of artificial intelligence in taxation. *American Journal of Industrial and Business Management*, *8*(08), 1817–1824. DOI: 10.4236/ajibm.2018.88123

Institute of Internal Auditors. (1947). *Statement of Responsibilities of Internal Auditing*. IIA.

Institute of Internal Auditors (IIA). (2017). Intelligence artificielle: Le futur de l'audit interne. Tone at the top, N°85. https://docs.ifaci.com/wp-content/uploads/2018/03/tone-at-the-top-85-ia.pdf

Institute of Internal Auditors-Morocco. (2019). Définition de l'audit interne. Retrieved February 2, 2025, from https://www.iiamaroc.org/definition-de-laudit-interne/

INTOSAI. (2023). The use of artificial intelligence (AI) in the execution of audits. Science and Technology in Audit, 50(2). Retrieved January 5, 2025, from https://intosaijournal.org/journal-entry/the-use-of-artificial-intelligence-ai-in-the-execution-of-audits/

Karaa, M., Bentahar, O., & Benzidia, S. (2016). Les facteurs d'adoption d'une innovation appliquée aux flux de patients: Le cas d'un centre hospitalier au Luxembourg. *Logistique & Management, 24*(2), 98–109. DOI: 10.1080/12507970.2016.1249527

Kaziba Mpaata, A., Lubogoyi, B., & Okiria, J. C. (2017). The effect of internal audit department function on the performance of the internal control system of a public hospital in Uganda.

Kefi, H. (2010). Mesures perceptuelles de l'usage des systèmes d'information : Application de la théorie du comportement planifié. Humanisme et Entreprise, 297(2), 45-64. Cairn.info. DOI: 10.3917/hume.297.0045

Kimberly, J. R., & Evanisko, M. J. (1981). Organizational innovation: The influence of individual, organizational, and contextual factors on hospital adoption of technological and administrative innovations. *Academy of Management Journal, 24*(4), 689–713. DOI: 10.2307/256170 PMID: 10253688

Kok, J. N., Boers, E. J., Kosters, W. A., Van der Putten, P., & Poel, M. (2009). Artificial intelligence: definition, trends, techniques, and cases. Artificial intelligence, 1(270-299), 51.

Kokina, J., & Davenport, T. H. (2017). The emergence of artificial intelligence: How automation is changing auditing. *Journal of Emerging Technologies in Accounting, 14*(1), 115–122. DOI: 10.2308/jeta-51730

Kotter, J. P. (1996). *Leadership and Leading Change*. Harvard Business Review Press.

Lafon, L. (2016). L'audit légal des établissements publics de santé. Gestion et management.

Laskawiec, A., & Lizot, J. (2014). Fiabilisation et certification des comptes des établissements publics de santé. Gestion & Finances Publiques, 3-4.

Le Roy, F., Robert, M., & Giuliani, P. (2013). L'innovation managériale. Revue française de gestion, 235(6), 77-90.

Makridakis, S. (2017). The forthcoming Artificial Intelligence (AI) revolution: Its impact on society and firms. *Futures, 90*, 46–60. DOI: 10.1016/j.futures.2017.03.006

Markaoui, K., & Hassine, M. (2018). Définition de la performance des services hospitaliers: enquête au sein du chu mohammed VI d'oujda. Revue du contrôle, de la comptabilité et de l'audit, 2(3).

McCarthy, J. (2007). From here to human-level AI. *Artificial Intelligence, 171*(18), 1174–1182. DOI: 10.1016/j.artint.2007.10.009

Menant, L. (2021). L'acceptabilité de l'intelligence artificielle appliquée aux systèmes d'information des ressources humaines: cas d'un agent conversationnel. Psychologie. Université Paul Valéry - Montpellier III, Français. ffNNT: 2021MON30091ff. fftel-03697429f

Luo, J., Meng, Q., & Cai, Y. (2018). Analysis of the impact of artificial intelligence application on the development of accounting industry. *Open Journal of Business and Management*, *6*(4), 850–856.

Mighiss, S., & Kabbaj, S. (2021). L'audit à l'ère de la transformation digitale. Revue du contrôle, de la comptabilité et de l'audit, 5(3).

Minvielle, E., Sicotte, C., Champagne, F., Contandriopoulos, A. P., Jeantet, M., Préaubert, N., Bourdil, A., & Richard, C. (2008). Hospital performance: Competing or shared values? *Health Policy (Amsterdam)*, *87*(1), 8–19. DOI: 10.1016/j.healthpol.2007.09.017 PMID: 18035448

Mohr, L. B. (1969). Determinants of innovation in organizations. *The American Political Science Review*, *63*(1), 111–126. DOI: 10.2307/1954288

Munro, L., & Stewart, J. (2011). External auditors' reliance on internal auditing: Further evidence. *Managerial Auditing Journal*, *26*(6), 464–481. DOI: 10.1108/02686901111142530

Nistor, N. (2014). When technology acceptance models won't work : Non-significant intentionbehavior effects. *Computers in Human Behavior*, *34*, 299–300. DOI: 10.1016/j.chb.2014.02.052

Obermeyer, Z., Powers, B., Vogeli, C., & Mullainathan, S. (2019). Dissecting racial bias in an algorithm used to manage the health of populations. *Science*, *366*(6464), 447–453. DOI: 10.1126/science.aax2342 PMID: 31649194

OECD. (2024). AI In Health: Huge Potential, Huge Risks. https://www.oecd.org/en/publications/ai-in-health_2f709270-en.html

Organisation for Economic Co-operation and Development (OECD). (2024). L'IA dans le domaine de la santé, un immense potentiel, d'énormes risques. Retrieved Februry 4, 2025, from https://www.oecd.org/content/dam/oecd/fr/publications/reports/2024/01/ai-in-health-huge-potential-huge-risks_ff823a24/ebfdeb50-fr.pdf

Pesqueux, Y. (2004). La notion de performance globale. 5ème forum international sur la performance Globale de l'entreprise. Université Tunis Carthage, 1-2 décembre.

Rodrigues, L., Pereira, J., da Silva, A. F., & Ribeiro, H. (2023). The impact of artificial intelligence on audit profession. *Journal of Information Systems Engineering & Management*, *8*(1), 19002. DOI: 10.55267/iadt.07.12743

Rogers, E. M. (1995). *Diffusion of Innovations* (4th ed.). ACM The Free Press.

Rogers, E. M., & Scott, K. L. (1997). The diffusion of innovations model and outreach from the National Network of Libraries of Medicine to Native American communities. Retrieved March, 22, 2006.

Sabae, G. U. E. L. D. I., & Mohammed Chakib, H. I. M. M. I. C. H. (2024). La réglementation des avancées technologiques au Maroc: Un pivot du développement. International Journal Of Advanced Research In Innovation, Management &. *Social Sciences*, *7*(1). Advance online publication. DOI: 10.57109/223

Safety Summit, A. I. (2023). AI Safety Summit 2023: Roundtable Chair's Summaries. www.gov.uk/government/publications/ai-safety-summit-1-november-roundtable -chairs summaries.

Saulquin, J. Y., & Schier, G. (2007). Responsabilité sociale des entreprises et performance. *La Revue des Sciences de Gestion*, *223*(1), 57–65. DOI: 10.3917/rsg.223.0057

Sawyer, L. B. (1973). *The practice of modern internal auditing: appraising operations for management*. No Title.

Schumpeter, J. A. (1939). *Business cycles: A theoretical, historical and statistical analysis of the capitalist process*. McGraw-Hill.

Segouin, C., & Perret, F. (2001). L'audit et l'amélioration continue de la qualité à l'hôpital. ADSP (AP-HP), 35, 34-8.

Swinney, L. (1999). Consideration of the social context of auditors' reliance on expert system output during evaluation of loan loss reserves. *International Journal of Intelligent Systems in Accounting Finance & Management*, *8*(3), 199–213. DOI: 10.1002/(SICI)1099-1174(199909)8:3<199::AID-ISAF160>3.0.CO;2-A

US White House. (2023). Executive Order on the Safe, Secure, and Trustworthy Development and Use of Artificial Intelligence. www.whitehouse.gov/briefing -room/presidential actions/2023/10/30/executive-order-on-the-safe-secure-and-trustworthy-development-and use-of-artificial-intelligence/

Veale, M., & Zuiderveen Borgesius, F. (2021). Demystifying the Draft EU Artificial Intelligence Act. *Computer Law & Security Review*, *42*, 105635. DOI: 10.1016/j.clsr.2021.105635

Venkatesh, V., & Bala, H. (2008). Technology Acceptance Model and a Research Agenda on Interventions. *Decision Sciences*, *39*(2), 273–315. DOI: 10.1111/j.1540-5915.2008.00192.x

Venkatesh, V., Morris, M. G., Davis, G. B., & Davis, F. D. (2003). User acceptance of information technology: Toward a unified view. *Management Information Systems Quarterly*, *27*(3), 425–478. DOI: 10.2307/30036540

Venkatesh, V., Morris, M. G., Davis, G. B., & Davis, F. D. (2003). User Acceptance of Information Technology : Toward a Unified View. MIS Quarterly, 27(3), 425-478. JSTOR. DOI: 10.2307/30036540

Venkatesh, V., Thong, J. Y., & Xu, X. (2016). Unified theory of acceptance and use of technology: A synthesis and the road ahead. *Journal of the Association for Information Systems*, *17*(5), 328–376.

Wahbi, A., Khaddouj, K., & Lahlimi, N. (2023). Study of the relationship between chatbot technology and customer experience and satisfaction. International Journal of Accounting, Finance, Auditing, Management and Economics, 4(6-1), 758-771.

World Health Organization. (2023), Regulatory considerations on artificial intelligence for health, https://iris.who.int/bitstream/handle/10665/373421/9789240078871-eng.pdf?sequence=1

World Health Organization Europe. (2007). Performance Assessment Tool for Quality Improvement in Hospitals.

Wu, I. L., & Hsieh, P. J. (2011). Understanding hospital innovation enabled customer-perceived quality of structure, process, and outcome care. *Total Quality Management & Business Excellence*, *22*(2), 227–241. DOI: 10.1080/14783363.2010.532343

Yusof, M., Kuljis, J., Papazafeiropoulou, A., & Stergioulas, L. K. (2008). An evaluation framework for Health Information Systems : Human, organization and technology-fit factors (HOT-fit). *International Journal of Medical Informatics*, *77*(6), 386–398. DOI: 10.1016/j.ijmedinf.2007.08.011 PMID: 17964851

Zarai, M.A., & Bettabai, W. (2007). Impact de l'efficacité des comités d'audit sur la qualité des bénéfices comptables divulgués. Revue gouvernance, 4(1).

Zarhloul, Z., & Mrani Zentar, S. (2022). La contribution de l'audit interne dans la performance du système de contrôle interne: cas du secteur bancaire marocain. International Journal of Accounting, Finance, Auditing, Management and Economics, 3(2-2), 354-368.

APPENDIX

Table 4. Some examples of AI applications in the Internal Audit department

Example of AI applications in the Internal Audit	Contributions
Predictive analysis of risks and anomalies	Early identification of risk areas within business processes. AI learns from historical audit data to detect abnormal patterns or trends suggesting a potential problem. AI could also identify atypical transactions that would not have been detected by a traditional audit, thereby reducing the risk of fraud or error.
Automating the collection and analysis of documents	The extraction and processing of data from documents, using optical character recognition (OCR), makes it possible to automate the collection and analysis of financial documents (invoices, bank statements, contracts). AI can not only digitize these documents but also extract the key data and structure it to facilitate analysis.
Continuous monitoring of compliance and security	AI can analyze internal communications (emails, chats) to detect inappropriate language or potential non-compliance issues. It can also monitor databases for unauthorized access or suspicious modifications, thereby strengthening system security. AI could also detect the presence of illicit or dangerous content on company media to ensure better protection.
Optimizing audit processes with natural language processing	Natural language processing (NLP), including text and summary generation, can optimize audit report creation and communication tasks. AI can generate draft reports based on the data analyzed, reducing drafting time. It can also summarize long, complex documents to help auditors quickly identify key points
Improving field auditing with computer vision	Computer vision, with image classification and recognition, object detection and multi-object tracking, can improve field auditing. As part of a physical inventory, AI can automatically identify and count objects in images or videos, which is faster and more accurate than a manual inventory.
Automating the drafting of audit questions with text generation	AI-assisted text generation can be used to automate the drafting of audit questions. AI can analyze business processes, potential risks and audit objectives to generate relevant questions. This saves auditors time in preparing for the audit and ensures that no crucial points are missed.
Real-time tracking and counting to analyze flows and operations	Real-time tracking and counting, for example with computer vision technologies and advanced analytics, can monitor flows and operations in real time. AI can analyze flows of people or products/services, identifying congestion points, inefficiencies or anomalies.

Source: Démarre ton avenir, Consulting firm, 2025

Table 5. AI tools specific to the auditing

AI Tool/ company	Specifics
AuditFile AI	is a cloud-based program made to automate regular auditing duties. The application reduces the amount of time needed for repetitive operations like data classification and report production by using machine learning techniques. The "roll-forward" feature, which facilitates the transition between audit periods and increases process efficiency, is one of its primary features. Notwithstanding its benefits, there are drawbacks, such as the potential for algorithmic mistakes to result in inaccurate classifications and the tool's limited flexibility in unusual audit situations.
Thomson Reuters	offers AI tools that enable auditors to spot anomalies and potential risks instantly, as well as managing massive data and automating tasks.
KPMG	The firm uses artificial intelligence tools such as predictive analysis and machine learning in its audit procedures. These tools are capable of detecting and identifying anomalies on the basis of massive data. However, algorithmic biases can lead to problems, which require specific technical know-how.
AppZen	This is AI-powered software for automating compliance management and expense audit procedures. Using machine learning and natural language processing, the software is used to review accounting and financial documents to identify potential risks and detect fraud.
MindBridge AI Auditor	It is a risk rating system, based on machine learning and pre-established rules, which enables auditors to categorize risks. This tool can generate learning that contains errors, requiring human intervention and supervision.

Source: Authors, 2025

Table 6. Examples of popular software and auditing practices using AI in hospitals

AI Tool/ company	Specifics
CernerPowerChart	This is software that enables hospitals to monitor and analyze patient data. It uses artificial intelligence algorithms to detect medical errors, non-compliance with protocols and various risks in the management of medical records.
TruCode Encoder	Based on artificial intelligence, this software enables medical data and procedures to be coded to improve the accuracy and speed of medical diagnosis.
McKesson Audit Management	This software makes it easier to identify fraud and anomalies in the administrative and financial management of hospitals, and enables ongoing monitoring and verification of compliance with the standards and regulations in force.
IBM Watson Health	This platform merges artificial intelligence and massive data analysis. It facilitates the detection of patient safety risks and financial reporting anomalies and irregularities.

Source: Authors, 2025

Chapter 10
AI for the Environmental Performance of Moroccan Public Organizations:
A Comparative Analysis of Random Forests and XGBoost

Saida Ifiss
https://orcid.org/0009-0001-3491-0104
Abdelmalek Essaâdi University, Morocco

ABSTRACT

This study examines the application of Machine Learning (ML) to evaluate and predict the environmental performance of Moroccan public organizations. It compares the performance of Random Forests (RF), XGBoost, Support Vector Machines (SVM) and Partial Least Squares (PLS) regression on a dataset collected from 270 organizations between 2018 and 2022. Key variables include total solid waste production, energy consumption and the rate of achievement of National Sustainable Development Strategy (NSDS) targets. Our results, evaluated using accuracy, F1 score, R^2 and mean square error (MSE), indicate that Random Forests offer better performance for predicting environmental performance. This research contributes to the literature on the application of AI to sustainable development in the public sector, and highlights the importance of environmental policies for optimizing resource management. Practical implications suggest that public organizations can use these models to guide their strategic decisions and improve their contribution to national sustainable development goals.

DOI: 10.4018/979-8-3373-1737-3.ch010

INTRODUCTION

Today, the 21st century, really, is detectable by a global awareness of the major environmental problems which humanity faces. No more a concern but a threat in fact to ecosystem stability and human well-being, threats to these dimensions are climate change, biodiversity depletion, pollution, and the depletion of natural resources. Quite certainly confronting such an ecological emergency, the transition toward more sustainable lifestyles and development becomes an imperative. Management of resources, reduction of adverse effects on the environment, and promotion of planet-friendly practices are now priorities at every level of society.

It is in this scenario that public organisations have a major responsibility. Public organisations are, after all, the key players in society, for they are the implementers of all environmental policies and developers for sustainability. They manage infrastructure and public services and regulate economic activity. Hence, it is necessary for them to adopt responsible management of the environment as well as work taking sustainable development principles into account in all their operations and decisions. Hence, it will necessarily require the active commitment and exemplarity of the public sector to realize the Sustainable Development Goals (SDGs) as they are laid out by the United Nations Agenda 2030 (United Nations, 2015). Additionally, the Agenda 2030 stresses concerted efforts on the part of governments, public institutions, and citizens to achieve sustainable development in its economic, social, and environmental dimensions.

This is true in Morocco. The country has embarked on a proactive path towards sustainable development as demonstrated in the National Sustainable Development Strategy (SNDD) adopted in 2016. The Ministry of Energy Transition and Sustainable Development (2021) broadly encourages Moroccan public organizations to embrace this approach, by innovating and sustainable uses of its available resources, and to diminish their environmentally damaging impacts by adopting applicable practices. These public organizations, whether they be central government institutions, local authorities health establishments or educational establishments, are expected to take the lead in terms of environmental management and in achieving national sustainable development goals.

Unfortunately, traditional forms of environmental management (largely based on description and linear processes) could be limiting, because they sometimes lack good large and complex data systems, of waking up to non-linear relationships between variables, and who could forecast the ramifications of decisions. For example, we need much more sophisticated qualitative processing tools to analyse issues such as waste, energy usage optimization, or greenhouse gas emissions reductions, where researchers have a lot of existing complexity to deal with.

There are prospects for machine learning (ML), one of the artificial intelligence (AI) disciplines, as the future alternative for overcoming these limitations. Aggregated data can be analyzed, heterogeneous data understood, hidden patterns revealed, trends even emergently produced, thereby identifying key factors in environmental performance. More importantly, complex algorithms are used for modeling non-linear relationships, making predictions, and drawing rational conclusions. Therefore, AI, especially AA, can enable sound environmental benefits management decision making because organizations can identify actions that are relevant, improve practices, and anticipate actions (Jordan & amp; Mitchell, 2015; García-Martínez et al., 2022).

In this sense, research on the application of AA to Moroccan public organizations' environmental performance occupies a key perspective in this area. Unfortunately, notwithstanding prospects that AA could prove promising for investigations in this area, there are few studies that have specifically addressed this topic (Mokhtari & Ait Saadi, 2021). Most studies within the scientific literature emphasize the applications of AA in developed economies or the private sector and other international influences. This gap indeed calls for urgent attention in this field. Study focusing on the particularities of the Moroccan public organizations, their regulatory constraints, the available resources, and specificities the environmental challenges that they face, will help raise the knowledge that can be fed to this body of literature..

This study thus sets out to explore the application of AI to the environmental performance of Moroccan public organizations, proposing a comparative analysis of two machine learning techniques: Random Forests (RF), XGBoost (Extreme Gradient Boosting), Support Vector Machines (SVM), and Partial Least Squares (PLS) regression. The objective is to assess how these algorithms can be applied to evaluate and predict environmental performance with respect to relevant criteria such as total solid waste production, energy consumption, and actual achievement of National Sustainable Development Strategy (NSDS) targets. By addressing this gap in scientific literature, the current research intends to arm Moroccan public organizations with tools and recommendations for better environmental management and a more robust involvement in national sustainable development objectives. This study, therefore, sees itself as especially innovative in explicitly comparing the four AA algorithms' performance regarding the one that is most appropriate to the context of Moroccan public organizations, in parallel analyzing the relative importance of key environmental factors.

The research centers on the following principal question: To what extent could machine learning methodologies including Random Forests, XGBoost, Support Vector Machines (SVM), and Partial Least Squares (PLS) regression be employed in assessing and predicting the environmental performance of Moroccan public organizations? In response to this question and therefore toward the realization of our goal, the following hypotheses were formulated:

- H1: Machine learning models (Random Forests, XGBoost, SVM and PLS) will be able to predict the environmental performance of Moroccan public organizations, using data relating to waste production, energy consumption and the rate of achievement of SNDD targets.
- H2: Machine learning models, i.e. Random Forests, XGBoost and SVM, will show a better ability to predict the environmental performance of Moroccan public organizations, than the PLS model.
- H3: Total solid waste production, energy consumption and the rate of achievement of SNDD objectives will have a statistically significant influence on the environmental performance of Moroccan public organizations.
- H4: The Random Forests (RF) model will perform significantly better than the XGBoost, SVM models in terms of accuracy, F1 score, coefficient of determination (R^2) and mean square error (MSE) in predicting performance.

The above question should consider three major factors: total solid waste production, total energy consumption, and the rate of achievement of targets of the National Sustainable Development Strategy (SNDD). It aims to provide insight as to the ability of the AA to improve understanding and management of environmental performance in a given public context with the constraining features of Moroccan organizations.

To achieve this objective, we defined three specific objectives. First, we will compare the performance of the Random Forest and XGBoost algorithms, as well as Support Vector Machines (SVM) and Partial Least Squares (PLS) regression for predicting the environmental performance of Moroccan public organizations. Performance metrics such as accuracy, F1 Score, coefficient of determination (R^2), and mean square error (MSE) will be used to determine which algorithm is the most suitable for the given context. Second, we will attempt to identify the most important issues influencing environmental performance in Moroccan public organizations. Our analysis will determine the extent to which the production of waste, production and consumption of energy, the number of sustainable development processes and initiatives undertaken, and the existence of a formal environmental policy influence environmental performance. Thirdly, this research aims to contribute to the scientific literature on the use of artificial intelligence with regard to sustainable development in the public sector specifically. By investigating the area of AA in a little-studied manner, we will aim to advance current knowledge on this topic, identify future research opportunities, and make meaningful recommendations for Moroccan public organizations and other similar contexts.

Essentially, this research will also help fill this gap in literature by examining the application of AA in detail to the environmental performance of Moroccan public organizations. Our intention is also to characterize the important factors that affect this performance and compare the performance of the RF algorithm with the XG-Boost -- to provide tools and perspectives for better environmental management. This would provide both consolidation for Moroccan public organizations' transition to improved sustainability practices, but may also initiate further applications in alternative national or sectoral contexts.

1. LITERATURE REVIEW

1.1 Key Definitions and Concepts

In this research study, it is imperative that we define a few relevant terms to get a clearer picture of the issues we have discussed. First, we are looking at environmental performance. Environmental performance is an organization's ability to manage its impact on the environment. Dyllick and Hockerts (2002) state that environmental performance includes the efficient use of natural resources, minimizing pollution and waste and being sustainable. Environmental performance can be calculated with a number of indicators such as energy consumption, water consumption, the amount of waste produced and greenhouse gas emissions produced from their operations. Environmental performance is an important indicator of an organization's sustainable practices and environmental responsibility.

Of these indicators, total solid waste production is of primary concern. Waste management is a key sustainability issue, and minimizing waste at source, recycling, and recovery are some of the central principle environmental management practices. Waste production is quantifiable, thus allowing organizations to determine how well it has reduced waste production and maintained effective waste management practices (Hoornweg and Bhada-Tata, 2012). Energy consumption is another primary measure of the ecological footprint. Whether advancing energy consumption efficiency or harnessing renewable energy, energy consumption is knowingly an indicative factor of environmental performance (Amasyali and El-Gohary, 2018). As outlined by Amasyali and El-Gohary (2018), to the extent that energy consumption is reduced demonstrates their efforts to reduce greenhouse gas emissions and ensure resource protection. The rate of achieving the National Sustainable Development Strategy (NSDS) objectives indicates the commitment of public organizations to national sustainability commitments. This rate pertains to how organizations design and implement operations integrating the Principles of the SNDD, and assist with achieving national objectives (Ministry of Energy Transition and Sustainable Development, 2021). Overall, these indicators offer a more multidimensional view of the environmental performance of public organizations in terms of their contribution to sustainability.

At the core of our approach is machine learning (ML), a sub-system of artificial intelligence through which the computer systems learn from data without being explicitly programmed. This capacity for learning opens doors to analytical techniques for the emerging analysis of wider datasets and the much more difficult connection identification between variables that typically escape traditional analyses. In this study, we will use two machine learning algorithms in particular.

The first of these is Random Forests. This is a set of tree classifiers, each of which is trained on a random part of the data. Random forests are very famous for being very robust against overlearning, as well as very effective in the performance of classification and even regression tasks (Hastie et al., 2009). Random forests are often considered to be distinguished by performance in classification and regression tasks, thus supporting our hypothesis H4 that random forest models should indeed perform as well as or even better than other models. Random forests especially show superiority in their ability to handle very complex non-linear data sets, thus qualifying them as relevant tools in our analysis of environmental performance.

The second algorithm is XGBoost (Extreme Gradient Boosting) - an algorithm that is a "gradient boosting" algorithm that combines a number of weak decision trees to create a stronger predictive model. Typically XGBoost is recognized for its effectiveness, ability to handle more complex data sets, and speed (Chen and Guestrin, 2016). For many, XGBoost is considered one of the glorified leaders of the machine learning space.

The third is Support Vector Machines (SVMs), created by *f* and Vapnik in 1995. SVM is a supervised learning algorithm that performs well in classification and regression tasks. SVMs fit an optimal hyperplane to the dataset, while ensuring a small margin separation between classes. SVMs are also able to use different kernels (i.e., linear, polynomial, or radial basis function - RBF), which allows them to handle non-linear relationships in the data, and extend their use.

Fourth, Partial Least Squares (PLS) regression, which was developed by Wold (1984), is another form of linear regression that is especially useful with multicolinearity in the data. PLS develops a relationship between the explanatory variables and the dependent variable through projecting the data in two sets into lower dimensional space while maximizing the covariance between those two sets of variables. Therefore, it works well with data that is complicated and multidimensional.

Finally, artificial intelligence (AI) and machine learning, in particular, are becoming increasingly influential facilitators of sustainable development. The use of AI is rising, in terms of optimizing resource use, reducing pollutant emissions and waste management, and more generally, achieving sustainable development goals. Accordingly, AI can help improve the efficiency in management of environmental systems, and assist organizations in reaching sustainability objectives (Vinuesa et al., 2020).

1.2 Analysis of existing literature

The scholarly [scientific] literature suggests a growing interest in the application of artificial intelligence (AI) and machine learning (ML) within environmental management, which recognizes the usefulness of AI and ML technologies for sustainability challenges. However, careful review of the existing literature demonstrates patterns and gaps that require investigation. In this section we conduct a critical review of the existing literature in the topical areas of research, organized by major themes, and highlight the pros and cons of the existing research and our work in context.

1.2.1 Applications in the Private Sector: Effectiveness and Motivation

A significant amount of research has concentrated on the role of AA for enhancing environmental performance in private companies, at least in the industrial sector. These studies have emphasized many different applications, some of which include energy consumption optimization, waste reduction, and process optimization. For instance, Amasyali and El-Gohary (2018) applied AA algorithms, including neural networks, to model and predict building energy consumption under various scenarios, with the objective of optimizing their energy management and mitigating carbon footprint. This study demonstrates explicitly how AA can be used to improve energy management in the building sector, as well as provide predictive tools for better resource efficiencies, but is limited to the private sector and disregards the peculiarities of the public sector. This study, along with similar studies, supports our hypothesis H1 suggesting that machine learning models can predict environmental performance.

Other researchers, such as Kaza et al. (2018), applied AA to leverage industrial waste management with the aim of identifying sources of waste, as well as leading to improved activities for recycling. They demonstrated that AA can be applied for the purpose of waste identification, sorting and recycling, as well as forecasting the rate of waste generation. The studies also established the possible application of AA to improve corporate environmental efficiency, producing both economic and ecological benefits, although the results are not transferable to public organizations due to structural and organizational differences.

It is important to note that the applications in the private sector are often driven by a fear of losing competitiveness or a desire to reduce costs, in contrast to public organizations which have public service and social responsibility objectives. For some companies, the adoption of sustainable environmental practices is viewed as a competitive advantage, but other companies are simply trying to comply with regulatory requirements from the government or pressure from stakeholders. This motivation may or may not align with the mission of public organizations which are distinctly oriented toward objectives based on public good and social responsibility.

1.2.2. AA for Sustainable Natural Resource Management: Challenges and Opportunities

There is a growing use of AI for the sustainable management of natural resources, which is a critical platform for conserving biodiversity and ecosystem services. An example of this is precision agriculture, where AI algorithms analyze satellite, sensor and meteorological data to better optimize the use of agricultural inputs (water, fertilizers and pesticides). Shen et al. (2021) provide a broad review of AI applied to agriculture. In their summary, they explain how the use of AI will improve efficiencies in the use of many resources, specifically water and fertilizers. A related area is water management, which is also a key component of natural resource management, including forecasting demand, leak detection and optimizing irrigation practices. Willard et al. (2021) framed the application of AI to predict water temperature dynamics in lakes with no monitoring database using transfer learning techniques. The example provided by Willard et al. is illustrative of AI's potential to optimize water management and enhance resource management efficiencies in conjunction with water-intensive work activities. Although the studies highlighted the capacity of AI to optimize the management of our natural resource systems, they focus specifically on environmental applications and none of the studies targeted applications in organizations.

1.2.3. Modeling and Forecasting Environmental Impacts: A Tool for Preventive Assistance

Modeling and forecasting environmental impacts is another important area of application for AA. Whether through identifying relationships between human activities and changes in the environment, or undertaking similar issues on a more macro scale, AA methods have the potential to analyze complex data sets. For instance, several studies have applied AA approaches to characterize air and water quality forecasting, utilizing monitoring and meteorological data. In their research, Li et al. (2016) built a deep learning architecture to predict air quality forecasts as their outcome. The authors showed that their model was able to capture complex relationships that are present between environmental variables and concentrations of air pollutants. In doing so, the study highlighted AI's potential, using deep learning, to deliver more accurate air pollution forecasts that would support public health initiatives. In the same vein, Najah Ahmed et al. (2019), also applied machine learning methods to assess and forecast water pollution, which created better opportunities to manage water resources. AA has even been used to model climate change impacts on ecosystems/populations to allow risks to be anticipated, and adapt, as was done in Runge et al. (2016) study on spatial prioritization for conservation actions. The studies cited above demonstrate the potential of AA tools to model complex environmental processes as exemplified through their approaches, but do not explicitly present the use of these tools within public organizations.

1.2.4 Contributions of Management Sciences and Public Policies: Theoretical Frameworks and Relevant Concepts

To increase understanding of the complexities of environmental performance in the public sector we must turn to the fields of management science and public policy as sources of relevant theoretical frameworks and concepts for analyzing the components of environmental performance in public organizations and the strategies for improving it.

- **Stakeholder Theory:** Stakeholder theory was created by Freeman (1984) and focuses on the nature of the relationship between an organization and its stakeholders (citizens, NGOs, businesses, governments, etc.). Stakeholder theory asserts that an organization's environmental performance is a function of the pressures related to the expectations of its various stakeholders. Therefore, public organizations must recognize and take account of the interests of all stakeholders when making environmental decisions.
- **Environmental Management Theory**: Environmental management theory draws on the work of Porter and van der Linde (1995) in which they argue that sustainable environmental practices can improve environmental performance and competitiveness. Therefore, public organizations can view environmental management from an innovative and efficiency-seeking perspective.
- **Environmental Governance Theory:** This theory emphasizes the role of institutions, policies, and processes that guide environmental management. Given this, it is essential that public organizations develop clear environmental policies; develop monitoring and evaluation, and cooperate with other actors to achieve their environmental goals.
- **Circular Economy Framework:** The concept of a circular economy is a more recent and emerging framework as it relates to the broad notion of how resources or waste need to be managed. This conceptual framework involves an integrated waste management approach that is grounded in the reduction, reuse, recycling and recovery of materials where possible in order to minimize the environmental effects associated with economic activity. Public organizations can formally apply circular economy practices in their own op-

erations to improve their sustainability commitments and actions while also contributing to society's transition towards a sustainable economy.

1.2.5. Gaps and Positioning of the Study

Although research focused on AI/ML for environmental management is on the rise, it has mostly focused on the private sector by ignoring the not-for-profit goals, regulatory constraints, and service mandates associated with public organizations (Wirtz et al., 2019). Models that are created for profit-seeking firms may not simply develop in the same way for public organizations, which is why we will compare Random Forests, XGBoost, SVM and PLS to test hypothesis H2. One major limitation is that existing work has not included Moroccan public institutions, which follow a different adoption pathway due the constraints of their budgets, their technical capacity, and their policy priorities. Our study contributes to existing work on ML, using Random Forests and XGBoost specifically to assess and improve environmental performance in the context of Moroccan public sector organizations. Existing research suggests that waste management (Hoornweg & Bhada-Tata, 2012; Zaman, 2016) and strong environmental policy (Darnall et al., 2005; Porter & van der Linde, 1995) improve performance, and provides the basis for hypothesis H3, as well as evidence related to efficiency (Wilson et al., 2015), sustainability (Liakos et al., 2018), and policy frameworks (Kaza et al., 2018) to inform the indicators that we will use. Our analysis will cover total solid-waste generation, final energy use and progress towards the Stratégie Nationale de Développement Durable, and from there we will provide contextually sensitive actionable recommendations. The next subsections describe data collection processes, analytical processes, as well as algorithm application.

1.2.6. Model Interpretability for Policy Contexts

Strong predictive performance alone will not suffice if public-sector managers are unable to explain the logic underpinning an AI model. For example, when environmental officers can see the effect of various variables such as per capita waste or energy intensity on how recommendations are generated to shape policy advice, they can defend their decisions to the public, auditors and other watchdogs, and they can satisfy transparency and accountability requirements in accordance with OECD principles (2019), Doshi-Velez & Kim (2017) and the EU act on Artificial Intelligence (in development).

We used two explanation methods in this research. For the nonlinear, machine-learning models—Random Forest, XGBoost, and SVM—we applied the SHapley Additive exPlanations (SHAP) method that provides consistent marginal contribution attribution to each predictor variable, thus providing both a global ranking of importance and local, case-based justifications for decisions. For the Partial Least Squares model we provide Variable-Importance-in-Projection scores, a linear approach that is always capable of being audited via classic statistics.

Our explanatory output have been configured to appear as colour-coded bar charts that rank drivers by mean influence, along with SHAP dependence plots that associate each contribution and A and B with the raw predictor values. All figures are rendered to high aspect ratio definitions; legends sit outside plotting regions, and captions are written in plain language. An interactive HTML dashboard (online appendix) allows the user to hover over any observation and reveal the explanatory outputs, copy the output, or export mini-reports.

2. METHODOLOGY

2.1 Data Description

Working from national data provided by Morocco's Haut-Commissariat au Plan (HCP) and the Agence Nationale des Déchets Solides (AND), we examined the environmental performance of 270 public organisations (2018-2022). The sample includes education (35%), health (25%), administration (20%), and social services (20%) to guarantee sectoral diversity, with the following performance indicators: annual solid-waste output in kg, total energy consumption, and progress on National Sustainable Development Strategy targets by employing the United Nations monitoring methodology (United Nations, 2015). By relying on comprehensive and reputable datasets, we ensure representativeness (and temporal comparability) (Fowler, 2014).

2.2 Data Processing: Managing Bias and Uncertainty

Bias was addressed by cleaning the dataset in accordance with Groves et al (2009)'s recommendations. Apart from replacing missing values using median imputation for numerics (Rubin, 1976), we checked a limited number of records containing duplicate entries for consistencies, and in alignment with generalised variables—e.g., the estimated volumes wasted—there was some chance of bias due to misperception, or mis-measurements (taking appropriate precautions, therefore we corroborated with primary and secondary sourced public reports wherever possible). Within each variable, we applied additional cross validation to confirm internal consistency (Tourangeau, Rips & Rasinski, 2000). Further, all variables were robustly standardised to maintain valid mean(s) that reduced the influence of outliers/influential points (Johnson & Wichern, 2007). The ML algorithms we used, are tolerant of moderate noise bias, and further limit the risk of saliency and reject over-fitting (Hastie et al., 2009).

2.3 Machine Learning Techniques and Parameterization

We have chosen four algorithms from the machine learning (ML) family to evaluate and predict the environmental performance of Moroccan public entities: Random Forest (RF), XGBoost (Extreme Gradient Boosted), Support Vector Machine (SVM), and Partial Least Squares (PLS) regression.

- Random Forest (RF): Random forests (Breiman, 2001) are ensemble models that consist of bags of decision trees trained on subsets of the data, chosen randomly. They can handle non-linear data and are generally more robust to overfitting. The random forests used in this analysis consisted of 100 trees, a maximum depth of 10, and utilized $\sqrt{}$features for split choices, which we judged balanced accuracy and generalizability as Breiman suggested.
- **XGBoost (Extreme Gradient Boosting):** XGBoost (Chen & Guestrin, 2016) is a fast and flexible method for gradient boosting ensembles - aggregating shallow decision trees. As it is effective for modeling complex environmental data, we specify 100 trees of depth 10 and a learning rate of 0.1 to provide a compromise between speed of convergence and generalization ability while capturing non-linear relationships and reducing bias.
- **Support Vector Machines (SVM):** Support Vector Machines (Cortes & Vapnik, 1995) separates classes using a maximal-margin hyperplane. An RBF kernel captures non-linear patterns. For this stage of analysis, we set $C = 1$ and configure γ automatically, following guidance from the documentation. Given the non-flexibility of $C = 1$, this should balance flexibility and generalisation, making SVM a good candidate for our heterogeneous environmental dataset.
- **Partial Least Squares (PLS):** Partial Least Squares regression (Wold et al., 1984) mitigates multicollinearity by projecting predictors onto latent components that maximize covariance with responses (Abdi & Williams, 2010). According to Abdi and Williams (2010), PLS is appropriate for high-dimensional mixed data, and the number of PLS dimensions is determined through cross-validation. Therefore, we kept the number of PLS dimensions that produced the best model performance.

These parameters were chosen after a first hyperparameter optimization phase, using a cross validation approach (Kohavi, 1995; Stone, 1974). We assessed the performance of the algorithms with different combinations of parameters to select the ones that produced the best results for accuracy and generalizability.

2.4 Evaluation of Models and Tools

We reviewed Random Forest, XGBoost, SVM and PLS based on Morocco's public-sector data set using scikit-learn (Pedregosa et al., 2011) and XGBoost (Chen & Guestrin, 2016) in Python. The algorithms were evaluated with four standard metrics: accuracy and F1 for classification, R^2 and mean-squared error for waste-quantity regression. We applied thorough preprocessing, bias checks and hyper-tuning across models and ensured all models were tuned with cross-validation, as advised in previous studies, to give us a fair comparison. By completing a systematic, rigorous and accountable approach using sourced data, we provided a systematic and transparent benchmark of environmental-performance prediction through multiple algorithms and detailed the results and implications upon us in the section forthcoming.

3. RESULTS

3.1. Descriptive Statistics

This section presents a descriptive analysis of the main variables studied, based on a sample of 270 Moroccan public organizations.

3.1.1. Total Solid Waste Production

A temporal analysis, illustrated in **Figure 1**, highlights a notable trend in solid waste production per organization. In 2018, the average production was 2250 kg/year (standard deviation = 1150 kg/year). The following year, in 2019, an increase in average production was observed, reaching 2500 kg/year (standard deviation = 1270 kg/year). A peak was recorded in 2020, with an average production of 2850 kg/year (standard deviation = 1320 kg/year). From 2021 onward, a decrease was observed, with an average production of 2650 kg/year (standard deviation = 1230 kg/year). Finally, in 2022, this downward trend was confirmed, with an average production of 2450 kg/year (standard deviation = 1180 kg/year).

This evolution reveals a complex dynamic in waste production within Moroccan public organizations. The significant increase observed between 2018 and 2020 warrants further analysis. Several factors could explain this initial rise:

- **Growth in organizational activity**: During this period, some public organizations may have experienced an expansion of their activities, mechanically leading to an increase in waste production. For example, an increase in the number of pupils in schools, patients in hospitals, or services offered by public administrations could have contributed to this rise.
- **Changes in consumption patterns:** Changes in consumption patterns, such as an increase in the use of packaged or disposable products, could also have played a role.
- **Exogenous factors:** Certain external events, such as large-scale awareness campaigns or government initiatives, could have temporarily led to an increase in waste production.

The peak in waste production observed in 2020 coincides with the onset of the COVID-19 pandemic. This global health crisis may have had a significant impact on waste production:

- **Increased medical waste:** The pandemic led to a considerable increase in the production of medical waste, such as masks, gloves and personal protective equipment (PPE), in healthcare establishments.
- **Changes in consumption practices:** Containment and social distancing measures may have led to an increase in home consumption and the production of packaging waste.
- **Disruptions to waste management systems:** The pandemic may have disrupted waste management systems, leading to delays in waste collection and processing.

The gradual decline in waste production observed from 2021 onward suggests an improvement in waste management practices within Moroccan public organizations. This reversal of the trend could be attributed to several factors:

- **Implementing waste reduction policies:** Public organizations have been able to implement waste reduction policies, such as promoting recycling, reducing the use of disposable products, and optimizing internal processes.
- **Staff awareness and training:** Staff awareness and training programs in good waste management practices have helped to reduce waste production.
- **Impact of the Stratégie Nationale de Développement Durable (SNDD)**: The alignment of public organizations with the objectives of the SNDD, particularly in terms of sustainable resource management, may have encouraged the adoption of more environmentally-friendly practices.

However, the significant variability (standard deviation > 1000 kg/year) underlines that some organizations still face major challenges in this environmental dimension. This heterogeneity can be attributed to a number of factors, such as differences in available infrastructure, employee awareness levels or uneven adoption of environmental policies. These observations support our hypothesis **H3** that waste generation is a key factor influencing environmental performance.

Figure 1. Total solid waste production (kg/year)

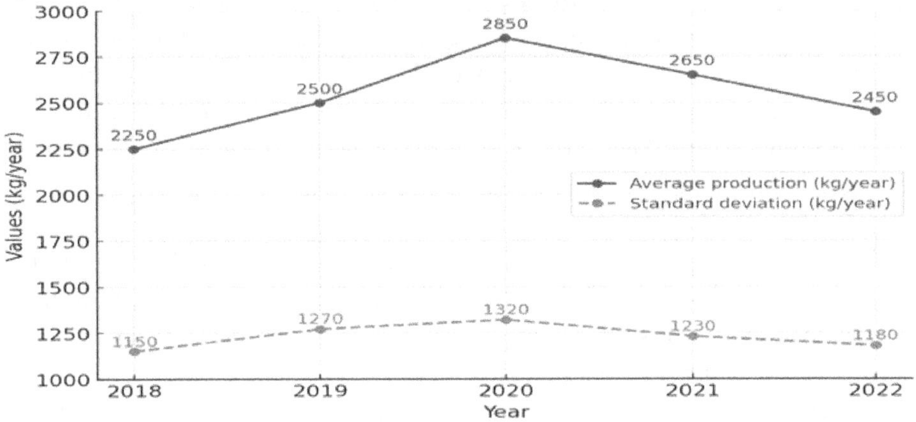

3.1.2. Energy consumption

Figure 2 presents the annual evolution of the average energy consumption of Moroccan public organizations from 2018 to 2022. This analysis reveals interesting trends that reflect both the challenges and progress made in energy management, as well as the contextual factors that may have influenced these changes.

In 2018, the average energy consumption stood at 14,500 kWh per year, with a standard deviation of 6,000 kWh, highlighting significant variability among organizations from the beginning of the study period. This variability can be attributed to differences in the size of the organizations, the nature of their activities, the age of their infrastructure, and their level of commitment to energy efficiency.

A gradual increase is then observed until 2020, when consumption peaks at 16,300 kWh per year, with a standard deviation of 6,500 kWh. This rise can be attributed to several combined factors:

- **Expansion of organizational activities:** As mentioned above, some public organizations may have experienced an expansion of their activities, leading to an increase in energy demand. For example, the construction of new buildings, the opening of new classrooms or an increase in the number of hospital beds may have contributed to this increase.

- **Introduction of more energy-intensive technological equipment:** The introduction of more modern technological equipment, such as computers, servers, medical devices or air-conditioning systems, may have led to an increase in energy consumption, particularly if this equipment is not optimized for energy efficiency.
- **Less Optimal Energy Efficiency in Certain Structures:** Some public organizations may operate in old or poorly insulated buildings, resulting in significant energy losses. Lack of investment in energy renovation or the absence of energy efficiency policies can also contribute to higher energy consumption.
- **Climatic factors:** Year-on-year climatic variations can also influence energy consumption, particularly for heating and cooling.

However, starting in 2021, a notable decrease is observed, potentially suggesting an improvement in energy efficiency practices. This reversal of the trend could be linked to the adoption of stricter environmental policies, such as those advocated by the National Sustainable Development Strategy (SNDD), or the integration of green technologies into operational processes. Several initiatives may have contributed to this decline:

- **Implementing the SNDD:** The SNDD encourages public organizations to adopt energy efficiency practices, invest in renewable energies and raise staff awareness of energy savings.
- **Investment in Green Technologies:** Some public organizations have been able to invest in green technologies, such as solar panels, LED lighting systems, energy management systems or more efficient equipment.
- **Awareness-raising and training campaigns:** Awareness-raising campaigns and staff training in energy conservation have encouraged more responsible behavior and more efficient use of energy.
- **Energy audits and action plans**: Energy audits and action plans to improve energy efficiency have helped organizations identify sources of waste and implement corrective measures.

According to 2022 Data, average energy consumption has stabilized at around 15,000 kWh/year, and a decline in standard deviation (at 6,200 kWh) indicates the gradual homogenization of energy performance among organizations. The stabilization of average energy consumption, in particular, suggests that energy efficiency activities are (hopefully) beginning to have an observable impact, although the possibility of enhanced energy performance remains.

In summary, the discussion on the evolution of energy consumption indicates a multi-faceted phenomenon influenced by many factors, from increases in the growth of the organizations' activities, to variability (and changes) in climates and energy efficiency measures. The decline since 2021 is promising; however, the continued variability among organizations demonstrates the importance of continuing to promote more sustainable energy management practices within the Moroccan Public Sector.

Figure 2. Energy consumption trend (kWh/year)

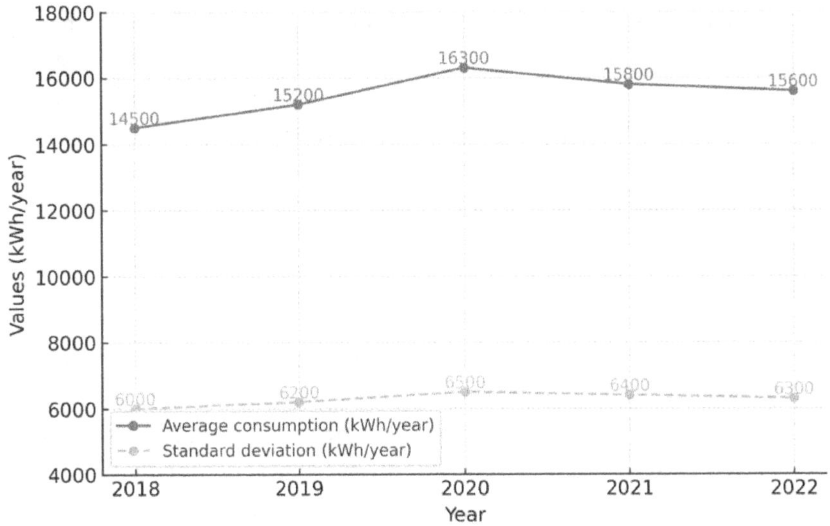

3.1.3. Rate of Achievement of SNDD Objectives

Sustainable Development Strategy (SNDD) objectives among the studied organizations, highlighting significant disparities in terms of commitment and progress toward sustainable development.

Indeed, a minority of them are at the extremes of the scale, with 3.7% showing an achievement rate between 0% and 20%, suggesting a lack of commitment or major challenges in implementing the SNDD objectives. On the other hand, 18.5% achieve rates between 80% and 100%, indicating strong commitment and successful integration of sustainable development principles into their operations.

The majority of organizations fall between 40% and 80% achievement, with a significant concentration of 33.3% in the 60%-80% range. This clustering in the 60%-80% range can be interpreted as a sign that most Moroccan public organizations have begun a transition toward sustainable development but still face challenges in achieving the more ambitious goals of the SNDD.

It is worth noting that over 60% of the organizations have an SNDD objective achievement rate above 60%, suggesting an overall positive commitment to implementing sustainable development practices. However, this average mask significant disparities and underscores the need for additional efforts to help the lower-performing organizations progress.

Several factors may explain this heterogeneous distribution:

- Level of Management Awareness and Commitment: The level of management awareness and commitment to sustainable development is a key success factor. Organizations with strong management commitment tend to allocate more resources to implementing the NSSD and encouraging the adoption of sustainable practices.
- Availability of Financial and Human Resources: Implementing the SDS requires investment in financial and human resources. Organizations with limited resources may find it difficult to implement sustainable development projects.
- Technical capacity and expertise: Implementing the NSSD requires technical capacity and expertise in sustainable development. Organizations lacking this capacity may find it difficult to identify and implement effective solutions.
- Organizational culture: Organizational culture can also influence the adoption of sustainable development practices. Organizations with a culture of innovation, collaboration and social responsibility tend to perform better when it comes to sustainability.
- **Monitoring and evaluation:** Organizations that set up systems to monitor and evaluate their progress towards sustainable development are more likely to achieve their objectives. Monitoring and evaluation make it possible to identify strengths and weaknesses, measure the impact of implemented actions and adjust strategies accordingly.

In conclusion, analysis of the rate of achievement of SNDD objectives reveals significant progress in the commitment of Moroccan public organizations to sustainable development, but also highlights the need to reduce disparities and help the least successful organizations to progress. Targeted efforts in awareness-raising, capacity-building and monitoring and evaluation are essential to accelerate the transition to more sustainable development.

Figure 3. Distribution of the rate of achievement of SNDD objectives

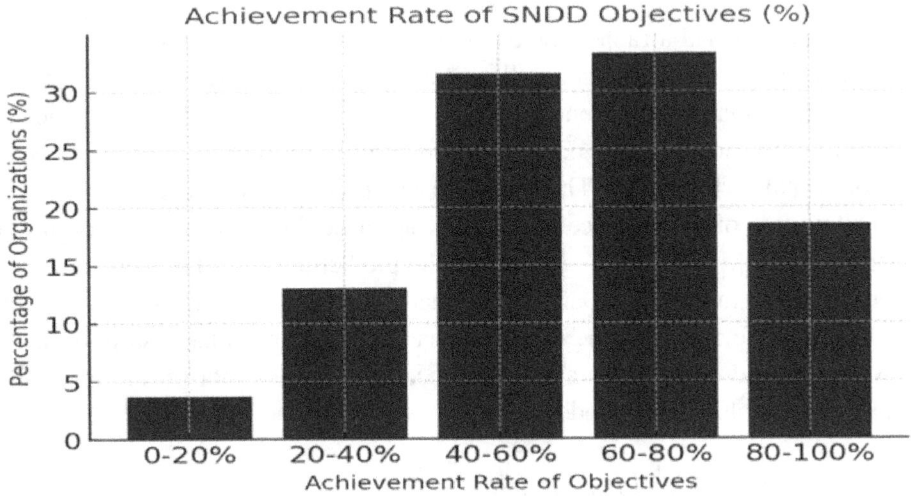

3.2. Model Performance

In this section, we will compare the performance of the four machine learning models used in this study: Random Forests (RF), XGBoost, Support Vector Machines (SVM), and Partial Least Squares (PLS), using the F1 score, the 'coefficient of determination' R^2, and mean squared error (MSE), because they provide the reader with an overall and detailed understanding of the models' predictive ability regarding the environmental performance of Moroccan public organizations.

Table 1. Comparison of performance between models

Model	Score F1	R^2	MSE
Random Forest (RF)	0.77	0.67	0.083
XGBoost	0.75	0.62	0.092
SVM	0.73	0.59	0.10
PLS	0.66	0.45	0.15

The results in this **Table 1** validate hypothesis **H1**, indicating that all tested models are capable of predicting the environmental performance of Moroccan public organizations, although their effectiveness varies.

- **Least Performant Models:**

- **Partial Least Squares (PLS)**

These models had a rather low F1 score of 0.66, which suggests that they do not balance precision and recall well, and a low F1 score may be a result of low precision (i.e., inability to identify most organizations with good environmental performance) or low recall (i.e., inability to identify all organizations with good environmental performance). The R^2 of 0.45 suggests the models explain a relatively small portion of the variance in the data and make these models less useful for prediction. The MSE (0.15) suggests that the predictions have large errors which emphasizes that these models are wholly inadequate when precision is important. The limited performance of PLS suggests that the predictive relationships between the variables and environmental performance are complex, not linear, and likely require more sophisticated models.

- **Moderate Performance Model:**
  - **Support Vector Machines (SVM):**

This model does achieve a little better performance than the previous ones, with an F1 score of 0.73, but still far from being accepted as a sophisticated model. The score of R^2 of 0.59 hints that this model at least captures some relationships in the data better than classical regression approaches, lacking when it comes to complexity in the task at hand. An MSE of 0.1 signifies that this model also produces a fair share of prediction errors. The performances of SVMs depend heavily on the chosen kernel and hyperparameters, and further arrangements may well improve its results.

- **Highly Performant Models:**
  - **Random Forests (RF) and XGBoost:**

Random Forests (Breiman, 2001) and XGBoost (Chen & Guestrin, 2016) return F1 = 0.77/0.75, R^2 = 0.67/0.62 and low MSEs (0.083, 0.092) through nonlinear interactions without over-fitting; both clearly outperform SVM and, especially, PLS thus supporting hypothesis H2 that ML better performs than linear PLS. While both RF and XGBoost have similar F1 and R^2 scores; RF edges ahead with the best precision recall balance, explained variance and lower error. As a result, Moroccan public bodies can use RF as a diagnostic and forecasting tool for environmental performance to improve evidence-based resource allocation an targeted improvements with respect to sustainability.

3.3 Variable Importance Analysis

This section provides an assessment of the variables' importance (total solid waste production, energy consumption, and SNDD objectives achievement) for each machine learning model (RF, XGBoost, SVM, and PLS). To achieve this, we utilize p-values to assess the statistical significance of each variable's influence on model accuracy and analyze the relative importance of the factors when predicting environmental performance.

3.3.1. Variable P-values by Model

Table 2 presents the p-values obtained for each variable across the different models:

Table 2. P-values of Variables in Various Machine Learning Models

Variable	Random Forests (RF(RF)	XGBoost	SVM	PLS
Total solid waste production	0.00005	0.00008	0.002	0.005
Energy consumption	0.01	0.005	0.02	0.01
Rate of achievement of SNDD objectives	0.00002	0.00001	0.001	0.001

The comprehensive examination of the p-values of different machine learning models (Random Forests, XGBoost, and SVM) provides the following important information. It shows that total solid waste production, energy consumption, and the achievement of the National Sustainable Development Strategy (SNDD) objectives were all statistically significantly associated with environmental performance, with p-values less than 0.05 across all models under study. The finding suggests that these variables have a real and non-negligible effect on environmental performance, thereby confirming hypothesis **H3**.

In other words, these results suggest that:

- An increase in solid waste production is associated with a decrease in environmental performance.
- An increase in energy consumption is associated with a decrease in environmental performance.
- An increase in the rate of achievement of SNDD objectives is associated with an improvement in environmental performance.

The p-value analysis also allows us to distinguish the relative importance of each variable. It appears that waste production and the rate of achievement of SNDD objectives are distinguished by particularly low p-values (in the range of 0.00001 to

0.0008) in the Random Forest and XGBoost models. These very low values indicate that these two variables play a major role in predicting and explaining environmental performance. In other words, they are the most important variables in these models.

Energy consumption, although statistically significant, shows higher p-values (around 0.01 to 0.03). This suggests that its impact on environmental performance, while real, is relatively weaker compared to waste production and the achievement rate of the SNDD objectives. In summary, this analysis demonstrates that waste production, energy consumption, and the achievement of SNDD objectives are key factors in environmental performance. Moreover, waste production and the achievement of SNDD objectives appear to be the most influential variables in the Random Forests and XGBoost models, while the influence of energy consumption is slightly less pronounced.

These results have important implications for the environmental management of Moroccan public organizations:

- **Priority to Waste Management**: Public organizations should prioritize waste management by implementing policies and practices aimed at reducing waste production, promoting recycling, and improving the management of hazardous waste.
- **Commitment to the SNDD:** Public organizations should fully commit to implementing the SNDD by integrating sustainable development objectives into their strategies, policies, and operations. Monitoring and evaluating progress toward achieving SNDD objectives are essential to ensure the effectiveness of efforts.
- **Energy Efficiency**: Although energy consumption has a relatively weaker impact compared to waste production and the achievement of SNDD objectives, it remains important to continue promoting energy efficiency in public organizations by investing in green technologies, raising staff awareness about energy savings, and implementing sustainable procurement policies.

Considering the overall results, particularly the superior performance of the Random Forests (RF) model in terms of F1 score (0.77), coefficient of determination R^2 (0.67), and mean squared error MSE (0.083) compared to the XGBoost and SVM models, we validate hypothesis **H4**, which posited that the Random Forests model would have significantly superior performance.

4. DISCUSSION

This study's results accentuate the importance and opportunities in using machine learning (ML) to evaluate and predict the environmental performance of Moroccan public organizations. Equally important, they show the significant value of sophisticated analytical techniques to address the multidimensional challenges of sustainability in this context.

Moreover, the key finding from the comparative assessments of the ML models is that, in terms of F1 score, R^2, and MSE, Random Forests (RF) outperformed all alternate models of XGBoost, Support Vector Machines (SVM), and Partial Least Square (PLS) regression. This may be due to RF's unique ability to accommodate the inherent complexity and non-linearity of the data, while being resilient to the overfitting that commonly arises in modeling settings, and thus RF was overall most appropriate for modeling environmental performance at an organizational level. Our results are consistent with a number of studies that cite RF as one of the best approaches to predict complex phenomena (Hastie et al., 2009).

While less performant, XGBoost also showed high effectiveness, demonstrating the utility of gradient boosting algorithms for this sort of analysis. The slight inferiority of the later in performance could be explained by the properties of the data, which may either have a lower noise threshold or lack proper hyperparameter tuning.

XGBoost can be thought of as state of the art because of its performance in so many classification and regression problems, but there are plenty of reasons to expect RF to perform better in this scenario:

- Nature of the Data: Random Forests tend to perform well with data that exhibit complex non-linear relationships and strong interactions between variables. It is possible that the relationships between waste production, energy consumption, the achievement rate of SNDD objectives, and the environmental performance of Moroccan public organizations are complex and non-linear, favoring RF. In contrast, XGBoost may be more sensitive to noise and outliers in the data.
- Complexity of the Problem: XGBoost can be particularly effective when data exhibit complex structures and require fine-grained modeling. If the problem of predicting environmental performance is not excessively complex, the simplicity and robustness of RF could give them an advantage. XGBoost, with its many adjustable parameters, can also be prone to overfitting if the sample size is not sufficiently large or if hyperparameters are not properly optimized.
- Hyperparameter Optimization: Although we optimized the hyperparameters of all models, it is possible that the hyperparameters of RF were better suited

to the specific data of our study than those of XGBoost. A more exhaustive search of XGBoost hyperparameters might have improved its performance, but this would require greater computational resources.

- Correlation Between Variables: Random Forests can effectively handle correlated variables, while XGBoost may require a feature selection or dimensionality reduction step to avoid collinearity issues. If our variables were highly correlated, this could have disadvantaged XGBoost.
- Robustness: Random Forests are known for their robustness against overfitting, which can be an advantage when the dataset is relatively small or noisy. In our case, with a sample of 270 organizations, RF's ability to generalize may have been a determining factor.

It is important to note that the relative performance of machine learning algorithms is often problem- and data-specific. The results of our study suggest that, in the context of Moroccan public organizations and with the variables considered, Random Forests proved to be the most effective approach.

The more modest performance of SVM and PLS suggests that these methods, while relevant in other contexts, are less suited to modeling the environmental performance studied here, potentially due to limitations in their ability to handle the complexity of non-linear relationships between variables. This result supports our hypothesis H2, which posited that machine learning models such as RF and XGBoost would show better predictive capabilities than the PLS model.

The analysis of variable importance confirmed that total solid waste production, energy consumption, and the achievement rate of the National Sustainable Development Strategy (SNDD) objectives are all significantly associated with environmental performance, thereby validating our hypothesis H3. Nevertheless, waste production and achieving SNDD objectives were also the dominant ER factors, especially in the RF and XGBoost models where p-values were extremely low. This result highlights the importance of waste management and commitment to sustainable development objectives in enhancing the environmental performance of public organizations in Morocco. Energy consumption was also significant, but its relative weight was smaller; therefore, while management of energy use is essential, targeted waste management and SNDD implementation initiatives could inform best practice. These conclusions are consistent with other studies focusing on best practice in waste management (Hoornweg & Bhada-Tata, 2012), and integrated environmental policy (Ministry of Energy Transition and Sustainable Development, 2021). In addition, our findings relate back to stakeholder theory (Freeman, 1984) as achieving the SNDD objectives considers the needs of multiple stakeholders.

The results of our study are consistent with previous research that underscores the significance of waste management (Hoornweg & Bhada-Tata, 2012) and integrating environmental policies (Ministry of Energy Transition and Sustainable Development, 2021) to help boost environmental performance. However, we have gone a step further by measuring the relative importance of these attributes and demonstrating the applicability of ML models to facilitate decisions based on data.

The substantive implications of the findings above are considerable. Moroccan public organizations can employ ML models, (e.g., RF), to evaluate and predict the consequences of environmental practices. Principle components should be aiding waste minimization, achieving SNDD targets while ultimately enhancing energy efficiency. ML models could also be employed to evaluate the effects of environmental policy scenarios and prioritize resource allocations. For example, it would be possible to model the impact of introducing new recycling technologies, promoting sustainable transportation modes, or implementing environmental awareness programs.

However, it is important to note that this study has certain limitations. The analysis is based on data collected from Moroccan public organizations, which limits the generalizability of the results to other contexts. The institutional, cultural, and economic specificities of Morocco could influence the relationships between the studied variables.

Moreover, we examined three key variables, but other factors (e.g., staff awareness levels, adoption of green technologies, etc.) could also influence environmental performance. Including these additional variables could improve the accuracy of ML models.

Furthermore, the use of administrative data carries potential biases. The data could be incomplete, inaccurate, or subject to measurement errors. The assessment of the achievement rate of SNDD objectives, in particular, could be subjective and dependent on organizational interpretations.

Many Moroccan public institutions possess only nascent analytical teams, yet they face growing pressure to harness advanced modelling for environmental policy. To bridge this capability gap without over-stretching resources, the chapter proposes a phased implementation roadmap that respects organisational constraints while progressively embedding explainable AI into routine decision processes.

The starting point is a data-readiness audit. Each agency assembles an inventory of the environmental indicators it already collects—energy consumption, water use, waste volumes—as well as metadata on measurement frequency, ownership and quality controls. Missing values, inconsistent units and siloed storage are documented, and a corrective plan is agreed with IT and domain experts. By completing this diagnostic exercise first, the organisation secures a clean, well-governed dataset that underpins every subsequent step and builds early cross-departmental cohesion.

Once the data foundation is secured, the institution launches a low-code pilot powered by AutoML with native explainability features. Platforms such as Google AutoML Tables or Microsoft Azure AutoML allow non-specialists to generate and benchmark multiple algorithms through a graphical interface, while automatically producing SHAP-based explanations for each prediction. Running a three-month pilot on a modest cloud budget enables the agency to validate model accuracy, user comprehension and governance safeguards without committing to expensive long-term contracts.

If the pilot confirms both technical soundness and managerial appetite, the agency progresses to the procurement of cloud-hosted model dashboards. Rather than licensing opaque turnkey solutions, the tender specification emphasises open APIs, embedded interpretability widgets and compliance with Morocco's forthcoming Responsible-AI Charter. Hosting the dashboards in a government-approved cloud environment ensures scalability, while single sign-on integration lets frontline managers consult live performance scores alongside existing e-government portals.

Finally, sustainable impact depends on continuous capability building through public-private partnerships. The roadmap recommends pairing civil-service analysts with university data-science labs and local start-ups in rolling three-month fellowships. Joint hackathons and mentoring sessions transform tacit knowledge into reusable code modules and foster a community of practice that endures beyond any single project. Over time, this partnership model diffuses expertise across ministries, reduces vendor lock-in and anchors explainable AI in Morocco's broader digital-transition agenda.

Future research should strive to overcome these limitations and deepen our understanding of the application of ML to the environmental management of public organizations. We recommend the following research directions:

- **Expand the Sample and Include Other Contexts:** It would be interesting to extend the study to other countries, particularly those with contexts similar to Morocco, in order to assess the generalizability of the results.
- **Making Use of Additional Variables**: The inclusion of variables such as employee awareness, uptake of green technology, the quality of environmental governance, and formal environmental policies, could improve the accuracy and appropriateness of the AA models.
- **Using More Objective Data**: The use of more objective and verifiable data, such as sensor data, satellite, or environmental audit data, could resolve potential biases associated with administrative data.
- **Using more comprehensive AoA methods**: Using more comprehensive AoA methods, such as reinforcement learning or deep neural networks, could provide more accurate and robust models.

- **Conducting Qualitative Case Studies**: In-depth qualitative case studies could enhance our understanding of contextual factors impacting the uptake of, and performance of, environmental management practices.

Finally, it is essential to consider the ethical implications of applying ML to environmental management. Care must be taken to ensure that ML models are used fairly, transparently, and responsibly. This involves avoiding biases and discrimination in data and algorithms, ensuring model transparency, and safeguarding data privacy.

CONCLUSION

This investigation has examined the potential application of machine learning to evaluate and forecast the environmental performance of Moroccan public organizations. The results (provided in section 5) confirm that Random Forests (RF) perform better than XGBoost, SVM, and the PLS model. It has shown that total solid waste, energy consumption, and level of achievement of the SNDD objectives are all significantly correlated with environmental performance, but total solid waste and the level of devotion to the SNDD objectives are the most significant.

In accordance with the principal objectives of the research, it provides a meaningful contribution to the emerging body of literature on the application of artificial intelligence for sustainable development in the public sector by offering an empirical analysis, based in Morocco, of the key levers influencing environmental performance, while identifying waste management and commitment to sustainable development objectives as critical issues, and highlights the potential contribution of ML tools for informing environmental policy and decisions.

These recommendations resulting from this study are simple: Moroccan public organizations should go from data-poor to data-rich in relation to their environmental performance and be mindful of their waste management and the implementation of the SNDD objectives. Machine Learning models such as, Random Forests, could introduce an important tool for Moroccan public organizations to evaluate their actions, improve their allocation of resources, and move toward behavior that is more sustainable.

Consequently, there are many research directions resulting from this study such as: across other variables that could be included; exploring the adaptability of the ML models in different contexts; developing models to evaluate scenarios; and potentially exploring some more advanced techniques for interpreting results. In all, we believed that it is important to continue generating tools and knowledge to support public organizations in being a catalyst for the transition to sustainable development.

REFERENCES

Abdi, H., & Williams, L. J. (2010). Partial least square methods: Regression and structural equation models. *Journal of Computational Statistics, 1*(2), 1–21.

Agence Nationale des Déchets Solides (AND). (2023). Statistiques sur la Production et la Gestion des Déchets Solides au Maroc. https://www.environnement.gov.ma/fr/dechets?utm_source=chatgpt.comhttps://www.environnement.gov.ma/fr/etat-de-l-environnement?utm_source=chatgpt.com

Amasyali, K., & El-Gohary, N. M. (2018). A review of data-driven building energy consumption prediction studies. *Renewable & Sustainable Energy Reviews, 81*(P1), 1192–1205. DOI: 10.1016/j.rser.2017.04.095

Breiman, L. (2001). Random Forests. *Machine Learning, 45*(1), 5–32. DOI: 10.1023/A:1010933404324

Chen, T., & Guestrin, C. (2016). XGBoost: A scalable tree boosting system. In *Proceedings of the 22nd ACM SIGKDD International Conference on Knowledge Discovery and Data Mining* (pp. 785-794).

Cortes, C., & Vapnik, V. (1995). Support-vector networks. *Machine Learning, 20*(3), 273–297. DOI: 10.1007/BF00994018

Darnall, N., Henriques, I., & Sadorsky, P. (2005). Adopting proactive environmental strategy: The influence of stakeholders and firm size. *Journal of Management Studies, 47*(6), 1072–1094. DOI: 10.1111/j.1467-6486.2009.00873.x

Dyllick, T., & Hockerts, K. (2002). Au-delà de l'analyse de rentabilité pour la durabilité de l'entreprise. *Stratégie commerciale et environnement, 11*(2), 130-141.

Fowler, F. J. (2014). *Survey research methods*. Sage Publications.

Freeman, R. E. (1984). *Strategic Management: A Stakeholder Approach*. Pitman.

García-Martínez, A., Pérez-Moreno, S., & Sánchez-Cuesta, A. (2022). Artificial intelligence for the management of environmental sustainability: An overview. *Environmental Science and Pollution Research International, 29*(30), 45128–45147.

Groves, R. M., Fowler, F. J., Couper, M. P., Lepkowski, J. M., Singer, E., & Tourangeau, R. (2009). *Survey methodology*. John Wiley & Sons.

Hastie, T., Tibshirani, R., & Friedman, J. (2009). *The Elements of Statistical Learning: Data Mining, Inference, and Prediction*. Springer. DOI: 10.1007/978-0-387-84858-7

Hoornweg, D., & Bhada-Tata, P. (2012). *What a Waste: A Global Review of Solid Waste Management*. Urban Development Series. World Bank., DOI: 10.1596/17388

Johnson, R. A., & Wichern, D. W. (2007). *Applied Multivariate Statistical Analysis*. Pearson Education India.

Jordan, M. I., & Mitchell, T. M. (2015). Machine learning: Trends, perspectives, and prospects. *Science, 349*(6245), 255–260. DOI: 10.1126/science.aaa8415 PMID: 26185243

Kaza, S., Yao, L., Bhada-Tata, P., & Van Woerden, F. (2018). *What a Waste 2.0: A Global Snapshot of Solid Waste Management to 2050*. Urban Development Series. World Bank., DOI: 10.1596/978-1-4648-1329-0

Kohavi, R. (1995). A study of cross-validation and bootstrap for accuracy estimation and model selection. *IJCAI (United States), 14*(2), 1137–1145.

Li, X., Peng, L., Hu, Y., Shao, J., & Chi, T. (2016). Deep learning architecture for air quality prediction. *Environmental Science and Pollution Research International, 23*(22), 22408–22417. DOI: 10.1007/s11356-016-7812-9 PMID: 27734318

Liakos, K. G., Busato, P., Moshou, D., Pearson, S., & Bochtis, D. (2018). Machine learning in agriculture: A review. *Sensors (Basel), 18*(8), 2674. DOI: 10.3390/s18082674 PMID: 30110960

Ministère de la Transition Énergétique et du Développement Durable (MTE DD). (2021). *Stratégie Nationale de Développement Durable (SNDD)*. Gouvernement du Royaume du Maroc. https://mtedd.gov.ma/images/Rapport_Strategie_Nationale_DD_juin2017_Mai_2017_Web.pdf

Najah Ahmed, A., Binti Othman, F., Abdulmohsin Afan, H., Khaleel Ibrahim, R., Ming Fai, C., Shabbir Hossain, M., Ehteram, M., & Elshafie, A. (2019). Machine learning methods for better water quality prediction. *Journal of Hydrology (Amsterdam), 578*, 124084. DOI: 10.1016/j.jhydrol.2019.124084

Pedregosa, F., Varoquaux, G., Gramfort, A., Michel, V., Thirion, B., Grisel, O., & Vanderplas, J. (2011). Scikit-learn: Machine learning in Python. *Journal of Machine Learning Research, 12*, 2825–2830.

Porter, M. E., & van der Linde, C. (1995). Green and competitive: Breaking the stalemate. *Harvard Business Review, 73*(5), 120–134.

Rubin, D. B. (1976). Inference and missing data. *Biometrika, 63*(3), 581–592. DOI: 10.1093/biomet/63.3.581

Runge, C. A., Tulloch, A. I. T., Possingham, H. P., Tulloch, V. J. D., & Fuller, R. A. (2016). Incorporating dynamic distributions into spatial prioritization. *Diversity & Distributions*, *22*(3), 332–344. DOI: 10.1111/ddi.12395

Stone, M. (1974). Cross-validatory choice and assessment of statistical predictions. *Journal of the Royal Statistical Society. Series B, Statistical Methodology*, *36*(2), 111–133. DOI: 10.1111/j.2517-6161.1974.tb00994.x

Tourangeau, R., Rips, L. J., & Rasinski, K. (2000). *The Psychology of Survey Response*. Cambridge University Press. DOI: 10.1017/CBO9780511819322

United Nations. (2015). *Transforming Our World: The 2030 Agenda for Sustainable Development.* New York. https://docs.un.org/en/A/RES/70/1

Vinuesa, R., Azizpour, H., Leike, J., Tegmark, M., & Fuso Nerini, F. (2020). The role of artificial intelligence in achieving the Sustainable Development Goals. *Nature Communications*, *11*(1), 1–10. DOI: 10.1038/s41467-019-14108-y PMID: 31932590

Willard, J. D., Read, J. S., Appling, A. P., Oliver, S. K., Jia, X., & Kumar, V. (2021). Predicting water temperature dynamics of unmonitored lakes with meta-transfer learning. *Water Resources Research, 57*, e2021WR029579. DOI: .DOI: 10.1029/2021WR029579

Wilson, D. C., Rodic, L., Cowing, M. J., Velis, C. A., Whiteman, A. D., Scheinberg, A., Vilches, R., Masterson, D., Stretz, J., & Oelz, B. (2015). Wasteaware benchmark indicators for integrated sustainable waste management in cities. *Waste Management (New York, N.Y.)*, *35*, 329–342. DOI: 10.1016/j.wasman.2014.10.006 PMID: 25458855

Wirtz, B. W., Weyerer, J. C., & Geyer, C. (2019). Artificial Intelligence and the Public Sector—Applications and Challenges. *International Journal of Public Administration*, *42*(7), 596–615. DOI: 10.1080/01900692.2018.1498103

Wold, S., Ruhe, A., Wold, H., & Dunn, W. J.III. (1984). The collinearity problem in linear regression. *SIAM Journal on Scientific and Statistical Computing*, *5*(3), 735–743. DOI: 10.1137/0905052

Zaman, A. U. (2016). A comprehensive review of the development of zero waste management. *Journal of Cleaner Production*, *91*, 12–25. DOI: 10.1016/j.jclepro.2014.12.013

Chapter 11
Artificial Intelligence and Operational Risk Management:
A Qualitative Analysis in the Moroccan Banking Sector

Hajar El Haji
https://orcid.org/0009-0006-7737-4504
Mohammed First University, Morocco

Oumayma Aitmoussa
https://orcid.org/0000-0002-3355-4742
Mohammed First University, Morocco

ABSTRACT

This paper explores the impact of artificial intelligence (AI) on operational risk management in the Moroccan banking sector through a qualitative case study conducted at Banque Populaire. The objective is to understand how AI, particularly in front-office operations, contributes to risk reduction, improved operational efficiency, and process automation. The results reveal a growing integration of AI, particularly through chatbots and automated services, helping to limit human error and reduce workload. However, challenges remain, related to both technical aspects (outages, cybersecurity, system interoperability) and human aspects (resistance to change, uneven adoption across customer segments). The study also highlights that the post-Covid context and accelerated digital transformation require banks to continually adapt their governance, information systems, and training practices. AI thus appears to be a major strategic lever for strengthening banks' operational resilience, provided it is accompanied by appropriate organizational preparation.

DOI: 10.4018/979-8-3373-1737-3.ch011

1. INTRODUCTION

Artificial intelligence (AI) represents a major advancement in the digital transformation of banks. It plays a vital role in improving operational efficiency, personalizing services, and managing risks. According to Brynjolfsson and McAfee (2017), AI reduces human intervention in repetitive processes, thus limiting operational errors and increasing productivity.

Well before the emergence of generative AI applications, financial institutions had already been relying on artificial intelligence technologies to address a variety of strategic and operational challenges.

Banks, for example, have used AI to streamline internal processes, enhance operational efficiency, and strengthen risk management frameworks. Today, the rapid democratization of AI tools—driven by technological innovation, reduced costs, and broader accessibility—is accelerating their widespread adoption across the financial sector. This momentum is also drawing increasing attention from regulatory authorities, who are examining the prudential, behavioral, ethical, and systemic implications of AI deployment within complex financial ecosystems.

Among the most widely adopted historical applications are customer service chatbots, fraud detection systems—particularly for anti-money laundering (AML) and counter-terrorist financing (CTF) purposes—as well as the automation of credit and insurance underwriting. Although these use cases are not entirely new, they have been significantly transformed and enhanced by recent technological advances, notably in data processing, machine learning algorithms, and predictive analytics.

In this context, financial institutions are making substantial investments in the development and deployment of AI-based solutions.

This investment momentum reflects strong expectations in terms of efficiency gains, cost reduction, and productivity improvements. According to McKinsey (2024), generative AI could generate between $200 billion and $340 billion in annual value creation—representing approximately 2.7% to 4.7% of the total revenue of the financial industry. For instance, banking sector spending on generative AI is projected to increase from $3.86 billion in 2023 to nearly $85 billion by 2030, with a significant portion allocated to infrastructure development and the recruitment of specialized talent in AI and data science.

However, despite the enthusiasm surrounding these innovations, institutions are adopting a relatively cautious approach when it comes to implementing generative AI in highly sensitive services or those with significant customer exposure. This cautious stance is driven by multiple factors, including regulatory uncertainty, reliance on third-party model providers, concerns about customer impact, and the need to safeguard data privacy and confidentiality.

Finally, the expanding use of AI raises significant risk-related challenges. While most identified risks—such as operational risks—are already monitored by financial regulators, AI tends to exacerbate their complexity. Critical issues such as model explainability, algorithmic bias, data security, and overall governance frameworks require heightened vigilance and proactive engagement from all sector stakeholders.

In Moroccan banks, particularly retail banks, AI is primarily integrated at the front office level, through tools such as chatbots, virtual assistants, and customer service automation. This development is in line with the work of Makridakis (2017), who highlights the role of AI in transforming customer interactions by providing fast and accurate solutions. This technological adoption leads to a reduction in manual tasks for front-office staff, as observed by Autor and Salomons (2018) in their analysis of the impacts of automation on the labor market. This also optimizes back-office tasks, particularly with regard to the reliability of processed and transferred data.

This development directly contributes to minimizing operational risks, defined by the Basel Committee as losses resulting from the failure or malfunction of processes, systems, or people (BCBS, 2004). AI plays a central role in mitigating these risks by improving the accuracy and speed of operations while limiting human error.

However, as Davenport (2018) noted, although banks are at the forefront of AI adoption, its use remains limited to certain processes such as customer service and predictive analytics, leaving untapped opportunities in strategic areas such as operational risk management.

This study addresses a central issue in the modern banking sector: To what extent does this technology contribute to reducing operational risks? This question is particularly important in a context where human error and process failures are determining factors in the emergence of these risks. The adoption of AI thus opens up interesting prospects for risk reduction by automating certain tasks and optimizing process management.

The central hypothesis we formulate in this study is the following: minimizing repetitive and manual tasks through artificial intelligence would significantly reduce banking operational risks by limiting human error and improving the traceability of actions. This hypothesis raises specific questions about the mechanisms of this technological contribution and its actual effects, particularly in the specific context of Moroccan retail banks.

- How does automating front-office processes through AI reduce operational risks related to human error?
- What impact has AI had on daily front-office tasks?

The objective of this study is to qualitatively explore the impact of AI on operational risk management in Moroccan banks, focusing in particular on the case of Banque Populaire. The aim is to analyze both the concrete contributions of AI in front-office operations, the perceptions of banking employees, as well as the organizational, technical, and human challenges related to this integration.

The methodology adopted is based on a qualitative approach, through the conduct of semi-structured interviews with professionals at Banque Populaire, an exploratory approach aimed at analyzing the dynamics of integrating artificial intelligence (AI) into operational risk management. The banking sector, and more specifically retail banking, is particularly well-suited to the adoption of AI due to its heavy reliance on digital operations and intensive information exchange (Rania EL OUIDANI, Brahim OUL-CAID, 2023). The choice of this bank, a major player in the Moroccan banking system, is justified by its commitment to digital transformation and its proven experience in risk management. Interviews were conducted in various representative branches to capture the diversity of contexts and perceptions related to the use of AI.

The article is divided into two parts. The first part provides a theoretical framework around the concept of operational risk and the contributions of artificial intelligence in the banking sector. The second part presents an analysis of the results of the field survey, highlighting concrete practices, employee perceptions, and the organizational implications of the use of AI in risk management.

1. LITERATURE REVIEW

1.1. Operational Risk Management

Operational risk is defined by the Basel Committee as "...the risk of loss resulting from a deficiency or failure inherent in procedures, people, internal systems, or external events. This definition includes legal risk, but excludes strategic and reputational risk." (Christophe J. Godlewski, 2004).

Operational risk, by definition, concerns numerous stakeholders, activities, and operations, at all levels of a bank's organizational structure and across all its business lines.

Indeed, the Basel Committee's work defined a risk segmentation into eight business lines, namely: Financial Engineering; Trading and Sales; Retail Banking; Wholesale Banking; Payments and Settlements; Agency Services; Asset Management; Retail Brokerage, and seven event categories, namely: Internal Fraud; External Fraud; Inadequate internal practices regarding human resources and workplace safety; (Non-deliberate) neglect of customer, product, and business practice rules; Damage to tangible assets; Business interruption and system malfunctions; Process malfunctions (execution, handover, delivery, finished products) (Christian Jimenez 2008).

Furthermore, unlike other banking risks, operational risk has the particularity of starting from the consequences and effects (losses in this case) and then tracing back to the causes. In other words, the starting point for the prudential treatment of this risk is based on the concept of loss.

However, beyond this interesting characteristic, operational risk also presents specific challenges that complicate its management within banks. A culture of vigilance and control must be built and disseminated among as many employees as possible, particularly those in "peripheral" entities (small branches located far from decision-making and control centers, etc.) (H. Agourrame 2022).

Faced with these challenges, operational risk management saw the entry into force of the Basel II Committee's work in 2007, integrating operational risk with the two pre-existing types of banking risks. The Committee proposed three pillars to appropriately measure and manage operational risk. The first pillar aims to ensure that banks have adequate capital to cover all risks related to their activities (8% Basel Committee 2006); A second Pillar, which complements the first pillar by introducing a new concept, namely "economic capital," encouraging banks to develop and use better techniques for monitoring and managing operational risks. " through a set of mechanisms implemented in the relevant business line. (Jean-Charles ROCHET 2008).

Finally, a third Pillar, which aims to complement the other two pillars, is by disciplining the stakeholders through the development of a set of communication requirements that are both quantitative and qualitative (strategies and procedures for monitoring the ongoing effectiveness of hedges or mitigation techniques) (Basel Committee 2006).

The reform of operational risk management methods will continue through the developments introduced by Basel III and Basel IV. Indeed, Basel III, implemented in 2010, led to the elimination of the internal models proposed by Basel II to address the risk of banks manipulating internal models to artificially reduce capital requirements (Basel Committee 2011). This reform will be further developed in 2017 by the work of Basel IV through the introduction of a new standardized approach (SA) for banking operational risk management (H. Agourrame 2022), the implementation of which remains a subject of debate among authors and analysts.

Consequently, the Moroccan regulatory framework has established a set of standards relating to operational risk management that Moroccan credit institutions must comply with to ensure better risk management. Therefore, based on the Basel II and III directives, the online publication of a set of circulars is necessary, as this will ensure the continued operation of the institution's activities, thus limiting losses in the event of disruptions due to major events related to operational risks (O. AIT MOUSSA 2023).

Faced with the evolving regulatory framework and the increasing complexity of operational risks, Moroccan banks are forced to rethink their risk management models. In this context, digital transformation is emerging as a major strategic lever, promoting process automation and improving operational performance. Moreover, in the case of Moroccan banks, Bank Al-Maghrib has placed digital technology at the heart of its latest 2019-2023 strategic plan. In 2022, according to Wali of Bank Al-Maghrib, “This concerns both the transformation of our internal processes and activities as well as the evolution of the digitalization of financial services and the emergence of a Fintech ecosystem.”

Currently, the growing integration of artificial intelligence in the Moroccan banking sector represents a response to these challenges, providing powerful tools to more effectively identify, prevent, and manage operational risks, particularly fraud and human error (R. EL OUIDANI1, B. OUL-CAID 2023).

Artificial intelligence (AI) is playing a growing role in the transformation of the banking sector, particularly in operational risk management. Its integration allows for the automation of processes, improved traceability and compliance, while introducing new challenges related to cybersecurity and algorithmic bias.

The emergence and growing adoption of artificial intelligence (AI) by financial institutions give rise to specific challenges in risk management, particularly in relation to operational risks.

While AI holds the promise of increased efficiency, service personalization, and process automation, it also introduces new vulnerabilities into financial systems. In response, regulatory authorities have gradually developed guidelines aimed at overseeing the responsible and secure use of this technology within the financial sector.

At the outset, it is important to emphasize that regulatory orientations concerning AI are largely aligned with pre-existing principles established in the financial domain. Indeed, the cross-cutting themes found in AI-related guidance—such as governance, risk management, accountability, and consumer protection—broadly mirror the prudential standards that have long governed financial activities. This regulatory continuity partly explains why many financial supervisory bodies have not yet issued AI-specific regulations, opting instead to reiterate foundational principles through broader supervisory frameworks or general-purpose policy documents.

In parallel, international and national authorities have issued cross-sectoral guidelines emphasizing core principles such as reliability, accountability, transparency, fairness, and ethics.

More recently, greater attention has been given to personal data protection, cybersecurity, and system integrity. These orientations are intended to establish a trusted framework for AI usage, while simultaneously encouraging responsible and controlled innovation across sectors, including finance.

Within this evolving landscape, financial regulators are adopting a technology-neutral stance, guided by a risk-based and proportionate approach. Rather than imposing rigid, prescriptive rules, they require financial institutions to demonstrate their ability to identify, assess, and manage the specific risks associated with their use of AI. This flexible approach provides institutions with a degree of interpretative freedom but also underscores the need for clearer guidance to ensure harmonization, consistency, and comparability in the implementation of existing regulatory standards.

Finally, although cross-cutting guidelines provide a relevant and foundational regulatory baseline, the use of AI in the core activities of financial institutions—or in high-stakes use cases—may require more specific and targeted regulatory mechanisms.

As a result, some authorities are considering introducing clarifications, and in some cases even revisions or entirely new rules, in particularly sensitive areas such as:

- AI system governance, especially regarding the accountability of boards of directors and executive management, as well as the need for a clear allocation of responsibilities across the entire AI system lifecycle;
- Model risk management, with a particular focus on the explainability of algorithms and the rigorous selection of appropriate explanation techniques that align with the models' complexity and intended use;
- Human intervention mechanisms, which are essential to mitigating adverse outcomes associated with certain automated decisions and ensuring a minimum level of human oversight.

1.2. AI and Operational Risk Reduction

As digital banking grows, so do customer expectations (Biswas & Carson, 2020). Customers now demand seamless, fast, and highly secure banking experiences, with personalized services and 24/7 accessibility. Banks must continuously innovate to meet these growing expectations, leveraging AI and other advanced technologies.

A theoretical study demonstrates the ability of artificial intelligence to foster new forms of customer interaction, understand customer expectations, and adapt to robust services offered by companies to remain competitive. Furthermore, it facilitates rapid responses to customer requests in many use cases. This research also shows that the appropriate adoption of AI technologies can redefine traditional banking processes. The study focuses on Mastercard (United States), Royal Bank of Scotland (Scotland), and Caixa Bank (Spain). (Gallego-Gomez & De-Pablos-Heredero, 2020).

There is a significant relationship between customer service and offers and discounts. It has been shown that if a customer uses a chatbot for customer service-related assistance, they are also likely to use it to get recommendations on offers and discounts. Improving chatbot functionality in these two areas could not only increase customer engagement but also boost the bank's business performance (Bhattacharya, C., & Sinha, M. (2022)).

AI enables the automation of many repetitive and error-prone tasks, such as transaction processing, customer data management, and transaction monitoring. This automation significantly reduces the risk of manual errors, improves operational efficiency, and allows staff to focus on higher-value tasks. For example, the use of AI in robotic process automation (RPA) has helped reduce operational costs and risks associated with human error.

Numerous concrete use cases already demonstrate how financial institutions are leveraging AI to enhance operational efficiency and mitigate risks associated with human-driven activities. As shown in Table 1 below provides a summary of selected practical examples, categorized by their primary objectives:

Table 1. Effectiveness of AI utilization in the banking and insurance sectors

Objective	Use case	Description	Example
Improve productivity and efficiency	Internal administrative • Human resource management • Virtual reality training on customer interaction Bank of America	• Summarise documents or internal meetings • Classify documents	Tasks Standard Chartered Axa Secure GPT
	Customer support	Chatbots to respond to customer queries • Automate email response to clients	Bank of America Erica customer chatbot DBS CSO Assistant Ping An2 AI service representatives JPMorgan Chase email classification system
	Human resource management	• Virtual reality training on customer interaction	Bank of America
	Coding applications	• Facilitate coding of IT	Goldman Sachs
	Insurance claims	• Use of AI to estimate property damage	MS&AD use of Tractable
	Reinsurance claims	• Automate identification of reinsurance claims	Zurich Catastrophe Insurance Agent

Source: FSI Insights no 63 Regulating AI in the financial sector: recent developments and main challenges and possible December 2024

One of the benefits of artificial intelligence in internal auditing is the automation of routine tasks. AI can automate repetitive and time-consuming tasks such as data entry, reconciliation, and documentation, allowing auditors to focus on higher-value activities (Chatterjee, et. al., 2022).

Artificial intelligence has fundamentally changed auditors' approach, providing them with new insights and previously unattainable capabilities (Costanza-Chock, Raji, & Buolamwini, 2022).

AI facilitates regulatory compliance management by automating monitoring and reporting, ensuring better traceability of operations. AI systems can analyze large data sets in real time to detect anomalies or suspicious behavior, strengthening internal controls and reducing compliance risks. Artificial intelligence-based fraud detection strengthens system security by identifying fraudulent transactions, scams, fake insurance claims, and anomalies (Bhattacharya, C., & Sinha, M. 2022).

AI and ML could be used to anticipate and detect fraud, suspicious transactions, payment defaults, and the risk of cyberattacks, which could improve risk management (Milojević, N., & Redzepagic, S. 2021).

Regarding the application of AI and machine learning to operational and related risk management, significant results have been achieved worldwide in the following areas: cybersecurity, fraud prevention, and anti-money laundering.

It has been found that with the use of artificial intelligence, banks can reduce risk, strengthen payment security, automate compliance-related operations, and generally improve their business. This study examines the capabilities of AI in facilitating consumer acceptance by ensuring transparency, confidentiality, and proper documentation (Bhattacharya, C., & Sinha, M. 2022).

Despite its benefits, the adoption of AI introduces new risks, particularly regarding cybersecurity and algorithmic bias. AI systems can be vulnerable to sophisticated attacks, such as algorithm hacking or exploiting flaws in machine learning models. Furthermore, biases in training data can lead to discriminatory or unfair decisions, affecting the reputation of financial institutions and leading to legal risks. For example, errors or biases in AI models can become systematic and lead to a loss of customer trust.

The adoption of automated monitoring systems has strengthened banks' ability to detect and mitigate risks more effectively (Ogboi & Unuafe, 2013). However, these technological advances also introduce new risks, particularly in cybersecurity and data management (Adeusi et al., 2014). As banks expand their digital footprint, managing these risks becomes imperative to maintain operational stability.

The rapid growth of digital financial services has necessitated new regulations to address issues such as money laundering, fraud, and data protection. The regulatory environment is still evolving, with ongoing efforts to strike a balance between promoting innovation and protecting consumers (Ofodile et al., 2024).

2. RESEARCH METHODOLOGY

2.1. Epistemological Stance

The epistemological stance adopted in this research is interpretivist, also referred to as comprehensive. This approach considers that the integration of artificial intelligence (AI) in operational risk management is not an objective and measurable fact independent of stakeholders, but that it is socially constructed by their experiences, perceptions, and interactions within a specific organizational context (Burrell & Morgan, 1979; Schwandt, 1994).

From this perspective, we do not seek to verify predefined hypotheses or produce statistical generalizations; rather, we aim to gain an in-depth understanding of the meaning that banking professionals attribute to AI tools, through their narratives, judgments, and daily practices. This is an inductive stance, open to the emergence of new concepts from the field, and based on immersion in the lived experiences of stakeholders. This approach is particularly justified in the context of a complex, evolving, and underexplored research topic, such as the appropriation of AI in a Moroccan banking sector undergoing a digital transformation. The interpretive approach thus allows us to grasp subjective dynamics (representations, resistance, levers of acceptance) that elude quantitative or positivist methods.

Furthermore, the adoption of an interpretivist approach is part of a constructivist epistemology, according to which knowledge is contextual, situated, and co-constructed between the researcher and the respondents (Lincoln & Guba, 1985). Here, we assume an active role in data interpretation by placing participants' comments in perspective with existing theoretical frameworks and fieldwork issues. This methodological reflexivity constitutes an additional guarantee of interpretive validity (Charmaz, 2006).

2.2. Data Collection Method

The use of an in-depth case study (Yin, 2018) focused on several bank branches in the eastern region of Morocco proved appropriate for exploring the research subject in its contextual complexity. Semi-structured interviews were chosen as the primary data collection tool, as they allow for a combination of methodological rigor and exploratory flexibility (Miles, Huberman, & Saldaña, 2019). This type of interview is based on a thematic framework developed from the literature (benefits of AI, barriers to its adoption, effects on risk management), while allowing participants the freedom to spontaneously explore certain unexpected aspects.

The interviews were conducted with front-office agents (branch managers, tellers, customer service representatives), selected using a purposive sampling approach. This choice was based on the relevance of their roles in terms of direct links to operational processes and banking technologies. This diversity of profiles allows for a multidimensional view of AI-related practices and the positions adopted.

Each interview lasted between 45 minutes and 1 hour 15 minutes, and took place in a setting conducive to confidentiality and freedom of expression. Data collection continued until thematic saturation was reached: by the 10th interview, emerging elements became redundant, indicating that the major categories of discourse had been covered (Guest, Bunce, & Johnson, 2006).

2.3. Data Analysis

The analysis followed an inductive interpretive approach, based on understanding the meaning that stakeholders attribute to their experiences. Rather than relying on automated or software coding, we favored a detailed reading of the discourses through their internal coherence and contextual anchoring (Paillé & Mucchielli, 2012).

The interviews were analyzed using an open thematic approach: points of convergence were identified, as well as dissonances and contradictions, revealing the tensions between the technological promises of AI and its actual appropriation in the field.

We also used triangulation between field data and theoretical frameworks to construct robust interpretations. For example, findings related to automation and error reduction were compared with the contributions of Davenport & Ronanki (2018) and Brynjolfsson & McAfee (2017), while resistance to adoption was put into perspective with the work of Arner, Barberis & Buckley (2016) on the human and regulatory issues related to AI in finance.

Finally, analytical traceability was ensured by the creation of field memos, interview summary tables, and cross-analysis grids to track interpretative reasoning and strengthen the reliability of the results (Saldaña, 2016). As shown in Table 2:

Table 2. Schematic summary of the methodology

Element	Detail
Epistemological stance	Interpretivist / Comprehensive
Research logic	Inductive, grounded in empirical data and informed by the literature
Method	Qualitative case study
Fieldwork	Banks operating in the Oriental region of Morocco
Data collection tool	Semi-structured interviews
Sampling	Purposive sampling based on the relevance of job roles
Analysis	Interpretative thematic analysis (Miles, Huberman & Saldaña, 2019; Paillé & Mucchielli, 2012)
Objective	To understand the actual effects of AI on operational risk management

Note. *Created by the authors.*

2.4. Justification for Choosing Banque Populaire as a Case Study

The selection of Banque Populaire Régionale de l'Orientale as a case study is based on several strategic criteria:

- Commitment to digital transformation:

This bank is among the Moroccan financial institutions that have implemented AI solutions to improve the efficiency of their operations.

According to Banque Populaire's 2023 report, the success of the digital bank was confirmed in 2023, with more than 11 million active digital customers (web & mobile) and the threshold of 10 million customers using Secur'Pass (enhanced authentication) having been crossed. The year 2023 was marked by numerous innovations in the various areas of expertise of the Digital & Payments division. The ratings of the group's mobile applications remain among the best on the market, with 4.7/5 on the App Store.

In the field of data and artificial intelligence, work to improve commercial performance generated 2.9 million business opportunities. Initiatives to improve operational efficiency continue: data enabled the automatic collection and monitoring of more than 5.8 million documents over the year (+30% compared to 2022). In the field of generative AI, the first work on business applications has been launched.

- Experience in Operational Risk Management:

As part of its overall risk management strategy, Banque Populaire aligns itself with the Risk Assessment Statement (RAS) and Risk Assessment Framework (RAF) developed by the BPCE Group. These methodological frameworks are adapted and implemented within each institution and subsidiary to ensure consistency in the identification, assessment, monitoring, and control of operational risks.

The management of these risks encompasses all consolidated entities within the Group, including outsourced activities that are considered essential or significant, in accordance with applicable regulations (Decree of November 3, 2014, amended in 2021). Governance is organized at two levels: on one hand, the Group Non-Financial Risk Committee (CRNFG), which defines strategic directions; and on the other hand, the Group Operational Risk Department (DROG), which ensures the operational implementation of these directions.

Each institution has an Operational Risk Department supported by business line correspondents who are functionally linked to the department. These individuals play a key role in the deployment of the Group's tools, the quality control of recorded data, incident monitoring, the updating of risk indicators, and the preparation of reports. They also participate in the regular risk mapping process and the implementation of corrective actions approved in committee.

More specifically, Banque Populaire Auvergne Rhône Alpes has established a centralized framework, supported by quarterly committees dedicated to operational risks, as well as systematic communication to executive management in the event of major incidents. The operational risk manager is responsible for several key functions: defining the risk management policy, developing procedures, assessing exposures, and producing risk reports.

The OSIRISK tool serves as the cornerstone of the operational system. It enables continuous risk assessment, incident management, regular updates to risk mapping, and tracking of action plans. This tool supports a forward-looking approach that incorporates emerging risks, information technology and cybersecurity threats, as well as risks related to third-party providers and regulatory non-compliance.

Finally, the bank relies on an operational risk dashboard that is updated quarterly, along with a reporting system powered by an internal data mart. To calculate its capital requirements, the BPCE Group applies the standardized approach set out by the Basel II regulatory framework.

- Mixed Organizational Structure:

Its governance model combines regional autonomy with strategic centralization.

Figure 1. Organizational Structure of the Case Study – "Crédit Populaire du Maroc"

Figure 1

Organizational Structure of the Case Study – "Crédit Populaire du Maroc"

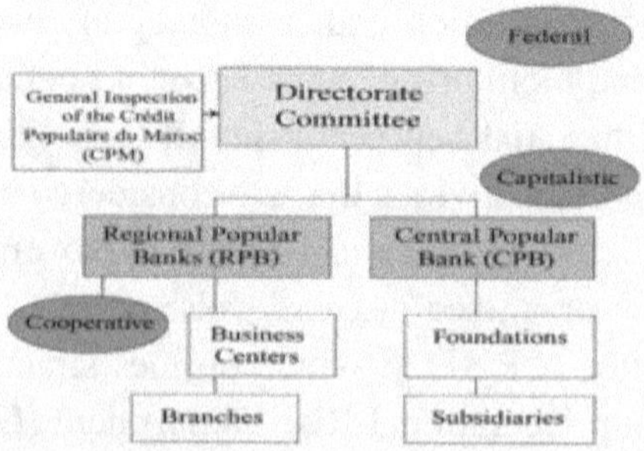

Note. Created by the authors.

Note. Created by the authors.

The first diagram highlights the federative structure of the Crédit Populaire du Maroc (CPM), organized around a Directorate Committee, the central governing body, which operates under the supervision of the General Inspectorate of the Crédit Populaire du Maroc. This hybrid structure combines two approaches: cooperative and capital-based.

The cooperative branch is represented by the Regional Popular Banks (BPR), which are autonomous entities operating at the local level. They maintain close proximity to customers through a network of business centers, branches, and agencies.

In parallel, the capital-based branch is embodied by the Central Popular Bank (BCP), the umbrella institution of the group. It plays a key role in strategic planning, coordination, and the management of subsidiaries and foundations. This duality—between regional logic and centralized governance—serves as a balancing mechanism between local presence and global oversight.

Figure 2. Operational Risk Governance – Crédit Populaire du Maroc

Figure 2

Operational Risk Governance – Crédit Populaire du Maroc

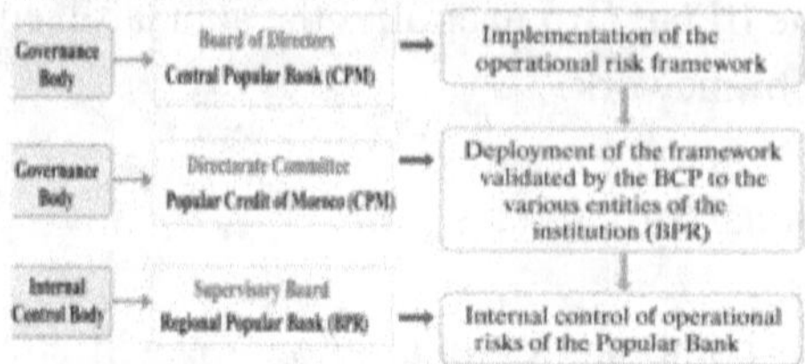

Note. Created by the authors.

Note. Created by the authors.

The second figure illustrates the various governance and internal control bodies involved in the implementation and monitoring of the operational risk management framework.

At the central level, the Board of Directors of the BCP serves as the strategic governance body responsible for designing and implementing the operational risk management framework. This framework is then operationalized by the Directorate Committee of the CPM, which ensures the translation of strategic directives into concrete actions across the group's various entities, particularly the Regional Popular Banks (BPRs).

At the regional level, the Supervisory Boards of the BPRs represent the internal control bodies responsible for ensuring the proper application of the risk management systems. This includes the monitoring of operational risks in a manner adapted to local specificities.

2.5. Data Collection and Analysis Method

The semi-structured interviews were conducted with a targeted sample of front-office employees. Participants were selected based on their level of interaction with AI tools and their involvement in operational risk management. The bank branches studied were strategically selected to best reflect the diversity of situations and customer profiles.

Semi-structured interviews were conducted with a targeted sample of front-office employees. Participants were selected based on their level of interaction with AI tools and their involvement in addressing operational risk management. The selected bank branches were strategically chosen to best reflect the diversity of situations and customer profiles, considering both geographical location and client typology: one branch located in a university area (young clients), another in a working-class residential zone (seniors), and a third in a commercial area (civil servants and retirees).

In each branch, three interviews were conducted, totaling nine interviews in all, each involving a branch manager, a teller, and a customer advisor.

Table 3. Distribution of agencies surveyed according to geographic location and customer segment

Codes	Profiles	Branch Location	Customer Segment
A	Branch Manager/ Cashier/ Customer Service Representative	University area	Young people
B	Branch Manager/ Cashier/ Customer Service Representative	Popular residential area	Seniors
C	Branch Manager/ Cashier/ Customer Service Representative	Commercial area	Civil Servants/ Retirees

Note. Created by the authors.

Table 3 presents the typology of bank branches that were the subject of the qualitative research, dividing them according to two key dimensions: the branch's geographic location and the dominant customer profile. Three codes (A, B, C) were assigned to anonymize the branches while preserving their distinctive characteristics. This classification aims to ensure the representativeness of the results by integrating a diversity of location contexts and customer types, which is essential in exploratory qualitative research.

The first category of branches (A) is located near university areas. The staff profiles interviewed in these branches include branch managers, tellers, and customer service representatives. These branches primarily serve a young clientele, composed of students, young professionals, and graduates at the beginning of their careers. This customer segment is often perceived as tech-friendly or even tech-enthusiastic, meaning they are comfortable with digital tools and likely to quickly adopt technological innovations such as artificial intelligence (AI). This specificity provides fertile ground for observing advanced or emerging uses of AI tools, particularly in automated interactions (chatbots, remote services), the use of mobile banking applications, or the acceptance of intelligent transaction monitoring solutions. In this sense, Type A branches constitute a privileged window on the future of the customer-AI relationship in the Moroccan banking sector.

The second category of branches (B) is located in so-called "working-class" residential areas, often characterized by high urban density, socio-professional diversity, and a significant presence of elderly populations. These branches are frequented primarily by senior or retired customers, whose relationship with technology is generally more distant, and sometimes even suspicious. Interviews conducted in these branches highlighted usage dynamics that differ markedly from those observed in the A branches. These include a greater need for support, a preference for human interaction, and a greater resistance to automated tools, particularly when it comes to operations perceived as sensitive (transfers, account management, complaints). This segment highlights the limitations of AI, which is perceived as cold or impersonal, and underscores the importance of a contextualized and inclusive deployment of technological innovations. The third category of agencies (C) is located in busy commercial areas, frequented by professionals, traders, and civil servants. This customer segment is described as hybrid, insofar as it combines a requirement for reliability, often associated with regular income and budgetary structuring, with a relative openness to digital innovations. Customers in this segment are often users of mobile applications, but at the same time demand a high level of security, traceability, and control. AI is seen here as a tool for simplification and efficiency, provided that its uses remain understood, controlled, and supervised. Type C agencies thus make it possible to grasp the conditions for a balance between automation and trust, constituting a relevant space for observing intermediate use cases, sometimes in transition between the traditional model (based on human interaction) and the advanced digital model.

Overall, this geographical and sociological distribution of branches allows for coverage of a wide variety of usage contexts, customer profiles, and attitudes toward AI. It thus gives the study a stronger analytical scope, avoiding the bias of focusing on a single type of customer or region. The diversity of the segments represented allows for an understanding of the plurality of behaviors, expectations, and resistance to intelligent tools. By integrating young, connected, and tech-savvy populations (branch A), older, cautious populations (branch B), and mixed users who are moderate but open to innovation (branch C), the study highlights the differentiated logics of artificial intelligence adoption in the Moroccan banking sector.

This sampling strategy is based on a logic of maximum variation, in accordance with the principles of the qualitative method, which aims to multiply points of view to identify invariants, but also significant dissonances. It also allows us to test the initial exploratory hypothesis that the effects of AI on operational risk management vary depending on user profiles, their exposure to digital tools, and the nature of their interactions with the banking institution.

Finally, this territorial segmentation offers significant interpretative value in that it sheds light on the social, technological, and organizational conditions of AI implementation. It allows us to contextualize the empirical results, compare them with existing literature on the digital transformation of banks (McKinsey, 2023; Bhattacharya & Sinha, 2022; Brynjolfsson & McAfee, 2017), and identify differentiated levers for action in terms of training, communication, and technological design.

3. ANALYSIS OF RESULTS

3.1. Use of AI in the Front Office

At the outset, the interviewee was asked whether AI was integrated within their bank. This initial question paved the way for a series of interviews with several banking professionals at the same level of the organization, in order to gain a broader perspective on this technological tool. Two central questions were addressed during our visits, with increasing degrees of detail: 'Does your bank use AI in its operations?' and 'Can you tell us your scope of intervention via the AI tool in the front office?'

However, despite these questions, it appeared that employees had limited, if any, knowledge of AI and its specific applications. "At the moment, there is no AI. It is still under development and represents a significant investment for the bank," Respondent A.

The responses revealed a lack of familiarity with the specific AI tools used within the organization. Indeed, participating employees did not show any awareness of which specific AI tools were integrated into the application. Their knowledge was limited to a general awareness of the existence of an application, but without details on the underlying technologies or specific AI functionalities. "My involvement with the application is limited to four tasks: subscription; cancellation; granting access to customers; and unsubscribing customers," Respondent Branch Manager C. However, they were unable to link these actions to the use of AI in their processes. This finding highlights a gap between the general perception of AI in the bank and the reality of its daily use.

3.2. Reduction of Repetitive Tasks and Impact on Human Error

Although respondents lack a precise understanding of the AI tools deployed, their operational integration raises significant issues, particularly in terms of operational risk management. We then focused our interviewee's discussion on the automation of daily tasks performed by banking business unit staff. This analysis will help us better understand the true scope of AI and identify potential levers for optimizing operational risk management. To this end, three questions were raised during our branch visits: What tasks have been automated by the back office? Have you noticed a reduction in human error through task automation? What impact has this automation had on your work?

- Task automation

The Banque Populaire bank integrates several solutions to improve efficiency, reduce human error, and better meet customer needs. Among these, account opening is facilitated by the use of digital tools to record customer information. He also mentioned that the processing of credit applications is now analyzed automatically, allowing for a faster and more accurate response. Regarding everyday banking transactions, such as money transfers, transfers, and bill payments, these are carried out via online platforms or ATMs. Regarding balance inquiries and account statements, these operations are accessible automatically via mobile applications (Zone A Cashier).

- Reduction of repetitive tasks

Our interviewees' responses were varied, revealing two important criteria differentiating the use of the new tools integrated by the bank: the "customer segment" and the "geographical area" of the bank branches, as mentioned in Table 3.

AI has reduced the workload by automating simple and repetitive operations (e.g., data entry, responding to customer queries). "Customer-facing banking applications have helped automate various operations, providing greater fluidity in the execution of services. Previously, we were handling up to 130 transactions per day from 8 a.m. to 1 p.m.; a workload that affected our mental health as well as that of my colleagues within the branch." Branch Manager A. This automation has not only reduced employee workload but also transformed the pace and nature of banking operations. This shift is particularly felt at the branch level, where branch managers report a direct impact on productivity and work comfort. "The current trend reveals a greater adoption of banking applications by younger users." Branch Manager A.

However, the adoption of banking applications is not limited to younger customers. Other customer segments are also showing growing adoption of digital tools, contributing to more widespread automation of operations. "Given our location, civil servant customers using the banking application contribute to reducing daily manual tasks." Branch Manager C.

The automation of transactional processes has had a considerable impact on operational risks; "This is the example of large companies, before employees entered mass transfers into the system on their own, now we give access to the manager to validate the order numbers of employees' accounts to minimize errors" Branch Manager C. This observation is reinforced by the feedback from the banking employees we met, who clearly highlight the positive impact of automation on reducing operational errors, "200 customers per day is not 50 customers…the machine is very important; Fewer withdrawals per day compared to before". Cashier at Branch C.

3.3. Challenges of Using AI

While AI generally contributes to reducing operational risks, it can also create challenges in terms of customer adaptation and satisfaction. Respondents report that some customers still prefer human interaction, whether for simple transactions or even for complex transactions requiring a more personalized approach. These nuances are clearly evident in the responses collected from banking employees: "Given our location in a working-class neighborhood, our client portfolio is primarily made up of senior clients whose adaptation to the use of the application is almost nonexistent; which increases the workload." » Branch Manager B.

"Manual work is still present at our branch; our customers prefer to contact our branch for assistance, even for the simplest transactions such as withdrawals." Teller at Branch B. "Retired customers are reluctant to use new technical tools, and most of them prefer mediation, especially when it comes to purchasing and communicating on the stock market." Account Manager at Branch A.

These results highlight that the adoption of AI is not limited to purely technological aspects, but also involves organizational and human challenges.

4. DISCUSSION OF RESULTS

The analysis of semi-structured interviews conducted with employees of Banque Populaire Régionale de l'Orientale reveals significant structural trends regarding the perception and use of artificial intelligence (AI) in operational risk management. This interpretation phase aims to compare empirical data from the field with the theoretical concepts used in the literature review, in order to enrich our understanding of the phenomenon studied.

The main objective of this discussion is therefore twofold: first, to identify points of convergence between the representations of the interviewed stakeholders, and second, to highlight the divergences or nuances that reflect the diversity of experiences and levels of technological appropriation. In this sense, the discussion goes beyond a simple descriptive restitution of the remarks to engage in a critical reflection on the organizational, human, and technological implications of the introduction of AI into banking processes.

This approach is part of a qualitative interpretative logic, where the meaning attributed by individuals to their practices constitutes essential data. By drawing on the contributions of authors such as Davenport and Ronanki (2018), Brynjolfsson and McAfee (2017), and McKinsey (2023), the aim is to analyze to what extent the feedback collected in the field confirms, qualifies or contradicts the lessons of existing literature.

Furthermore, this discussion allows us to test the exploratory hypothesis that the integration of AI would reduce banking operational risks, notably by minimizing human error, automating repetitive tasks, and improving traceability. Interviews conducted in various branches—particularly those with a high youth clientele—provide contextualized insights into the conditions for success and the limitations of this digital transformation in terms of risk management.

Thus, this section does not limit itself to describing agents' perceptions, but aims to connect qualitative data with theoretical frameworks in order to identify robust interpretations and informed recommendations for financial institutions undergoing digitalization.

4.1. Convergence of Responses

Several major points of agreement emerged from the respondents' discussions, corroborating the theories identified in the literature review.

- AI as a lever for optimizing operational processes

A majority of participants (75%) agreed that the introduction of AI, particularly through the automation of internal processes, has reduced human error, improved operational traceability, and strengthened control mechanisms. This perception is consistent with the conclusions of Davenport and Ronanki (2018), for whom AI not only allows for the systematization of certain critical tasks, but also for the generation of real-time analyses that facilitate the detection of operational anomalies.

Complementarily, Brynjolfsson and McAfee (2017) emphasized that the benefits of AI are only fully realized when organizations integrate these tools into a comprehensive process transformation by rethinking decision-making chains.

- Gradual integration focused on the front office

Interviews reveal that AI use is primarily visible in customer interfaces, particularly through chatbots and virtual assistants. This observation is part of an international trend highlighted by McKinsey (2023), which indicates that the deployment of AI in the banking sector generally begins with low-risk use cases such as customer support, before expanding to more sensitive functions such as compliance or risk management.

- Persistent technical and human barriers

Respondents nevertheless point to several obstacles to AI adoption, including resistance to change, training gaps, and a lack of awareness of available tools. This finding confirms the work of Brynjolfsson and McAfee (2017), who assert that technological adoption relies more on organizational factors (culture, support, training) than on the availability of the technology alone.

4.2. Divergences in Perceptions

Beyond these convergences, several differences in assessment were noted, illustrating the diversity of employees' experiences and perceptions of AI.

- Complexity or Simplification of Tasks

While 60% of respondents believe that AI makes their work easier by reducing repetitive tasks, 30%, on the contrary, cite an increase in complexity due to the familiarity with new tools. This ambivalence can be linked to the observations of Metawa et al. (2022), who show that the perception of AI is closely linked to employees' level of technological familiarity, their role within the organization, and their exposure to new tools.

- Customer Acceptability of AI

Participants' responses demonstrate a divergence in customer acceptability. Some note a positive reception of automated tools for simple operations, while others report a persistent preference for human interaction in complex operations. This duality is echoed in the work of Farazi (2024), who emphasizes the importance of matching technological solutions to customer profiles. Young urban customers, according to him, demonstrate a greater appetite for digital tools, unlike other, more conservative segments.

4.3. Contributions of AI in Operational Risk Management

The results obtained confirm several dimensions highlighted in the literature:

- Automation of critical tasks

As Bhattacharya and Sinha (2022) indicate, AI enables fine-grained automation of transaction processing, reducing the risks associated with manual errors while increasing processing speed.

- Strengthening internal audit

Chatterjee et al. (2022) highlight that AI can alleviate auditors' routine tasks (reconciliations, documentation), freeing up time for more analytical tasks.

- Continuous monitoring and fraud detection

Thanks to its massive data processing capabilities, AI enables proactive detection of risky behaviors. Costanza-Chock, Raji, and Buolamwini (2022) emphasize the growing role of algorithmic audit technologies in financial institutions' internal control.

- Cyber risk prevention and regulatory compliance

Milojević and Redzepagic (2021) highlight the role of AI in combating fraud, detecting cyberattacks, and ensuring automatic compliance (regtech). This capability is essential in a context of increasing regulation.

Finally, these results corroborate the initial hypothesis, according to which the automation of repetitive tasks allows a significant reduction in operational risks, particularly in branches serving a young and connected clientele (branches A and C). AI therefore appears not only as a technological tool, but also as a strategic lever for securing and optimizing banking operations.

5. CONCLUSION

Artificial intelligence is now emerging as an essential lever in operational risk management within the Moroccan banking sector. This qualitative study conducted at Banque Populaire reveals that AI is well integrated into front-office operations, particularly through the use of chatbots and the automation of customer service. This integration has significantly reduced human error, while improving operational fluidity and the quality of service provided. However, some employees still encounter adaptation difficulties, revealing a need for increased support in the adoption of these technological tools.

The results confirm that AI represents a major opportunity for operational risk management. It allows for the minimization of staff assigned to repetitive tasks, improved process traceability, and the strengthening of control mechanisms. However, this digital transformation also brings new challenges. Technical aspects such as outages, system malfunctions, and IT infrastructure vulnerability are compounded by human challenges: customer acceptability of tools, generational disparities, and ongoing staff training.

Rapid digitalization, accelerated in particular by the Covid-19 crisis, has revealed and amplified trends toward hybrid work and the increased use of connected technologies (cloud, big data, smartphones, tablets, etc.). Banque Populaire's 2024 report highlights the continued expansion of information systems' external access, further exposing institutions to cyber risks. In this context, system security is becoming a crucial issue, and the expectations of regulators, such as those of Groupe BPCE, require constant vigilance in the face of increasingly sophisticated attacks.

Thus, while the benefits of AI are tangible, its implementation requires rigorous organizational preparation. This includes human resource training, adapting governance structures, managing technological risks, and raising customer awareness. Only through a comprehensive vision and an integrated strategy will Moroccan banks be able to maximize the benefits of AI while managing its risks. This research thus paves the way for future work on the quantitative assessment of these impacts and on interbank comparisons at the national level.

REFERENCES

Adeusi, S. O., Akeke, N. I., Adebisi, O. S., & Oladunjoye, O. (2014). Risk management and financial performance of banks in Nigeria. *Risk Management*, *6*(31), 123–129.

Agourrame, H. (2021). *International banking regulation: Origins, evolution, and impact on bank business models*. Harmattan.

Aït Moussa, O. (2023). Effectiveness of internal control systems for operational risk in banks: Development of a conceptual model. [IJESM]. *International Journal of Economic and Management Studies*, *3*(3), 814–833.

Arner, D. W., Barberis, J., & Buckley, R. P. (2016). The evolution of Fintech: A new post-crisis paradigm? *SSRN*, *47*(4), 1271–1319. DOI: 10.2139/ssrn.2676553

Autor, D., & Salomons, A. (2018). *Is automation labor-displacing? Productivity growth, employment, and the labor share (No. w24871)*. National Bureau of Economic Research., DOI: 10.3386/w24871

Bhattacharya, C., & Sinha, M. (2022). The role of artificial intelligence in banking for leveraging customer experience. Australasian Accounting, Business and Finance Journal, 16(5). https://doi.org/10.xxxx

Biswas, S., Carson, B., Chung, V., Singh, S., & Thomas, R. (2020). AI-bank of the future: Can banks meet the AI challenge? McKinsey & Company. https://www.mckinsey.com

Brynjolfsson, E., & McAfee, A. (2017). Artificial intelligence, for real. *Harvard Business Review*, *1*(1), 1–31.

Burrell, G., & Morgan, G. (1979). *Sociological paradigms and organisational analysis: Elements of the sociology of corporate life*. Heinemann.

Charmaz, K. (2006). *Constructing grounded theory: A practical guide through qualitative analysis*. Sage Publications.

Chatterjee, M., Ahmed, A., Dadure, P., & Pakray, P. (2022, April). Inclination of NLP applications towards stereotypical and gender biased results. In *Proceedings of the International Conference on Innovative Computing & Communication (ICICC)*. DOI: 10.2139/ssrn.4096410

Comité de Bâle sur le contrôle bancaire. (2006). International convergence of capital measurement and capital standards: A revised framework (June 2006). Basel Committee on Banking Supervision.

Comité de Bâle sur le contrôle bancaire. (2010). Basel III: A global regulatory framework for more resilient banks and banking systems (revised version June 2011). Basel Committee on Banking Supervision.

Costanza-Chock, S., Raji, I. D., & Buolamwini, J. (2022, June). Who audits the auditors? Recommendations from a field scan of the algorithmic auditing ecosystem. In *Proceedings of the 2022 ACM Conference on Fairness, Accountability, and Transparency* (pp. 1571–1583). DOI: 10.1145/3531146.3533213

Crisanto, J. C., Ehrentraud, J., Fabian, M., & Monteil, A. (2024). *Perspectives of the Financial Stability Institute*. Bank for International Settlements.

Davenport, T. H., & Ronanki, R. (2018). Artificial intelligence for the real world. HBR's 10 Must Reads, 67.

Dupont, L., Fliche, O., & Yang, S. (2020). *Governance of artificial intelligence in finance*. Banque de France.

El Ouidani, R., & Oul-Caid, B. (2023). The adoption of AI in the Moroccan banking sector: Between economic and legal issues. Journal of Economics, Management [JEMED]. *Environmental Law (Northwestern School of Law), 6*(1).

Farazi, M. Z. R. (2024). Exploring the role of artificial intelligence in managing emerging risks: An in-depth study of AI applications in financial institutions' risk frameworks. *The American Journal of Management and Economics Innovations, 6*(10), 20–40. DOI: 10.37547/tajmei/Volume06Issue10-04A

Gallego-Gomez, C., & De-Pablos-Heredero, C. (2020). Artificial intelligence as an enabling tool for the development of dynamic capabilities in the banking industry. [IJEIS]. *International Journal of Enterprise Information Systems, 16*(3), 20–33. DOI: 10.4018/IJEIS.2020070102

Godlewski, C. J. (2004). Consistency of bank ratings with profitability and default in emerging countries. Management and Economics Research Laboratory, University Robert Schuman. Working Paper No. 65.

Guest, G., Bunce, A., & Johnson, L. (2006). How many interviews are enough? An experiment with data saturation and variability. *Field Methods, 18*(1), 59–82. DOI: 10.1177/1525822X05279903

Huberman, A. M. (2019). *Qualitative data analysis: A methods sourcebook*. Sage Publications.

Lincoln, Y. S., & Guba, E. G. (1985). *Naturalistic inquiry*. Sage Publications. DOI: 10.1016/0147-1767(85)90062-8

McKinsey & Company. (2023). Scaling Gen AI in banking: Choosing the best operating model. https://www.mckinsey.com/industries/financial-services/our-insights/scaling-gen-ai-in-banking-choosing-the-best-operating-model

Metawa, N., Xu, Z., Zhu, G., & Zhou, Q. (2022). Machine learning-based customer meta-combination brand equity analysis for marketing behavior evaluation. *Information Processing & Management, 59*(1), 102800. DOI: 10.1016/j.ipm.2021.102800

Milojević, N., & Redzepagic, S. (2021). Prospects of artificial intelligence and machine learning application in banking risk management. *Journal of Central Banking Theory and Practice, 10*(3), 41–57. DOI: 10.2478/jcbtp-2021-0023

Ofodile, O. C., Odeyemi, O., Okoye, C. C., Addy, W. A., Oyewole, A. T., Adeoye, O. B., & Ololade, Y. J. (2024). Digital banking regulations: A comparative review between Nigeria and the USA. *Finance & Accounting Research Journal, 6*(3), 347–371. DOI: 10.51594/farj.v6i3.897

Ogboi, C., & Unuafe, O. K. (2013). Impact of credit risk management and capital adequacy on the financial performance of commercial banks in Nigeria. Journal of Emerging Issues in Economics. *Finance and Banking, 2*(3), 703–717.

Ononiwu, M. I., Onwuzulike, O. C., Shitu, K., & Ojo, O. O. (2024). Operational risk management in emerging markets: A case study of Nigerian banking institutions. *World Journal of Advanced Research and Reviews, 23*(3), 446–459. DOI: 10.30574/wjarr.2024.23.3.2705

Paillé, P., & Mucchielli, A. (2012). L'analyse qualitative en sciences humaines et sociales (3e éd.). Armand Colin.

Rochet, J.-C. (2008). The future of banking regulation. (If a publisher is available, add it here. If unpublished, note as such.)

Saldaña, J. (2016). *The coding manual for qualitative researchers* (3rd ed.). Sage Publications.

Wali of Bank Al-Maghrib. (2022, November 9). Digital transformation: Between regulation and competitiveness [Speech]. *International Conference*, Marrakech.

Xu, Z., Zhu, G., Metawa, N., & Zhou, Q. (2022). Machine learning-based customer meta-combination brand equity analysis for marketing behavior evaluation. *Information Processing & Management, 59*(1), 102800. DOI: 10.1016/j.ipm.2021.102800

Yin, R. K. (2017). *Case study research and applications: Design and methods* (6th ed.). Sage Publications.

Chapter 12
The Role of AI-Driven Decision Support Systems (DSS) in Enhancing Organizational Performance:
A Qualitative Study of Morocco's Automotive Industry

Sara Mantouzi
https://orcid.org/0009-0001-3732-8232
The National School of Business and Management of Casablanca, Hassan II University, Morocco

Said Youssef
The National School of Business and Management of Casablanca, Hassan II University, Morocco

ABSTRACT

The rapid advancement of Artificial Intelligence (AI) necessitates its integration into decision-making, particularly through AI-driven Decision Support Systems (DSS). These systems enhance efficiency, automate analytical tasks, and provide predictive insights to improve decision accuracy. This chapter examines the impact of AI-powered DSS within Morocco's automotive industry, a sector marked by rapid growth, increasing data complexity, and evolving market dynamics. Using a qualitative methodology, the study analyzes interviews with DSS users, employing Nvivo for thematic analysis, word frequency mapping, and cross-tabulation. Findings indicate

DOI: 10.4018/979-8-3373-1737-3.ch012

that AI-enhanced DSS improve resource allocation, organizational responsiveness, and innovation capacity, strengthening overall performance and competitiveness. By contributing to AI-driven business transformation discourse, this chapter highlights AI's role in fostering industrial competitiveness. Future research should explore AI's long-term implications and conduct cross-sectoral analyses to refine AI-driven decision-making frameworks.

INTRODUCTION

Because technology is developing so quickly, organizations must constantly adapt by incorporating new technologies like artificial intelligence (AI) (Taherdoost, 2023). The incorporation of AI through business roles reveals its increasing role in restructuring processes, decreasing manual effort, and pushing measurable gains in corporate efficiency (Mantouzi et al., 2024; Mantouzi & Said, 2023). The increasing incorporation of artificial intelligence (AI) into business plans highlights its importance in optimizing processes and boosting output. Because of AI's ability to process enormous amounts of data and turn it into insights that can be employed, organizations can lower risks and uncertainties related to both internal and external environments. (Mantouzi et al., 2024; Mantouzi & Said, 2023).

According to (Russell & Norvig, 2010), Artificial Intelligence (AI) is a subfield of information technology that focuses on creating machines that can perform tasks that are typically associated with human cognitive processes, like learning, perception, decision-making, and natural language interpretation. (Nilsson, 2005) adds that mechanizing human intelligence in the long run is AI's ultimate goal. AI greatly improves organizational performance, changes business models, and strengthens human decision-making (Ali et al., 2018; Chi et al., 2020; Lugano, 2017; Mettler et al., 2017).

Decision Support Systems (DSS) serve as essential technological tools that organize and analyze large datasets to help managers make decisions. (Inmon, 1996) defines DSS as organized databases of integrated, time-sensitive, non-volatile, and thematic data that aid in managerial decision-making. These systems serve as essential management tools, encouraging the creation of control mechanisms and analytical dashboards to maximize organizational decision-making. DSS are sophisticated instruments that use data-driven analysis to deliver customized operational solutions. They are crucial in overseeing decision-making processes and can combine information from various sources to support choices in a range of operational contexts (Terribile et al., 2015; Yazdani et al., 2017; Zhai et al., 2020). The integration of AI into DSS significantly increases its utility by improving data processing efficiency and enabling the analysis of vast and complex datasets (Asolo et al., 2024). AI-driven

DSS improve decision-making speed, accuracy, and adaptability by automating repetitive tasks and using predictive analytics to anticipate trends. This makes them essential in dynamic business environments (Anumandla, 2018).

Morocco's automotive sector has experienced consistent expansion, establishing the country as an emerging manufacturing and exporting hub in the global automotive value chain (Jaidi & Msadfa, 2017). Morocco is now more competitive through the arrival of significant foreign automotive manufacturers, which has also encouraged industrial diversification and foreign direct investment. This expansion offers important chances for technological innovation, job creation, and increased investment within the sector. Automotive companies must efficiently manage complex networks of suppliers and customers as the industry expands, which calls for strong data management and decision-making skills (Amachraa, 2023). The automotive industry benefits greatly from DSS as it enables manufacturers to manage massive amounts of data efficiently. Through facilitating automated data analysis and decision-making procedures, DSS enables organizations to maximize quality control, production planning, and supply chain management (Brotcorne et al., 2019; Perboli et al., 2018). These benefits are further increased by integrating AI-driven DSS, which improves operational optimization, real-time analytics, and predictive capabilities (Dwivedi et al., 2020; Guerlain et al., 2000; Renfrew et al., 2024; Waqar, 2024). AI-driven DSS improves operational effectiveness while tackling the automotive industry's sustainability issues. They encourage circular economy and decarbonization initiatives like supply chain transformation and energy-efficient manufacturing. AI-driven DSS are essential for strategic decision-making in Morocco's automotive sector, enhancing competitiveness, productivity, and innovation while supporting environmental objectives.

This study investigates the influence of AI-driven DSS on organizational efficacy, efficiency, and competitiveness in Morocco's automotive industry. Organizations can optimize resource allocation, boost operational efficiency, and improve decision-making processes by utilizing AI-driven DSS. The central research question guiding this study is: **How does the integration of AI-driven DSS influence organizational performance in Morocco's automotive industry?** This inquiry aims to generate empirical insights into the transformative potential of AI-driven DSS in enhancing decision-making and operational outcomes. Building on the results of the literature review and qualitative analysis, we aim to identify the relevant variables, develop a conceptual model, and establish the relationships between these variables. The primary objective of this study is to address the following key research questions:

What is the impact of technical variables on user usage and satisfaction?
What is the impact of managerial variables on user usage and satisfaction?

How do user usage and satisfaction impact individual and organizational performance?

To achieve this, we first outline the main concepts addressed in the literature review, followed by an introduction to the mobilized theories. The methodology employed is then thoroughly described. Finally, we explore the results and findings, offering a deeper understanding of the connection between AI-driven DSS and organizational performance.

LITERATURE REVIEW AND MOBILIZED THEORIES

Decision Support Systems (DSS)

The development of Business Intelligence (BI) in the 1990s was catalyzed by rapid advancements in information technology and the proliferation of large-scale data-sharing networks. Within this domain, Decision Support Systems (DSS) have emerged as a fundamental component, conceptualized through various scholarly perspectives. (Le Moigne, 1977) defines DSS as a structured and accessible system of information specifically designed to facilitate managerial decision-making. (Kimball, 1996) characterizes DSS as an organized replication of transactional data, optimized for querying and analytical processing. Expanding on this view, (Inmon, 1996) conceptualizes DSS as subject-oriented, time-sensitive, integrated, and non-volatile data structures that provide critical support for strategic and operational decision-making.

DSS are now widely regarded as indispensable management tools, enabling the development of dynamic dashboards and real-time performance monitoring mechanisms. Their core function is to enhance organizational decision-making processes by ensuring data-driven insights, thereby reinforcing strategic planning, operational efficiency, and overall corporate governance. DSS are becoming more widely acknowledged as intelligent systems that improve decision-making and enable operational responses by utilizing gathered data to address particular needs and difficulties (Terribile et al., 2015).

(Yazdani et al., 2017) claim that DSS are essential in managing decision-making activities, while (Zhai et al., 2020) assert that these systems integrate data from multiple sources to support decision-making across various contexts. As stated by (Irawan, 2020), DSS provides crucial insights for intricate strategic and operational decisions, helping decision-makers tackle semi-structured and unstructured issues within organizations. Data management, model management, knowledge management, and user interface subsystems are among the interconnected subsystems that make up DSS, according to (Ramathilagam & Pitchipoo, 2022). These elements facilitate the three main phases of a DSS's implementation: data storage, data extraction from transactional systems, and the conversion of processed data into useful insights for decision-making. The strategic value of DSS resides in its ability to guarantee that companies make decisions based on accurate, well-structured, and contextually relevant data, which improves managerial efficacy and long-term competitive advantage.

AI-driven DSS in Morocco's Automotive Industry

Morocco has become a major force in the global automotive industry over the last ten years, especially in the production of automotive components and vehicle assembly. This development is mainly attributed to the tactical assistance of government procedures, which have inaugurated the necessary infrastructure for fast industry growth (Amachraa, 2023). The Emergence Plan, which centered on the construction of a logistical platform, including the Tangier Med port, and auxiliary projects like specialized training facilities, marked the beginning of the government's efforts. This was further supported by The National Pact for Industrial Emergence and the Industrial Acceleration Plan, which have been crucial in bolstering Morocco's industrial base (Amachraa, 2023; Jaidi & Msadfa, 2017). With production rising from 60,000 units in 2010 to 535,825 units in 2023, the Kingdom has experienced impressive growth and prepares to reach its goal of 1 million units by 2030 (Japan International Cooperation Agency (JICA), BCG, 2022). As stated by the Moroccan Association of Automotive Industry and Trade (AMICA), a production capacity of 700,000 vehicles in 2022 has helped the country reach a 65% integration rate in its automotive production.

In order to stay competitive, companies need to adopt cutting-edge solutions like artificial intelligence (AI) due to the rapid development of technology (Taherdoost, 2023). AI has drawn a lot of interest in the last ten years from both academia and industry, and it has become a disruptive force in a number of business functions. Its extensive use goes beyond data analytics to include task automation, process optimization, and productivity improvement (Mantouzi et al., 2024; Mantouzi & Said, 2023). The capacity of AI to process large datasets and produce useful insights reduces uncertainty and minimizes risks related to dynamic internal and external environments (Mantouzi et al., 2024; Mantouzi & Said, 2023). Empirical studies demonstrate how AI can improve decision-making, increase organizational agility, and maximize performance results. (Collins et al., 2021; Duan et al., 2019; Dwivedi et al., 2020; Wilson & Daugherty, 2018).

The automotive industry has seen a significant transformation due to technological advancements, especially the incorporation of advanced AI systems. The automotive industry uses AI in a wide range of areas, including design, supply chain management, after-sales services, and support services, in addition to production procedures and assembly lines (Suhaib Kamran et al., 2022). According to (Shah et al., 2023), the adoption of AI might significantly impact the automobile industry by increasing innovation, productivity, and competitiveness. (Chai & Nizam, 2021) noted its profound impact on marketing and sales tactics, smart manufacturing, autonomous vehicles, and leadership transformation. AI-driven DSS are essential for tackling new trends in the automotive industry, such as the manufacturing of electric vehicles (EVs), the circular economy, and Industry 4.0 integration. These systems promote sustainable practices, increase supply chain transparency, and improve operational efficiency. Furthermore, AI-DSS facilitates supplier diversification and guarantees adherence to international sustainability standards, allowing the sector to innovate, maximize efficiency, and accomplish environmental objectives.

AI-driven developments have the potential to assist the Moroccan automotive sector, particularly in the areas of predictive maintenance services and logistical network optimization. AI integration into Decision Support Systems (DSS) has become essential for enhancing managerial decision-making due to the inherent uncertainty in the global business environment (Gupta et al., 2022; Renfrew et al., 2024). Through the analysis of enormous volumes of historical data, real-time information, and predictive analytics, DSS uses AI-driven algorithms to help professionals by producing incredibly accurate insights. By identifying possible risks, automating repetitive tasks, and guaranteeing optimal resource allocation, these intelligent systems help to optimize projects, boost productivity, and reduce expenses (Waqar, 2024). Ultimately, the automotive industry has a strategic chance to attain sustainable growth, operational resilience, and improved competitive advantage as a result of the convergence of AI and DSS.

Mobilized Theories for Assessing the Impact of AI-driven DSS on Organizational Performance

This study examines how social and technological factors affect the performance of AI-driven Decision Support Systems (DSS) by combining the socio-technical framework and the updated DeLone and McLean IS Success Model. It emphasizes the importance of the combination and interaction between human and technical factors in defining DSS effectiveness within businesses.

Socio-technical theory has been widely used in a variety of fields, including engineering, organizational studies, and information systems. (Morris, 2009), providing a thorough framework for qualitative and quantitative analysis of complex systems.

From micro-level organizational structures to macro-level societal systems, this theory covers a wide range of levels (Geels, 2010; Griffith & Dougherty, 2001; Trist, 1981). In healthcare DSS, (Coiera et al., 2006) argue that system efficacy should be evaluated by taking into account cognitive and socio-technical interactions in addition to usability and performance. Similarly, (Mackrell et al., 2009) discovered that the success of DSS adoption in Australia's cotton sector can be attributed to the participants' capacity to modify technology to meet changing demands. The socio-technical approach offers a more comprehensive perspective on DSS implementation by highlighting the interdependence of technology and human actors. This approach increases system acceptability and benefits stakeholders. (Baxter & Sommerville, 2011), avoiding technological determinism and acknowledging the interdependence of social and technical subsystems. (Palvia et al., 2001) and (Serafeimidis & Smithson, 1995) highlight the importance of viewing DSS as socio-technical entities that are a part of their organizational environments. This theoretical framework provides a strong basis for investigating the creation, uptake, and efficacy of DSS in intricate organizational contexts.

A number of variables can be distinguished from a sociotechnical standpoint. (Mumford, 1993, 1995) highlights the significance of user participation in the development and deployment of information systems. User participation and involvement in the sociotechnical design process are the foundation of Mumford's ETHICS model. Several studies emphasize the importance of user participation in the success of information systems. According to (McKeen et al., 1994) complexity serves as a moderating variable in the positive relationship between user satisfaction and participation in complex projects. (Mckeen & Guimaraes, 1997) underscore that the type of participation affects satisfaction levels, while (Garrity, 1994) views participation as a critical factor in determining system success. As stated by (Michel, 2011; Michel & Cocula, 2014), the quality of training is observed as an antecedent variable to other quality factors. Training is a methodical process that helps users gain the skills and knowledge required to use information systems effectively, which helps them do their jobs more effectively. As underlined by (Palvia et al., 2001), one of the main components of the social subsystem is managerial support. Support from management is essential for promoting system adoption and reducing user rejection to adopt new technologies. The degree of managerial involvement has a significant impact on the success of new information systems since it not only makes it easier to implement technological change but also shapes user acceptance and perceptions.

The updated Information Systems (IS) Success Model (DeLone & McLean, 2003a) was chosen for our study because it provides a comprehensive and reliable framework for assessing the complex success of information systems. DeLone and McLean's seminal work (2003) intended to incorporate prior research on Information Systems (IS) success into a consistent framework, identifying six essential dimensions: system quality, information quality, use, user satisfaction, individual impact, and organizational impact. This framework, which was developed from empirical research, offers an organized method for comprehending IS success and is highly pertinent to our study. Although the model's clarity has led to widespread acceptance, previous research has identified certain limitations (Hu, 2003; Urbach & Müller, 2012), implying that more improvement is required. The model has been updated or expanded over time by academics, who have added new dimensions or different frameworks (Ballantine et al., 1996; P. B. Seddon, 1997; P. Seddon & Kiew, 1996). DeLone and McLean revised their model in 2003 by including service quality, combining organizational and individual impact into "net benefits," and using "intention to use" as a measure of user attitude. The six dimensions are still present in the revised model, which also emphasizes the connections among these factors.

METHODOLOGY

Qualitative research is indispensable for exploring a defined group's attitudes and actions regarding particular subjects. As articulated by (Poisson, 1983), instead of quantifying phenomena to create statistical correlations, qualitative research seeks to describe the lived experiences of the participants. Researchers are able to gain a solid understanding of the variables and how they interact in the environment under study by carefully analyzing the observed context. In the context of the automotive manufacturing industry, this method is especially beneficial because it fosters rich, interactive interactions with participants, which facilitate the identification and contextualization of important dimensions. These insights then serve as the foundation for the development of pertinent theories.

The choice of semi-structured interviews is influenced by our research question as well as our epistemological position, related to positivism, which highlights the use of empirical data to support theoretical observations. This methodological approach permits us to improve our conceptual framework and formulate hypotheses considering all of the interviewees' views, arguments, and confirmations (Albarello, 2004). By incorporating these insights, we expect to improve the complexity and pertinence of our analysis and guarantee a comprehensive and contextually conscious investigation of the research topic.

Our study's sample selection process followed a purposive strategy, depending on the researcher's choice to find pertinent elements (Thiétart, 2014). In order to interview a significant number of companies, the selection criteria for respondents and companies were based on sector-specific data. By using this approach, we were able to evaluate the way variables from our theoretical model were applied in the real-world context. Additionally, to guarantee a wide range of perspectives and increase the diversity of insights, we gave priority to diversification by choosing respondents with different profiles. Additionally, we followed the theoretical saturation principle (Glaser et al., 1968), confirming that the sample size was adequate in order to prevent new information from emerging through further data collection. After the 12th interview, saturation was reached in our study. Twelve managers were interviewed in total, using both telephone and face-to-face methods, and each interview lasted an average of one hour. The interview locations were selected according to the participants' availability.

Table 1. The Characteristics of the Respondents

Respondent	Age	Gender	Job Title	Job Profile	Experience Level
Respondent 1	30-35 years	Male	Manager	IT Department	6-10 years
Respondent 2	25-30 years	Female	Manager	After-Sales Recovery	6-10 years
Respondent 3	40-45 years	Male	Service Manager	Maintenance	> 10 years
Respondent 4	30-35 years	Male	Manager	Accounting Department	6-10 years
Respondent 5	30-35 years	Male	Service Manager	IT Department	> 10 years
Respondent 6	30-35 years	Female	Manager	Quality Department	6-10 years
Respondent 7	25-30 years	Male	Manager	IT Department	2-5 years
Respondent 8	30-35 years	Male	Manager	Supply Chain	6-10 years
Respondent 9	25-30 years	Male	Manager	IT Department	6-10 years
Respondent 10	40-45 years	Male	Manager	Production Department	> 10 years
Respondent 11	30-35 years	Male	Manager	Production Department	6-10 years
Respondent 12	30-35 years	Female	Service Manager	Accounting Department	6-10 years

Source: Generated from Nvivo

In order to support a comprehensive and rigorous analysis of AI-driven DSS, the interview guide was carefully constructed around five central thematic dimensions. In order to provide insights into the overall strategic implications of AI-driven DSS, the first dimension examines how it affects internal organizational processes as well as the external business environment. The second dimension identifies the essential elements of AI-driven DSS that are essential to the assessment procedure, ensuring the creation of a strong analytical framework. The third focuses on measuring user satisfaction by describing their opinions and experiences to assess the usability and efficiency of the system. The fourth observes the tangible advantages of using AI-driven DSS, emphasizing how they aid in performance optimization and organizational decision-making. Finally, the fifth dimension contextualizes the use of AI-driven DSS in the automotive industry by examining its distinctive features. This methodical approach guarantees a theoretically and methodologically sound evaluation of AI-driven DSS, thereby ensuring its applicability in both academic and real-world contexts.

A detailed thematic analysis of the 12 conducted interviews was carried out through a meticulous transcription and coding process (Evrard et al., 2003). Until the theoretical saturation principle was achieved, an iterative process that involved constant improvement between interview execution and coding was used. We employed NVivo QSR 12, a software program that facilitates systematic data organization and interpretation, to improve the thematic analysis's efficiency and consistency. Following accepted best practices in qualitative research, this methodological approach guarantees a systematic and comprehensive evaluation of the data.

This study is the initial stage of a research project, where the conceptual framework and important variables were defined. The objective is to contextualize the important dimensions within the Moroccan automotive industry, validate variables, find new ones for the conceptual framework, and match interview insights with existing literature.

RESULTS

General Overview from the Interviews

According to the word frequency analysis (Figure 1), important terms like: "decision-making," "system," "data," "users," "quality," "satisfaction," "information," "tasks," "performance," and "organizational" are prominently shown in the dataset. Two separate sections can be distinguished in this analysis. The first section focuses on how AI-driven DSS supports users to complete tasks, with a focus on individual performance outcomes and user satisfaction. The second section turns its attention to organizational performance, emphasizing the key role that information quality plays in the decision-making process. Furthermore, the system's technical quality component is positioned strategically at the intersection of organizational and individual performance. This structure implies that the implementation of AI-driven DSS, distinguished by exceptional technical quality, gives users the information they need to make wise decisions and improves organizational and individual performance.

Based on pertinent theoretical frameworks, we used a thematic content analysis methodology and the "word frequency" query in the Nvivo coding process. The terms "quality," "system," "information," and "service" were used frequently in the interviews, leading to the development of thematic nodes: "technical quality," "information quality," and "service quality." Interviewees consistently referred to these variables, either explicitly or implicitly.

Other significant concepts were also discovered during the first stage of analysis, including "management," "support," "participation," and "training." Consequently, more nodes were created to record these dimensions: "top management support," "participation," and "training quality." In addition, we coded the variables "usage" and "satisfaction," which illustrate users' attitudes and behaviors. These factors are crucial for assessing how AI-driven DSS influences organizational and individual performance, especially in the context of Morocco's automotive industry.

Figure 1. Word Frequency Query

Source: Generated from Nvivo

The Impact of AI-driven DSS Quality Factors on Behavioral and Attitudinal Variables

To assess the relationship between various quality-related factors and user satisfaction, a matrix cross-tabulation analysis was conducted. As presented in Table 2, the association between the technical quality of AI-driven DSS and user satisfaction was identified 17 times. Interviewees consistently emphasized that their satisfaction is largely driven by technical quality, which encompasses ease of use, system responsiveness, accessibility, security, data processing and analytical capabilities, information presentation quality, flexibility, integration of artificial intelligence, and adaptability to technological advancements.

Moreover, the relationship between service quality and user satisfaction was referenced 12 times, underscoring the pivotal role of the Information Systems (IS) department in meeting user needs, addressing DSS-related issues, providing ongoing training, and involving users in various phases of AI-driven DSS implementation. Additionally, the connection between information quality and satisfaction was cited 8 times. According to the interviewees, satisfaction is largely dependent on the availability of relevant, reliable, clear, precise, and concise information, which facilitates effective decision-making.

Table 2. Matrix Cross-Tabulation Query Between Quality Variables and Satisfaction

Satisfaction	Frequency
Information Quality	8
Service Quality	12
Technical Quality	17

Source: Generated from Nvivo

To investigate the relationship between the quality dimensions of AI-driven DSS and its usage, a matrix cross-tabulation analysis was performed (Table 3). The link between system usage and the technical quality of AI-driven DSS was cited 12 times in the interviews. Participants emphasized that ease of use is a key factor influencing productivity, autonomy, and user efficiency. Additionally, they highlighted that superior technical quality enhances the frequency and extent of AI-driven DSS utilization.

Similarly, the relationship between system usage and service quality was mentioned four times, with interviewees stressing the crucial role of the Information Systems (IS) department in supporting DSS adoption. This finding underscores the importance of IS support in promoting user engagement with the system. However, a weak association was observed between system usage and information quality, with only one reference to this relationship in the dataset.

Table 3. Matrix Cross-Tabulation Query Between Quality Variables and System Usage

System Usage	Frequency
Information Quality	1
Service Quality	4
Technical Quality	12

Source: Generated from Nvivo

The Influence of Managerial Variables on Behavioral and Attitudinal Factors

The relationship between managerial variables and behavior- and attitude-related variables was examined using a matrix cross-tabulation analysis (Table 4). The association between user participation and satisfaction was referenced 11 times across the interviews. The majority of interviewees emphasized that involving users in AI-driven DSS implementation process enhances both satisfaction and motivation, particularly highlighting the pivotal role of user participation within AI-driven

DSS project teams. Top management support, identified as both a precursor and a key driver of satisfaction, was cited 4 times. Additionally, the relationship between training quality and satisfaction was mentioned 12 times. Interviewees underscored the necessity of providing continuous, adequate, and contextually tailored training. They emphasized that training content must be designed to meet the specific needs of the users.

Table 4. Matrix Cross-Tabulation Query Between Managerial Variables and Satisfaction

Satisfaction	Frequency
User Participation	11
Top Management Support	4
Training Quality	12

Source: Generated from Nvivo

We sought to understand the impact of managerial variables on system usage. To this end, a matrix cross-tabulation analysis was conducted (Table 5). The relationship between user participation and system usage was cited 8 times. Interviewees indicated that user involvement indirectly enhances the level of system usage. Additionally, top management support—through motivating supervisors to encourage AI-driven DSS usage—was found to improve system usage by providing users with the necessary resources. This relationship was mentioned 3 times in the interviews. Furthermore, interviewees referenced the connection between training quality and system usage 7 times. They emphasized that high-quality training enhances system usage by improving users' technical capabilities and enabling more effective interaction with the AI-driven DSS.

Table 5. Matrix Cross-Tabulation Query Between Managerial Variables and System Usage

System Usage	Frequency
User Participation	8
Top Management Support	3
Training Quality	7

Source: Generated from Nvivo

The Influence of Behavioral and Attitudinal Variables on Net Benefits

The interviewees underscored the relationship between two behavior- and attitude-related variables and individual user performance. In particular, the use of AI-driven DSS and high levels of satisfaction were identified as pivotal factors that drive user motivation, enhance task execution efficiency, and improve autonomy and productivity. Additionally, these variables promote increased innovation and creativity among users, which ultimately contributes to the enhancement of individual performance (Table 6).

Table 6. Matrix Cross-Tabulation Query Between Behavior- and Attitude-Related Variables and Individual Performance

Individual Performance	Frequency
System Usage	14
Satisfaction	13

Source: Generated from Nvivo

The relationship between individual and organizational performance was referenced 12 times in the interviews (Table 7). According to the interviewees, individual user performance directly contributes to organizational performance, suggesting that AI-driven DSS can drive organizational change both internally and externally. This change manifests in enhanced decision-making, achievement of organizational objectives, more efficient resource allocation, improved customer satisfaction, monitoring of the external environment, and effective internal management.

Table 7. Matrix Cross-Tabulation Query Between Net Benefits Variables

Organizational Performance	Frequency
Individual Performance	12

Source: Generated from Nvivo

DISCUSSION

An in-depth review of the literature, coupled with a critical examination of the theoretical frameworks related to the evaluation of organizational performance through Decision Support Systems (DSS), enabled the identification of the principal conceptual dimensions underlying performance measurement. The conceptual model developed in this study seeks to assess the influence of DSS adoption on organizational outcomes. Accordingly, the model incorporates a range of variables, including those related to system quality variables, managerial variables, behavioral and attitudinal variables, as well as variables related to net benefits, including both individual and organizational performance. This model aims to evaluate the impact of Decision Support Systems (DSS) on organizational performance in Morocco's automotive industry by identifying causal relationships between technical and managerial variables.

A qualitative approach was initially employed to engage with participants and contextualize the key dimensions within the Moroccan automotive sector, forming the basis for hypothesis development and a subsequent quantitative study. Our goal is to align the insights gathered from the interviewees with the existing literature to identify areas of convergence and divergence, validate the variables to be included, and/or uncover new variables that should be integrated into our conceptual framework.

Figure 2. Conceptual Framework of the Study

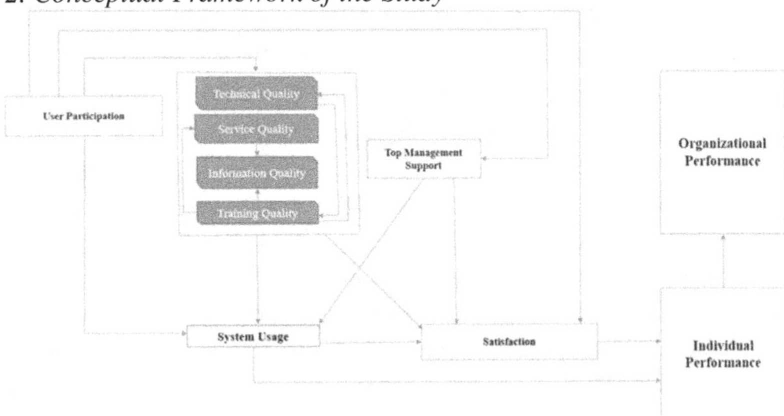

Source: Authors

The study investigates the evaluation of AI-driven DSS across dimensions related to system quality: technical quality, service quality, and information quality. Technical quality is assessed based on indicators such as system availability, incident frequency, and response times, all of which significantly influence user satisfaction and individual performance. The result obtained from the qualitative analysis allows us to corroborate the intrinsic link documented in the literature (DeLone & McLean, 2003a; Kettinger & Lee, 1994). Respondents emphasized that effective AI-driven DSS must be intuitive, adaptable to business needs, capable of handling large datasets, and secure (Respondent 1, Respondent 5). Additionally, some respondents highlighted the importance of incorporating artificial intelligence (AI) into DSS to improve real-time data processing and accuracy (Respondent 2). Regarding service quality, the evaluation is focused on IT support, with respondents stressing the significance of prompt responses and tailored user assistance to ensure a positive user experience. Several researchers have demonstrated this relationship (Kettinger & Lee, 1994; Parasuraman et al., 1988). Resistance to AI adoption and technical limitations, such as integrating AI with legacy systems, are common challenges faced by organizations, as revealed in interview excerpts. A phased implementation, supported by stakeholder engagement and public-private partnerships to enhance digital infrastructure, can facilitate smoother and more sustainable AI integration.

AI-driven DSS evaluation places a high priority on information quality, particularly when it comes to decision-making. As stated by (DeLone & McLean, 1992, 2003b), information quality is a direct consequence of the system's data generation and dissemination procedures. According to respondents, high-quality, current, and accurate information is essential for decision-making because it helps users to spot business opportunities, monitor market trends, and keep a competitive edge (Rai et al., 2002). Users are empowered by such information to take well-informed actions, such as implementing corrective actions and making smart investments (Respondent 4). Additionally, AI-driven DSS systems assist users to target clients more precisely and maximize operational effectiveness (Respondent 4). These results highlight the significance of information quality in improving user satisfaction and organizational performance.

The study further examines how managerial factors, like training quality, top management support, and user participation, affect the performance of AI-driven DSS. Active user participation during the implementation stage encourages system enhancements, produces innovative solutions, and facilitates problem detection, as stated by (Hwang & Thorn, 1999). Top management support is essential to overcome opposition to new technologies and guarantee the adoption of AI-driven DSS, as elucidated by (Bailey & Pearson, 1983; Legge, 1989). Additionally, effective system navigation requires high-quality training, and well-designed training programs leading to improved system usage and success (Mykytyn, 1988; Sabherwal et al., 2006). The study establishes a direct link between user satisfaction and the technical, service, and information quality of the AI-driven DSS, highlighting a positive correlation between system quality and user satisfaction. The results of our qualitative study are consistent with the literature (Cyert & March, 1963; Khalifa & Liu, 2003). Respondents also emphasized the significance of AI-driven DSS in industries such as automotive, where these systems play a critical role in process optimization and strategic decision-making, particularly in the context of technological advancements like AI integration and vehicle electrification (Respondent 1, Respondent 5).

Also, this study examines the impact of AI-driven DSS on both individual and organizational performance, using the concept of net benefits, which combines individual and organizational gains as defined by (DeLone & McLean, 2003b). In terms of individual performance, previous research (DeLone & McLean, 2003b; Igbaria et al., 1997) highlights the importance of system-task compatibility and user satisfaction, which positively influence perceived performance. The majority of respondents stated that by improving user skills, AI-driven DSS improves individual performance and satisfaction while also increasing efficiency, productivity, creativity, and innovation. Respondents also underlined how AI-driven DSS promotes the creation of innovative managerial techniques and work practices, which in turn improves organizational performance. AI-driven DSS influences organizational decision-making by offering tools for planning, control, and reporting, as mentioned by (Mirani & Lederer, 1998) and (Bradley et al., 2006). The authors recognized the informational, transactional, and strategic advantages. Interviewees frequently emphasized the benefits of AI-driven DSS for enhancing resource management, accomplishing corporate goals, and promoting organizational transformation. Additionally, AI-driven DSS improves internal and external environments by offering insightful information about consumer demands, market trends, and risks, which increases responsiveness and competitiveness (Respondent 1; Respondent 4). As a result, AI-driven DSS support improved operational efficiency, well-informed decisions, and a competitive advantage.

CONCLUSION

This study investigates the success of AI-driven DSS in the automotive industry via a qualitative analysis of 12 interviews with system users. Utilizing Nvivo software, the analysis identifies important factors that impact AI-driven DSS efficacy, emphasizing technical, service, and information quality, all of which are essential for system performance, reliability, and user satisfaction. The study also emphasizes how important managerial elements are to successful system adoption and use, including user participation, managerial support, and training quality.

The results show that behavioral and attitudinal factors have a significant impact on organizational and individual performance. AI-driven DSS improves decision-making processes to achieve organizational goals while boosting individual productivity, creativity, and decision quality. In order to attain the best results, system quality must be matched with the organizational context, with the assistance of active managerial involvement and user participation. The study emphasizes how technological innovation and organizational success are dynamically related, particularly in volatile industries like the automotive industry.

The study offers valuable insights, but it is limited by a number of factors, including the sample size, qualitative biases, and its emphasis on a particular sectoral and cultural context. Future studies could use larger and more varied samples. This study is the first part of a larger project that will use a mixed-methods approach. In the following phases, the developed hypotheses will be tested primarily through quantitative analysis.

Even though advanced AI has the potential to produce substantial business value, industry leaders still face a number of ethical dilemmas, such as algorithmic bias, public safety, data privacy, and possible job displacement. Organizations are encouraged to use structured AI ethics frameworks to guide strategic decision-making in order to manage these complexities in the development and integration of AI technologies. In order to promote responsible AI development, UNESCO's 2021 Recommendation on the Ethics of Artificial Intelligence lays out important guidelines that prioritize human rights, accountability, transparency, safety, equity, and sustainability. It aims to reduce ethical risks and global inequality while ensuring AI benefits to all societies.

Future studies should look into how businesses apply AI ethics frameworks—like UNESCO's 2021 Recommendation—in real-world scenarios. Assessing their impact on user engagement, trust, and long-term results should be the main goal. Such research will improve understanding of responsible AI adoption in a range of industries.

REFERENCES

Albarello, L. (2004). *Devenir praticien chercheur*. De Boeck.

Ali, O., Shrestha, A., Soar, J., & Wamba, S. F. (2018). Cloud computing-enabled healthcare opportunities, issues, and applications : A systematic review. *International Journal of Information Management*, *43*, 146–158.

Amachraa, A. (2023). Driving The Dream : Morocco's Rise In The Global Automotive Industry. *Policy Center for the New South.*, *9/23*, 1–21.

Anumandla, S. K. R. (2018). AI-enabled Decision Support Systems and Reciprocal Symmetry : Empowering Managers for Better Business Outcomes. *International Journal of Reciprocal Symmetry and Theoretical Physics*, *5*, 33–41.

Asolo, E., Gil-Ozoudeh, I., & Ejimuda, C. (2024). AI-Powered decision support systems for sustainable agriculture using AI-Chatbot solution. *Journal of Digital Food, Energy & Water Systems, 5*(1).

Bailey, J. E., & Pearson, S. W. (1983). Development of a tool for measuring and analyzing computer user satisfaction. *Management Science*, *29*(5), 530–545.

Ballantine, J., Bonner, M., Levy, M., Martin, A., Munro, I., & Powell, P. L. (1996). The 3-D model of information systems success : The search for the dependent variable continues. [IRMJ]. *Information Resources Management Journal*, *9*(4), 5–15.

Baxter, G., & Sommerville, I. (2011). Socio-technical systems : From design methods to systems engineering. *Interacting with Computers*, *23*(1), 4–17.

Bradley, R. V., Pridmore, J. L., & Byrd, T. A. (2006). Information Systems Success in the Context of Different Corporate Cultural Types : An Empirical Investigation. *Journal of Management Information Systems*, *23*(2), 267–294. DOI: 10.2753/MIS0742-1222230211

Brotcorne, L., Perboli, G., Rosano, M., & Wei, Q. (2019). A managerial analysis of urban parcel delivery : A lean business approach. *Sustainability*, *11*(12), 1–23.

Chai, T. Y., & Nizam, I. (2021). Impact of Artificial Intelligence In Automotive Industries Transformation. *International Journal of Information System and Engineering*, *9*(1), 1–35. DOI: 10.24924/ijise/2021.04/v9.iss2/01.35

Chi, M., Huang, R., & George, J. F. (2020). Collaboration in demand-driven supply chain : Based on a perspective of governance and IT-business strategic alignment. *International Journal of Information Management*, *52*(C), 1–40.

Coiera, E., Westbrook, J. I., & Wyatt, J. C. (2006). Section 1 : Health and Clinical Mangement: The Safety and Quality of Decision Support Systems. *Yearbook of Medical Informatics*, *15*(1), 20–25. DOI: 10.1055/s-0038-1638469

Collins, C., Dennehy, D., Conboy, K., & Mikalef, P. (2021). Artificial intelligence in information systems research : A systematic literature review and research agenda. *International Journal of Information Management*, *60*, 1–17. DOI: 10.1016/j.ijinfomgt.2021.102383

Cyert, R. M., & March, J. G. (1963). A behavioral theory of the firm. *Englewood Cliffs, NJ, 2*(4), 169-187.

DeLone, W. H., & McLean, E. R. (1992). Information systems success : The quest for the dependent variable. *Information Systems Research*, *3*(1), 60–95.

DeLone, W. H., & McLean, E. R. (2003a). The DeLone and McLean model of information systems success : A ten-year update. *Journal of Management Information Systems*, *19*(4), 9–30.

DeLone, W. H., & McLean, E. R. (2003b). The DeLone and McLean model of information systems success : A ten-year update. *Journal of Management Information Systems*, *19*(4), 9–30.

Duan, Y., Edwards, J. S., & Dwivedi, Y. K. (2019). Artificial intelligence for decision making in the era of Big Data–evolution, challenges and research agenda. *International Journal of Information Management*, *48*, 63–71.

Dwivedi, A., Agrawal, D., & Madaan, J. (2020). Identification and prioritization of issues to implementation of information-facilitated product recovery system for a circular economy. *Modern Supply Chain Research and Applications*, *2*(4), 247–280.

Evrard, Y., Pras, B., Roux, E., & Desmet, P. (2003). *Market : Études et recherches en marketing*. Dunod.

Garrity, E. J. (1994). User participation, management support and system types. [IRMJ]. *Information Resources Management Journal*, *7*(3), 34–43.

Geels, F. W. (2010). Ontologies, socio-technical transitions (to sustainability), and the multi-level perspective. *Research Policy*, *39*(4), 495–510.

Glaser, B. G., Strauss, A. L., & Strutzel, E. (1968). *The discovery of grounded theory; strategies for qualitative research*. Nursing research. https://journals.lww.com/nursingresearchonline/Citation/1968/07000/The_Discovery_of_Grounded_Theory__Strategies_for.14.aspx

Griffith, T. L., & Dougherty, D. J. (2001). Beyond socio-technical systems : Introduction to the special issue. *Journal of Engineering and Technology Management, 18*(3-4), 207–218.

Guerlain, S., Brown, D. E., & Mastrangelo, C. (2000). Intelligent decision support systems. *Conference proceedings. International conference on systems, man and cybernetics.'cybernetics evolving to systems, humans, organizations, and their complex interactions, 3*, 1934-1938. https://ieeexplore.ieee.org/abstract/document/886396/

Gupta, S., Modgil, S., Bhattacharyya, S., & Bose, I. (2022). Artificial intelligence for decision support systems in the field of operations research : Review and future scope of research. *Annals of Operations Research, 308*(1), 215–274. DOI: 10.1007/s10479-020-03856-6

Hu, P.-H. (2003). Evaluating telemedicine systems success : A revised model. *36th Annual Hawaii International Conference on System Sciences, 2003. Proceedings of the*, 8-pp. https://ieeexplore.ieee.org/abstract/document/1174379/

Hwang, M. I., & Thorn, R. G. (1999). The effect of user engagement on system success : A meta-analytical integration of research findings. *Information & Management, 35*(4), 229–236.

Igbaria, M., Zinatelli, N., Cragg, P., & Cavaye, A. L. (1997). Personal computing acceptance factors in small firms : A structural equation model. *MIS quarterly. JSTOR, 21*(3), 279–305.

Inmon, W. H. (1996). The data warehouse and data mining. *Communications of the ACM, 39*(11), 49–51.

Irawan, Y. (2020). Decision support system for employee bonus determination with web-based simple additive weighting (SAW) method in PT. Mayatama Solusindo. [JAETS]. *Journal of Applied Engineering and Technological Science, 2*(1), 7–13.

Jaidi, L., & Msadfa, Y. (2017). *La Complexité de la Remontée des Chaînes de valeur Mondiale : Cas des Industries Automobile et Aéronautique au Maroc et en Tunisie/ The Complexity of the Rise of Global Value Chains: The Case of Automotive and Aeronautics Industries in Morocco and Tunisia* (Policy Paper, p. 1-48). OCP Policy Center.

Japan International Cooperation Agency (JICA), BCG. (2022). *Study for the promotion of the African automotive industry : Post-COVID 19 supply chain and mobility reform.*

Kettinger, W. J., & Lee, C. C. (1994). Perceived service quality and user satisfaction with the information services function. *Decision Sciences, 25*(5-6), 737–766.

Khalifa, M., & Liu, V. (2003). Determinants of successful knowledge management programs. *Electronic Journal of Knowledge Management*, *1*(2), 101–110.

Kimball, R. (1996). *The data warehouse toolkit : Practical techniques for building dimensional data warehouses*. John Wiley & Sons, Inc.

Le Moigne, J.-L. (1977). La dynamique de l'homme au travail. Une nouvelle approche par l'analyse de système. *Revue Française de Sociologie, JSTOR*, *18*(3), 528–530.

Legge, K. (1989). Information technology : Personnel management's lost opportunity? *Personnel Review*, *18*(5), 2–61.

Lugano, G. (2017). Virtual assistants and self-driving cars. *15th International Conference on ITS Telecommunications (ITST)*, 1-5. https://ieeexplore.ieee.org/abstract/document/7972192/

Mackrell, D., Kerr, D., & von Hellens, L. (2009). A qualitative case study of the adoption and use of an agricultural decision support system in the Australian cotton industry : The socio-technical view. *Decision Support Systems*, *47*(2), 143–153. DOI: 10.1016/j.dss.2009.02.004

Mantouzi, S., & Said, Y. (2023). Intelligence artificielle et performance du secteur de l'enseignement supérieur marocain : Enjeux et interactions. *Revue Française d'Economie et de Gestion*, *4*(11), 21–42.

Mantouzi, S., Youssef, S., El Mouatassim, A., Ourahou, Y., Jafi, H., Zouhouredine, I., & Hamliri, M. (2024). Leveraging AI for business intelligence : A pathway to improved organizational performance in Morocco's manufacturing sector. *Multidisciplinary Science Journal, Accepted Articles*. https://malque.pub/ojs/index.php/msj/article/view/7254

Mckeen, J. D., & Guimaraes, T. (1997). Successful Strategies for User Participation in Systems Development. *Journal of Management Information Systems*, *14*(2), 133–150. DOI: 10.1080/07421222.1997.11518168

McKeen, J. D., Guimaraes, T., & Wetherbe, J. C. (1994). The relationship between user participation and user satisfaction : An investigation of four contingency factors. *Management Information Systems Quarterly*, *18*(4), 427–451.

Mettler, T., Sprenger, M., & Winter, R. (2017). Service robots in hospitals : New perspectives on niche evolution and technology affordances. *European Journal of Information Systems*, *26*(5), 451–468. DOI: 10.1057/s41303-017-0046-1

Michel, S. (2011). *Contribution à l'évaluation du système d'information bancaire* [Thèse de doctorat, Université Montesquieu]. https://www.theses.fr/2011BOR40047

Michel, S., & Cocula, F. (2014). L'évaluation des systèmes d'information : Un état de l'art à la lumière des approches de la variance et processuelles. *Management & Avenir, 74*(8), 33–51.

Mirani, R., & Lederer, A. L. (1998). An Instrument for Assessing the Organizational Benefits of IS Projects. *Decision Sciences, 29*(4), 803–838. DOI: 10.1111/j.1540-5915.1998.tb00878.x

Morris, A. (2009). Socio-technical systems in ICT : A comprehensive survey. *Technical Report, Information Engineering and Computer Science, DISI-09-054*, 1-16.

Mumford, E. (1993). The ETHICS approach. *Communications of the ACM, 36*(6), 82–83. DOI: 10.1145/153571.214824

Mumford, E. (1995). *Effective systems design and requirements analysis approach : The Ethics Approach*. Macmillan.

Mykytyn, P. P. (1988). An empirical investigation of DSS usage and the user's perception of DSS training. *Information & Management, 14*(1), 9–17. DOI: 10.1016/0378-7206(88)90063-8

Nilsson, N. J. (2005). Human-level artificial intelligence? Be serious! *AI Magazine, 26*(4), 68–68.

Palvia, S. C., Sharma, R. S., & Conrath, D. W. (2001). A socio-technical framework for quality assessment of computer information systems. *Industrial Management & Data Systems, 101*(5), 237–251.

Parasuraman, A., Zeithaml, V. A., & Berry, L. (1988). SERVQUAL : A multiple-item scale for measuring consumer perceptions of service quality. *1988, 64*(1), 12-40.

Perboli, G., Musso, S., & Rosano, M. (2018). Blockchain in logistics and supply chain : A lean approach for designing real-world use cases. *IEEE Access : Practical Innovations, Open Solutions, 6*, 62018–62028.

Poisson, Y. (1983). L'approche qualitative et l'approche quantitative dans les recherches en éducation. *Revue des Sciences de l'Education, 9*(3), 369–378.

Rai, A., Lang, S. S., & Welker, R. B. (2002). Assessing the validity of IS success models : An empirical test and theoretical analysis. *Information Systems Research, 13*(1), 50–69.

Ramathilagam, A., & Pitchipoo, P. (2022). Modeling and development of fuzzy logic-based intelligent decision support system. *Romanian Journal of Information Science and Technology, 25*(1), 58–79.

Renfrew, D., Vasilaki, V., & Katsou, E. (2024). Indicator based multi-criteria decision support systems for wastewater treatment plants. *The Science of the Total Environment, 915*, 1–18. DOI: 10.1016/j.scitotenv.2024.169903

Russell, S., & Norvig, P. (2010). *Intelligence artificielle : Avec plus de 500 exercices*. Pearson Education.

Sabherwal, R., Jeyaraj, A., & Chowa, C. (2006). Information System Success : Individual and Organizational Determinants. *Management Science, 52*(12), 1849–1864. DOI: 10.1287/mnsc.1060.0583

Seddon, P., & Kiew, M.-Y. (1996). A partial test and development of DeLone and McLean's model of IS success. *AJIS. Australasian Journal of Information Systems, 4*(1), 90–109.

Seddon, P. B. (1997). A respecification and extension of the DeLone and McLean model of IS success. *Information Systems Research, 8*(3), 240–253.

Serafeimidis, V., & Smithson, S. (1995). Requirements for an IT investment appraisal framework for the 1990s : Towards a more rigorous solution. *European Conference on Information Technology Investment Evaluation*, 146-160.

Shah, J. M., & Natraj, N. A., Hallur, Giri. G., & Aslekar, A. (2023). Artificial Intelligence (AI) in the Automotive Industry and the use of Exoskeletons in the Manufacturing Sector of the Automotive Industry. *2023 International Conference on Sustainable Computing and Data Communication Systems (ICSCDS)*, 428-432. https://doi.org/DOI: 10.1109/ICSCDS56580.2023.10105009

Suhaib Kamran, S., Haleem, A., Bahl, S., Javaid, M., Prakash, C., & Budhhi, D. (2022). Artificial intelligence and advanced materials in automotive industry : Potential applications and perspectives. *Materials Today: Proceedings, 62*(6), 4207–4214. DOI: 10.1016/j.matpr.2022.04.727

Taherdoost, H. (2023). An Overview of Trends in Information Systems : Emerging Technologies that Transform the Information Technology Industry. *Cloud Computing and Data Science, 4*(1), 1–16. DOI: 10.37256/ccds.4120231653

Terribile, F., Agrillo, A., Bonfante, A., Buscemi, G., Colandrea, M., D'Antonio, A., De Mascellis, R., De Michele, C., Langella, G., & Manna, P. (2015). A Web-based spatial decision supporting system for land management and soil conservation. *Solid Earth, 6*(3), 903–928.

Thiétart, R.-A. (2014). *Méthodes de recherche en management-4ème édition*. Dunod.

Trist, E. L. (1981). *The evolution of socio-technical systems* (Vol. 2). Ontario Quality of Working Life Centre.

Urbach, N., & Müller, B. (2012). The Updated DeLone and McLean Model of Information Systems Success. In Dwivedi, Y. K., Wade, M. R., & Schneberger, S. L. (Eds.), *Information Systems Theory* (Vol. 28, pp. 1–18). Springer New York., DOI: 10.1007/978-1-4419-6108-2_1

Waqar, A. (2024). Intelligent decision support systems in construction engineering : An artificial intelligence and machine learning approaches. *Expert Systems with Applications*, *249*, 123503. DOI: 10.1016/j.eswa.2024.123503

Wilson, H. J., & Daugherty, P. R. (2018). Collaborative intelligence : Humans and AI are joining forces. *Harvard Business Review*, *96*(4), 114–123.

Yazdani, M., Zarate, P., Coulibaly, A., & Zavadskas, E. K. (2017). A group decision making support system in logistics and supply chain management. *Expert Systems with Applications*, *88*, 376–392.

Zhai, Z., Martínez, J. F., Beltran, V., & Martínez, N. L. (2020). Decision support systems for agriculture 4.0 : Survey and challenges. *Computers and Electronics in Agriculture*, *170*, 1–16. DOI: 10.1016/j.compag.2020.105256

KEY TERMS AND DEFINITIONS

Artificial intelligence: It refers to machines performing tasks that typically require human intelligence, such as learning and problem-solving. Defined by John McCarthy in 1956, AI aims to replicate human cognition, with its full potential still unfolding.

Decision support system: A Decision Support System (DSS) is a structured and accessible information system designed to aid managerial decision-making by organizing and processing transactional data for analytical use.

System usage: In the context of DSS refers to the extent and frequency with which users interact with the system to support decision-making activities.

Satisfaction: It is defined as a global evaluation—both cognitive and affective—of the user's pleasant fulfillment derived from interacting with an information system.

Individual performance: It refers to the improvements in work outcomes through better decision-making, problem-solving, and contextual understanding, leading to higher productivity, efficiency, and job performance.

Organizational performance: It refers to a company's competitiveness, productivity, and efficiency in maintaining its market presence and achieving its objectives.

Compilation of References

Aayog, N. (2018). National strategy for artificial intelligence. *Paper. June*, 2019-01. https://niti.gov.in

Ab Hamid, M. R., Sami, W., & Sidek, M. M. (2017). Discriminant validity assessment : Use of Fornell & Larcker criterion versus HTMT criterion. *Journal of Physics: Conference Series*, *890*(1), 012163. DOI: 10.1088/1742-6596/890/1/012163

Abbas, G., Rafiq, S., & Gul, M. (2023). Unraveling dividend payouts: a comprehensive analysis of cash flow and earnings approaches in the listed manufacturing companies. FiTUA. DOI: 10.51380/gujr-39-02-10

Abdelrahman, H. (2023). Artificial Intelligence in Human Resource Management: Advanced Computing Systems for Talent Analytics and Decision Making. *Journal of Advanced Computing Systems*, *3*(6), 1–11.

Abdi, H., & Williams, L. J. (2010). Partial least square methods: Regression and structural equation models. *Journal of Computational Statistics*, *1*(2), 1–21.

Abebe, R., Barocas, S., Kleinberg, J., Levy, K., Raghavan, M., & Robinson, D. (2021). Roles for computing in social change. *Communications of the ACM*, *64*(3), 62–71. DOI: 10.1145/3430368

Acemoglu, D. mname, & Restrepo, P. mname. (2018). Artificial Intelligence, Automation and Work. SSRN *Electronic Journal*. DOI: 10.2139/ssrn.3098384

Acemoglu, D., & Restrepo, P. (2019). Automation and New Tasks: How Technology Displaces and Reinstates Labor. *The Journal of Economic Perspectives*, *33*(2), 3–30. DOI: 10.1257/jep.33.2.3

Adadi, A., & Berrada, M. (2018). Peeking inside the black-box: A survey on explainable artificial intelligence (XAI). *IEEE Access : Practical Innovations, Open Solutions*, *6*, 52138–52160. DOI: 10.1109/ACCESS.2018.2870052

Adeusi, S. O., Akeke, N. I., Adebisi, O. S., & Oladunjoye, O. (2014). Risk management and financial performance of banks in Nigeria. *Risk Management*, *6*(31), 123–129.

Agence Nationale des Déchets Solides (AND). (2023). Statistiques sur la Production et la Gestion des Déchets Solides au Maroc. https://www.environnement.gov.ma/fr/dechets?utm_source=chatgpt.comhttps://www.environnement.gov.ma/fr/etat-de-l-environnement?utm_source=chatgpt.com

Aggarwal, C. C. (2018). *Neural networks and deep learning: A textbook*. Springer. DOI: 10.1007/978-3-319-94463-0

Agourrame, H. (2021). *International banking regulation: Origins, evolution, and impact on bank business models*. Harmattan.

Agrawal, A., Gans, S. J., & Goldfarb, A. (2019). Artificial Intelligence: The Ambiguous Labor Market Impact of Automating Prediction. *The Journal of Economic Perspectives*, *33*(2), 31–50. DOI: 10.1257/jep.33.2.31

Agrawal, V. (2022). Demystifying the Chinese Social Credit System: A Case Study on AI-Powered Control Systems in China. *Proceedings of the AAAI Conference on Artificial Intelligence*, *36*(11), 13124–13125. DOI: 10.1609/aaai.v36i11.21698

Agresti, A. (2010). *Analysis of Ordinal Categorical Data* (2nd ed.). Wiley., DOI: 10.1002/9780470594001

Aguinis, H., Beltran, J. R., & Cope, A. (2024). How to use generative AI as a human resource management assistant. *Organizational Dynamics*, *53*(1), 101029. DOI: 10.1016/j.orgdyn.2024.101029

Ahmad, N., Ullah, Z., & Arshad, H. (2021). Artificial intelligence for sustainable finance in low-income countries. *Journal of Cleaner Production*, *310*, 127385.

Aiken, M., & Hage, J. (1971). The organic organization and innovation. *Sociology*, *5*(1), 63–82. DOI: 10.1177/003803857100500105

Ait Lemqeddem, H., & Chouay, J. (2020). Le rôle de la digitalisation dans l'efficacité de l'audit interne. *Revue Française d'Economie et de Gestion*, *1*(5).

Aït Moussa, O. (2023). Effectiveness of internal control systems for operational risk in banks: Development of a conceptual model. [IJESM]. *International Journal of Economic and Management Studies*, *3*(3), 814–833.

Ajzen, I. (1991). The theory of planned behavior. *Organizational Behavior and Human Decision Processes*, *50*(2), 179–211. DOI: 10.1016/0749-5978(91)90020-T

Akram, S., Buono, P., & Lanzilotti, R. (2024). Recruitment chatbot acceptance in a company: A mixed method study on human-centered technology acceptance model. *Personal and Ubiquitous Computing*, *28*(6), 961–984. DOI: 10.1007/s00779-024-01826-4

Alarcón, D., Sánchez, J. A., & De Olavide, U. (2015). Assessing convergent and discriminant validity in the ADHD-R IV rating scale : User-written commands for Average Variance Extracted (AVE), Composite Reliability (CR), and Heterotrait-Monotrait ratio of correlations (HTMT). *Spanish STATA meeting, 39*, 1-39. https://www.academia.edu/download/50804454/convergent_validity_with_average_variance_extracted.pdf

Albahri, A. S., Duhaim, A. M., Fadhel, M. A., Alnoor, A., Baqer, N. S., Alzubaidi, L., Albahri, O. S., Alamoodi, A. H., Bai, J., Salhi, A., Santamaría, J., Ouyang, C., Gupta, A., Gu, Y., & Deveci, M. (2023). A systematic review of trustworthy and explainable artificial intelligence in healthcare: Assessment of quality, bias risk, and data fusion. *Information Fusion*, *96*, 156–191. DOI: 10.1016/j.inffus.2023.03.008

Albarello, L. (2004). *Devenir praticien chercheur*. De Boeck.

Ali, O., Shrestha, A., Soar, J., & Wamba, S. F. (2018). Cloud computing-enabled healthcare opportunities, issues, and applications : A systematic review. *International Journal of Information Management*, *43*, 146–158.

Allen, C., Wallach, W., & Smit, I. (2022). *Moral machines: Teaching robots right from wrong*. Oxford University Press.

Almaqtari, F. A., Farhan, N. H., Al-Hattami, H. M., & Elsheikh, T. (2023). The moderating role of information technology governance in the relationship between board characteristics and continuity management during the Covid-19 pandemic in an emerging economy. *Humanities & Social Sciences Communications*, *10*(1), 1–16. DOI: 10.1057/s41599-023-01552-x PMID: 36938575

Alshake Theep, K., Mansour, A. M., Al-Ma'aitah, I. M., Dabaghia, M. N., & Dabaghie, Y. M. (2024). Leveraging AI predictive analytics for marketing strategy : The mediating role of management awareness. *Journal of System and Management Sciences*, *14*(2), 71–89. DOI: 10.33168/JSMS.2024.0205

Alsheiabni, S., Cheung, Y., & Messom, C. (2019). Factors inhibiting the adoption of artificial intelligence at organizational-level : A preliminary investigation. *Americas Conference on Information Systems 2019*, 2. https://research.monash.edu/en/publications/factors-inhibiting-the-adoption-of-artificial-intelligence-at-org

Altukhi, Z. M., Pradhan, S., & Aljohani, N. (2025). A Systematic Literature Review of the Latest Advancements in XAI. *Technologies*, *13*(3), 93. DOI: 10.3390/technologies13030093

Alzoubi, Y. I., & Mishra, A. (2024). Green artificial intelligence initiatives: Potentials and challenges. *Journal of Cleaner Production*, *468*, 143090. DOI: 10.1016/j.jclepro.2024.143090

Amachraa, A. (2023). Driving The Dream : Morocco's Rise In The Global Automotive Industry. *Policy Center for the New South.*, *9/23*, 1–21.

Amasyali, K., & El-Gohary, N. M. (2018). A review of data-driven building energy consumption prediction studies. *Renewable & Sustainable Energy Reviews*, *81*(P1), 1192–1205. DOI: 10.1016/j.rser.2017.04.095

Amiot, C. E., Terry, D. J., Jimmieson, N. L., & Callan, V. J. (2006). A longitudinal investigation of coping processes during a merger: Implications for job satisfaction and organizational identification. *Journal of Management*, *32*(4), 552–574. DOI: 10.1177/0149206306287542

Amiri, I., Sekaki, Y., Hainous, M., & Zaam, H. (2021). Déterminants de la qualité de l'audit interne: Que dit la littérature académique et professionnelle? *Revue Française d'Economie et de Gestion*, 2(6).

AMMC. (2023). Guide de la gouvernance d'entreprise au Maroc.

Ananny, M., & Crawford, K. (2018). Seeing without knowing: Limitations of the transparency ideal and its application to algorithmic accountability. *New Media & Society*, *20*(3), 973–989. DOI: 10.1177/1461444816676645

Andaloussi, S., Mohamed, H., El Akkili, H., & Fahmi, Y. (2024). Digital Transformation in Morocco Public Health Sector: Survey of the Telemedicine in the Fez-Meknes Region. In International Conference on Digital Technologies and Applications (pp. 542-550). Cham: Springer Nature Switzerland. Springer 2023. DOI: DOI: 10.1007/978-3-031-68653-5_51

Anderson, D., & Anderson, L. A. (2021). *Beyond Change Management: How to Achieve Breakthrough Results Through Conscious Change Leadership* (2nd ed.). Wiley.

Andrieux, P., Johnson, R. D., Sarabadani, J., & Van Slyke, C. (2024). Ethical considerations of generative AI-enabled human resource management. *Organizational Dynamics*, *53*(1), 101032. DOI: 10.1016/j.orgdyn.2024.101032

Androniceanu, A. (2023). The new trends of digital transformation and artificial intelligence in public administration. *Administratie Si Management Public, 2023*(40), 147-155. *Scopus.* Advance online publication. DOI: 10.24818/amp/2023.40-09

Androutsopoulou, A., Karacapilidis, N., Loukis, E., & Charalabidis, Y. (2019). Transforming the communication between citizens and government through AI-guided chatbots. *Government Information Quarterly*, *36*(2), 358–367. DOI: 10.1016/j.giq.2018.10.001

Angelov, P., & Buswell, R. (2002). Identification of evolving fuzzy rule-based models. *IEEE Transactions on Fuzzy Systems*, *10*(5), 667–677. DOI: 10.1109/TFUZZ.2002.803499

Anumandla, S. K. R. (2018). AI-enabled Decision Support Systems and Reciprocal Symmetry : Empowering Managers for Better Business Outcomes. *International Journal of Reciprocal Symmetry and Theoretical Physics*, *5*, 33–41.

An, Z., Gao, W., Li, D., & Ye, D. (2022). Dividend payouts, Cash-Flow uncertainty, and the role of Institutions. *Journal of Business Finance & Accounting*, *49*(7–8), 1356–1390. DOI: 10.1111/jbfa.12595

Appelbaum, S. H., Degbe, M. C., MacDonald, O., & Nguyen-Quang, T. S. (2022). Organizational Change: A Review of Theory and Research in the 21st Century. *Journal of Organizational Change Management*, *35*(3), 421–437.

Araujo, T., Helberger, N., & de Vreese, C. H. (2023). AI in organizations: From automation to augmentation. *Journal of Business Research*, *161*, 113807.

Armenakis, A. A., & Harris, S. G. (2022). Reflections: Organizational Change Management in the Age of Digital Transformation. *Journal of Change Management*, *22*(1), 12–29.

Arner, D. W., Barberis, J., & Buckley, R. P. (2016). The evolution of Fintech: A new post-crisis paradigm? *SSRN*, *47*(4), 1271–1319. DOI: 10.2139/ssrn.2676553

Arshad, N., Waseem, F., & Abbas, S. F. (2022). Factors Affecting Dividend Payout Ratio of Dividend Paying Firms Listed on KSE-100 Index. iRASD. *Journal of Management*, *4*(2), 162–181. DOI: 10.52131/jom.2022.0401.0071

Arthur, P. (2015). l'audit dans le secteur public: Tenir compte des attentes, être performant. CBOK, IFACI

Arun, T., & Kamath, R. (2022). Interpretable credit scoring using SHAP values: A regulatory perspective. *Journal of Financial Regulation and Compliance*, *30*(4), 421–436.

Arya, V., Bellamy, R. K. E., Chen, P. Y., Dhurandhar, A., Hind, M., Hoffman, S. C., . . . Zhang, Y. (2019). One explanation does not fit all: A toolkit and taxonomy of AI explainability techniques. arXiv preprint arXiv:1909.03012. https://arxiv.org/abs/1909.03012

Aschbacher, K. (2024). The Uncertain Promise of HR Analytics: A Comprehensive Analysis of Data Utilised in Predictive Models for Employee Turnover (Doctoral dissertation, University of Graz).

Asolo, E., Gil-Ozoudeh, I., & Ejimuda, C. (2024). AI-Powered decision support systems for sustainable agriculture using AI-Chatbot solution. *Journal of Digital Food, Energy & Water Systems, 5*(1).

Asongu, S. A., & Nwachukwu, J. C. (2022). Financial development, governance, and artificial intelligence in Africa. *Technological Forecasting and Social Change, 177*, 121499.

Autor, D. H. (2015). Why Are There Still So Many Jobs? The History and Future of Workplace Automation. *The Journal of Economic Perspectives*, *29*(3), 3–30. DOI: 10.1257/jep.29.3.3

Autor, D., & Salomons, A. (2018). *Is automation labor-displacing? Productivity growth, employment, and the labor share (No. w24871)*. National Bureau of Economic Research., DOI: 10.3386/w24871

Avolio, B. J., Kahai, S. S., & Dodge, G. E. (2003). E-leadership: Implications for theory, research, and practice. The Leadership Quarterly, 11(4), 615–668. (00)00062-X

Azam, M. S. (2023). How can we build human resources (HR) that deliver value? A systematic literature review of traditional and transformational HR roles. *Global Business and Organizational Excellence*, *42*(4), 81–92. DOI: 10.1002/joe.22191

Baars, B. J. (1988). *A cognitive theory of consciousness*. Cambridge University Press.

Bailey, J. E., & Pearson, S. W. (1983). Development of a tool for measuring and analyzing computer user satisfaction. *Management Science*, *29*(5), 530–545.

Baker, T., & Smith, L. (2019). *Educ-AI-tion rebooted? Exploring the future of artificial intelligence in schools and colleges.*

Baker, H. K., & Jabbouri, I. (2016). How Moroccan managers view dividend policy. *Managerial Finance*, *42*(3), 270–288. DOI: 10.1108/MF-07-2015-0211

Baker, H. K., & Jabbouri, I. (2017). Dividend policy in Morocco: Survey evidence from Casablanca Stock Exchange. *International Journal of Managerial Finance*, *13*(3), 347–365.

Baker, M., & Wurgler, J. (2006). Investor sentiment and the cross-section of stock returns. *The Journal of Finance*, *61*(4), 1645–1680. DOI: 10.1111/j.1540-6261.2006.00885.x

Balcioğlu, Y. S., & Artar, M. (2024). Artificial intelligence in employee recruitment. *Global Business and Organizational Excellence*, *43*(5), 56–66. DOI: 10.1002/joe.22248

Ballantine, J., Bonner, M., Levy, M., Martin, A., Munro, I., & Powell, P. L. (1996). The 3-D model of information systems success : The search for the dependent variable continues. [IRMJ]. *Information Resources Management Journal*, *9*(4), 5–15.

Bankins, S. (2021). The ethical use of artificial intelligence in human resource management: A decision-making framework. *Ethics and Information Technology*, *23*(4), 841–854. DOI: 10.1007/s10676-021-09619-6

Bannister, F., & Connolly, R. (2020). Administration by algorithm : A risk management framework. *Information Polity*, *25*(4), 471–490. DOI: 10.3233/IP-200249

Barberis, N., & Thaler, R. (2003). A survey of behavioral finance. In *Handbook of the Economics of Finance* (Vol. 1, pp. 1053–1128). Elsevier.

Barodi, M., & Lalaoui, S. (2025). Civil servants' readiness for ai adoption: The role of change management in morocco's public sector. *Problems and Perspectives in Management, 23*(1), 63-75. *Scopus.* Advance online publication. DOI: 10.21511/ppm.23(1).2025.05

Barredo Arrieta, A., Díaz-Rodríguez, N., Del Ser, J., Bennetot, A., Tabik, S., Barbado, A., Garcia, S., Gil-Lopez, S., Molina, D., Benjamins, R., Chatila, R., & Herrera, F. (2020). Explainable Artificial Intelligence (XAI): Concepts, taxonomies, opportunities and challenges toward responsible AI. *Information Fusion*, *58*, 82–115. DOI: 10.1016/j.inffus.2019.12.012

Baruch, Y., & Holtom, B. C. (2008). Survey response rate levels and trends in organizational research. *Human Relations*, *61*(8), 1139–1160. DOI: 10.1177/0018726708094863

Baxter, G., & Sommerville, I. (2011). Socio-technical systems : From design methods to systems engineering. *Interacting with Computers*, *23*(1), 4–17.

Beck, K., Beedle, M., van Bennekum, A., Cockburn, A., Cunningham, W., Fowler, M., & Thomas, D. (2001). *Manifesto for Agile Software Development*. Agile Alliance.

Bell, E., Bryman, A., & Harley, B. (2022). *Business research methods.* Oxford university press., DOI: 10.1093/hebz/9780198869443.001.0001

Bel, M. (2016). *Prédire l'utilisation d'une nouvelle technologie: Le cas des Systèmes de Transports Intelligents Coopératifs*. GRENOBLE ALPES.

Benabou, A., Touhami, F., & Demraoui, L. (2024, May). Artificial intelligence and the future of human resource management. In *2024 International Conference on Intelligent Systems and Computer Vision (ISCV)* (pp. 1-8). IEEE. DOI: 10.1109/ISCV60512.2024.10620146

Bencsik, A. (2024). The opportunities of digitalisation in public administration with a special focus on the use of artificial intelligence. *Studia Iuridica Lublinensia, 33*(2), 11-23. *Scopus.* Advance online publication. DOI: 10.17951/sil.2024.33.2.11-23

Besson, P., & Rowe, F. (2012). Strategizing information systems-enabled organizational transformation: A transdisciplinary review and new directions. *The Journal of Strategic Information Systems*, *21*(2), 103–124. DOI: 10.1016/j.jsis.2012.05.001

Bhat, R. (2010). Corporate governance and dividend policy in India. *Journal of Emerging Market Finance*, *9*(1), 55–70.

Bhattacharya, C., & Sinha, M. (2022). The role of artificial intelligence in banking for leveraging customer experience. Australasian Accounting, Business and Finance Journal, 16(5). https://doi.org/10.xxxx

Bhattacharya, S. (1979). Imperfect information, dividend policy, and "the bird in the hand" fallacy. *The Bell Journal of Economics*, *10*(1), 259–270. DOI: 10.2307/3003330

Bigoness, W. J., & Perreault, W. D.Jr. (1981). A conceptual paradigm and approach for the study of innovators. *Academy of Management Journal*, *24*(1), 68–82. DOI: 10.2307/255824

Binns, R., Veale, M., Van Kleek, M., & Shadbolt, N. (2018). 'It's reducing a human being to a percentage': Perceptions of justice in algorithmic decisions. In *Proceedings of the 2018 CHI Conference on Human Factors in Computing Systems* (pp. 1–14). ACM. DOI: 10.1145/3173574.3173951

Bird & Bird. (2025). *GCC : Navigating AI Regulations - the Current Landscape*. https://www.twobirds.com/en/insights/2025/united-arab-emirates/gcc-navigating-ai-regulations---the-current-landscape

Birkinshaw, J. M., & Mol, M. J. (2006). How management innovation happens. *MIT Sloan Management Review*, *47*(4), 81–88.

Birkinshaw, J., Hamel, G., & Mol, M. J. (2008). Management innovation. *Academy of Management Review*, *33*(4), 825–845. DOI: 10.5465/amr.2008.34421969

Bishop, C. M., & Nasrabadi, N. M. (2006). *Pattern recognition and machine learning* (Vol. 4). Springer.

Biswas, S., Carson, B., Chung, V., Singh, S., & Thomas, R. (2020). AI-bank of the future: Can banks meet the AI challenge? McKinsey & Company. https://www.mckinsey.com

Bizarro, P. A., & Dorian, M. (2017). Artificial intelligence: The future of auditing. *Internal Auditing*, *5*(1), 21–26.

Booth, H. (2024). *Faisal Al Bannai. TIME*. https://time.com/7012755/faisal-al-bannai/

Borissov, B., & Hristozov, Y. (2024). Potential for Using Artifical Intelligence in Public Administration. *ECONOMICS - Innovative and Economics Research Journal*, *12*(3), 409-423. *Scopus*. Advance online publication. DOI: 10.2478/eoik-2024-0034

Botsman, R. (2017). *Who Can You Trust?: How Technology Brought Us Together and Why It Might Drive Us Apart*. PublicAffairs.

Bouckaert, G., Peters, B. G., & Verhoest, K. (2010). *The Coordination of Public Sector Organizations*. https://doi.org/DOI: DOI: 10.1057/9780230275256

Bradley, R. V., Pridmore, J. L., & Byrd, T. A. (2006). Information Systems Success in the Context of Different Corporate Cultural Types : An Empirical Investigation. *Journal of Management Information Systems*, *23*(2), 267–294. DOI: 10.2753/MIS0742-1222230211

Brangier, É., Dufresne, A., & Hammes-Adelé, S. (2009). Approche symbiotique de la relation humain-technologie : Perspectives pour l'ergonomie informatique. Le travail humain, 72(4), 333-353. Cairn.info. DOI: 10.3917/th.724.0333

Breiman, L. (2001). Random forests. *Machine Learning*, *45*(1), 5–32. DOI: 10.1023/A:1010933404324

Brislin, R. W. (1970). Back-translation for cross-cultural research. *Journal of Cross-Cultural Psychology*, *1*(3), 185–216. DOI: 10.1177/135910457000100301

Brock, A., Donahue, J., & Simonyan, K. (2018). *Large Scale GAN Training for High Fidelity Natural Image Synthesis*. http://dx.doi.org//arXiv.1809.11096DOI: 10.48550

Brotcorne, L., Perboli, G., Rosano, M., & Wei, Q. (2019). A managerial analysis of urban parcel delivery : A lean business approach. *Sustainability*, *11*(12), 1–23.

Brown, K., & Coulter, P. B. (1983). Subjective and objective measures of police service delivery. *Public Administration Review*, *43*(1), 50–58. DOI: 10.2307/975299

Bryniolfsson, E., & McAfee, A. (2014). *The second machine age: Work, progress, and prosperity in a time of brilliant technologies.* WW Norton & company.

Brynjolfsson, E., Rock, D., & Syverson, C. (2018). Artificial Intelligence and the Modern Productivity Paradox: A Clash of Expectations and Statistics. In *The Economics of Artificial Intelligence: An Agenda* (pp. 23–57). National Bureau of Economic Research.

Brynjolfsson, E., & McAfee, A. (2017). Artificial intelligence, for real. *Harvard Business Review, 1*(1), 1–31.

Brynjolfsson, E., & McAfee, A. (2017). *Machine, Platform, Crowd: Harnessing Our Digital Future.* W. W. Norton & Company.

Bryson, J. M., Crosby, B. C., & Bloomberg, L. (2014). Public Value Governance : Moving Beyond Traditional Public Administration and the New Public Management. *Public Administration Review, 74*(4), 445–456. DOI: 10.1111/puar.12238

Buchanan, D., & McCalman, J. (2023). *High-Impact Change Management: Principles and Practices.* Routledge.

Budhwar, P., Malik, A., De Silva, M. T., & Thevisuthan, P. (2022). Artificial intelligence–challenges and opportunities for international HRM: A review and research agenda. *International Journal of Human Resource Management, 33*(6), 1065–1097. DOI: 10.1080/09585192.2022.2035161

Bughin, J., Seong, J., Manyika, J., Chui, M., & Joshi, R. (2018). *Notes from the AI frontier: Modeling the impact of AI on the world economy.* McKinsey Global Institute.

Burnes, B., & Bargal, D. (2023). Complexity and Uncertainty: Revisiting Stacey's Matrix in a Post-Pandemic World. *Management Decision, 61*(1), 101–117.

Burnes, B., & Cooke, B. (2022). Re-evaluating Lewin's Legacy: Contemporary Relevance of the Three-Step Model. *Human Relations, 75*(1), 5–27.

Burrell, G., & Morgan, G. (1979). *Sociological paradigms and organisational analysis: Elements of the sociology of corporate life.* Heinemann.

Caine, K., & Han, Y. (2021). Ethical implications of AI-enabled workplace monitoring: A review. *Ethics and Information Technology, 23*(3), 399–414. DOI: 10.1007/s10676-021-09603-4

Calay, V. (2019). Une administration 4.0 ? Les enjeux du développement d'une stratégie digitale pour le Service public de Wallonie. *Reflets et perspectives de la vie économique, Tome LVII*(3), 55-71. Cairn.info. DOI: 10.3917/rpve.583.0055

Camburn, D. (1993). Organizational learning and ethical decision making. *Journal of Business Ethics, 12*(8), 607–616.

Carucci, R. (2016). Why Organizations Don't Learn. *Harvard Business Review.*

Castells, M. (2010). Globalisation, Networking, Urbanisation: Reflections on the Spatial Dynamics of the Information Age. *Urban Studies (Edinburgh, Scotland), 47*(13), 2737–2745. DOI: 10.1177/0042098010377365

Cawsey, T. F., Deszca, G., & Ingols, C. (2023). *Organizational Change: An Action-Oriented Toolkit* (4th ed.). SAGE Publications.

CESE. (2022). *Pour une intelligence artificielle responsable au service du développement humain.* Conseil Économique, Social et Environnemental du Maroc. Retrieved from.

Chaddad, A., Katib, Y., & Hassan, L. (2021). Future artificial intelligence tools and perspectives in medicine. *Current Opinion in Urology, 31*(4), 371–377. DOI: 10.1097/MOU.0000000000000884 PMID: 33927099

Chai, T. Y., & Nizam, I. (2021). Impact of Artificial Intelligence In Automotive Industries Transformation. *International Journal of Information System and Engineering, 9*(1), 1–35. DOI: 10.24924/ijise/2021.04/v9.iss2/01.35

Chamola, V., Hassija, V., Sulthana, A. R., Ghosh, D., Dhingra, D., & Sikdar, B. (2023). A review of trustworthy and explainable artificial intelligence (xai). *IEEE Access : Practical Innovations, Open Solutions, 11*, 78994–79015. DOI: 10.1109/ACCESS.2023.3294569

Char, D. S., Shah, N. H., & Magnus, D. (2018). Implementing Machine Learning in Health Care—Addressing Ethical Challenges. *The New England Journal of Medicine, 378*(11), 981–983. DOI: 10.1056/NEJMp1714229 PMID: 29539284

Charmaz, K. (2006). *Constructing grounded theory: A practical guide through qualitative analysis.* Sage Publications.

Chatterjee, M., Ahmed, A., Dadure, P., & Pakray, P. (2022, April). Inclination of NLP applications towards stereotypical and gender biased results. In *Proceedings of the International Conference on Innovative Computing & Communication (ICICC).* DOI: 10.2139/ssrn.4096410

Chatterjee, S. (2020). AI strategy of India : Policy framework, adoption challenges and actions for government. *Transforming Government: People. Transforming Government, 14*(5), 757–775. DOI: 10.1108/TG-05-2019-0031

Chebrolu, A., Sasmal, S. K., Behera, R. N., & Das, S. K. (2020). Prediction of factor of safety for slope stability using advanced artificial intelligence techniques. In Advanced Engineering Optimization Through Intelligent Techniques: Select Proceedings of AEOTIT 2018, 173-181. DOI: 10.1007/978-981-13-8196-6_16

Cheng, L., Liu, F., & Yao, W. (2020). Data cleaning for financial machine learning: A practical guide. *The Journal of Financial Data Science*, *2*(3), 22–39.

Chen, T., & Guestrin, C. (2016). XGBoost: A scalable tree boosting system. *Proceedings of the 22nd ACM SIGKDD International Conference on Knowledge Discovery and Data Mining*, 785–794.

Chen, Z. (2023). Ethics and discrimination in artificial intelligence-enabled recruitment practices. *Humanities & Social Sciences Communications*, *10*(1), 1–12. DOI: 10.1057/s41599-023-02079-x

Cheong, B. C. (2024). Transparency and accountability in AI systems : Safeguarding wellbeing in the age of algorithmic decision-making. *Frontiers in Human Dynamics*, *6*, 1421273. DOI: 10.3389/fhumd.2024.1421273

Chernov, A. V., Chernova, V. A., & Komarova, T. V. (2020). The Usage of Artificial Intelligence in Strategic Decision Making in Terms of Fourth Industrial Revolution. *Proceedings of the 1st International Conference on Emerging Trends and Challenges in the Management Theory and Practice (ETCMTP 2019)*. DOI: 10.2991/aebmr.k.200201.005

Chesterman, S. (2019). Artificial Intelligence and the Problem of Autonomy. SSRN *Electronic Journal*. DOI: 10.2139/ssrn.3450540

Cheung, G. W., Cooper-Thomas, H. D., Lau, R. S., & Wang, L. C. (2024). Reporting reliability, convergent and discriminant validity with structural equation modeling : A review and best-practice recommendations. *Asia Pacific Journal of Management*, *41*(2), 745–783. DOI: 10.1007/s10490-023-09871-y

Chicco, D., Tötsch, N., & Jurman, G. (2021). The coefficient of determination R^2 is more informative than SMAPE, MAE, MAPE, MSE and RMSE in regression analysis evaluation. *PeerJ. Computer Science*, *7*, e623. DOI: 10.7717/peerj-cs.623 PMID: 34307865

Chi, M., Huang, R., & George, J. F. (2020). Collaboration in demand-driven supply chain : Based on a perspective of governance and IT-business strategic alignment. *International Journal of Information Management*, *52*(C), 1–40.

Chin, Y. S., Mohamad, A. A., & Lo, M. C. (2024). Harnessing the power of artificial intelligence (AI): A paradigm shift in HRM practices for employee sustainable performance. *Global Knowledge, Memory and Communication.* Advance online publication. DOI: 10.1108/GKMC-06-2024-0355

Chivu, I., Popescu, D. I., & Ciulu, R. (2023). Human-Centered Change Management in the Digital Era: A Review of the ADKAR Model. *Procedia: Social and Behavioral Sciences, 299*, 87–94. DOI: 10.1016/j.sbspro.2023.02.011

Chomiak, K., Miktus, M., Chomiak, K., & Miktus, M. (2021, August 10). Harnessing value from data science in business: ensuring explainability and fairness of solutions. Consensus. https://consensus.app/papers/harnessing-value-from-data-science-in-business-ensuring-chomiak-miktus/68bfffc21b1d52a2936bf14a0f073a48/

Chouaib, A. (2014). The impact of ethical behavior on organizational performance. *Revue des Sciences de Gestion, 41*(3), 123–135.

Chouaya, M., & Jarboui, A. (2017). Determinants of dividend policy in Tunisia. *International Journal of Business and Management Studies, 6*(1), 38–52.

Chukwuani, V. N., & Egiyi, M. A. (2020). Automation of accounting processes: Impact of artificial intelligence. [IJRISS]. *International Journal of Research and Innovation in Social Science, 4*(8), 444–449.

Clampitt, P. G., DeKoch, R. J., & Cashman, T. (2000). A strategy for communicating about uncertainty. *The Academy of Management Perspectives, 14*(4), 41–57. DOI: 10.5465/ame.2000.3979815

Coiera, E., Westbrook, J. I., & Wyatt, J. C. (2006). Section 1 : Health and Clinical Mangement: The Safety and Quality of Decision Support Systems. *Yearbook of Medical Informatics, 15*(1), 20–25. DOI: 10.1055/s-0038-1638469

Collins, C., Dennehy, D., Conboy, K., & Mikalef, P. (2021). Artificial intelligence in information systems research : A systematic literature review and research agenda. *International Journal of Information Management, 60*, 1–17. DOI: 10.1016/j.ijinfomgt.2021.102383

Comité de Bâle sur le contrôle bancaire. (2006). International convergence of capital measurement and capital standards: A revised framework (June 2006). Basel Committee on Banking Supervision.

Comité de Bâle sur le contrôle bancaire. (2010). Basel III: A global regulatory framework for more resilient banks and banking systems (revised version June 2011). Basel Committee on Banking Supervision.

Commission européenne. (2021). Proposal for a regulation laying down harmonised rules on artificial intelligence (Artificial Intelligence Act). COM/2021/206 final. https://eur-lex.europa.eu/legal-content/EN/TXT/?uri=CELEX%3A52021PC0206

Cortes, C., & Vapnik, V. (1995). Support-vector networks. *Machine Learning*, *20*(3), 273–297. DOI: 10.1007/BF00994018

Costanza-Chock, S., Raji, I. D., & Buolamwini, J. (2022, June). Who audits the auditors? Recommendations from a field scan of the algorithmic auditing ecosystem. In *Proceedings of the 2022 ACM Conference on Fairness, Accountability, and Transparency* (pp. 1571–1583). DOI: 10.1145/3531146.3533213

Crauser, C., Delorme, J., & Perret, B. (1989). *Initiation aux méthodes quantitatives appliquées à l'économie*. La Découverte.

Criado, J. I., Dias, T. F., Sano, H., Rojas-Martín, F., Silvan, A., & Filho, A. I. (2021). Public Innovation and Living Labs in Action : A Comparative Analysis in post-New Public Management Contexts. *International Journal of Public Administration*, *44*(6), 451–464. DOI: 10.1080/01900692.2020.1729181

Criado, J. I., Sandoval-Almazan, R., & Gil-Garcia, J. R. (2013). Government innovation through social media. *Government Information Quarterly*, *30*(4), 319–326. DOI: 10.1016/j.giq.2013.10.003

Crisanto, J. C., Ehrentraud, J., Fabian, M., & Monteil, A. (2024). *Perspectives of the Financial Stability Institute*. Bank for International Settlements.

Crowder, J. A., Carbone, J., & Friess, S. (2020). Human–AI Collaboration. In *Artificial Psychology* (pp. 35–50). Springer International Publishing., DOI: 10.1007/978-3-030-17081-3_4

Curtin, D., & Mendes, J. (2011). Transparence et participation : Des principes démocratiques pour l'administration de l'union européenne: *Revue française d'administration publique, n° 137-138*(1), 101-121. DOI: 10.3917/rfap.137.0101

Cusumano, A. M., Gawer, A., & Yoffie, B. D. (2019). *The Business of Platforms: Strategy in the Age of Digital Competition, Innovation, and Power*. Harper Business.

Cyert, R. M., & March, J. G. (1963). A behavioral theory of the firm. *Englewood Cliffs, NJ, 2*(4), 169-187.

da Costa Nunes, E. H., de Oliveira, J. C. B., de Queiroz Melo, L. M., Feitosa, C. E. A., & Monteiro, I. T. (2024). Democracy out-of-the-box : Analysis of compliance with constitutional principles in tax policies that use Artificial Intelligence. *Journal on Interactive Systems*, *15*(1), 333–348. DOI: 10.5753/jis.2024.3879

Daft, R. L. (1978). A dual-core model of organizational innovation. *Academy of Management Journal, 21*(2), 193–210. DOI: 10.2307/255754

Damanpour, F. (1988). Innovation type, radicalness, and the adoption process. *Communication Research, 15*(5), 545–567. DOI: 10.1177/009365088015005003

Damanpour, F., & Aravind, D. (2012). Managerial innovation: Conceptions, processes and antecedents. *Management and Organization Review, 8*(2), 423–454. DOI: 10.1111/j.1740-8784.2011.00233.x

Dang, C., Li, F., & Yang, C. (2018). Measuring firm size in empirical corporate finance. *Journal of Banking & Finance, 86*, 159–176. DOI: 10.1016/j.jbankfin.2017.09.006

Darnall, N., Henriques, I., & Sadorsky, P. (2005). Adopting proactive environmental strategy: The influence of stakeholders and firm size. *Journal of Management Studies, 47*(6), 1072–1094. DOI: 10.1111/j.1467-6486.2009.00873.x

Datta, A. (2022). The digitalising state : Governing digitalisation-as-urbanisation in the global south. *Progress in Human Geography, 47*(1), 030913252211417. DOI: 10.1177/03091325221141798

Davenport, T. H., & Ronanki, R. (2018). Artificial intelligence for the real world. HBR's 10 Must Reads, 67.

Davenport, T. H., & Ronanki, R. (2018). Artificial Intelligence for the Real World. *Harvard Business Review, 96*(1), 108–116.

Davis, F. D. (1989). Perceived usefulness, perceived ease of use, and user acceptance of information technology. *Management Information Systems Quarterly, 13*(3), 319–340. DOI: 10.2307/249008

Davison, R. M., Martinsons, M. G., & Kock, N. (2009). Ethical decision making in software piracy: Initial development and test of a four-component model. *Management Information Systems Quarterly, 33*(1), 167–180.

De Almeida, P. G. R., dos Santos, C. D., & Farias, J. S. (2021). Artificial intelligence regulation: A framework for governance. *Ethics and Information Technology, 23*(3), 505–525. DOI: 10.1007/s10676-021-09593-z

De Boer, N., & Raaphorst, N. (2023). Automation and discretion : Explaining the effect of automation on how street-level bureaucrats enforce. *Public Management Review, 25*(1), 42–62. DOI: 10.1080/14719037.2021.1937684

DeAngelo, H., DeAngelo, L., & Stulz, R. M. (2006). Dividend policy and the earned/contributed capital mix: A test of the lifecycle theory. *Journal of Financial Economics, 81*(2), 227–254. DOI: 10.1016/j.jfineco.2005.07.005

Delgado, C., & Zeller, F. (2023). Emotion recognition and the ethics of AI in organizational change. *AI & Society*, *38*(1), 177–194. DOI: 10.1007/s00146-022-01384-9

Dell Technologies & IDC. (2022). *The Digital Transformation Index Morocco*. Retrieved from.

DeLone, W. H., & McLean, E. R. (1992). Information systems success : The quest for the dependent variable. *Information Systems Research*, *3*(1), 60–95.

DeLone, W. H., & McLean, E. R. (2003a). The DeLone and McLean model of information systems success : A ten-year update. *Journal of Management Information Systems*, *19*(4), 9–30.

Dewasiri, N. J., Yatiwelle Koralalage, W. B., Azeez, A. A., Jayarathne, P. G. S. A., Kuruppuarachchi, D., & Weerasinghe, V. A. (2019). Determinants of dividend policy: Evidence from an emerging and developing market. *Managerial Finance*, *45*(3), 413–429. DOI: 10.1108/MF-09-2017-0331

Dhinakaran, D., Thenmozhi, D., & Karthikeyan, P. (2020). AI-powered chatbots for organizational support: Roles and use cases. *Journal of Organisational Transformation & Social Change*, *17*(3), 243–258.

Digiampietri, L. A., Roman, N. T., Meira, L. A., Jambeiro Filho, J., Ferreira, C. D., Kondo, A. A., Constantino, E. R., Rezende, R. C., Brandao, B. C., & Ribeiro, H. S. (2008). Uses of artificial intelligence in the Brazilian customs fraud detection system. *DG. O*, 181-187. https://www.academia.edu/download/84397920/digiampietri-dgo08.pdf

Digiposte. (2024). *Digital trust : Traceability of dematerialized documents*. https://business.digiposte.fr/blog/ressources-humaines/confiance-numerique-comment-est-assuree-la-tracabilite-des-documents-dematerialises/

Dima, J., Gilbert, M. H., Dextras-Gauthier, J., & Giraud, L. (2024). The effects of artificial intelligence on human resource activities and the roles of the human resource triad: Opportunities and challenges. *Frontiers in Psychology*, *15*, 1360401. DOI: 10.3389/fpsyg.2024.1360401 PMID: 38903456

Djafer, B. M., & Reda, S. M. (2020). *L'Administration Electronique levier de Modernisation de l'Administration Publique. N°15*, 405-425.

Dodig-Crnkovic, G., Basti, G., & Holstein, T. (2024). *Delegating Responsibilities to Intelligent Autonomous Systems: Challenges and Benefits*. DOI: 10.20944/preprints202411.1179.v1

Dong, J. J., Yan, S. M., & Yang, X. W. (2024). Influencing Factors and Mechanisms of Value Co-Creation in Artificial Intelligence-Driven Human Resource Management: A System Dynamics Simulation. *Systems, 12*(9), 352. DOI: 10.3390/systems12090352

Doshi-Velez, F., & Kim, B. (2017). Towards a rigorous science of interpretable machine learning. arXiv preprint arXiv:1702.08608. https://arxiv.org/abs/1702.08608

Duan, Y., Edwards, J. S., & Dwivedi, Y. K. (2019). Artificial intelligence for decision making in the era of Big Data–evolution, challenges and research agenda. *International Journal of Information Management*, *48*, 63–71.

Du, J. (2024). Ethical and Legal Challenges of AI in Human Resource Management. *Journal of Computing and Electronic Information Management, 13*(2), 2024. DOI: 10.54097/83j64ub9

Du, J., Cai, H., & Jin, X. (2024). Exploring the Association Between Artificial Intelligence Management and Green Innovation: Expanding the Research Field for Sustainable Outcomes. *Sustainability (Basel), 16*(21), 9315. DOI: 10.3390/su16219315

Dupont, L., Fliche, O., & Yang, S. (2020). *Governance of artificial intelligence in finance*. Banque de France.

Dwivedi, D. (2023). Algorithmic Bias : A Challenge for Ethical Artificial Intelligence (AI). In *Immersive Technology and Experiences* (p. 67-84). Springer Nature Singapore. https://doi.org/DOI: 10.1007/978-981-99-8834-1_5

Dwivedi, A., Agrawal, D., & Madaan, J. (2020). Identification and prioritization of issues to implementation of information-facilitated product recovery system for a circular economy. *Modern Supply Chain Research and Applications*, *2*(4), 247–280.

Dyllick, T., & Hockerts, K. (2002). Au-delà de l'analyse de rentabilité pour la durabilité de l'entreprise. *Stratégie commerciale et environnement, 11*(2), 130-141.

Easterbrook, F. H. (1984). Two agency-cost explanations of dividends. *The American Economic Review*, *74*(4), 650–659.

El Mesbahi, M., & Alaoui, A. (2022). Le changement organisationnel au Maroc: Entre rationalité managériale et contraintes culturelles. *Revue Marocaine de Gestion et d'Économie, 13*(1), 45–62.

El Mesbahi, M., & Alaoui, A. (2022). Les dynamiques culturelles de la transformation numérique au Maroc. *Revue Marocaine de Gestion*, *18*(1), 45–59.

El Ouidani, R., & Oul-Caid, B. (2023). The adoption of AI in the Moroccan banking sector: Between economic and legal issues. Journal of Economics, Management [JEMED]. *Environmental Law (Northwestern School of Law)*, *6*(1).

El-Ghoul, M., Almassri, M. M., El-Habibi, M. F., Al-Qadi, M. H., Abou Eloun, A., Abu-Nasser, B. S., & Abu-Naser, S. S. (2024). *AI in HRM: Revolutionizing Recruitment*. Performance Management, and Employee Engagement.

Elliot, V. H., Paananen, M., & Staron, M. (2020). Artificial Intelligence for Decision-Makers. *Journal of Emerging Technologies in Accounting*, *17*(1), 51–55. DOI: 10.2308/jeta-52666

Eloundou, T., Manning, S., Mishkin, P., & Rock, D. (2023). GPTs are GPTs: An early look at the labor market impact potential of large language models. OpenAI Technical Report.

Errabih, F. (2020). Individual ethics and organizational ethics: Two facets of ethical decision-making. *Revue des Sciences de Gestion*, *45*(2), 89–102.

Etalab. (2021). *Supporting administrations in the use of public algorithms*. https://www.etalab.gouv.fr/algorithmes-publics

Etikan, I., Musa, S. A., & Alkassim, R. S. (2016). Comparison of convenience sampling and purposive sampling. *American Journal of Theoretical and Applied Statistics*, *5*(1), 1–4. DOI: 10.11648/j.ajtas.20160501.11

Eubanks, V. (2018). *Automating inequality : How high-tech tools profile, police, and punish the poor*. St. Martin's Press.

European Commission. (2023). Hiroshima Process International Code of Conduct for Advanced AI Systems, https://digital-strategy.ec.europa.eu/en/library/hiroshima-process international-code-conduct-advanced-ai-systems.

European Commission. (2023). *Proposal for a Regulation laying down harmonised rules on artificial intelligence*. https://eur-lex.europa.eu/legal-content/EN/TXT/HTML/?uri=CELEX:52021PC0206

European Commission. (2024). *AI adoption in the public sector : A new study on key influencing factors and two frameworks for competencies and governance. AI Watch*. https://ai-watch.ec.europa.eu/news/ai-adoption-public-sector-new-study-key-influencing-factors-and-two-frameworks-competencies-and-2024-11-25_en

Evrard, Y., Pras, B., & Roux, E. (2003). Market: études et recherches en marketing (3e éd.). Paris: Dunod.

Evrard, Y., Pras, B., Roux, E., & Desmet, P. (2003). *Market : Études et recherches en marketing*. Dunod.

Faheem, M. A., Anwer, S., Rayhan, Z., Ullah, M. A., Paudel, R., Ahmed, M. F., & Khan, H. (2024). AI-Driven Innovation In HRM And Its Impact On Business Management: An In-Depth Study Of Technology Advancement And Strategic Implementation. *Nanotechnology Perceptions*, *20*, 1174–1204.

Fama, E. F., & French, K. R. (2001). Disappearing dividends: Changing firm characteristics or lower propensity to pay? *Journal of Financial Economics*, *60*(1), 3–43. DOI: 10.1016/S0304-405X(01)00038-1

Farazi, M. Z. R. (2024). Exploring the role of artificial intelligence in managing emerging risks: An in-depth study of AI applications in financial institutions' risk frameworks. *The American Journal of Management and Economics Innovations*, *6*(10), 20–40. DOI: 10.37547/tajmei/Volume06Issue10-04A

Farinu, U. (2025). Fairness, Accountability, and Transparency in AI: Ethical Challenges in Data-Driven Decision-Making. Available at *SSRN* 5128174. DOI: 10.2139/ssrn.5128174

Farooq, M., Ramzan, M., & Yen, Y. Y. (2025). Artificial Intelligence in Business and Law.

Fenwick, A., Molnar, G., & Frangos, P. (2024). The critical role of HRM in AI-driven digital transformation: A paradigm shift to enable firms to move from AI implementation to human-centric adoption. *Discover Artificial Intelligence*, *4*(1), 34. DOI: 10.1007/s44163-024-00125-4

Fernández-Delgado, M., Cernadas, E., Barro, S., & Amorim, D. (2014). Do we need hundreds of classifiers to solve real world classification problems? *Journal of Machine Learning Research*, *15*(1), 3133–3181.

Fernandez, T., & Gupta, S. (2022). Smart leadership: The impact of AI-based personalization on digital leadership effectiveness. *Journal of Leadership & Organizational Studies*, *29*(4), 457–472.

Ferrell, O. C., & Gresham, L. G. (1985). A contingency framework for understanding ethical decision making in marketing. *Journal of Marketing*, *49*(3), 87–96. DOI: 10.1177/002224298504900308

Ferrell, O. C., Johnston, M. W., & Ferrell, L. (1989). A synthesis of ethical decision models for marketing. *Journal of Macromarketing*, *9*(2), 55–64. DOI: 10.1177/027614678900900207

Fiegler-Rudol, J., Lau, K., Mroczek, A., & Kasperczyk, J. (2025). Exploring Human–AI Dynamics in Enhancing Workplace Health and Safety: A Narrative Review. *International Journal of Environmental Research and Public Health*, *22*(2), 199. DOI: 10.3390/ijerph22020199 PMID: 40003424

Fielt, E. (2024). Digital Business Model Innovation: An External Enablement Perspective and Research Agenda. *Journal of Business Models*, *12*(3), 19–41. DOI: 10.54337/jbm.v12i3.8470

Figoli, F. (2022, June 16). AI in design idea development: A workshop on creativity and human-AI collaboration. *Proceedings of Design Research Society*. DOI: 10.21606/drs.2022.414

Firoz, M. (2024). IT in HRM: Enhancing efficiency and employee engagement.

Fischer, T., & Krauss, C. (2018). Deep learning with long short-term memory networks for financial market predictions. *European Journal of Operational Research*, *270*(2), 654–669. DOI: 10.1016/j.ejor.2017.11.054

Flanagan, O. (2004). *The science of the mind*. MIT Press.

Floridi, L., & Cowls, J. (2022). A unified framework of five principles for AI in society. *Harvard Data Science Review*, *4*(1). Advance online publication. DOI: 10.1162/99608f92.8cd550d1

Floridi, L., Cowls, J., Beltrametti, M., Chatila, R., Chazerand, P., Dignum, V., & Vayena, E. (2018). AI4People-an ethical framework for a good AI society: Opportunities, risks, principles, and recommendations. *Minds and Machines*, *28*(4), 689–707. DOI: 10.1007/s11023-018-9482-5 PMID: 30930541

Fonds Monétaire International. (2021). *Fiscal Monitor : Digitalization and Public Finances*. Fonds Monétaire International. https://www.imf.org/en/Publications/FM/Issues/2021/10/13/fiscal-monitor-october-2021

Forat Yazdi, E., Chitsaz, E., & Etemadi, M. (2024). *Demystifying Artificial Intelligence (AI) in Human Resource Management (HRM): A Bibliometric Analysis of Explainable Artificial Intelligence (XAI)(2013-2023)*. Sciences and Techniques of Information Management.

Ford, J. D., Ford, L. W., & D'Amelio, A. (2008). Resistance to change: The rest of the story. *Academy of Management Review*, *33*(2), 362–377. DOI: 10.5465/amr.2008.31193235

Ford, R. C., & Richardson, W. D. (1994). Ethical decision making: A review of the empirical literature. *Journal of Business Ethics, 13*(3), 205–221. DOI: 10.1007/BF02074820

Fornell, C., & Larcker, D. F. (1981). Evaluating Structural Equation Models with Unobservable Variables and Measurement Error. *JMR, Journal of Marketing Research, 18*(1), 39–50. DOI: 10.1177/002224378101800104

Fowler, F. J. (2014). *Survey research methods*. Sage Publications.

Freeman, R. E. (1984). *Strategic Management: A Stakeholder Approach*. Pitman.

Fremeaux, S., & Noel, G. (2015). Moral development according to Kohlberg: An application in an organizational context. *Journal of Responsible Organization, 10*(2), 45–60.

Frost, J. (2021). *Regression analysis: An intuitive guide for using and interpreting linear models*. Statistics By Jim Publishing.

Fui-Hoon Nah, F., Zheng, R., Cai, J., Siau, K., & Chen, L. (2023). Generative AI and ChatGPT: Applications, challenges, and AI-human collaboration. *Journal of Information Technology Case and Application Research, 25*(3), 277–304. DOI: 10.1080/15228053.2023.2233814

Gallego-Gomez, C., & De-Pablos-Heredero, C. (2020). Artificial intelligence as an enabling tool for the development of dynamic capabilities in the banking industry. [IJEIS]. *International Journal of Enterprise Information Systems, 16*(3), 20–33. DOI: 10.4018/IJEIS.2020070102

Gandomi, A., & Haider, M. (2015). Beyond the hype: Big data concepts, methods, and analytics. *International Journal of Information Management, 35*(2), 137–144. DOI: 10.1016/j.ijinfomgt.2014.10.007

Gao, L., Chen, Z., & Wen, J. (2023). Trust and transparency in AI-mediated communication: Empirical evidence from workplace settings. *Computers in Human Behavior, 141*, 107614.

García-Martínez, A., Pérez-Moreno, S., & Sánchez-Cuesta, A. (2022). Artificial intelligence for the management of environmental sustainability: An overview. *Environmental Science and Pollution Research International, 29*(30), 45128–45147.

Garg, S., Sinha, S., Kar, A. K., & Mani, M. (2022). A review of machine learning applications in human resource management. *International Journal of Productivity and Performance Management, 71*(5), 1590–1610. DOI: 10.1108/IJPPM-08-2020-0427

Garrity, E. J. (1994). User participation, management support and system types. [IRMJ]. *Information Resources Management Journal, 7*(3), 34–43.

Geels, F. W. (2010). Ontologies, socio-technical transitions (to sustainability), and the multi-level perspective. *Research Policy, 39*(4), 495–510.

Geloune, R. B. (2024). Predictive Accuracy of Performance in Knowledge Work: Comparison of Human Judgment, Regression and Artificial Intelligence Models (Doctoral dissertation, Case Western Reserve University).

General Data Protection Regulation (GDPR). (2018). *Article 22 - Automated individual decision-making*. Official Journal of the European Union.

Gentsch, P., van Geenen, D., & Schmid, B. (2021). AI and human decision-making: A hybrid approach for ethical outcomes. *Journal of Artificial Intelligence Research, 70*, 1–25.

Ge, Y., Tan, J., Zhu, Y., Xia, Y., Luo, J., Liu, S., Fu, Z., Geng, S., Li, Z., & Zhang, Y. (2022). Explainable fairness in recommendation. *Proceedings of the 45th International ACM SIGIR Conference on Research and Development in Information Retrieval*, 681–691. DOI: 10.1145/3477495.3531973

Ghosh, S., Das, A., Sanyal, S., & Srivastava, A. (2023). AI-powered communication analytics in enterprise systems: Framework and case applications. *Journal of Organizational Computing and Electronic Commerce, 33*(1), 45–62. DOI: 10.1080/10919392.2022.2139034

Gilpin, L. H., Bau, D., Yuan, B. Z., Bajwa, A., Specter, M., & Kagal, L. (2018). Explaining Explanations: An Overview of Interpretability of Machine Learning. 2022 IEEE 9th International Conference on Data Science and Advanced Analytics (DSAA), 80–89. DOI: 10.1109/DSAA.2018.00018

Girard, J. P. (2007). Organizational culture and its impact on ethical decision-making. *Management, 32*(3), 45–58.

Glaser, B. G., Strauss, A. L., & Strutzel, E. (1968). *The discovery of grounded theory; strategies for qualitative research.* Nursing research. https://journals.lww.com/nursingresearchonline/Citation/1968/07000/The_Discovery_of_Grounded_Theory__Strategies_for.14.aspx

Glickman, J., & Jordan, C. (2024). *How AI Can Support Cities' Sustainability Goals. National League of Cities.* https://www.nlc.org/article/2024/04/08/how-ai-can-support-cities-sustainability-goals/

Glover, S. M., Prawitt, D. F., & Spilker, B. C. (1996). The influence of decision aids on user behavior: Implications for knowledge acquisition and inappropriate reliance. *Organizational Behavior and Human Decision Processes, 72*(2), 232–255. DOI: 10.1006/obhd.1997.2735

Godlewski, C. J. (2004). Consistency of bank ratings with profitability and default in emerging countries. Management and Economics Research Laboratory, University Robert Schuman. Working Paper No. 65.

Goleman, D., Boyatzis, R., & McKee, A. (2013). *Primal Leadership: Unleashing the Power of Emotional Intelligence*. Harvard Business Press.

Goodfellow, I., Pouget-Abadie, J., Mirza, M., Xu, B., Warde-Farley, D., Ozair, S., Courville, A., & Bengio, Y. (2014). Generative adversarial nets. *Advances in neural information processing systems, 27*. https://proceedings.neurips.cc/paper/5423-generative-adversarial-nets

Goodfellow, I. (2016). *Deep learning* (Vol. 196). MIT press.

Goodwin, T. (2015). *The Battle is for the Customer Interface*. Https://Techcrunch.Com/2015/03/03/in-the-Age-of-Disintermediation-the-Battle-Is-All-for-the-Customer-Interface/

Graham, J. R., & Harvey, C. R. (2001). The theory and practice of corporate finance: Evidence from the field. *Journal of Financial Economics, 60*(2–3), 187–243. DOI: 10.1016/S0304-405X(01)00044-7

Griffith, T. L., & Dougherty, D. J. (2001). Beyond socio-technical systems : Introduction to the special issue. *Journal of Engineering and Technology Management, 18*(3-4), 207–218.

Groves, R. M., Fowler, F. J., Couper, M. P., Lepkowski, J. M., Singer, E., & Tourangeau, R. (2009). *Survey methodology*. John Wiley & Sons.

Guerlain, S., Brown, D. E., & Mastrangelo, C. (2000). Intelligent decision support systems. *Conference proceedings. International conference on systems, man and cybernetics.'cybernetics evolving to systems, humans, organizations, and their complex interactions, 3*, 1934-1938. https://ieeexplore.ieee.org/abstract/document/886396/

Guest, G., Bunce, A., & Johnson, L. (2006). How many interviews are enough? An experiment with data saturation and variability. *Field Methods, 18*(1), 59–82. DOI: 10.1177/1525822X05279903

Gulson, K. N., & Webb, P. T. (2017). Mapping an emergent field of 'computational education policy' : Policy rationalities, prediction and data in the age of Artificial Intelligence. *Research in Education*, *98*(1), 14–26. DOI: 10.1177/0034523717723385

Gunning, D., & Aha, D. (2019). DARPA's explainable artificial intelligence (XAI) program. *AI Magazine*, *40*(2), 44–58. DOI: 10.1609/aimag.v40i2.2850

Gupta, R. (2024). Impact of Artificial Intelligence (AI) on Human Resource Management (HRM). International Journal For Multidisciplinary Research, doi, 10.

Gupta, D., & Ranjan, P. (2022). Machine learning in finance: Data quality, preprocessing, and applications. *International Journal of Finance & Economics*, *27*(1), 1–20.

Gupta, S., Modgil, S., Bhattacharyya, S., & Bose, I. (2022). Artificial intelligence for decision support systems in the field of operations research : Review and future scope of research. *Annals of Operations Research*, *308*(1), 215–274. DOI: 10.1007/s10479-020-03856-6

Haenlein, M., & Kaplan, A. (2019). A brief history of artificial intelligence: On the past, present, and future of artificial intelligence. *California Management Review*, *61*(4), 5–14. DOI: 10.1177/0008125619864925

Hair, J. F., Black, W. C., Babin, B. J., & Anderson, R. E. (2010). *Multivariate data analysis : Pearson College division*. Person.

Hair, J. F., Risher, J. J., Sarstedt, M., & Ringle, C. M. (2019). When to use and how to report the results of PLS-SEM. *European Business Review*, *31*(1), 2–24. DOI: 10.1108/EBR-11-2018-0203

Hair, J., Hult, G. T. M., Ringle, C., & Sarstedt, M. (2022). *A Primer on Partial Least Squares Structural Equation Modeling*. PLS-SEM.

Hall, P., Gill, N., Kurka, T., & Pham, H. (2021). A unified view of model interpretability: Shapley values and beyond. *Communications of the ACM*, *64*(8), 59–66. DOI: 10.1145/3453192

Hamel, G. (2006). The why, what, and how of management innovation. *Harvard Business Review*, *84*(2), 72. PMID: 16485806

Hamet, P., & Tremblay, J. (2017). *Artificial Intelligence in Medicine (A. ten Teije* (Popow, C., Holmes, J. H., & Sacchi, L., Eds.). Vol. 10259). Springer International Publishing., DOI: 10.1007/978-3-319-59758-4

Hanna, M., Pantanowitz, L., Jackson, B., Palmer, O., Visweswaran, S., Pantanowitz, J., Deebajah, M., & Rashidi, H. (2024). Ethical and Bias considerations in artificial intelligence (AI)/machine learning. *Modern Pathology*, •••, 100686. PMID: 39694331

Hantem, A. (2019). L'introduction d'une Comptabilité D'exercice Au Sein Des Centres Hospitaliers Universitaires Au Maroc: Caractéristiques Et Analyse Des Facteurs D'adoption Et De Succès (Doctoral dissertation, Université Hassan II Casablanca).

Hantem, A. (2023). Le Recours aux Nouveaux Outils du Management Public: Vers Un Systeme Comptable Fiable Et Transparent. *Revue D'Etudes en Management et Finance D'Organisation*, *8*(1).

Hantem, A., Emzi, K., Youssoufi, N., Emzi, K., Mkik, M., & Outaaza, K. (2024). Factors Influencing Patient Satisfaction with the Use of Teleconsultation in Morocco. In Bansal, J. C., Borah, S., Hussain, S., & Salhi, S. (Eds.), *Computing and Machine Learning. CML 2024. Lecture Notes in Networks and Systems* (Vol. 1108). Springer., DOI: 10.1007/978-981-97-6588-1_33

Hantem, A., Soussi, H., Emzi, K., & Emzi, K. (2024). Analysis of the Perception of Innovations Adoption in Public Health Establishments in Morocco: Crossed Perspectives of Healthcare Professionals. In Motahhir, S., & Bossoufi, B. (Eds.), *Digital Technologies and Applications. ICDTA 2024. Lecture Notes in Networks and Systems* (Vol. 1098). Springer., DOI: 10.1007/978-3-031-68650-4_53

Han, Y. (2022). The Impact of Industrial Robots on the Skill-Based Wage Gap. *American Journal of Industrial and Business Management*, *12*(04), 571–602. DOI: 10.4236/ajibm.2022.124031

Haque, A. B., Islam, A. N., & Mikalef, P. (2023). Explainable Artificial Intelligence (XAI) from a user perspective: A synthesis of prior literature and problematizing avenues for future research. *Technological Forecasting and Social Change*, *186*, 122120. DOI: 10.1016/j.techfore.2022.122120

Harrison, C., Tomás, C., & Crook, C. (2014). An e-maturity analysis explains intention– behavior disjunctions in technology adoption in UK schools. *Computers in Human Behavior*, *34*, 345–351. DOI: 10.1016/j.chb.2013.10.042

Harter, J. K., Schmidt, F. L., & Hayes, T. L. (2002). Business-unit-level relationship between employee satisfaction, employee engagement, and business outcomes : A meta-analysis. *The Journal of Applied Psychology*, *87*(2), 268–279. DOI: 10.1037/0021-9010.87.2.268 PMID: 12002955

Hassija, V., Chamola, V., Mahapatra, A., Singal, A., Goel, D., Huang, K., Scardapane, S., Spinelli, I., Mahmud, M., & Hussain, A. (2024). Interpreting black-box models: A review on explainable artificial intelligence. *Cognitive Computation*, *16*(1), 45–74. DOI: 10.1007/s12559-023-10179-8

Hastie, T., Tibshirani, R., & Friedman, J. (2009). *The Elements of Statistical Learning: Data Mining, Inference, and Prediction*. Springer. DOI: 10.1007/978-0-387-84858-7

Hatch, N. W., Mackey, T. B., Freeman, C., & Louca, F. (2002). As Time Goes by: From the Industrial Revolutions to the Information Revolution. *Academy of Management Review*, *27*(2), 306. DOI: 10.2307/4134358

Hayes, J. (2022). *The Theory and Practice of Change Management* (6th ed.). Palgrave Macmillan.

Heidemann, A., Hülter, S. M., & Tekieli, M. (2024). Machine learning with real-world HR data: Mitigating the trade-off between predictive performance and transparency. *International Journal of Human Resource Management*, *35*(14), 2343–2366. DOI: 10.1080/09585192.2024.2335515

Heifetz, R. A., & Linsky, M. (2022). *Leadership on the Line: Staying Alive through the Dangers of Leading*. Harvard Business Press.

Heinrich, C. J. (2002). Outcomes–Based Performance Management in the Public Sector : Implications for Government Accountability and Effectiveness. *Public Administration Review*, *62*(6), 712–725. DOI: 10.1111/1540-6210.00253

Henseler, J., Ringle, C. M., & Sarstedt, M. (2015). A new criterion for assessing discriminant validity in variance-based structural equation modeling. *Journal of the Academy of Marketing Science*, *43*(1), 115–135. DOI: 10.1007/s11747-014-0403-8

Heron, J. (1996). Ethical decision-making in business: Issues and dilemmas. *Revue Française de Gestion*, *22*(109), 78–89.

Hiatt, J. (2006). *ADKAR: A Model for Change in Business, Government and Our Community*. Prosci Learning Center.

Hiatt, J. (2021). *ADKAR: A Model for Change in Business, Government, and Our Community*. Prosci Learning Center Publications.

High-Level Expert Group on Artificial Intelligence. (2019). *Ethics guidelines for trustworthy AI*. European Commission.

Highsmith, J. (2009). *Agile Project Management: Creating Innovative Products* (2nd ed.). Addison-Wesley Professional.

Hill, C. J., & Lynn Jr, L. E. (2016). *Public management : Thinking and acting in three dimensions. CQ Press*. 39-65. http://dx.doi.org/DOI: 10.4135/9781483395814.n2

Hofeditz, L., Clausen, S., Rieß, A., Mirbabaie, M., & Stieglitz, S. (2022). Applying XAI to an AI-based system for candidate management to mitigate bias and discrimination in hiring. *Electronic Markets*, *32*(4), 2207–2233. DOI: 10.1007/s12525-022-00600-9 PMID: 36568961

Hoornweg, D., & Bhada-Tata, P. (2012). *What a Waste: A Global Review of Solid Waste Management*. Urban Development Series. World Bank., DOI: 10.1596/17388

Horney, N., Pasmore, B., & O'Shea, T. (2021). Agile Leadership and Change: Building Organizational Adaptability. *OD Practitioner*, *53*(2), 7–14.

Hu, P.-H. (2003). Evaluating telemedicine systems success : A revised model. *36th Annual Hawaii International Conference on System Sciences, 2003. Proceedings of the*, 8-pp. https://ieeexplore.ieee.org/abstract/document/1174379/

Huang, C., Zhang, Z., Mao, B., & Yao, X. (2023). An Overview of Artificial Intelligence Ethics. *IEEE Transactions on Artificial Intelligence*, *4*(4), 799–819. DOI: 10.1109/TAI.2022.3194503

Huang, M.-H., & Rust, R. T. (2021). Artificial intelligence in service. *Journal of Service Research*, *24*(1), 3–20.

Huang, Z. (2018). Discussion on the development of artificial intelligence in taxation. *American Journal of Industrial and Business Management*, *8*(08), 1817–1824. DOI: 10.4236/ajibm.2018.88123

Huberman, A. M. (2019). *Qualitative data analysis: A methods sourcebook*. Sage Publications.

Hwang, M. I., & Thorn, R. G. (1999). The effect of user engagement on system success : A meta-analytical integration of research findings. *Information & Management*, *35*(4), 229–236.

Iansiti, M., & Lakhani, R. K. (2020). *Competing in the Age of AI: Strategy and Leadership When Algorithms and Networks Run the World*. Harvard Business Press.

Ibrahim, A. K., & Benabdelhadi, A. (2021). La transformation digitale de l'administration publique : Revue de littérature systématique. *International Journal of Accounting, Finance, Auditing. Management and Economics*, *2*(5), 5. Advance online publication. DOI: 10.5281/zenodo.5528289

Igbaria, M., Zinatelli, N., Cragg, P., & Cavaye, A. L. (1997). Personal computing acceptance factors in small firms : A structural equation model. *MIS quarterly. JSTOR*, *21*(3), 279–305.

Inmon, W. H. (1996). The data warehouse and data mining. *Communications of the ACM*, *39*(11), 49–51.

Institute of Internal Auditors (IIA). (2017). Intelligence artificielle: Le futur de l'audit interne. Tone at the top, N°85. https://docs.ifaci.com/wp-content/uploads/2018/03/tone-at-the-top-85-ia.pdf

Institute of Internal Auditors. (1947). *Statement of Responsibilities of Internal Auditing*. IIA.

Institute of Internal Auditors-Morocco. (2019). Définition de l'audit interne. Retrieved February 2, 2025, from https://www.iiamaroc.org/definition-de-laudit-interne/

International Organization for Standardization. (2023). ISO/IEC 42001:2023 – Artificial intelligence management system (AIMS) – Requirements with guidance. https://www.iso.org/standard/81230.html

INTOSAI. (2023). The use of artificial intelligence (AI) in the execution of audits. Science and Technology in Audit, 50(2). Retrieved January 5, 2025, from https://intosaijournal.org/journal-entry/the-use-of-artificial-intelligence-ai-in-the-execution-of-audits/

Irawan, Y. (2020). Decision support system for employee bonus determination with web-based simple additive weighting (SAW) method in PT. Mayatama Solusindo. [JAETS]. *Journal of Applied Engineering and Technological Science*, *2*(1), 7–13.

Islam, M. R. (2024). *Explainable Artificial Intelligence for Enhancing Transparency in Decision Support Systems*. Malardalen University.

Ismail, I. A., & Aloshi, J. M. (2025). Data Privacy in AI-Driven Education : An In-Depth Exploration Into the Data Privacy Concerns and Potential Solutions. In *AI Applications and Strategies in Teacher Education* (p. 223-252). IGI Global. https://www.igi-global.com/chapter/data-privacy-in-ai-driven-education/358899

Ismatullaev, U. V. U., & Kim, S. (2022). Review of the factors affecting acceptance of AI-Infused Systems. *Human Factors*, *66*(1), 126–144. DOI: 10.1177/00187208211064707 PMID: 35344676

Jafri, S., Upreti, S., Saiyad, F. B. J., Madhukar, K. S., Chaturvedi, V. M., & Divakaran, P. (2024, March). Effectiveness of Artificial Intelligence for Enhancing Decision-Making Process of Recruitment in HRM Process. In 2024 IEEE International Conference on Contemporary Computing and Communications (InC4) (Vol. 1, pp. 1-6). IEEE. DOI: 10.1109/InC460750.2024.10649327

Jaidi, L., & Msadfa, Y. (2017). *La Complexité de la Remontée des Chaînes de valeur Mondiale : Cas des Industries Automobile et Aéronautique au Maroc et en Tunisie/ The Complexity of the Rise of Global Value Chains: The Case of Automotive and Aeronautics Industries in Morocco and Tunisia* (Policy Paper, p. 1-48). OCP Policy Center.

Jain, R. (2024). Transparency in AI Decision Making: A Survey of Explainable AI Methods and Applications. *Advances of Robotic Technology*, *2*(1), 1–10. DOI: 10.23880/art-16000110

Jamal, A., Aissaoui, K., & Kassal, S. (2024, December). Enhancing Recruitment Transparency and Efficiency with Explainable AI (XAI). In 2024 3rd International Conference on Embedded Systems and Artificial Intelligence (ESAI) (pp. 1-6). IEEE.

Jangphanish, K., Boonyanet, W., & Tongkong, S. (2025). Analyzing robust dividend payout policy with dynamic panel regression: Application of speed of adjustment to half-life. *PLoS One*, *20*(1), e0316478. DOI: 10.1371/journal.pone.0316478 PMID: 39813290

Janiesch, C., Zschech, P., & Heinrich, K. (2021). Machine learning and deep learning. *Electronic Markets*, *31*(3), 685–695. DOI: 10.1007/s12525-021-00475-2

Janssen, M., & Kuk, G. (2016). The challenges and limits of big data algorithms in technocratic governance. *Government Information Quarterly*, *33*(3), 371–377. DOI: 10.1016/j.giq.2016.08.011

Japan International Cooperation Agency (JICA), BCG. (2022). *Study for the promotion of the African automotive industry : Post-COVID 19 supply chain and mobility reform.*

Jarrahi, M. H. (2023). Artificial Intelligence and the Future of Work: Human-AI Symbiosis in Organizational Decision-Making. *International Journal of Information Management*, *68*, 102620.

Jena, B., Saxena, S., Nayak, G. K., Saba, L., Sharma, N., & Suri, J. S. (2021). Artificial intelligence-based hybrid deep learning models for image classification: The first narrative review. *Computers in Biology and Medicine*, *137*, 104803. DOI: 10.1016/j.compbiomed.2021.104803 PMID: 34536856

Jensen, M. C. (1986). Agency costs of free cash flow, corporate finance, and takeovers. *The American Economic Review*, *76*(2), 323–329.

Jensen, M. C., & Meckling, W. H. (1976). Theory of the firm: Managerial behavior, agency costs, and ownership structure. *Journal of Financial Economics*, *3*(4), 305–360. DOI: 10.1016/0304-405X(76)90026-X

Johnson, G. M. (2021). Algorithmic bias : On the implicit biases of social technology. *Synthese*, *198*(10), 9941–9961. DOI: 10.1007/s11229-020-02696-y

Johnson, R. A., & Wichern, D. W. (2007). *Applied Multivariate Statistical Analysis*. Pearson Education India.

Jones, T. M. (1991). Ethical decision making by individuals in organizations: An issue-contingent model. *Academy of Management Review*, *16*(2), 366–395. DOI: 10.2307/258867

Jordan, M. I., & Mitchell, T. M. (2015). Machine learning: Trends, perspectives, and prospects. *Science*, *349*(6245), 255–260. DOI: 10.1126/science.aaa8415 PMID: 26185243

Ju, J., Meng, Q., Sun, F., Liu, L., & Singh, S. (2023). Citizen preferences and government chatbot social characteristics : Evidence from a discrete choice experiment. *Government Information Quarterly*, *40*(3), 101785. DOI: 10.1016/j.giq.2022.101785

Kacprzyk, J. (2022). AI-enabled Decision Aid and Decision Support for Symbiotic Autonomous Systems. IEEE, 4–5. DOI: 10.1109/ICCICC57084.2022.10101649

Kamal, S. M., & Qour, T. E. (2024). La transformation digitale des administrations publiques et la performance des services publics : Définition, compréhension du processus et agenda de recherche. *Revue Française d'Economie et de Gestion*, *5*(7), 7. https://www.revuefreg.fr/index.php/home/article/view/1673

Kapiriri, L., Norheim, O. F., & Martin, D. K. (2008). Fairness and accountability for reasonableness. Do the views of priority setting decision makers differ across health systems and levels of decision making? *Social Science & Medicine*, *68*(4), 766–773. DOI: 10.1016/j.socscimed.2008.11.011 PMID: 19070414

Kaplan, A. M., & Haenlein, M. (2016). Higher education and the digital revolution: About MOOCs, SPOCs, social media, and the Cookie Monster. *Business Horizons*, *59*(4), 441–450. DOI: 10.1016/j.bushor.2016.03.008

Kaplan, A. M., & Haenlein, M. (2020). Rulers of the world, unite! The challenges and opportunities of artificial intelligence. *Business Horizons*, *63*(1), 37–50. DOI: 10.1016/j.bushor.2019.09.003

Kaplan, A., & Haenlein, M. (2019). Siri, Siri, in my hand : Who's the fairest in the land? On the interpretations, illustrations, and implications of artificial intelligence. *Business Horizons*, *62*(1), 15–25. DOI: 10.1016/j.bushor.2018.08.004

Karaa, M., Bentahar, O., & Benzidia, S. (2016). Les facteurs d'adoption d'une innovation appliquée aux flux de patients: Le cas d'un centre hospitalier au Luxembourg. *Logistique & Management*, *24*(2), 98–109. DOI: 10.1080/12507970.2016.1249527

Kaur, J. (2024). Responsible Artificial Intelligence (AI) Governance: Ethical Frameworks for Business Decision-Making. In Ethical Quandaries in Business Practices: Exploring Morality and Social Responsibility (pp. 337-368). IGI Global.

Kaur, A., & Wadhawan, K. (2023). AI : Job Creator or Jobless Future. *International Journal For Multidisciplinary Research*, *5*(4), 4520. Advance online publication. DOI: 10.36948/ijfmr.2023.v05i04.4520

Kaza, S., Yao, L., Bhada-Tata, P., & Van Woerden, F. (2018). *What a Waste 2.0: A Global Snapshot of Solid Waste Management to 2050*. Urban Development Series. World Bank., DOI: 10.1596/978-1-4648-1329-0

Kaziba Mpaata, A., Lubogoyi, B., & Okiria, J. C. (2017). The effect of internal audit department function on the performance of the internal control system of a public hospital in Uganda.

Kefi, H. (2010). Mesures perceptuelles de l'usage des systèmes d'information : Application de la théorie du comportement planifié. Humanisme et Entreprise, 297(2), 45-64. Cairn.info. DOI: 10.3917/hume.297.0045

Kéfi, M. K., & Sarr, M. (2014). Cultural influences on ethical decision making: A comparative study. *Journal of Business Ethics*, *123*(4), 573–586.

Kettinger, W. J., & Lee, C. C. (1994). Perceived service quality and user satisfaction with the information services function. *Decision Sciences*, *25*(5-6), 737–766.

Khafif, H., & Touhami, N. O. (2024). Les conséquences de l'exclusion socio-économique des jeunes sous la perspective de la croissance inclusive. *International Journal of Accounting, Finance, Auditing, Management and Economics*, *5*(7), 583-599. https://ijafame.org/index.php/ijafame/article/view/1642

Khair, M. A., Mahadasa, R., Tuli, F. A., & Ande, J. R. P. K. (2020). Beyond human judgment: Exploring the impact of artificial intelligence on HR decision-making efficiency and fairness. *Global Disclosure of Economics and Business*, *9*(2), 163–176. DOI: 10.18034/gdeb.v9i2.730

Khalifa, M., & Liu, V. (2003). Determinants of successful knowledge management programs. *Electronic Journal of Knowledge Management, 1*(2), 101–110.

Kimball, R. (1996). *The data warehouse toolkit : Practical techniques for building dimensional data warehouses*. John Wiley & Sons, Inc.

Kimberly, J. R., & Evanisko, M. J. (1981). Organizational innovation: The influence of individual, organizational, and contextual factors on hospital adoption of technological and administrative innovations. *Academy of Management Journal, 24*(4), 689–713. DOI: 10.2307/256170 PMID: 10253688

Kim, Y., Myeong, S., & Ahn, M. J. (2023). Living labs for AI-enabled public services : Functional determinants, user satisfaction, and continued use. *Sustainability (Basel), 15*(11), 8672. DOI: 10.3390/su15118672

Kingma, D. P. (2013). *Auto-encoding variational bayes*.

Kitchin, R. (2014). The real-time city? Big data and smart urbanism. *GeoJournal, 79*(1), 1–14. DOI: 10.1007/s10708-013-9516-8

Kohavi, R. (1995). A study of cross-validation and bootstrap for accuracy estimation and model selection. *IJCAI (United States), 14*(2), 1137–1145.

Kohlberg, L. (1969). Stage and sequence: The cognitive-developmental approach to socialization. In Goslin, D. A. (Ed.), *Handbook of socialization theory and research* (pp. 347–480). Rand McNally.

Kok, J. N., Boers, E. J., Kosters, W. A., Van der Putten, P., & Poel, M. (2009). Artificial intelligence: definition, trends, techniques, and cases. Artificial intelligence, 1(270-299), 51.

Kokina, J., & Davenport, T. H. (2017). The emergence of artificial intelligence: How automation is changing auditing. *Journal of Emerging Technologies in Accounting, 14*(1), 115–122. DOI: 10.2308/jeta-51730

König, P. D., & Wenzelburger, G. (2020). Opportunity for renewal or disruptive force? How artificial intelligence alters democratic politics. *Government Information Quarterly, 37*(3), 101489. DOI: 10.1016/j.giq.2020.101489

Kotler, P., Kartajaya, H., & Setiawan, I. (2017). *Marketing 4.0: Moving from traditional to digital*. Wiley.

Kotter, J. P. (1996). *Leadership and Leading Change*. Harvard Business Review Press.

Kotter, J. P. (2014). *Accelerate: Building Strategic Agility for a Faster-Moving World*. Harvard Business Review Press.

Kotter, J. P., & Schlesinger, L. A. (1979). Choosing Strategies for Change. *Harvard Business Review*, *57*(2), 106–114. PMID: 10240501

Kouki, M., & Guizani, M. (2009). Ownership structure and dividend policy in the context of the Tunisian stock market. *Journal of Business Finance & Accounting*, *36*(7–8), 861–885.

Ko, Y., & Leem, C. S. (2021). The Influence of AI Technology Acceptance and Ethical Awareness towards Intention to Use. *Journal of Digital Convergence*, *19*(3), 217–225. DOI: 10.14400/jdc.2021.19.3.217

Krauss, C., Do, X. A., & Huck, N. (2017). Deep neural networks, gradient-boosted trees, random forests: Financial prediction at Nasdaq. *European Journal of Operational Research*, *259*(2), 689–702. DOI: 10.1016/j.ejor.2016.10.031

Kuhfeld, W. F. (2010). Logistic regression modeling using SAS: Theory and application. SAS Institute. https://support.sas.com/resources/papers/proceedings10/264-2010.pdf

Kuhn, M., & Johnson, K. (2013). *Applied predictive modeling*. Springer. DOI: 10.1007/978-1-4614-6849-3

Kumar, A., & Sinha, P. (2024). Changing dividend payout behavior and predicting dividend policy in emerging markets: Evidence from India. *Investment Management & Financial Innovations*, *21*(1), 259–274. DOI: 10.21511/imfi.21(1).2024.20

Kurmangali, M., Yeraliyeva, Y., & Beimisheva, A. (2024). Digitalization and artificial intelligence in central asia: Governmental responses and further implications. *Public Policy and Administration, 23*(2), 146-159. *Scopus.* Advance online publication. DOI: 10.13165/VPA-24-23-2-03

Kuswara, Z., Pasaribu, M., Fitriana, F., & Santoso, R. A. (2024). Artificial Intelligence in Financial Reports : How it Affects the Process's Effectiveness and Efficiency. *Jurnal ilmu keuangan dan perbankan (jika), 13*(2), 257-272. https://doi.org/DOI: 10.34010/jika.v13i2.12730

Kwok, K. (2024). *Gulf's AI strategy is built on more than sand. Reuters Breakingviews.* https://www.reuters.com/breakingviews/gulfs-ai-strategy-is-built-more-than-sand-2024-11-13/

La Porta, R., Lopez-de-Silanes, F., & Shleifer, A. (1999). Corporate ownership around the world. *The Journal of Finance*, *54*(2), 471–517. DOI: 10.1111/0022-1082.00115

Lafon, L. (2016). L'audit légal des établissements publics de santé. Gestion et management.

Lainey, P. (2015). Ethics in business: A developmental perspective. *Management, 40*(4), 67–78.

Landers, R. N., & Behrend, T. S. (2023). Auditing the AI auditors: A framework for evaluating fairness and bias in high stakes AI predictive models. *The American Psychologist, 78*(1), 36–49. DOI: 10.1037/amp0000972 PMID: 35157476

Lane, J. E. (2014). Method, Theory, and Multi-Agent Artificial Intelligence. *Journal for the Cognitive Science of Religion, 1*(2), 161–180. DOI: 10.1558/jcsr.v1i2.161

Langer, M., & König, C. (2022). Explainability of artificial intelligence in human resources. In *Handbook of research on artificial intelligence in human resource management* (pp. 285–302). Edward Elgar Publishing.

Langer, M., König, C. J., Back, C., & Hemsing, V. (2023). Trust in artificial intelligence: Comparing trust processes between human and automated trustees in light of unfair bias. *Journal of Business and Psychology, 38*(3), 493–508. DOI: 10.1007/s10869-022-09829-9

Larsson, S., & Heintz, F. (2020). Transparency in artificial intelligence. *Internet Policy Review, 9*(2). Advance online publication. DOI: 10.14763/2020.2.1469

Laskawiec, A., & Lizot, J. (2014). Fiabilisation et certification des comptes des établissements publics de santé. Gestion & Finances Publiques, 3-4.

Le Moigne, J.-L. (1977). La dynamique de l'homme au travail. Une nouvelle approche par l'analyse de système. *Revue Française de Sociologie, JSTOR, 18*(3), 528–530.

Le Roy, F., Robert, M., & Giuliani, P. (2013). L'innovation managériale. Revue française de gestion, 235(6), 77-90.

Leben, D. (2023). Explainable AI as evidence of fair decisions. *Frontiers in Psychology, 14*, 1069426. Advance online publication. DOI: 10.3389/fpsyg.2023.1069426 PMID: 36865358

LeCun, Y., Bengio, Y., & Hinton, G. (2015). Deep learning. *Nature, 521*(7553), 436–444. DOI: 10.1038/nature14539 PMID: 26017442

Lee, M. K., Jain, A., Cha, H. J., Ojha, S., & Kusbit, D. (2019). Procedural justice in algorithmic fairness. Proceedings of the ACM on Human-Computer Interaction, 3(CSCW), 1–26. DOI: 10.1145/3359284

Lee, J. D., & See, K. A. (2004). Trust in automation: Designing for appropriate reliance. *Human Factors, 46*(1), 50–80. DOI: 10.1518/hfes.46.1.50.30392 PMID: 15151155

LegalProd. T. (2024). Transparence Des Algorithmes. *LEGALPROD*. https://www.legalprod.com/transparence-des-algorithmes/

Legge, K. (1989). Information technology : Personnel management's lost opportunity? *Personnel Review*, *18*(5), 2–61.

Lewicka, D., Starowicz-Rajca, H., Blbas, R., & Wilczewski, A. (2024). Cultivating Success: A Practical Exploration Of Applying Artificial Intelligence In Human Resources Management. Scientific Papers of Silesian University of Technology. Organization & Management/Zeszyty Naukowe Politechniki Slaskiej. Seria Organizacji i Zarzadzanie, (199).

Liakos, K. G., Busato, P., Moshou, D., Pearson, S., & Bochtis, D. (2018). Machine learning in agriculture: A review. *Sensors (Basel)*, *18*(8), 2674. DOI: 10.3390/s18082674 PMID: 30110960

Liberal Forum. (2020). *Predictive Analytics and AI in Governance*. https://liberalforum.eu/wp-content/uploads/2021/07/PUBLICATION_AI-in-e-governance.pdf

Lincoln, Y. S., & Guba, E. G. (1985). *Naturalistic inquiry*. Sage Publications. DOI: 10.1016/0147-1767(85)90062-8

Lintner, J. (1956). Distribution of incomes of corporations among dividends, retained earnings, and taxes. *The American Economic Review*, *46*(2), 97–113.

Lipton, Z. C. (2018). The mythos of model interpretability. *Communications of the ACM*, *61*(10), 36–43. DOI: 10.1145/3233231

Li, X., Peng, L., Hu, Y., Shao, J., & Chi, T. (2016). Deep learning architecture for air quality prediction. *Environmental Science and Pollution Research International*, *23*(22), 22408–22417. DOI: 10.1007/s11356-016-7812-9 PMID: 27734318

Logsdon, J. M., & Yuthas, K. (1997). Corporate social performance, stakeholder orientation, and organizational moral development. *Journal of Business Ethics*, *16*(12), 1213–1226. DOI: 10.1023/A:1005741931995

Louziri, I., & Oubal, M. (2022). Determinants of dividend policy in Morocco: An empirical study of listed companies. *Moroccan Journal of Finance and Management*, *8*(1), 31–47.

Lugano, G. (2017). Virtual assistants and self-driving cars. *15th International Conference on ITS Telecommunications (ITST)*, 1-5. https://ieeexplore.ieee.org/abstract/document/7972192/

Lundberg, S. M., & Lee, S.-I. (2017). A unified approach to interpreting model predictions. Advances in Neural Information Processing Systems, 30, 4765–4774. https://proceedings.neurips.cc/paper_files/paper/2017/file/8a20a8621978632d76c43dfd28b67767-Paper.pdf

Lundberg, S. M., Erion, G., Chen, H., DeGrave, A., Prutkin, J. M., Nair, B., Katz, R., Himmelfarb, J., Bansal, N., & Lee, S.-I. (2020). From local explanations to global understanding with explainable AI for trees. *Nature Machine Intelligence*, *2*(1), 56–67. DOI: 10.1038/s42256-019-0138-9 PMID: 32607472

Lundberg, S. M., & Lee, S. (2017). A unified approach to interpreting model predictions. *Advances in Neural Information Processing Systems*, *30*, 4765–4774.

Luo, J., Meng, Q., & Cai, Y. (2018). Analysis of the impact of artificial intelligence application on the development of accounting industry. *Open Journal of Business and Management*, *6*(4), 850–856.

Machkour, B., & Abriane, A. (2020). Industry 4.0 and its Implications for the Financial Sector. *Procedia Computer Science*, *177*(1), 496–502. DOI: 10.1016/j.procs.2020.10.068

Mackrell, D., Kerr, D., & von Hellens, L. (2009). A qualitative case study of the adoption and use of an agricultural decision support system in the Australian cotton industry : The socio-technical view. *Decision Support Systems*, *47*(2), 143–153. DOI: 10.1016/j.dss.2009.02.004

Magatef, S., Al-Okaily, M., Ashour, L., & Abuhussein, T. (2023). The impact of electronic customer relationship management strategies on customer loyalty : A mediated model. *Journal of Open Innovation*, *9*(4), 100149. DOI: 10.1016/j.joitmc.2023.100149

Makridakis, S. (2017). The forthcoming Artificial Intelligence (AI) revolution: Its impact on society and firms. *Futures*, *90*, 46–60. DOI: 10.1016/j.futures.2017.03.006

Maleka, S. (2023). *Enhancing efficiency and decision-making in government through AI in Strategic Planning and Strategic Management Processes*. ResearchGate. https://www.researchgate.net/profile/Stevens-Maleka-2/publication/372516160_Enhancing_Efficiency_and_Decision-Making_in_Government_through_AI_in_Strategic_Planning_and_Strategic_Management_Processes/links/64bb7d42b9ed6874a5389331/Enhancing-Efficiency-and-Decision-Making-in-Government-through-AI-in-Strategic-Planning-and-Strategic-Management-Processes.pdf

Mantouzi, S., Youssef, S., El Mouatassim, A., Ourahou, Y., Jafi, H., Zouhouredine, I., & Hamliri, M. (2024). Leveraging AI for business intelligence : A pathway to improved organizational performance in Morocco's manufacturing sector. *Multidisciplinary Science Journal, Accepted Articles*. https://malque.pub/ojs/index.php/msj/article/view/7254

Mantouzi, S., & Said, Y. (2023). Intelligence artificielle et performance du secteur de l'enseignement supérieur marocain : Enjeux et interactions. *Revue Française d'Economie et de Gestion*, *4*(11), 21–42.

Maqsudi, A., Rachmawati, T., & Hwihanus, H. (2022). Influencing Factors Dividend Policy: Empirical Evidence From Different Parts Of The World. *Eduvest*, *2*(7). Advance online publication. DOI: 10.59188/eduvest.v2i7.527

Margetts, H., & Dorobantu, C. (2019). Rethink government with AI. *Nature*, *568*(7751), 163–165. DOI: 10.1038/d41586-019-01099-5 PMID: 30967667

Markaoui, K., & Hassine, M. (2018). Définition de la performance des services hospitaliers: enquête au sein du chu mohammed VI d'oujda. Revue du contrôle, de la comptabilité et de l'audit, 2(3).

Marketscreener. (2024). Morocco Listed Companies Financial Data. https://www.marketscreener.com/stock-exchange/shares/africa/morocco-95/

Marsh, D., & McConnell, A. (2010). TOWARDS A FRAMEWORK FOR ESTABLISHING POLICY SUCCESS. *Public Administration*, *88*(2), 564–583. DOI: 10.1111/j.1467-9299.2009.01803.x

Martin, D. K., Giacomini, M., & Singer, P. A. (2002). Fairness, accountability for reasonableness, and the views of priority setting decision-makers. *Health Policy (Amsterdam)*, *61*(3), 279–290. DOI: 10.1016/S0168-8510(01)00237-8 PMID: 12098521

Martins, A., & Wu, H. (2021). Emotional intelligence in AI-assisted change management. *Journal of Organizational Psychology*, *21*(5), 92–104.

McCarthy, J. (2007). From here to human-level AI. *Artificial Intelligence*, *171*(18), 1174–1182. DOI: 10.1016/j.artint.2007.10.009

McCullagh, P. (1980). Regression models for ordinal data. *Journal of the Royal Statistical Society. Series B, Statistical Methodology*, *42*(2), 109–142. https://www.jstor.org/stable/2984952. DOI: 10.1111/j.2517-6161.1980.tb01109.x

McDavid, J. C., Huse, I., & Hawthorn, L. R. (2018). *Program evaluation and performance measurement : An introduction to practice*. Sage Publications.

Mckeen, J. D., & Guimaraes, T. (1997). Successful Strategies for User Participation in Systems Development. *Journal of Management Information Systems*, *14*(2), 133–150. DOI: 10.1080/07421222.1997.11518168

McKeen, J. D., Guimaraes, T., & Wetherbe, J. C. (1994). The relationship between user participation and user satisfaction : An investigation of four contingency factors. *Management Information Systems Quarterly*, *18*(4), 427–451.

McKinsey & Company. (2021). The State of AI in 2021.

McKinsey & Company. (2023). Scaling Gen AI in banking: Choosing the best operating model. https://www.mckinsey.com/industries/financial-services/our-insights/scaling-gen-ai-in-banking-choosing-the-best-operating-model

Mehrabi, N., Morstatter, F., Saxena, N., Lerman, K., & Galstyan, A. (2021). A Survey on Bias and Fairness in Machine Learning. *ACM Computing Surveys*, *54*(6), 1–35. DOI: 10.1145/3457607

Menant, L. (2021). L'acceptabilité de l'intelligence artificielle appliquée aux systèmes d'information des ressources humaines: cas d'un agent conversationnel. Psychologie. Université Paul Valéry - Montpellier III, Français. ffNNT: 2021MON30091ff. fftel-03697429f

Men, L. R., & Bowen, S. A. (2021). *Excellence in internal communication management*. Business Expert Press.

Mergel, I., Rethemeyer, R. K., & Isett, K. (2016). Big Data in Public Affairs. *Public Administration Review*, *76*(6), 928–937. DOI: 10.1111/puar.12625

Metawa, N., Xu, Z., Zhu, G., & Zhou, Q. (2022). Machine learning-based customer meta-combination brand equity analysis for marketing behavior evaluation. *Information Processing & Management*, *59*(1), 102800. DOI: 10.1016/j.ipm.2021.102800

Mettler, T., Sprenger, M., & Winter, R. (2017). Service robots in hospitals : New perspectives on niche evolution and technology affordances. *European Journal of Information Systems*, *26*(5), 451–468. DOI: 10.1057/s41303-017-0046-1

Mhlambi, S. (2020). From rationality to relationality: Ubuntu as an ethical framework for AI. Carr Center for Human Rights Policy Working Paper Series. Harvard Kennedy School. https://carrcenter.hks.harvard.edu/publications/ubuntu-ethical-framework-ai

Michel, S. (2011). *Contribution à l'évaluation du système d'information bancaire* [Thèse de doctorat, Université Montesquieu]. https://www.theses.fr/2011BOR40047

Michel, E. J., By, R. T., & Burnes, B. (2022). Leading and managing change: Revisiting Kotter's 8-step change model. *Journal of Change Management*, *22*(1), 19–36.

Michel, S., & Cocula, F. (2014). L'évaluation des systèmes d'information : Un état de l'art à la lumière des approches de la variance et processuelles. *Management & Avenir*, *74*(8), 33–51.

Mighiss, S., & Kabbaj, S. (2021). L'audit à l'ère de la transformation digitale. Revue du contrôle, de la comptabilité et de l'audit, 5(3).

Miller, M. H., & Rock, K. (1985). Dividend policy under asymmetric information. *The Journal of Finance*, *40*(4), 1031–1051. DOI: 10.1111/j.1540-6261.1985.tb02362.x

Miller, T. (2019). Explanation in artificial intelligence: Insights from the social sciences. *Artificial Intelligence*, *267*, 1–38. DOI: 10.1016/j.artint.2018.07.007

Milojević, N., & Redzepagic, S. (2021). Prospects of artificial intelligence and machine learning application in banking risk management. *Journal of Central Banking Theory and Practice*, *10*(3), 41–57. DOI: 10.2478/jcbtp-2021-0023

Ministère de la Transition Énergétique et du Développement Durable (MTE DD). (2021). *Stratégie Nationale de Développement Durable (SNDD).* Gouvernement du Royaume du Maroc. https://mtedd.gov.ma/images/Rapport_Strategie_Nationale_DD_juin2017_Mai_2017_Web.pdf

Minvielle, E., Sicotte, C., Champagne, F., Contandriopoulos, A. P., Jeantet, M., Préaubert, N., Bourdil, A., & Richard, C. (2008). Hospital performance: Competing or shared values? *Health Policy (Amsterdam)*, *87*(1), 8–19. DOI: 10.1016/j.healthpol.2007.09.017 PMID: 18035448

Mirani, R., & Lederer, A. L. (1998). An Instrument for Assessing the Organizational Benefits of IS Projects. *Decision Sciences*, *29*(4), 803–838. DOI: 10.1111/j.1540-5915.1998.tb00878.x

Mittelstadt, B. D., Allo, P., Taddeo, M., Wachter, S., & Floridi, L. (2016). The ethics of algorithms: Mapping the debate. *Big Data & Society*, *3*(2), 1–21. DOI: 10.1177/2053951716679679

Mittelstadt, B., Russell, C., & Wachter, S. (2019). Explaining explanations in AI. In *Proceedings of the Conference on Fairness, Accountability, and Transparency* (pp. 279–288). DOI: 10.1145/3287560.3287574

Mohamed, A., Puteh, M., & Ariffin, A. (2020). Natural Language Processing (NLP) in sentiment analysis: A review. *Indonesian Journal of Electrical Engineering and Computer Science*, *17*(1), 51–59.

Mohr, L. B. (1969). Determinants of innovation in organizations. *The American Political Science Review*, *63*(1), 111–126. DOI: 10.2307/1954288

Molnar, C. (2022). *Interpretable Machine Learning: A Guide for Making Black Box Models Explainable* (2nd ed.)., https://christophm.github.io/interpretable-ml-book/

Morris, A. (2009). Socio-technical systems in ICT : A comprehensive survey. *Technical Report, Information Engineering and Computer Science, DISI-09-054*, 1-16.

Mousa, M., & Mahmood, M. (2022). AI and internal communication in digital transformation: A relational approach. *Journal of Communication Management (London)*, *26*(2), 145–162.

Mrzygłód, U., & Nowak, S. (2017). Market reactions to dividends announcements and payouts: Empirical evidence from the Warsaw Stock Exchange. *Contemporary Economics*, *11*(2), 187–204. DOI: 10.5709/ce.1897-9254.236

Mühlhoff, R. (2023). Predictive privacy : Collective data protection in the context of artificial intelligence and big data. *Big Data & Society*, *10*(1), 20539517231166886. DOI: 10.1177/20539517231166886

Mujtaba, D. F., & Mahapatra, N. R. (2024). Fairness in AI-driven recruitment: Challenges, metrics, methods, and future directions. arXiv preprint arXiv:2405.19699.

Mujtaba, B. G. (2025). Human-AI Intersection: Understanding the Ethical Challenges, Opportunities, and Governance Protocols for a Changing Data-Driven Digital World. *Business Ethics and Leadership*, *9*(1), 109–126. DOI: 10.61093/bel.9(1).109-126.2025

Mumford, E. (1993). The ETHICS approach. *Communications of the ACM*, *36*(6), 82–83. DOI: 10.1145/153571.214824

Mumford, E. (1995). *Effective systems design and requirements analysis approach : The Ethics Approach*. Macmillan.

Munro, L., & Stewart, J. (2011). External auditors' reliance on internal auditing: Further evidence. *Managerial Auditing Journal*, *26*(6), 464–481. DOI: 10.1108/02686901111142530

Mwita, K. M., & Kitole, F. A. (2025). Potential benefits and challenges of artificial intelligence in human resource management in public institutions. *Discover Global Society*, *3*(1), 1–19. DOI: 10.1007/s44282-025-00175-8

Myers, S. C., & Majluf, N. S. (1984). Corporate financing and investment decisions when firms have information that investors do not have. *Journal of Financial Economics*, *13*(2), 187–221. DOI: 10.1016/0304-405X(84)90023-0

Mykytyn, P. P. (1988). An empirical investigation of DSS usage and the user's perception of DSS training. *Information & Management, 14*(1), 9–17. DOI: 10.1016/0378-7206(88)90063-8

Nadimpalli, M. (2017). Artificial Intelligence Risks and Benefits. *International Journal of Innovative Research in Science, Engineering and Technology, 6*(6), 6–6.

Najah Ahmed, A., Binti Othman, F., Abdulmohsin Afan, H., Khaleel Ibrahim, R., Ming Fai, C., Shabbir Hossain, M., Ehteram, M., & Elshafie, A. (2019). Machine learning methods for better water quality prediction. *Journal of Hydrology (Amsterdam), 578*, 124084. DOI: 10.1016/j.jhydrol.2019.124084

Nguyen, T. H., & Kim, Y. (2022). Personalized content generation and employee engagement: The role of AI in internal communication. *Information & Management, 59*(7), 103661. DOI: 10.1016/j.im.2022.103661

Nguyen, T. H., & Kim, Y. (2022). The role of conversational AI in organizational resilience and learning. *Journal of Business Research, 145*, 412–421. DOI: 10.1016/j.jbusres.2022.02.037

Nilsson, N. J. (2005). Human-level artificial intelligence? Be serious! *AI Magazine, 26*(4), 68–68.

Nistor, N. (2014). When technology acceptance models won't work : Non-significant intentionbehavior effects. *Computers in Human Behavior, 34*, 299–300. DOI: 10.1016/j.chb.2014.02.052

Nleya, S. M., & Velempini, M. (2024). Industrial Metaverse: A Comprehensive Review, Environmental Impact, and Challenges. *Applied Sciences (Basel, Switzerland), 14*(13), 5736. DOI: 10.3390/app14135736

Noureddine, B., Said, G., Mohamed, C., & Abdelhak, M. (2024). L'intégration de l'IA dans l'administration des douanes marocaine : Approche prospective stratégique. *American Scientific Journal, 3*(25), 25. Advance online publication. DOI: 10.5281/zenodo.13381535

Ntim, C. G. (2012). Corporate governance and dividend policy in South Africa. *International Review of Applied Economics, 26*(2), 157–174.

Nzobonimpa, S. (2023). Artificial intelligence, task complexity and uncertainty : Analyzing the advantages and disadvantages of using algorithms in public service delivery under public administration theories. *Digital Transformation and Society, 2*(3), 219–234. DOI: 10.1108/DTS-03-2023-0018

O'Neill, A. (2024a, November 7). Inflation rate in Morocco 2029. Statista. https://www.statista.com

O'Neill, A. (2024b, November 7). Gross domestic product (GDP) in Morocco 2029. Statista. https://www.statista.com

Obermeyer, Z., Powers, B., Vogeli, C., & Mullainathan, S. (2019). Dissecting racial bias in an algorithm used to manage the health of populations. *Science*, *366*(6464), 447–453. DOI: 10.1126/science.aax2342 PMID: 31649194

Odilla, F. (2024). Unfairness in AI Anti-Corruption Tools : Main Drivers and Consequences. *Minds and Machines*, *34*(3), 28. DOI: 10.1007/s11023-024-09688-8

OECD. (2020). *Employment Outlook*. Https://Www.Bollettinoadapt.It/Wp-Content/Uploads/2020/07/Document.Pdf.

OECD. (2022). Enhancing SME Transparency and Formalization in the MENA Region.

OECD. (2024). AI In Health: Huge Potential, Huge Risks. https://www.oecd.org/en/publications/ai-in-health_2f709270-en.html

OECD. (2025). *Artificial intelligence*. OECD. https://www.oecd.org/en/topics/artificial-intelligence.html

Ofodile, O. C., Odeyemi, O., Okoye, C. C., Addy, W. A., Oyewole, A. T., Adeoye, O. B., & Ololade, Y. J. (2024). Digital banking regulations: A comparative review between Nigeria and the USA. *Finance & Accounting Research Journal*, *6*(3), 347–371. DOI: 10.51594/farj.v6i3.897

Ogboi, C., & Unuafe, O. K. (2013). Impact of credit risk management and capital adequacy on the financial performance of commercial banks in Nigeria. Journal of Emerging Issues in Economics. *Finance and Banking*, *2*(3), 703–717.

Olaoye, F., & Potter, K. (2024). AI-DRIVEN PREDICTIVE ANALYTICS IN BUSINESS DECISION- MAKING. *Journal of Artificial Intelligence*.

Ononiwu, M. I., Onwuzulike, O. C., Shitu, K., & Ojo, O. O. (2024). Operational risk management in emerging markets: A case study of Nigerian banking institutions. *World Journal of Advanced Research and Reviews*, *23*(3), 446–459. DOI: 10.30574/wjarr.2024.23.3.2705

Oreg, S., Bartunek, J. M., Lee, G., & Do, B. (2021). An affect-based model of recipients' responses to organizational change events. *Academy of Management Review*, *46*(2), 327–346.

Oreg, S., Michel, A., & By, R. T. (2021). *The Psychology of Organizational Change: Viewing Change from the Employee's Perspective*. Cambridge University Press.

Organisation de coopération et de développement économiques. (2019). Principes de l'OCDE sur l'intelligence artificielle. https://www.oecd.org/fr/intelligence-artificielle/principes/

Organisation for Economic Co-operation and Development (OECD). (2024). L'IA dans le domaine de la santé, un immense potentiel, d'énormes risques. Retrieved Februry 4, 2025, from https://www.oecd.org/content/dam/oecd/fr/publications/reports/2024/01/ai-in-health-huge-potential-huge-risks_ff823a24/ebfdeb50-fr.pdf

Orr, J., & Dutta, A. (2023). Multi-Agent Deep Reinforcement Learning for Multi-Robot Applications: A Survey. *Sensors (Basel)*, *23*(7), 3625. DOI: 10.3390/s23073625 PMID: 37050685

Osborne, S. P., Cucciniello, M., Nasi, G., & Zhu, E. (2022). Digital transformation, artificial intelligence and effective public services : Challenges and opportunities. *Global Public Policy and Governance*, *2*(4), 377–380. DOI: 10.1007/s43508-022-00058-7

Ouboumlik, A., & Touhami, N. O. (2024). Digitalization of Public Finances and Public Procurement in Morocco : Impacts on Business Climate. [IJPADA]. *International Journal of Public Administration in the Digital Age*, *11*(1), 1–26. DOI: 10.4018/IJPADA.359178

Ouboumlik, A., & Touhami, N. O. (2024). La transformation digitale de l'administration publique : Revue de littérature systématique. *American Scientific Journal*, *3*(25), 25. Advance online publication. DOI: 10.5281/zenodo.13366459

Oxford Business Group. (2023). Morocco explores opportunities for AI integration across key sectors.

Paillé, P., & Mucchielli, A. (2012). L'analyse qualitative en sciences humaines et sociales (3e éd.). Armand Colin.

Palvia, S. C., Sharma, R. S., & Conrath, D. W. (2001). A socio-technical framework for quality assessment of computer information systems. *Industrial Management & Data Systems*, *101*(5), 237–251.

Papagiannidis, E., Enholm, I. M., Dremel, C., Mikalef, P., & Krogstie, J. (2023). Toward AI governance: Identifying best practices and potential barriers and outcomes. *Information Systems Frontiers*, *25*(1), 123–141. DOI: 10.1007/s10796-022-10251-y PMID: 35464171

Papagiannidis, E., Mikalef, P., Conboy, K., & Van de Wetering, R. (2023). Uncovering the dark side of AI-based decision-making: A case study in a B2B context. *Industrial Marketing Management*, *115*, 253–265. DOI: 10.1016/j.indmarman.2023.10.003

Paramita, D., Okwir, S., & Nuur, C. (2024). Artificial intelligence in talent acquisition: Exploring organisational and operational dimensions. *The International Journal of Organizational Analysis*, *32*(11), 108–131. DOI: 10.1108/IJOA-09-2023-3992

Parasuraman, A., Zeithaml, V. A., & Berry, L. (1988). SERVQUAL : A multiple-item scale for measuring consumer perceptions of service quality. *1988, 64*(1), 12-40.

Park, H., Ahn, D., Hosanagar, K., & Lee, J. (2021, May). Human-AI interaction in human resource management: Understanding why employees resist algorithmic evaluation at workplaces and how to mitigate burdens. In *Proceedings of the 2021 CHI conference on human factors in computing systems* (pp. 1-15). DOI: 10.1145/3411764.3445304

Park, H., Lee, J., & Kim, S. (2023). The role of AI in adaptive communication and leadership behavior. *Technological Forecasting and Social Change*, *190*, 122411.

Parlement européen & Conseil de l'Union européenne. (2016). Règlement général sur la protection des données (RGPD). Règlement (UE) 2016/679. https://eur-lex.europa.eu/legal-content/FR/TXT/?uri=CELEX%3A32016R0679

Pavlidis, G. (2024). Unlocking the black box: Analysing the EU artificial intelligence act's framework for explainability in AI. *Law, Innovation and Technology*, *16*(1), 293–308. DOI: 10.1080/17579961.2024.2313795

Pedregosa, F., Varoquaux, G., Gramfort, A., Michel, V., Thirion, B., Grisel, O., & Vanderplas, J. (2011). Scikit-learn: Machine learning in Python. *Journal of Machine Learning Research*, *12*, 2825–2830.

Peng, S., Kalliamvakou, E., Cihon, P., & Demirer, M. (2023). *The Impact of AI on Developer Productivity: Evidence from GitHub Copilot*.

Perboli, G., Musso, S., & Rosano, M. (2018). Blockchain in logistics and supply chain : A lean approach for designing real-world use cases. *IEEE Access : Practical Innovations, Open Solutions*, *6*, 62018–62028.

Perconti, P., & Plebe, A. (2020). Deep learning and cognitive science. *Cognition*, *203*, 104365. DOI: 10.1016/j.cognition.2020.104365 PMID: 32563082

Percy, S. L. (1980). Response time and citizen evaluation of police. *Journal of Police Science and Administration*, *8*(1), 75–86.

Perez, C. (2002). *Technological Revolutions and Financial Capital.* Edward Elgar Publishing., DOI: 10.4337/9781781005323

Pesqueux, Y. (2004). La notion de performance globale. 5ème forum international sur la performance Globale de l'entreprise. Université Tunis Carthage, 1-2 décembre.

Phillips-Wren, G. (2012). AI TOOLS IN DECISION MAKING SUPPORT SYSTEMS: A REVIEW. *International Journal of Artificial Intelligence Tools, 21*(02), 1240005. DOI: 10.1142/S0218213012400052

Piaget, J. (1932). *The moral judgment of the child.* Free Press.

Picard, R. W. (1997). Affective computing. In *PsycEXTRA Dataset.* DOI: 10.1037/e526112012-054

Piper, D. L. A. (2024). *China-releases-AI-safety-governance-framework.* https://www.dlapiper.com/en-us/insights/publications/2024/09/china-releases-ai-safety-governance-framework

Poisson, Y. (1983). L'approche qualitative et l'approche quantitative dans les recherches en éducation. *Revue des Sciences de l'Education, 9*(3), 369–378.

Polanyi, K. (2001). *The Great Transformation: The Political and Economic Origins of Our Time* (2nd ed. édition). Beacon Press.

Pomahač, R. (2024). Artificial public administration - myth or reality? *Acta Universitatis Carolinae Iuridica, 70*(2), 133-143. *Scopus.* Advance online publication. DOI: 10.14712/23366478.2024.27

Porter, E. M., & Heppelmann, E. J. (2014). How Smart, Connected Products Are Transforming Competition. *Harvard Business Review, 92*, 1–18.

Porter, M. E., & van der Linde, C. (1995). Green and competitive: Breaking the stalemate. *Harvard Business Review, 73*(5), 120–134.

Powell, J. R. (2024). Human Resource Professionals' Perceptions of Trust in Explainable Artificial Intelligence Hiring Software (Doctoral dissertation, National University).

Prikshat, V., Islam, M., Patel, P., Malik, A., Budhwar, P., & Gupta, S. (2023). AI-Augmented HRM: Literature review and a proposed multilevel framework for future research. *Technological Forecasting and Social Change, 193*, 122645. DOI: 10.1016/j.techfore.2023.122645

Probst, P., Wright, M. N., & Boulesteix, A. L. (2019). Hyperparameters and tuning strategies for random forest. *Wiley Interdisciplinary Reviews. Data Mining and Knowledge Discovery*, *9*(3), e1301. DOI: 10.1002/widm.1301

Prosci (2023). Best Practices in Change Management: 12th Edition Benchmarking Report.

Pulapaka, S., Godavarthi, S., & Ding, S. (2024). *Empowering the Public Sector with Generative AI : From Strategy and Design to Real-World Applications*. https://doi.org/DOI: 10.1007/979-8-8688-0473-1

PwC. (2024). *Data and AI-driven urban planning*. https://www.pwc.com/m1/en/publications/documents/2024/data-and-ai-driven-urban-planning.pdf

Radford, A. (2018). *Improving language understanding by generative pre-training*.

Radonjić, A., Duarte, H., & Pereira, N. (2024). Artificial intelligence and HRM: HR managers' perspective on decisiveness and challenges. *European Management Journal*, *42*(1), 57–66. DOI: 10.1016/j.emj.2022.07.001

Rai, A., Constantinides, P., & Sarker, S. (2021). Next-generation digital platforms: Toward human–AI hybrids. *Management Information Systems Quarterly*, *45*(1), iii–ix. DOI: 10.25300/MISQ/2021/16276

Rai, A., Constantinides, P., & Sarker, S. (2022). Next-Generation Digital Platforms: Toward Human-AI Hybrids. *Information Systems Research*, *33*(1), 1–18. DOI: 10.1287/isre.2013.0495

Rai, A., Lang, S. S., & Welker, R. B. (2002). Assessing the validity of IS success models : An empirical test and theoretical analysis. *Information Systems Research*, *13*(1), 50–69.

Raji, I. D., Smart, A., White, R., & Mitchell, M. (2020). Closing the AI accountability gap: Defining an end-to-end framework for internal algorithmic auditing. In *Proceedings of the 2020 Conference on Fairness, Accountability, and Transparency* (pp. 33–44). DOI: 10.1145/3351095.3372873

Ramathilagam, A., & Pitchipoo, P. (2022). Modeling and development of fuzzy logic-based intelligent decision support system. *Romanian Journal of Information Science and Technology*, *25*(1), 58–79.

Ransbotham, S., Kiron, D., Gerbert, P., & Reeves, M. (2017). *Reshaping Business with Artificial Intelligence: Closing the Gap Between Ambition and Action*. MIT Sloan Management Review & The Boston Consulting Group.

Rathi, P., Shringarpure, K., Unnikrishnan, B., Pandey, A., & Nair, A. (2021). *Patient treatment pathways of multidrug-resistant tuberculosis cases in coastal South India : Road to a drug resistant tuberculosis center* (8:498). F1000Research. https://doi.org/DOI: 10.12688/f1000research.17743.5

Renfrew, D., Vasilaki, V., & Katsou, E. (2024). Indicator based multi-criteria decision support systems for wastewater treatment plants. *The Science of the Total Environment, 915*, 1–18. DOI: 10.1016/j.scitotenv.2024.169903

Řepová, H., Zouhar, J., & Král, P. (2024). Attractiveness of firms with chatbot as job interviewers: Does the interviewer-type matter in the first contact with candidates? *International Journal of Communication Networks and Distributed Systems, 30*(6), 711–732. DOI: 10.1504/IJCNDS.2024.141672

Ribeiro, M. T., ... (2016). "“Why should I trust you?”: Explaining the predictions of any classifier." Proceedings of the 22nd ACM SIGKDD International Conference on Knowledge Discovery and Data Mining.

Ribeiro, M. T., Singh, S., & Guestrin, C. (2016). "Why should I trust you?": Explaining the predictions of any classifier. Proceedings of the 22nd ACM SIGKDD International Conference on Knowledge Discovery and Data Mining, 1135–1144.

Ribeiro, M. T.. "Why Should I Trust You? Explaining the Predictions of Any Classifier." *Proceedings of the 22nd ACM SIGKDD International Conference on Knowledge Discovery and Data Mining*, 2016. DOI: 10.18653/v1/N16-3020

Rigotti, C., & Fosch-Villaronga, E. (2024). Fairness, AI & recruitment. *Computer Law & Security Review, 53*, 105966. DOI: 10.1016/j.clsr.2024.105966

Robles, P., & Mallinson, D. J. (2025). Artificial intelligence technology, public trust, and effective governance. *The Review of Policy Research, 42*(1), 11–28. DOI: 10.1111/ropr.12555

Rochet, J.-C. (2008). The future of banking regulation. (If a publisher is available, add it here. If unpublished, note as such.)

Rodrigues, L., Pereira, J., da Silva, A. F., & Ribeiro, H. (2023). The impact of artificial intelligence on audit profession. *Journal of Information Systems Engineering & Management, 8*(1), 19002. DOI: 10.55267/iadt.07.12743

Rogers, E. M., & Scott, K. L. (1997). The diffusion of innovations model and outreach from the National Network of Libraries of Medicine to Native American communities. Retrieved March, 22, 2006.

Rogers, E. M. (1995). *Diffusion of Innovations* (4th ed.). ACM The Free Press.

Rubin, D. B. (1976). Inference and missing data. *Biometrika*, *63*(3), 581–592. DOI: 10.1093/biomet/63.3.581

Rudin, C. (2019). Stop explaining black box machine learning models for high stakes decisions and use interpretable models instead. *Nature Machine Intelligence*, *1*(5), 206–215. https://www.nature.com/articles/s42256-019-0048-x. DOI: 10.1038/s42256-019-0048-x PMID: 35603010

Rudnicka, P., Nowicki, M., & Grabowski, A. (2023). AI in change management: Predictive analytics and behavioral modeling for employee engagement. *The International Journal of Organizational Analysis*.

Runge, C. A., Tulloch, A. I. T., Possingham, H. P., Tulloch, V. J. D., & Fuller, R. A. (2016). Incorporating dynamic distributions into spatial prioritization. *Diversity & Distributions*, *22*(3), 332–344. DOI: 10.1111/ddi.12395

Russell, S. J., & Norvig, P. (2016). *Artificial intelligence : A modern approach*. Pearson.

Russell, S., & Norvig, P. (2010). *Intelligence artificielle : Avec plus de 500 exercices*. Pearson Education.

Russell, S., & Norvig, P. (2020). *Artificial Intelligence: A Modern Approach* (4th ed.). Pearson.

Sabae, G. U. E. L. D. I., & Mohammed Chakib, H. I. M. M. I. C. H. (2024). La réglementation des avancées technologiques au Maroc: Un pivot du développement. International Journal Of Advanced Research In Innovation, Management &. *Social Sciences*, *7*(1). Advance online publication. DOI: 10.57109/223

Sabherwal, R., Jeyaraj, A., & Chowa, C. (2006). Information System Success : Individual and Organizational Determinants. *Management Science*, *52*(12), 1849–1864. DOI: 10.1287/mnsc.1060.0583

Sachan, S., Yang, J., Xu, D., Benavides, D. E., & Li, Y. (2019). An explainable AI decision-support-system to automate loan underwriting. *Expert Systems with Applications*, *144*, 113100. DOI: 10.1016/j.eswa.2019.113100

Safety Summit, A. I. (2023). AI Safety Summit 2023: Roundtable Chair's Summaries. www.gov.uk/government/publications/ai-safety-summit-1-november-roundtable-chairs summaries.

Sainila, S. (2024). Shaping Tomorrow's Workplace with AI-Driven HRM: Bridging the Gap Between Technology and Human Capital.

Saldaña, J. (2016). *The coding manual for qualitative researchers* (3rd ed.). Sage Publications.

Saulquin, J. Y., & Schier, G. (2007). Responsabilité sociale des entreprises et performance. *La Revue des Sciences de Gestion, 223*(1), 57–65. DOI: 10.3917/rsg.223.0057

Sawyer, L. B. (1973). *The practice of modern internal auditing: appraising operations for management.* No Title.

Schnackenberg, A. K., & Tomlinson, E. C. (2016). Organizational Transparency: A New Perspective on Managing Trust in Organization-Stakeholder Relationships. *Journal of Management, 42*(7), 1784–1810. DOI: 10.1177/0149206314525202

Scholta, H., & Lindgren, I. (2023). Proactivity in digital public services : A conceptual analysis. *Government Information Quarterly, 40*(3), 101832. DOI: 10.1016/j.giq.2023.101832

Schumann, C., Foster, J., Mattei, N., Dickerson, J. P., Schumann, C., Foster, J., Mattei, N., & Dickerson, J. P. (n.d.). We need fairness and explainability in algorithmic hiring. Consensus. https://consensus.app/papers/we-need-fairness-and-explainability-in-algorithmic-hiring-schumann-foster/440873588e61537fa785e50cec2a50b2/

Schumpeter, J. A. (1935). *Théorie de l'évolution économique* (Dalloz, Ed.).

Schumpeter, J. A. (1939). *Business cycles: A theoretical, historical and statistical analysis of the capitalist process.* McGraw-Hill.

Schumpeter, J. A. (1983). *The Theory of Economic Development: An Inquiry Into Profits.* Capital, Credit, Interest, and the Business Cycle.

Schwepker, C. H., & Good, D. J. (2019). Marketing control and ethical decision-making: A comparison of managers. *Journal of Business Ethics, 156*(2), 337–351.

Seabold, S., & Perktold, J. (2010). Statsmodels: Econometric and statistical modeling with Python. In 9th Python in Science Conference. DOI: 10.25080/Majora-92bf1922-011

Seddon, P. B. (1997). A respecification and extension of the DeLone and McLean model of IS success. *Information Systems Research, 8*(3), 240–253.

Seddon, P., & Kiew, M.-Y. (1996). A partial test and development of DeLone and McLean's model of IS success. *AJIS. Australasian Journal of Information Systems, 4*(1), 90–109.

Segouin, C., & Perret, F. (2001). L'audit et l'amélioration continue de la qualité à l'hôpital. ADSP (AP-HP), 35, 34-8.

Selbst, A. D., Boyd, D., Friedler, S. A., Venkatasubramanian, S., & Vertesi, J. (2019). Fairness and abstraction in sociotechnical systems. Proceedings of the Conference on Fairness, Accountability, and Transparency (FAT*), 59–68. DOI: 10.1145/3287560.3287598

Senadheera, S., Yigitcanlar, T., Desouza, K. C., Mossberger, K., Corchado, J., Mehmood, R., Li, R. Y. M., & Cheong, P. H. (2024). Understanding Chatbot Adoption in Local Governments : A Review and Framework. *Journal of Urban Technology*, •••, 1–35. DOI: 10.1080/10630732.2023.2297665

Serafeimidis, V., & Smithson, S. (1995). Requirements for an IT investment appraisal framework for the 1990s : Towards a more rigorous solution. *European Conference on Information Technology Investment Evaluation*, 146-160.

Shah, J. M., & Natraj, N. A., Hallur, Giri. G., & Aslekar, A. (2023). Artificial Intelligence (AI) in the Automotive Industry and the use of Exoskeletons in the Manufacturing Sector of the Automotive Industry. *2023 International Conference on Sustainable Computing and Data Communication Systems (ICSCDS)*, 428-432. https://doi.org/DOI: 10.1109/ICSCDS56580.2023.10105009

Shefrin, H. (2007). *Behavioral Corporate Finance: Decisions that Create Value*. McGraw-Hill.

Shin, D. (2021). The Effects of Explainability and Causability on Human–AI Interaction Trust and Reliance. *Computers in Human Behavior*, *123*, 106878. DOI: 10.1016/j.chb.2021.106878

Shlezinger, N., Eldar, Y. C., & Boyd, S. P. (2022). Model-Based Deep Learning: On the intersection of deep learning and optimization. *IEEE Access : Practical Innovations, Open Solutions*, *10*, 115384–115398. DOI: 10.1109/ACCESS.2022.3218802

Shlezinger, N., Whang, J., Eldar, Y. C., & Dimakis, A. G. (2023). Model-Based Deep learning. *Proceedings of the IEEE*, *111*(5), 465–499. DOI: 10.1109/JPROC.2023.3247480

Shum, H.-Y., He, X., & Li, D. (2018). From Eliza to XiaoIce: Challenges and opportunities with social chatbots. *Frontiers of Information Technology & Electronic Engineering*, *19*(1), 10–26. DOI: 10.1631/FITEE.1700826

Simon, H. A. (1957). *Models of man: Social and rational*. Wiley.

Sivakumar, K., Chakrabarty, S., & Roy, S. (2016). The role of ethical climate on salesperson's role stress, job attitudes, turnover intention, and job performance. *Journal of Personal Selling & Sales Management*, *36*(4), 297–312.

Smith, B. C. (2019). *The promise of artificial intelligence : Reckoning and judgment.* https://doi.org/DOI: 10.7551/mitpress/12385.001.0001

Soares, E., Angelov, P. P., Costa, B., Castro, M. P. G., Nageshrao, S., & Filev, D. (2020). Explaining deep learning models through Rule-Based approximation and Visualization. *IEEE Transactions on Fuzzy Systems*, *29*(8), 2399–2407. DOI: 10.1109/TFUZZ.2020.2999776

Soleimani, M., Intezari, A., Arrowsmith, J., Pauleen, D. J., & Taskin, N. (2025). Reducing AI bias in recruitment and selection: An integrative grounded approach. *International Journal of Human Resource Management*, •••, 1–36. DOI: 10.1080/09585192.2025.2480617

Souza, M. J., Lima, F. G., & Pereira, J. R. (2024). Earnings, leverage, and dividend payouts: Empirical evidence from Latin America. *Journal of Financial Stability*, *67*, 101187.

Sovrano, F., Hine, E., Anzolut, S., & Bacchelli, A. (2025). Simplifying software compliance: AI technologies in drafting technical documentation for the AI Act. *Empirical Software Engineering*, *30*(3), 91. DOI: 10.1007/s10664-025-10645-x PMID: 40191404

Stacey, R. D. (2022). *Strategic Management and Organisational Dynamics: The Challenge of Complexity to Ways of Thinking about Organisations*. Pearson Education.

Stone, P., Brooks, R., Brynjolfsson, E., Calo, R., Etzioni, O., Hager, G., Hirschberg, J., Kalyanakrishnan, S., Kamar, E., Kraus, S., Leyton-Brown, K., Parkes, D., Press, W., Saxenian, A., Shah, J., Tambe, M., & Teller, A. (2022). *Artificial Intelligence and Life in 2030: The One Hundred Year Study on Artificial Intelligence*.

Stone, D. L., Deadrick, D. L., Lukaszewski, K. M., & Johnson, R. (2015). The influence of technology on the future of human resource management. *Human Resource Management Review*, *25*(2), 216–231. DOI: 10.1016/j.hrmr.2015.01.002

Stone, M. (1974). Cross-validatory choice and assessment of statistical predictions. *Journal of the Royal Statistical Society. Series B, Statistical Methodology*, *36*(2), 111–133. DOI: 10.1111/j.2517-6161.1974.tb00994.x

Stone, M. D., & Woodcock, N. D. (2014). Interactive, direct and digital marketing: A future that depends on better use of business intelligence. *Journal of Research in Interactive Marketing*, *8*(1), 4–17. DOI: 10.1108/JRIM-07-2013-0046

Suhaib Kamran, S., Haleem, A., Bahl, S., Javaid, M., Prakash, C., & Budhhi, D. (2022). Artificial intelligence and advanced materials in automotive industry : Potential applications and perspectives. *Materials Today: Proceedings*, *62*(6), 4207–4214. DOI: 10.1016/j.matpr.2022.04.727

Sundararajan, M., Taly, A., & Yan, Q. (2017). *Axiomatic Attribution for Deep Networks*.

Sun, T. Q., & Medaglia, R. (2019). Mapping the challenges of Artificial Intelligence in the public sector : Evidence from public healthcare. *Government Information Quarterly*, *36*(2), 368–383. DOI: 10.1016/j.giq.2018.09.008

Swinney, L. (1999). Consideration of the social context of auditors' reliance on expert system output during evaluation of loan loss reserves. *International Journal of Intelligent Systems in Accounting Finance & Management*, *8*(3), 199–213. DOI: 10.1002/(SICI)1099-1174(199909)8:3<199::AID-ISAF160>3.0.CO;2-A

Taddeo, M., & Floridi, L. (2018). How AI can be a force for good. *Science*, *361*(6404), 751–752. DOI: 10.1126/science.aat5991 PMID: 30139858

Taherdoost, H. (2023). An Overview of Trends in Information Systems : Emerging Technologies that Transform the Information Technology Industry. *Cloud Computing and Data Science*, *4*(1), 1–16. DOI: 10.37256/ccds.4120231653

Tambe, P., Cappelli, P., & Yakubovich, V. (2019). Artificial intelligence in human resources management: Challenges and a path forward. *California Management Review*, *61*(4), 15–42. DOI: 10.1177/0008125619867910

Tang, Y., & Li, Q. (2021). Transparency in AI-powered internal campaigns: Implications for employee engagement. *Journal of Business Research*, *134*, 683–694.

Tanwar, M., Prasad, A., & Dhir, S. (2023). Big data and predictive analytics in change management: A bibliometric analysis. *Journal of Organizational Change Management*, *36*(4), 758–775.

Taouabit, O., Touhami, F., & Elmoukhtar, M. (2023). Transformation digitale de l'administration publique au Maroc et son impact sur l'expérience utilisateur : Cas des services rendus aux notaires par l'Agence Nationale de la Conservation Foncière du Cadastre et de la Cartographie. *International Journal of Accounting, Finance, Auditing, Management and Economics*, *4*(3-2), Article 3-2. DOI: 10.5281/zenodo.8054810

Taslim, W. S., Rosnani, T., & Fauzan, R. (2025). Employee involvement in AI-driven HR decision-making: A systematic review. *SA Journal of Human Resource Management*, *23*, 1–10. DOI: 10.4102/sajhrm.v23i0.2856

Tayazime, J., & Moutahaddib, A. (2021). La Transformation Digitale de l'Administration Publique au Maroc : La Perception des Usagers Particuliers. *Revue de Gestion et d'Économie, 9*(1 & 2), Article 1 & 2. DOI: 10.34874/PRSM.jbe.31604

Terribile, F., Agrillo, A., Bonfante, A., Buscemi, G., Colandrea, M., D'Antonio, A., De Mascellis, R., De Michele, C., Langella, G., & Manna, P. (2015). A Web-based spatial decision supporting system for land management and soil conservation. *Solid Earth, 6*(3), 903–928.

Terzidou, K. (2023). The Evolution of the Perception of Artificial Intelligence in the EU: The Case of Judicial Administration. *Journal of Intellectual Property, Information Technology and E-Commerce Law, 14*(3), 365-375. *Scopus*. Advance online publication. DOI: 10.2139/ssrn.4633945

Thiétart, R.-A. (2014). *Méthodes de recherche en management-4ème édition*. Dunod.

Toreini, E.. (2020). "The relationship between trust in AI and trustworthy machine learning technologies." *Proceedings of the ACM on Human-Computer Interaction* DOI: 10.1145/3351095.3372834

Tourangeau, R., Rips, L. J., & Rasinski, K. (2000). *The Psychology of Survey Response*. Cambridge University Press. DOI: 10.1017/CBO9780511819322

TradingEconomics. (2024). Morocco Interest Rate. https://tradingeconomics.com/morocco/interest-rate

Treviño, L. K. (1986). Ethical decision making in organizations: A person-situation interactionist model. *Academy of Management Review, 11*(3), 601–617. DOI: 10.2307/258313

Trischler, M. F. G., & Li-Ying, J. (2023). Digital business model innovation: Toward construct clarity and future research directions. *Review of Managerial Science, 17*(1), 3–32. DOI: 10.1007/s11846-021-00508-2

Trist, E. L. (1981). *The evolution of socio-technical systems* (Vol. 2). Ontario Quality of Working Life Centre.

Tschang, F. T., & Almirall, E. (2021). Artificial intelligence as augmenting automation: Implications for employment. *The Academy of Management Perspectives, 35*(4), 642–659. DOI: 10.5465/amp.2019.0062

Tursunbayeva, A., Franco, M., & Pagliari, C. (2023). AI in HR and organizational development: Opportunities for personalization and adaptation. *AI & Society, 38*(1), 125–141. DOI: 10.1007/s00146-022-01356-z

Tursunbayeva, A., Franco, M., & Pagliari, C. (2023). The evolving role of AI in human resources and organizational communication. *AI & Society*, *38*(1), 111–127. DOI: 10.1007/s00146-021-01235-1

Uhl-Bien, M., Arena, M. J., & Zoller, T. D. (2022). Leadership for organizational adaptability: A theoretical synthesis and integrative framework. *The Leadership Quarterly*, *33*(2), 101579.

United Nations. (2015). *Transforming Our World: The 2030 Agenda for Sustainable Development.* New York. https://docs.un.org/en/A/RES/70/1

Upmann, P. (2024). Localized Ethical Frameworks : Aligning AI with Regional Cultural and Societal Norms. *AIGN*. https://aign.global/ai-ethics-consulting/patrick-upmann/localized-ethical-frameworks-aligning-ai-with-regional-cultural-and-societal-norms

Urbach, N., & Müller, B. (2012). The Updated DeLone and McLean Model of Information Systems Success. In Dwivedi, Y. K., Wade, M. R., & Schneberger, S. L. (Eds.), *Information Systems Theory* (Vol. 28, pp. 1–18). Springer New York., DOI: 10.1007/978-1-4419-6108-2_1

US White House. (2023). Executive Order on the Safe, Secure, and Trustworthy Development and Use of Artificial Intelligence. www.whitehouse.gov/briefing-room/presidential actions/2023/10/30/executive-order-on-the-safe-secure-and-trustworthy-development-and use-of-artificial-intelligence/

van Ark, B. (2015). Productivity and Digitilization in Europe: Paving the Road to Faster Growth. *DigiWorld Economic Journal*, *100*(4), 107.

Van Der Voet, J., Kuipers, B. S., & Groeneveld, S. (2016). Implementing Change in Public Organizations : The relationship between leadership and affective commitment to change in a public sector context. *Public Management Review*, *18*(6), 842–865. DOI: 10.1080/14719037.2015.1045020

Van der Voort, H. G., Klievink, A. J., Arnaboldi, M., & Meijer, A. J. (2019). Rationality and politics of algorithms. Will the promise of big data survive the dynamics of public decision making? *Government Information Quarterly*, *36*(1), 27–38. DOI: 10.1016/j.giq.2018.10.011

van Haeften, W., Zhang, R., Boesen - Mariani, S., Lub, X., Ravesteijn, P., & Aertsen, P. (2024). Bridging the AI Skills Gap in Europe: A Detailed Analysis of AI Skills and Roles. *Resilience Through Digital Innovation: Enabling the Twin Transition*, 385–402.

Vaswani, A., Shazeer, N., Parmar, N., Uszkoreit, J., Jones, L., Gomez, A. N., Kaiser, Ł., & Polosukhin, I. (2017). Attention is all you need. In Advances in neural information processing systems (Vol. 30, pp. 5998–6008).

Veale, M., & Zuiderveen Borgesius, F. (2021). Demystifying the Draft EU Artificial Intelligence Act. *Computer Law & Security Review*, *42*, 105635. DOI: 10.1016/j.clsr.2021.105635

Venkatesh, V., & Bala, H. (2008). Technology Acceptance Model and a Research Agenda on Interventions. *Decision Sciences*, *39*(2), 273–315. DOI: 10.1111/j.1540-5915.2008.00192.x

Venkatesh, V., Morris, M. G., Davis, G. B., & Davis, F. D. (2003). User acceptance of information technology: Toward a unified view. *Management Information Systems Quarterly*, *27*(3), 425–478. DOI: 10.2307/30036540

Venkatesh, V., Thong, J. Y., & Xu, X. (2016). Unified theory of acceptance and use of technology: A synthesis and the road ahead. *Journal of the Association for Information Systems*, *17*(5), 328–376.

Vereb, D., Krajcsák, Z., & Kozák, A. (2025). The importance of positive employee experience and its development through using predictive analytics. *Journal of Modelling in Management*, *20*(1), 51–69. DOI: 10.1108/JM2-02-2024-0057

Vinuesa, R., Azizpour, H., Leike, J., Tegmark, M., & Fuso Nerini, F. (2020). The role of artificial intelligence in achieving the Sustainable Development Goals. *Nature Communications*, *11*(1), 1–10. DOI: 10.1038/s41467-019-14108-y PMID: 31932590

Vishwanath, B., & Vaddepalli, S. (2023). The future of work: Implications of artificial intelligence on hr practices. Tuijin Jishu/Journal of Propulsion Technology, 44(3), 1711-1724.

Wahbi, A., Khaddouj, K., & Lahlimi, N. (2023). Study of the relationship between chatbot technology and customer experience and satisfaction. International Journal of Accounting, Finance, Auditing, Management and Economics, 4(6-1), 758-771.

Wali of Bank Al-Maghrib. (2022, November 9). Digital transformation: Between regulation and competitiveness [Speech]. *International Conference*, Marrakech.

Wallach, W., Allen, C., & Smit, I. (2010). A model of moral judgment in artificial agents. In *AAAI Fall Symposium: Machine Ethics* (pp. 50–55).

Wang, X., Li, Z., Xu, Q., & Zhao, Y. (2023). Real-time adaptation of transformation strategies via AI analytics. *International Journal of Information Management*, *73*, 102596. DOI: 10.1016/j.ijinfomgt.2023.102596

Wang, Y. (2021). Artificial intelligence in educational leadership: A symbiotic role of human-artificial intelligence decision-making. *Journal of Educational Administration, 59*(3), 256–270. DOI: 10.1108/JEA-10-2020-0216

Waqar, A. (2024). Intelligent decision support systems in construction engineering : An artificial intelligence and machine learning approaches. *Expert Systems with Applications, 249*, 123503. DOI: 10.1016/j.eswa.2024.123503

Waterman, R. H., Peters, T. J., & Phillips, J. R. (2021). The McKinsey 7-S Framework: Linking Strategy and Structure. *The McKinsey Quarterly*.

West, D. M. (2021). *How robotic process and intelligent automation are altering government performance. Brookings Institution.* https://www.brookings.edu/articles/how-robotic-process-and-intelligent-automation-are-altering-government-performance/

White & Case. (2025). *AI Watch : Global regulatory tracker - United Kingdom.* https://www.whitecase.com/insight-our-thinking/ai-watch-global-regulatory-tracker-united-kingdom

Willard, J. D., Read, J. S., Appling, A. P., Oliver, S. K., Jia, X., & Kumar, V. (2021). Predicting water temperature dynamics of unmonitored lakes with meta-transfer learning. *Water Resources Research, 57*, e2021WR029579. DOI: .DOI: 10.1029/2021WR029579

Willmott, C. J., & Matsuura, K. (2005). Advantages of the mean absolute error (MAE) over the root mean square error (RMSE) in assessing average model performance. *Climate Research, 30*(1), 79–82. DOI: 10.3354/cr030079

Wilson, D. C., Rodic, L., Cowing, M. J., Velis, C. A., Whiteman, A. D., Scheinberg, A., Vilches, R., Masterson, D., Stretz, J., & Oelz, B. (2015). Wasteaware benchmark indicators for integrated sustainable waste management in cities. *Waste Management (New York, N.Y.), 35*, 329–342. DOI: 10.1016/j.wasman.2014.10.006 PMID: 25458855

Wilson, H. J., & Daugherty, P. R. (2018). Collaborative intelligence : Humans and AI are joining forces. *Harvard Business Review, 96*(4), 114–123.

Windmann, A., Wittenberg, P., Schieseck, M., & Niggemann, O. (2024). Artificial Intelligence in Industry 4.0: A Review of Integration Challenges for Industrial Systems. *The 22nd IEEE International Conference on Industrial Informatics, 4*.

Winfield, A. F., Michael, K., Pitt, J., & Evers, V. (2019). Machine Ethics: The Design and Governance of Ethical AI and Autonomous Systems [Scanning the Issue]. *Proceedings of the IEEE, 107*(3), 509–517. DOI: 10.1109/JPROC.2019.2900622

Wirtz, J., & Lovelock, C. (2021). *Services marketing : People, technology, strategy* (8e éd.). World Scientific Publishing Company.

Wirtz, B. W., Weyerer, J. C., & Geyer, C. (2019). Artificial Intelligence and the Public Sector—Applications and Challenges. *International Journal of Public Administration*, *42*(7), 596–615. DOI: 10.1080/01900692.2018.1498103

Wirtz, J., Hofmeister, J., Chew, P. Y. P., & Ding, X. (2023). Digital service technologies, service robots, AI, and the strategic pathways to cost-effective service excellence. *Service Industries Journal*, *43*(15–16), 1173–1196. DOI: 10.1080/02642069.2023.2226596

Wold, S., Ruhe, A., Wold, H., & Dunn, W. J.III. (1984). The collinearity problem in linear regression. *SIAM Journal on Scientific and Statistical Computing*, *5*(3), 735–743. DOI: 10.1137/0905052

Wooldridge, J. M. (2009). *Introductory Econometrics: A Modern Approach* (4th ed.). South-Western College Publishing.

World Health Organization Europe. (2007). Performance Assessment Tool for Quality Improvement in Hospitals.

World Health Organization. (2023), Regulatory considerations on artificial intelligence for health, https://iris.who.int/bitstream/handle/10665/373421/9789240078871-eng.pdf?sequence=1

Wu, I. L., & Hsieh, P. J. (2011). Understanding hospital innovation enabled customer-perceived quality of structure, process, and outcome care. *Total Quality Management & Business Excellence*, *22*(2), 227–241. DOI: 10.1080/14783363.2010.532343

Wu, W., Huang, T., & Gong, K. (2020). Ethical Principles and Governance Technology Development of AI in China. *Engineering (Beijing)*, *6*(3), 3. Advance online publication. DOI: 10.1016/j.eng.2019.12.015

Yanamala, K. K. R. (2023). Transparency, privacy, and accountability in AI-enhanced HR processes. *Journal of Advanced Computing Systems*, *3*(3), 10–18. DOI: 10.69987/JACS.2023.30302

Yang, A. Z. (2024). A Comparative Analysis of AI Governance Frameworks. *Washington Journal of Law, Technology & Arts*. https://wjlta.com/2024/07/09/a-comparative-analysis-of-ai-governance-frameworks/

Yaseen, H., & Dragotă, V. (2021). *Forecasting the Dividend Policy Using Machine Learning Approach: Decision Tree Regression Models*. Springer., DOI: 10.1007/978-3-030-71869-5_2

Yazdani, M., Zarate, P., Coulibaly, A., & Zavadskas, E. K. (2017). A group decision making support system in logistics and supply chain management. *Expert Systems with Applications*, *88*, 376–392.

Yehia, H. (2021). Dividend payout in Egypt. *Corporate Ownership and Control*, *18*(2), 112–125.

Yigitcanlar, T., Li, R. Y. M., Beeramoole, P. B., & Paz, A. (2023). Artificial intelligence in local government services : Public perceptions from Australia and Hong Kong. *Government Information Quarterly*, *40*(3), 101833. DOI: 10.1016/j.giq.2023.101833

Yin, R. K. (2017). *Case study research and applications: Design and methods* (6th ed.). Sage Publications.

Yin, Y., Zhang, L., & Du, X. (2022). Digital trace data and behavioral analytics for transformation management. *Information Systems Frontiers*, *24*(2), 415–430.

Yosra, J., & Abdelkrim, Z. (2024). Artificial Intelligence in the Service of Education in Morocco: Opportunities, Challenges, and Perspectives. *International Journal Of Applied Management And Economics*, *2*(09), 09. Advance online publication. DOI: 10.5281/zenodo.12772245

Yu, L., & Li, Y. (2022). Artificial intelligence decision-making transparency and employees' trust: The parallel multiple mediating effect of effectiveness and discomfort. *Behavioral Sciences (Basel, Switzerland)*, *12*(5), 127. DOI: 10.3390/bs12050127 PMID: 35621424

Yun, L., Yun, S., & Xue, H. (2024). Improving citizen-government interactions with generative artificial intelligence : Novel human-computer interaction strategies for policy understanding through large language models. *PLoS One*, *19*(12), e0311410. DOI: 10.1371/journal.pone.0311410 PMID: 39689162

Yusof, M., Kuljis, J., Papazafeiropoulou, A., & Stergioulas, L. K. (2008). An evaluation framework for Health Information Systems : Human, organization and technology-fit factors (HOT-fit). *International Journal of Medical Informatics*, *77*(6), 386–398. DOI: 10.1016/j.ijmedinf.2007.08.011 PMID: 17964851

Zaman, A. U. (2016). A comprehensive review of the development of zero waste management. *Journal of Cleaner Production*, *91*, 12–25. DOI: 10.1016/j.jclepro.2014.12.013

Zamora, M., & Zerbini, F. (2022). Smart collaboration platforms and AI in hybrid work environments. *Journal of Organizational Computing and Electronic Commerce*, *32*(3), 192–212.

Zarai, M.A., & Bettabai, W. (2007). Impact de l'efficacité des comités d'audit sur la qualité des bénéfices comptables divulgués. Revue gouvernance, 4(1).

Zarhloul, Z., & Mrani Zentar, S. (2022). La contribution de l'audit interne dans la performance du système de contrôle interne: cas du secteur bancaire marocain. International Journal of Accounting, Finance, Auditing, Management and Economics, 3(2-2), 354-368.

Zengul, F. D., Oner, S., & Yildiz, M. (2023). Artificial intelligence in organizational information management: Opportunities and ethical challenges. *Information Systems Frontiers*, *25*(1), 219–237. DOI: 10.1007/s10796-022-10258-3

Zhai, Z., Martínez, J. F., Beltran, V., & Martínez, N. L. (2020). Decision support systems for agriculture 4.0 : Survey and challenges. *Computers and Electronics in Agriculture*, *170*, 1–16. DOI: 10.1016/j.compag.2020.105256

Zhang, F., Klonek, F. E., Li, X., Ge, X., Song, S., Liu, Y., Zhu, X., Yang, M. M., Zhong, Y., Tian, A. W., Hirschi, A., Wu, S., Ruan, M., & Chen, S. (2024). Navigating the AI Revolution: AI's Impact on Business Practices and Employee Experiences. *Academy of Management Proceedings*, *2024*(1). DOI: 10.5465/AMPROC.2024.17622symposium

Zhang, H. (2024). *Exploring the Impact of AI on Human Resource Management: A case study of organizational adaptation and employee dynamics*. IEEE Transactions on Engineering.

Zhang, K., & Aslan, A. B. (2021). AI technologies for education: Recent research & future directions. *Computers and Education: Artificial Intelligence*, *2*, 100025. DOI: 10.1016/j.caeai.2021.100025

Zhang, Y., & Siau, K. (2024). Meta-Entrepreneurship: An Analysis Theory on Integrating Generative AI, Agentic AI, and Metaverse for Entrepreneurship. *Journal of Global Information Management*, *32*(1), 1–21. DOI: 10.4018/JGIM.364094

Zhou, J., Gao, S., & Chen, W. (2022). Conversational AI in corporate communication: Current trends and future implications. *Journal of Business Research*, *152*, 186–197.

Zhou, J., Gao, S., & Chen, W. (2022). The future of AI in employee engagement and change communication. *Journal of Business and Psychology*, *37*(6), 1173–1191. DOI: 10.1007/s10869-021-09785-5

Zhou, Z., Wang, Y., & Wu, Y. (2022). Machine learning for financial prediction: An empirical evaluation of interpretability and performance. *Expert Systems with Applications*, *193*, 116435.

Zhu, M., & Ma, Y. (2023). Artificial empathy and the limits of AI in leadership communication. *The Leadership Quarterly*, *34*(1), 101653.

Zuboff, S. (2019). Surveillance Capitalism and the Challenge of Collective Action. *New Labor Forum*, *28*(1), 10–29. DOI: 10.1177/1095796018819461

About the Contributors

Abdelfattah Jamal is an Associate Professor with Habilitation in Management Sciences at the Faculty of Legal, Economic and Social Sciences, University Cadi Ayyad Marrakech, Morocco. He holds a Ph.D. in Economics and Management from Sidi Mohammed Ben Abdellah University Fez and a Habilitation to Direct Research. His research focuses on organizational change management, managerial and social innovation, agility and resilience, digital transformation, and the integration of artificial intelligence in HR management and marketing. A permanent researcher at the Laboratory of New Management Practices (NPG) at Cadi Ayyad University, he supervises doctoral theses on digital transformation, corporate social responsibility (CSR), and AI. He actively participates in national and international conferences on digital-era management. Author of scientific publications in peer-reviewed journals and conference proceedings, he is a member of several scientific committees of academic journals and professional associations. He also contributes as a reviewer for recognized journals in management and organizational psychology.

Karima Aissaoui is an Associate Professor at the Faculty of Sciences, University Mohammed I, Oujda, Morocco, specializing in Computer Science. With extensive expertise in Artificial Intelligence, e-Learning, Security, and Systems Engineering, Pr. Aissaoui has made significant contributions to these fields, focusing on innovative solutions and interdisciplinary approaches. Her research interests include developing intelligent systems, enhancing online learning platforms, improving cybersecurity measures, and optimizing complex systems. Pr. Aissaoui's work has contributed to advancing both academic knowledge and practical applications in these rapidly evolving areas of technology.

lLhoussaine Alla is a professor in management sciences at the National School of Applied Sciences, and a researcher at the LAREMEF laboratory, Sidi Mohamed Ben Abdellah University, Fez, Morocco. He is a permanent professor of various marketing management modules at Sidi Mohamed Ben Abdellah University in

Fez (Morocco) and in several public and private business graduate schools. He is an accredited professional expert in Training Engineering, Professional Coaching and Mentoring young entrepreneurs. After a PhD thesis on creating value for the customer and its impact on the overall performance of companies, Prof. Lhoussaine Alla invested more in scientific research in marketing, through various scientific contributions in the form of participation in international conferences and symposia and scientific publications, in various themes inherent to Marketing (customer value creation, customer behaviour, e-marketing, customer experience, sales performance, Marketing Data Analytics, territorial marketing, territorial attractiveness, territorial economic intelligence, ...), finance (stock market performance, financial analysts, financing package,...), entrepreneurship (entrepreneur profile, startups, entrepreneurial resilience,...), tourism (tourist attractiveness, visitor behaviour, tourism, performance of tourist destinations,...), logistics (SC, SCM, SSCM, Green SCM, logistics performance,...). Prof. Lhoussaine ALLA is also (co)editor of the e-book "Integrating Intelligence and Sustainability into supply chains. IGI Global. DOI: 10.4018/979-8-3693-0225-5" and Editor-in-chief of the scientific journal Alternatives Managériales et Economiques (AME), indexed by IMIST-CNRST and Cairn. Prof. Lhoussaine ALLA is also (co)coordinator of many scientific events devoted to marketing research. As a scientific and educational accumulation, in his capacity as editor of numerous books, especially in collaboration with IGI Global, Prof ALLA has been able to mobilize a large community of imminent researchers and experts on a global scale, to share the fruits of their relevant and innovative research in the implementation, supervision, evaluation, control and reinvention of innovative solutions developed through data engineering and AI in marketing. He is co-editor of several collective works including: "Integrating Intelligence and Sustainability in Supply Chains", "AI and Data Engineering Solutions for Effective Marketing", "Data Collection and Analysis in Scientific Qualitative Research", Applying Qualitative Research Methods to Management Science, Utilizing Technology to Manage Territories, Sustainable and Intelligent Territorial Marketing and Entrepreneurship. Prof ALLA is the coordinator of a team of young researchers very dynamic and talented, with complementary profiles, creating a friendly space for high-level scientific research.

Bouchra Alj is a professor and researcher in management sciences, with more than 22 years of experience, having gained international recognition through her contributions to the management of organizations, public finances and taxation. After obtaining her PhD at the Mohammed V University, Faculty of Legal, Economic and Social Sciences (FSJES) in Rabat-Agdal, she joined the Cadi Ayyad University in Marrakech before joining the Hassan II University in Casablanca, where she is currently working for the FSJES in Mohammedia. She coordinates the Accounting –

Finance – Taxation course and teaches specialized modules covering bachelor's, master's and doctoral degrees, such as management of organizations, corporate taxation, tax audit, entrepreneurship and management science research methodology. Prof. Bouchra ALJ is also the head of a research team within the Research Laboratory in Economics, Management and Strategies of Organizations (LAREMSO), where she leads innovative research projects and supervises doctoral theses as well as graduate and master's degree projects. Under his direction, the team explores a variety of topics related to finance, economics, management and econometrics, focusing on an interdisciplinary approach to address concrete and current issues. In addition to her academic responsibilities, Prof. Bouchra ALJ is the author of several books, including on income taxation in Morocco and management of organizations. As the Director of Publication for The Economics & Management Review (), a journal indexed on IMIST, she is actively contributing to the dissemination of original research, Strengthening links between Moroccan researchers and the international scientific community. She is also a member of several scientific and editorial committees for renowned academic journals. Her work as a private sector consultant allows her to integrate the latest developments in management and taxation into an international context, bridging the gap between theory and practice. Prof. Bouchra ALJ regularly publishes in national and international academic journals, and her research is presented at renowned conferences around the world. His research is oriented towards management, public finance and taxation, with a particular interest in tax psychology and tax justice. She is also co-author of articles published in English and French, thus broadening the scope of her contributions. Very active on the national and international academic scene, Prof. Bouchra ALJ is frequently invited to sit on juries and panels of national and international conferences and plays a key role in organizing and hosting seminars, seminars and study days for committed researchers. She frequently participates in scientific and project evaluation committees, thus strengthening her influence in the field of management sciences.

Badr Bentalha teaches Supply Chain and Operations Management at National School Of Business and Management – Fez, Sidi Mohamed Ben Abdellah University – Morocco. Dr. Bentalha investigates the structural dynamics and control of complex networks, applying his findings to supply chain management, Industry 4.0, risk analysis, and digital supply chains. His pioneering research has established seminal academic and practical approaches for sustainable and intelligent supply chain optimization. Using optimization, simulation, control theory, and AI, he tackles real-world supply chain and operations challenges. His work emphasizes the intersection of supply chain management, operations research, industrial engineering, and digital technology. As a professor, he teaches undergraduate, graduate, and, doctoral courses in operations management, supply chain management, logistics, management information systems, and strategic management. Through guest lectures, webinars, and scholarly presentations, he engages students and fosters an active learning environment. He aims to equip future industry leaders with the management knowledge and technological skills to build more resilient, adaptable, and sustainable supply chain operations. Dr. Bentalha's academic background includes management and economics, operations research, and supply chain management. He studied management operations and supply chain management, graduating with honors. He earned PhD degrees and completed an aggregation in economics and management. Before entering academia, he primarily worked in industry and consulting, focusing on process optimization in manufacturing, logistics, and ERP systems. His practical experience includes numerous operations research and process optimization projects for operations design, logistics, scheduling, and supply chain management. Before joining the Fez National School of Business and Management, he was a professor of economics and management preparatory classes since 2009. Dr. Bentalha's influential research is cited in supply chain management and logistics. His publication record includes over 60 papers in prestigious academic journals such as the International Journal of Logistics Systems and Management, International Journal of Business Performance Management, International Journal of Business and Technology Studies, Journal of Environmental Issues and Climate Change, and Economical Managerial Alternatives. He is also the author of three books: Netnography: Principles, Method, and Ethics, Internal Audit of Treasury and Cash Management: Report on the Audit of Treasury and Integrating Intelligence and Sustainability in Supply Chains. Professor Bentalha specializes in supply chain and operations management, operations research, and service management. He is passionate about integrating knowledge across disciplines to solve real-world problems. He has delivered numerous invited plenary talks, keynotes, and panel discussions at conferences and global webinars. He serves as Associate Editor of the Economical Managerial Alternatives journal and is on the editorial boards and advisory committees of several other publications. He regularly presents his research and has chaired organized program committees, and served on advisory boards for over 60 international conferences in supply chain management, operations, management studies, control theory, and information science. He is a member of numerous scientific committees of international journals and conferences. Since 2009, Mr. Bentalha has helped sundry companies implement an audit system, resolve issues, and improve performance.

***

Hassane Amaazoul, a Doctor of Economics and Management, is a lecturer and researcher at ENCG Dakhla, Ibn Zohr University, Agadir (Morocco). He teaches, among other things, HRM, Strategic Management, and Intercultural Management. His research focuses on CSR, Sustainable Development, and Performance. He is a member of several associations and academic circles: ORSEM at ISCAE (Casablanca), RIODD (Montpellier), and ADERSE (Lyon). On January 18, 2023, I received the Best Article Award from the Sustainable Finance Competition for researchers from French-speaking emerging countries. This Award is organized by the United Nations-Francophone PRI Network (Principles for Responsible Investment), the Forum for Responsible Investment (FIR) and the African Chair in Innovations and Sustainable Management at Mohammed VI Polytechnic University (CAIMD-UM6P), for my article entitled "CSR and financial performance: a study of 107 Moroccan companies" published in 2021 in the Journal "Recherches en Sciences de Gestion" (France). Author of several contributions to the "Regards Croisés" section of the journal "Question(s) de Management"

Malika Asbayou holds a PhD in Management Sciences with a specialization in Human Resource Management. She is the Training Strategy Coordinator at the University Hospital Center Ibn Sina in Rabat and a research associate with the Governance, Information, and Organizational Communication Research Team at the National School of Business and Management (Agadir). Her research interests include innovation, wellbeing, digital transformation and human resource management.

Intissar Baiza is a doctoral student in economics, Management, Information and Governance Research Laboratory (LARMIG) Research team: Economy, Territory, Organization and Governance (ETOG) Faculty of Legal, Economic and Social Sciences Ain Sebaâ Hassan II University of Casablanca, Morocco

Latifa Boumalk is a PhD student in Management Sciences and Techniques at the Research Laboratory in Tourism, Innovation and Sustainable Development (LARTI2D) of the National School of Business and Management (ENCG Agadir), under the Ibnou Zohr University of Agadir (Morocco). Her research is part of the Management of Organizations axis, with a focus on digital transformation, public administration, quality of services, users and artificial intelligence.

Rita El Guermai is currently a PhD candidate at Cadi Ayyad University in Marrakech, Morocco. Her research focuses on the impact of Artificial Intelligence on customer loyalty in the telecommunications sector. She holds a Master's degree in Marketing and Business Strategy, and a Bachelor's degree in International Trade. Her academic interests include digital transformation, predictive marketing, and AI-driven customer relationship management. She has contributed to several academic conferences and collective publications in the fields of marketing innovation and emerging technologies.

Mohamed Amine is a PhD candidate in Management, specializing in Finance, at Cadi Ayyad University in Morocco.

Aziz Hantem, who holds a doctorate in Management Sciences from Hassan II University in Casablanca, is a Professor-Researcher at the Ecole Nationale de Commerce et de Gestion (ENCG)-Dakhla, part of Ibn Zohr University, Morocco. He is a member of the University Council and a member of the School Council at ENCG-Dakhla. As a Professor and Researcher, Aziz HANTEM works with public and private higher education establishments. His research interests and most recent publications focus on innovation and management in the healthcare sector. He coordinates scientific events and leads numerous projects, some of which have been used in national and international scientific work.

Saida Ifiss holds a doctorate in Management Sciences from Abdelmalek ESSAADI University. Her research focuses on governance models aimed at increasing the effectiveness of public public organisations. She is the author of a dozen articles published in peer-reviewed journals. peer-reviewed journals. She has over three years' experience in university teaching. Saida IFISS continues to make an active contribution to the field of public management through her academic work and her commitment to teaching.

Soukaina Jouad is a research professor at the National School of Commerce and Management (ENCG) in Dakhla, affiliated with Ibn Zohr University. With a PhD in Management Sciences from ENCG Agadir, Dr. Jouad has built a strong academic and professional career, combining research and teaching. Specializing in audit, management control, and logistics, Dr. Jouad is passionate about preparing future business leaders with the knowledge and critical thinking skills necessary to succeed in a competitive global economy. In addition to her academic responsibilities, Dr. Jouad participates in national and international conferences, publishes scholarly articles, and collaborates with local economic actors to promote sustainable business practices in the southern regions of Morocco.

Priya Kadyan is a highly accomplished professional with a robust educational background and extensive experience in the field of Human Resources. She holds a postgraduate degree in Business Administration from Pune University, specializing in HR and BA. Presently, she is diligently pursuing her PhD at Chandigarh University, focusing on HR-related research.

Hassan Khafif is a doctoral student in economics, Management, Information and Governance Research Laboratory (LARMIG) Research team: Economy, Territory, Organization and Governance (ETOG) Faculty of Legal, Economic and Social Sciences Ain Sebaâ Hassan II University of Casablanca, Morocco

Mohamed Lahmouchi is a Professor in university Hassan II – Casablanca.

Sara Mantouzi is a distinguished doctor and lecturer in Management Science at the National School of Business and Management (ENCG) of Hassan II University, Morocco. With a Doctorate in Management Science, she specializes in decision support systems, organizational performance management, and financial control. Her research focuses on implementing analytical tools that enhance strategic decision-making, improve performance evaluation, and optimize financial reporting processes. Dr. Mantouzi has contributed to international peer-reviewed journals and participated in multidisciplinary projects linking management science, technology, and organizational behavior.

Naoual Ouazzani Touhami is a researcher-Professor, Management, Information and Governance Research Laboratory (LARMIG) Research team: Economy, Territory, Organization and Governance (ETOG) Faculty of Legal, Economic and Social Sciences Ain Sebaâ Hassan II University of Casablanca, Morocco.

Ayoub Ouboumlik is a doctoral student in economics, Management, Information and Governance Research Laboratory (LARMIG) Research team: Economy, Territory, Organization and Governance (ETOG) Faculty of Legal, Economic and Social Sciences Ain Sebaâ Hassan II University of Casablanca, Morocco

Ikrame Ouhnine is currently a PhD candidate at Abdelmalek Essaâdi University in Tangier, Morocco.

Charaf Saidi is a research professor at cadi ayyad university, marrakech, Faculty of Legal, Economic and Social Sciences of Marrakech.

Rohan Singh currently holds the Associate Professor in Management position at Chandigarh University, Punjab. His primary focus in research lies within the domains of Human Resource Management, delving into the complex dynamics shaping HR strategies and their adaptation in the era of AI, gig workers, and hybrid work practices and also exploring the relation between HRM and various performance metrics. Additionally, he engages in various academic activities, including serving as a guest faculty, keynote speaker, session chair, acting as a resource person for FDP sessions and participating as an external examiner (Master's and Research

Scholars), among others. He has showcased his research prowess by publishing in esteemed international journals and conferences, accumulating an impressive citation count of over 500. In addition to his academic role, Dr. Singh boasts over 14 years of comprehensive experience in the field of Overall Project Management at the Sponsored Research & Industrial Consultancy Cell of the esteemed Indian Institute of Technology Kharagpur. He has extensive experience in evaluating scholarly manuscripts. Over the years, he has contributed to the peer-review process for numerous prestigious journals, ensuring the integrity and quality of published research as Associate Editor, Editorial Review Board Member, Advisory Board Member, Reviewer Board Member, Advisory-cum-Reviewers' Board Member and National Member.

Index

A

C

D

E

F

G

P

R

S

T

www.ingramcontent.com/pod-product-compliance
Lightning Source LLC
LaVergne TN
LVHW080349011026
849161LV00009B/2239